Sixteenth-Century Italian Art

BLACKWELL ANTHOLOGIES IN ART HISTORY ———

The *Blackwell Anthologies in Art History* series presents an unprecedented set of canonical and critical works in art history. Each volume in the series pairs previously published, classic essays with contemporary historiographical scholarship to offer a fresh perspective on a given period, style, or genre in art history. Modeling itself on the upper-division undergraduate art history curriculum in the English-speaking world and paying careful attention to the most beneficial way to teach art history in today's classroom setting, each volume offers ample pedagogical material created by expert volume editors – from substantive introductory essays and section overviews to illustrations and bibliographies. Taken together, the *Blackwell Anthologies in Art History* will be a complete reference devoted to the best that has been taught and written on a given subject or theme in art history.

Sixteenth-Century Italian Art

Edited by *Michael W. Cole*

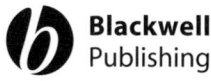
Blackwell
Publishing

BLACKWELL PUBLISHING
350 Main Street, Malden, MA 02148-5020, USA
9600 Garsington Road, Oxford OX4 2DQ, UK
550 Swanston Street, Carlton, Victoria 3053, Australia

First published 2006 by Blackwell Publishing Ltd

1   2006

Library of Congress Cataloging-in-Publication Data

Sixteenth-century Italian art / edited by Michael W. Cole.
        p. cm. — (Blackwell anthologies in art history ; 3)
    Includes index.
    ISBN-13: 978-1-4051-0840-9 (hardback : alk. paper)
    ISBN-10: 1-4051-0840-1 (hardback : alk. paper)
    ISBN-13: 978-1-4051-0841-6 (pbk. : alk. paper)
    ISBN-10: 1-4051-0841-X (pbk. : alk. paper) 1. Art, Italian—16th century.
2. Architecture—Italy—16th century. I. Title: 16th century Italian art. II. Cole,
Michael Wayne, 1969–   III. Series.

    N6915.S62 2006
    709.45′09031—dc22

                                                                    2006001998

A catalogue record for this title is available from the British Library.

Set in 10.5/13pt Galliard
by Graphicraft Limited, Hong Kong
Printed and bound in the United Kingdom
by T.J. International Ltd, Padstow, Cornwall

The publisher's policy is to use permanent paper from mills that operate
a sustainable forestry policy, and which has been manufactured from pulp
processed using acid-free and elementary chlorine-free practices. Furthermore,
the publisher ensures that the text paper and cover board used have met
acceptable environmental accreditation standards.

For further information on
Blackwell Publishing, visit our website:
www.blackwellpublishing.com

Contents

Illustrations

Picture research: Kitty Bocking

Series Editor's Preface

The *Blackwell Anthologies in Art History* series is intended to bring together writing on a given subject from a broad historical and historiographic perspective. The aim of the volumes is to present key writings in the given subject area whilst at the same time challenging their canonical status through the inclusion of less well-known texts, including contemporary documentation and commentaries, that present alternative interpretations or understandings of the period under review.

Sixteenth-Century Italian Art presents the reader with a wide-ranging selection of texts that vividly convey how the art history of this period has evolved and why it remains an active field of study. Alongside painting, sculpture, architecture, this anthology also includes material on drawing, printmaking, and the decorative arts to give a fuller picture of artistic production across the whole of the sixteenth century in northern Italy as well as Florence and Rome. The texts chart the changing preoccupations and views of both Anglo-American and continental European art historians to give a very clear sense of the processes and methods involved in the study of sixteenth-century Italian art.

The anthology provides a thorough introduction to *Sixteenth-Century Italian Art* through a synthesis of historical writings and contemporary texts which combine to make a significant contribution to the field. It will be invaluable to students and teachers, as well as those with a general interest in the period. This is one of the first volumes to appear and it makes a very pleasing addition to the series.

Dana Arnold
2005

Acknowledgments

The editor and publisher gratefully acknowledge the permission granted to reproduce the copyright material in this book:

1. Tilmann Buddensieg, "Raffaels Grab" ["Raphael's Tomb"], pp. 45–60 from Tilmann Buddensieg and Matthias Winner (eds.), *Munuscula Discipulorum: Kunsthistorische Studien, Hans Kauffmann zum 70. Geburtstag 1966.* Berlin: Verlag Bruno Hessling Berlin, 1968. Translation by Madeleine Viljoen and Michael Cole © 2006 by Blackwell Publishing Ltd.

2. Christof Thoenes, "St. Peter als Ruine: Zu einigen Veduten Heemskercks" ["St. Peter's as Ruins: On Some *vedute* by Heemskerck"], pp. 481–500 from *Zeitschrift für Kunstgeschichte* 49:4 (1986). Translation by Michael Cole © 2006 by Blackwell Publishing Ltd.

3. Edgar Wind, "Virtue Reconciled with Pleasure," pp. 81–96 from *Pagan Mysteries in the Renaissance*, new and enlarged edition. London: Faber and Faber Ltd, 1968. © 1958, 1968, by Edgar Wind. Reprinted by permission of W. W. Norton & Company, Inc.

4. Robert W. Gaston, "Love's Sweet Poison: A New Reading of Bronzino's London *Allegory*," pp. 249–288 from *I Tatti Studies: Essays in the Renaissance*, vol. 4. Florence: The Harvard University Center for Italian Renaissance Studies, 1991. © 1991 by Robert W. Gaston. Reprinted by permission of the author.

5. Martin J. Kemp, "Leonardo da Vinci: Science and the Poetic Impulse," pp. 196–213 from *Royal Society for the Encouragement of Arts, Manufactures & Commerce Journal* (February 1985). © 1985 by The Royal Society of Arts. Reprinted by permission of The Royal Society of Arts and the author.

6. Philippe Morel, excerpts from *Les Grottes maniéristes en Italie au XVIe siècle* [Mannerist Grottos in Sixteenth-Century Italy]. Paris: Macula, 1998. © 1998 by Macula. Translation by Michael Cole © 2006 by Blackwell Publishing Ltd.

7. Nicola Courtright, "Imitation, Innovation, and Renovation in the Counter-Reformation: Landscapes *all'antica* in the Vatican Tower of the Winds," pp. 126–142 from Alina Payne, Ann Kuttner, and Rebekah Smick (eds.), *Antiquity and Its Interpreters*. Cambridge: Cambridge University Press, 2000. © 2000 by Cambridge University Press. Reprinted by permission of the publisher and author.

8. Pamela M. Jones, "Landscapes and Still Lifes," pp. 76–84 from *Federico Borromeo and the Ambrosiana: Art, Patronage and Reform in Seventeenth Century Milan*. Cambridge: Cambridge University Press, 1993. © 1988 by Cambridge University Press. Reprinted by permission of the publisher and author.

9. Elizabeth Cropper, "Preparing to Finish: Portraits by Pontormo and Bronzino around 1530," pp. 499–504 from Klaus Bergdolt and Giorgio Bonsanti (eds.), *Opere e giorni: studi su mille anni di arte europea*. Venice: Marsilio, 2001. © 2001 by Elizabeth Cropper. Reprinted by permission of the author.

10. Nancy J. Vickers, "The Mistress in the Masterpiece," pp. 19–41 from Nancy K. Miller, *The Poetics of Gender*. New York: Columbia University Press, 1986. © 1986 by Columbia University Press. Reprinted by permission of the publisher.

11. Leo Steinberg, "Michelangelo's Florentine Pietà: The Missing Leg," pp. 343–353 from *The Art Bulletin* 50:4 (1968). © 1968 by Leo Steinberg.

12. Alina Payne, "Reclining Bodies: Figural Ornament in Renaissance Architecture," pp. 94–113, 340–342 from George Dodds and Robert Tavernor (eds.), *Body and Building: Essays on the Changing Relation of Body and Architecture*. Cambridge, Mass.: MIT Press, 2002. © 2002 by The MIT Press. Reprinted by permission of the publisher.

13. Catherine Wilkinson, "The New Professionalism in the Renaissance," pp. 124–160 from S. Kostof (ed.), *The Architect: Chapters in the History of the Profession*. Berkeley: University of California Press, 1977. © 1977, 1986 by Oxford University Press, Inc. Reprinted by permission of Oxford University Press, Inc.

14. Michael Bury, "On Some Engravings by Giorgio Ghisi Commonly Called 'Reproductive'," pp. 4–19 from *Print Quarterly* 10:1 (1993). © 1993 by Print Quarterly. Reprinted by permission of Print Quarterly Publications.

15. Marco Collareta, "L'historien et la technique. Sur le rôle de l'orfèvrerie dans les *Vites* de Vasari" ["The Historian and Technique: On the Role of Goldsmithery in Vasari's *Lives*"], pp. 165–176 from *Histoire de l'histoire de l'art*. Paris:

Klincksieck, Musée du Louvre, 1995. Translation by Irene Gates and Michael Cole © 2006 by Blackwell Publishing Ltd.

16. Charles de Tolnay, "Michelangelo and Vittoria Colonna," pp. 51–69 from *Michelangelo V: The Final Period*. Princeton: Princeton University Press, 1960. © 1960 by Charles de Tolnay. Reprinted by permission of Rainer Kretschmann.

17. Alexander Nagel, "Gifts for Michelangelo and Vittoria Colonna," pp. 647–668 from *The Art Bulletin* 79:4 (1997). © 1997 by Alexander Nagel. Reprinted by permission of the author.

18. James S. Ackerman, "The Gesù in the Light of Contemporary Church Design," pp. 15–28 from Rudolf Wittkower and Irma B. Jaffe (eds.), *Baroque Art: The Jesuit Contribution*. New York: Fordham University Press, 1972. © 1972 by Fordham University Press. Reprinted by permission of the publisher.

19. Charles Dempsey, "The Carracci and the Devout Style in Emilia," pp. 75–87 from National Gallery of Art, Washington, Center for Advanced Study in the Visual Arts, *The Age of Correggio and the Carracci: Emilian Painting of the 16th and 17th Centuries: A Symposium*. Washington, DC: National Gallery of Art, Washington, 1987. © 1987 by Charles Dempsey. Reprinted by permission of the National Gallery of Art, Washington and the author.

20. John Shearman, "Leonardo's Colour and Chiaroscuro," pp. 13–47 from *Zeitschrift für Kunstgeschichte* (1962). © 1962 by Zeitschrift für Kunstgeschichte. Reprinted by permission of Deutscher Kunstverlag.

21. Mary Pardo, "The Subject of Savoldo's *Magdalene*," pp. 67–91 from *The Art Bulletin* 71:1 (1989). © 1989 by Mary Pardo. Reprinted by permission of the author.

22. David Summers, "*Figure come fratelli*: A Transformation of Symmetry in Italian Renaissance Painting," pp. 59–88 from *The Art Quarterly* NS 1:1 (1977). © 1977 by David Summers. Reprinted by permission of the author.

23. Ingrid D. Rowland, "Raphael, Angelo Colocci, and the Genesis of the Architectural Orders," pp. 81–104 from *The Art Bulletin* 76:1 (1994). © 1994 by Ingrid Rowland. Reprinted by permission of the author.

Every effort has been made to trace copyright holders and to obtain their permission for the use of copyright material. The publisher apologizes for any errors or omissions in the above list and would be grateful if notified of any corrections that should be incorporated in future reprints or editions of this book.

Introduction

My brief, in assembling this anthology, was to collect a group of "classic" and recent texts on Italian art in the sixteenth century that could supplement a textbook in introducing beginning students and interested general readers to the period and the subject. The idea was both to convey the degree to which the history of sixteenth-century Italian art, as a living field of study, depends on argument and changing views, and, more basically, to give students a better sense than a textbook can about what scholars who work in the area really *do*. Read alongside a textbook, the envisioned anthology would, ideally, not retell the "story of art," but would rather help students think about the ways in which that story has been and can be told – how art historians have approached the field, what their dominant interests have been, where the questions they have been asking have moved.

Among the challenges the assignment and the project presented, the most difficult was perhaps that of settling on an appropriate scope. The present volume, which will eventually have companions on fifteenth- and on seventeenth-century art, was to cover the period of roughly 1500–1600, what Italianists refer to as the "Cinquecento." But is the Cinquecento a "period" in any meaningful sense of the term? Both in the United Kingdom and in the United States, art history courses that deal broadly with sixteenth-century topics tend to be taught under the rubrics of "Renaissance" art, which includes the first decades of the century, of "Baroque" art, which begins with the last, and of "Mannerism," which falls in between. A reader on the Cinquecento, if its chronological markers were to be respected, would cover too little of both the first and the last topics to serve as an introduction to either. To judge from the available textbooks, moreover, courses devoted to Mannerism are rare, perhaps because the very idea of Mannerism has so fallen out of favor as to make any non-critical introduction to its literature unappealing.

The decision to devote separate volumes at least to the fifteenth and sixteenth centuries might well be defended by pointing to the historical and cultural factors that make the years around 1500 seem a real watershed for the visual arts: one could point to shifting court patronage, marked by events like the exiling of the Medici from Florence in 1493 and of the Sforza from Milan in 1499, as well as by the rise of French and Spanish influence on the peninsula; to the emergence of major reform movements, represented in the first place by Savonarola and the *piagnoni*, in the same years; to the rebuilding of St. Peter's and the expansion and decoration of the Vatican palaces, which contributed to lending Rome as a city a new gravitational force; to the success of new media, such as the print, the oil-on-canvas painting, and the small bronze, all of which, being portable, contributed to new interregional exchange; and even to the rise of internationally renowned superstar artists like Raphael, Michelangelo, and Titian. In many cases, the stories that begin with these events find their conclusions only at the end of the century, with, for example, the institutionalization of reform in conciliar decrees and published treatises, the movement and in some cases migration of major Italian artists to France and Spain, and the advent of academies that would make Michelangelo's and Raphael's lessons into a sort of dogma. In the end, the usefulness of these or other period divisions must be left to the judgment of those teaching the courses. One might note, nevertheless, that a basic English-language introductory literature, including Sydney Freedberg's *Painting in Italy 1500–1600*, in the Pelican History of Art series, and Robert Klein and Henri Zerner's *Italian Art 1500–1600: Sources and Documents*, has long bracketed the Cinquecento as a coherent artistic period. In Italy itself, the sense that the Cinquecento constitutes a period is, if anything, even more current: it guides exhibitions, like the 1997 *Il Cinquecento da Praga a Cremona*, the 2000 *Cinquecento lombardo, da Leonardo a Caravaggio*, the 2002 *Cinquecento a Bologna*, and the 2004 *Tiziano e la pittura del Cinquecento a Venezia*, as well as books, of which the volumes in the UTET *Storia dell'arte in Italia* series and the classic anthologies, edited by Paola Barocchi, of sixteenth-century *Scritti* and *Trattati*, are but the most well-known examples.

An equally troublesome question has been that of how, in putting together a volume such as this, one should go about selecting its texts. Inasmuch as the objective of the volume is to introduce students to highlights from the history of Italian art, it might seem to make sense simply to identify the best work that has been done in the field – to assemble a top ten, as it were, of Italian Renaissance art history essays. Amusing as it can be to try to compile such a list, however, the approach strikes me as misguided. To begin, it is difficult to imagine that any two art historians today, asked independently to list a few relatively short, "classic" articles on sixteenth-century Italian art, would end up with the same selections (indeed, the numerous lists of suggestions that Blackwell solicited from my colleagues at other universities contained little overlap). The same is still more true when it comes to recent studies, where the vast literature reflects varying interests and specializations in period, geographical region, and medium, not to mention varying methods of teaching and study. There are even questions, I think, about whether such a compilation, could it be agreed upon, would serve the purposes to which the present anthology is directed: if one were to list the best things written on Cinquecento painting in the last one hundred years, one would, I expect, end up with a book overly narrow in subject, with much on Michelangelo, little on Raphael, and still less on works that have not traditionally counted as "masterpieces."

In view of all of this, my own aim has not been to present a roster of the "best" recent contributions to the field, but rather to think about the volume more collectively, to find studies that, while exceptionally good in their own right, also present different perspectives on common questions, thus allowing readers to think about both the implications and the limitations of any individual piece within the book. The texts included here no doubt reflect my own tastes and prejudices, though I have, in selecting them, made every effort at diversity, including pieces on painting, sculpture, architecture, drawing, printmaking, and the decorative arts, on early, middle, and late sixteenth-century topics and issues, on northern Italy as well as Florence and Rome, by both Anglo-American and continental European scholars. It seemed to me that this book should not aim to replace a textbook or lectures. It neither could nor should *survey* the art of the cultures it concerns; where choices were necessary, therefore, quality of writing and power of ideas were always given precedence over chronological or geographical comprehensiveness. Nor did it seem terribly necessary to provide beginning students with a capsule historiography of the field. For this reason, I have avoided articles that deal explicitly with the definition or relevance of such terms as "High Renaissance," "Mannerism," or "Counter-Reformation." Survey books, focusing as they do on style, offer this already, and instructors will have their own sense of the relative importance of such questions.

Throughout, I have attempted to include essays that, while they may focus on a small group of artworks, have considerably larger implications. While all of the pieces are rigorous in their scholarship, I have been more interested in finding essays that pose important questions effectively, or illuminate the larger period, than in finding studies the primary contribution of which is to interpret an isolated work. I have made a point of avoiding both pieces that are too general or basic and excerpts from books so readily available in paperback versions that students may already be expected to purchase them in another form (Rudolf Wittkower's *Architectural Principles in the Age of Humanism* or John Shearman's *Mannerism*, for example). Four of the pieces here have never appeared previously in English; a number of others are important studies that first appeared in journals, conference proceedings, or anthologies that some readers may have missed. With the exception of one article and a few excerpts from longer books, all pieces have been included here in their entirety (albeit, in many cases, with a reduced program of illustrations). In no case have I included more than one piece by the same author.

My aims for the volume, in sum, have been to collect an array of perspectives on themes that, as I see it, are central to the field of sixteenth-century art history as it is taught today. Instructors and students alike should find that the themes that frame the book's six parts bear on much of the art that students in introductory courses see. The section topics are broad; they are topics to which writers over the last century have repeatedly returned. The pieces in those sections exemplify different approaches that writers over the last half-century, and especially over the last two decades, have taken to late- and post-Renaissance art; ideally, they will both illuminate the range of questions one might put to artworks from the period today and introduce arguments that can serve as the basis for class discussion or debate. Though teachers may wish to assign only selected essays from the volume, and to assign them in a different order than they appear here – the index points to some other topics around which the collection might alternatively have been structured – the book's thematic organization should also allow the essays to play more readily off one another, even where the material those essays cover is different.

Part I
Pagan Mysteries

Introduction

Among the most venerable topics in the historiography of sixteenth-century Italy is how that culture engaged the legacy of classical Antiquity. The question gets raised in view of myriad contemporary phenomena: archaeological unearthings of masterworks from the distant past; translations and philological discoveries that exposed readers to new kinds of thinking; the rise, partially inspired by hieroglyphics, of a sophisticated emblematics; the empowerment and patronage of political figures who took ancient imperial leaders as their models. Part of what makes all of this important is that it figures not just into the high culture of the period but also into periodization itself. The very term "Renaissance" implies a return to or recovery of some aspect of the ancient past, and scholars have long used the idea of such a return to counterpose a period of "rebirth" to a "Middle Ages," the values of which were severely qualified or rejected.

One question that such a schema raises has to do with the room it leaves for and sense it makes of non-secular Renaissance works: these, after all, constitute the vast majority of the material culture associated with the period. What points of friction emerge when ancient, non-Christian forms are revivified in a post-classical Catholic context? How does the meaning of Christian art – whether figurative or architectural – change when fused with pagan types?

The essays by Buddensieg and Thoenes tackle these questions directly. Buddensieg, whose article focuses on a once (but no longer) popular sculpture, commissioned by Raphael to serve as the primary ornament for his tomb, illustrates the degree to which we have lost the taste for a version of the "classical" that artists in the early years of the sixteenth century were trying to recapture. Central to Buddensieg's essay are the matters of how, in Raphael's day, classical imagery could be reconciled with modern cult practices, and of how the possibility of this reconciliation differentiated Raphael's moment from what had come before. Though it focuses on what many today would regard as a minor work, Buddensieg's piece sheds light on the status of other early Cinquecento sculptures made in its idiom (Andrea Sansovino's *Virgin and Child with St. Anne*, for example, or Jacopo Sansovino's *Madonna del Parto*, both of which became "cultic" in novel ways), on Raphael's own stylistic exemplarity (especially inasmuch as the subject of the sculpture at issue, the Madonna and Child, is the subject we now associate most readily with Raphael's own "classicism"), and on that artist's own double role as an antiquarian and as a member of Rome's artistic avant-garde.

While Buddensieg's article is about High Renaissance restoration practices and about the implications these could have, Thoenes's looks at something like the reverse of this: the significance that ruins carried *as ruins*. Formulating bold proposals about architectural patronage in the early sixteenth century – that, for example, the grandiose visions of the first Cinquecento Popes compelled them, out of rivalry with the ancients, to commission things that they knew couldn't be made, and that, in the period's most important architecture, destruction could be as important as creation – Thoenes also, and more elaborately, shows how the repeatedly abortive works that resulted from such commissions might be perceived by reflective visitors to the city. In Maerten van Heemskerck's drawings of St. Peter's, Thoenes demonstrates, the ancient and modern are fused in ways we might not expect: the old and the new come, paradoxically, to be inverted, with the most recent building looking the most ruinous. The article shows a sometimes neglected side to the contemporary reputation of Bramante, the man we associate virtually with the invention of High Renaissance architecture. It offers a fascinating perspective on the problem of the *non-finito*, the unfinished work so characteristic of the period (and not just in architecture). Finally, it encourages reflection on the complex role drawings increasingly came to have in the sixteenth century: as documents of what their makers witnessed around them, but also as critiques and satires of a sort that only the most personal of media could allow.

Both the Buddensieg and Thoenes articles deal with the making of modern works for environments dominated by the relics of the ancients. The second pair of readings, by contrast, treats a different set of issues, now raised not by antiquarian architectural projects, but by the recovery, absorption, and reworking of ancient pictorial and literary themes. Here the problem is not so much that of the special demands presented by the Renaissance's invariably Christian promoters, but of the content that recovered "pagan" forms could carry and of the questions that we, their latter-day interpreters, might ask of them. The first piece, a chapter from the classic book by Edgar Wind that gives the section as a whole its title, draws attention to the frequency with which Renaissance paintings were structured through principles of counterposition. Opening with a suggestion about the ways that patrons of sixteenth-century paintings might find a kind of surrogate within the pictures they commissioned, Wind argues that one widespread genre of sixteenth-century images, a genre keyed to pairings of ancient Roman characters, conveyed a new conception of virtue, one that turned on the harmonizing of antithetical impulses. Wind's emphasis on the theme of "reconciliation" brings out the period's preoccupation with the dynamics of aesthetic harmony, union, and moderation – a preoccupation inspired by ancient literature and conveyed through renewed versions of ancient forms.

Methodologically, Wind's piece also exemplifies its author's inimitable facility in moving from the particular to the general, from content to form, from the classical to the early modern world. The ostensible advantage to making his case in the broad strokes he does is that his arguments thereby extend beyond the evidence he happens to cite; the *kind* of interpretation Wind illustrates might be undertaken for any number of pictures that he himself does not consider. As such, however, Wind's essay also provides illuminating counterpoint to both the approach and the argument of the final piece in the section, Robert Gaston's "Love's Sweet Poison." Gaston begins by challenging some of the premises that earlier writers like Wind often took for granted: that the "Renaissance" was a unified phenomenon, making it reasonable to compare evidence from different geographical centers, even where contacts between them were not clear; that "pagan" ideas were unproblematically accessible, regardless of the presence of texts in any particular place and of the relevant actors' command of the languages in which they were written; or that motifs of classical origin need really, by the Late Renaissance, be treated as distant in any meaningful way, when, in many cases, they had by this time been fully assimilated into current vernacular poetics. Imposing on himself a set of stringent ground rules, Gaston offers a brilliant reading of one picture, a reading that, like Wind's, relates the literary to the visual, and content to style, but does so by examining in the first place the cultural milieu out of which its artist came, and the likely viewers for which it was made. In the process, he points to ways that painterly style could reflect the concerns of contemporary poetic discourses, and to how a widely shared visual language could be used to pursue distinctly local concerns.

1

Raphael's Tomb

Tilmann Buddensieg

Qual tomba!
Francesco Gasperoni 1837

Probably no other artist's death was as deeply mourned and lamented as that, on April 6, 1520, of the 37-year-old Raphael. His corpse was bewailed *con universal dolore de tutti et maximamente de li docti*.[1] For days, Rome spoke of nothing else. There was not an artist in Rome who failed to shed tears at his coffin; even Leo X wept with *ismisurato dolore*.[2]

From various first-hand accounts, we are familiar with the arrangements Raphael made, in view of his death, for his tomb and for his very considerable estate.[3] He divided his worldly possessions among his pupils and his relatives. He made it the responsibility of his students, with funds specifically reserved for the purpose, to restore one of the ancient tabernacles in the Pantheon, to erect an altar in it, to place a marble statue of the Madonna above this, and to lay his body there to rest, under the statue and behind the altar.[4] Raphael was not, that is, buried in the altar, nor in front of it or below it, but inside the pedestal of the statue of the Madonna that the altar itself hid (fig. 1.1). For the maintenance of the *capella* and for the reading of masses, Raphael allocated the hefty sum of 1000 ducats, and on top of this, the income from a house he bequeathed to the church of Santa Maria ad Martyres, the Pantheon.[5]

After the death of the master, his students went about executing his will. To judge from an overlooked remark by Pirro Ligorio, it would seem that Baldassare Peruzzi directed the construction of the tabernacle.[6] The main task, the execution of an over life-size sculpture of the Madonna, fell to Raphael's student and friend, the brother-in-law of Giulio Romano, Lorenzo Lotti, called Lorenzetto.[7] Until Raphael's death, Lorenzetto had worked under Raphael's supervision on the sculptural decoration for the funerary chapel of Agostino Chigi in Santa Maria del Popolo.

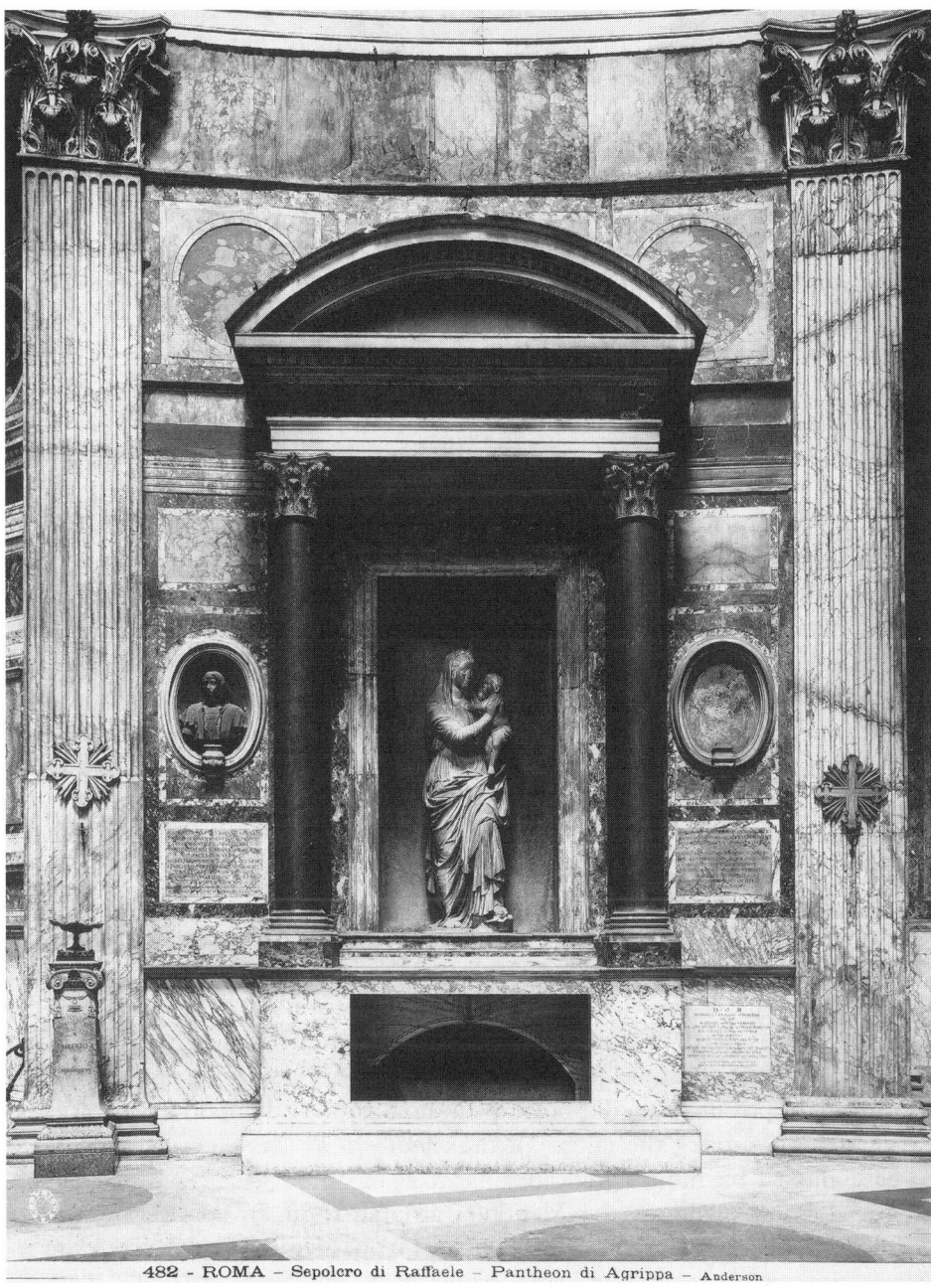

482 - ROMA – Sepolcro di Raffaele – Pantheon di Agrippa – Anderson

Figure 1.1 Raphael's tomb, Pantheon, Rome. Archivio Anderson / Alinari Archives-Florence.

Surveying the comments about the shape Raphael's tomb took in the hands of his students between 1524 and 1525, one cannot fail to notice that its centerpiece, the *Madonna del Sasso*, has almost never met with undiluted approval from its viewers. Once the tomb's pernicious 1911 restoration, in striking contrast to Raphael's wishes, exposed a sarcophagus that he did not want, and once the candles and votive offerings before the Madonna, formerly one of the most venerated in Rome, were cleared away, the *Madonna del Sasso* seemed to withdraw into the shadow of the tabernacle.[8] It is no longer a cult image, the altar has been destroyed, and Raphael's coffin has been untethered from its material connection with the statue, torn away from the concealment that Raphael had expressly desired.

In the modern art-historical literature, Lorenzetto's work has found little appreciation. The Florentine youths of the Cinquecento are more popular than the richly draped Roman matron. Quâtremère de Quincy and Carlo Fea, in 1820 and 1822, called the statue *goffa*.[9] Passavant, in 1839, perceived in the figure the lofty qualities of the artistic flowering of the first half of the sixteenth century, but also found it lacking in original invention and skillful execution.[10] Ernst Platner, in his 1840 description of Rome, wrote that the work was much weaker than Lorenzetto's *Jonas* in the Chigi Chapel.[11] Compared to this, Jacob Burckhardt's judgment seems more carefully weighed. In the first edition of his *Cicerone*, in 1855, he likewise praised the *Jonas* but added that "the prophet *Elijah*, by contrast, reveals Lorenzetto's duller execution, as does the Madonna statue, thought to be rather beautiful, on the altar in the Pantheon that hides Raphael's tomb." Burckhardt, that is, took there to be a gap between the statue's worthy design and "dull execution." With the publication of the fifth edition of the *Cicerone*, Wilhelm von Bode's appraisal of the statue came to the fore: he held it to be "no better than the spiritless *Elias*."[12] Eugène Müntz at least granted the work *un certain charme*; the drapery *ne manque pas de style*.[13] John Pope-Hennessy, in his 1965 book on the sculpture of the high Renaissance, did not deem the work worthy of a single word.[14]

Now, there is hardly a building, statue, or picture in Rome that is so trivial that some viewer, at some point, for reasons of art theory, art history, local patriotism, or private taste, did not explain how good and important it was. The two exceptions among the judges of the *Madonna del Sasso*, nevertheless, have to be granted a bit more significance.

Pirro Ligorio mentions the Madonna around 1560, in connection with a detailed consideration of the Pantheon, in his massive work, the *Antichità di Roma*, now preserved in the state archive in Turin.[15] He provides a fleeting sketch of the statue in the tabernacle, and in his description calls it the *bella figura di marmo della Santissima Vergine*. This word, *bella*, does not seem to me to be an arbitrary judgment of taste; rather, it appears to hold documentary value, for it comes from a man who, despite his slight and infelicitous talent, must in some respects be considered the heir to Raphael – at least, by way of Peruzzi, as a student-descendent of the Urbinate he so glowingly praises. In this wholly unpolemical appraisal of Lorenzetto's statue, expressed by Ligorio as if it were self-evident, there may be preserved the opinion that was generally accepted among Raphael's students and in the generation after Raphael, the judgment that the sculpture, whatever else, was fitting within the framework Raphael had designed. The testimony from Ligorio can be placed alongside the generally laudatory *Vita* that Vasari dedicated to Lorenzetto, a biography that we cannot yet otherwise fill out, especially with regard to his activity as an architect. Like Ligorio, the painter Vasari appears to have esteemed the *Madonna del Sasso*, for he used it for his figure of *Religio* in the *Sala di cento giorno* in the Cancelleria.[16]

Two hundred years after Ligorio, Winckelmann discussed Lorenzetto's Madonna statue in a most remarkable manner. In his *Abhandlung von der Fähigkeit der Empfindung des Schönen in der Kunst*, which appeared in 1763, he contrasted the "perfect" Lorenzetto with the "deficient" Bernini. Bernini could only produce good drawing, without feeling, "which nature had denied him." He was skilled only at imitating beauty, not at discovering or creating it. Lorenzetto, however, was gifted with both "correct drawing and sensitivity, more than the other sculptors of modern times." Winckelmann then proceeded to place the *Madonna del Sasso*, a "perfect work," even above the *Jonas* of the Chigi Chapel, and he lamented that "it is not noticed by anybody." He names Lorenzetto's Madonna and the "even lesser known" *St. Anne*, also in the Pantheon, by the "worthy" Lorenzo Ottone, as "two of the best modern statues."[17] Winckelmann and Ligorio clearly both admired in Lorenzetto's statue that dominant element of the antique that led viewers of the last 100 years to condemn it for lack of fantasy, for a "spiritless" cold classicism.

Given such differences of opinion, a renewed study of Lorenzetto's sculpture seems necessary, in the first place because the question of whether his work is very good, less good, or bad distracts us from Raphael's tomb as a whole, and from the problem of the *Madonna del Sasso* as a Raphael commission. Why was it precisely this form of Madonna that seemed, to the collaborating Raphael pupils Giulio Romano, Penni, Peruzzi, and Lorenzetto, to be the fitting fulfillment of the master's commission? Can we condemn the result, as has the entirety of the modern scholarship – overhastily, it seems to me – as an artistic failure?

Lorenzetto's statue is an astonishingly faithful replica of an ancient statue of Venus in the Vatican, one that today appears as a nymph, with restored arms, with an ancient head that does not belong to it, and with the addition of a partially antique boy Bacchus (fig. 1.2).[18] It is a clothed version of the Aphrodite of Melos – a figure that has best come down to us in the so-called Madrid Venus – with one curious feature that distinguishes it from the large number of variants, the doubled girdle around the hips and under the breast. Not only the composition as a whole, but also the ancient Venus's rich drapery, fold for fold, went into Lorenzetto's Madonna.

[…]

Lorenzetto's statue is not a more or less accurate, more or less veiled or secret adaptation of an ancient statue. The *Madonna del Sasso* must be seen as a

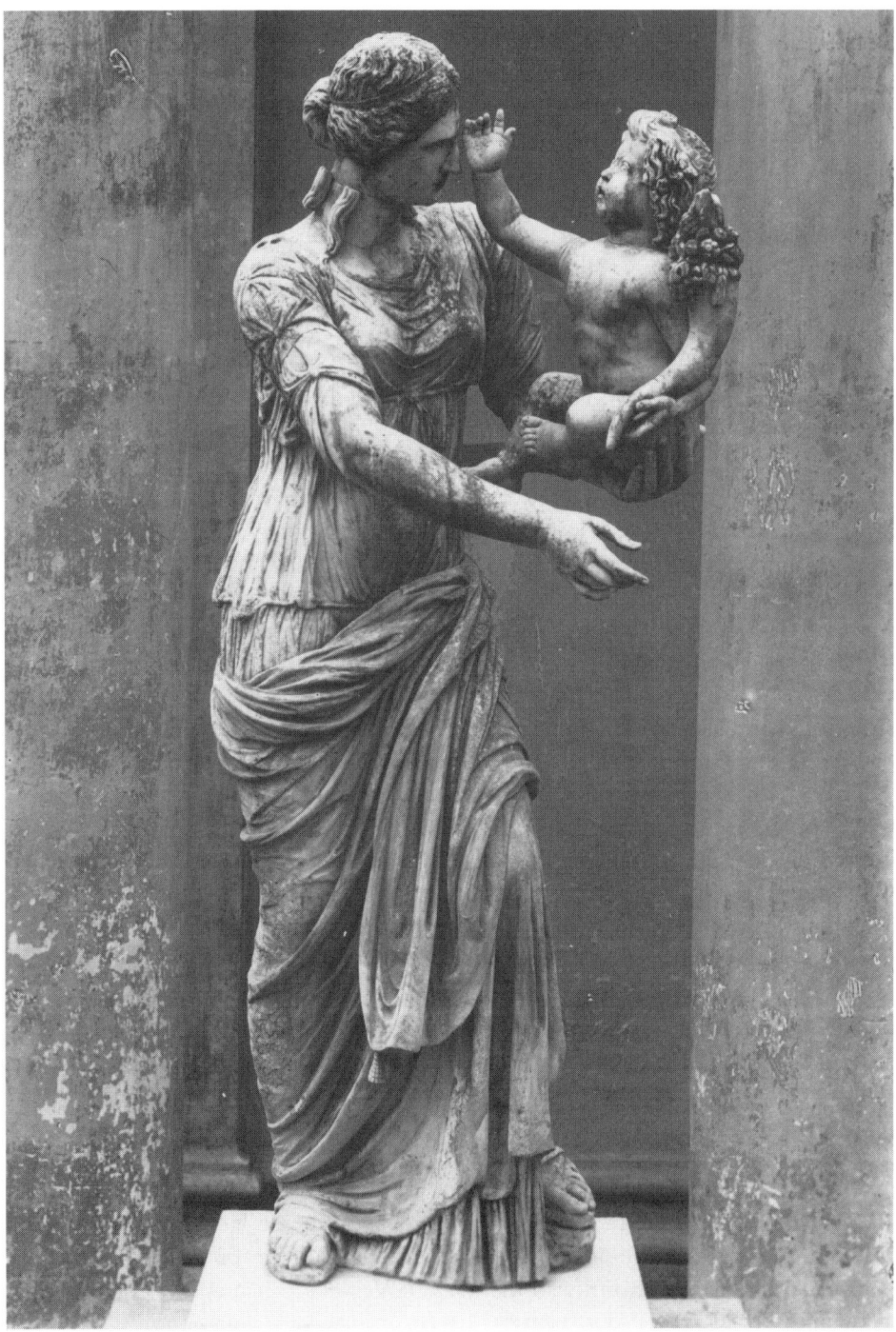

Figure 1.2 Statue of Nymph, Vatican, Cortile della Pigna. Deutsches Archäologisches Institut, Rome.

conscious and undisguised reproduction of an ancient statue, in the same material, at roughly the same size, and with a minimum of personal *maniera*. Its deviations from the ancient model do not serve to cancel out this model from Lorenzetto's work, but rather represent that minimum of change that enabled perhaps for the first time the balancing of example and imitation, of ancient and Renaissance statue. Even the head of the Madonna bears the features of an ancient, at present not yet identifiable female portrait, and the Christ child is individualized as little as possible.

It is worth emphasizing that this circumstance, the copying of a nearly life-size ancient sculpture as a very prominent Christian statue in a church (i.e. not on the roof of a palace or in a park) in the same material and at approximately the same size, is, to my knowledge, without parallel before Lorenzetto. Such a state-ment may provoke objections, but it must in any event be conceded that the effect of the antique, say, in Reims, or with the Pisani, or with Antico, Riccio, or the Lombardi, is fundamentally different from that in Lorenzetto. With Lorenzetto, the moment of the veiling of the ancient model, a model trans-formed and used only for inspiration, is missing, as is the intention of simulating an authentic antiquity.[19] Lorenzetto's artistic pioneering results in a quite per-sonal accomplishment, that of keeping the ancient sculpture of a goddess visible in the image of the Mother of God.[20] Is it possible to explain the premises of this creation with what has been said up to now?

The conclusion that Lorenzetto, for lack of inspiration, sought refuge in an ancient model seems impermissible to me. The fact that in other works he showed himself fully capable of creating his own designs speaks against this. It would, furthermore, have been easy for, say, Giulio Romano to help his brother-in-law with a drawing, had he thought this necessary. One should rather assume that Lorenzetto and the other Raphael students were of the opinion that the unusual merging of the statue of an ancient goddess with the image of the Mother of God was appropriate to Raphael's commission. Raphael must have demanded a *Madonna all'antica* from Lorenzetto. Perhaps Raphael even illus-trated his wishes for the design of his tomb with a sketch of the Madonna.

To this point, we have not explained Raphael's extraordinary wish to be buried in the Pantheon, nor have we commented on the form of Raphael's sepulcher within the conservative history of the Renaissance tomb.

When Raphael died, he was the master builder responsible for St. Peter's, the successor to his promoter, Bramante, in the office. What would have been more obvious than to be laid to rest, like Bramante, in the basilica, close to the papal palace that held his most important paintings? The Pantheon, before Raphael, had never been a preferred burial place for anyone but the canons of the Rotonda.[21]

The tomb's design ultimately adds to the existing complex only a statue of the Madonna, an altar, a distich, and an epitaph. The rich figural and decorative ornamentation common on prominent Renaissance tombs has been omitted. We find neither an allegory of fame, immortality, or redemption – which are at hand in the presence of the Virgin – nor a pictorially expounded biography of the deceased, nor pictures or emblems of sorrow and transience.[22] Raphael's arrangements apparently averted his students from any allegorizing, monumental glorification of his person and his fame, from anything like what Michelangelo's disciples celebrated on the catafalque reconstructed by Wittkower.[23] One might counter that an artist, even the most acclaimed artist, was not entitled, as spiritual and worldly dignitaries were, to elaborate tomb decorations. The Pope's highly unusual permission for Raphael to erect his tomb in the Pantheon, though, means that Raphael would have been given a certain amount of freedom with its figural program. Finally, Raphael had formulated his critique of the traditional, highly figured Renaissance sepulcher – and with this, surely, also his critique of Michelangelo's project for Julius II – in the extremely sober Chigi tomb; the criticism was directed not only at the formal and figural arrangements of these works, but also at their endless production process.

The conjunction of niche, statue, altar, inscription, and tabernacle, which was already offered by the Roman Rotunda, was proper to it; these were not imposed foreign bodies. The elements of Raphael's tomb are found in ancient burial constructions: suffice here a reference to a drawing made by Bramantino around 1500 of an ancient tomb near S. Sebastiano in Rome, where one sees, in a tabernacle, a tomb altar with an inscribed tablet and, immediately above it, a statue in a rectangular niche.[24] Raphael's plan for his tomb focused exclusively on inserting the tomb into the existing setting. His commission to his students avoided all elements alien to the ancient building. The *Madonna del Sasso* appears in the form of an ancient goddess, and it thus accommodates itself to the ancient niche. From this point of view, one should take Vasari's report about Raphael's commission quite literally. Vasari specifies that the builders "restored" a tabernacle of the Rotonda. "Restoration" is surely not only to be understood as the repair of the building's damaged parts.[25] The Madonna enters an empty niche of the Pantheon and does so, simultaneously, as an ancient goddess. One of the ancient tabernacles, which had stood empty since the year 609, was thereby restored; one of the wounds that early Christianity had inflicted on the pagan building was healed. The gods that had been chased out of the temple returned, transmuted, into the church, in the form of a cult image of the Mother of God.

In the year 609, the pagan temple had been converted by Pope Boniface IV into a church; from a house of the Devil was made first a church consecrated to all saints and then one dedicated to the Madonna.[26] For medieval chroniclers after Bede and for visiting pilgrims, the splendor of the ancient sculptural decorations turned into a host of devils and demons, which, at the moment the church was dedicated, fled through the hole that opened in the vault.[27] There is no more telling illustration of this medieval notion of the Pantheon as the *Templum omnium idolum* than the oldest representation of the building known to me, in the Apocalypse commentary in Cambridge by the Minorite Alexander from the middle of the thirteenth century.[28] It shows the moment when the pagan temple was rededicated as a Christian church by Boniface IV. While the pope swings his holy water baton and raises his left hand, the deacon next to him, the *Romani stantes et factum respicientes* and the *Imperator Focas*, with his companion outside the building, all look in amazement at two devils who slip out of tabernacles and seek to flee through the opening, which itself looks like damage done to the circle and quatrefoil. Given that his means of representation remain so thoroughly within the realm of the medieval imagination, the painter's art must be admired here, for he is able to illustrate, in perfect Gothic style, the circle, the quatrefoil, the tabernacles, the opening, and the foyer: all of the main features of the building.

Petrarch brought about a fundamental change in the understanding of the Pantheon, one that could be described as a reconciliation with the pagan building that the church of Santa Maria ad Martyres had subjugated. In his late work, the 1366 "De remediis utriusque fortunae," Petrarch mentions the Pantheon in a memorable manner. While the ruins of the famous buildings of ancient Rome appear to him as *exempla* of the vanity of all human accomplishment, he nevertheless praises the Madonna because she, through the marvelous power of her sacred name, preserved the venerable Pantheon as the single famous intact building of Antiquity.[29] Behind the poetic image of the building saved by the Madonna lies a feeling of wonder at the preservation of the huge ancient edifice – a feeling that, so far as we know, was alien to the medieval encounter with the Pantheon, but which, after Petrarch, would become a universally accepted judgment to the Renaissance and to Modernity.

Around the same time, a student of Petrarch, Fazio degli Uberti, even outstrips his master. In his "Dittamondo," Fazio celebrates the Mother of God's succession to the presumed ancient mistress of the Pantheon, the gods' mother Cybele, as a harmonious *translatio* of power. His play on words with the pagan "gods' mother" and the Christian "mother of God" conceptualizes a concord between paganism and Christianity like the one that would later be seen in Lorenzetto's Madonna, above Raphael's tomb.[30]

The Roman and Florentine humanists began to lament the circumstances that led to the early Christians' destruction of ancient statues.[31] The early Christian image of the Madonna was cut down to a small panel, submerged under numerous repaintings, and surrounded by a bright Cosmatesque tabernacle.[32] Beginning with Flavio Biondo, antiquarians examined the ancient texts for information about which statues could have stood in the empty niches, then decorated with bad paintings. Probably in 1513, Domenico de Clarellis, called Menichantonio, an architect from the Bramante circle, drew the interior of the Pantheon.[33] As if obvious, he filled the empty niches with ancient sculptures. The medieval history of the Pantheon was erased. With his tomb, Raphael completed this thought. The *Madonna del Sasso* appears in the image of an ancient statue. The early Christian icon is as foreign to this classicizing Madonna as it is to the statues of the gods it displaced.

Lorenzetto's works do not show the pallor of the Antiquarian, because Raphael did not trouble himself with an archaeological reconstruction of the building's ancient condition. The statue above his tomb is simultaneously an ancient goddess and one of the most venerated cult images of the Madonna in Rome, the statue's tabernacle simultaneously a *capella* in front of which masses for the soul were to be read. Christian church and ancient temple merge with one another: the medieval dominance and prepotency of the church over the temple vanishes, the classicisizing detachment of the temple from the church is avoided. This vivid synthesis is one of the most moving achievements of that short epoch that Wölfflin called "classic art." With Raphael's death, seven years before the sack of Rome, this epoch had already come to an end.

How completely Raphael's thoughts could be misunderstood and indeed destroyed is demonstrated by the restoration of the tomb that Muñoz oversaw in 1911.[34] The *Madonna del Sasso* was extracted from its cult context, a sarcophagus that was not even part of the original construction was brought into the open and the altar was destroyed. This created a hybrid of tomb and monument, and it spurred an aesthetic beatification of Raphael of a sort that had scared off the classicism prevailing at the elevation of his bones in 1833. While Raphael had declined any reference to his person, and while his friends had added just his name in an inscription, the Baroque first intervened in the original composition of the tomb, when Maratta had a portrait bust inserted to the left of the tabernacle in 1674. Bellori describes clearly the motivation for this: almost 150 years had passed without the visitors who had come to the tomb to pray for Raphael's salvation and to honor his memory being able to take consolation by looking at his picture. One visited the tomb *per pregarli requie e venerare la sua memoria.*[35]

Nothing about this character of Raphael's tomb changed in 1833 either. All that was erected was a powerful, temporary catafalque after a sketch by Pietro Camporese the Younger, and it was decided, after some discussion, to return things to their original condition.[36] Today Raphael's tomb is broken into two parts; of these, at least the sarcophagus, with incidental organ and choir music, will remain a tourist attraction.

[. . .]

Raphael's unimaginably rich activities in his last years included not only the Chigi Chapel, the rebuilding of St. Peter's, the completion of the Stanze, the Loggie, the Loggetta, the Farnesina frescoes and numerous panels, but also Leo X's commission for a painted and drawn reconstruction of ancient Rome. Nothing from this enormous undertaking has come down to us; we know about it only from Raphael's letter to Leo X and from the testimony of Raphael's friends and contemporaries. After Raphael's death, these witnesses did not so much lament the interruption of work on St. Peter's, on the Stanze, on the *Transfiguration* or other undertakings. Such things could be completed by his pupils or continued by successors. What they unanimously regarded as the greatest and most irredeemable cultural loss was that Raphael could no longer carry out this reconstruction of ancient Rome.[37]

The observations assembled above allow us to see only in a general way the previously unappreciated extent to which such an image of *Roma antica* might have driven Raphael to realize his architectural works on paper. His drawing in the Uffizi of the interior of the Pantheon, however, offers the most unmediated impression of his concrete work on the project.[38] Here, for the first time, after a century of labors by earlier draftsmen, we find the architectonic space of a historical building drawn in such a way that the observer supposes himself to be standing inside the structure. The number of copies made after this drawing testifies to the admiration contemporaries had for the accomplishment. Two closely related drawings in Vienna[39] and Kassel[40] of the interior of the Pantheon, to judge from their pictorial and spatial composition, originated in Raphael's ambit. These may document the work of Raphael's collaborators on the Master Plan of Rome.

In Raphael's Pantheon drawing, we can still feel what the Venetian Marcantonio Michiel wrote from Rome to Marsilio in Venice five days after Raphael's death: Raphael had begun a plan of ancient Rome that was so extraordinary that everyone who saw it supposed himself to be standing in *Roma antica*. The city's cadaver had been brought back to life.

With his tomb, Raphael wanted to do in and for the Pantheon what Castiglione, in his epigram on the death of his friend, set into verse:

> *Te dudum extinctis reddere posse animam.*
> [You were able to bring the dead back to life.]

As Wilhelm Heinse wrote in a letter to Gleim, "Raphael's beauty lay more in his mind than in his colors." Accordingly, we should understand Raphael's tomb as his last work.

Notes

I presented the findings of this essay in preliminary form in my inaugural lecture, on November 10, 1965, at the Freie Universität in Berlin, at a session at the Bibliotheca Hertziana in Rome, at the Art Historians' Club at Harvard University, and at New York University's Institute of Fine Arts. I owe thanks for many leads to the possibility I had of working in the Hertziana, and to discussions there. Carlo Bertelli was especially helpful to me in making new photos of the *Madonna del Sasso*.

1 Letter from Marcantonio Michiel to Antonio Marsilio in Venice, 11 April 1520, in Jacopo Morelli, *Notizia d'opere di disegno, da un Anonimo* (Bassano, 1800), 210 n. 128; published also by P. E. Visconti, *Notizie risguardanti il testamento di Raffaello, il luogo della sua sepoltura e la Maria Bibiena a lui fidanzata* – a very rich study, which appeared together with the most important source on the opening of the tomb on 14 September 1833: Pietro Odescalchi, *Istoria del ritrovamento delle spoglie mortali di Raffaello Sanzio* (Rome, 1836), 146ff. J. D. Passavant, *Rafael von*

    Urbino und sein Vater Giovanni Santi, vol. 1 (Leipzig, 1839), 321ff. and (Paris, 1860), 281ff. Vincenzo Golzio, *Raffaello nei documenti, nelle testimonianze dei contemporanei e nella letteratura del suo secolo* (Vatican City, 1936), 120ff. (cited in what follows as "Golzio").

2   Same letter, loc. cit.; see also Golzio, 115 and 230 for Vasari's testimony.

3   The text of Raphael's orally recorded will is published in Visconti, 91ff., Passavant 1860, 278ff. and 368ff., Golzio, 116ff.; see also Vasari, *Vite*, ed. Milanesi, vol. IV, 382 and 579, and Golzio, 229ff.

4   Golzio, 154ff., publishes the "supplica di Baldassare da Pescia, esecutore testamentario di Raffaello a Clemente VII," from 20 November 1520: ". . . in ecclesia beate Marie rotunde de Urbe, in qua sepulturam eligerat (sic), unam capellam et sibi sepulturam fieri et fabricari voluit et mandavit." Letter from Pandolfo Pico in Rome to the Duchess of Mantua, from 7 April 1520, in Golzio, 114ff.: "Detto Raphaello honoratissimamente e stato sepulto a la Rothunda ove lui ha ordinate chel se ghe fazi a sua memoria una sepoltura da mille ducati et altri ha lassato per dottare la capella ove sarà detta sepoltura." Vasari's testimony is the most elaborate; *Vita*, ed. Golzio, 229ff.: "Per che fece testamento; e prima, come cristiano, mandò l'amata sua fuor di casa e le lasciò modo di vivere onestamente; dopo divise le cose sue fra' discepoli suoi, Giulio Romano, il quale sempre amò molto, Giovanni Francesco Fiorentino detto il Fattore, ed un non so chi prete da Urbino suo parente. Ordinò poi che delle sue facultà in Santa Maria Ritonda si restaurasse un tabernacolo di quegli antichi di pietre nuove, ed un altare si facesse con una statue di Nostra Donna di marmo; la quale per sua sepoltura e riposo dopo la morte s'elesse; e lasciò ogni suo avere a Giulio e Giovan Francesco, facendo esecutore del testamento messer Baldassare da Pescia, allora datario del papa."

5   Cf. the letter from Pandolfo Pico, cited in n. 4.

6   Pirro Ligorio, "Antichita di Roma," Turin, State Archive, Cod. I a. III. 15 (vol. 13), fol. 48v: "Et uno d'essi (that is, one of the interior tabernacles) sendo stato ristaurato da M. Baldassar Peruzzo Architetto senese, et da Raphael d'Urbino pittore miracoloso in natura, è stata cagione si fatta rinovatione, che alcune altri hanno fatto il simile, e nelli Fianchi dell'Altare prima ristaurato, dove è la Bella Figura di Marmo della santissima Vergine col figliuolo in braccio Bambino, sono le intitulationi delli sudetti ristauratori quivi appiedi sepulti di Raphael et di Baldassar." On Ligorio's Pantheon studies, see now the exhaustive essay by Howard Burns, "A Peruzzi Drawing in Ferrara," *Mitteilungen des kunsthistorischen Institutes in Florenz* 12 (1966), 246ff. and esp. 260ff. See also Lanciani, *Storia di Scavi* II, 237.

7   Vasari, *Vite*, ed. Milanesi, IV, 579; Golzio, 239: "Dovendosi poi esseguire il testamento di Raffaello, gli (i.e., Lorenzetto) fu fatto fare una statua di marmo alta quattro braccia d'una Nostra Donna per lo sepolcro di esso Raffaello nel tempio di Santa Maria Ritonda, dove per ordine suo fu restaurato qual tabernacolo." On Lorenzetto, cf. F. Schottmüller's 1929 article in Thieme and Becker's *Künstlerlexikon*; Adolfo Venturi, *Storia dell'arte italiana* 10 (1935), 312ff. An encomiastic but not very productive discussion of the statue can also be found in Carlo Astolfi, *Raffaello Sanzio Scultore* (Rome, 1935), 29ff. (also in *Rassegna Marchigiana* 12 [1934], 315ff.). For an overview, see now John Pope-Hennessy, *Italian High Renaissance and Baroque Sculpture* (London, 1963), text volume, 43ff. (with no mention of the *Madonna del Sasso*). New material is in Michael Hirst, "The Chigi Chapel in

S. Maria della Pace," *Journal of the Warburg and Courtauld Institutes* 24 (1961), 275ff. The height of the statue is 2.77 m.

8   See Golzio, 121, and Antonio Muñoz, *La tomba di Raffaello nel Pantheon* (Rome, 1920).

9   Quâtremère de Quincy, *Istoria della vita e delle opere di Raffaello Sanzio* (Milan, 1829; first edition Paris, 1820), 287. Carlo Fea, *Notizie intorno Raffaele Sanzio da Urbino* (Rome, 1822), 6.

10 Passavant (Paris, 1860), 533.

11 E. Platner, C. Bunsen et al., *Beschreibung der Stadt Rom*, vol. 3 (Stuttgart and Tübingen, 1842), 355.

12 Jacob Burckhardt, *Der Cicerone* (Basel, 1855), 642 (reprint of the first ed. Stuttgart, 1953, 607). Bode's judgment in the 10th edition (Leipzig, 1910), 555.

13 Eugène Müntz, *Histoire de l'art pendant la Renaissance*, vol. 3 (Paris, 1895), 434.

14 J. Pope-Hennessy, op. cit. (cf. n. 7).

15 Cf. n. 6.

16 Most recently, Armando Schiavo, *Il palazzo della Cancelleria* (Rome, n.d.), plates 16, 18.

17 J. J. Winckelmann, *Abhandlung von der Fähigkeit der Empfindung des Schönen in der Kunst, und dem Unterrichte in derselben* (Dresden, 1763), in *Winckelmanns Werke*, ed. C. L. Fernow, vol. 2 (Dresden, 1808), 394ff. Italian ed., ed. Carlo Fea, vol. 6 (Prato, 1831), 539ff.

18 The statue stands today in the portico of the Braccio Nuovo, on the southern side of the Giardino della Pigna. Here, too, I would like to thank Frau Dr. Speier for her help in locating the statue. The oldest illustration of the statue is that in the Codex Escurialensis, ed. H. Egger (Vienna, 1906), fol. 31, 94ff. A. Michaelis recognized the Venus statue in the Nike drawn there. On de Cavealleriis's engraving, see Johannes Baptista de Cavealleriis, *Antiquae Statuae urbis Romae* (Rome, 1561/62), plate 35, ed. 1584/85, plate 44, and on this, Thomas Ashby, "Antiquae Statuae Urbis Romae," *Papers of the British School in Rome* 9 (1920), 106ff., esp. 147, as well as Hülsen, *Antikengärten*, no. 109. The statue also appears (without mention in the text) in Erasmo Pistolesi, *Il Vaticano descritto ed illustrato*, vol. 4 (Rome, 1829), plate LVII. Having been moved frequently in the 19th and 20th centuries, the statue, so far as I can see, has not appeared in any of the Vatican catalogues. See also A. Reinach, *Répertoire de la Statuaire*, vol. 2 (Paris, 1897), 338, and E. Ravaisson, "Vénus de Milo," *Mémoires de l'Académie des Inscriptions et Belles-Lettres* 34 (1892), 72, plate 6, 2. The height of the statue is 2.05 m. Cf. the measurements of the *Madonna del Sasso*, n. 7.

19 A discussion of the problem of the copy and its different possibilities and limits can be found in Heinz Ladendorf, *Antikenstudium und Antikenkopie* (Berlin, 1953), 62ff., without reference to Lorenzetto.

20 Matthias Winner is wholly correct in referring me to Dürer's equation of Apollo with Christ, Venus with Mary, and Hercules with Samson, which the artist voiced when sketching the introduction to his *Lehrbuch der Malerei*: "Thus, in the same way that they (that is, the artists of Antiquity) allotted the most beautiful human form to their idol Abblo, do we want to use the same measurement for Christ, the man who was the most beautiful in all the world. And as they used Venus as the most beautiful women, so do we want chastely to set forth the same delicate form

in the purest Virgin Mary, the Mother of God. And out of Samson, we want to make Hercules, and to do the same with all the others. See K. Lange and F. Fuhse, *Dürers schriftlicher Nachlass* (Halle, 1893), 316; Hans Rupprich, *Dürer, Schriftlicher Nachlass*, vol. 2 (Berlin, 1966), 104.

21 The tomb inscriptions are in Vincenzo Forcella, *Iscrizioni delle Chiese e d'altri edificii di Roma*, vol. 1 (Rome, 1873), 287ff., and Giovanni Eroli, *Raccolta generale delle Iscrizioni pagane e cristiane etc. nel Pantheon di Roma* (Narni, 1895), 415ff.

22 Erwin Panofsky, *Grabmalplastik* (Cologne, 1964), esp. 74ff. Also André Chastel, "La glorification humaniste dans les monuments funéraires de la Renaissance," in *Umanesimo e Scienza politica. Atti del Congresso internaz. di Studi umanistici 1949* (Milan, 1951), 477ff.

23 Rudolf and Margot Wittkower, *The Divine Michelangelo* (London, 1964), fig. 8, 9, and the reconstruction on p. 148. See also Hans Ost, "Ein Ruhmesblatt für Raphael bei Maratti und Mengs," *Zeitschrift für Kunstgeschichte* 28 (1965): 288ff.

24 Giuseppe Mongeri, *Le rovine di Roma, Studi del Bramantino* (Milan, 1880), plate 3.

25 Here it should be noted that Ligorio names Raphael and Peruzzi as the two *ristauratori* of the Pantheon. See n. 6.

26 In what follows, I depend on my unpublished *Habilitationsschrift*, "Studien zum Nachleben antiker Architektur und Skulptur in Rom," Berlin, 1965. Cf. above all the short synopsis of the first chapter in the *Sitzungsberichten der kunstgeschichtlichen Gesellschaft zu Berlin* 13 (1964/65), 3ff. ("Das Pantheon in der Renaissance").

27 In the *Kaiserchronik* from ca. 1150, ed. E. Schröder, MGH, D. Chron. I (1892), it says that, with Bonface IV, "dem wâren gote gemahelte er daz hûs, / die Tievel brâsten oben uz, / sumelîche in daz abgrunde. / des ist ze Rôme noch hiute urchunde." Hermann von Fritzlar depicted the reconsecration of the Pantheon still more drastically in his 1343–49 Lives of the Saints: "Dô vorstôrete der bâbist di apgote. Der wâren zwêne und sibentzic, und di tûvele furen ûz den bilden, und der Rômer apgot, der tûvel, nam den tynaphel obene von der Kirchen, der ist von erze gegozzen un ist kunstic heidenisch werc und ist wol alsô grôz alsô ein bakoven. Disen furte her vor sente Pêters munster, dâ her noch hûte dises tages stêt, und daz loch an der Kirchen, dô der tynaphel ûffe stunt, daz stêt noch offen, unde enmac nimant vorbûwen. Wanne die Kirche ist gar grôz und enhât nirgen kein sule in ir." Franz Pfeiffer, *Deutsche Mystiker des 14. Jahrhunderts*, vol. 1 (Leipzig, 1845), xiv, text pp. 230ff. This text includes a remarkable and extremely rare medieval description of an ancient building from the perspective of Gothic architecture. Compare this story with the representation of the Pantheon, discussed here, by the Minorite Alexander.

28 Cambridge, University Library, MS. Mm V 31, fol. 74, North German, after the middle of the 13th century. See M. Huggler, "Der Bilderkreis in den Handschriften der Alexander-Apocalypse," *Antonianum* 9 (1934), 85ff., 269ff. (without illustrations of the Pantheon scene), and Alois Wachtel, "Alexander Minorita, Expositio in Apocalypsim," MGH, *Quellen zur Geistesgeschichte des Mittelalters*, vol. 1 (Weimar, 1955), xiv ff. and 257. I owe thanks to Christian Klamt for the reference to this manuscript.

29 De remediis I, 118, *Opera Omnia* (Basel, 1554), 42: "Nec vero solum templa Deorum quae paraverat, in ipsos aedificantes ruere, sed pia etiam loca hac ipsa aetate

in eadem urbe alia ceciderunt, alia tremuerunt, et nunc vix ponderibus suis stant, praeter unum Pantheon Agrippae, quod diis erectum sancti possident, et Maria, quae antiquissimam illam domum sui nominis virtute sustentat. Crede mihi aliis quam lapideis fundamentis eget gloria ut mansura sit." See Prince d'Essling and Eugène Müntz, *Pétrarque, ses études d'art, son influence sur les artistes etc.* (Paris, 1902), 24ff.

30 Fazio degli Uberti, "Il Dittamondo," ed. G. Corsi, *Scrittori d'Italia* 206–7, (Bari, 1952), I, 104ff. (II, VI, 52ff.): "Il Pantheon dentro dal grembo mio / allor fu fatto in nome d'una dia / la qual si disse madre d'ogni dio. / Di questa cosi bella profezia / non m'accorsi io allora, ma or ne godo, / Ché veggio s'intese di Maria."

31 Tilmann Buddensieg, "Gregory the Great, the Destroyer of Pagan Idols etc." *Journal of the Warburg and Courtauld Institutes* 28 (1965), 44ff.

32 Carlo Bertelli, "La Madonna del Pantheon," *Bollettino d'Arte* 46 (1961), 24ff. Antonio Muñoz, "La decorazione medioevale del Pantheon," *Nuovo Bullettino di Archeologia Cristiana* 18 (1912), 25ff., plate vi.

33 Sketchbook in the Mellon Collection, Washington, fol. 33. Hans Nachod, "A Recently Discovered Architectural Sketchbook etc.," *Rare Books*, published for the Friends and Clients of H. P. Kraus, New York, VIII, June 1955, 1, fig. 1.

34 Antonio Muñuz, *La tomba di Raffaello nel Pantheon* (Rome, 1920). The reconfiguration of the tomb seems immediately to have provoked criticism; cf. Muñoz, 29: "Qualche anima pia espresse i suoi dubii sulla convenienza di esporre sotto un altare il corpo di un personaggio, degnissimo si di venerazione, ma non santificato dalla Chiesa. Ma è bene ricordare che ciò fu fatto col pieno consentimento delle autorità ecclesiastiche." Cf. also Golzio, 120f.

35 Giovanni Pietro Bellori, *Descrizzione delle imagini dipinte da Raffaelle d'Urbino etc.* (Rome, 1695), 102: "Ma era quasi compito il giro di cento cinquanta anni dalla morte di Raffaelle, senza che quelli, che visitavano il suo sepolcro per pregarli requie, e venerare la sua memoria, potessero consolar la vista con l'effigie dei quell venerabil volto, quando l'anno 1674 il Signor Carlo Maratti con animo grato, e generoso verso sì gran Maestro . . . e per sodisfare insieme al commune desiderio de gli studiosi di esso, fece il modello del suo ritratto cavato dalla scuola di Atene, scolpito dopo nel marmo per mano di Paolo Naldi sino al busto, e collocato in un nicchio al monumento in Santa Maria Rotonda." See also Hans Ost, "Ein Ruhmesblatt für Raffael bei Maratti und Mengs," in *Zeitschrift für Kunstgeschichte* 28 (1965), 281ff.

36 The catafalque is in Muñoz, op. cit., 17, illustrated 23; Camporese's words on his sketch are cited in n. 1. For a fuller discussion see Francesco Gasparone, *Sul ritrovamento delle obbliate Reliquie di Raffaelle Sanzio e sul progetto di funebre Catafalco ideato in quella occasione al Cav. Pietro Camporese Architetto* (Rome, 1837). Sarti, Canina and P. Anzani also made sketches; cf. Golzio, 121. Antonio Sarti's sketch, as Manfred F. Fischer alerted me, is preserved in the Cooper Union Museum in New York. The question of whether the sarcophagus containing Raphael's mortal remains should be left visible or should be re-enclosed was also discussed in 1833; see Pietro Odescalchi, op. cit. (n. 1), 58f. The founding of the Presidents of the Virtuosi del Pantheon, which led to the restoration of the Pantheon to its old condition, deserves to be cited briefly here, as it indicates a deep understanding of Raphael's tomb: "Piacque a Raffaello (e fu sublime l'idea) che la statua di Nostra

Donna del Sasso fosse parte principale del suo sepolcro, nè altro, da quella statua in fuori, ci mostrasse agli occhi de' riguardanti. Ora sarebbe cosa disconvenevole, per non dire irreligiosa, opporsi al volere di lui . . . Ad un sacro tabernacolo che invita a devozione e a preghiere per l'anima di quell grande [sarebbe surrogate] un luogo tutto profane: imperocchè il render sacra quella cella, divenuto unicamente sepolcrale, terrebbe all'idolatria. La beata Vergine . . . che Raffaello si elesse per suo sepolcro, quella che forma il vero e parlante coperchio della ossa di lui . . . sarebbe indecorosamente negata alla vista di coloro che visitassero l'urna . . . essendochè alle sole ossa de' santi condedasi sì fatto onore."

37 The most recent overview is Oskar Fischel, *Raphael* (Berlin, 1962), pp. 151ff. See the literature cited in note 1 for the texts.

38 Wolfgang Lotz, "Das Raumbild in der italienischen Architekturzeichnung der Renaissance," *Mitteilungen des Kunsthistorischen Institutes in Florenz* VII (1956), pp. 215ff., with references to the older literature. An extensive discussion of this and the following Pantheon drawings can be found in my *Habilitationsschrift*; see n. 26.

39 Hermann Egger, *Kritisches Verzeichnis der stadtrömischen Architekturzeichnungen* I, Vienna 1905, AH 7, attributed by him to a "Master C from 1515." The correct date of 1519 is given in my essay on the Constantinian basilica in the *Münchner Jahrbuch der bildenden Kunst* 15 (1962), 44, no. 11.

40 Unfortunately, heavy overdrawing and wash was added to the sheets by their later owner, the Dutch architect Pierre Jacques Roman (there is an entry in the codex from 1755). The Pantheon sheet is conceived in a similar way to that of the Viennese Master C and has been measured with the same rule (the Bolognese foot?). The Pantheon drawings in the Codex Coner (Ashby, plate 35, 56), along with those by Menichantonio, by Viennese Master C, and by the anonymous Kassel master, belong closely together and lead back to Raphael's Uffizi drawing. I take a woodcut exterior view of the Pantheon, which appeared in the *Epigrammata Antiquae Urbis* assembled in 1517 by Andrea Fulvio and published in 1521 by Mazochius, fol. 6v, to belong to the circle of Raphael. The perspectival distortion of the dome, the reduction of the porch to six columns, and the overly narrow Rotunda ought to be attributed to the woodcutter's indelicate cutting of the significant sketch. As has been frequently remarked (see Fischel, op. cit., p. 153), Andrea Fulvio mentions that Raphael often collaborated on his topographical studies.

2

St. Peter's as Ruins: On some *vedute* by Heemskerck

Christof Thoenes

Everyone who studies the building of New St. Peter's eventually develops feelings of gratitude towards Maerten van Heemskerck. Without Heemskerck and his *vedute*, and without those of his circle, the sixteenth-century history of the building could hardly be written. The same is not true, at least not to the same extent, for other contemporary building projects: we have a few individual sheets here and there, but only for St. Peter's is there – as there is for the great monuments of Antiquity – a complete and to a certain degree systematically built up series of drawn views.[1] One could understand this as a "homage to Bramante," the rediscoverer of the art of fine building, whose major Roman works were admitted to the ranks of classical exempla by Serlio and his predecessors. But the paradigm of the new style, the Tempietto of San Pietro in Montorio, which was studied and represented over and over again by architects, was not one of Heemskerck's subjects. And one must only see how he imagined the completed church of St. Peter's to recognize that his interests were not really in modern architecture, but much more in what was then the condition of the building, its part in a cityscape that – as his self-portrait in the Fitzwilliam Museum shows – presented itself to him fundamentally as a landscape of ruins. This was a topos in the description of Rome, one that involved criticism as much as admiration. "The modern things here are in a very sorry state," wrote Alberto degli Alberti, from Rome, to Giovanni de' Medici, "the things that have fallen to pieces are Rome's beauty"[2] – and in this, no city in the world was Rome's equal. This was roughly a century before Heemskerck, but there are, even today, plenty of places in the city where the truth in this sentence can still be appreciated.

Of course, the physiognomy of Rome had, over the course of the century, changed. The Mantuan plan from the end of the Quattrocento already shows Rome no longer to be a city of ruins, and emphasizes, above all, the buildings of the previous decades. The pontificates of Julius II and Leo X would bring new buildings that were much more magnificent yet. These go hand in hand with a new sense of the ruins, a sense of them not only as study objects for architects and topographers, but as parts of the city's image and as elements of Roman life. We owe to Raphael, in the background of the Attila fresco, one of the earliest and at the same time most profound pictorial paraphrases of the theme – profound insofar as the imagery reflects on threatening catastrophes, fires, and destruction, the ruins' historical causes. It is not coincidental that it is Raphael the architect who includes the ruins of an ancient tomb near the Piazza del Popolo as ruins in his city plan.[3]

It is not only the ruins of Antiquity that now shape the image of the city. Particularly with the end of Julius II's pontificate a new phenomenon comes to the fore: the "ruins of new building." All of the large undertakings of the pope's last years – St. Peter's and the Vatican Palace, the Palazzo dei Tribunali and S. Biaggio della Pagnotta, SS. Celso e Giuliano and many others – lay incomplete at his death, and some stayed that way forever. New projects, such as the Villa Madama, soon joined their company. These are not exceptional cases; indeed, one could demonstrate – I cannot do it here – that the fragmentary and the torso-like occupy a very conspicuous place in modern Roman building. This tends to be explained with reference to the rapid changes in the papacy and to the constant restructuring of economic and power relations that resulted from this. The monumental demands of patrons and architects, who competed with one another as well as with the ancient ruins, were raised to an extreme. If the ruins' gigantic size was felt to be an incentive and a moral duty,[4] though, so did their fragmentary condition – "ipsa ruina"[5] – teach that in architecture, at least in the view of posterity, having desired greatness counted for more than accomplishing it. In this way, the divergence of intention and capacity becomes a distinguishing feature of the Roman Renaissance.[6] "Architectural seams," cracks, edges breaking open testify everywhere to the reach and to the thwarting of ambitions.[7] Left aside by new planning, what was incomplete remained standing and survived the epoch, like the four bays of Pius II's loggia façade, which, into the seventeenth century, flanked the entrance to St. Peter's. Completed things, such as the gigantic niche of the Belvedere, appeared like a remnant from still more gigantic, broken-off structures. That which had been abandoned, or half destroyed, came to be accepted as a ruin, and was so incorporated, even in name – witness the "Ponte Rotto" – into the cityscape.[8] Ornamental motifs like rustication or the exploded pediment referred expressly to the impression of ruins.[9] Technical defects, too, most of them due to excessive haste in the execution of buildings, belong to this picture: the foundational buildings of the new style have a striking tendency – one that contemporaries already remarked – to break, as if they can't wait to reach the state of the classical ruin. James Ackerman has already assembled the witnesses for Bramante's "bad reputation" as an engineer;[10] we will soon return to the example of St. Peter's.

What unites old and new ruins is that the temporal dimension of building becomes visible. This is true not only with regard to the familiar ruin-themes of dilapidation and transience (which only really became topical again after the catastrophic experience of the Sack), but also with regard to the "growth" of architecture: becoming and passing away, construction and destruction appear as phases of a process in the views through the ruinous structures.[11] Thus, for the draftsman of the Coner Codex, no basic difference exists between a new construction *in statu nascendi* and an antique ruin. Cross-sections, such as those through rotundas, stood physically before one's eyes in the Roman world of rubble, and stimulated the development of analytical drawing methods. The argument can only be sketched here; one example is the representation of Bramante's never-completed rebuilding of SS. Celso e Giuliano, from the Mellon Codex, where the draftsman transforms the already completed corner chapel back into a sort of artful ruin so as to be able to present it in a cut-away view.

With all of this, it is no wonder that *vedutisti*, and history painters, too, drew no strict boundaries between the ancient and the modern world of ruins. Thus, Philipp Galle (after Heemskerck), sets the Adoration of the Shepherds in unspecified ruins, and the Adoration of the Magi in the basement of Bramante's spiral staircase near the Belvedere.[12] In both cases, naturally, the ruins are meant to be ancient, even though such structures, in their substance, seem closer to a real modern ruin than to one from Antiquity.[13] Ultimately, this had to do with the destruction motif – these things are, precisely, "cose disfacte." It was just this that astonished the Northerners, and it was doubtless also what they looked for.[14]

Let us, then, finally look at St. Peter's, the building more closely and frequently connected with the Roman ruins than any other new construction in the city. I will not linger over the much-discussed polemic against Bramante "il Ruinante," that is, the architect who did not build the church so much as he destroyed it, the old basilica that had not previously been a ruin. All that must be pointed out is that this was not a singular act of destruction, but a process, one that ran through the whole of the remaining building history. It did not progress simply and directly from west to east, but proceeded in such a way that fragments of the old building remained preserved in the midst of the new, which itself appeared, so to speak, to have grown into this, part of it forgotten and crumbled, part of it, though – including the old apse and a piece of the transept wall belonging to it – carefully preserved. When Maderno began his façade, parts of the old basilica's walls still stood. Occasionally, the roles of the old and the new buildings were exchanged: it was the preserved remainder of the basilica that, separated in 1539 from the building site by Sangallo's "muro divisorio," again offered shelter for church services, while Bramante's piers and arches still rose, uncovered, into the sky. For the architects of the new building, the confusion of the old and the new parts – which originally emerged in plans, and later became a reality – was both an impediment and a source of formal inspiration: this is the most illuminating explanation for the combination, frequently tested after Bramante, of large pilaster-piers with architrave-bearing columns of the sort used in the old nave.[15] The columns themselves – to the degree that Bramante's original *furia* had spared them – were collected, measured, and inventoried, at which point they wandered, as spolia, at least partially back into the new construction. In this way, demolition and reconstruction were, in principle, an

27

ongoing process, a sort of continual metamorphosis, one that lasted beyond the actual completion of the building and into the eighteenth century, until the erecting of the sacristy, which replaced the last standing remains of Old St. Peter's, the late antique Mausoleum of S. Maria della Febbre, with a modern structure.

A second aspect of the ruins has to do with the new building itself. Its history, too, is shot through with partial destructions, the demolition of already completed parts, from Michelangelo's halting of work on the south tribuna, begun under Raphael, to the tearing down of Bernini's bell towers, under Urban VIII.[16] The most spectacular of these was probably Sixtus V's demolition, in one stroke, of the Bramante choir first completed under Leo X, in order to rebuild the choir arm from Michelangelo's plan. Technically, this was an extremely complicated process, one which, to follow the sources, caused "molta spesa e gran fatica." What is less well known is that the demolition almost resulted in another ruin: Bramante's wall cracked, and Grimaldi describes a tremendous split that ran through the middle of the ceiling over the apse.[17] Similar and still more dangerous cracks had opened up in the walls of the great piers and arches; we shall come back to those. But even where it seemed intact, the Bramante choir must have been rather ruin-like, not only on account of its bare brick architecture, which contrasted with Michelangelo's travertine revetment, but also and especially for the large, empty window openings, through which one looked into the interior of the building. The sight of empty window sockets remained characteristic for Michelangelo's architecture, too; their deeply indented sections should, as we now know,[18] have led to an unclad attic. There, the bare core-masonry would have appeared almost ruin-like. And there, too, light openings gaped, leading shaft-like to the interior. The familiar *veduta* by Hubert Robert[19] very effectively brings out the somewhat uncanny pull of the whole, in the confrontation with the as yet still standing ancient rotunda.

Now, these are interpretations. There was, however, one moment in the history of the new building when it really was a ruin, and this was precisely Heemskerck's moment. In 1527, five years before his arrival in Rome, all activity at the building site had come to a standstill, and definitively so: this was the general conviction. The half-finished walls had been partially covered with emergency roofs, which soon rotted; plants grew over everything. In a certain way, one saw the expectations that skeptics had harbored from the beginning on fulfilled. "Apparve smisurato il concetto di Bramante," wrote Vasari, looking back over the origins of the building.[20] The first doubt about the possibility of its completion had already been voiced in the days of Leo X.[21] Serlio, in his third book, presented Bramante's dome project as an "invenzione bella et ornata," though not one that could be executed: anyone could see that Bramante's piers and arches collapsed under their own weight.[22] The reference here is to the cracks mentioned above, which, in fact, later necessitated extensive safeguarding; the south dome-bearing arch, according to Grimaldi, actually collapsed in the time of Sixtus V, and had to be rebuilt.[23] "Si sarebbe potuto sperare prima di veder l'ultimo giorno del mondo, che S. Pietro finito," Condivi remembered.[24]

There are surely several reasons why it was only at this moment, after the Sack of Rome, that the *vedute* appear – with the exception of one extraordinarily beautiful and interesting anonymous drawing in the Ashby collection, today in the Vatican library. Plainly datable before Heemskerck even on the basis of style, the drawing can be assigned on the basis of the building history to about 1524/5.[25] I leave open the question of whether, as has recently been suggested, Jan van Scorel can be considered as its author.[26] It was, in any case, a draftsman who not only belonged artistically to an older generation but also experienced Rome in a somewhat less desolate moment than had Heemskerck and his contemporaries. This is evident in its representation of St. Peter's as a building site:[27] one sees the large wheel of a freight elevator, one of the "ruote," payment for which was delivered in 1524; the adjacent barrel vault on the right rests on its empty scaffolding. This is, then, an edifice in the process of growth, and the point of view has been selected so as to make this apparent (a view from the north, at that time, would not have offered this impression). Indeed, reading the drawing from right to left produces the image of a process, one which, departing from the large, already completed parts in the foreground, will continue until the remaining parts of the old building, in the background on the right, have brought it to an end.

Now, it really could be a coincidence – I do not want to read too much into these drawings – that when Heemskerck, between 1532 and 1536, drew the things appearing in figure 2.1, he positioned himself a good 200 meters farther

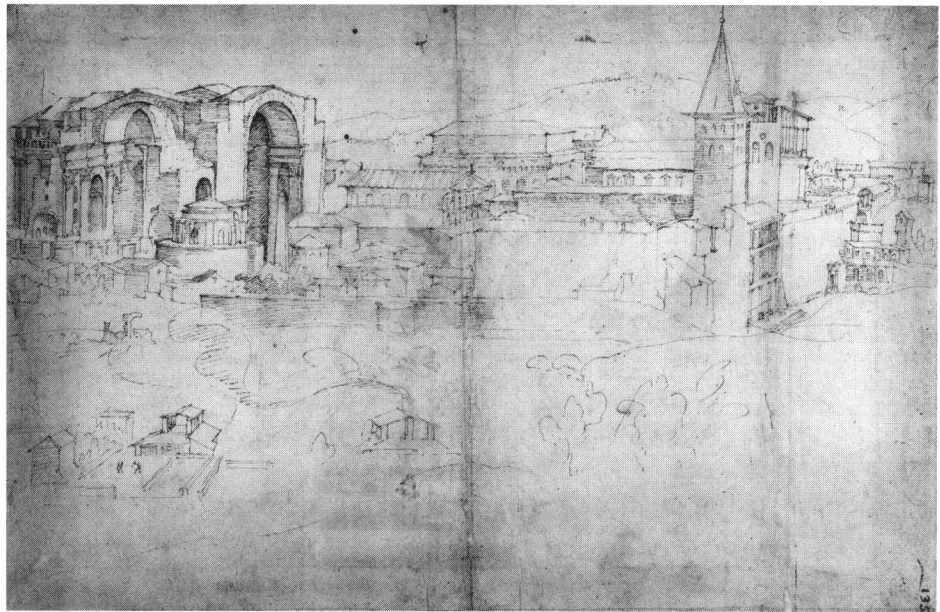

Figure 2.1 St. Peter's from the southeast, drawing by Maerten van Heemskerck, 1532–6. Berlin, Kupferstichkabinett, Heemskerck-Skizzenbücher, II, fol. 51r BPK 29.552. Staatliche Museen zu Berlin. Photo: Jörg P. Anders.

29

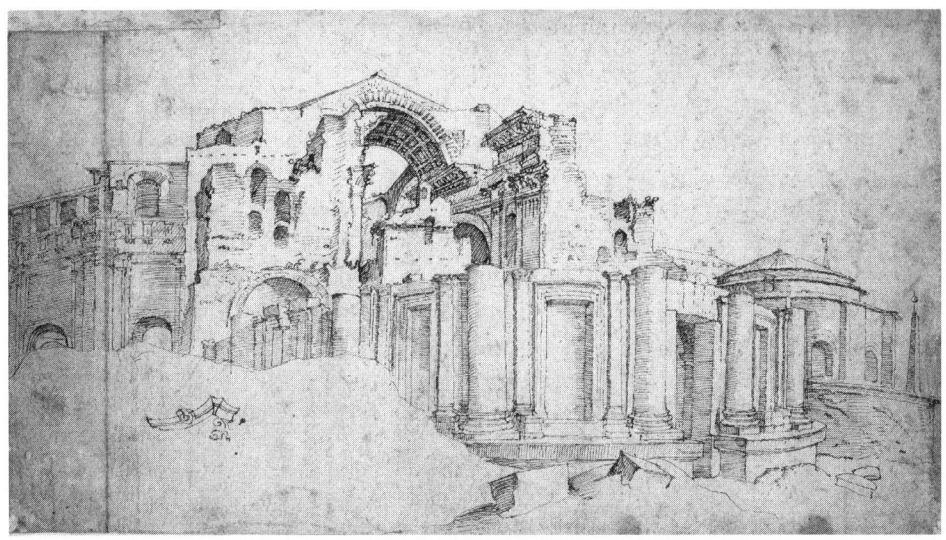

Figure 2.2 St. Peter's from the south, drawing by Maerten van Heemskerck, 1532–6. Berlin, Kupferstichkabinett, Heemskerck-Skizzenbücher, II, fol. 54r BPK 40.973. Staatliche Museen zu Berlin. Photo: Jörg P. Anders.

east. Whatever the case, the effect is exactly the opposite: the view now includes the entire complex of the old and new building, from the Bramante choir to the façade of the atrium on St. Peter's square. Here one realizes how much there remained to do. The first part stands there magnificently, colossal as a piece of bath architecture, but like such architecture, it also appears to have been pushed back in time; further building, let alone completion, is unthinkable. And this is now confirmed through close-ups of the building. I illustrate them here one after the other, so that they produce a roughly complete picture of the old and new building, for this could very well have been Heemskerck's intention, too.

First the exterior views. Figure 2.2 gives, again, the view from the south: on the left appears the Bramante choir, in the foreground Raphael and Sangallo's "Tribuna," as far as it had progressed by 1527. Anyone not familiar with the building history might think that the walls had collapsed, and had thus provided a clear view to the interior, where now in fact an authentic ruin appears: this is formed by the remains, still standing, of the old transept wall. But even the parts of the interior ornamentation that have already been transferred to the new building (capitals, entablatures) seem more like leftovers from a past splendor. In the mountains of rubble in the foreground additional individual pieces appear, as if they had fallen there from above. On the right, still just visible, is a portion of the old nave, S. Maria della Febbre; above it, as boundaries to the field of vision, are the tops of the bell tower and of the obelisk. Here too, then, the point of view has been selected so as to visualize the building in its whole complexity, in all its states of incompleteness and provisionality – but now as compactly as possible. This is brought about through the proximity of the viewpoint to the building, which results in a kind of wide-angle perspective. The viewing angle opens from the customary 60 degrees to something like 90 degrees; in this way the underside, too, is shown to its best advantage. None of this is necessitated by a lack of space; rather, it constitutes a stylistic means, one that Heemskerck also employed in other *vedute* in order to intensify the image of the world of ruins, transferring the viewer almost corporeally inside it, allowing him to look around.[28]

Figure 2.3 shows the opposite view, from the north. The point of view is directly across from that of the sheet just discussed, and opens into the same kind of angle. Again the draftsman stands extremely close by: on the actual site, one must turn one's head in order to see all of what is included here. It is for this reason that the two 40-palm-high niches (in the middle foreground and at the right edge) appear on different angles, though in reality they lie at the same level; the Bramante choir, on the right, shrinks to a mere profile, though it is still in the picture. Objectively the cropping is the same as that of the previous view – the obelisk now appears on the left border, as it formerly appeared on the right. This is without doubt the most expressive sheet in the series, the one that lends the most pathos to the ruins' character. The gigantic building seems quite frail here, as if collapsed, already ancient; the weathered walls, partly covered, partly bare, are strewn with holes for scaffolding and are raked with furrows and grooves. The large piers break off abruptly; the pendentive for the dome, which

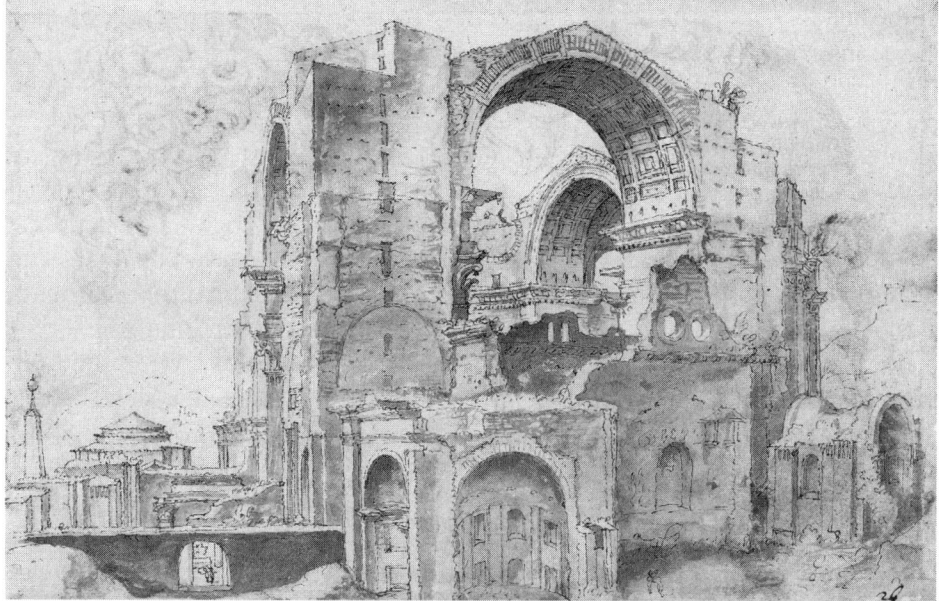

Figure 2.3 St. Peter's from the north, drawing by Maerten van Heemskerck, 1532–6. Berlin, Kupferstichkabinett, Heemskerck-Skizzenbücher, I, fol. 13r BPK 40.974. Staatliche Museen zu Berlin. Photo: Jörg P. Anders.

31

is starting to become visible, is only half-built; it stands serrated against the sky. Two tiny figures (through the arch of the darkly inked wall in the left foreground) stand baffled at the foot of this mountain.

It is tempting, of course, to connect such a view to critiques of Rome, especially the critiques made in those years by visitors from north of the Alps. If Martin Luther and others compared Rome with Babel, then the association with the great tower and its collapse must have been unavoidable, a "common proverbial example of Superbia rebelling against God."[29] I have not, however, been able to find comments that would corroborate this, and the question of Heemskerck's own confession has not yet, so far as I can tell, been answered.[30] In Rome, he drew what he saw – concretely, uncompromisingly, accurately, and, occasionally, with caustic humor. He abstained from criticism, though it is difficult not to perceive some satire when one sees antiquities represented as they are in the sketchbook: the Belvedere Torso, the Capitoline statues, or other assemblies of the Eternal City's gods.[31] In any case, it appears that, with his humanist-antiquarian interests, a sense of the comic, not to mention the laughable, in the situation, was not lost on the Netherlander (unlike his later commentators). Architecture does not allow itself to be brought so pointedly into the picture; indeed, one gains from Heemskerck's large *vedute*, as nowhere else, an idea of the absurdity with which the undertaking of the rebuilding of St. Peter's must have appeared in the eyes of contemporaries. One confirmation of this is offered in an engraving by Hieronymus Cock,[32] perhaps based on a Heemskerck design. This, wherever possible, exaggerates the ruinous condition of the building; it designates the structure as "aedes divi petri romanae deformatio" in the inscription along the upper edge of the sheet.

Quickly now let us glance at the other sheets. The view from the east should really have shown the atrium – Heemskerck did not draw it, perhaps because it represented an architectonically unified and still intact space. Instead of this we have two views of St. Peter's Square, the well-known panorama-*veduta* from the Albertina, and a less familiar, very fleetingly sketched view done from the opposite direction, in the Berlin sketchbooks. Heemskerck gave this the feeling of ruin through the addition of two repoussoir fragments in the foreground, a capital and a lion's head, which are extremely large and near, and which thus contrast with the distance view. This, too, is a procedure that we know from other sheets.[33]

It is similar to the procedure behind one of the interior views of the building. This shows a view from north to south at the start of the south tribuna (making it the complement to fig. 2.2), a representation that is difficult to take in spatially, since the wide-angle technique, applied once again here, leads to considerable distortions. I will abstain from explaining the building topography[34] and content myself with a comparison to Heemskerck's manner of seeing, as exemplified by a view of the Colosseum, looking out from the interior of the Arch of Constantine.[35] Here, as before, there is a surprising juxtaposition of near and far, which almost iconoclastically underscores the torn and the fragmentary aspects

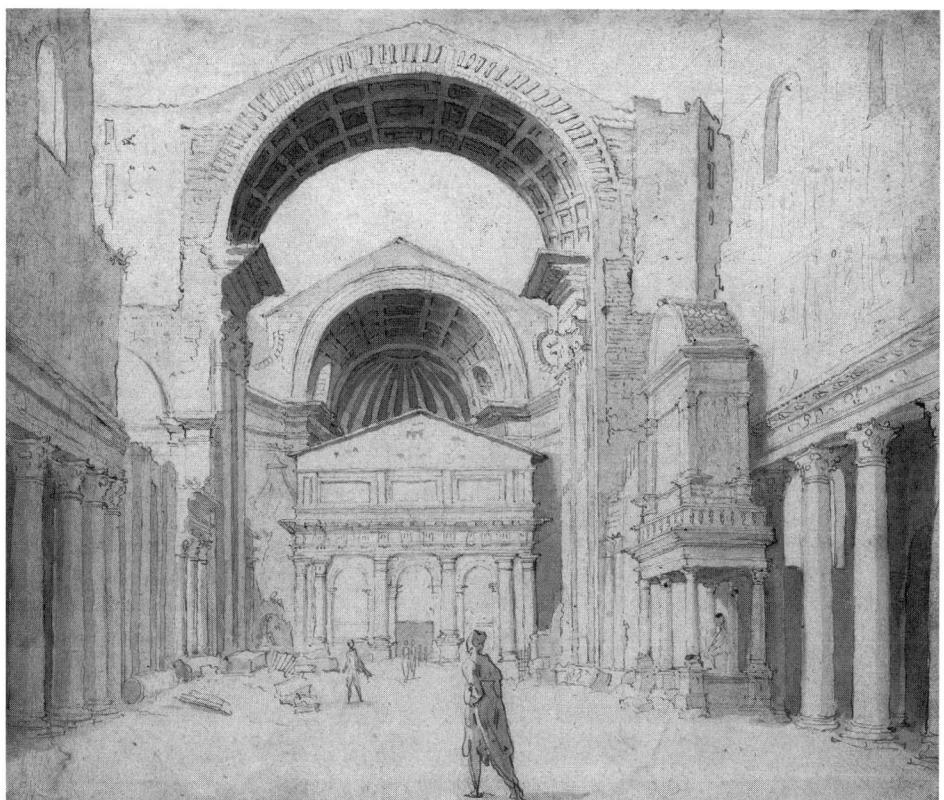

Figure 2.4 St. Peter's, interior, looking toward the west, copy after Maerten van Heemskerck. Berlin, Kupferstichkabinett, Heemskerck-Skizzenbücher, II, fol. 52r BPK 40.170. Staatliche Museen zu Berlin. Photo: Jörg P. Anders.

of the scenery. With loose but precise strokes, the condition of the wall is again characterized: the coffers of the vault, cast in pieces, the still bare front wall of the pier, parts of the decoration in the large niche, and, on the right, the start of the "Fra-Giocondo Niche," a wall core that has been laid open and in which plants have already settled themselves, just as they have in the stump of a gallery pier on the left.

The main view of the interior is fig. 2.4, a view through the nave from east to west.[36] The framing has again been chosen so that the old and new buildings, with all of their different parts and conditions, come into the picture; almost unnoticeably, their lightly shaking contours, like frayed edges, pass over into one another. Equally shocking is the view through the empty space of the dome to the protective building and the bare front wall of the Bramante choir. The perspective of the view is normal here; the position of the draftsman (as it can be reconstructed) lies not far from the old entrance to the nave, at about the level of the second pilaster. This would no longer have been possible after Sangallo, in 1538 (shortly after Heemskerck's departure from Rome), erected his dividing wall along the nave. The familiar *veduta* from the Kunsthalle in Hamburg shows the view from the door of this dividing wall outward (as the draftsman's inscription specifies).[37]

To this, finally, is added the view through the transept, made at a right angle to the previous one, from north to south. This is the *veduta* that Richard Krautheimer discovered in Stockholm,[38] and it must certainly be understood as a part of the cycle, perhaps even as the pendant to the large exterior view from the north. If, on that sheet, it was primarily the size of the building, and its desolation, that evoked Babylonian associations, so here the motif of confusion is foregrounded: the ruins of the old and of the new building are interconnected in a way that's scarcely transparent any more. Debris covers the floor, architectural pieces lie about, and there is rampant, jungle-like vegetation. A pair of figures wander about among these things, and convey a feeling of hopelessness: so, contemporaries must have imagined, did the pope and his priests in those days have to clear a path, in wind and rain, if they wanted to celebrate the mass at the tomb altar inside the protective building. This was the condition of the building when Heemskerck left Rome – doubtless knowing that this would be a lasting condition. Begun a lifetime earlier, it had become a part of the Roman world of ruins.

Today we know that history proceeded otherwise; had Heemskerck stayed in Rome for just a few more years, he could have seen what Vasari depicted in his Chancellery frescoes: out of the ruins new life bloomed, the abandoned torso began to transform itself back into a building site.[39] Its scale is reassuringly shrunken in the picture, especially by comparison to the large figures in the foreground; the point of view is elevated, and it has become possible to survey the whole – possible, at least, for the painter. At this point, Vasari could not yet have known what he would later so beautifully state: that only Michelangelo's reconception of the whole plan – "a minor forma, ma si bene a maggior grandezza" – would reduce the building to feasible dimensions.[40] Precisely those parts that arise newly here would then again fall victim to the pickaxe. The history of the ruins of St. Peter's was not yet over.

Notes

The following text was presented at a colloquium that the Bibliotheca Hertziana organized in April 1986 on the topic of "Roma quanta fuit, ipsa ruina docet," at which the figure of Heemskerck played an unexpected key role, thanks above all to the contributions from Ernst Gombrich, Nicole Dacos, and Matthias Winner. I have preserved the form and scope of the conference lecture, and have added source and literature references to the notes, along with several further considerations.

1   The *vedute* in this essay will be cited following Ch. Hülsen and H. Egger, *Die römischen Skizzenbücher von Marten van Heemskerck im kgl. Kupferstichkabinett zu Berlin*, 2 vols., Berlin, 1913, reprint Soest 1975; on this, compare Ilja Veldman,

"Notes occasioned by the publication of the facsimile edition of Hülsen/Egger," *Simiolus* (1977), 106–113. The author is much indebted to Frau Veldman, with whom he has for years been exchanging opinions over the question of Heemskerck's St. Peter's *vedute*. On Heemskerck, see also I. M. Veldman, *Maarten van Heemskerck and Dutch Humanism in the 16th Century*, Maarssen 1977; E. A. Saunders, "A commentary on iconoclasm in several print series by Maarten van Heemskerck," *Simiolus* (1978/79): 59–83; R. Grosshands, *Maerten van Heemskerck, Die Gemälde*, Berlin, 1980, esp. 39 (Ruinen bei Heemskerck). For questions connected with the building history of St. Peter's, consult Graf Wolff Metternich and Ch. Thoenes, *Die frühen St.-Peter-Entwürfe 1505–1514*, Tübingen, 1987, esp. the excursus "Zur Datierung der Veduten."

2 Letter "ex urbe delacerata" from March 1443: A. Fabroni, *Magni Cosmi Medicei Vita*, II, Pisa 1788, 165ff. The Florentine's sarcasm contrasts with Rome's inhabitants' pride in the ruins, as witnesses of their great past (see n. 4). On life with and in the ruins in medieval Rome, see the relevant passages in Gregorovius, *Geschichte der Stadt Rom im Mittelalter* and in R. Krautheimer, *Rome, Profile of a city, 312–1308*, Princeton, 1980; the so-called Casa dei Crescenzi (Krautheimer 197ff.) appears to be an earlier architectonic reflection of this. The literary evidence has recently been assembled by M. Greenhalgh, "'Ipsa ruina docet': l'uso dell'antico nel medioevo," in S. Settis (ed.), *Memoria dell'antico nell'arte italiana*, I, Turin, 1984: 113–167; on the humanists' new view of the ruins, see now also A. Esch, "Mauern bei Mantegna," *Zeitschrift für Kunstgeschichte* (1984): 293–319, esp. 310ff.

3 The "trullo" between Via della Ripetta and Via del Corso (Via Lata), called a "meta" on the Bufalini plan. See H. Günther, "Die Stadtplanung unter den Medici-Päpsten in Rom (1513–1534)," *Jahrbuch des Zentralinstituts für Kunstgeschichte*, I (1985): 237–293.

4 "Priscae excellentiae virtutisque monumenta" (inscription on the so-called *Statuenstiftung* of Sixtus IV); "quel poco che resta . . . per testimonio di quelli animi divini che pur talor con la memoria loro excitano et destano alle virtù gli spiriti che oggidì sono tra noi" (Castiglione and Raphael's letter to Leo X: *Raffaello Sanzio, Tutti gli scritti*, ed. E. Camesasca, Milan 1956, 53; cf. Ch. Thoenes in *Raffaello a Roma, il convegno del 1983*, Rome, 1986, 375 and 380). The formulation of this motif can be followed back as far as the Roman city statutes of 1363, book II, article 191, "De antiquis aedificiis non diruendis" (E. Rodocanachi, *Les institutions communales de Rome sous la papauté*, Paris 1901, 395: "les monuments anciennes qui, disent les statuts, perpétuent le souvenir de la gloire du peuple romain"). On the Roman Senate's concern for ancient monuments already in the 12th century, see Gregorovius, *Geschichte der Stadt Rom*, VIII, 7, 4.

5 The motto "Roma quanta fuit . . ." appears on the title page of Serlio's "Terzo Libro" (1540), and was presumably thence copied as the (subsequently added?) inscription on a view of the Septizonium in Heemskerck's Berlin albums (II, 85r/ 87v, acc. to Hülsen/Egger "Anonymus A"); it also appears in a somewhat different formulation on the Mantuan Rome plan (after 1538). On the history of the idea and its tradition cf. E. and J. Garms in *Storia d'Italia, Annali 5, Il paesaggio*, Turin 1982, 591ff., and Ch. Thoenes in *Römisches Jahrbuch für Kunstgeschichte* (1983): 368; significant is the change from a medieval topos of elegiac meditation on passing (Hildebert von Lavardin) to a methodological principle for the archaeological studies of the High Renaissance (a conclusion from the preserved fragments of a

lost whole: cf. Castiglione/Raphael, as in n. 4, 53ff.). The sentimental moment is revived again, however, in later examples; see, for instance, the inscription on the Theater of Sabbioneta (S. Mazzoni and O. Guaita, *Il Teatro di Sabbioneta*, Florence, 1985, 54).

6 Quattrocento architects already tried to convince their patrons that, in building, one should not think about means. Alberti read in Thucydides that the power of Athens had derived from the "astuteness of premonition," which was "far beyond its capacity to build" (*De re aed.*, Foreword; against this, however, the fatherly-commercial admonitions in Book II, ch. 1, are then directed). Never has a city been impoverished or destroyed through enormous building (Filarete, *Trattato di architettura*, ed. M. Finli and L. Grassi, Milan, 1972, I, 238, with examples from ancient history). Had the ancients, in building, paid attention to expense, their fame would have been long vanished (idem); decisive for all was the will to make what came into their minds ("par che mettessero ad effetto ciò che imaginarno, e che solo el volere rompesse ogni difficultate": Raphael to Leo X, ed. cit., 54). An anonymous Roman in the 17th century still thought it more valuable to "stabilire cosa sopra modo maestosa, e singolare, senza farla," than to plan too small (K. Güthlein in *Römisches Jahrbuch für Kunstgeschichte*, 1981, 211, in reference to St. Peter's). Corresponding to this on the patrons' side are the papal programs for the beautification of Rome, beginning with Nicholas V. Nevertheless there predominated in Roman building practice, until the end of the Quattrocento, a rather sober utilitarianism; cf. the unsurpassed characterization of Sixtus IV's architecture by Gregorovius, XIII, 7, 2. Most of these buildings were carried through to their end without any change in plan.

7 According to Kurt W. Forster (in a lecture in Vicenza, 1986) a design by Giulio Romano for his house in the Macel de' Corvi was laid out from the start as a fragment, from which one would have had to infer the total dimensions, which could not have been realized in the given location.

8 The open displays of incongruities resulting from the building history must especially have struck those traveling in northern Italy. The incomplete façades of such prominent new buildings as S. Petronio in Bologna or S. Croce, S. Lorenzo, and the cathedral in Florence already took on the character of historical ruins; on this, cf. Arnold Esch's descriptions of the ancient-medieval wall structures as bearers of historicity in the pictures of Mantegna (as in n. 2). On medieval communal palaces the incorporated older wall structures were revealed in a way that suggests historical documentary intentions.

9 Serlio's examples of the "ornamento rustico" appear to have been repeatedly demolished and overgrown with plants (Book IV, fol. 131ff. in the 1619 edition). It is not possible here to go into the "sketchbooks" of architects, which contain numerous examples of the fascination with the phenomenon of ruins, including some that are independent from their architectural archaeological interest (Codex Escurialensis, Libro of Giuliano da Sangallo, etc.).

10 James Ackerman, "Notes on Bramante's bad reputation," in *Studi bramanteschi, Atti del congresso internazionale 1970*, Rome 1974, 339–349; cf. also Thoenes, ibid., 395.

11 The ruins appear here as the complement to a style unfamiliar with the idea of developing, "growing" forms, and with the dimension of time: the homogeneity of the external appearance of the work suggests its "momentary" origin. Vasari formulates this in his praise of the Farnesina: "non murato ma veramente nato" (ed. Milanesi,

IV, 593; ibid., 157 Vasari speaks of the "voglia che tali fabbriche [Cortile del Belvedere] non si murassero, ma nascessero"). This look of the momentary is itself well-suited to large-scale architecture like St. Peter's, where the history of its origins, which dragged through generations, cannot be read from the building itself, since the plans did not continue their predecessors (as those for large buildings in the Middle Ages did) but interfered with, neutralized, and even destroyed them (witness Michelangelo's demolition of the Raphael/Sangallo south tribuna).

12 Grosshans (as in n. 1), 39, figs. 145, 204.

13 On Genezzano cf. Ch. L. Frommel, "Bramante's 'Ninfeo' in Genezzano," *Römisches Jahrbuch für Kunstgeschichte* (1969): 137–160; Ch. Thoenes, "Note sul 'Ninfeo' di Genezzano," in *Studi bramanteschi* (as in n. 10), 575–583. On Cornheert: Grosshans (as in n. 1), fig. 143.

14 Cf. Heemskerck's view of the Pantheon, Berlin II, 39r, which draws a look of ruin even out of such an exceptionally well-preserved building. The sight of ruins of massive stone buildings affected visitors to Rome in the early 16th century, when the development of modern weapons of mass destruction was only in its infancy, and seemed more exotic than we can imagine; on the other hand, the buildings' state of preservation, made possible by the Roman climate, also impressed people. The same was true of the "new building ruins" with their bare wall cores, unprotected by exterior walls and roofs (cf. the dome piers and arches of St. Peter's). Even today travelers from the north seem taken aback by the predominant Mediterranean custom of placing unfinished structures (concrete skeletons) openly in the landscape, on the reckoning that they will "grow."

15 On the question of the Old Basilica as a part of the "program" for the new building, see Metternich and Thoenes (as in n. 1).

16 The young Bernini, by his own confession, had also harbored demolition plans on a truly heroic scale: Maderno's entire nave, he thought, would be better put aside, and the Michelangelo design carried out in its place; unfortunately, the Popes would only come to power in an age when it was difficult to win them over any longer for undertakings of that sort (diary of the Lord of Chantelou, 15 July 1665).

17 Giacomo Grimaldi, *Descrizione della basilica antica di S. Pietro in Vaticano*, Cod. Barb. lat. 2733, ed. R. Niggl, Vatican City, 1972, 464.

18 H. A. Millon and C. H. Smyth, "Michelangelo and St. Peter's," *Burlington Magazine* (1969): 484–501.

19 H. Egger, *Römische Veduten*, 2nd ed., Vienna 1932, I, 48.

20 Vasari-Milanesi, IV, 163.

21 In 1517 appeared Andrea Guarna's dialogue "Simia," in which St. Peter made the dead Bramante wait before the gates of Heaven until Leo finished building New Saint Peter's (Andrea Guarna da Salerno, *Scimmia*, ed. E. and G. Battisti, Rome 1970); similar ideas were already present in the anonymous *Julius II dialogus post mortem* of 1513, ed. E. Thion, Paris, 1875, 168ff. (I thank H. Günther for the kind reference). In Germany there were rumors that stones meant for St. Peter's wandered in the night to the palace of the papal nephews, and that the Pope donated the incoming indulgence money to his sister (L. v. Pastor, *Geschichte der Päpste*, IV, I, Freiburg, 1906, 549).

22 S. Serlio, *Il terzo libro* . . . , Venice 1619, fol. 66r. In the introduction to Book 5 (ibid., fol. 202r), Serlio complained that people no longer built large churches, and that they left those that had been begun incomplete.

23 Grimaldi (as in. 17), 464ff.

24 A. Condivi, *Vita di Michelangelo Buonarroti*, ed. E. Spina Barelli, Milan, 1964, 79.

25 Metternich and Thoenes (as in n. 1), Excursus D; cf. H. Egger (as in n. 19), I, 38 ("before 1530"); H. A. Millon and C. H. Smyth, "Michelangelo and St. Peter's," *Römisches Jahrbuch für Kunstgeschichte* (1976): 144 ("before 1527").

26 Ch. L. Frommel in *Raffaello architetto* (exhibition catalogue), Rome, 1984, 303.

27 For this, cf. Raphael's *vedute* of building sites from the time of Julius II and Leo X: the Vatican Loggie and part of a sockel from a pier in St. Peter's in the background of the *Disputa* (Ch. L. Frommel, "Eine Darstellung der Loggien in Raffaels Disputa?" in *Festschrift Eduard Trier*, Berlin, 1981, 103ff.); Villa Madama in the background of the *Battle of Constantine* (idem in *Römisches Jahrbuch für Kunstgeschichte*, 1975, 62ff.; R. Quednau, *Die Sala di Costantino im Vatikanischen Palast*, Hildesheim and New York 1979, 351ff.).

28 Berlin I, 3r, shows a comparable view. In that case, the concern is for an empirical rather than a constructed view, as is shown by certain inconsistencies.

29 See K. Hoffmann, "Dürer's 'Melencolia',", in *Kunst als Bedeutungsträger, Gedenkschrift für Günter Bandmann*, Berlin, 1978, 251–77, 262, and ibid., 264, for the positive interpretation, dating back to Alberti, of the Tower of Babel, as well as further literature. For the 16th-century critique of Rome, see A. Chastel, *The Sack of Rome*, Princeton, 1983, esp. 49ff. ("Rome-Babylon") and 91ff. ("Urbis direptio"); figs. 41–44, Cranach's and Holbein's woodcuts of the destruction of Babylon, based on Hartmann Schedel's view of Rome; and in the Italian ed. (*Il sacco di Roma*, Turin, 1983), fig. 57, the graffito "Babilonia," dated 1528 on Peruzzi's view of Rome in the Sala della Prospettiva in the Farnesina. Further material can be found in P. Brezzi, "Tra condanne e esaltazioni, i giudizi sulla città e l'idea di Roma nel Quattrocento e Cinquecento," in *Roma e l'antico nell'arte e nella cultura del Cinquecento* (ed. M. Fagiolo), Rome, 1985, 11–22.

30 On this, cf., in addition to Saunders (as in n. 1), J. S. Bangs, "Maerten van Heemskerck's Bel and the Dragon and Iconoclasm," *Renaissance Quarterly* (1977): 8–10.

31 Berlin, I, 5r, 6v, 27r, 29v, 30v, 45r, 53v, 59r, 63r, 72r. There are no examples to be found among the sheets allotted by Hülsen and Egger to "Anonymous A."

32 Timothy A. Riggs, "Hieronymus Cock (1510–1570), Printmaker and Publisher in Antwerp at the sign of the Four Winds," Yale University, Ph.D., 1971, 298ff. no. 109. The position of the draftsman lay somewhat farther west than that of fig. 2.3; the view here is perspectively normal, which could support I. Veldman's suspicion that the Cock engravings are to be connected with a Heemskerck imitator (Anonymous A?) rather than with Heemskerck himself ("Disegni romani di Maerten von Heemskerck," lecture at the Kunsthistorisches Institut in Florence, 1979).

33 Sometimes this rises to the point of paradox: the detail in the foreground appears larger than the monument itself; cf. e.g. Berlin I, 28v, fallen composite capital and Colosseum; I, 32r, ancient colossal foot with strap sandal and Porticus Octaviae; I, 36r, marble crator from S. Cecilia and Temple of Serapis from the Quirinal. The capital on our sheet could be a damaged or incomplete, not yet positioned piece of work for the large order of pilasters inside St. Peter's, which lay on the ground in the north transept – if this, too, is not already to be understood as one of Heemskerck's emblematic elements; cf. the corresponding sketch in the foreground of fig. 2.2.

34 Cf. Metternich and Thoenes (as in n. 1), Excursus D.

35 The wide-angle principle is taken here to its extreme, as the background panorama stretches from the Colle Oppio to the Septizonium; this corresponds to an angle of nearly 180 degrees.

36 Presumably a copy from a missing Heemskerck original; cf. Hülsen and Egger, vol. II, 33.

37 Egger (as in n. 19), I, 32; attributed by James Ackerman to Ammanati (*The Cortile del Belvedere*, Vatican City, 1954, 216ff.). Inscription: "Questo e ritratto di Sto Pietro dalla porta della chiesa vecchia acanto all'organo verso la testa della croce di bramante."

38 R. Krautheimer, "Some Drawings of Early Christian Basilicas in Rome: St. Peter's and S. Maria Maggiore," *Art Bulletin* (1949): 211–215.

39 Paul III, as the building master of St. Peter's, wore an Old Testament priest's habit; Metternich's suspicion, that this alludes to the *re*building of the temple, after its destruction, under the leadership of the High Priest Zorobabel (or Joshua), is illuminating, though it cannot be substantiated by contemporary sources (F. Graf Wolff Metternich, *Bramante und St. Peter*, Munich, 1975, 24; cf. also *Tiberii Alpharani De Basilicae Vaticane antiquissima et nova structura*, ed. M. Cerrati, Rome, 1914, p. xxxiii). On the right, beside the scene of the building of the church, appears the figure of "Opulentia": she should, to follow Francesco Doni's text (for the reference to which I thank Julian Kliemann), allude to "l'entrate della chiesa," whose desired richness was first made possible by the rebuilding. Cf. also E. Steinmann in *Monatshefte für Kunstwissenschaft* (1910), 45ff., 52; R. Harprath, *Papst Paul III. als Alexander der Grosse*, Berlin, 1978, 45f.

40 Vasari–Milanesi, VV, 220f.

3

Virtue Reconciled with Pleasure

Edgar Wind

Among the most engaging paintings by the young Raphael is the little picture of the *Dream of Scipio* (fig. 3.1), now in the National Gallery, which was presumably painted for a young Scipione Borghese.[1] The young hero lies at the foot of a laurel tree,[2] apparently dreaming of his fame. Two women approach him. The sterner one presents him with a sword and a book, the more gracious offers a flower. These three attributes – book, sword, and flower – signify the three powers in the soul of man: intelligence, strength, and sensibility, or (as Plato called them) mind, courage, and desire. In the Platonic scheme of the "tripartite life", two gifts, the intellectual and moral, are of the spirit while the third gift (the flower) is of the senses. Together they constitute a complete man, but as they mingle in different proportions they produce different characters and dispositions: "The philosophers," wrote Fulgentius in copying out Plutarch, who in his turn restated a view of Plato, "have decided that the life of humanity consists of three parts, of which the first is called theoretical, the second practical, the third pleasurable: which in Latin are named *contemplativa, activa*, and *voluptaria*."[3]

In the *Dream of Scipio* by Macrobius, which ends with a discourse on *tripartita philosophia*, the hero is warned against the voluptuous life and urged to pursue the active and contemplative virtues – *perfectionis geminae praecepta*.[4] The "precepts of twofold perfection" are impressed upon him also in Raphael's picture, but not to the exclusion of Pleasure. While he is offered the sword and the book with which to pursue the arduous path of virtue, suggested in the background by the steep rock and the spire rising above it, he is also offered the pleasing flower: the landscape on the right is a friendly valley. His posture suggests that he inclines towards virtue, but the flower is also part of his dream; and in that he follows the morality of Ficino, for whom the *triplex vita* was a persistent subject of meditation. "No reasonable being doubts," he wrote to Lorenzo de' Medici,[5] "that there are three kinds of life: the contemplative, the active, and the pleasurable (*contemplativa, activa, voluptuosa*). And three roads to felicity have been chosen by men: wisdom, power, and pleasure (*sapientia, potentia, voluptas*)." To

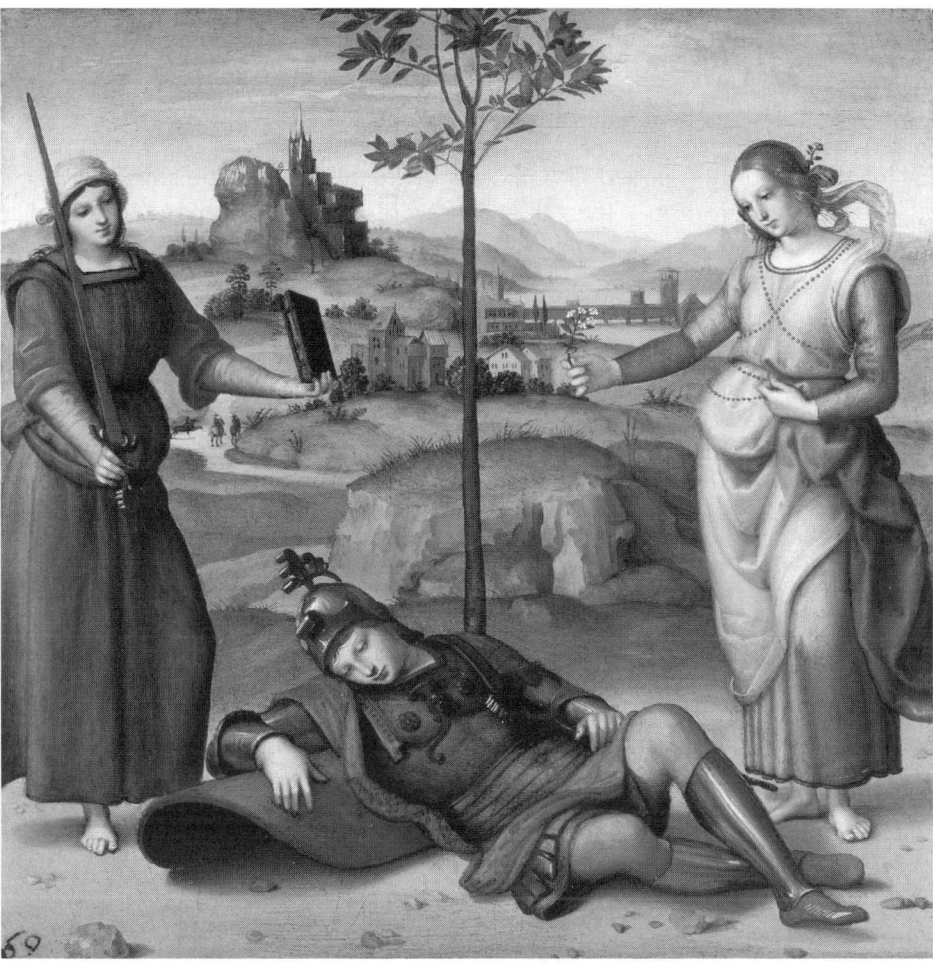

Figure 3.1 Raphael, *Allegory* ("Vision of a Knight") also sometimes known as "The Dream of Scipio." © National Gallery Collection; reproduced by kind permission of the Trustees of the National Gallery, London / CORBIS.

pursue any one of them at the expense of the others is, according to Ficino, wrong, or even blasphemous. Paris chose pleasure, Hercules heroic virtue, and Socrates chose wisdom rather than pleasure. All three were punished by the deities they had spurned, and their lives ended in disaster. "Our Lorenzo, however, instructed by the oracle of Apollo, has neglected none of the gods. He saw the three [that is, the three goddesses who had appeared to Paris], and all three he adored according to their merits; whence he received wisdom from Pallas, power from Juno, and from Venus grace and poetry and music." To compliment a prince on his universality by comparing his judgement to that of Paris became a fixed formula of Renaissance euphuism. In Lyly's *Euphues and his*

41

England (1580), Peele's *Arraignment of Paris* (1584), Sabie's *Pans Pipe* (1595), to name only a few,[6] the same compliment was addressed to Queen Elizabeth. It was carried to extremes in an allegorical portrait at Hampton Court in which the Queen puts the three goddesses to shame because, as the inscription fulsomely asserts, she combines in herself the gifts which they possess only separately.[7] The flattery is more subdued in Raphael's *Scipio*. He humbly dreams of the gifts he is to receive. No doubt, he will accept them all three, but prudently divided in the proportion of 2:1.

It is significant commentary on the painting that it had *The Three Graces* (fig. 3.2), now in Chantilly, as a companion piece. The two pictures are of the same size, and since they both came from the Borghese Collection, and are inscribed with consecutive numbers, there can be no doubt that they form a

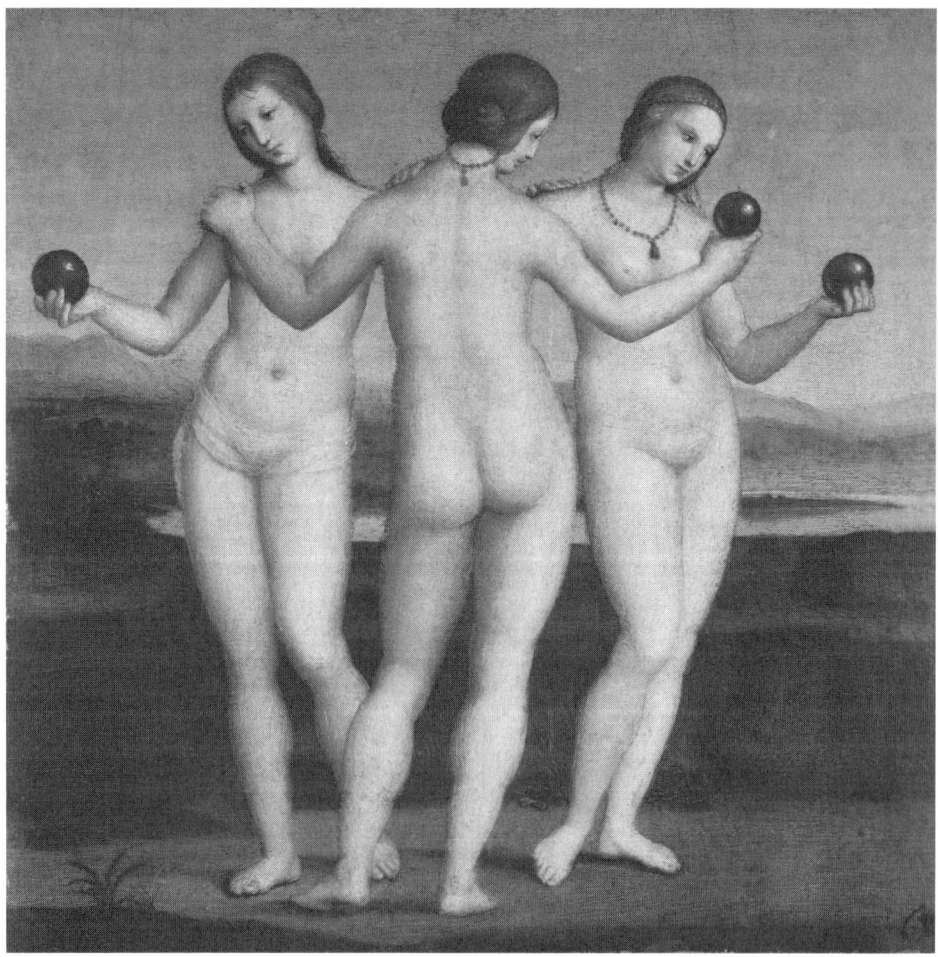

Figure 3.2   Raphael, *The Three Graces*. AKG-images / Erich Lessing.

pair;[8] and they were still together in the collection of Sir Thomas Lawrence.[9] But they must not be imagined as a diptych, which is excluded by their square shape, and also by the change of scale in the figures. It is more likely that they were placed back to back, the two parts being related to each other like the obverse and reverse of a medal.

Although the three Graces in the picture look indistinguishable, they are characterized very lightly by a certain difference of attributes. Castitas wears a loin-cloth, and has no jewels around her neck. Voluptas, on the opposite side, is distinguished by a long necklace with a sizeable jewel. The Grace in the centre is more modest. The chain hanging from her hair is shorter than the necklace of her neighbour, and also the jewel attached to it is smaller. Not quite so abstemious as Chastity, nor so liberally adorned as Pleasure, Beauty holds the balance between them, being chaste and pleasurable in one. She touches Chastity's shoulder as she turns towards Pleasure; and so subtle is the distribution of weights that, although the group retains its classical symmetry, the emphasis is decidedly on the right. Two apples are here offered, as against one;[10] and the two little chains also add their weight. Only one foot of the left figure is freely visible, so that her counter-movement has little support. And the landscape in the background sustains the asymmetrical action, the expanse of water flowing freely towards the right while it stops short behind the figure of Chastity. All these features combine to convey the same moral: Beauty inclines Chastity towards Love. The proportion of 2:1 is weighted on the side of Pleasure.

The golden apples in the hands of the Graces characterize them as the servants of Venus; for it is to her that the golden apples are sacred, and she is occasionally described as holding them herself: "Mala aurea tria ferebat."[11] In Politian's vision of the garden of Venus, the fruits it bears are *pomi d'oro*.[12] As attributes of the Graces, apples are not so unusual as has been claimed.[13] Cartari and Gyraldus described the Graces as *nexis manibus poma gestantes*,[14] and as they are supposed to unfold the unity of Venus, it is not unreasonable for them to hold her fruit.

In offering these gifts of love, the Graces counterbalance the demands of Scipio's heroic dream. Instead of two gifts of the spirit and one of the senses, they bring two delectable gifts and one of restraint. While the hero is advised to adopt a rule of action by which he subordinates his pleasure to his duties, he is here invited to soften those severities and allow virtue to come to fruition in joy. The discipline of Scipio is only one side of the picture; the other is his affectionate liberality. *Virtus* and *Amor* belong together:

> For what is noble should be sweet.
> [Ben Jonson, *Pleasure Reconciled to Virtue*]

The combination of a martial spirit with amiability, which is the moral of Raphael's *Scipio and the Graces*, was so essential and natural to the Renaissance code of chivalry that it would seem unnecessary to assign to it any hidden roots in an

43

antiquarian study of mysteries. Nor was the double life led by the average courtier, that of a warrior and of a lover, so novel as to require philosophers to propose it. Yet when it came to sanctioning these two lives, and to explaining their relation to each other, philosophers and antiquaries were much in demand; and as might be expected, they made the most of the opportunity to season glorification with paradox.

The ancient "mystery" upon which they seized was the unlawful union of Mars and Venus, from which issued a daughter named Harmony. Born from the god of strife and the goddess of love, she inherits the contrary characters of her parents: *Harmonia est discordia concors.*[15] But her illegitimate birth, far from being a blemish, was taken for a sign of mystical glory, according to a rule set forth very clearly in Leone Ebreo's *Dialoghi d'amore*. In discussing the love and procreation of the gods as metaphors for universal forces in nature, he explained that "when this union of the two parents occurs regularly in nature, it is called marriage by the poets, and the partners are called husband and wife; but when the union is an extraordinary one, it is styled amorous or adulterous, and the parents who bring forth are styled lovers."[16]

In reflecting on the extraordinary nature of Harmony, which became the core of his theory of beauty, Pico della Mirandola delved rather deeply into Plutarch's theory of Mars and Venus. "It is well known," wrote Plutarch in the essay *De Iside et Osiride*, "that, in the fables of the Greeks, Harmony was born from the union of Venus and Mars: of whom the latter is fierce and contentious, the former generous and pleasing. And see how philosophers have agreed with this. Heraclitus openly called war the father, king and master of all things, and declared that Homer, in wishing that discord would vanish from the councils of gods and men, had secretly blasphemed against the origin of all things because they are born from strife and adversity. . . . Empedocles calls the force effective of good by the name of love and friendship . . . and the destructive force he calls pernicious strife. . . . The Pythagoreans attach several names to each of these forces. . . . But Plato, concealing and foreshadowing his opinion in many places, calls the first of these contrary principles the Same, and the second the Other. . . . For mixed is the origin of this world, and its frame composed of contrarious powers. . . ."[17]

And in *De Homero*, included by Xylander in Plutarch's *Moralia*, we read again: "This is what the fable of Mars and Venus suggests, of whom the latter corresponds to Empedoclean friendship, the former to Empedoclean strife. . . . And with this agrees what is transmitted by other poets, that Harmony was born from the union of Mars and Venus: for when the contraries, high and deep, are tempered by a certain proportion, a marvellous consonance arises between them."[18]

In Plato's *Sophist* (242D–E) the doctrine of contraries uniting in concord is ascribed to "the Ionian and Sicilian muses" – according to Simplicius (also Schleiermacher and Diels)[19] an ironic reference to Heraclitus and Empedocles: Plato makes these "muses" say "that being is one and many, and is held together by enmity and friendship . . . ; peace and unity sometimes prevailing under the sway of Aphrodite, and then again plurality and war, by reason of a principle of strife".[20] Plotinus, who mentioned Heraclitus and Empedocles by name,[21] treated the doctrine with more solemnity: "How are enchantments produced? . . . through the natural concord of like principles and contrariety of unlike. . . . The true magic is the Love contained within the universe, and the Hate likewise. This is the original enchanter and master of potions. . . . In all the universe there is but one general harmony though it be formed of contraries."[22]

It is clear that Pico had such passages in mind when, writing "On the general nature of Beauty",[23] he defined beauty as a "composite" and inherently "contrarious" principle, without fearing the heresies that it might entail. His account may be said to go to the root of the matter, and despite its prolixity, it must be quoted at length:[24]

> And for this reason no simple thing can be beautiful. From which it follows that there is no beauty in God because beauty includes in it a certain imperfection, that is, it must be composed in a certain manner: which in no way applies to the first cause. . . . But below it [the first cause] begins beauty because there begins contrariety, without which there would be no creation but only God. Nor do contrariety and discord between various elements suffice to constitute a creature, but by due proportion the contrariety must become united and the discord made concordant; and this may be offered as the true definition of Beauty, namely, that it is nothing else than an amicable enmity and a concordant discord. For this reason did Heraclitus say that war and contention are the father and master[25] of all things, and, concerning Homer, that he who curses strife may be said to have blasphemed against nature. But Empedocles spoke more perfectly when he introduced discord not by itself but together with concord as the origin of all things, understanding by discord the variety of elements of which they are composed, and by concord their union; and therefore he said that only in God is there no discord because in him there is no union of diverse elements, but his unity is simple, without any composition. And since in the constitution of created things it is necessary that the union overcomes the strife (otherwise the thing would perish because its elements would fall apart) – for this reason is it said by the poets that Venus loves Mars, because Beauty, which we call Venus, cannot subsist without contrariety; and that Venus tames and mitigates Mars, because the tempering power restrains and overcomes the strife and hate which persist between the contrary elements. Similarly, according to the ancient astrologers, whose opinion Plato and Aristotle follow, and according to the writings of Abenazra the Spaniard and also of Moses, Venus was placed in the centre of heaven next to Mars, because she must tame his impulse which is by nature destructive and corrupting, just as Jupiter offsets the malice of Saturn. And if Mars were always subordinated to Venus, that is, the contrariety of the component elements to their due proportion, nothing would ever perish.

The many and famous Renaissance idylls in which the victorious Venus, having subdued the fearful Mars by love, is seen playing with his armour, or allowing her cupids and infant satyrs to play with it, all celebrate this peaceable hope: that Love is more powerful than Strife;[26] that the god of war is inferior in

45

strength to the goddess of grace and amiability. In Cossa's fresco of the *Triumph of Venus*, in the Palazzo Schifanoia, the vanquished Mars not only kneels before her but is actually chained to her throne as a prisoner. The fetter of love, an amiable reminiscence of the more sinister chain contrived through the cunning of Vulcan, is reduced in Veronese's allegory of Mars and Venus (fig. 3.3) to a

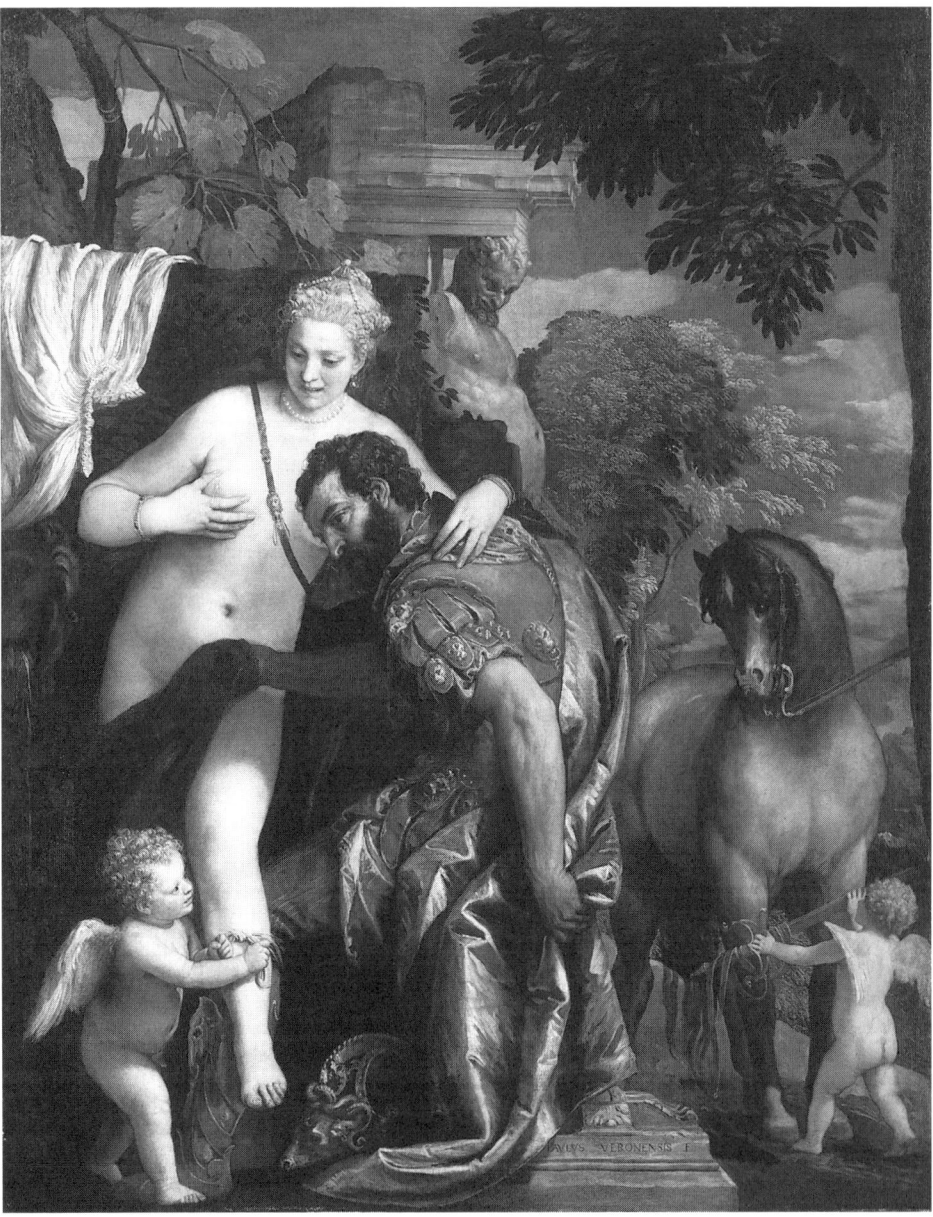

Figure 3.3 Paolo Veronese, *Mars and Venus*. The Metropolitan Museum of Art, John Kennedy Fund, 1910 (10.189). Photograph, all rights reserved, The Metropolitan Museum of Art.

knot tied by a winged cupid.[27] But in the idylls of the same subject painted by Botticelli and Piero di Cosimo no chain or ribbon is required to demonstrate the bondage of Mars. Venus has put his fierceness to sleep. While Cossa's fresco of her triumph belongs to an astrological cycle and should be interpreted accordingly, any thought of "sextile and trine aspects", which have occasionally been read into the paintings by Botticelli and Piero, would destroy their peculiar poetry. Since the planet Mars always retains, even when dominated by the planet Venus, a certain degree of boldness and bellicose fervour – a point clearly brought out by Ficino in *De amore* V, viii, and not neglected by Cossa – the reduction of Mars to a sleeping loving swain, surrounded by *amoretti* playing at war, is, with all due allowance for the wide influence of horoscopy, emphatically *not* an astrological image.[28]

Botticelli has added a further touch of bucolic raillery by transforming the cupids into infant satyrs who sneak impishly into the armour surrendered by Mars. His formidable weapons are reduced to toys.[29] Only the wasps that buzz round the head of the sleeper are a reminder of his pugnacious spirit: "quod per vespam . . . pugnacitatem et infestum adversos hostes ingenium ostendebant".[30] As a marginal comment on the scene, the wasps should not be underrated: for although Venus "tames and mitigates" the contentiousness of Mars, she also "loves Mars because Beauty, which we call Venus, cannot subsist without contrariety"; and thus a union of sweetness and sting remains implicit in the *discordia concors* of Mars and Venus.[31]

The discordant element becomes more prominent when, instead of putting Mars to sleep, Venus adopts the martial weapons for her own. Dressed in armour (ὅπλα Κυθήρης), the *Venus victrix* or *Venus armata* signifies the warfare of love:[32] she is a compound of attraction and rejection, fostering her gracious aims by cruel methods. Like the "bitter-sweet" pun of *amare–amaro*, to which Bembo devoted a whole book of the *Asolani*,[33] the threatening equation of *amare–armare* became indispensable to lovesick sonneteers. Michelangelo employed it for his *cavalier armato*,[34] and the ridiculous Armado recalled it in *Love's Labour's Lost*. Even Virgil's Diana-like Venus – *virginis os habitumque gerens et virginis arma* – is but a variant of the *Venus armata*: a bellicose Venus who has donned the weapons that normally belong to her opponent – either Diana, Minerva, or Mars.

But again, while appearing armed, Venus may give to the armour a peaceable motive. The martial Venus may stand for the strength that comes from love, for the fortitude that is inspired by charity,[35] or – in the reverse – for a sweetness derived from strength: *de forti dulcedo*.[36] In a poetical self-portrait by Navagero, *De imagine sui armata*, she introduces the rueful patriotism of a poet who accepts his martial calling with regret:

> *Quid magis adversum bello est bellique tumultu*
> *Quam Venus? ad teneros aptior illa jocos.*
> *Et tamen armatam hanc magni pinxere Lacones,*
> *Imbellique data est bellica parma Deae . . .*

> *Sic quoque, non quod sim pugna versatus in ulla,*
>   *Haec humeris pictor induit arma meis.*
> *Verum, hoc quod bello, hoc patriae quod tempore iniquo,*
>   *Ferre vel imbellem quemlibet arma decet.*[37]

Thus, in response to the perilous hour, the heroic warrior disguises his softness by a display of steel, and compares himself, although he is a man, with the ambiguous figure of the *Venus armata*.

No doubt, the incongruity of the simile was a deliberate device in Navagero.[38] He intended to perplex and surprise the beholder, and also perhaps to remind him that the martial Venus, originally a Spartan deity, was for Roman poets and orators a cryptic figure on which, Quintilian says, they exercised their wit: "cur armata apud Lacedaemonios Venus".[39] But side by side with the jocose tradition, which was inherited from the Greek epigrammatists, the Romans retained towards the armed Venus an attitude of religious respect. The ancestral goddess of the Julian house, she appears on gems and coins of Caesar and Augustus, as a martial figure of Roman peace, of victorious generosity relying on her strength.[40] The poets in the circle of the emperor Maximilian, in an attempt to revive the Augustan figure, called one of their poetic cycles *Die geharnischte Venus.*[41] But in the majority of Renaissance adaptations, of which Politian's witty epigram *In Venerem armatam* is perhaps the most ingenious,[42] she was allowed to drop the heroic style, presiding instead over scenes of domestic good humour which celebrate the inescapable triumphs of love, *omnia vincit amor.* Curiously decked out in martial trophies, like Omphale when she made Hercules attend to the spindle while she usurped his club and lion's skin, she may look slightly encumbered by her outfit;[43] but since she has conquered the rudest god by her wiles, a touch of bizarrerie is not unbecoming to the *victrix* in this unequal battle.

In comparing the pictures of the martial Venus with Navagero's self-portrait as an amiable warrior, we find that the roles of Mars and Venus, which would normally be divided between man and woman, both recur within man and woman as such. The principle of the "whole in the part" entails this rather baffling conclusion: that Venus is not only joined to Mars, but that his nature is an essential part of her own, and *vice versa.* True fierceness is thus conceived as potentially amiable, and true amiability as potentially fierce. In the perfect lover they coincide because he – or she – is the perfect warrior. But whenever their "infolded" perfection is "unfolded", the argument requires two opposing images which, by contrasting the martial with the amiable spirit, reveal their transcendent unity.[44]

It is curious to observe, and not irrelevant, that while these equations of fierce virtue and pliant love were playfully developed on Florentine medals in the pagan idiom of poetic theology, the medals designed for Savonarola expressed a similar contrast in images that were inspired by his prophetic visions: GLADIUS DOMINI SUPER TERRAM CITO ET VELOCITER, SPIRITUS DOMINI SUPER TERRAM COPIOSE ET ABUNDANTER.[45] The wrathful symbol of the God of vengeance whose sword or dagger hovers over the earth is not only contrasted in this medal with the burning love of the winged dove rising to heaven, but these are the contrary aspects of one deity: the God of vengeance is the God of love. His justice is mercy, His anger pity; His punishment itself is sent as a blessing because it purges the soul of sin. The famous conversions performed by Savonarola were helped by an inherent affinity of thought between pagan and Christian mysticism. The same tensions, conflicts, and contradictions which have so often been ascribed to the incompatibility between Renaissance paganism and Christianity prevailed actually within each of the rival attitudes; and this made communication between them so easy. The pagan courtier who thought of himself as inspired by a Venus–Diana or a Venus–Mars was quite accustomed to translate his ideal of action into a pair of Christian virtues: *carità* united with *fortezza*. For he would recall the divine identity of wrath and love which is the secret of the Bible. "There is," as we may remember from Pico,[46] "this diversity between God and man, that God contains in himself all things because he is their source, whereas man contains all things because he is their centre." In the centre the opposites are held in balance, but in the source they coincide. In so far as man therefore approaches his own perfection, he distantly imitates the deity. Balance is but an echo of divine transcendence.

The wise Federigo da Montefeltro who, as a successful *condottiere*, delighted in cultivating the arts of peace, expressed his faith in harmonious balance through the discordant symbol of a cannon-ball, which he placed under the protection of the thundering Jupiter. On his medal the three stars in the sky form a constellation of Jupiter between Mars and Venus, and their symmetry is repeated in the group of emblems below; the sword and cuirass belonging to Mars, the whisk-broom and myrtle to Venus, while the ball in the centre is dedicated to *Jupiter tonans*, whose flying eagle carries the unusual still-life on its wings.[47] Although the balance looks safe, it is not solid: for the slightest dip of the eagle's wings would set the cannon-ball rolling. The inscription says, however, that Venus "touches" the threatening Jupiter, who enables her to counterbalance Mars.[48] Yet contrary to other triumphs of Venus, the design suggests that her complete dominion over Mars might also set the cannon-ball rolling. The supreme god alone is the guardian of equity, the source and arbiter of the *discordia concors*, of which Mars and Venus are the component parts.

Notes

1 Panofsky, *Hercules am Scheidewege* (1930), pp. 76ff.; R. Eisler, *Revue archéologique* XXXII (1930), pp. 134f. Although not mentioned by these authors, it was surely Macrobius's commentary on Cicero's *Somnium Scipionis* that suggested the idea of a "dreaming Scipio", a subject genuinely antique and Neoplatonic (cf. Boyancé, *Études sur le songe de Scipion*, 1936, pp. 121–46, 173ff.), and not created *ad hoc* by Raphael's adaptation of a "dreaming Hercules" from a Northern woodcut illustrating

Sebastian Brant (Panofsky, op. cit., p. 79). On a marble relief in the Louvre, conceived as an ideal portrait of Scipio, see Bode, *Studien über Leonardo da Vinci* (1921), pp. 30f., where the design is ascribed to Leonardo, the stone work to Francesco di Simone, a pupil of Desiderio, working in Verrocchio's atelier.

2   "Lauri residens iuvenis viridante sub umbra" (Silius Italicus, *Punica* XV, 18). The derivation of the episode from the Choice of Hercules (Xenophon, *Memorabilia* II, i, after Prodicus) remained a favourite topic among eighteenth-century antiquaries; for example, Joseph Spence, *Polymetis* (1747), p. 142, who added an execrable poem of his own on The Choice of Hercules, twenty-seven stanzas long (pp. 155–62). Panofsky (op. cit., p. 38 note 1) cites G. A. Cubaeus, *Xenophontis Hercules Prodicius et Silii Italici Scipio* (1797), and T. C. Schmid, *De virtute Prodicia et Siliana* (1812).

3   Fulgentius, *Mythologiae* II, 1: "De iudicio Paridis." Cf. Plutarch, *De liberis educandis* 10 (*Moralia* 8A), which repeats Plato, *Republic* 441, 580Dff.

4   *In Somnium Scipionis* II, xvii, 183.

5   *Opera*, pp. 919f. See also *Supplementum Ficinianum* I, pp. 80–6: "De triplici vita et fine triplici."

6   Cf. E. C. Wilson, *England's Eliza* (1939), pp. 136, 147f., 239 note.

7   C. H. Collins Baker, *Catalogue of the Pictures at Hampton Court* (1929), p. 47, no. 635 (*Inv.* 301); R. C. Strong, *Portraits of Queen Elizabeth I* (1963), p. 79, no. 81. The Latin distichs and the early date (1569) recall the Queen's visits to Cambridge (1564) and to Oxford (1566), which occasioned volumes of complimentary verses "in Greek and Latin, Hebrew, Caldee, and English" (Wilson, op. cit., pp. 70, 72). One of the Latin poems, by Henry Bust, welcoming Elizabeth to Oxford (31 August 1566), is quoted in J. D. Reeves, "The Judgment of Paris as a device of Tudor Flattery", *Notes and Queries* CXCIX (1954), p. 8.

8   Panofsky, op. cit., pp. 142f.

9   Crowe and Cavalcaselle, *Raphael* I (1882), pp. 202 note, 209 note.

10   There is an interesting *pentimento* in the painting. The central Grace originally held no apple but touched the shoulders of the two other Graces. The alteration stresses the asymmetry.

11   Gyraldus, *Opera* I, 387; also Cartari, *Imagini*, s.v. "Venere": "con tre pomi d'oro in una mano". The three apples which Hercules got from the Hesperides were also "mala aurea Veneri consecrata" (*Libellus de deorum imaginibus* xxii, MS Vat. Reg. lat. 1290, fol. 6r), but the suggestion that because of these Herculean apples Raphael's picture of the Graces should be associated with the Hesperides is surely unfounded, particularly if the figure on the obverse is Scipio and not Hercules. In the Venus fresco of the Palazzo Schifanoia the Graces hold four apples, not three: which would also seem to rule out any necessary association of these apples with Hercules or the Hesperides. The golden apples of Atalanta were again apples of Venus, so described by Alciati, *Emblemata*, no. 61.

12   *Giostra* I, xciv, 2. On apples as general attributes of Venus, see Pierio Valeriano, *Hieroglyphica*, fols. 394ff., "De malo", with a long excursus on the ball game of apples, after Philostratus, *Imagines* I, 6. On lovers throwing apples, see also two epigrams ascribed to Plato (Diogenes Laertius III, 32; *Anthologia Graeca* V, 79f.) and a charming verse by Virgil (*Eclogues* III, 64f.). In one of the so-called Otto prints (Hind, *Early Italian Engraving*, no. A IV 10, pl. 139) the lovers are equipped with a large basket filled with apples which they throw at each other.

13   "Die goldenen Kugeln auf unserem Gemälde . . . freilich ein Unikum", Salis, op cit.,
     p. 154. The idea that the Graces might be imagined as playing ball goes back as far
     as Chrysippus. Seneca, *De beneficiis* II, xvii, 3 (also II, xxxii, 1): "Volo Chrysippi
     nostri uti similitudine de pilae lusu." Hence Ripa, *Iconologia*, s.v. "Gratie": "perciò
     Crisippo assimigliava quelli che danno e ricevono il benefitio, a quelli che giuocano
     alla palla. . . ." The same image in Plutarch, *De genio Socratis* 13 (*Moralia* 582F),
     trans. Xylander, p. 485: "Nam si pulchrum est amicis benefacere, non est turpe ab
     amicis beneficium accipere. Gratia enim non minus accipiente quam dante opus
     habet, ab utrisque perficitur ad pulchritudinem. Qui vero non accipit, tanquam
     pilam recte obiectam dedecorat, decidentem frustra." On the ex-libris of Johannes
     Cuspinianus, which derives from a Cranach portrait now in the Reinhart Collection,
     Winterthur (cf. H. A. von Kleehoven, "Cranachs Bildnisse des Dr Cuspinian und
     seiner Frau", *Jahrbuch der preussischen Kunstsammlungen* XLVIII, 1927, p. 231,
     fig. 1), the Graces, inscribed DO–ACCIPIO–REFERO, are represented in the act of
     playing ball.

14   The phrase in the Latin version of Cartari (1687, p. 219) is the same as in Gyraldus,
     loc. cit. I, 387. On the ancient concept of Graces as fruit-bearing deities, see Carl
     Robert, "De Gratiis Atticis", op. cit., p. 148; Jahn, *Die Entführung der Europa*,
     pp. 37–43.

15   Cf. Gafurius, *De harmonia musicorum instrumentorum*, frontispiece, also fols. 2v,
     97r. Among ancient sources see Horace, *Epistolae* I, xii, 19; Ovid, *Metamorphoses*
     I, 433; Lucan, *Pharsalia* I, 98; and above all Plutarch as quoted above, p. 44.
     Gafurius alternates between the classical formula *concordia discors* and its inversion,
     discordia concors (for which see Manilius, *Astronomica* I, 142; Augustine, *Epistolae*
     XVI, 4).

16   Leone Ebreo, *Dialoghi d'amore*, ed. S. Caramella (1929), p. 108; tr. F. Friedeberg-
     Seeley and J. H. Barnes (1937), p. 122. On the humorous illustration of the
     doctrine in the *Parnassus* by Mantegna see Wind, *Bellini's Feast of the Gods*, pp. 9–
     20; with further notes on Homeric laughter in "Mantegna's Parnassus", *Art
     Bulletin* XXXI (1949), pp. 224–31. It is interesting that Plato's censure of the
     laughter of the gods did not deter Proclus from reading a cosmogonic mystery into
     it, which he found foreshadowed in the *Timaeus*, the *Republic*, and the *Parmenides*.
     The relevant passages are cited by Koch, *Pseudo-Dionysius Areopagita*, pp. 253f.;
     for their interpretation see Lobeck, *Aglaophamus*, pp. 891f.; Dieterich, *Abraxas*,
     p. 28; also K. Preisendanz, *Die griechischen Zauberpapyri* II (1931), pp. 95ff.,
     110ff.

17   *De Iside et Osiride* 48 (*Moralia* 370D–371A).

18   *Moralia*, trans. Xylander, p. 25. Calcagnini paraphrased the passage in "De
     concordia", *Opera*, p. 414: ". . . quod in citharis maxime agnoscitur, ut ex dissonis
     fiat concentus. Sic enim prudenter veteres Harmoniam ex Marte et Venere genitam
     existimarunt, quod gravis et acuta seorsum opponi videantur: quom vero una
     componantur, incredibilem suavitatem auribus reddant." Another example in Codrus
     Urceus, *Orationes seu sermones* (1502), fol. G ir: "Fabula etiam quam de Venere et
     Marte coniunctis scripsit Homerus, amicitiam Empedoclis significat, quando vero
     dissolvuntur contentionem . . . unde ex Veneris et Martis coitu fingitur nata harmonia.
     . . . Hoc est quod ex contrariis sonis, gravibus scilicet et acutis simul proportione
     mixtis, nascitur consonantia."

51

19 Simplicius, *In Aristotelis Physicorum libros*, ed. H. Diels (1882), p. 50; see also Diels, *Die Fragmente der Vorsokratiker* I (1934), p. 288, no. 29; Schleiermacher, *Platons Werke* II, ii (1857), p. 94.

20 See also *Republic* 545D–E: "Shall we, after the manner of Homer, pray the Muses to tell us how discord first arose?" On Love and Strife in the Judgement of Paris, see Wind, *Pagan Mysteries in the Renaissance* (1968), Appendix 7, pp. 270ff.

21 *Enneads* IV, viii, 1ff.

22 Ibid. IV, iv 40f. (trans. Dodds).

23 *Commento* II, vi (ed. Garin II, viii, pp. 495f.).

24 The argument which follows is difficult to reconcile with *Enneads* I, vi, where Plotinus insists on the phenomenon of simple beauty, and with *Enneads* V, viii, and VI, vii, 33, where "intelligible beauty" is defined as pure and without parts. See also Ficino, *Opera*, pp. 1792f. Apparently Pico felt certain, to the point of Platonic heterodoxy, that if the One is assumed to be above Beauty (*Enneads* VI, ix, 11), it follows that Beauty must depend on composition. As in the case of intelligence and will, it suited his radicalism to stress the inapplicability of beauty to the supreme One more ruthlessly than Ficino, who had also treated of God's "intelligence" in positive terms *Theologia Platonica* II, ix f., *Opera*, pp. 103ff.), which Pico tended to ridicule. In *Commento* 1, i (ed. Garin, p. 462) he reflected with amusement that "a great Platonist" had felt disturbed because Plotinus seemed to deny intelligence to the supreme One – apparently a quarrel over *Enneads* VI, vii, 37.

25 The Italian text, which gives the word *genetrice*, is clearly faulty at this point, since Pico was transcribing Heraclitus fr. 53. Possibly a word like *governatore* for βασιλεύς was shortened in the first draft and then wrongly expanded by a copyist.

26 Compare Lucretius's famous invocation of Venus against Mars, *De rerum natura* I, 30–41. Also *Symposium* 196D, Mars "the captive and Love is the lord, for love, the love of Aphrodite, masters him . . . and the master is stronger than the servant."

27 The allegory is very involved. While Mars bends down in adoration and submission, his *fortezza* is characterized as a restraining *virtù* because it is he who holds up the garment of chastity that covers Venus; while she, by touching her breast from which milk flows, reveals *castità* as transformed into *carità* (a motive reminiscent of the *Caritas Romana*). The restraints of Love imposed by a noble *fortezza* are playfully imitated on the right by a cupid using the sword of Mars to restrain the horse, which is already bound by its bridle. In a curious painting by Veronese in Turin (Gualino Collection) the lovers turn in surprise towards the apparition of a horse's head whose bridle is held by Cupid. On the bridling of horses to signify the chastening of animal passion, see *Sacred and Profane Love* as discussed in Wind, *Pagan Mysteries*, p. 145.

28 Cast as a stucco relief, the figures of Venus awake and Mars asleep, surrounded by a swarm of playing cupids, frame a Renaissance mirror, reproduced in John Pope-Hennessy, *Catalogue of Italian Sculpture in the Victoria and Albert Museum* (1964), no. 129, fig. 151. The frame is set in an emblematic ring bearing the famous device of "diamond with foliage" (not confined to the Medici family, but used by the Este and others as well; cf. Hill, nos. 103, 120, 365). Applied to a mirror, it designates the owner as a woman both amiable and adamant, *Venus semper invicta*. One of the putti crowns Venus with a wreath, another rides a goose (a watchful as well as

amorous bird: see Valeriano, *Hieroglyphica*, fols. 174v, 175r). On the side of the vanquished Mars they are taming a dragon.

29 Cupids playing with the armour of Mars are common in ancient reliefs and epigrams which celebrate the triumphs of Amor, for example *Anthologia graeca* XVI, 214f. (Loeb Library V, p. 287, with illustration). In Lucian's *Herodotus*, cupids playing with martial weapons are introduced into Aëtion's painting of Alexander and Roxana; but instead of suggesting a triumph of love over war, their symbolic function is here the reverse: Lucian says that they signify Alexander's abiding "love of war".

30 Valeriano, *Hieroglyphica*, fol. 31v, s.v. "Pugnacitas"; also fol. 189v: "De vespa", with illustration inscribed *pugnacitas*.

31 In Alciati, *Emblemata*, no. 89, the amorous motto *dulce et amarum* is illustrated by the pseudo-Theocritean idyll (no. xix) of Cupid stung by bees while tasting honey, a subject which Melanchthon, Cranach, and Hans Sachs found singularly attractive (R. Förster, *Das Erbe der Antike*, 1911, pp. 6f.). Sting and sweetness are also combined in a pair of humorous paintings by Piero di Cosimo representing *Silenus stung by Wasps* as a sequel to *Bacchus's Discovery of Honey* (after Ovid, *Fasti* III, 735–60, cf. Panofsky, *Studies in Iconology*, pp. 59–63). Since these pictures were painted for a Vespucci, Gombrich was surely right in suspecting (*Journal of the Warburg and Courtauld Institutes* VIII, p. 49) that because of the *vespae* in their coat-of-arms, the Vespucci favoured paintings with wasps, and that Botticelli's *Mars and Venus* may have been one of them. But it is characteristic of Renaissance "inventions" that the heraldic subject would not be introduced flatly for its own sake, but as motivated by the theme of the painting.

32 The mythographical sources listed in Gyraldus, *Opera* I, 394 ("Venus armata") and I, 399 ("Venus victrix"); Cartari, *Imagini* (1571), pp. 544ff. On the ancient image and its revival see L. Curtius, "Zum Antikenstudium Tizians", *Archiv für Kulturgeschichte* XXVIII (1938), p. 236. In giving the armed Venus a shield with a Gorgoneion, more usually associated with Minerva or Mars (cf. the shield of Mars in Marcantonio Raimondi's engraving, Bartsch no. 945; or the shield of Minerva, Bartsch no. 337), Agostino Veneziano did not invent a new conflation of attributes for the *Venus victrix* (R. Wittkower, "Transformations of Minerva in Renaissance Imagery", *Journal of the Warburg Institute* II, 1939, p. 202, pl. 38a) but followed ancient precedent: see D. Le Lasseur, *Les déesses armées* (1919), p. 187, on a black-figured amphora in the British Museum (B. 254) inscribed "Aphrodite" and depicting her with aegis; likewise an ancient gem formerly in the Berlin antiquarium (no. 11362), illustrated in Furtwängler, *Die antiken Gemmen* III (1900), pp. 336f., figs. 183f. The cuirass placed at the feet of Venus in a drawing ascribed to Marco Zoppo, again far from representing "the corselet of Minerva" (Wittkower, loc. cit.), belongs to the martial equipment of the *Venus victrix*, on whose armour, employed in the warfare of love, see *Anthologia graeca* XVI, 173: ὅπλα Κυθήρης.

33 Book I is a plaintive declamation, with Petrarchan interludes, against *amore amaro* (cf. Plautus, *Trinummus* 260: "Amor amara dat").

34 *Rime*, ed. Girardi, no. 98 (= ed. Frey, no. 76).

35 Raphael's allegory of *Fortezza–Carità* in the Stanza della Segnatura (on which see Wind, "Platonic Justice designed by Raphael", *Journal of the Warburg Institute* I, 1937, pp. 69f.) was fittingly compared by O. Fischel, *Raphael* (1948), p. 91, to the

martial heroines of love in Ariosto, and he referred to Catarina Sforza as a historical embodiment of the type.

36 *Aenigma Sampsonis* (Judges xiv, 14) discussed by Gyraldus, "Aenigmata", *Opera* II, 621f., with reference to a coin of Alfonso d'Este inscribed DE FORTI DULCEDO and showing bees nesting in a helmet, *Corpus nummorum italicorum* X (1927), pl. xxx, 23. The same image in Alciati, no. 45, with the motto EX BELLO PAX.

37 Andreas Naugerius, *Orationes duae carminaque nonnulla* (Venice 1530), fol. 38r; cf. *Opera omnia*, ed. Vulpius (1718), pp. 218f.

38 Cf. the androgynous portrait of Francis I, discussed in Wind, *Pagan Mysteries*, p. 214.

39 *Institutio oratoria* II, iv, 26. The variety of answers may be gathered from *Anthologia graeca* XVI, 171–7; also IX, 321, which advises Venus to disarm, and IX, 320, a palinode like Stesichorus's *Helen*: "It is not true. . . ." Ausonius, *Epigrammata* 64, a verbal combat between the armed Venus and Minerva, is a translation of *Anthologia graeca* XVI, 174. Plutarch referred to the Spartan Venus in *De Fortuna Romanorum* 4 (*Moralia* 317F): "Even as the Spartans say that Aphrodite, as she crossed the Eurotas, put aside her mirrors and ornaments and her magic girdle, and took a spear and shield, adorning herself to please Lycurgus, even so Fortuna . . . when she was approaching the Palatine and crossing the Tiber . . . took off her wings, stepped out of her sandals, and abandoned her untrustworthy and unstable globe."

40 Furtwängler, *Die antiken Gemmen* III, p. 304, illustrated ibid. I, pl. xxxvii, 30; xliv, 77f.; lxiv, 65. H. Mattingly, *Coins of the Roman Empire in the British Museum* I (1923), pp. cxxiii, 98f., nos. 599ff.; II (1930), p. xlii. See also Winckelmann, *Description des pierres gravées du feu Baron de Stosch* (1760), p. 118, no. 564: "Jules César la portait ainsi gravée sur son cachet." The Rev. T. M. Parker drew my attention to Rutilius Namatianus, *De reditu suo* I, 67–70, in praise of the union of Mars and Venus.

41 Cf. Lessing, *Schriften*, ed. Lachmann, XVI, p. 451; XVIII, p. 321.

42 *Opera* II, fol. 102v.

43 Campbell Dodgson, *A Book of Drawings formerly ascribed to Mantegna* (1923) p. 25; now attributed to Marco Zoppo, cf. A. E. Popham and P. Pouncey, *Italian Drawings in the British Museum* (1950), no. 260. On the iconography see above, note 32.

44 Hill, no. 858, medal of Rodrigo de Bivar, inscribed QUORUM OPUS ADEST. Since the obverse shows the portrait of Rodrigo alone, the inscription and image of the reverse refer to the valour and grace combined in his person. Hill's assumption that the presence of Venus refers to Rodrigo's "matrimonial prospects" in Rome is iconographically inconclusive. Nor should the employment of an Italian medallist by the Spanish prince be cited in support of that hypothesis, since his Spanish castle La Calahorra, in a remote corner of the Sierra Nevada, was rebuilt by him in the Italian style with the help of Italian workmen, and trimmed in Carrara marble specially imported. See Carl Justi, "Die Einführung der Renaissance in Granada", *Miscellaneen aus drei Jahrhunderten spanischen Kunstlebens*, I (1908), pp. 218–23. Although much of the marble has been plundered, mythological and emblematic reliefs still adorn the window-frames of the splendid court, offering a natural parallel to the Italian workmanship of the medal. Justi calls the building "the earliest monument of pure Italian workmanship in this realm".

45 Hill, no. 1080. Inscription and image derive from a visionary dream recorded by Savonarola in his *Compendium revelationum* (1514, fol. 5).

46 See Wind, *Pagan Mysteries*, p. 48.

47 Hill, no. 304. Although it is known, and explicitly stated by Hill, that Federigo da Montefeltro used the emblem of a bombshell in other instances, the cannon-ball in the medal has not been recognized as such, despite the reference to *Jupiter tonans* in the inscription. Giehlow, who identified all the other emblems in the design, assumed that the sphere must refer to Jupiter but interpreted it as a symbol of the earth, "Die Hieroglyphenkunde des Humanismus in der Allegorie der Renaissance", *Jahrbuch der kunsthistorischen Sammlungen in Wien* XXXII (1915), p. 37. In a later medal, clearly posthumous (Hill, no. 1118), the globe is flanked by cornucopiae and surmounted by a triumphant eagle, while winged putti carry the whole affair on a shield. The allusion to the cannon-ball has been dropped. In its stead the design recalls Ficino's pun *Urbinas–Orbinas* (*Opera*, p. 1294).

48 In an engraving by Marcantonio Raimondi (Bartsch no. 345), which might have the title *Discordia concors*, Mars chides Venus for her amiable tricks. Having taken off his armour and laid it down at her feet (a clear sign that he is under her domination), he still hopes by admonition to forestall the sequel to his surrender: for it is evident that, pushed by Cupid, Venus will play the part of a goddess of Peace by putting her flaming torch to the trophies of war (cf. Hill, pl. 201, no. 872 bis). The contrived wit of Marcantonio's engraving is in the manner of Alexandrian epigrams: In consorting with Venus the apprehensive Mars tries to save his armour from her fire.

4

Love's Sweet Poison: A New Reading of Bronzino's London *Allegory*

Robert W. Gaston

Looking back over fifty years of publications on Bronzino's celebrated *Allegory* in the National Gallery, London (fig. 4.1) one cannot but be impressed by the tenacious power of research paradigms.[1] These models of explanation, made up of assumptions that determine which questions ought to be asked of the artist and the work of art, and which bodies of evidence are likely to yield responses to those questions, are often far from explicit in iconographic discourse. In the "classic" formulations of iconographic practice by Warburg, Saxl, Wind, and Panofsky, such methodological issues were either excluded from the exposition altogether or restricted to the parenthetical locations of foreword and afterword. By keeping questions of method outside the iconographic demonstration, the discourse could assume an hermetic quality that enhanced its rhetorical persuasiveness.[2]

In this paper I shall take a critical approach to questions of method arising from study of the *Allegory*, one which may seem unnecessary to some art historians. But if we ask why it is that the *Allegory* has remained somehow "resistant" to explanation, we cannot avoid dealing with the issue of paradigms. My offering a new interpretation implies that I regard it as being historically more probable than those advanced by my predecessors.[3] It will be clear, however, that my interpretation is indebted to the work of every scholar who has written on this picture.

Panofsky's model of iconographic research assumed that scholars would recognize relationships between "documents of civilization" and the subject matter of the representation.[4] If his theoretical range of "documents" sounded comprehensive, the kinds he actually consulted in his *Studies in Iconology* were both limited and determined by his assumptions about the sorts of connections he presumed to have existed between artists and contemporary humanistic scholarship, and between artists and patrons.

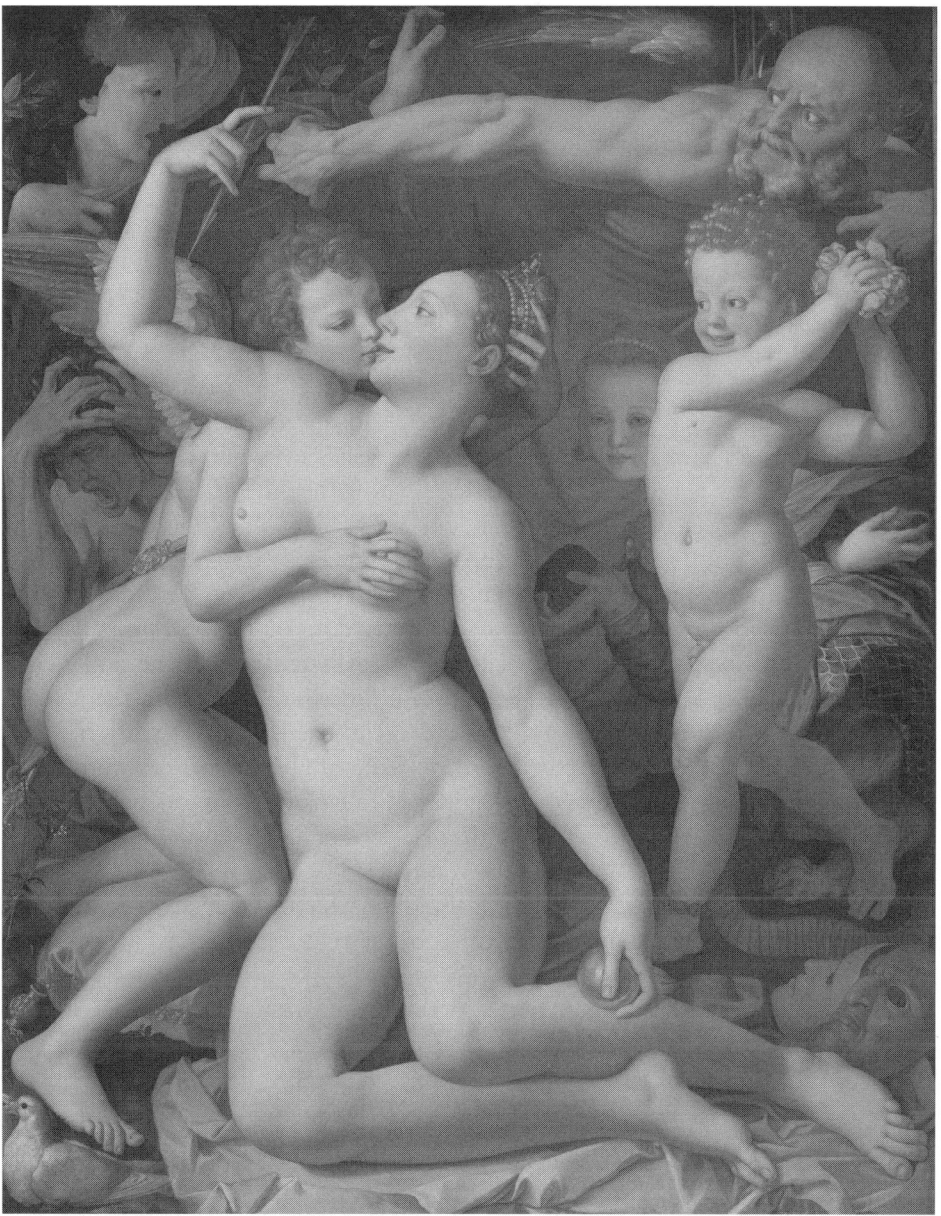

Figure 4.1 Agnolo Bronzino (1503–1572), *Allegory with Venus and Cupid*,
ca. 1540–50. Oil on panel. National Gallery, London, UK / The Bridgeman
Art Library.

Panofsky's exegesis of the *Allegory* seemed to arise from a sensitive response to the clues recorded in Vasari's description, in the 1568 edition of his *Vite*, of what was perhaps the same picture, which reads:

> Fece un quadro di singolare bellezza, che fu mandato in Francia al re Francesco; dentro al quale era una Venere ignuda con Cupido che la baciava, et il Piacere da un lato e il Giuoco con altri Amori, e dall'altro la Fraude, la Gelosia, et altre passioni d'amore.[5]

However, several of Panofsky's descriptive observations were demonstrably inaccurate. Venus' golden apple is not "tendered" to the eager Cupid. Why should the two masks beside Venus's feet in the foreground relate to the rose-bearing putto and the "girl in the green dress" in the middle and background? Are the hands of that strange girl-monster really switched to the opposite arms? Is the female figure at the top-left, whom he identified as Truth, the daughter of Time, actually drawing the curtain "from the whole spectacle" to uncover it? Each of these observations was "caused" by Panofsky's iconographic assumptions interfering with his visual perception. The need to "fit" the picture to Vasari's description was an obvious determinant for him. Superimposed on this was the interpretive force of Saxl's essay on Time and Truth (1936),[6] and the hermeneutical presuppositions that informed their joint work on the *Nachleben* of classical ideas and their Renaissance adaptation. Both scholars believed that classical, patristic and medieval literary sources were made accessible to artists in the sixteenth century principally through mythological and iconographic handbooks such as those of Cartari and Ripa. Just as Saxl explained Marcolini's *Veritas Filia Temporis* woodcut and legend of 1536 by reference to Cartari's gathering of disparate sources in 1556, so Panofsky explained much of the *Allegory*'s iconography by reference to Ripa's *Iconologia* of 1593.

The chronological discrepancy between the earliest use of Marcolini's *Veritas* woodcut and Cartari's *Imagini* did not trouble Saxl, because Marcolini also published the latter, and Saxl could visualize an intellectual continuum maintained by the publisher. But Panofsky's susceptibility to the charms of Ripa, when interpreting Bronzino, can only be accounted for by his conception of the spatio-temporal and intellectual unity of Renaissance culture. When Panofsky quoted the Paris, 1515, Latin edition of Pierre Bersuire's *Ovide moralisé* as a text relevant to Bronzino's image of Venus and Cupid kissing, he gave it the status of a passage that was "still unforgotten" in the sixteenth century. But to whom was it known or available? It was not proposed that any person acted as scholarly intermediary between the humanist erudition of Latin books and an artist who was probably ignorant of that language. For Panofsky it was enough to demonstrate that the requisite textual knowledge was "available" in European books. The processes by which it allegedly found its way into the picture did not require precise definition.

In following Vasari's description Panofsky found his iconographic options drastically narrowed. If "the head of an elderly woman madly tearing her hair" at the left seemed to correspond with Vasari's "label" Jealousy, then where was he to find visual confirmation of her identity? Ripa's image of *Gelosia* was patently irrelevant. He turned to Dürer's etching known as *The Desperate Man*. Here was a male figure apparently tearing his hair, but accompanied by other figures, two of them perhaps derived from the Nymph and Satyr woodcut in the *Hypnerotomachia Poliphili*. The etching at least predated Bronzino's picture, even if the hair-tearing man was the wrong gender for *Gelosia*.

Vasari also determined for Panofsky that the child throwing roses could represent the terms "Pleasure" and "Jest" with "almost equal correctness", and that the girl-monster behind that figure had to be Deceit (*Fraude*). In arguing that through this hybrid creature "Bronzino manages to give a summary of and almost visual commentary upon the qualities of hypocritical falsehood which are described by sixteenth-century iconologists," Panofsky was perpetrating his own gentle *fraude* on the reader. In truth, he could not find Bronzino's figure described in Ripa, or Cartari, or in any other iconologist of the century. Several of the attributes of her animal-reptile body did indeed have their parallels in aspects of Ripa's personifications of *Inganno*, *Hippocrisia*, and *Fraude*, but only Panofsky's suggestive prose made them seem accessible, in a specious unity, to the inventor of Bronzino's painting.

In a concluding note, Panofsky suggested that Bronzino's painting of Venus and Cupid with putti in Budapest repeated the main idea of the *Allegory* "in a less invective fashion". He sensed that Vasari may have confused his recollection of the *Allegory*'s subject "with his impression of the Budapest panel".

> This would account, (1) for the omission of "Time" and "Truth", (2) for the emphasis of a strict symmetry ("*da un lato – e dall'altro*") which is indeed maintained in the Budapest picture, (3) for the mention of "Giuoco" and "Piacere", which error would be explicable by the presence of *two* playful Putti in the Budapest version.

Panofsky's final observation in that note, that "both compositions are, of course, influenced by Michelangelo's Venus (cartoon made for Bartolomeo Bettini, executed in colors by Jacopo Pontormo, the teacher of Bronzino); it shows already the motif of the embrace in combination with that of the masks" – was to be the departure-point for several subsequent readings of the picture.

In 1967 Michael Levey proposed a new interpretation, supposing that the *Allegory* presented "an *invenzione* with echoes, conscious echoes of the great Florentine tradition" arising from "the active genius of Michelangelo". Touching on the observer's response to the "polished surfaces" of Bronzino's pictures and its hermeneutical consequences, on the relationship between his poetic activity and intended meaning in his pictorial inventions, Levey completely recast the terms in which the *Allegory* could be considered. He associated it with two other pictures by Bronzino treating "the subject", those at Budapest and the Galleria Colonna, Rome, regarding the former (as had Panofsky) as a variant of the *Allegory*, and the latter as a variant of the *Venus and Cupid* designed by Michelangelo ca. 1532–33 and painted by Pontormo. Levey cited Vasari's testimony that the commissioner of Pontormo's painting, Bartolomeo Bettini, intended to have the painting in a room accompanied by portraits of the Tuscan lyric poets, to be painted by Bronzino. "Thus the three artists were already brought into connection with the theme." Assuming that "the erotic power of Venus" was the dominant motif, with Dante, Petrarch, and Boccaccio "present as witnesses to the power and beauty of love", Levey went on to argue that Venus' seduction of Cupid, or the "Triumph of Venus" over the love to which even she is vulnerable, was the common subject of both Pontormo's *Venus and Cupid* and Bronzino's *Allegory*. Among his evidence was a poem addressed to Michelangelo, which, referring to his cartoon, describes Venus's power to "bring Cupid to her lips". Less convincing, chronologically, was his appeal to the subscription from an engraving by Saenredam after Goltzius.

Levey took Vasari's description of the *Allegory* even more seriously than Panofsky, reidentifying "Truth" as *Fraude* because Vasari said that she appeared on the same side of the picture as "Jealousy", and because closer visual analysis of her head indicated "a hollow mask attached to a neck". Therefore Time, in attempting to tear off *Fraude*'s drapery, seeks "to reveal her deceitful vacuity". Again following Vasari, Levey equated the girl monster with *Piacere*, the honey-comb and "sting of her tail" representing the "double aspect" of amorous pleasure. The "moral" signified in these attributes is "not for us but for Cupid", who is being robbed of his arrow "even while he enjoys the honeyed kiss offered so seductively by his mother". The putto is Vasari's *Giuoco*, and with Pleasure makes up the *passioni d'amore* mentioned by Vasari.

In closing, Levey suggested that Bettini may have been the *Allegory*'s original commissioner, but considered it likely that Cosimo I, by then owner of the Michelangelo–Pontormo *Venus*, "might well have been instigated by such possession to have his painter execute an elaborate variation on it".

In 1978 William Keach enlarged Levey's documentation of the Michelangelo cartoon, noting the "precarious position" of the arrows remaining in Cupid's quiver after Venus has surreptitiously removed one as she embraces him. Keach saw this "threat" to Venus as corresponding to the arrow Venus holds in Bronzino's *Allegory* having its point "perilously close to the inside of her arm". He interpreted "the central subject" of both Michelangelo and Bronzino as the wounding of Venus, "instead of, or in addition to, Venus Disarming Cupid", and nominated Ovid's *Metamorphoses*, X, 525–528, in which Cupid accidentally grazed Venus's breast with an arrow, causing her infatuation, as a likely source for both artists.[7]

Graham Smith's article of 1981 formed a pendant to Levey's, accepting that the *Allegory* represented a *Triumph of Venus*, but seeking to identify its sources in the writings of Bronzino's friend Benedetto Varchi, who lectured to literary academies in Padua and Florence on love and jealousy in the first half of the 1540s. Smith found that Bronzino's depiction of "Jealousy's" emotional turmoil, dark complexion, and close association with Cupid were explicable in terms of Varchi's describing how jealousy was essential to love, how it transformed love's sweetness into bitterness, and was a species of envy. He noted that Varchi's emphasis on the bittersweet aspect of love drew upon Latin and Italian poetic traditions, making special mention of Petrarch and Bembo. But he regarded Varchi's *Sulla Gelosia* as the key text establishing "the idea of the duplex nature of Pleasure in Florence at the time of the painting", and which "associates in a single text a number of the abstractions given visual form by Bronzino, and offers an explanation for their being gathered together". The honeycomb and sting held by the girl at the right "allude to the double aspect of pleasure". Searching for a "concrete" identity for the girl-monster, Smith opted for Cartari's lascivious, flesh-eating Lamia, but in doing so had to deny the visual significance of her clothing, claws, and reptile's tail. The rose-bearing putto similarly represented for Smith the dual aspect of love's pleasure, his happy disposition about to be pained by the sharp thorn visible under his foot. Noting that Varchi wrote a sonnet to Bronzino ca. 1546 praising his portrait of Eleonora of Toledo, and that the two exchanged sonnets over the next twenty years, Smith leaned to the view that Varchi was the author of the *Allegory*'s *concetto*, and had perhaps commissioned it. He concluded, however, that given the visual precedent of a seated Venus embraced by Cupid in Pontormo's drawing for the marriage decorations of Cosimo and Eleonora, the commission should be retained for Cosimo, who gave it away, finding the completed work "more suggestive than the written sketch on which it was based".

In 1982, Charles Hope, in a reprise of Levey's argument, advised students of the *Allegory* to ignore later iconographic compilations such as those of Cartari and Ripa. Bronzino would have drawn on "such visual precedents as he could find", and where there were none "devised figures" with self-explanatory attributes. He preferred to relate the girl-monster's iconography to the visual image of *Fraude* in the Marcolini woodcut which Bronzino presumably would have seen. For Panofsky's "Truth" and Levey's *Fraude*, he proposed a new identity, outside of Vasari's group, making her the personification of Oblivion. Her having no back to her head seemed consistent with contemporary belief that the memory resided in that part of the brain, its absence in Bronzino's figure denoting forgetfulness, *Oblivione*. Hope had to turn to early sixteenth-century France for a visual image of Oblivion in this form, but noted that the concept was present in the repertoire of Petrarch, whose poetry was familiar to Bronzino. He argued that the central group of Venus, Cupid and the putto representing *Il piacere* depicted "not love in general, but the incompletely reciprocated love of a man for a woman, the most familiar poetic theme of the Renaissance". The "screen of laurel" visible behind the figures denoted the Petrarchan conceit of poetic fame, and here he reiterated Levey's evidence about the Bettini commission.

Hope suggested that Oblivion and Time were collaborating "to obscure love and the disagreeable passions it engenders". Conway, in 1986, interpreted the *Allegory* as showing Time frustrating Oblivion's efforts to cover with her veil the figure beneath her, usually interpreted as Jealousy, but now meticulously described as a male suffering the effects of syphilis.

Iris Cheney's article of the same year read the *Allegory* as a rather complex *Psychomachia*, having "dense layering of overlappping meanings", some allegedly Medicean, others to do with virtues combating vices, and ages of love, and Neoplatonic philosophy. Cheney's description of the "conception of allegorical personification" that Bronzino supposedly employs in the *Allegory*, namely "synthetic, allusive, unstable rather than concrete, and static, as it would be a generation later in Ripa's *Iconologia*", gave a good indication of her flexible and eclectic approach to Bronzino's iconography.

It is clear that the clues offered by Vasari can be used to arrive at incompatible explanations, ones difficult to substantiate from the surviving visual sources. There is no consensus as to who devised the *Allegory*, although Vasari's testimony that it became a state-gift has led scholars to assume that a "learned adviser" was responsible for its subject. No contract or Medici correspondence substantiating its commissioning has come to light. Nor is there evidence that the *Allegory* was ever in the French royal collection in the sixteenth century.[8] As Panofsky first noted, Vasari confused its subject matter with the similar picture now in Budapest; the early provenance of this is equally mysterious.

Given the uncertainties in Vasari's account, and the doubtful benefits accruing from its application in iconographic analysis, I propose to put aside his text. In reinterpreting the *Allegory* I shall accept the validity of Hope's view that the woman at the top-left personifies Oblivion, and Conway's perception that the anatomy of the "hair-tearing" figure at the left is that of a mature male.

The formal structure of the painting is precisely organized so that the figures are displayed in three distinct spatial layers. Venus, Cupid, and the putto with the roses are distinguished by their foreground placement and strong lighting; the putto's mischievous gaze, his decisive movement towards Venus and Cupid, and his arm-gesture indicative of his intending to throw roses over the love-making couple, all serve to tie him in with them, even though he stands slightly deeper in the picture-space and very close to the girl-monster, over whose reptilian coil he steps. The girl, her hands framing the putto's body, is located in a middleground, closed off by the suspended blue cloth, a space shared at the left by the suffering male figure. Time and Oblivion stand or kneel behind the cloth they hold. The foreground figures interact with each other, but not with those behind them. The interlocked gazes of Time and Oblivion, and their mutual concern with the blue cloth, would separate them entirely from the middle and foreground figures were it not that the cloth extends beneath Venus, right to the picture-plane. The anguished man at the left is self-absorbed, and ignored by the others. The girl-monster, however, looks between the putto and the Venus–Cupid group and engages the eyes of the picture's beholder.

If we consider the appearance of her head and shoulders without prejudice, we shall have to admit that she resembles the young women of Bronzino's portraits and religious paintings from the 1540s. Even the coiffure and expensive clothing are fully in keeping with Bronzino's depictions of the self-presentation of young ladies at the Florentine court. The pearl-studded clasp that holds her diaphanous shawl, the gold satin sash that girds her waist, and her milk-white hands, are further visual clues that the girl-part of this hybrid creature is to be understood as a contemporary young beauty such as one could see at the court of Cosimo I. All that differs is that her gaze is more intense than was appropriate in either a female portrait, or in a figure looking out of a narrative picture in the Albertian manner. Her honeycomb and sting may well be, as Levey suggested, what Cupid will find in his dalliance with Venus; but her straining gaze at the picture's viewer indicates that he, too (presuming a male recipient), will experience the sweetness and bitter pain of love if he succumbs to the lure of those eyes.

The new interpretation to be offered below will be based on the belief that Bronzino could have read widely in the vernacular literature of his day. In putting this view I am aware of simply bringing into sharper focus and on the one picture ideas that have at least been foreshadowed by several contributors to the iconographic investigation of the *Allegory*, notably Graham Smith, and by scholars now exploring the connections between Cinquecento vernacular literature on deportment and poetic theory, and theory and practice in the visual arts, especially Elizabeth Cropper and Leatrice Mendelsohn. It seems reasonable to assume, however, that since Bronzino wrote several hundred pages of poetry – some of it published before he painted the *Allegory* – he may have shown a preference in his reading for vernacular verse. Moreover, I shall argue that a reading of Bronzino's poetry will suggest enough thematic connections to confirm that he was capable of the *invenzione* of the *Allegory*. Finally, it will be proposed that his poetic relationship with Benedetto Varchi should be explored in more detail.

Let us presume that the *Allegory* was completed in or about 1546, as stylistic comparison suggests. We shall exclude from consideration everything published after that date, forgetting about Cartari, Ripa, the learned Latin mythological handbooks of the late 1540s and 1550s (Giraldi, 1548; Conti, 1551; Valeriano, 1556), and indeed, everything else in Latin.[9] In several of his *rime in burla* Bronzino uses Latin words and phrases, some of which fragments seem to come from a single textbook on logic that he put to mock-scholarly use in crafting his poems.[10] Varchi translated some Ovid for him,[11] and also testified that, by 1539, Bronzino knew all of Dante and most of Petrarch by heart.[12] The then available parts of the classical authors named by Bronzino in his poetry – Aristotle, Cicero, Demosthenes, Donatus, Homer, Horace, Juvenal, Livy, Ovid, Plato, Plutarch, and Vitruvius[13] – were accessible in vernacular translations.[14]

He also cites Ariosto, Francesco Berni, Boccaccio, Annibal Caro, Della Casa, Il Lasca, Michelangelo, and Varchi.[15] These names indicate that he was an active reader, as one would expect of a man who says in his poetry that he could not eat, sleep, or rest until he had written some poems: who reserved a great part of his nights for writing his *rime*, making *castelli in aria*, as he put it.[16]

Ekphrasis, the rhetorical description of landscape, architecture, or works of visual art, was a topic of late-antique epigrams, love poetry and narrative prose.[17] Elements of it were adopted in Petrarch's *rime* and those of his imitators.[18] The Petrarchan poet might attempt vainly to "paint" (*depingere*) the remarkable beauty of his *donna* in words,[19] or compare her physical attributes with those of Venus sculpted or painted by famous classical artists. He did so, however, to demonstrate the superior evocation achieved in his verse in comparison with the universally admired, classical work of visual art.

There was a powerful erotic aspect to the ekphrastic prose romance in antiquity; in Longus's *Daphnis and Chloe* the writer's vision of a pictorial history of Eros, which arouses his desire (*pothos*), is the fictive stimulus for his rival narrative.[20] Petrarch and Boccaccio developed variants from such prototypes, and in the half-century before Bronzino's *Allegory* many erotic stories set in *all'antica* landscapes and architecture were composed in the vernacular. In these the writer attributes to the visual artist the invention of "classical" erotic scenes which he may then either describe in detail, or suggestively decline to do so, privately savoring what he "sees" and leaving it to the reader's imagination, thus observing a responsibility for decorum that exceeds that of the artist being fictively imitated. In the *Hypnerotomachia Poliphili* (1499), the best known of these inventions, the text outdoes the woodcuts in explicit eroticism.[21] Such literature employed fictive eroticism to denote the writer's control of his medium, therefore of his reader.[22] But in the Petrarchan tradition of love poetry in which Bronzino writes, classical erotic mythology was introduced into its poetic discourse as "purified" *exempla*, or *comparanda* which illuminate the fictive interaction of the poet and his unattainable lady.

When Bronzino's literary friends alluded, in their poetic discourses with him, to his being at once a new Apollo, and a new Apelles,[23] they were resorting to rhetorical cliché (Varchi used it for Michelangelo). But to overlook Bronzino's dual commitment to painting and poetry is to fail to comprehend the meaning of his work in either medium. When, in his poetry, he refers to maintaining the *decoro del cominciato stil*,[24] or describes a painted nude figure that is *quasi una natura nuova*,[25] he alludes to the interpenetration of, the inseparability of, the poetic and the pictorial. Bronzino's lifelong admiration for Michelangelo's artistic achievement, which is fittingly expressed in his poetry and painting, is a stylistic devotion in the most profound senses of both terms. The language in which Bronzino describes his "servitude" to Michelangelo is that of the latter's poetic vocabulary, which was drawn from the same Tuscan sources that nourished his own. For Bronzino to consecrate himself poetically to the "Archangel Michael", to "a terrestrial god", to dedicate his "hand" and "intellect"[26] to following Michelangelo up that "arduous pathway" to a pictorial style arising from *studio* and *disegno*,[27] was to acknowledge the exemplary impact of the great Florentine's simultaneous mastery of poetry and painting.

The Petrarchan poet's declaration of failure in his literary attempts to describe the living beauty of his lady, that "silent truth which surpasses every style",[28] is, of course, a conventional capitulation to artistic despair. Michelangelo's protestations of the feebleness of his sculptor's crafting simply transposed Petrarch's *penne, carte, enchiostri* into hammers and chisels.[29] The ironic tensions created in Petrarchan poetry written by the visual artist – the maker of two or three-dimensional forms having an existence like that "silent truth" of reality – were bound to be extreme. The artist-poet would appreciate that, although the poet might even allow (as did Niccolò da Correggio) that painting and poetry are rivals in representing respectively the *forma* and the *virtù* of his lady, and that both must fall short of perfection in their tasks,[30] nevertheless the poem's critique of both media has the last word. He would realize that while contemporary poets (like Marco da Lodi) may acknowledge that an artist of Raphael's skill might be ready and willing to represent "a worthy portrait" (*ritratto degno*) of his lady in any conceivable medium, the poetic tradition itself required that this visual image not succeed in disclosing her "true image" (*effigie vera*), which is already "well sculpted" in the poet's own heart.[31] Most testing of all for such an artist-poet would be the awareness that his poetry could achieve its representational aims in "depicting" his lover without having to resort to very specific description of her physical attributes: it sufficed to suggest that these were incomparable, or superior to those of a goddess whose imaging by visual artists had already become exemplary, but remained inadequate because of its visual definiteness, that is, by virtue of its not being poetry.

For the Petrarchan poet who is also a painter, the truth of representation is itself the most critical issue. If every paintbrush is necessarily *fallace* in its task of depicting the lover's beauty,[32] if only Petrarch can portray the subtlety of her colors,[33] what is left to the painter? We can explore this issue in looking more closely at Bronzino's literary relationship with Benedetto Varchi.[34] When he and Bronzino first met is not documented. Known for his republican views, Varchi left Florence with his Strozzi patrons after the murder of Alessandro de' Medici in 1536, to settle in Padua. There he stayed with Pietro Bembo, developed a local academy of *litterati*, and kept his literary ties with Florence through tutoring gifted young Florentines like Ugolino Martelli. Duke Cosimo, judging that the educational and propagandistic advantages in Florence's having Varchi back outweighed the political objections, invited him to return in 1543, and in March he entered the newly revamped Accademia Fiorentina, developed from that of the *Umidi*. As early as 1537, however, Bronzino's sculptor friend, Tribolo, had enlisted Varchi's scholarly advice in inventing the decorations for the Medici villa at Castello. When Bembo passed through Florence in 1539, Varchi arranged for this *Petrarca novello*[35] to meet with Bronzino and his friends.

In 1545, the year in which he was elected consul of the academy, Varchi was imprisoned briefly, charged with the rape of a twelve-year-old farm girl, but released with a fine after his literary friends intervened with the Duke. He was dogged by accusations of homosexual seduction of the aristocratic youths he tutored, and hated by many Florentine *litterati* who saw him promoting Bembo's strain of Petrarchan poetry over Dante. Bronzino maintained friendships with many of Varchi's enemies, Gelli and Giambullari, for example, while defending Varchi in his poetry against their "envious bites" (*invidi morsi*).[36] He hoped for "a sweet, honourable peace" for Varchi, far from the "vile, impious and lying" *volgo*.[37] For his part, Varchi saw Bronzino as "a wall" between himself and those who would destroy him.[38] The poems they exchanged are fascinating, because the discourse is so tightly woven, so profoundly complementary in the way Varchi constructs his *risposte* to each of Bronzino's poems addressed to him, using parts of Bronzino's vocabulary. The *vero amore* experienced by these two men is perfectly embodied in the way their poems share and speak each other's words.

In his poetry from the 1550s Bronzino defends Varchi's views on vernacular literature against the attacks of Castelvetro. There was, then, a prolonged and significant literary relationship between the two men, one which mirrors the seriousness of Bronzino's involvement with poetry as a persuasive means of effect-ing moral change in the reader.[39] Its pictorial analogue exists in the portrait-roles Bronzino gave to Varchi in his *Limbo* (*in restauro*, Florence), and *Deposition* (Accademia, Florence), where, respectively, Varchi carried Christ's cross as the Good Thief, and tenderly lifts Christ's body from the cross, as Nicodemus. These roles acknowledge Varchi's importance to Bronzino as a guide in theolo-gical issues after 1548, but also denote, in their representational vivacity, that the poet's friend and mentor, himself a poet, could not escape the skill of the painter's brush, nor the painter's judgement as a teacher of *i buoni costumi*.[40]

Varchi must have riveted Bronzino's attention when he read his *Lezioni due sopra la pittura e scultura* to the Accademia Fiorentina in March 1547.[41] The pretext for the first lecture, Michelangelo's sonnet, *Non ha l'ottimo artista alcun concetto*, allowed Varchi to present an exegesis in which the poet and philo-sopher vie for precedence in teaching humanity about *amore*. The second *Lezione* deals with the relative merits of painting and sculpture, but those are placed, with telling honesty, after architecture, medicine, and the higher arts of the word. Varchi speaks of the illusionistic power of painting and sculpture, but for him poetry alone can represent *il di dentro*, the interior experience of "the concepts and passions of the soul".[42]

One of his pictorial examples was Michelangelo's cartoon of *Venus and Cupid*, painted by Pontormo. This he related to the by then familiar recension of instances taken from Pliny of the painter's ability to deceive the eye. Birds and animals could be deceived by painted and sculpted images, just as men fell in love with marble statues like Praxiteles' *Venus*: "however the same thing still happens today all the time with the Venus that Michelangelo drew for

M. Bartolomeo Bettini".[43] This was a remarkable tribute to a living painter, and if Bronzino was aware of this opinion before he painted the *Allegory*, it may have been a factor in its genesis.

Varchi gives an account, in his treatise *Della generazione de' mostri* (1548), of how, in 1536, Bronzino had made a splendid representation (*fu ritratto egregiamente*) of female Siamese twins born at the Porta al Prato, before they were separated and dissected by surgeons at the garden of Palla Rucellai.[44] Explaining the different meanings of the term *mostro*, Varchi noted that the description *mostri dell'animo* applied to those who surpassed all others in their works of hand or mind. In this sense Bembo had called Michelangelo *un mostro della natura*, and Petrarch himself had called his Laura *altero, e raro mostro* among women. Even an outstanding ruler like Duke Cosimo could be so designated, Varchi observed.[45] Bronzino himself used the concept in an early poem addressed to Varchi, celebrating his presence in Florence as a champion of the vernacular (*la lingua nostra*), when he called him *divino quasi huom, ch'e pur dipinto, e vivo mostro*.[46]

The poetic dialogue between Varchi and Bronzino is about their sharing in this canon of Florentine *mostri*. Bronzino writes to praise and protect this *Nuovo Pegaso* of the Florentine Parnassus,[47] created under Duke Cosimo's patronage of the Accademia Fiorentina. He admires, as should the world, the *chiaro stil* of Varchi's vernacular poetry and prose.[48] Varchi, in turn, praises the *doppio stile* of Bronzino, poet and painter: his *chiaro pennello* represents *il bello di fuor*, and the *altro stile* of his poetry, *il buon di dentro*.[49] The adjective *chiaro* (from the Latin *clarus)* was frequently used (83 times) by Petrarch in his verse to denote fame, but more often a beautiful property of clarity or brightness in substances like water or light, the eyes of Laura, or the poet's own vision.[50] Bronzino and Varchi surely knew by heart the stanza of Petrarch's *canzone, Si è debile il filo a cui s'attene*, which compared the clarity with which the color in crystal or glass made by human hand shines forth, with the incomparable clarity with which "my disconsolate soul shows forth through my eyes the cares and savage sweetness that are in my heart".[51]

Bronzino actually explored the meanings of the term *chiaro* in one of his late humorous poems, *Dell'Esser chiaro*. Beginning with the query, why the ancient poets and theorists of poetry (*color ch'anticamente poetaro*) never said anything about "being clear" (*dell'esser chiaro*) when every kind of philosophy is concerned with nothing else, Bronzino personifies his *Esser chiaro* and describes ironically how confusing life would be without him. One would never know *il ver dalla bugia* (truth from deception), *l'esser dal sogno* (reality from a dream). Things would be *sempre in ambiguo* (always ambiguous), *senza risoluzion* (unresolved), *sempre in pendente* (always suspended); being something (*qualcosa*) would seem mixed up with (*mescolato*) being nothing (*niente*). These ontological and epistemological doubts are related here to a major theme of Bronzino's poetry: despairing of being able to know whether friendship, i.e. love, is *vera o finta*, whether there is *l'amaro nel petto e 'l dolce in mano* (bitterness in the breast and sweetness in the hand).[52] What is presented to the eye in human interaction is assumed to be fraudulent. Simple souls (*semplici*) are always *traditi o ingannati* (betrayed or deceived).[53] The court, in particular, is riddled with deception. Among the women there is so much *cortesia senza onesta*. A woman who is *cortese*, beautiful, wise and dutiful (*pia*), is "a large part of all that is good in the world", but she is a rare phenomenon. At court there is so much covering of real thoughts *sotto contrario ammanto* (under turned coat).[54] One possible solution was to "leave the mob to its false pleasure, and enjoy the truth in secret" (*lasci al volgo / Il piacer falso, e'l ver goda in secreto*).[55]

Being unable to see beneath the appearances of things greatly troubled Bronzino, at least in the rhetoric of his poetry. In the absurd, upside-down world of his *rime in burla* none of the human sciences or pseudo-sciences is of avail. Even physiognomy, which *guarda i volti* (studies faces), and should enable one "to know the thieves, and assassins from the sodomites, the sad from the fools", is not reliable.[56] The *finto riso* (counterfeit smile) is the means to worldly success and money. To follow its call is to enter a world of horror, a "sick and blind life" (*inferma vita, e cieca*) "deprived of the *sanita d'amici*".[57] Bronzino can begin an early sonnet with the half-hopeful words *Se l'occhio non m'inganna, e 'l ver mi dice* (If my eyes don't deceive me, and tell me the truth), but within a few lines Amor is there, playing and smiling (*mentre ei gioca, e ride*), and the suffering is about to begin.[58]

Does the notion of a *chiaro stil*, common to poetry and painting, throw any light on Bronzino's approach to representation, and on the *Allegory* in particular? Its potential ambiguity – it can mean both "distinguished" in the sense of being famous, and "clear" – is an obvious clue to its purely verbal, associative significance. Bronzino was doubtless acquainted with Bembo's *Prose della volgar lingua* (1525), where Michelangelo and Raphael were greatly praised, but also faintly praised, in comparison with the *antichi buoni maestri* in their "much lesser arts" (*arti molto minori*). Bembo called the two modern masters *eccellenti e cosi chiari*, but stated that they, and indeed all other men who were *chiari e illustri*, were only so because of writing (*scrivere*), without which no art could be *bella e chiara*. Phidias, Apelles, Vitruvius, even Alberti, would be unknown had they not written themselves or been celebrated in ink.[59]

In his facetious poem, *Del Dappoco* (On the Good-for-Nothing), written in the 1550s, Bronzino's poetic voice declares that he "scribbles a few sheets" (*scombiccerarmi / qualche foglio*) to pass the time and to rest his brain. In speaking of his pictorial *lavoro*, he specifies that it "wearies the soul and the brain" (*di affatica l'anima e 'l cervello*). There is more, he says, to the *padre universal disegno* than "using rule and compasses" (*ch'oprar regolo o seste*).[60] In making this defence of the intellectual dimension of his painting, Bronzino was certainly aligning himself with Leonardo's distinction between *fatica del corpo* and *fatica dell'ingegno*, as a way of separating painting and sculpture from the purely mechanical arts, a position further exploited by Varchi in his *Due lezioni*.[61] But the poem was probably reacting to a paragraph of Mario Equicola's description of painting in the *Discorso della pittura*, which formed part of his *Institutioni* of 1541.

> E la pittura opera & fatica piu del corpo che dell'animo, da gli idioti esercitati il piu delle volte, d'una delle quattro Mathematice discipline contenta, d'altra cognitione non ha mestiere, se non al natural farsi simile con colori diversamente proprij, con lineamenti, ombre, & prospettive. La sua cura è rendere al visivo senso il vero. Il poeta tutte le discipline brama, con figure, tropi, & numeri a stupire i periti costringe, & in ammiratione gl'indotti adduce. Con parole atte servando il decoro delle introdutte persone l'intelletto del poeta s'affatica.[62]

The sneering tone of this would have cut Bronzino deeply, particularly in that he himself had used the phrase *ritrar al naturale* to denote pictorial representation in his early poem *Del Pennello* (published in 1538). There he takes the ekphrastic motive of the skillful representation (*un buon ritratto*) of a nude couple engaged in sexual intercourse as a poetic device for exploring the visual impact of a representation, to judge the illusionistic power of the artist's brush (*giudicare / il pennel*). The brush (*pennello*) doubles throughout for the artist's penis, and that Bronzino engages poetically with Giulio Romano's *I modi*, and equally with Aretino's verse commentaries on them, is clear enough. He does not bother to list the thousand-and-one *diversi atti e modi stravaganti* that could be represented, from different viewpoints, in foreshortening, or in perspective. The artist's *pennello* is the means by which "art arrives at nature" (*l'arte alla natura arriva*). Beneath the layers of irony of this there lurks an acute sensitivity to the limits of decorum, and to the issue of artistic genius, poetic and pictorial. The *faticose attitudin* (tiring poses) of the sexual protagonists may be *ben lavorato* (technically clever), and look natural to the eye, but this is an easy victory for representation. How can the eye resist such allurement? Does it require *un gran cervello* (a huge brain), *un grande ingegno* (a great genius), to represent such things? In order to be able to paint what he himself plans, or designs (*far quella cosa, ch'io disegno*), it is appropriate that he "sharpens his genius" (*aguzzi l'ingegno*), and that he attempts to "heighten his style" (*alzar questo mio stile*). The intellectual, that is, poetic, dimension of *disegno*, is what Bronzino alludes to here;[63] his "learned hand" (*dotta mano*), as Varchi called it.[64]

What does Bronzino's *Allegory* represent? What is it about? To reply that it is "about representation" may seem to be a perversely modern interpretation. This is to ignore, however, that the Petrarchan poetic vocabulary had already subsumed and absorbed the classical visual representation of love. When Petrarch wrote of *Amore*: "Not at all blind I see him, but bearing a quiver, naked except where shame veils him; a boy with wings, not depicted but alive" (*non pinto ma vivo*),[65] he asserts that his Cupid has a representational "truth" that is explicitly "more real" than that achieved by any painter. Even in Il Burchiello's playful parody of the inability of both the ancient poets and a modern painter (Orcagna) to describe accurately the nature of *Amore*,[66] the poet's "truer" description that pretends to substitute for those others achieves an ironic victory. Bronzino's profound know-ledge of such poetic discourse makes it very likely that his *Allegory* was conceived as a pictorial "answer" to the problem of visual representation, as it was framed for him by the poets and their critics. This approach can account for the fact that art historians have had difficulty in finding visual sources for the *Allegory*.

If the *Allegory*'s purpose was to represent more alluringly, more truthfully, the phenomenon of human erotic love and its consequences than poetry itself could do, then Bronzino's sources were just as likely to be poetic as visual. Pre-existing pictorial "attempts" could be regarded as already vanquished by poetry. He eschews close imitation of Michelangelo's *Venus and Cupid*, itself a *risposta* to the classical and vernacular love-poem, because visual originality is crucial to his struggle with the vividness of poetry. There may be some now-lost fragment of classical art that suggested to Bronzino his poses for Venus and Cupid. Caraglio's prints showing the loves of the gods do seem germane.[67] But I shall argue that the intense, incestuous erotic encounter between Cupid and his mother that we view in the *Allegory* is more the figuration of a poetic conceit than a reflection of a visual tradition. Not that Bronzino was simply imitating the words of Petrarch, or those of any other vernacular poet, even himself, in the *invenzione* of his *Allegory*. This would be to misunderstand that the picture *is*, in its representa-tional ontology, the poem about love.

For any Italian artist or poet interested in the iconography of love in the 1530s and 1540s, Mario Equicola's *Libro di natura d'amore* (1525)[68] afforded an exhaustive encyclopedia of the subject, ranging from the prose and poetry of Greek and Roman antiquity to that of the early Cinquecento. Equicola's *Libro* is richly allusive in the precision of its descriptions of protagonists for the visual artist, and in its concern with pictorial representation as a *topos* of the literary tradition on love.

His compilation shows so lucidly how, in Boccaccio, a Lucretian and partly Christian misogynist attitude to woman emerges to develop alongside the *dolce stil nuovo* conception of the pain and pleasure of unrequited love.[69] This Boccaccian strain identified women as *animali*, physically disgusting and full of deceptions (*piene d'inganni*). They use the sweet poison of sexual pleasure, and poisonous words, to lead men into states of acute suffering.[70] But, as Equicola notes, these male "victims" do not really struggle to free themselves from such *infermita*, "so sweet is the suffering and so *suavo 'l veneno*".[71] There were, in fact, venomous motives in Petrarch's *rime* – the venomous arrows of *amore*, his *dolce veneno*, the slow poison of Time, the poet's lady as a deaf adder or viper among the flowers – which facilitated the later adaption into Petrarch's imitators of the image of the desired woman as herself the venomous serpent.[72] Two stanzas of Rosello Roselli's (1399–1452) sonnet will suffice as a Quattrocento example of this image:

> O falsa, pien d'inganni e sanza fede,
> femina maledetta,

> bene e pazo chi aspetta
> poter trovare in te, crudel, merzede.
> . . .
> Piu ti rivolti, non fa al vento foglia,
> bestial furia rissosa,
> superba e venenosa:
> ch'ognior cerchi ingannar chi piu ti crede.[73]

His friend Burchiello composed a bizarre version of this type, pretending to attack some "filthy" (*sozze*) "saucy" (*sfacciate*) young male buglers, who expose their chests to his gaze, and whom he transforms into whorish Satanesses, dragging their tails behind them.[74]

Serafino l'Aquilano (1505) complained that his lady was the Hydra, with seven heads (*& cum si gran veneno / che nha septe altre*) signifying the *sdegno, disperation, vivace morte, sospecto, gelosia, dubio,* and *timore* that he suffers with her.[75] Pietro Bembo, in his *Gli Asolani* (1505, 1530), reasoned that Amore is a *potentissimo veneno*. It is not possible to love without experiencing bitterness, this being "that venom with which the feelings poison it". Excessive desire, the passion of the mind that is proper to Love, drives lovers into incestuous embraces.[76]

Iacopo Sannazaro in his *Sonetti e canzoni* of 1531 made *gelosia*, the sister of "bitter death", into a *crudel mostro,* a *serpente* hidden in the sweet bosom: *Tra soavi vivande*, there is *aspro veneno*.[77] Vittoria Colonna, for her part, creates a sense of her poetic identity with the Sirens whose songs seduce men, with that *rio pestifero angue* who participated in the *primo inganno* of the Fall.[78] But the most sustained textual representation of the conceit of woman as poisonous serpent occurs in a series of prose works published by the Venetian doctor and scholar, Michelangelo Biondo (1500–ca. 1565).[79] Using two unhappy marriages as a literary pretext, together with teachings attributed to Socrates and his humanist tutor, Agostino Nifo, Biondo launched his diatribes against women with his *Angitia Cortigiana* of 1540. His courtier hero, a man *pieno di cortesia,* but skilled in *l'arte d'ingannare,* who knows that *il veneno* lies *di sotto il melle,* owes much to Castiglione's prototype. Courtiers are, for Biondo, the dirtiest, filthiest, most evil of men. The courtesan is the female equivalent; she is not a *cosa humana*. Her love is a "bitter fruit", causing the spread of syphilis, a disease on which he was an authority. She is *mastra d'inganno,* her poison (*veneno*) hidden in her "sweet words". At the close of *Angitia,* his participants find themselves in a garden resplendent with flowers and fruits which hang there perfectly ripe, to deceive the passerby with *quel dolce veneno ascosto in mezo il corpo loro fabricato in modo di fabrica di Mele*.[80]

In 1542 the first two parts of his trilogy, *Angoscia, Doglia, e Pena,* "the three furies of the world", appeared, the last following in 1546.[81] It is not merely coincidental that these works are posed as philosophical commentaries on verse, because much of the vocabulary of suffering exploited here is drawn from Petrarch. It is supplemented with some of the most vicious denigration of the female mind and body anywhere in print, partly taken from Boccaccio's *Corbaccio,* the rest from Biondo's own miserable experience as lover. His male protagonist in *Angoscia*, believing that his lady is *il piu perfetto animale al mondo*, realizes that he is deceived, and seeks help from his guides to redefine her. In this process, all the poetic clichés positively defining woman's beauty, moral qualities and desirability, are systematically destroyed. Substituted is a composite image of woman as a wild, crazy, venomous animal with an angel's face, *un viso angelico*. She is not even an animal, but a *bestia*, a deformed, ugly animal whose mind is the source of *fraude* and *inganno*. She administers her sweet poison (*dolce veneno*), the honeyed nectar, to her lover, with "a flicker of her tongue" (*un vibrar di lingua*), like the venomous serpent she is. She seduces her lover also by the visual beauty of her *vestito francese*, and by the ornamentation of her head – fashionable coiffure (*foggia di scuffiotti*), decorated with enamelled gold medallions, *fatte alla antica*, like those used in the triumphs of the ancient Caesars. Her purpose is to *triomphare del cuore humano*. Man must flee from her, like the lamb from the wolf, as he instinctively does from the snake. If not, he will be drawn into her *profondissimo fonte*, the dark cave, full of her deceiving *liquore*, a fetid, toxic and horrible place, whose nature is disguised by *diversi drappi*. Passion for this creature led to the ruin of Hercules, Achilles, Ulysses, and many gods and poets. Her male lover will suffer the living death of *angoscia*, which, "afflicting the heart, consumes the body".[82]

In *Doglia*, Biondo explains how the male's flesh, bones, and marrow are consumed through his contracting this *morbo feminile*. The subterranean habits, and frigidity of snakes, are discussed. Woman is equated with the Hydra, the Basilisk, the Scorpion, and the horned viper. The various colors of woman's clothing correspond with those in snakes. Her poison, too, is secreted in the mouth, and injected by the tongue, through the voice; but also through the kiss, in the sucking and licking of the tongue. Man, however, remains ignorant of the *veneno* of his *donna*, even though he may have his eyes open, because her poison is hidden away. Woman is, moreover, a pricking thorn (*spino pungente*), not that of a rose but the kind that *per disgratia ponge il scalzo viatore*. She pricks most painfully with her tongue, the sharpest of all thorns. The only way to free woman from her state of enmity with *fede* would be to remake her, like Pygmalion did his statue, or "to carve her more perfectly in silver than Mentor sculpted Capitoline Jove".[83]

There is more in these strange works of Biondo that could be pursued in the search for parallels with the subject matter of Bronzino's *Allegory*. The dark color of the suffering man's skin may be related to Biondo's description of how the male lover becomes "smoked" to *un color nero* by the *fumo amaro, e scuro* emitted by his lady, a stinking black vapor that obscures the moon and the stars; Biondo's unfortunate lover's *pomposa donna* also has scaly feet caused by her *venenoso amore*.[84] Here was sufficient textual stimulation for Bronzino to have conceived the form of his "girl-monster", even if he had not already visualized her from hints in the poetic tradition. The importance of the tongue's role in the kiss of Bronzino's Venus and Cupid can now be appreciated. Bronzino had perhaps also read Leone Ebreo's *Dialoghi d'amore* (1535), where the penis is linked with the tongue in a manner that would interest a poet:

> The male member is analogous to the tongue in position, shape and power of erection and retraction: it is placed amid the rest, and as to activity – even as the movements of the other beget progeny of the body, so motions of the tongue bring forth progeny of the spirit in speech, that invests learning with expression, and gives birth to spiritual offspring. And they have another thing in common: the kiss – that of the one provoking that of the other.[85]

The tongue's being synonymous with the word, spoken or written, allowed Michelangelo to say that he loved *con la lingua* when his *penna* failed him, and the paper resisted his efforts.[86] Bronzino must have known that Michelangelo's *Venus and Cupid* cartoon was the representation of a poetic *concetto*, drawn originally from Ovid, as Keach noted, but more accessibly from Dante's *Purgatorio*, XXVIII, 64–66, where Venus's loving gaze unleashed accidentally by Cupid's arrow, is surpassed by Metelda's gaze directed at the poet. The anonymous poet who "responded" to the cartoon, in praise of its representation, tried to create the sonnet Michelangelo had made visible.[87]

It is in this competitive spirit that Bronzino, in his *Allegory*, extends the physical interaction of Venus and Cupid beyond Michelangelo's poetic *and* visual *concetti*. Taking as his visual model of Cupid the eroticized, adolescent type developed by Parmigianino[88] (which had its physical, if not its erotic precedents in two centuries of illustrations to Petrarch's *Trionfi*),[89] Bronzino shows Cupid himself experiencing the kind of seduction that the "victims" of this cruel, pitiless, boy-god enjoyed before their inevitable suffering began. That Cupid is in a state of acute sexual excitation is suggested not only by his kneeling pose, with its implication of his vulnerability to homosexual penetration, but also by the way that pose hides his likely erection from the viewer. While Cupid gazes, transfixed, into the black eyes of the classical goddess Venus, she gives him, with her flickering tongue, the honeyed poison that Bronzino's girl-monster will give her contemporary lover, if he submits to the power of her gaze. In the Latin and Italian vernacular tradition of love-poetry it was Cupid who "used the poet cruelly", whose fiendish insensitivity to the pain caused by his arrows made him the object of the poet's admiring hatred. To watch Cupid undergoing his own seduction, and the theft of his arrow, ought to be a source of satisfaction to the poet nourished on Petrarch's *Trionfi*, were it not that the *concetto* merely confirms the irresistible power of woman's sexuality.

Sannazaro had attempted something analogous to Bronzino's transformation of small poetic clues into a developed conceit, in his poem, published in the 1530s, describing how Cupid makes Venus suffer. Venus complains that this "lying youth" (*garzon bugiardo*) lacks "respect" (*reverenza*) for her: he consumes her, burns her, afflicts and tortures her, leaving her naked and pale. What hope, she complains, have the other gods, if he can do this to me? Women are warned not to let him under their guard, not to let him use his poison (*veneno*).[90] Such imaginative recasting of the familiar personages of poetic tradition constituted a large part of Renaissance originality. The explicitly priapic Cupids, and equally priapic Polifilo of the *Hypnerotomachia* are representative of this. So was the Cupid in the anonymous *capitoli* in praise of madness (*pazzia*) (1543), who plays "between the sweet apples of the ivory breast" of the poet's lady.[91] Caio Baldassare Olimpo degli Alessandri eroticized the *profilato naso* (such as Bronzino's *Venus* displays) of his beautiful Venus-lady, a nose made by the *divin pennello*, a *monticello* whence Cupid fires his arrow into the poet's heart.[92]

A notable and neglected source of such re-workings is Galeotto dal Carretto's *Tempio de Amore* (1518),[93] an amusing tour of the kingdom of Love, parodying Dante's *Divina Commedia* and Petrarch's *Trionfi*, but also the *Hypnerotomachia*, which it seeks to outdo in its *ekphrasis* of classicizing works of art. Vividly described personifications of virtues, vices, emotions and mental states inhabit its verse. Time, *maestro d'ogni cosa*, and Oblivion, play substantial roles, as do Innocence, Justice, and the vices that threaten them. *Amor* is accompanied by *Gioco*. In the *Tempio de Amore* itself the love-afflicted hero, Phileno, who begs for release from his unrequited love through the intercession of Time and Oblivion, is shown Venus and Amor enthroned, with two white doves beneath. *Dolore* in the form of a tearful man rending his hair, is among the group of suffering victims of love pointed out to the hero. There are descriptions of ancient pictures of the Calumny of Apelles, of Parnassus, of statues of Dante, Petrarch and the modern poets. The classical gods have their attributes minutely recounted. In one of two chapels flanking the *altare grande* of Venus and Cupid there is *la concupiscentia ingannatrice*, who lures her victims with false promises of pleasure.[94]

It is easy for art historians to ignore these long-winded works in verse, but we do so at our peril. In a tedious invention by Antonio Fregoso, his *Dialogo de fortuna* (1519), one encounters what is unquestionably the literary source for Marcolini's *Veritas Filia Temporis* woodcut. The protagonists, two men erudite in Greek and Latin, are walking in *un bel prato* near a fountain, when a beautiful, nude young woman rises up from the *ombrose acque*, her face *si fulgente e pura*. She explains that she is *Verita*, the *figlia del tempo*, and of her mother *Experientia*. She complains of being rejected by the *vulgo ignaro*, of being persecuted by *Odio* (hatred), by *Ignorantia*, who makes a person who looks human, a *bestia* within. Having more enemies than friends, Truth has submerged herself in this fountain to flee their *bestial furore*. She has recognized friendly souls in the two learned travellers and rises to tell them, at considerable length, about the manifold errors of humankind, of the effects of *mala fortuna*, and, most interestingly for us, how *ceca opinion* (blind opinion) *in forma de la . . . fraude . . . depinta* is most responsible for her being buried in the fountain. Only when men cease to believe that *fortuna* rules their lives and that *experientia* should teach them responsibility for their actions, will her "immortal father", Time, draw her from the waters so that she might dwell again *fra gente humana*. Fregoso's *Dialogo* had appeared in eight editions before Marcolini's woodcuts saw the light in 1536,[95] and rather than appealing to Cartari as Saxl did, I would suggest that both Marcolini and Aretino had read Fregoso and either drew the woodcuts themselves or employed an artist to work from Fregoso's text. There is no reason why diffusion of the *Dialogo* in Germany and England should not account for similar, but not identical, images arising there before Marcolini's.

Bronzino probably knew both Fregoso's text and the Marcolini woodcut showing Truth, Time and *Fraude*. This last figure doubtless influenced the way he painted the reptilian lower body of his girl-monster in the *Allegory*, a happy solution, given that his poetic model of the serpent-lover embodied deception, which was kept hidden from view. Another contemporary image of *Fraude* may be relevant to the *Allegory*. One of Marcolini's most beautiful books is his *Le ingeniose sorti* of 1540. This elaborate game of chance was graced with one hundred woodcuts, and a frontispiece invented by Giuseppe Porta (Salviati).[96] Subtitled *Giardino di Pensieri*, the game had intellectual appeal, and the fifty named allegorical woodcuts must have caught many an artist's attention in the days before Cartari. The image of *Fraude* has a bearing on Bronzino's *Allegory* because it represents a partly disrobed woman feeling with her hand in the man's purse while she distracts him with a kiss. Her zigzag pose, and the way the man is held in rapt attention to her eyes, while his right hand explores her breast, are aspects not dissimilar to the poses and actions of Venus and Cupid in the *Allegory*. At the right, a Herm with erect penis, and draped with a heavy curtain, specifies the sexual nature of this act of *fraude*.

It is not without interest that the *Veritas Filia Temporis* woodcut also features in *Le sorti*, and yet another that I believe was drawn from this book by Bronzino, the figure of *Dolore*. Conway noticed some similarity between this image and the suffering man at the left of the *Allegory*.[97] Marcolini's *Dolore* is a male figure, like Carretto's of 1524, because the word is masculine. The other most frequently used terms to denote the male lover's suffering in the Renaissance poetic discourse of unrequited love – *angoscia, doglia, pena, gelosia, tristitia* – were feminine, and normally required female personifications. Varchi had paused to define *dolor* in the two senses of *corporale* and *intelletuale* in his 1545 lectures on Petrarch to the Accademia Fiorentina,[98] which Bronzino doubtless heard. Marcolini's *Dolore* has in common with Bronzino's suffering man a tightly flexed forearm culminating in unruly, tufted hair on the head, of which a single lock falls free. The downward tilt of the heads is similar, and although Bronzino's man has his mouth wide in a silent groan, or scream, and the two hands joined in the hair, the images are close enough to suggest a direct influence.

I have argued against Jealousy's being one of Bronzino's personifications, though the sufferings experienced by his *Dolore* could encompass jealousy. The blue cloth held by Time and Oblivion may represent Jealousy in its color, if Bronzino was prepared to disagree with Equicola, who noted that the French wanted *ceruleo* (sky blue) to denote Jealousy, whereas the Italians made better sense by having it signify *Fede*.[99] Carretto, however, preferred Jealousy dressed in *turchino* (dark blue).[100] The strong pink flush given to the cheek of Bronzino's Cupid, stronger than the "milk and roses" tinge that was poetically proper for Venus, was surely dictated by his knowledge that Boccaccio and more recent poets like Fregoso and Carretto had described *Amore*'s face as "hot" and "burning" because, as Leone Ebreo put it, Cupid "signified burning and inordinate love and desire which knows no restraint".[101] The hint of laurel in the gloom behind Time and Oblivion, can, as Hope has suggested, refer to Petrarch's notion of poetic fame; but Bronzino may also have known Fregoso's poetic account of the "small wood of green laurels", a *triomphante bosco* of Love in which the hero of his popular *Cerva biancha* (1510 – eleven eds. by 1540), found rest after a frightening journey through the land of Anteros.[102]

Elements of misogyny are evident in Bronzino's facetious poetry.[103] Although the vocabulary of fish, cheese and vegetable *double-entendres* was formally essential to *rime in burla*, there is reason to suspect that Bronzino was homo-erotic in his leanings.[104] He never married, and late in 1543, some time after the death of his close friend and former guardian, the swordmaker Cristofano Allori, he brought his mother and niece together with Allori's widow and three children, and became the "pastor" of this new flock. Bronzino had moved under Allori's protection in 1518, when he was fifteen,[105] but also maintained his long association with Pontormo, who was probably homosexual. We can only speculate about the *amore* that existed between Bronzino and Varchi, who, incidentally, began his affair with the courtesan-poet Tullia of Aragon in the winter of 1545–46.[106]

Bronzino's misogyny may have become more learned under the tutelage of Varchi, in whose 1543 treatise *Sulla generazione del corpo*, the Aristotelian concept of woman as an imperfect, diminutive version of man, as the "first monster", was fully expounded.[107] Varchi had read Fracastoro's Latin work on syphilis, and also Pietro d'Abano on snakes and poisons.[108] Michelangelo Biondo's *Dialogus de Invidia* (Rome, 1539) was surely read by Varchi for his lecture *Sopra l'Invidia* in 1545.[109] Biondo's treatise on physiognomy, *De cognitione hominis per aspectum* (Rome, 1544), was the sort of work that Bronzino might have wanted translated. Biondo's son, Scipione, dedicated his *Rime* in 1545 to the *spiriti gloriosi* of the Accademia Fiorentina, in the hope of snaring patronage from Duke Cosimo. His *Nova Prudentia*, a heavily ironic prose work in the manner of his father, transferred the venomous serpent motive to Prudentia; he commented that his own mother was nourished by Circe.[110]

Elizabeth Cropper is surely correct in suggesting that Bronzino, in his portraits from the 1530s and 1540s,

> sought to answer the challenges of poetry concerning painting's ability to express not only outer beauty but also inner virtue, and, in the process, accomplished the same kind of definition of a Florentine style, the expressive power of which relied exclusively neither on the canons of antiquity nor on straightforward naturalism, that Bembo had provided for literature.[111]

I have argued that the *Allegory* also should be approached as a work "naturally expressive of Florentine culture", arising not only from the *exempla* of Michelangelo's works in *disegno* – in this case especially the *Venus and Cupid* cartoon – but also from his paradigmatic role as the Florentine poet-artist.

There is no reason to assume that anyone but Bronzino himself conceived the *Allegory*. The probability that it came into Cosimo's possession and was given away by him, need not indicate that he commissioned it and had a scholar write the *invenzione*. Cosimo need only have seen it, and need not have understood what it was about, to have taken it from Bronzino and disposed of it as he wished. Duchess Eleonora's own *Deposition* by Bronzino, from her private chapel, was commandeered and given away in 1545 by Cosimo. Bronzino was greatly in need of money at the time. In 1546 he was mid-way through his financial supporting of the Allori family and their business.[112]

It is my feeling that Bronzino may have painted the *Allegory* as a demonstration to Varchi, and the members of the Accademia Fiorentina, that Michelangelo's *Venus and Cupid*, painted by his beloved master, Pontormo, could be rivalled and surpassed by a representation that *showed* the artist's mastery of the language of poetic love. Varchi's affair with the poet-courtesan Tullia may have stung Bronzino into jealous action. Vasari was not close to Bronzino and seems not to have understood the intellectual forces that shaped his painting. He could recall some details of such a remarkable picture, but was certainly not privy to its meaning.

That meaning hovers between the personal, the poetic, and the pictorial. The lover-beholder of the picture is shown, in the exquisitely erotic, incestuous love of Venus and Cupid, and the playful participation of *Giuoco*, how he will be drawn into and will enjoy the embrace of his *cortigiana*. She, with the honey-poison of her words and body, and especially with her serpent's tongue, will create such a state of simultaneous pleasure and pain in the lover that he will rend his hair and beg for deliverance from Time and Forgetfulness, who will heed his cries with such agonizing slowness that his suffering will seem eternal. But who can resist the direct gaze of such a beautiful creature, monster though she be?

Notes

Research for this paper was carried out while the author was Samuel H. Kress Senior Research Fellow at the Center for Advanced Study in the Visual Arts at the National Gallery of Art, Washington D.C., in 1989. All of the sixteenth-century books mentioned in the paper were, except where specified, consulted at the Folger Shakespeare Library, and I am deeply grateful to the staff for their assistance. Patricia Stablein Harris, Scholar in Residence, who is preparing a book on the theme of woman-as-serpent in medieval and Renaissance literature, was especially generous in sharing her thoughts with me. It is my hope that some of the evidence I have noticed independently will prove useful in her larger project. My thanks go also to Tony Pagliaro, to the editors of *I Tatti Studies*, whose suggestions have improved the essay in many respects, and to Mrs. Jennie Rowntree for preparing the typescript.

A note on orthography and dating: no attempt has been made to modernize the Italian texts quoted in this study from manuscripts and sixteenth-century books: dates, however, have been given in the modern style, rather than the Florentine.

1   The studies consulted are: E. Panofsky, *Studies in Iconology*, New York, 1939, pp. 69–91, and New York, 1962, pp. vii, 83–91; H. Lossow "Das Londoner Venus-und-Cupido Bild des Agnolo Bronzino", *Das Werk des Kunstlers*, n.p., 1939, I, pp. 162–168; A. H. Gilbert and H. W. Janson, reviews of Panofsky, *Art Bulletin*, 22, 1940, pp. 174–175; C. Gould, *National Gallery Catalogues. The Sixteenth-Century Italian Schools*, London, 1962, pp. 21–24, 1975 ed., pp. 41–44; M. Levey, "Sacred and Profane Significance in Two Paintings by Bronzino", *Studies in Renaissance and Baroque Art Presented to Anthony Blunt on his Sixtieth Birthday*, London, 1967, pp. 30–33; W. Keach, "Cupid Disarmed or Venus Wounded? An Ovidian Source for Michelangelo and Bronzino", *Journal of the Warburg and Courtauld Institutes*, 41, 1978, pp. 327–331; C. McCorquodale, *Bronzino*, New York, 1981, pp. 97–90; G. Smith, "Jealousy, Pleasure and Pain in Agnolo Bronzino's 'Allegory of Venus and Cupid'", *Pantheon*, 39, 1981, pp. 250–258; C. Hope, "Bronzino's *Allegory* in the London National Gallery", *Journal of the Warburg and Courtauld Institutes*, 45, 1982, pp. 239–243; J. F. Conway, "Syphilis and Bronzino's London Allegory", *Journal of the Warburg and Courtauld Institutes*, 49, 1986, pp. 250–255; I. Cheney, "Bronzino's London *Allegory*: Venus, Cupid, Virtue, and Time", *Source*, 6, no. 2, 1987, pp. 13–18; L. M. F. Bosch, "Bronzino's London *Allegory*: Love versus Time", *Source*, 9, 1990, pp. 31–35; the latter was kindly drawn to my attention by Prof. Janet Cox-Rearick after this article was completed. My summaries of and comments on these studies are selective and do not pretend to completeness. I have intentionally overlooked the questions raised by X-ray examination of the picture.

2   Cf. D. Carrier, "Erwin Panofsky, Leo Steinberg, David Carrier: The Problem of Objectivity in Art Historical Interpretation", *Journal of Aesthetics and Art Criticism*, 47, 1989, pp. 322–347.

3   Ibid., p. 335, rightly observes ". . . to treat interpretations as discoveries of facts makes it difficult to understand how original interpretations are debated".

4   Panofsky, *op. cit.* (see note 1), 1962, p. 16.

5   G. Vasari, *Le vite de' più eccellenti pittori, scultori ed architettori*, Florence, 1568, II, Part III, p. 864; cf. Vasari, *Le vite*, ed. G. Milanesi, Florence, 1878–81, VII, 1881, pp. 598–599; *Le vite*, ed. P. Della Pergola, *et al.* VIII, Novara, 1967, p. 14 (the 1568 text, with useful annotations). "He made a picture of singular beauty which was sent to King Francis. It was a nude Venus with Cupid who kissed her, and Pleasure was on one side as well as Jest and other Cupids, and on the other side was Deceit, Jealousy and other passions of love."

6   "Veritas Filia Temporis", in R. Klibansky and H. J. Paton (eds.) *Philosophy and History. Essays Presented to Ernst Cassirer*, Oxford, 1936, pp. 197–222.

7   Smith, *op. cit.* (see note 1), p. 257 correctly notes that Keach's sources do not support his idea that Venus's wound is self-inflicted.

8   Gould, *op. cit.* (see note 1), p. 43.

9   In this I would differ from L. M. F. Bosch, "Time, Truth and Destiny: Some Iconographic Themes in Bronzino's 'Primavera' and 'Giustizia'", *Mitteilungen des*

Kunsthistorischen Institutes in Florenz, 27, 1983, pp. 73–82, who finds the Latin handbooks relevant to those tapestry designs from 1546.

10 [Angiolo Bronzino], *Li Capitoli faceti editi ed inediti di Mess. Agnolo Allori detto il Bronzino*, ed. P. Magrini, Venice, 1822 (henceforth as Bronzino, *Capitoli*), pp. 47, 234, 242, 333, 341, 349; cf. Agnolo Bronzino, *Rime in burla*, ed. F. P. Nardelli, Rome, 1988 (henceforth as Nardelli, *Rime*), p. 59, *Esortazione del Bronzino pittore alle Zanzare*, vs. 142: *Ho sempre udito dir "principiis osta"*, [*recte "obsta"*]; proverbial, but perhaps also known to Bronzino from Ovid's *Remedia amoris*, vs. 91; p. 66, *In lode della Galea*, vs. 64: *Ergo, per questo che vuoi tu inferire?*; here the philosophical context is clear; p. 96, *La padella*, vs. 244–246: *Il Filosofo dice ed io lo scrivo: / "Nemo dat quod non habet", adunque ergo, / convien che la padella abbia del vino.*; p. 116, *Della Cipolla*, cap. 2, vs. 175–176: *Basta, che chi la cipolla compose / bisognò ch' egl'avesse l'icche e l'ocche*; p. 124. Ibid., cap. 3, vs. 124: *Loica, idest . . .*; p. 387, *Capitolo dell'Esser Chiaro*, vs. 280–281: *Venga or tutto lo stuol latino e'l greco / e confessi con Socrate "Unum scio"*; Nardelli, p. 438, notes that this is drawn from Plato's *Apology of Socrates*. These fragments clearly do not constitute evidence of a reading knowledge of Latin on Bronzino's part.

11 M. Plaisance, "Une première affirmation de la politique culturelle de Cosme Ier: la transformation de l'Académie des 'Humidi' en Académie florentine (1540–1542)", in A. Rochon (ed.), *Les écrivains et le pouvoir en Italie a l'époque de la Renaissance*, Paris, 1973, pp. 361–438, esp. 377.

12 Varchi, in a letter of May 1539, edited in part by D. Heikamp, "Rapporti fra accademici ed artisti nella Firenze del '500", *Il Vasari*, N.s. 9, 1957, pp. 139–150 at p. 148, note 3.

13 Bronzino, *Capitoli, op. cit.* (see note 10), pp. 87, 92, 133, 234, 334, 345, 356, 384; Nardelli, *Rime, op. cit.* (see note 10), p. 46 (Plato, Homer, Aristotle), 124 (Demosthenes, Cicero, Plutarch, Livy), 125 (Homer), 128 (Horace, Ovid, Homer), 197 (Vitruvius), 328 (Horace). Virgil is obviously used in *Delle Scuse*, ch. 2, pp. 201–202.

14 See F. Argelati, *Biblioteca degli volgarizzatori*, Milan, 1776. Donatus' primer of Latin grammar, called the *Ars Minor*, may have been introduced to Bronzino by Pontormo, who, as Vasari records, was taught the "first principles of Latin grammar" by his grandmother (Vasari, *Vite*, 1568, III, II, p. 475); at least one of the Latin citations in note 10, above, derives from Donatus. The use of *Ergo* with *dunque* indicates that Bronzino was using Mancinelli's interlinear bilingual *Donato al senno* (Venice, 1492, etc.): see P. F. Grendler, *Schooling in Renaissance Italy. Literacy and Learning, 1300–1600*, Baltimore, 1989, pp. 184–185.

15 Bronzino, *Capitoli, op. cit.* (see note 10), pp. 59, 86, 171, 344, 345; Nardelli, *Rime, op. cit.* (see note 10), pp. 126–127, 358 (Petrarch, Dante, Boccaccio), 137 (Berni, Varchi, Della Casa), 196 (Michelangelo); Nardelli, in her notes, also identifies Bembo (p. 419), Castelvetro (pp. 418, 420ff.), Doni (pp. 403, 406, 410, 424), and several possible sources for the giant motive in *Il Piato* (p. 426). An index of sources is a curious omission from Nardelli's edition. For Bronzino's lyric poetry I have used the MS. prepared by an amanuensis (as Nardelli has noted), "Delle Rime del Bronzino", Biblioteca Nazionale Centrale di Firenze (henceforth BNF), MS. Magl. II, IX, 10; some of these were edited, inaccurately, by D. Moreni in *Rime inedite di Raffaello Borghini e di Angiolo Allori detto Il Bronzino*, Florence, 1822.

16 Bronzino, *Capitoli, op. cit.* (see note 10), *Il Caparbio*, p. 24; *Delle Scuse*, ch. I, p. 79; Nardelli, *Rime, op. cit.* (see note 10), p. 162 vs. 196: *Ond'io d'allora in qua non ho potuto / né mangiar, né dormir, né riposarmi, / fin ch'io non sono a scrivere venuto*; p. 190, vs. 337: *Sta ben, tutto confesso, ma s'io veglio / gran parte della notte e poco dormo / e sol quel tempo alle mie rime sceglio, / che debb'io fare allor? fabbrico e formo / castelli in aria?*

17 Among the important studies are: G. Downey, "Ekphrasis", *Reallexikon für Antike und Christentum*, IV, Stuttgart, 1959, cols. 921–944; E. C. Harlan, *The Description of Paintings as a Literary Device and its Application in Achilles Tatius*, Ph. D. diss., Columbia University, 1965; A. Holweg, "Ekphrasis", *Reallexikon zur byzantinischen Kunst*, IX, Stuttgart, 1967, cols. 33–75; S. Alpers, "Ekphrasis and Aesthetic Attitudes in Vasari's *Lives*", *Journal of the Warburg and Courtauld Institutes*, 23, 1960, pp. 190–215; M. Shapiro, *The Poetics of Ariosto*, Detroit, 1988, ch. 6, "Ecphrasis and Encomium"; N. E. Land, "Titian's *Martyrdom of St. Peter Martyr* and the 'limitations' of ekphrastic art criticism", *Art History*, 13, 1990, pp. 293–317.

18 A. Frey-Sallmann, *Aus dem Nachleben antiker Gottergestalten*, Leipzig, 1931, is still useful; as are several papers in A. Franceschetti (ed.), *Letteratura italiana e arti figurative*, I, Florence, 1988, particularly that of L. Mendelsohn, "Boccaccio, Betussi e Michelangelo: ritratti delle donne illustri come *Vite parallele*", pp. 323–334; see also M. Rogers, "The decorum of women's beauty: Trissino, Firenzuola, Luigini and the representation of women in sixteenth-century painting", *Renaissance Studies*, 2, 1988, pp. 47–88.

19 Petrarch uses the verb nineteen times in his *Rime*: K. McKenzie, *Concordanza delle Rime di Francesco Petrarca*, Oxford, 1912, p. 121; see the thoughtful papers by E. Cropper, "On Beautiful Women, Parmigianino, *Petrarchismo*, and the Vernacular Style", *The Art Bulletin*, 58, 1976, pp. 374–394, and "The Beauty of Woman: Problems in the Rhetoric of Renaissance Portraiture", in M. W. Ferguson, *et al.* (eds.), *Rewriting the Renaissance. The Discourses of Sexual Difference in Early Modern Europe*, Chicago, 1986, pp. 175–190.

20 See A. Carson, *Eros the Bittersweet*, Princeton, 1986, p. 86; Longus's and similar texts are gathered conveniently in W. A. Hirshig (ed.), *Erotici Scriptores*, Paris, 1856.

21 Francesco Colonna (?), *Hypnerotomachia Poliphili*, Venice, 1499, repr. 1969; in the text the marble relief depicting the sleeping nymph is compared with Praxiteles' Venus that moved the men of Cnidos to sacrilegious masturbation: the satyr who stands behind her sleeping form in the woodcut, in the text looks between her drawn up knees at her *stristi petali* (cf. *stricti petioli* in *Hypnerotomachia*, ed. G. Pozzi and L. Ciapponi, I, 1964, p. 64) which invite the viewer's touch; this is one of several such examples. Cf. M. Calvesi, *Il sogno di Polifilo prenestino*, Rome, 1980.

22 Here I follow P. S. Harris, review of L. Kendrick, *The Game of Love: Troubadour Wordplay*, Berkeley, 1988, in *Speculum*, 65, 1990, at p. 1006, where she notes that sexuality is used as a "mask" to "assert the generative and ordering power" of the poet.

23 For example, Varchi's sonnet to Bronzino, Bronzino, *ove si dolce ombreggia, e suona*, vs. 9, MS. BNF *cit.* (see note 15), II, X, fol. 116v.

24 Bronzino, *Capitoli, op. cit.* (see note 10), *Il Caparbio*, p. 36; Nardelli, *Rime, op. cit.* (see note 10), p. 172.

25 Bronzino, *Capitoli, op. cit.* (see note 10), *Delle Scuse*, ch. II, p. 83; Nardelli, *Rime, op. cit.* (see note 10), p. 194.

26 MS. (see note 15), fols. 138v, 140r: *O stupor di Natura, Angelo eletto*, and *Come l'alto Michele Angel, con forte*.

27 Bronzino, *Capitoli, op. cit.* (see note 10), *Delle Scuse*, ch. II, p. 86; Nardelli, *Rime, op. cit.* (see note 10), p. 196; see R. Clements "Eye, mind and hand in Michelangelo's poetry", *Publications of the Modern Language Association*, 69, 1954, pp. 324–336.

28 Petrarch, *Rime sparse*, 309: *il ver tacito estime / ch'ogni stil vince*, in *Petrarch's Lyric Poems*, ed. and trans. R. M. Durling, Cambridge, Mass., 1976, pp. 488–489.

29 See G. Cambon, *Michelangelo's Poetry. Fury of Form*, Princeton, 1985.

30 Niccolò Da Correggio (1450–1508): *Laudo il pictor, ma più laudo un che scriva . . . Ma como excede tua forma il pennello, / exederan le tue virtu la penna, e restarà imperfecto e questo e quello: Opere*, ed. A. T. Benvenuti, Bari, 1969, no. 51, p. 132; cf. no. 77, p. 145 on *l'occhio interior* and *l'altro de fuori*.

31 Marco da Lodi (Cadamosto), *Sonetti et altre rime di M. Marco da Lodi*, Rome, 1544, *Piu che certo teng'io che Raphaele*, p. 27r.

32 Ibid.: *E trovera fallace ogni pennello.*

33 Giovangiorgio Trissino, *Di M. Giovangiorgio Trissino, La Sophonisba, Li Retratti, Epistola, Oracion al Serenissimo Principe di Vinegia*, [Venice, 1525]; *I ritratti*, p. 43r: Mantegna and Leonardo, Apelles and Euphranor are defeated by *il nobilissimo di tutti e pittori Messer Francesco Petrarcha*.

34 On Varchi, see G. Manacorda, *Benedetto Varchi, l'uomo, il poeta, il critico*, Pisa, 1903; U. Pirotta, *Benedetto Varchi e la cultura del suo tempo*, Firenze, 1971; M. Plaisance, *op. cit.* (see note 11), and his "Culture et politique à Florence de 1542 à 1551", in A. Rochon (ed.), *Les écrivains et le pouvoir en Italie à l'époque de la Renaissance*, II, Paris 1974, pp. 149–242.

35 See Manacorda, *op. cit.* (see note 34), p. 59. See also F. Piovan, "Per la datazione del sonetto del Bembo al Varchi", *Italia medioevale e umanistica*, 27, 1984, pp. 311–329.

36 Varchi, sonnet to Bronzino, MS. (see note 15), fol. 35v: *Quel cortese, che già gran tempo, scorsi / Affetto in voi, caro BRONZIN, cui furo / Tutti altri secondi, quasi muro / Tra me s'oppone, e mille invidi morsi* (vs. 1–4).

37 Bronzino, sonnet to Varchi, MS. (see note 15), fol. 36v: *VARCHI il cui bel pensier sovrano, e saggio / Sol'accompagnia dolce honesta pace: Lunge dal volgo vile empio, e fallace* (vs. 1–3).

38 Varchi, sonnet to Bronzino, MS. (see note 15), fol. 35v.

39 See Manacorda, *op. cit.* (see note 34), p. 39 for Varchi's views on the moral and social ends of poetry. See Nardelli, *Rime, op. cit.* (see note 10), pp. 204–217, 418–426 for a new edition of the *Saltarelli*, which deals with the Varchi, Caro, Castelvetro dispute.

40 See my article, "Iconography and Portraiture in Bronzino's 'Christ in Limbo'", *Mitteilungen des Kunsthistorischen Institutes in Florenz*, 27, 1983, pp. 41–72; the phrase *i buoni costumi* is Varchi's (see Manacorda, *op. cit.* [see note 34], note 39).

41 L. Mendelsohn, *Paragoni: Benedetto Varchi's Due Lezzioni and Cinquecento Art Theory*, Ann Arbor, 1982, makes an exhaustive study of these.

42 B. Varchi, *Opere*, II, Trieste, 1859, pp. 627–647; here I concur with F. Quiviger, "Benedetto Varchi and the Visual Arts", *Journal of the Warburg and Courtauld Institutes*, 50, 1987, pp. 219–224.

43 Varchi, *op. cit.* (see note 42), p. 643; Bettini was a friend of Varchi's: see Plaisance, *op. cit.* (see note 11), p. 368, note 17.

44 Varchi, *op. cit.* (see note 42), p. 665, *Della generazione de' mostri*; the drawing seems not to have survived. *Quanti sono in questo luogo che si ricordano d'aver veduto quel mostro, che nacque dalla Porta al Prato circa dodici anni sono, il quale fu ritratto egregiamente dallo eccellentissimo Bronzino? . . . Facesi sparare nell'orto di Palla Rucellai alla presenza di maestro Alessandro da Ripa e di maestro Francesco da Monte Varchi, e d'alcuni medici e pittori eccellentissimi.*

45 Ibid., pp. 662–664.

46 Bronzino, sonnet to Varchi, MS. (see note 15), fol. 34v.

47 Ibid., fol. 35r; one of the several vices threatening Varchi as Pegasus in the poem is Invidia: the printer's mark in Michelangelo Biondo's *Dialogus de invidia*, Rome, 1539 (*Per Valerium D'Oricum Brixiensem*, at B iv r) shows Pegasus perched on a mountainside, with the legend *Nulla est via invidia virtuti*. Smith, *op. cit.* (see note 1), p. 257 and Hope, *loc. cit.* (see note 1), p. 243 plausibly connect the iconography of the Budapest *Allegory* with Bronzino's sonnet beginning *Poi, ch'in terra odio, e 'n Cielo Invidia, e Ira / Scorse Venere bella, al santo Figlio / Rivolto il vago, e luminoso Ciglio . . .* (ibid. fol. 69r); it should be noted that Bronzino elsewhere in his poetry brings together *Amore, Invidia and Gelosia* (in the *canzon, Candida, fresca, e leve*, ibid. fol. 83v, and cf. 80r and in the sonnet *A' la dole' ombra amata Pianta*, ibid. fol. 48r), and gives a strikingly pictorial description of Invidia's "angry eyes and sour muzzle" (*biechi occhi e muso arcigno*) in *Dello Starsi*, cap. 3, vs. 25, Nardelli, *Rime, op. cit.* (see note 10), p. 374.

48 Bronzino, sonnet to Varchi, MS. (see note 15), fol. 54v.

49 Varchi, sonnet to Bronzino, ibid., fol. 76v. *Voi, che nel fior della sua verde etate / Coll'alto vostro, e si chiaro pennello, / A nome mio BRONZIN formaste il bello / Di fuor cui par non fu mortal beltate: / Se di me punto calvi, o'se curate / Di Voi, coll'altro stile, e non men bello / Formate il buon di dentro, che con ello / Posta vitio saria mortal bontate* (vs. 1–8).

50 McKenzie, *op. cit.* (see note 19), pp. 84–85.

51 Durling, *op. cit.* (see note 28), p. 98.

52 Bronzino, *Capitoli, op. cit.* (see note 10), pp. 224–236; Nardelli, *Rime, op. cit.* (see note 10), pp. 379, 381, 385.

53 Bronzino, *Capitoli, op. cit.* (see note 10), *Lo Sdegno*, p. 170; Nardelli, *Rime, op. cit.* (see note 10), p. 385.

54 Bronzino, *Capitoli, op. cit.* (see note 10), *Il Caparbio*, pp. 26, 36; Nardelli, *Rime, op. cit.* (see note 10), pp. 164, 172.

55 Bronzino, *Capitoli, op. cit.* (see note 10), *Dell'Esser chiaro*, p. 236; Nardelli, *Rime, op. cit.* (see note 10), p. 388.

56 Bronzino, *Capitoli, op. cit.* (see note 10), *In lode della galea*, ch. 1, p. 356; Nardelli, *Rime, op. cit.* (see note 10), p. 72.

57 Bronzino, sonnet, MS. (see note 15), fol. 115r.

58 Ibid., fol. 3r.

59 P. Bembo, *Prose della volgar lingua*, III, 1, in *Prose e rime di Pietro Bembo*, ed. C. Dionisotti, Turin, 1978, pp. 183–185.

60 Bronzino, *Capitoli, op. cit.* (see note 10), pp. 2, 7, 11; Nardelli, *Rime, op. cit.* (see note 10), pp. 145, 149, 152.

61 For Leonardo's thoughts on the *paragone* see P. Barocchi, *Scritti d'arte del Cinquecento*, I, Milan, 1971, pp. 475–488; cf. Mendelsohn, *loc. cit.* (see note 41) on Varchi.

62 M. Equicola, *Institutioni di Mario Equicola al comporre in ogni sorte di Rima della lingua volgare, con uno eruditissimo Discorso della Pittura, & con molte segrete allegorie circa le Muse & la Poesia*, Milan, 1541, B iv v; cf. B iv r: *La pittura chi somamente non lauda, e illaudibile, per esser arte della natura imitatrice, & che essa natura quasi in tutto ripresenta.*

63 Bronzino, *Capitoli, op. cit.* (see note 10), pp. 394–398; Nardelli, *Rime, op. cit.* (see note 10), pp. 23–26. On *disegno* see M. Poirier, "The Role of the Concept of *Disegno* in Mid-Sixteenth-Century Florence", in *The Age of Vasari*, Notre Dame, 1970, pp. 53–66. On Giulio's *Modi* and their context, see M. Tafuri, "Giulio Romano: linguaggio, mentalità, committenti", in *Giulio Romano*, Milan, 1989, pp. 15ff.; for examples of explicit eroticism in Florentine art before 1550, see P. Webb, *The Erotic Arts*, London, 1983; Bronzino, given his strong interest in northern prints, may have been acquainted with Lucas van Leyden's sensual engravings of 1528–30, on which see L. Silver and S. Smith, "Carnal knowledge: the late engravings of Lucas van Leyden", *Nederlands Kunsthistorisch Jaarboek*, 29, 1978, pp. 239–298.

64 Varchi, sonnet to Bronzino, MS. (see note 15), fol. 57r, vs. 9.

65 Durling, *op. cit.* (see note 28), pp. 296–297. Here I must acknowledge my debt to the two remarkable studies by E. Cropper, *op. cit.* (see note 19), where the view that representations of female beauty are always "about representation" in the Petrarchan tradition is subtly argued; in the latter paper she summarizes as follows (p. 190): "in the Renaissance *paragone* of painting and poetry, the portrayal of a beautiful woman is not merely an example. It is the test the poet sets the painter, and the primary figure for the truthfulness of the representation of beauty itself." Prof. Cropper shows convincingly that Leonardo attempted, through painting itself, to refute the poet's denial of the validity of painted appearance.

66 Domenico di Giovanni (Burchiello), *Rime del Burchiello comentate dal Doni*, Venice, 1553 (the *Rime* first publ. 1472), VI, p. 184: *Molti poeti han gia descritto Amore*. See A. J. Smith, *The Metaphysics of Love*, Cambridge, 1985; T. Hyde, *The Poetic Theology of Love*, Newark, 1986.

67 See G. Smith, "Bronzino's use of prints: some suggestions", *The Print Collector's Newsletter*, 9, 1978, pp. 110–113.

68 Here I cite *Libro di natura d'amore di Mario Equicola novamente stampato et con somma diligentia corretto*, Venice, 1526.

69 Ibid., pp. 16r–19v.

70 Ibid., p. 17r, summarizing from *Fiammetta: vedere che cosa sono come animali spiacevoli et abbominevoli*; Boccaccio's *Corbaccio* is his most sustained misogynist diatribe (G. Boccaccio, *Opere in versi. Corbaccio*, etc., ed. P. G. Ricci, Milan, 1965; *The Corbaccio. Giovanni Boccaccio*, trans. A. K. Cassell, Urbana, 1975, with a useful introduction and bibliography on the antifeminist tradition); for background, J. A. Phillips, *Eve, The History of an Idea*, New York, 1984; B. S. Anderson and J. P. Zinsser, *A History of Their Own*, I, New York, 1988, pp. 26–51.

71 Equicola, *op. cit.* (see note 68), p. 174v.

72 McKenzie, *op. cit.* (see note 19), pp. 488, 490, *s.v. veleno, veneno*. On the idea, see N. M. Penzer, *Poison-Damsels and other essays in Folklore and Anthropology*, London,

1952, pp. 3–71; M. Hallisy, *Venomous Woman. Fear of the Female in Literature*, New York, 1987, which has its merits, but is thin and unreliable on the Renaissance material; Dr Stablein Harris' book will, one hopes, meet this need.

73 In C. Muscetta and D. Ponchiroli (eds.), *Poesia del Quattrocento e del Cinquecento*, Turin, 1959, p. 19. "O false accursed woman, deceitful and faithless; indeed the lover who expects to find recompense in you, cruel one, is mad . . . You turn about more than a leaf before the wind, you bestial, quarrelsome fury, proud and venomous. You are ever trying to deceive the one who trusts you most."

74 Burchiello, *op. cit.* (see note 66), pp. 191–192.

75 *Poeme di Seraphino. Novamente cum diligentia . . . Impresso cum molte cose adiuncte*, n.p., 1505 (1st publ. 1502), no. LVI, p. B vii r; cf. no. II, p. A i r, where the lady's *dolce aspecto angelico* is a *mortal veneno*; XXIII, A vi v; *Capitulo de l'odio*, III, p. G vi v–vii v, on the *dolce veneno* of *gelosia*; Serafino's numerous poems entitled *Col tempo*, about woman's aging, are an obvious source for Giorgione's picture with the *Col tempo* motive inscribed; on Serafino, see A. Rossi, *Serafino Aquilano e la poesia cortigiana*, Brescia, 1980, pp. 78ff.

76 P. Bembo, *Gli Asolani*, I, xxi–xxii, in Bembo, *Prose e rime, op. cit.* (see note 59), pp. 351–355; cf. Pietro Bembo's *Gli Asolani*, trans. R. Gottfried, New York, 1971, pp. 34–44, to be used with care.

77 Here cited from *Sonetti e canzoni di M. Giacomo Sannazaro nobile napoletano, Nuovamente corretti e ristampati*, Venice, 1549; 13r: *O gelosia, d'amanti horribil freno*; cf. I. Sannazaro, *Opere volgari*, ed. A. Mauro, Bari, 1961, p. 155.

78 In her *Rime*, first ed. 1538; here quoted from V. Colonna, *Rime*, ed. A. Bullock, Rome, 1982, no. 27, p. 69; cf. J. Gibaldi, "Child, Woman, and Poet: Vittoria Colonna", in K. M. Wilson (ed.), *Women Writers of the Renaissance and Reformation*, Athens, Ga., 1987, pp. 22–46. The woman-as-serpent motive had diffused into Florentine political rhetoric as early as 1433. The *signoria*'s sumptuary legislation of that year noted that the responsible officials had attempted "to restrain the barbarous and irrepressible bestiality of women, who, not considering the fragility of their nature, but rather with that reprobate and diabolical nature, . . . force their men, with their honeyed poison, to submit to them. But it is not in accordance with nature for women to be burdened by so many expensive ornaments, and on account of these unbearable expenses, men are avoiding matrimony . . ." (G. Brucker [ed.], *The Society of Renaissance Florence. A Documentary Study*, New York, 1971, p. 181; cf. Anderson and Zinsser, *op. cit.* [see note 70], p. 434).

79 See G. Stabile, *s.v.* "Biondo, Michelangelo", *Dizionario biografico degli Italiani*, 10, Rome, 1968, pp. 560–653; Schlosser's derision for his *Della nobilissima pittura* of 1549 has helped to distract art historians from his other works: J. Schlosser Magnino, *La letteratura artistica*, ed. O. Kurz, Florence, 1964, pp. 243ff.

80 M. Biondo, *Angitia Cortigiana, de natura, del cortigiano*, Rome, 1540, *passim*; his *De origine morbi gallici*, was published at Venice, 1542: he was a medical theorist of considerable standing, working on pediatrics, wounds, and pharmacology, as well as syphilis.

81 The three are edited together by G. Zonta, *Trattati del Cinquecento sulla donna*, Bari, 1913, but inaccurately, so I cite the first eds. of *Angoscia* and *Doglia*, *Pena* being less relevant for this study: *Angoscia, la prima furia del mondo*, Venice, 1542; *Doglia, la seconda furia del mondo*, Venice, 1542.

82 Biondo, *Angoscia, op. cit.* (see note 81), pp. A v r, B iii r–vi v, C iii r–iv r, C vi r–D vii v. Cf. B. Castiglione, *Il Cortegiano*, I, *ix*, ed. V Cian, Florence, 1894, p. 26. Biondo's debt to Nifo is evident in the latter's *De amore liber*, chs. XXVII–XLI, and Platina's *Contra amores* (publ. together as *Veneres et cupidines venales, Augustini Niphi, Itali. Accedit Babtista Platina de remediis Amoris*, Leiden, 1646). Of the classical sources, most pertinent is Xenophon, *Memorabilia*, I, iii, 10–14, where Socrates compares a lover's kiss to a venomous tarantula's bite.

83 Biondo, *Doglia, op. cit.* (see note 81), pp. A v v–vi r, B v r, D i v, D vi r–viii v.

84 Biondo, *Angoscia, op. cit.* (see note 81), A vi r–v.

85 L. Ebreo, *The Philosophy of Love* (*Dialoghi d'Amore*), trans. F. Friedeberg-Seeley and J. H. Barnes, London, 1937, p. 94. Cf. E. D. Harvey, "Speaking in tongues: the poetics of the feminine voice in Chaucer's *Legend of Good Women*", in E. E. DuBrock (ed.), *New Images of Medieval Women*, Lewiston-Queenston, 1989, pp. 47–60.

86 M. Buonarroti, *Rime*, ed. E. N. Girardi, Bari, 1960, no. 87, p. 51; cf. no. 17, p. 9, on Time's *pessimo veneno*.

87 For the sonnet, see, *Die Dichtungen des Michelangiolo Buonarroti*, ed. C. Frey, 2nd ed. Berlin, 1964, p. 271.

88 The debt to Parmigianino was first noticed by H. W. Janson, *op. cit.* (see note 1); cf. his *Cupid Carving his Bow*, Vienna, Kunsthistorisches Museum.

89 See G. Carendente, *I Trionfi nel primo Rinascimento*, Naples, 1963. We may pause to consider here Bronzino's poem *Della Cipolla* (On the Onion). Nardelli has argued persuasively that the *cipolla* represents the phallus. At the beginning of the second *capitolo* Bronzino presents an elaborate parody of the catalogue of attributes of Cupid as they were described by the vernacular poets and by scholars like Equicola. He proposes that *Amore*, who had his earthly abode (*stanza in Terra*) in Cyprus, is really an onion himself (*è proprio una cipolla stessa*). Bronzino then systematically compares Cupid with the onion-penis: the latter's bared head with the (fore)skin retracted (*senza cappa*) is equated with Cupid's nudity (*amore è ignudo*). The catalogue continues through covert images of fellation of the penis, masturbation and homosexual intercourse, emphasizing the bitter-sweet (*amore è dolce e amaro*) taste of the Cupid-onion. The motive of pederasty with Cupid, or with boys of his age and beauty, dominates this part of the poem, which regrettably cannot be precisely dated. The locating of Cupid in his *stanza* on Cyprus clearly evokes the setting of Michelangelo's cartoon of *Venus and Cupid* that the sculptor had drawn from the poetic tradition, but may also relate to Boccaccio's *Genealogia de gli dei*, translated from Latin by G. Betussi in 1547, where Venus is said to dwell on Cyprus in *l'albergo, la stanza, & il nido delle lascivie, & di tutti gli piaceri* (here cited from the Venice, 1627 edition, p. 52v). The *nido*, Venus' love-nest, is presumably what Bronzino seeks to portray in his setting of the *Allegory*. If the *Allegory* were datable as late as 1547 (this is stylistically plausible, but Vasari's *re Francesco* is an obstacle) I should want to adduce as a source Boccaccio's entry on *Frode*, based on Dante's Gerione (*Inf.*, XXVII), a male prototype for Bronzino's serpent-girl; Boccaccio's paraphrase of Dante (ed. 1627, p. 19r) is clearly adapted by Bronzino in his *rime in burla*, e.g.: *Sotto benigna adunque, & simil faccia d'huomo giusto comprende l'Autore l'estrinseco de gli huomini fraudolenti. Percioche sono di volto, & di parlar benigni, nell'habito modesti, nel passo gravi, di costumi notabili, & per pietà riguardevoli. Nelle opre poi, nascosto sotto compassionevole zelo*

Robert W. Gaston

d'iniquità, sono di contraria pelle, d'astutia armati, & tinti di macchie di scelerità, talmente ch'ogni loro operatione alla fine si conchiude tutta ripiena di mortal veneno; cf. also Boccaccio's account of Scorpio in his entry on *Venere maggiore* (ed. cit. p. 50v), a *venenoso* animal, *pieno di frode*, representing the *amarezza* experienced by lovers desirous of *un poco di dolcezza.*

90 I. Sannazaro, *Farsa di Venere che cerca il figluolo Amore*, in *Opere, op. cit.* (see note 77), esp. pp. 259–260.

91 *Tre bellissimi capitoli in lode della pazzia, con alcune stanze Amorose di novo stampate*, Venice, 1543, B v v.

92 *Gloria d'amore*, Venice, 1544, A vi r; cf. his *Delle tremolante poppe*, A viii r, and poem on Time, B v r; his *Trambotti de comparitione* abound with woman-as-serpent motives: see his *Libro de amore chiamato Ardelia*, Venice, 1544, *Strambotti*, A iii v–A vi v.

93 I have used *Comedia nuova del magnifico et celeberrimo poeta signor Galeotto Marchese dal Carretto intitulata Tempio de Amore*, Venice, 1524; on the author, see Rossi, *op. cit.* (see note 75), pp. 114–115.

94 Carretto, *op. cit.* (see note 93), for Innocente and Justice, pp. N iii v–O iii v, Time, A v r–ix r, O iii v, Oblivion, C ii r, vi r, F iv v, *Giuoco*, I iii r, white doves, N iii r, Calumny of Apelles and Parnassus, E iii v–iv v, poet statues, E vi v, *Concupiscentia*, F iii v.

95 I quote from *Dialogo De Fortuna Del Magnifico Cavalliero Antonio Phileremo Fregoso*, Venice, 1521, B iii r–v r; cf. A. F. Fregoso, *Opere*, ed. G. Dilemmi, Bologna, 1976, pp. xliii ff. on the editions. Cf. also, on *fraude*, Iacopo Caviceo, *Libro del Peregrino*, Venice, 1520, p. M i r: the woodcut (AA i r) shows a lover tied to a tree like St. Sebastian, taunted by two Satyrs. On Fregoso's *Dialogo*, see M. Santoro, *Fortuna, ragione e prudenza nella civiltà letteraria del Cinquecento*, 2nd ed., Naples, 1978.

96 See C. L. L. E. Witcombe, "Giuseppe Porta's frontispiece for Francesco Marcolini's *Sorti*", *Arte Veneta*, 37, 1983, pp. 170–174, with bibliography: see esp. S. Casali, *Annali della tipografia veneziana di Francesco Marcolini*, Forli, 1861, repr. 1953, pp. 119ff., A. Quondam, "Nel giardino del Marcolini. Un editore veneziano tra Aretino e Doni", *Giornale Storico della Letteratura Italiana*, 157, 1980, pp. 83–116. Library of Congress has the rare first edition.

97 Conway, *op. cit.* (see note 1), p. 251, noting that Enea Vico also engraved it in reverse.

98 Varchi, *Opere, op. cit.* (see note 43), II, p. 455.

99 Equicola, *op. cit.* (see note 68), p. 164r.

100 Carretto, *op. cit.* (see note 93), p. viii v.

101 For Boccaccio, see Equicola, *op. cit.* (see note 68), p. 19v; Fregoso, *Opera nova intitulata Cerva Biancha*, Venice, 1510, here citing the 1525 ed. p. I vi r; Carretto, *op. cit.* (see note 93), p. H i r; Ebreo, *op. cit.* (see note 85), p. 340.

102 Fregoso, *op. cit.* (see note 102), p. G vi V.

103 This is argued persuasively by Nardelli, *Rime, op. cit.* (see note 10).

104 A lyric poem, MS. *loc. cit.* fol. 32v seems relevant: *Deh, come spesso di novello Amico / Falle la speme a chi soverchia pone / Ne lascia il tempo a la sua bella Figlia / Scoprire il Velo?* Here Time unveils Truth to expose an insincere love between men. For the background to Bronzino's erotic vocabulary, see J. Toscan, *Le Carnaval du langage. Le lexique érotique des poètes de l'équivoque de Burchiello à*

86

Marino (XVe–XVIIe siècles), 4 vols., Lille, 1981; E. B. Weaver, "Erotic language in Francesco Berni's *Rifacimento*", *Modern Language Notes*, 99, 1984, pp. 80–100; F. Berni, *Rime*, ed. D. Romei, Milan, 1985; P. Floriani, "La poesia tolta in gioco", *Rivista di Letteratura Italiana*, 5, 1987, pp. 161–179; A. Corsaro, *Il poeta e l'eretico. Francesco Berni e il "Dialogo contra i poeti"*, Florence, 1988; C. Mutini, introduction to Nardelli, *op. cit.* (see note 10), pp. 1–20.

105 I draw these biographical details from Archivio di Stato di Firenze, Notarile Antecosimiano, MS. A 223, fols. 202r–203v; A. Furno, *La vita e le rime di Angiolo Bronzino*, Pistoia, 1902, p. 31 (followed by Nardelli, *Rime, op. cit.* [see note 10], p. 441) placed Cristofano's death in 1555, but did not know these and other legal documents which I shall publish in detail elsewhere; four of Bronzino's lyric poems (MS. [see note 15], fols. 10v–12r) mourn Cristofano and should probably be dated in the early 1540s: Bronzino becomes *Nuovo Pastor d'abbandonato Ovile*. The MS. cited, which is dated *D[ie] XXI mensis Januarij 1548* (1549 modern style), reads at 202v: *Et trovando che il detto Agnolo per mesi 19, cioè da di 17 di Ottobre 1543 fino a dj 22 di Maggio 1545, tenne continuamente conto di tutto [quello che] spendeva nel vitto, nel qual tempo vivevano a una medesima spesa luj, la madre, una sua nipote, et di loro Ma Dianora, Bastiano, Corozo et Alessandro suo figliuoli, et cosi in tutto boche 7, cioè 3 per conto d'Agnolo et 4 per conto loro ... Et trovando massime, perchè cosi afferma la detta Ma Dianora et i detti suoi figlioli, che il detto Agnolo per anni 7 et mezzo continuamente ha fatto tutto le spese che sono occorse in detta casa per conto del vitto di suo proprio, le quali spese alla detta ragione ascenderebbono alla somma di ducati 62 per ciascuno anno ...;* and at 202r: *Et havando prima notitia che intra il detto Agnolo et il detto Christofano mentre vissono per più et più anni fu grandissima amicizia, et che il detto Agnolo l'anno 15 cominciò ad habitare in casa del detto Christofano et in quella habita insino che visse.* My thanks are due to Christiane Günther for leading me to this document, and to Gino Corti for clarifying the transcription.

106 See Manacorda, *op. cit.* (see note 34), p. 78.

107 Varchi, *op. cit.* (see note 42), pp. 289, 301, 304.

108 Ibid., pp. 359, 668.

109 See note 47, above.

110 Scipione Biondo, *Rime leggiadre de gli academici novi*, Venice, 1545; *Nova Prudentia et e il Ragionamento ironico Novo et Raro al mondo Contra la gran schiera delle sceleraggini*, Venice, 1546, esp. C iv r.

111 E. Cropper, "Prolegomena to a new interpretation of Bronzino's Florentine portraits", in A. Morrogh, *et al.* (eds.), *Renaissance Studies in Honor of Craig Hugh Smyth*, II, Florence, 1985, pp. 149–160, quotation p. 150.

112 As the documents cited in note 105 indicate.

Part II
Nature and Artifice

Introduction

Among the most familiar, if fugitive, ways of characterizing the art of the Italian Renaissance is in terms of its "naturalism." From the time of Vasari, one conventional narrative of the period has described how Quattrocento painters and sculptors made their pictures and figures increasingly life-like; they differed from their predecessors precisely in that they seemed newly equipped or committed to imitating what they saw before them. The new naturalism, what Jacob Burckhardt famously described as "The Discovery of the World and of Man," could be motivated and enabled by any number of factors: by an informative encounter with the expressive forms of ancient statuary or with the "descriptive" pictorial modes characteristic of northern European art; by a new empiricism, embodied, for example, in the increasingly common practices of dissection and life-study; by new technical means, like linear and atmospheric perspective; or even by newly recovered texts that changed readers' perceptions of the world in which they lived.

When we think, though, about what naturalism could have meant before the scientific revolution, or even about what, in the Renaissance, constituted "nature" – we are still, after all, in a world with four elements, where the cosmos centered on the Earth and where "spirits" played an active part in most natural operations – it becomes clear that the very notion of pre-modern naturalistic painting requires examination. Adding complications, moreover, especially where the sixteenth century is concerned, are the aims of the arts themselves: by this time, naturalism was no longer an unqualified pictorial end. Vasari himself argued that the artists of his time, having already mastered the rendering of nature, pushed their style beyond this, toward something more graceful, adorned, and finely finished, and twentieth-century accounts of the era, which saw the Renaissance culminating or terminating in an age of conspicuous artfulness, drew similar conclusions. Histories of the Renaissance that make room for "mannerism" suggest that, where the problem of naturalism in sixteenth-century Italian art is to be investigated, the investigation must treat that naturalism as part of a dialectic, as a mode adopted always with an awareness of a self-conscious artifice that both sustained and qualified it.

This section focuses on the forms that the imitation of nature could take and the ends to which that imitation was put in different regions in Italy at different moments in the sixteenth century. The first essay, a paper by Martin Kemp on the painter-scientist Leonardo da Vinci, introduces the general problem at issue by asking what science itself would have meant for a painter at the height of the Renaissance. As Kemp points out, those in Leonardo's day who were considered most expert on naturalistic matters were frequently as interested in poetics as in what we would now call research; the two domains, seemingly antithetical today, then both informed and reflected one another. In Leonardo's time, even the idea of scientific proof relied on a different kind of thinking from that to which we are accustomed, depending as it did on principles of affinity and analogy, principles no less relevant to those involved with the visual arts. *Fantasia*, the mental function associated with artistic invention, could be subjected to scientific investigation; poetry, meanwhile, could serve as a vehicle for presenting facts and discoveries about the physical world. The very techniques that artists used could be the siblings to those employed in fields we would now call chemistry, astronomy, or physics.

The second piece, an excerpt from Philippe Morel's important book on the Renaissance grotto, looks at a different kind of material entirely, and accordingly frames the issue of naturalism in different terms. Seeking to set out the natural-historical ideas that served as the conceptual basis for a type of architectural construction that commonly featured in Renaissance gardens, Morel concerns himself not so much with scientific procedure as with the idea of nature's own invention, nature's function as a creator whose generative powers might be imitated. Morel forces us to attend to the materiality of the artwork in the mid-sixteenth century, for the materials of things, their origins, and the transformations to which they could be submitted were, as Morel shows, *staged*, to the extent that what the naturalistic artwork might imitate was not a natural thing so much as a natural process. Human artifice itself was implicated in the actions of "nature" that the garden put on display – a fact that was underscored when four of the most important sculptures Michelangelo had left in Florence, the *Prisoners* originally intended for the Tomb of Julius II, were incorporated into the walls of a grotto in the Boboli gardens.

The remaining selections deal with two distinct genres of European painting, both of which took something close to their modern form in sixteenth-century Italy. Nicola Courtright's "Imitation, Innovation, and Renovation in the Counter-Reformation" looks at Matthijs Bril's landscape inventions for the Tower of the Winds in the Vatican in the early 1570s. As Courtright shows, these paintings fall into the tradition of the *veduta*, the topographical view of a specific place, yet they amplify their descriptions of the city through the addition both of imaginary elements and of small figures, ostensibly carrying out activities appropriate to their place. As landscape compositions alone, the paintings would have provided an important model for later artists like Domenichino and Claude Lorrain; in context, however, they also relate closely to the reform program of their patron, Pope Gregory XIII, and to the function of the building they decorate. Courtright's study illustrates how ancient models – in this case literary ones – continued to inspire inventions for prominent, Church-sponsored projects even in the years after the Council of Trent, and it demonstrates the degree to which traditions of sacred imagery could contribute to the rise of what might now seem the most secular of painted subjects.

Pamela Jones's piece, which is excerpted from her book on the Milanese Archbishop Federico Borromeo, considers the interests of a patron closely associated with the rise of still-life painting in Italy. Borromeo, who was resident in Rome from 1586 to 1601, who was a founding sponsor of that city's painters' academy, and who probably commissioned Caravaggio's ca. 1598 *Basket of Fruit*, was one of the late sixteenth century's most important reformers, a Jesuit-trained theologian who, in the early seventeenth century, went on to write a major treatise on devotional painting. Jones shows the surprising value that humble subjects like Caravaggio's could have for meditative clerics of Borromeo's bent, the way that seemingly neutral objects could stand at the center of devotional images, even without the addition of figures or of overtly Christian motifs. Borromeo's ideas about the natural order, no less than his interests as a collector, contributed to the origin of the pictorial genres, an ordering of painterly subjects that would not be formalized until the following century, but the core imagery of which depended on the new artistic ideas associated with the reformed Church.

5

Science and the Poetic Impulse

Martin J. Kemp

Have you ever wondered what Leonardo's paintings would look like if all evidence of his writings had been lost? In one obvious sense, they would not look different at all, in that their physical configuration would not be affected. However, if we take "looking" to be a process actively conditioned and directed by established frames of reference and expectation, the way we approach them would be very altered. Without the writings, I suspect Leonardo would less obviously and incontrovertibly be seen as a natural heir to the Florentine tradition of rational naturalism. On the visual evidence of the paintings and drawings alone a case could be made for his having subverted that tradition in the direction of ambiguity, mystery and fantasy; in other words, towards qualities often associated with poetic expression rather than scientific empiricism. We would, I think, see more of the Leonardo of Pater and less of the Leonardo of Ritchie Calder.

However, we do possess a substantial body of authentic writings, and these quite properly colour our view of his art. Can the picture painted by the written legacy be reconciled with my hypothetical picture of the wordless Leonardo as a purveyor of visual poesy? This is one way of framing the question I want to ask in this paper. A more historical way of approaching the question would be: how far was Leonardo consciously or unconsciously affected by poetic values as understood and manifested in his intellectual and social context? I intend to argue not only that important facets of Leonardo's creative activity can best be viewed in a specifically poetic context but also that his poetic impulse exhibits a deep continuity with what we would define as the scientific aspects of his work. I hope I will avoid forcing a false unity between *intelletto* and *fantasia*, but rather show their complementary natures in Leonardo's practice.

Before such a case can be made, it is necessary to establish with some care the nature of his relationship with poetry and imaginative literature, since this has been less clearly accomplished in earlier writing on Leonardo – my own included – than his involvement with scientific discovery and invention. The evidence ranges from the most specific, in the form of books he owned, to the more general sense of the communicative context in which his paintings were created.

His two most substantial booklists – that in the *Codice atlantico* dating apparently from the 1490s, and that in the Madrid Codices from *c.* 1503–5 – certainly do not paint a picture of a man single-mindedly concerned with natural philosophy.[1] There is an almost equal balance between literary and scientific works, if I may be permitted to use that anachronistic classification for the moment. And within the literary area we find the main branches of vernacular writing fairly equally represented. Chivalric romances of the kind so popular in Renaissance courts are well represented, not least by the work of the brothers Luca and Luigi Pulci.[2] Moralizing, didactic poetry is present in works from the fourteenth and fifteenth centuries.[3] Romantic poetry as practised at the Sforza court is represented by the sonnets of Gasparo Visconti and by the great master, Petrarch, alongside poems by Burchiello in a robustly non-Petrarchian vein. He also owned collections of *facetie* (jests), *novelle* and fables, the pithy and not infrequently ribald tales which he imitated in his own writings.[4]

The booklists need to be used with caution, both because they do not necessarily provide a complete or even a balanced record of what he read and owned, and because, as many of us have cause to know, the ownership of a book should not be taken as evidence that its owner has read it. The many other explicit and implicit references to literary sources in his notebooks, which supplement the booklists, need to be used with similar caution, since a quotation from or reference to an author may not come first-hand. Indeed, Leonardo owned a *Zibaldone*, one of those scrap-book collections of literary, historical and philosophical snippets which provided a form of instant learning. The aphoristic statements which head a number of pages from his early *Codice trivulziano* have the nature of prospective entries in a *Zibaldone*.[5]

In addition to the evidence in Leonardo's own writings, we can illustrate the literary environment in which he was directly immersed, above all during his employment at the Sforza court in Milan. We have already noted that he owned a book of sonnets by Visconti, who appears to have been on particularly friendly terms with Bramante, and we will see later that Leonardo was the butt of a humorously critical poem composed by Gasparo in Milan. He was also on the receiving end of laudatory poems by Bernardo Bellincioni, then the most prominent of the Sforza poets. One of these speaks of Leonardo, Giorgio Merula the humanist, Caradosso the medallist, and Gieronimo *bombadiere* as four "divine stars" of Ludovico's court.[6] Bellincioni had come to Milan, like Leonardo, from Medicean Florence, and retained strong links with Lorenzo Il Magnifico's circle, including Luigi Pulci, Poliziano and Lucrezia Tornabuoni.[7] Leonardo for his part provided costume and set designs for theatrical compositions by the court poets, including Bellincioni.[8]

If any evidence should be required of the impact of poetry as a force with which he had to reckon, we need look no further than his *paragone*, which goes to considerable lengths to combat the particular claims of each of the branches of poetry we have found represented in his library. His criticisms do reflect a considerable knowledge of the Renaissance poetic genres. When he referred more generally to the self-praise which poetry accords itself, he may well have been thinking both of the claims of his colleagues competing for Ducal attention and to written claims such as those provided by Luigi Pulci in his *Morgante* (a book owned by Leonardo), where the author expressed his hope to satisfy all varieties of taste with his poetic *fantasia*.[9]

The manner in which Leonardo often forced his arguments against poetry towards untenable extremes reflects the seriousness with which he took the challenges of the word-smiths; and he was not averse to challenging them on their own terms in his own literary and literary-based compositions. He shared the humanists' delight in puns and verbally conceded meanings. His pictograms, which spell out aphorisms in a form of picture-writing, rely upon a variety of references: straight puns (e.g. a *col*, a hill, as "with the"), symbolic references (e.g. a lady with a sail = *fortuna*), musical notations (e.g. the note *fa* on a stave) and animals from his emblematic bestiary. He also turned his hand to purely verbal manipulations, as in "O moro, io moro se con tua moralità non mi amori tanto il vivere m'é amaro".[10] This play on a word, in this case the nickname of Ludovico, Il Moro, can be paralleled in the work of Poliziano:

> Quel che tu ami amil tu solo? – Solo
> Chi t' ha levata da mio amore? – Amore
> Che fa quello a chi porti amore? – Ah more[11]

Of all the major branches of Renaissance literature, the ubiquitous and conventionalized love poetry, which was given fresh impetus by the Neoplatonizing attitudes of Lorenzo de'Medici's circle, might seem on the surface to have least appeal for Leonardo. However, he was touched by its underlying philosophy, and at least one aspect of his pictorial practice was deeply informed by its conventions. One of the *Zibaldone*-like excerpts in the *Codice trivulziano* reads:

> The lover is moved by the beloved object as the senses are by sensory impressions [*sensibile*], and they unite with each other and become one and the same thing . . .[12]

The generally Neoplatonic flavour of this has long been recognized – corresponding to the Dionysian tag, *amore est virtus unitiva*.[13] A more immediate source may well be Dante's *Convivio*, which seems to have provided Leonardo with regular intellectual nourishment:

> Love . . . is nothing other than the spiritual union of the soul and the beloved object.[14]

A related echo of the Neoplatonism current in the Medicean environment of his early career occurs in Leonardo's explanation of the oft-repeated axiom that "every painter paints himself":

Because judgement is one of the powers of the soul, by which it composes the form of the body in which it resides ... having to reproduce with the hands a human body, it naturally reproduces that body which it first invented. From this it follows that he who falls in love, naturally loves things similar to himself.[15]

The philosophy behind this is related to an idea commonly expressed in scholastic philosophy that "omne agens agit sibi simile" ("every agent performs its acts in its own image").[16] Perhaps Dante again provides an intermediary.[17]

It seems that Leonardo aired this idea at the Sforza court, because in a poem by Visconti it is used to attack an unnamed target, identifiable as Leonardo. The sonnet is entitled "Against a bad painter":

> Formerly there was a painter
> who could draw nothing but a cypress tree,
> According to what Horace tells us
> where he teaches us to understand poetry.[18]
>
> There is one nowadays who has so fixed
> in his conception the image of himself
> that when he wishes to paint someone else
> he often paints not the subject but himself.
>
> And not only his face, which is beautifully fair
> according to himself, but in his supreme art
> he forms with his brush the manners and customs of men.
>
> It is true that he neglects important matters,
> that is to say that his brain goes wandering
> each time the moon wanes:
> hence, when it comes to making a good poem
> and to make paintings which work well as a whole,
> he lacks the fetters, restraints and chains.[19]

In addition to such reciprocal echoes between Leonardo's thought and Renaissance poetry, there do seem to be clear references to love poetry in his practice of painting, above all in his portraits. I will choose here to speak of the *Cecilia Gallerani* (figure 5.1), because its court context is explicit, but I could equally well refer to the *Ginevra de'Benci* or the *"Mona Lisa"*. The brilliant freshness of Leonardo's portrayal has tended to mask the close correspondence between his imagery and the often tired stereotypes of Petrarchian love sonnets. The standard focuses of attention in such poetry are (in this order), the eyes, the mouth, the hair and the hands. Examples of radiant eyes, sweetly smiling mouths, beguiling coiffures and pure white hands, are so legion that it is hard to know which to cite. I could quote the great masters, Dante and Petrarch, or Leonardo's Florentine contemporaries, Lorenzo de'Medici and Poliziano.[20] But it is probably more germane to look to Leonardo's Sforza colleagues. When Bellincioni was called to praise the Milanese Duchess, we are asked to "admire the face so full of beauty, with eyes of such beauty as to move rocks and mountains".[21] Their distinguished relative, Isabella d'Este (portrayed, incidentally, by Leonardo), has eyes which put the sun into shade.[22] While Visconti, in a set of sonnets dedicated to Bianca Maria Sforza, talks of "luminous eyes . . . or rather sweet and radiant suns"; of sweet speech; of the "graceful hand which steals me away from myself"; and of "sweet and lustrous" hair, plaited and bound in decorative knots (like the coiffure of Leonardo's *Leda*),[23] Lorenzo had comparably spoken of the lady's "beautifully white and delicate hand" which has "tied his heart in a million knots".[24] Love knots were all the rage amongst the d'Este ladies, and may, as I have argued elsewhere, explain the knotted cord in the Sala delle Asse.[25]

That Leonardo's *Cecilia* thrived in such a context is confirmed by Bellincioni's laudatory sonnet. Almost inevitably, "beside her beautiful eyes, the sun appears darkly shaded".[26] The portrait shows that Leonardo knew full well the language in which to speak to his intended audience, and has translated the *dolce stil nuovo* into paint in a manner unmatched by his predecessors. Indeed, in his *paragone*, he was not shy to claim that he had outstripped the poet in this respect:

> If the poet says that he can inflame men with love, . . . the painter has the power to do the same, and to an even greater extent in that he can place in front of the lover the true likeness of that which is beloved, often making him kiss it and speak to it.[27]

The impact of such poetic imagery did not fade in Leonardo's later career, and continued to be expressed in a deeply personal manner, most notably in the famous *Pointing Lady*. It has already been suggested that she should be identified as the beautiful Matelda of the *Divina Commedia*, who conducts Dante from Purgatory to Paradise.[28] Whether or not the identification is specific, the presentation and emotional context is very close:

> As a dancing lady turns with her feet together,
> Foot by foot set close and close to the ground,
> And scarcely putting one before the other,
>
> So she to me . . . turned round . . .
>
> So when she'd come to where the crystalline
> Clear water bathes the grasses, she at once
> Did the grace to lift her eyes to mine . . .
>
> So upright, on the other bank she smiled.[29]

The Dantesque image of the beloved in a sylvan setting, typically in a beautiful floral grove watered by gurgling streams and stirred by murmuring breezes, became another commonplace of Renaissance poetry. Often the sylvan image is used to soothe the fevered brow of the lover who is freezing in fire or burning

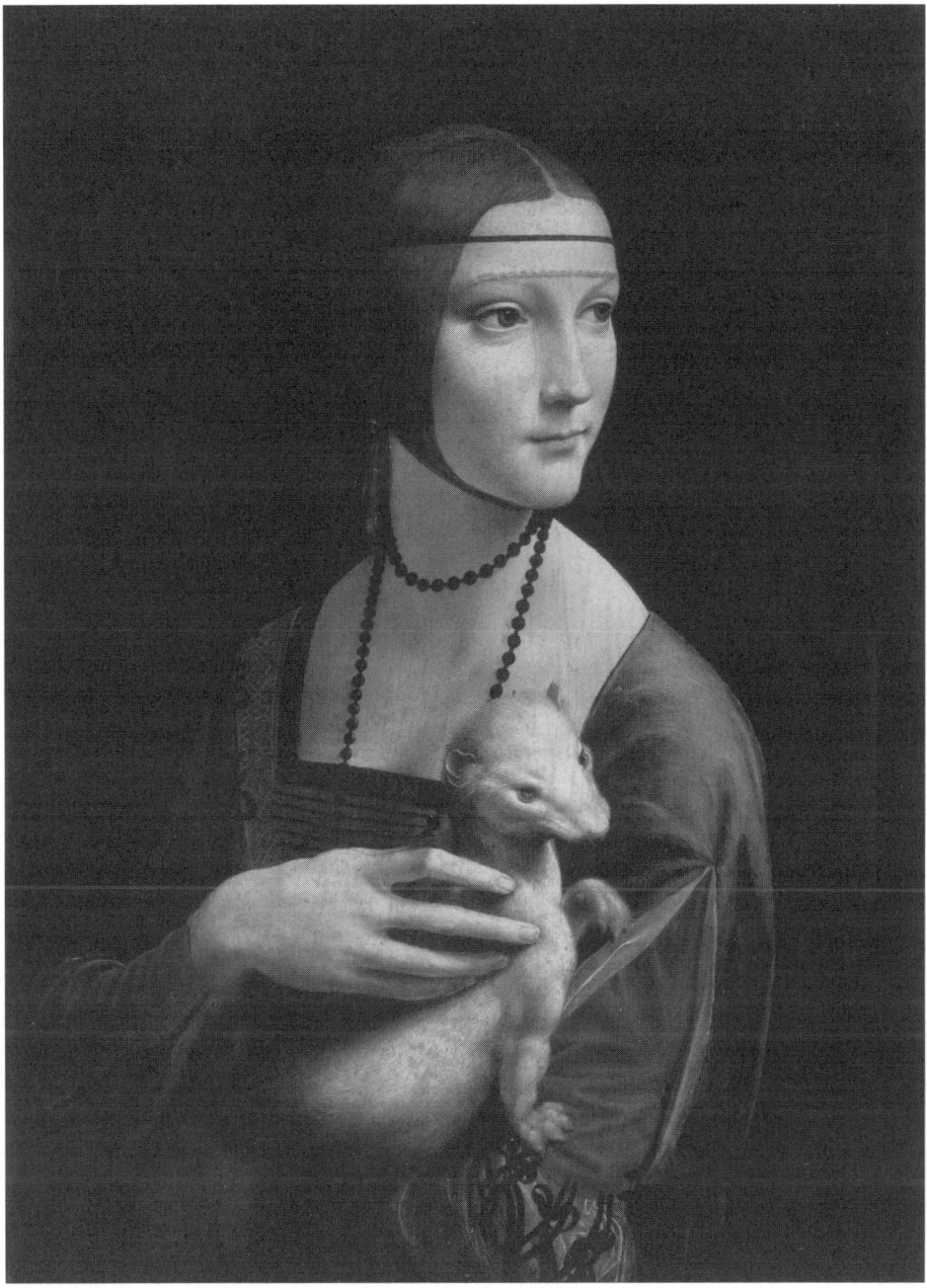

Figure 5.1 Leonardo da Vinci, *Cecilia Gallerani*, ca. 1490. Oil on walnut wood. Muzeum Czartoryski, Cracow; AKG-images / Erich Lessing.

in ice. Once again Leonardo claimed to outdo the poet in pastoral imagery. In painting "you will be able to see yourself again as a lover with your beloved in flowering meadows beneath the sweet shade of verdant trees".[30] The painter can conjure up "shady and cool places in hot weather . . . and similarly warm places in cold weather. If he wants valleys, if he wants to disclose great expanses of countryside from the summits of high mountains . . . he is lord of them."[31]

One of the standbys of love poetry is antithesis – the setting of contrasting qualities side by side to achieve a heightened effect. Lorenzo de'Medici provided a compound example:

> Contrasting voices make a sweet song,
> And diverse colours a new beauty:
> The sharp tone pleases in conjunction with the flat.
> In black, white finds its grace.[32]

Similarly, Visconti tells us that:

> The wise merchant who wishes to sell
> A beautiful white pearl of the Orient,
> Contrives to show it in a black sandal.[33]

This technique of dark-light contrast is, of course, just that recommended by Leonardo for obtaining effects of relief in painting. Thus for portraiture he specifically recommended tinting the walls of his studio black.[34] He advised the painter that he should:

> so arrange that the part which is illuminated should border upon a dark object, and correspondingly the shaded part should border upon a light object.[35]

The tonal contrasts which help give the *Cecilia* such an outstanding sense of relief are brilliant manifestations of the harmony of contrasts in creative action.

Antithesis reflected the paired powers of nature – lightness and darkness, heat and coldness, sweetness and bitterness, joy and sorrow, goodness and evil, and so on. On the back of his drawing of Aristotle and Phyllis, he listed examples of what he called "companies":

> voluptuousness-grief
> love-jealousy
> happiness-envy
> fortune-suffering.[36]

This expresses the idea that a virtue is born in the inevitable company of its consequent vice. In a sense, the one defines the other: "no sooner is virtue born than envy is conceived, and sooner will a solid body lack shadow than virtue lack envy". This sentence is accompanied by a drawn allegory of a typically elaborate kind. The beautiful, naked Virtue "gives birth from her body to Envy, a scrawny, ugly and pale woman", with a scorpion's tail, who tries to steal Virtue's arrows, incinerates her hair and attacks her with a tongue in the form of a serpent. Virtue responds by blinding Envy with a branch of olive (for peace) and renders her deaf with a sharp arrow.[37]

Such complexly obscure allegories, designed for courtly consumption, represent one of Leonardo's ways of answering the writer's challenge to "signify great things", consciously emulating the great Grecian Apelles, who had painted an elaborate allegory of Calumny.[38] Often the general allegorical message was pressed into the specific service of contemporary needs, as when he devised schemes showing Ludovico Il Moro protecting a young man from the "hideous figure" of poverty, and joining forces with Justice to rout Slander and Envy.[39] Concern with the critical tongues of slander reached a high level in the Sforza court, particularly at the time of the death in 1494 of the young Gian Galeazzo, the legitimate Duke, in circumstances which gave natural rise to suspicion. The regular instances of Leonardo drawings from the mid 1490s showing ill-report at work may owe their origins to this. Ultimately, as one of Leonardo's simpler drawings suggests, the fame which arises from Virtue provides weapons to combat Envy. The tongue-tipped arrow of Envy is impeded by a large volume – of laudatory sonnets, dare we suggest? – and she retreats before Fame's lance.

This kind of composition finds a close counterpart in the propagandist poetry of Bellincioni. In addition to general praise of Ludovico's virtue and fame, Bellincioni also turned his pen "Against Detractors", the title of one of his published works. The French king is allusively characterized as "that which already recorded the error of Peter"; that is to say as the crowing cock which signalled St. Peter's disowning of Christ, and therefore as the Gallic cock which symbolized France. "But if envy makes to silence truth", Bellincioni says, Ludovico will act with the force of a sledgehammer. Mixing his metaphors, just as Leonardo did, he characterized Il Moro as "all ermine" – that is moderation and unstained virtue – "even if his name is black".[40] We may recall that an animal which appears to be an unnaturally large ermine symbolizes Cecilia's pure virtues as well as making a pun on her surname. Milanese manuscript illuminations speak the same symbolic language, one of them depicting Il Moro as a sturdy black mulberry providing essential support for a willowy young Duke Gian Galeazzo.[41]

Where Leonardo differed from the conventional allegorist is that he preferred not to be constricted by the traditional, recognizable range of symbolic reference. He sought what we might call a form of natural allegory, based upon his study of the essence or natures of particular objects and forces in nature. To some extent this was derived from the medieval readings of the book of nature with which he was familiar – Aesop's fables, the bestiary and Cecco d'Ascoli's *L'Acerba*. But Leonardo tended to draw his *own* allegorical meaning out of his scientific understanding of the phenomena. An example is his splendid evocation of a small piece of glowing charcoal from which arises a vigorous fire:

> ... then the fire rejoicing at the dried logs placed upon it, began to rise, driving out the air from the gaps between the logs, twining itself about them in vivacious and joyous progress. Having begun to puff out from the apertures between the logs, through which it has made delightful windows for itself, and to send out gleaming and shining flames, it rapidly disperses the gloomy darkness of the enclosed kitchen. Once the flames have grown they gambol with the air surrounding them, and singing with sweet murmurs, they create a mellifluous sound.[42]

But this joyous progress may be halted. The proud fire, "king of the elements," resents the water in the cauldron above it, endeavouring to boil the water away. However, the water boils over, dousing the fire, and extinguishing its pride.[43]

The problem with this kind of natural allegory is that the same natural element may behave quite differently in different contexts. As Ovid realized (in a passage paraphrased by Leonardo), "flame is killed by a strong wind and nourished by a moderate one."[44] Lorenzo de'Medici similarly drew contrasts between the beneficial and destructive effects of moderate and excessive amounts of water, wind and fire.[45] The human equivalent is that temperate love can delight, but intemperate love is a source of distress.

If we look at the range of allegorical uses of fire by Leonardo, we will find a bewildering variety of often contrasting meanings. Fire is variously: a source of destruction, when used in war; a source of vainglorious temptation, as when a moth flies into a candle; a source of life, since it gives warmth; a victim of ingratitude, as it is extinguished by man when daylight comes; a manifestation of the benefits of moderation, because it is sustained by a modest breeze; a false threat, as in a swinging censer of incense; a revealer of truth, since it is used to refine gold, and can melt the mask of falsehood; a symbol of ingratitude, devouring the wood which gives it life; a supreme nutritive power, in that nothing grows without it; a manifestation of misplaced pride, as in the cauldron allegory; and a sign of short-lived life, devouring a candle.[46] The observational variety and allegorical inventiveness is awesome, but the sheer open-endedness of "natural allegory" ultimately destroys the signifying codes which are necessary if a visual composition is to be read coherently and unambiguously.

It was precisely the stereotyped quality necessary for allegorical coherence which Leonardo mocked when he wrote: "If Petrarch was so fond of laurel, it was because it has a good taste with sausages and roast thrush: I cannot set any store by their twaddle."[47] The grindingly monotonous word-play on the name of Petrarch's beloved Laura as the virtuous "laurel" was taken up no less tediously in the circle of Lorenzo il Magnifico who, as *il Lauro*, grew afresh from a severed branch.[48] Leonardo's mockery conforms to a vigorously acid brand of anti-Petrarchian burlesque, which coexisted humorously in the courts alongside the sweet cadences of unrequited love. Luigi Pulci, whose work was well-known to Leonardo, worked a comparable pun on fennel (*finocchio*), as a flavouring for sausages, and the verb "to bamboozle" (*infinocchiare*), which takes the normal place of "to inflame" (*infocare*):

> Tu gl' infinocchi come le salsicce,
> E con l'occhietto gli vai infinocchiano.

This occurs in a poem satirizing Lorenzo's praise of the lovely Nencia. The subject of Pulci's attentions was a "beloved" whose squint has to be seen to be believed.[49] Leonardo also possessed a book of poems by Il Burchiello, the Florentine barber Domenico di Giovanni, who uncompromisingly set about deflating the pomposity of courtly Petrarchism. As antidotes to the marble brows and cupid's-bow mouths of the conventional beloved, such poets paint pictures of grotesque characters. Il Pistoia (Antonio Camelli) provides a good example:

> To nothing on earth my face conforms,
> It measures up to neither triangle nor circle.
> My nose accosts the point of my chin.
> My face is coloured by night.
> My breast is found where my shoulders should be.[50]

Leonardo's grotesque characters inhabit just such a world of physiognomic nonconformity. Bellincioni also turned his hand to burlesque verse, writing in "praise" of a notable glutton and a famous buffoon.[51]

When such grotesques are grouped together in a kind of narrative they belong to the word of the *facetie* and *novelle*. Leonardo owned a copy of the *Facetie* by the great humanist Poggio Braccionini, and the major *quattrocento* collection of *novelle* by Masuccio Salernitano.[52] No stratum of society is left unscathed, from the stupid peasant to the myopic man of learning, from the humblest vassal to the grandest prince. Priests are frequent butts of the tales, short and long, as they were in Leonardo's own *facetie*.[53]

Leonardo's own literary efforts embraced a range of standard types – jests in the Poggio manner, fables in imitation of Aesop, word-painting of exotic locations as in Ovid, Luca Pulci and Antonio Pucci, descriptions of battles in line with the chivalric epic, spurious letters in an epistolary tradition, and descriptions of storms to rival those by narrative poets. Like Poliziano, and using much the same kind of image of rich architecture and cunningly designed gardens, he painted a beguiling word-picture of the "Site of Venus". In my judgement – and I should stress it is an inexpert judgement in literary matters – Leonardo's own compositions fall short in verbal skill of the best of his contemporaries. What seems to redeem at least some of them is his ability to draw on his rich reservoir of natural causes and effects to compose what we may call visually credible fantasies, as when he verbally resurrected a long dead fossil whale:

O mighty and once animated instrument of creative nature. To you, your vast strength availed you not . . . Availed you not the branched and sturdy fins with which you pursued your prey, ploughing the salt waves tempestously asunder with your breast.[54]

Sometimes scientific theory is directly involved in a meditation on the meaning of nature:

Look at the light and consider its beauty.
Blink your eyes and look again.
That which you see there was not,
And that which was there is no more.
Who is it that re-makes it if the maker continually dies?[55]

This relates closely to one of the arguments in favour of the intramission theory of vision which Leonardo adopted from the Arabian, Alhazen, via the medieval tradition. According to this argument, if a ray *from* the eye was responsible for vision – as maintained by the rival intramission theory – there should be a time delay in seeing a distant light when the eye is shut and then opened, which is clearly not the case.[56]

Poetic speculation and fantasy, for Leonardo, was founded on a bedrock of natural causes and effects. This was not intended to limit the exercise of fantasy or the scope for invention. Indeed, Leonardo delighted in the painter's ability to rival a poet such as Dante in evoking terrible visions:

If the painter wishes to fabricate images of animals or devils in the inferno, with what abundance of *inventione* his mind teems.
If poetry terrifies people with fictional hells, painting can do likewise by actually producing the same thing.[57]

To understand Leonardo's attitude, we would do well to remember that Dante's great fictions were commonly seen, with good reason, to be founded upon a prodigious grasp of natural philosophy in the Aristotelian tradition. Dante's use of poetic simile – comparing a spiritual or emotional experience to a natural phenomenon – was stated by Landino, the great commentator in Lorenzo's circle, to "reveal the workings of some natural cause [*causa naturale*] or provide the reader with knowledge and the rules of some natural effect [*cognizione e dottrina d'alcuna cosa naturale*]".[58] Dante, like Leonardo, was an avid student of medieval optics, and the *Paradiso* in particular contains some overt displays of his optical learning.

When Leonardo instructed the painter how to compose an infernal monster he recommended that it should be founded on a compound of parts from animals known to exist in nature. The principle is that a monster could only exist or have existed if it was formed in obedience to natural law, and the parts of known animals provide a repertoire of forms which have been so designed. Thus, when we look at one of his marvellously compelling sketches of dragons, we sense an understanding of animal structure and motion which raises it far above the heraldic commonplace of dragons in fifteenth-century art. The arched neck, drawn back with the recoiled motion of an enraged swan, the snarling mongrel's head, the braced wings of a terrified bird and the splayed legs of a fighting cat, all draw upon his deep grasp of nature.

It is often difficult to tell where actual and feigned observation begin and end. The sheet of cats at Windsor (figure 5.2) contains a number of images which surely bespeak direct scrutiny of an actual cat, lying with its limbs in a contented tangle, while other cats seem to be invented – if plausibly – and begin to look somewhat like lionesses. The freer process of invention then embraces a curly-tailed dragon, and a threatened if out-of-scale mouse, both drawn on a "natural base" though not from nature.

A good example of the free and often unexpected way in which his *fantasia* created new conjunctions is the sketch of Michelangelo's *David* on the page containing his word-picture of the "Site of Venus". At the feet of the figure he has added what appear to be sea-horses, thus transforming the image into a "Neptune". Elsewhere he approached the designs of a Neptune from a different angle, taking as his starting point his *Battle of Anghiari* studies. The latter approach gives a more rhythmically integrated effect, but Neptune (evolved from a seated rider) is now oddly truncated at high level. At the top of the sheet Leonardo instructs himself to "lower the horses", which would give an arrangement closer to the David variation.

Leonardo recognized the process at work here as a special form of inventive imagination or *fantasia*. This is characterized in the terms of medieval faculty psychology, which assigned different mental capacities to each of the ventricles of the brain. Leonardo worked his own idiosyncratic variations on the location and functions of the so-called "inner senses" of the medieval theory. One of the characteristics commonly assigned to *fantasia* was that of combining images to make new compounds, inventing endless permutations on the raw data of sense impressions. He explained that "nature is concerned only with the production of elementary things, but man from these elementary things produces an infinite number of compounds."[59] Where he departed from the medieval norm was in his location of *fantasia* in the second ventricle rather than the first. The ventricle was the home of rational intellect and seat of the soul. *Fantasia* was thus moved to the centre of mental activity, and could accordingly act in close liaison with the higher powers of thought.

I think it is relatively easy to see how Leonardo's upgraded form of *fantasia* can be reconciled with the Renaissance view of Dantesque poetry as a vehicle of natural and divine wisdom. It is perhaps harder to see what reciprocal rôle imagination might possess in science – but it is only harder if we cling to our modern preconceptions of what constitutes science. I have argued elsewhere that Leonardo's science is best understood in a context of scientific thought which

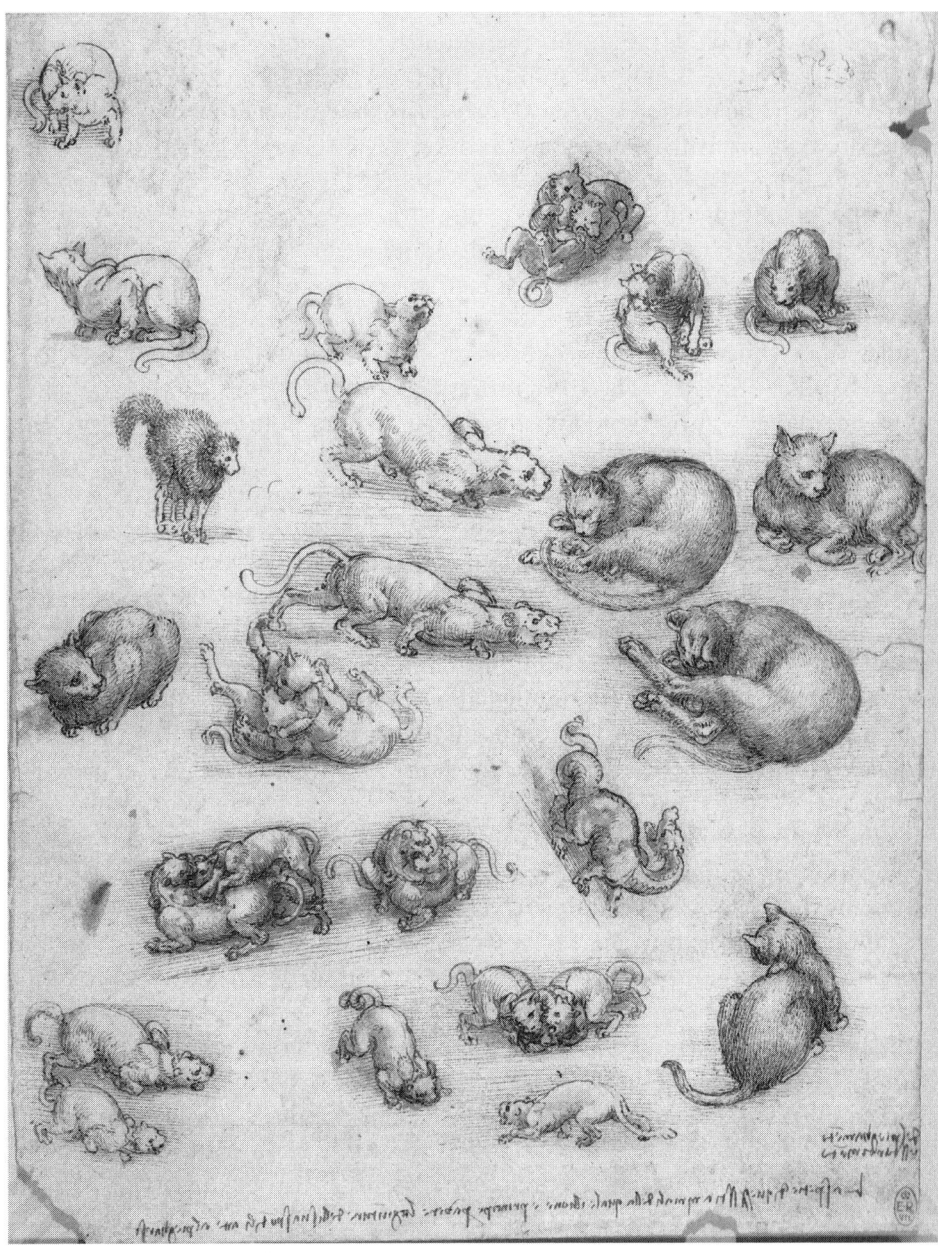

Figure 5.2 Leonardo da Vinci, study sheet with cats and a dragon. Windsor, Royal Library, 12363. The Royal Collection © 2005, Her Majesty Queen Elizabeth II.

assigned a high value to methods of proof largely foreign to modern stereotypes of science. One of these methods of proof was the composite building of explanations, in which a limited set of regular causes are made to explain a variety of diverse effects. Such explanations were seen to have a value approaching that

106

of mathematical proof, and provided a goal to which Leonardo was attracted no less than many of his medieval predecessors. Ultimate proofs of a mathematical nature can be seen as the supreme goal of his physiological anatomy.[60]

Another closely related method of explanation in this scheme is argument by analogy. A particularly nice instance is his interpretation of the heart as the "seed" from which the vascular system arises, making his point by means of two comparative drawings beside his demonstration of the main vessels of the thorax. This is not simply a question of the germinating plant providing a convenient analogy but rather reflects his conviction that there is a deep affinity between the natures of all created forms. The most all-embracing of the analogies was the theory of the microcosm and macrocosm, which stated that the constitution of man mirrored the world as a whole – to use Leonardo's words, that man is "a lesser world".[61] It was around this theory that he attempted to build his explanation of the movement of fluids in the body of the earth, not only in the seas, rivers and springs, but also in a hypothetical network of underground veins.[62]

Aristotle himself had expressed reservations about the method of argument by analogy:

> It is absurd for anyone to think, like Empedocles, that he has made an intelligible statement where he says that the sea is the sweat of the earth. Such a statement is perhaps satisfactory in poetry, for a metaphor is a poetic device, but it does not advance our knowledge of nature.[63]

However, Aristotelian science in the Middle Ages exercised little of the caution recommended by their mentor, and analogy became an established method of demonstration. It was this method which Landino rightly recognized as having a prominent rôle in the *Divina Commedia*.

A particularly spectacular exposition of how man is built on the model of nature as a whole is Statius's discourse in the 25th canto of Dante's *Purgatory*. Statius described the way in which the implanted soul in the womb progresses through stages corresponding to plants and brutes, before the "Prime Mover" infuses the soul with a self-aware human consciousness. If we want an instance from Leonardo's own time, we can look towards Lorenzo de'Medici's invocation of God as the "Bellissimo Architetto" of the human microcosm.[64]

The microcosm is simultaneously a poetic image and a scientific cause, and no easy separation can be made between the two uses.

This vision gives the world and its contents an animistic quality, and it is not surprising to find Leonardo talking of elements and forces in terms of "longings" and "desires". The elements – earth, water, air and fire – all "desire" to return to their natural place in the order of things. All forces "wish" to expand themselves in their assigned time and distance. Man is part of this scheme:

> The hope and desire of returning to one's origins and returning to the primal chaos is analagous of the moth to the light. The man who with perpetual longing

desires with joyous expectation each new spring, each new summer, each new month and new year . . . does not perceive that he is longing for his own destruction. But this longing in its quintessence is an integral part of nature, and man is the model of the world.[65]

The image is closely related to the opening of Ovid's *Metamorphoses*, in which the "shapeless and disorganized mass" of Chaos is organized by the supreme artificer into the orderly spheres of the four elements. Henceforth, an element out of its place will desire to return to its due location, just as man's soul desires to return to his maker.

The visual images by Leonardo which obviously spring to mind in this context are the *Deluge* drawings (figure 5.3), although they are separated from the Ovidian quotation by more than thirty years. If the early quotation has something of the literary and philosophical bravado of a young man, the late drawings manifest a lifetime's experience of the darker forces of nature. The drawings have all the power of Dante's "blast of hell that never ceases whirling":

> Then o'er that dull tide came the crash and roar
> Of an enormous and appalling sound,
> So that the ground shuddered from shore to shore;

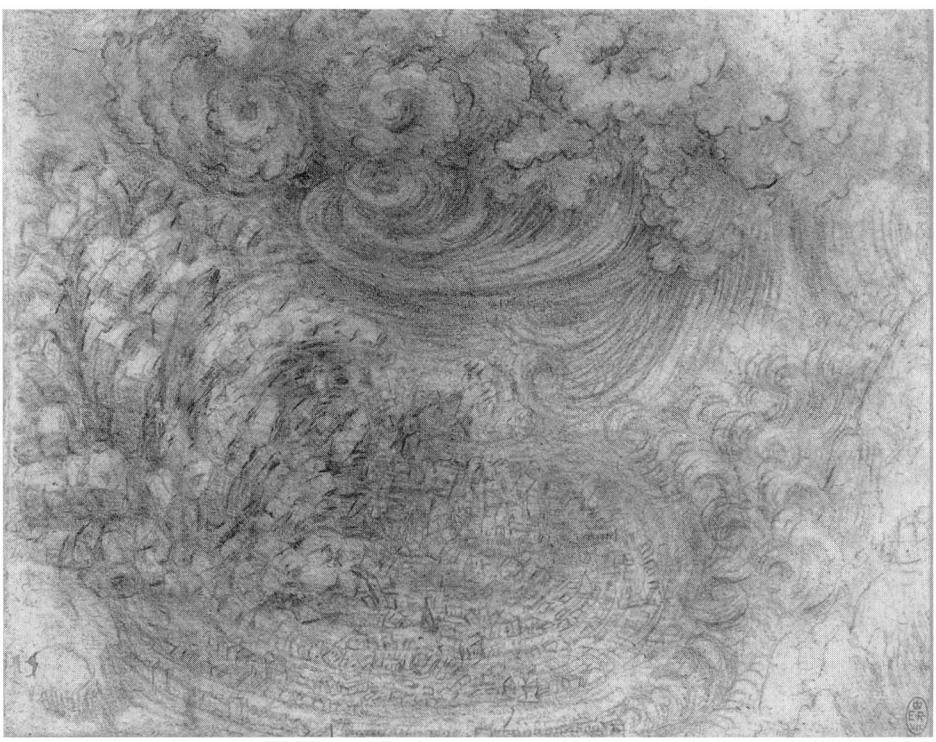

Figure 5.3 Leonardo da Vinci, *Deluge*. Windsor, Royal Library, 12378. The Royal Collection © 2005, Her Majesty Queen Elizabeth II.

> A sound like the sound of a violent wind, around
> The time of opposing heats and the parched weather,
> When it sweeps on the forest and leaps with a sudden bound,
>
> Shattering and scattering the boughs hither and thither;
> Proud with a tower of dust for harbinger
> It goes, while the wolves and herdsmen flee together.[66]

The imagery of Leonardo's own written description of a deluge is very similar. He speaks of "the course of diverse winds . . . bearing hither and thither infinite numbers of branches stripped from trees", and "various species of animals terrified and reduced to tameness".[67]

The poetic power of the verbal and visual images is undeniable, but we should note that both poet and painter richly inform such images with their scientific understanding. When Dante talks of the movement of water he uses a remarkable variety of descriptive verbs in a manner which resembles Leonardo's attempts to classify the motion of vortices. Dante used *meare, descendere, fluere, effluere, influere, defundere, decurrere, manare, emanare*.[68] Leonardo, in a typically profligate manner, listed more than sixty terms, including: ". . . *declinazione, elevazione, cavamento, consummamento, percussione, reuinamento, discenso, impetuità, retrosi* . . .".[69] Although the terms are not the same, both authors are similarly attempting to forge a vernacular vocabulary for the description of natural phenomena equivalent to that which had been evolved in Latin science. One of the key terms in Leonardo's vocabulary of motion, *percussione*, was also well-used by Dante, and reflects the shared base of their dynamic theory. One of Dante's many analogies drew upon what we may fairly term a hydrodynamic observation:

> From centre to circumference, and again from circumference to centre,
> Moves the water in a round bowl
> According to whether it is percussed from outside or in.

Dante called this an "apt simile" for the impact of the words of St. Thomas on the poet's senses in the *Paradiso*.[70] This image of the concentric transmission of percussive waves exercised Leonardo's attention not a little, with respect to water, sound and light.[71]

I should stress that I am not saying that Dante necessarily provides the source for Leonardo's general conceptions or even the source for individual ideas – though there are particular instances which suggest that this may have been so. Rather, I am saying that, in spite of their very different visions and ultimately different ends, they founded their imaginative constructs on a comparable base of natural philosophy and empirical knowledge – that their *fantasia* and *scientia* stand in a similar relationship to each other. Leonardo's description of a deluge is more obsessively thoroughgoing than Dante's in its use of the vocabulary of medieval impetus theory, but the difference is one of degree rather than one of kind.[72]

Dante's image of circular transmission has already been compared by Sir Ernst Gombrich to one of Leonardo's speculations:

> Water percussed by water makes circles around the point of percussion; similarly the voice in the air over a longer distance; and even longer through the fire; and still greater the mind through the universe, but because the mind is finite, it does not extend to infinity.[73]

This suggests that the parallel with Dante may go even further than the basic affinity between their fantasy and science. One of the insistent messages of Matelda and Beatrice in the later stages of *Purgatorio* and in the *Paradiso* is the dullness and limited nature of man's wits when faced with the infinite. Matelda – perhaps our *Pointing Lady* – promises to

> . . . tell the reason why
> These things are so, which cause perplexities,
> And thus I'll make the offending mists to fly.[74]

While Beatrice even more pointedly says:

> . . . You make yourself dull
> With false fancies [*falso imaginar*] so that you can not see
> As you would if you had cast them off.[75]

Neither the poet's unaided intellect nor his imagination can grasp the infinite majesty of divine glory. The rôle of the mysterious, smiling, all-knowing and smugly superior ladies is to transcend these limits.

Clearly Leonardo's theology was not developed to the pitch of Dante's – nor would he have wished it to be – but he did increasingly come to realize the finite limits of rational comprehension. Leonardo declared that he would not attempt to "write or give information of these things of which the human mind is incapable and which cannot be proved by any instance of nature."[76] But, equally, his view of the universal machine required some supreme designer, some motive force – even if its ultimate nature was indefinable.

I should like to suggest that it is possible in this light not only to see the *Pointing Lady* as possessing the aura of the Dantesque ladies, but also to see such figures as *St. John the Baptist* and the St. Annes in the Louvre painting and London cartoon as divinely favoured intermediaries "who", in Leonardo's words, "possess the secrets by inspiration".[77] Their sweet smiles, knowing looks, pointing gestures and paradoxical aura of intimate remoteness align them perfectly in mood with the sublimated subjects of Dante's divine love.

I hope I have suggested, during the course of our journey from the secular devices of the Sforza court to the transcendental realm of ineffable divinity, that Leonardo's relationship to comtemporary poetry is not simply a matter of shared conventions – a superficial if interesting question of iconographical me-chanics – but rather a matter of deeply shared habits of mind. These habits of mind embrace such specific points as the position of the courtly woman in the Renaissance and the limits of rational knowledge, as well as the more general if less clearly defined sense of the way imagination feeds on science and vice versa. The personal balance which Leonardo struck between science and the poetic impulse, and the resulting expression in his paintings and drawings, manifests the individuality of his genius. But it is a balance which can be more fully understood within the intellectual and social contexts shared by Renaissance poets, whether great or minor, whether Dante or Bellincioni.

Notes

Reference to Leonardo's manuscripts is by the standard abbreviations as in *The Literary Works of Leonardo da Vinci*, 3rd ed., (2 vols., London, 1970), II, p. 400 (with B.L. for Br. M., and Forster for S.K.M.), and M. Kemp, *Leonardo da Vinci. The Marvellous Works of Nature and Man* (London and Cambridge (Mass.) 1981), pp. 21–2. Abbreviations are as follows: R. for paragraph nos. in Richter; Pedretti for C. Pedretti, *A Commentary to Jean Paul Richter's Edition* (2 vols., Oxford, 1977).

1   C.A. 210r (R. 1469) and Madrid II 2 v (Pedretti, II, pp. 355ff).
2   On the C.A. booklist: Luca Pulci, *Il Driadeo* (various printed eds. in 1480s). Luigi Pulci, *Morgante* (numerous 15th century eds.). Additionally on Madrid booklist: Luca Pulci, *Ciriffo Calvaneo* (Venice, 1479, or Florence, 1490). He also owned A. da Barberino, *Guerino Meschino* (various eds.), and possibly B. da Imola, *Il Romuleo* (see Pedretti, II, p. 356).
3   Moralizing and didactic works on the C.A. booklist: *Fiore di Virtù* (Venice, 1488); Cecco d'Ascoli, *L'Acerba* (various eds.); F. Frezzi, *Quadriregio* (probably Milan, 1488); a *Zibaldone*, authorship unknown. Additionally on Madrid booklist: S. Brandt, *Ship of Fools* (various Latin and French eds.).
4   On the C.A. Booklist: Aesop's *Fables* (one of the two copies mentioned in the Madrid list is one of the French eds.); P. Bracciolini, *Facetie* (3 eds. in Italian trans.). Additionally on Madrid booklist: Masuccio Salernitano, *Il Novellino* (various eds.). He also knew F. Sacchetti's *Novelle* and L. Carbone's *Cento trenta novelle* (Kemp, *Leonardo*, p. 156).
5   A *Zibaldone* is listed in both booklists. For a good discussion of such sources see C. Dionisotti, "Leonardo uomo di lettere", *Italia Medioevale e Umanista*, V, 1962, pp. 183–216. The Codice trivulziano in the Biblioteca Trivulziana in Milan is the earliest of Leonardo's intact surviving notebooks and can be dated to the second half of the 1480s. A selection of the aphorisms is in Richter, II, pp. 237–50.
6   B. Bellincioni, *Le Rime*, ed. P. Fanfani (Bologna, 1876), LXXVII, p. 106. See also pp. 26 and 72 for other references to Leonardo. "Giannino Bombadieri" is mentioned by Leonardo on CA. 225rb (see Kemp, *Leonardo*, p. 105).
7   For a sonnet addressed to Luigi Pulci by Bellincioni, see *Rime*, LI, pp. 81–2 (and see note 9 below).

8 Leonardo's involvement with theatrical design is discussed by C. Steinitz, "Leonardo Architetto Teatrale e Organizzatore di Feste", *IX Lettura Vinciana* (Florence, 1970); and M. Angiolillo, *Leonardo. Feste e Teatri*, with intro. by C. Pedretti (Naples, 1979).

9 L. Pulci, *Morgante*, ed. F. Ageno, in *La Letteratura Italiana* (Milan-Naples, n.d.), XVIII, 140ff. See also XVIII, 143 for an admiring reference to Bellincioni.

10 Madrid, II, 141r.

11 A. Poliziano, *Rispetti spicciolati*, I, "Pan ed Eco", *Rime*, ed. N. Sapegno (Rome, 1965), p. 23.

12 Triv. 6r (R. 1202).

13 Dionysius, *De divinis nominibus*, V, 12.

14 Dante, *Convivio*, III, ii, 3. See P. Boyde, *Dante. Philomythes and Philosopher. Man in the Cosmos*, Cambridge, 1981, pp. 256ff.

15 Libro A, 15 (II), see C. Pedretti, *Leonardo da Vinci On Painting: A Lost Book (Libro A)* (London, 1965), p. 35; and M. Kemp, "'Ogni Dipintore Dipinge Se': A Neoplatonic Echo in Leonardo's Art Theory", *Cultural Aspects of the Italian Renaissance. Essays in Honour of P. O. Kristeller*, ed. C. H. Clough (Manchester and New York, 1976), pp. 300–11.

16 Boyde, op. cit., p. 225.

17 Boyde, ibid, p. 256.

18 Horace, *Ars Poetica*, 19–21.

19 G. Visconti, *I Canzonieri per Beatrice d'Este e per Bianca Maria Sforza*, ed. P. Bongrani (Milan, 1979), CLXVIII, pp. 117–18. I have omitted the last three lines, which refer back to Horace. This poem was kindly drawn to my attention by Paul Holberton (Warburg Institute). Dr. Paolo Rossi of the University of Lancaster provided valuable assistance in the translation of what is a far from lucid piece of writing.

20 For Dante's *Convivio*, III, viii, in relation to the *"Mona Lisa"* see Kemp, *Leonardo*, p. 267. A. Poliziano, *La Giostra*, 45f., *Ballate*, V, *Rispetti spicciolati*, XII and XV; Petrarch, *Sonetti*, LXXV, CCCXLVIII; Lorenzo de'Medici, *Canzone*, VII; *Selve d'Amore*, I; and "Comento sopra alcuni de' suoi sonetti", *Opere*, ed. A. Simioni, 2 vols (Bari, 1913), pp. 43 and 47; amongst many other examples.

21 Bellincioni, *Rime*, X, p. 39.

22 Bellincioni, XXXIV, p. 62, and LXX, p. 95.

23 Visconti, *Canzoniere*, VI (3), p. 11.

24 Lorenzo de'Medici, "Comento . . .", *Opere*, ed. Simioni, I, p. 58.

25 Kemp, *Leonardo*, pp. 186–7 for the Sala delle Asse; and P. Marani, "Leonardo e le colonne *ad tronchonos*: tracce di un programma iconologico per Ludovico il Moro", *Raccolta Vinciana*, XXI, 1982, pp. 94–102.

26 Bellincioni, *Rime*, XLV, pp. 72–3.

27 Urb. 13v–14r.

28 For the identification of the "Pointing Lady" as Matelda, see P. Meller, "Leonardo da Vinci's Drawings to the Divine Comedy", *Acta Historiae Artium Academiae Scientiarum Hungaricae*, II, 1955, pp. 135–66.

29 *Purgatorio*, XXVIII, 52–67 (trans. based on D. L. Sayers, *Penguin Classics*, Harmondsworth, 1949).

30 Urb. 12r–v.

31 Urb. 5r.

32 Lorenzo, *Selve d'Amore*, I, 28, *Opere*, ed. Simioni, I, p. 250.

33 Visconti, *Canzoniere*, XI (8), p. 14.

34 B.N. 2038 20v (R. 520).

35 B.N. 2038 31r (R. 563).

36 Hamburg, Kunsthalle (Pedretti, I, p. 385).

37 A full exposition of the meaning of the figures is provided in Lomazzo's *Trattato*, which clearly relies upon direct knowledge of an account by Leonardo himself; see Pedretti, I, p. 385.

38 Urb. 9r, B.N. 2038, 19v.

39 I^2 138v (R. 672), and the drawing in the Musée Bonnat, Bayonne, illustrated in A. E. Popham, *The Drawings of Leonardo da Vinci* (London, 1946), no. 109B.

40 Bellincioni, *Rime*, XXVII, pp. 55–6.

41 Paris, Bibliothèque Nationale, Vélins, 724. The same MS also contains an allegory with Il Moro as a black man piloting a boat bearing his nephew, under the guidance of St. Ludovic. For a later Leonardo allegory along these lines see M. Kemp, "*Navis Ecclesiae*: an Ambrosian Metaphor in Leonardo's Allegory of the Nautical Wolf and Imperious Eagle", *Bibliothèque d'Humanisme et Renaissance*, XLIII, 1981, pp. 257–68.

42 C.A. 116vb (Pedretti II; p. 271).

43 Forster, III, 30r (Pedretti II, p. 269).

44 Ovid, *Remedia Amores*, 807–8: "Nutritur vento, vento restinguitur ignis;/lenis alit flammas, grandior aura necat." Cf. Leonardo, C.A. 270ra: "Il superchio vento uccide la fiamma e il temperato la nutrica" (Pedretti, I, p. 398).

45 Lorenzo, *Selve d'Amore*, I, 3–8, *Opere*, ed. Simioni, pp. 243–5.

46 Listed in corresponding order: B.L. 42v (R. 1297); C.A. 67r (R. 1268) and Trn. l7v (Pedretti, II, p. 244); C.A. 116vb (Pedretti, II, p. 270) and C.A. 307r (R. 1295, p. 298); B.L. 173r (R. 687); C.A. 270ra (Pedretti, I, p. 398); B.L. 212v (R. 1310); Windsor 12700v (R. 684); B.N. 2038 34v (R. 686); C.A. 67r (R. 1273); Forster III 30r (Pedretti, II, p. 269).

47 Triv. lv (R. 1332).

48 Forster II^1 63r (R. 697) for Leonardo's emblematic drawing of the Medicean "*broncone*". Cf. Poliziano, *Stanze*, XV.

49 Luigi Pulci, *Beca di Dicomano*, 1–22, in *Il Poliziano, Il Magnifico, Lirici del Quattrocento*, ed. M. Bontempelli, Florence, 1922, p. 311.

50 Antonio Camelli, *Autoritratto*, 7–11, ibid., p. 316.

51 Bellincioni, *Rime*, CXXVI, pp. 175–6, and CXXXIII, p. 184.

52 See note 4.

53 For Leonardo's anticlerical *facetie*, see R. 1280 and 1284, and Pedretti, II, p. 272. Pedretti (272–5) also transcribes the vulgar *facetie* suppressed by Richter.

54 B.L. 156r (R. 1217).

55 F49v (Pedretti II, p. 243).

56 For Leonardo and the intramission theory, see M. Kemp, "Leonardo and the Visual Pyramid", *Journal of the Warburg and Courtauld Institutes*, XL (1977), pp. 128–49; and J. Ackerman, "Leonardo's Eye", *JWCI*, XII (1978), pp. 108–46.

57 Urb. 13v–14r and Ash. II, 24v.

58 *Proemio al commenti dantesco* in *Scritti critici e teorici*, ed. R. Cardini (Rome, 1974), I, p. 142.

59 Windsor 19045. See M. Kemp, "From Mimesis to Fantasia", *Viator*, VIII (1977), pp. 377ff.

60 Kemp, *Leonardo*, pp. 293–5.

61 A. 55v (Kemp, *Leonardo*, pp. 117–18).

62 M. Kemp, "The Crisis of Received Wisdom in Leonardo's Late Thought", *Leonardo e l'Età della Ragione*, ed. E. Bellone and P. Rossi (Milan, 1981), pp. 33ff., for "veins of water" etc.

63 Aristotle, *Meteorologica*, III, 3.

64 Lorenzo, *Rimi Spirituali*, Capitoli, I, *Opere*, ed. Simioni, II, p. 119.

65 B.L. 156v (R. 1162).

66 *Inferno*, V, 31, and IX, 64–72 (trans. based on Sayers).

67 W. 12665v (R. 608).

68 Boyde, op. cit., p. 215.

69 I 72r–v; see E. H. Gombrich, "The Form of Movement in Water and Air", *Leonardo's Legacy*, ed. C. D. O'Malley (Berkeley and Los Angeles, 1969), p. 178.

70 *Paradiso*, XIV, 103.

71 K. D. Keele, *Leonardo da Vinci's Elements of the Science of Man* (New York and London, 1983), pp. 58ff.

72 Kemp, *Leonardo*, pp. 319–20, for the "scientific" language of the Deluge description.

73 H. 67r. See Gombrich op. cit., p. 199. Gombrich translates the last line as: "but since the universe is finite, the impulse does not extend to the infinite". I take "*finita*" to refer to "*la mente*" rather than "*l'universo*".

74 *Purgatorio*, XXVIII, 88–90 (trans. Sayers).

75 *Paradiso* I, 88–90 (trans. based on Sayers and Reynolds).

76 Windsor 19084r (Kemp, *Leonardo*, p. 342).

77 Windsor 19115r (ibid. p. 343).

6

Mannerist Grottos in Sixteenth-Century Italy

Philippe Morel

Studies from the last few years of the Italian grottos of the sixteenth century have often been as attentive to detail as they have been stimulating and varied. Among the problems these studies have raised, two, which seem closely related, particularly interest me: the representation of *natura naturans* and the relationship of the grotto to the natural sciences.

Detlef Heikamp concluded his last article on the Grotto Grande in the Boboli Gardens in Florence (1583–93) in these terms: "The grotto reflects a pessimistic vision of the destructive forces of nature, but also an intimate connection to nature's secrets, as well as to the laws on which its creations are based. This is the moment when the natural sciences begin a new development."[1] The idea is only sketched. Similarly, in a short but suggestive study, Cristina Acidini introduced certain aspects of the question, without precisely confronting them.[2] I would like, for my part, to delve into problems relating to the generation of stones, to the petrifaction of non-mineral bodies, and to the theme of the Flood or of immersion.

The Revetment of Grottos: The Influence of Antiquity

Far from being, like the walls of a palace or villa, a neutral ground against which a fresco, tapestry, or painting stands out – a ground that demands no particular attention – the wall surface constitutes a fundamental point of departure for the decoration of artificial grottos. It is the product of a specific choice (the mineral substance generally being applied to masonry), it participates decisively in the rustic and naturalistic characterization of the space, and it can partially cover the plastic elements (landscapes, figures, painted and sculpted objects) that are the traditional components of the setting, to the point of being inseparable from them, making itself their body and material.

This basic observation, unfortunately, leads to a group of difficulties that impede analysis. Since the artificial grottos have, for the most part, been destroyed – only a few more or less well-preserved examples survive – we find ourselves essentially forced to rely on written documents, be they brief references or more in-depth descriptions. Such texts, however, are ordinarily voluble and detailed only with regard to painted or sculpted images, automata, or precious and noteworthy materials like coral and mother-of-pearl. When the surface as a whole is at issue, the vocabulary is manifestly imprecise and general.

"On the walls of grottos and caverns," Alberti explains, "the Ancients used to apply a revetment, which they made artificially rough by mixing in small fragments of pumice stone, also called 'froth of travertine,' what Ovid called *vivum pumicem*."[3] Ovid actually described the interiors of two grottos: the sacred grotto of Diana, in Book III of the *Metamorphoses*, is a

> forest lair, the construction of which owed nothing to art: nature, with her genius alone, had given it the illusion of art, for, with living pumice and light tufa, she had drawn the curve of a natural vault.[4]

A similar revetment is found in the grotto where Hercules and Omphale go to repose, in Book II of the *Fasti*: "She entered into a grotto of which the vault had been lined with tufa and with living rock."[5] The appearance and the use of these two grottos give them an ambiguous position between natural chance and human artifice, between a wild place and an inhabited one.

The literature bears witness to a growing taste for rustic grottos in the gardens of imperial Rome. Was pumice (*pumex*) used in artificial grottos? This is what seems to emerge in a passage from Pliny's *Natural History*: "That is what we call the eroded stones, suspended in the edifices known as 'museums' [nymphaea] in order to artificially imitate grottos."[6] In his *De lapidibus*,[7] Theophrastus had earlier insisted on the diversity of pumice stones, and had declared that there existed at least two categories of these: those formed by combustion and those formed from sea foam. The volcanic origin of pumice stone was reaffirmed by Vitruvius, who did not mention the second type, but did remark that Pompeian pumices had an unusual quality that one did not find in other spongy stones.[8]

Some semantic confusion was doubtless inherited from Antiquity. Witness an observation by Agricola, from the middle of the sixteenth century: "Being full of holes, like *spogna*, pumice was called by the same name, as emerges in Vitruvius's text."[9] The term *spogna* (or *spugna*) thus covers rather diverse geological and mineralogical actualities (volcanic or sedimentary rocks, composed respectively of volcanic glass and of calcite). Ovid's *pumex vivus* might not have been volcanic in nature, and ought rather be allied with what Alberti more justly called "froth of travertine" (an extremely vacuolar, sedimentary, calcite-based rock), the travertine of Tivoli being, as Agostino Del Riccio specified, "whitish in color and very spongy in appearance."[10] This confusion had a long life, since we still mention pumice stone among the materials used in ancient nymphaea,[11] when in fact these appear to be deposits or concretions of calcium.[12]

Such a digression on *pumex vivus* is not gratuitous, for this porous, flaky, friable stone is found in various grottos in Latium, at Tivoli, at Bagnaia, at Caprarola, and in Tuscany. At the same time, Ovid's "light tufa" might remind us of *asprone*, the black and spongy tufa that appeared at the entrance of the grotto of the Villa Gaddi, which Annibale Caro described in a 1538 letter.[13] The probable (but partial) similarity of materials results at once from the availability of these substances in the region, and from a will to imitate the Antiquity known from texts and from a few surviving nymphaea.[14] The manner of applying this rock-work could itself also evoke ancient decorations when it was divided by trellises or by rows of shells, or when it was associated with a mosaic depicting various forms (geometric figures, plants, animals, personages, etc.).[15]

In effect, the development of a fashion for grottos, in Rome in the first half of the sixteenth century, picks up on an antiquarian taste that took as its model the nymphaeum, the theme of the source and of its protective divinity. This grotto *à l'antique* would have seemed like an extension of the rustic fountain, where the humanist motif of the sleeping nymph was frequently repeated.[16] The antiquarian characterization of the artificial grotto in Rome in this period – setting for a statue, pastoral evocation, humanist cult of muses – equally affected the type of rock-work that was employed. But the humanist preoccupation soon underwent a change that translated into a concern for novelty and diversity in the choice and composition of materials.

The Staging of the *spugne*

It is at this point that another form of *spugna* arises, one totally distinct from tufa and volcanic pumice: a calcareous concretion with no scaly or friable appearance. In the mid-1520s, Vasari recounts, Giovanni da Udine executed a *fontana selvatica* for the Villa Madama:

> In the hollow of a dale surrounded by woods, he made droplets of water and tiny jets pour from concretions and stalactites, such that the whole seemed truly to be a natural spectacle. In the upper part of these hollows and among these spongy rocks, he placed a lion's head, ringed with maidenhair fern and other grasses, all arranged with great art.[17]

What is, at first glance, only a fountain *à l'antique* in the genre of "natural fonts encountered in the woods" is enriched with *tartari e pietre di colature d'acqua* (stalactites), from which the water flows.[18] A letter by Claudio Tolomei, where the fountains in the garden of Agabito Bellhuomo in Rome are described, puts still more of an accent on the art–nature dialectic, on the ambivalence of these

117

fountains, which, seemingly made "by nature herself, not by chance but with exceptional art," come as close to being artificial nature as they do to being natural artifice:[19]

> The spongy concretions that one finds in Tivoli ornament and embellish [these fountains], for, being formed by water, they return to the service of water as if they were its own creation. With their variety and beauty, they adorn [the water] much better than they did in their place of origin.[20]

No description or evocation of the ancient grotto gives evidence of such a revetment. When Tolomei talks of the "ingenious, recently rediscovered artifice, consisting in the fabrication of fountains," the rediscovery, qualified in a positive way by being antiquarian, concerns the rustic appearance of the fountains more than the materials used in the garden. Consequently, it is less a reference to the past than a real innovation, one that will soon gain the allure of an investigation, with nature as its object. *Spugne*, Agostino Del Riccio wrote toward the end of the century, "are the adornment of fountains, and it is for this reason that we frequently decorate beautiful gardens with *spugne*."[21] As the letter of Tolomei reveals, his reference is to the calcareous concretions otherwise called *tartari* or *congelazioni d'acqua*, which result from the dripping of waters and from the depositing of mineral substances they may contain. It is in Florence and in the surrounding region, but equally at Genoa, that frequent, if not systematic, use of such materials will be made. Del Riccio continues:

> I believe that Grand Dukes Cosimo I and Francesco I de' Medici liked to decorate fountains, as is evident from the very beautiful and famous villa at Pratolino, where one sees numerous *spugne*, mounted together, such that they seem to have been assembled by Mother Nature.[22]

The few grottos and fountains from Pratolino that have come down to us, those that we know through engravings, drawings, or descriptions, and the better-preserved Castello or Boboli grottos confirm Agostino Del Riccio's comments, which find an extension in the grottos that he himself imagined for a royal garden, where *spugne* are omnipresent. Those of the grottos in Rome and in that region essentially originate from Tivoli or from the lake of Piediluco (Piè-di-Lupo), near Terni. The Genoese took their own supplies from the natural caves along the Ligurian coast, particularly from those in the Finalese, and the Florentines had a wealth of options. The calcareous concretions at Castello were taken from a place not far from there, on Mount Morello. The Volterra region offered a different variety of these, near its salt mines, as illustrated by the material covering one of the nymphs personifying the city during a spectacle given at the wedding of Cosimo I:

> She was entirely white, and crowned with branches of weeping willow and other trees, with a coiffure [. . .] adorned with many colors, which, overflowing,

congealed and became fixed to her clothes, where they made one think of white roots.[23]

Spugne are variable in color: "[Those] that one finds in the valley of Marina [. . .] show a grayish color," writes Del Riccio, "but one also encounters other colors, notably bright yellow."[24] They were employed in the first chamber of the grotto by Buontalenti at Boboli:

> *Spugne* from the Radicofani region [. . .] tend towards red, and one sees these [. . .] in the fountains at Pratolino. [. . .] The white *spugne* that form in the underground conduits at Siena are especially beautiful, and they have been used extensively in the Pratolino grottos.[25]

White or grey, yellowish, pinkish or brownish, these *spugne* vary equally in their size, form, and placement. Small or in patches, they partially cover the walls and the pillars, as in the Grotto of Cupid at Pratolino. *Congegniate insieme* ("agglutinated"), they form a small mountain, a *monte di spugne* similar to those that one would see at Pratolino in one of the niches of the Grotto of the Flood or at the center of the red marble basin in the Grotto of the Steam Room.[26] Often, they carpet the back of the niches or hang from the vaults in the form of stalactites – one can, looking at the Grotto Pavese at Genoa (fig. 6.1), get an idea of how the vault of the Grotto of the Flood (the most beautiful of them all, according to Montaigne) would have been.[27] Then there are the stalagmites of slightly more significant dimensions, which, notably, were imported from Corsica, and which constitute the essential ornamentation of some grottos and fountains: in the Grotto of the Spugna at Pratolino, one would see "a very large *spugna* surrounded by small white *spugne*";[28] another, six meters high, was offered by the Luchese to Francesco I de Medici, who had it placed near the Fountain of Jupiter;[29] another, finally, according to Del Riccio the most beautiful of all, with a milky whiteness and a Hungarian provenance, would have been found at the back of the Boboli grotto.[30]

Spugne and Water: The Imitation of *natura naturans*

These *pietre spugnose*, writes Tolomei, "being formed by water, return to the service of water."[31] They are, in effect, constantly associated with water, which washes them, streams along their surface, or falls drop by drop from the stalactites. In the Grotto of the Spugna, according to Sgrilli, "a great quantity of water emerges from every part, and it is a beautiful sight to behold this multitude of water jets falling on the central *spugna*, which is further beautified by the effect of this permanent stream."[32] The first chamber of the Grotto Grande in the Boboli Gardens lacks its water today, but originally multiple jets would have shot from the ground, bathing the walls and their *spugne*, along

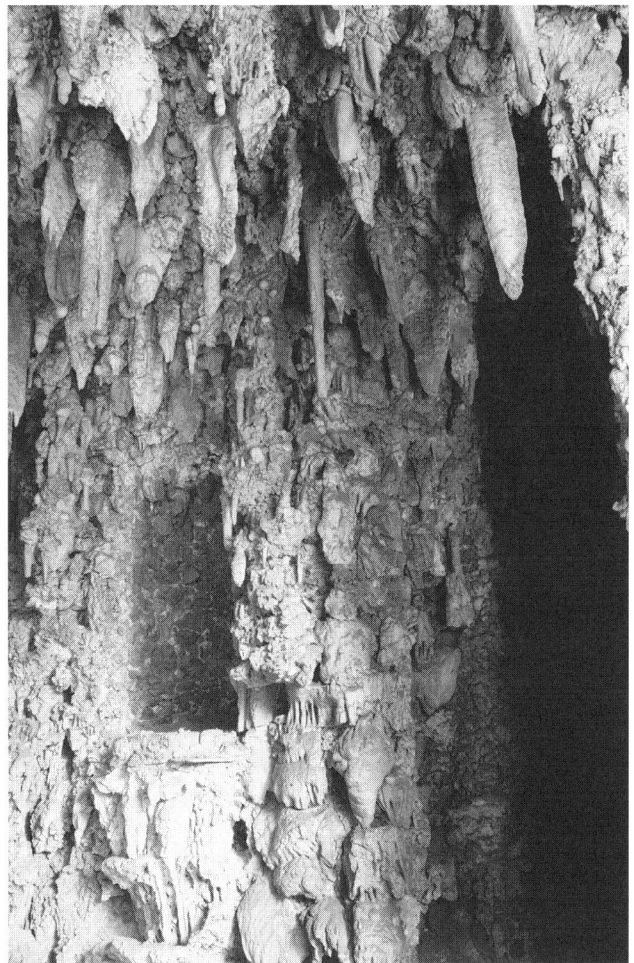

Figure 6.1   Stalactites caught on the vaults of the Grotto Pavese, Genoa, ca. 1594. Photo by Philippe Morel / courtesy Macula, Paris.

which the water passing through the pipes inserted into the mineral vegetation also streamed. All of this water was gathered in the basins that line the walls.[33] This continuous stream would have fostered the lustrous look of the calcareous concretions, which now appear rather faded and desiccated. In the grotto-pergola of the Villa Gaddi in Rome, tiny drops traverse the vaults of two niches before passing through the *tartari bianchi di acqua congelata* ("white stalactites made of congealed water"), which one would have believed to have been formed naturally, by the calcareous deposits of the seeping water.[34]

These *gromme* or *tartari* consist of *colature d'acque petrificate* ("drips of petrified water"), *congelazioni d'acque* which one also encounters in the Apennines, as Vasari tells us in the fifth chapter of his "Introduction to Architecture" in the *Lives*. To the ancients' inventions in the domain of the artificial grotto, he says, the moderns added "compositions of a Tuscan type, decorated with stalactites, resembling large roots, formed over time by the seepage of calcareous waters."[35] Taken from the place where nature had produced them, the stalactites were arranged in the vaults of grottos, sometimes with iron and leather tenons, so that tiny, carefully hidden, perforated lead pipes could allow drops of water, gliding along the *colature di questi tartari* ("drips of these stalactites"), hanging from the vaults, to escape.[36]

In Antiquity, water was part of the grotto setting, which often served as a sacred place, dedicated to the nymphs. Thus we can deduce from several verses of Propertius that the artificial grottos in the gardens of Maecenas were sprinkled by water from the Marcia.[37] In the sixteenth century, however, water intervenes in a different way: it is directly associated with the *spugne*, which were themselves engendered by waters. This return to origins, to the process responsible for the formation of stone, is made explicit by Caro and Vasari. To be sure, we remain here within the framework of the dialectic between natural artifice and artificial nature (between art that imitates nature and nature that imitates art), but there is now a displacement of imitation, an imitation that is transferred from the object back onto its genesis. It is nature in gestation, more than the brute nature beneath the rocky, irregular revetments, that is represented in the generation of the mineral substances that are the *spugne*.

The texts of Caro and Vasari are equally valuable for the terms they use: the *spugne* are variously qualified as *tartari* and as *gromme*. With the *colature d'acque petrificate* and the *congelazioni d'acque*, then, there is a question of encrustation, but also one of petrification and congelation. These pours, these morphologies of precipitation along the trickles, this dripping, suggest at once the physical mechanisms of formation or transformation and the nature of movement.

There seems, then, to be a slippage over the course of the century: from the first grottos, marked by a humanist and antiquarian spirit, we pass on to solutions in which there begins to appear a "naturalist" preoccupation, which subsequently becomes the characteristic and predominant trait of the Florentine grottos of the last third of the century. In the wake of Antiquity, art was able to imitate nature passively, even in its crudest aspect; now it manages to reflect nature in its becoming and to compete with it in its effects. This attitude, typically Mannerist, leads, in the case of the grotto, to a truly analytic approach, an investigation into the internal mechanisms of nature, and an exegesis of its hidden laws. The Mannerist grotto invites us to penetrate *into* nature, with all the mystery and estrangement that that in the Renaissance can imply.

The Formation of Stones: Ancient and Medieval Theories   –

But the problem posed for us by these grottos, where earth and water are staged in an act of union and metamorphosis, must first be formulated in

121

scientific terms. It is, to say the least, symptomatic that the evolution that marks the art of the grotto around the middle of the century is, on the whole, contemporary with the appearance and development of a scientific literature largely dedicated to the origins, qualities, and utilization of stones and metals. Before tackling these writings, and, more particularly, those that deal with the generation of stones, it seems necessary to examine briefly the ancient and medieval texts that gave Renaissance writers inspiration – if sometimes only for criticism, guided by a knowledge based more on observation and experimentation than on Aristotelian or alchemical axioms. Four natural philosophers ought to occupy our attention: Aristotle, Theophrastus, Avicenna, and Albertus Magnus.

The rather brief passage in the *Meteorologica* where Aristotle considers the problem of the formation of stones and metals enjoyed a certain fortune on account of the theory of exhalations formulated there, a theory that would still be topical at the beginning of the seventeenth century, in the writings of Ferrante Imperato.[38] Enclosed in the ground, where they are compressed by dryness, exhalations (which have the heat of the sun as their efficient cause) underwent a process of congelation. Dry and smoky, they produced "fossils" – that is to say stones, to follow the meaning that the Renaissance gave this word. Wet and vaporous, they were the material cause of metals, which were fusible or ductile.

Written around 315 BCE, Theophrastus's treatise on stones offered a more thorough account of the question and moved away a bit from the Aristotelian point of view. The material causes of stones and metals were, respectively, earth and water. In the case of metals, Theophrastus simplified things: Aristotle talked of wet exhalations, and Plato of "fusible varieties of water."[39] With regard to earth, from which stones were born, this, mixed with water, became a pure, uniform substance, the product of a filtering (*percolatio*) or of a deposit-forming discharge (*confluxus*): a filtering in the subterranean "veins" or a deposit at the base of rock cavities. This pure and uniform material hardened or solidified under the action of heat or cold, which produced "fossils."[40]

At the beginning of the eleventh century, Avicenna somewhat revitalized these theoretical premises in a small treatise, *De congelatione et conglutinatione lapidum*, the first chapter of which was dedicated to the origin of stones. These were made of water and earth, either through the solidification of an essentially liquid substance (*congelatio*) or through the piling up and agglutination of solid particles (the liquid substance furnishing the mineral cement that assured those particles' cohesion), all of this being produced under the influence of a special *vis mineralis*, present in the places where stones form.[41]

Avicenna's ideas received a lengthy commentary from Albertus Magnus in the *De mineralibus* (ca. 1250–1260). From the Arab philosopher Albertus borrowed the alchemical hypothesis that metals were a mixture of sulfur and quicksilver, while turning back to the Aristotelian theory of exhalations (the efficient causes of minerals, dry exhalations corresponding to sulfur and wet exhalations to quicksilver). Stones originate either from a *conglutinatio* of dry particles, or from a *congelatio* of liquid substances: *conglutinatio* is accomplished by means of humidity, with a viscous and unctuous humor that induces the adhesion and the mixture of sand grains, powders, or small pebbles; *congelatio* takes place through the action of a hot or cold dryness on the liquid substance, which falls drop by drop or drains in some other way.[42]

Having reviewed and refuted the theses of Empedocles (all stones are produced by a boiling heat) and Democritus (stones have a vegetative soul, which is the principle of their formation), Albertus vehemently critiques the opinion of certain alchemists who deny the existence of a mineral power in the earth, and who affirm that there is no particular principle behind stones' origins. According to him, the *virtus lapidum generativa* intervenes in two ways, using two instruments – heat and cold – which, by making the adhesive humor evaporate, effects the consolidation of the stones born from *conglutinatio* and which, compacting the liquid substance, brings the process of solidification through *congelatio* to its conclusion. This power, which determines and regulates the formation of minerals, is only present in certain places, where it has been infused by adequate astral influences. These influences constitute the formal cause on which the magnetic and chemical characteristics of stones, and thus their curative and magical power, depend.[43]

After Albertus Magnus, speculation on the origin of stones seems no longer to have occupied thinkers, as there predominated on the one hand an alchemical reflection interested only in metals and their transmutation, and on the other, a purely encyclopedic propensity for lists of stones, often precious or engraved, from which one could study medicinal virtues and magical powers.[44] We must wait for the sixteenth century and the new popularity of agriculture and mining for the revival of such a problematic. Indeed, it is within the framework of writings on agriculture or on the extraction and working of minerals that we find accounts of the formation of mineral substances, as can be seen in Georgius Agricola, Bernard Palissy, and Giovanni Vittore Soderini. Agricola's treatises, to a certain extent, herald the encyclopedias of minerals elaborated by Aldrovandi, Cesalpino, and Mercati at the end of the sixteenth century, encyclopedias in which the problem of the origin and the formation of stones is no longer central, and no longer provides room for really new interpretations. The texts of Soderini and Palissy, for their part, merit our attention for their close connection to the art of gardens and artificial grottos.

The Formation of Stones: Sixteenth-Century Theories

Agricola's best-known book is the *De re metallica* (1556), a richly illustrated work on mining and on the processing of materials. But it is his compendium of treatises, beginning with the *De ortu et causis subterraneorum*, that ought to hold our attention here.[45] The Latin edition appeared in Basel in 1546, and the

Italian translation was published in Venice in 1550. Here, the opinions of Aristotle, Theophrastus, Avicenna, and Albertus Magnus are repeatedly adduced and compared. Agricola pursues the biological analogy, alchemical in origin, introduced by Albertus, who compared the mineralizing power with animalian sperm. Thus, the canals of the earth "conceive the substance of fossil things, just as the female womb produces the egg of generation."[46] It is the "veins," "fibers," or "commissures" of rocks that are the vases and receptacles for the matter out of which mineral substances are made. Even when every animistic reference is excluded, the earth in gestation is presented as a sort of organism, endowed with the internal circulation and cavity-receptacles that are the physical conditions (allowing space and movement) of the generative process.

After demonstrating the impossibility of the Aristotelian theses concerning the formation of stones through dry exhalations, Agricola, seeing in pure and uniform matter the results of a *percolatio* or *confluxus*, backs Theophrastus.[47] He thus takes over the idea of Avicenna and Albertus, that stones are generated from a mixture of earth and water. To each of the two processes described by the medieval philosophers, the *conglutinatio* and the *congelatio*, he assigns a corresponding transitional material state of that mixture: the *luto* or *fango* for earth bathed in water, and the *sugo* for water enriched with earth. Heat and cold are the actual efficient causes:

> Stones that water can dissolve show us that heat has conglutinated and fabricated them by drying them out: those which, inversely, are liquefied in the heat of fire, as is the case with silica, show themselves to have been united and generated by the action of coldness. For union and conglutination, along with their contrary qualities, liquefaction and dissolution, derive and are born from contrary causes. Heat hardens material by extracting its wetness, while coldness, by driving out most of its air, forcefully unites and compresses this same humor.[48]

Where Agricola disagrees with Albertus Magnus and Avicenna, then, is that the latter see in heat and cold only the instruments of the *vis mineralis* infused in the material by celestial influences, a theory that Agricola refutes, just as he refutes everything that touches closely or distantly on astrology and alchemy:[49] "The virtue that gives stones their form does not reside in their matter [. . .], and there are no other virtues in the place where stones form than those inherent in its qualities."[50] In doing this, Agricola equally dismisses the thesis of Democritus – which would be revived by Girolamo Cardano in his *De subtilitate* – according to which stones could be born and could grow thanks to the virtue of a vegetative soul.[51] The German naturalist withdraws, in this way, to an orthodox Aristotelian position, recognizing heat and coldness as the only active causes, variations of which depend on the force of solar rays and on the heat present in the subsoil.

A third efficient cause consists in the *sugo congelato* which, being a simple material cause, can serve in the formation of stalactites and stalagmites. The *sughi*, Agricola explains, "differ from waters in their density."[52] They are the product of a mixture of "something dry with something wet," or of the erosion worked by waters on earth or metals. The *sughi congelati* are of various types: they can contain salt or niter, aluminum or *atramento sutorio*, sulfur or bitumen, verdigris or rust,[53] substances that were, for the most part, qualified as "intermediate" (between stones and metals) by Albertus Magnus. They could equally involve a *sugo atto a diventare pietra* – the only one that directly interests us for grottos – a "substance apt to become stone," which

> drips from commissures, fibers or veins in the caverns' womb; it hardens and becomes stone before falling to the ground; it is thus that drops remain suspended; [. . .] it also happens that the drops become stone after having been distilled and having fallen to the floor [. . .]; the two processes can happen simultaneously [. . .] and can form white or variegated columns, as Pliny the Elder writes [. . .].[54]

On the basis of a certain experience (one manifest in the *De re metallica*) and from a detailed consideration of the ancient and medieval theories, Agricola proposes a morphogenesis of stalactites and stalagmites, linking this to a "congelative humor," a *sugo atto a diventare pietra* about which we will have to speak again, once we turn to the question of the petrifaction of non-mineral bodies.

In one passage from his treatise on agriculture, composed in the 1570s or 1580s but published only in 1811, the Florentine Giovanni Vittore Soderini presents a peculiar juxtaposition and a curious blend of the diverse opinions formulated previously.[55] His text is interesting in many respects: it is contemporary with the grottos that we are studying and it originates from an author who was directly concerned with the art of gardens. His approach to the problem, more accumulative, confused and second-hand than truly erudite and critical, shows that all of the hypotheses, ancient, medieval or modern, could still, at the end of the century, be adopted – at the price, doubtless, of some amalgamation and theoretical adjustment.

Soderini begins with Aristotle: hot and dry exhalations, smoky and earthy, are the origin of stones, and it is necessary to distinguish fossils from metals (the latter being fusible and ductile). Trapped in the ground, the exhalations congeal and are converted into mud (from Aristotle, we pass now to Theophrastus, by way of Agricola) which, cooked by heat, will become stone. The author slips an allusion to the efficient virtue of celestial bodies (Avicenna and Albertus) into the passage, and he continues by paraphrasing Agricola on the generation of subterranean things. Declaring that matter can be united and collected *per un concorso di molti parti insieme e per via di lambiccamento* ("through the coming together of many parts and through distillation"), he refers to the *confluxus* and *percolatio* about which Theophrastus speaks. He again takes up Agricola, evoking the *sugo atto a farsi pietra* (the "liquid apt to become stone") that is the origin of the petrification of wood and of bones, and the origin of the generation of stalactites and calcareous formations: "[. . .] dripping within the caverns and along the crevices, fibers and veins of the earth, it falls, hardens, and becomes stone, unless the drops remain suspended."

Soderini then names several places where one encounters masses of such calcareous formations (notably the grottos of Finalese, which provide the material for the artificial grottos of Genoa): "concretions engendered in this manner, which serve as fountain decorations in gardens and in villa courtyards." From scientific discourse he thus moves on naturally to the decoration of fountains and grottos, before making a wholly rhetorical concession to the Counter-Reformation: all of this seems terribly contradictory and uncertain, and therefore the clearest and firmest opinion is that which Genesis teaches us – all the stones appeared at the moment of Creation.

Though they probably exercised no direct influence on the Italian grottos of the sixteenth century, the writings of Bernard Palissy, which are bound up with a creative reflection concerning the grotto and which are extremely rich in information, ought to be taken into consideration. Let us recall briefly that the "inventor of the King's rustic little figures" conceived several grottos: some of these were executed, like the one at the château of Écouen, for Anne de Montmorency, and the one at the Tuileries, for Catherine de Médicis; others remained on paper, like the one for the great *écuyer* Claude Gouffier, and, above all, like the ideal garden grottos described at length in the *Recette véritable*.[56]

Published in 1563, this first work is dedicated primarily to agricultural problems: manure, vegetables, and the nature of stones. Here Palissy formulated his basic theory in natural scientific matters: that there is salt in all things, animals, trees, stones, and metals. Under this generic term are united gem salt, vitriol, ammoniac, tartar, niter, alum, saltpeter, and "salicor" – salts that belong to "intermediate bodies" and to *sughi congelati*. It is salt that originates the congelation of stones and the petrifaction of bones and shells.

This point of view is only really developed in the *Discours admirable*,[57] where Palissy returns to the material of lectures he had given in 1575 and 1576. Here he claims to have searched through the entrails of the earth and to have "dissected" its womb over the course of forty years. The author also formed a cabinet, "in which," he says, "I placed several wonderful and monstrous things that I took from the womb of the earth."[58] Returning to the problem of the generation of stones, he explains that this begins with a salt dissolved in water: qualified as "essencive," "congelative," and "germinative," this water is distinct from common water, which is "exhalative," though in this one nevertheless finds the former water mixed.[59] Salt serves for cohesion and generation: without it, everything – human bodies and plants, like stones and metals – would fall into powder.[60] It is "the adhesive and the generative and conservative mastic of all things," a congelative material without which nothing would be – what Palissy calls the "fifth element."[61] The author would also write: "the beginning and origin of all natural things is water."[62] Or again: "Like all species of plants, all animated things are in their first essence made of liquid materials; similarly, all types of stones, metals and minerals are formed of liquid materials."[63] Lapidary materials "are, in their first essence, liquid, fluid and aqueous."[64]

In the case of the formation of stones, the salt is picked up by streaming waters, the rain running across ground where it is found in abundance. At this point distillation intervenes, before the decoction and the congelation of the "salsitive" water.[65] It is thus that stones grow, not by vegetative action (an allusion to the theory of the *vis mineralis*) but by congelative addition.[66] The rocks are

> augmented by some fall of rain that carried with it a stony [i.e. saline] material. But the true and most certain building up of stones is that which happens in the stones that are still in the stomach of the earth. For just as I said of metals, [. . .] that it was necessary for them to be enclosed in humid and aqueous places, as the forma- tion of human nature happens, so, similarly, the quarry stones cannot be generated except in hollow places, hidden in the womb of the earth.[67]

These are gestation processes that Palissy could himself have observed with the "mesches pendants" (stalactites) under the earth. Already in the *Recette véritable*, he speaks of caves found on the banks of the Loire, where "there was a rock from which water fell very slowly in little drops: and in distilling, it congealed and was reduced to a mass of white stone."[68] This distillation is even more visible in the stalactites he could have examined and later collected:

> having looked closely at their natures, I recognized, in the forms of several stones made like the icicles that hang from the gutters of houses when it freezes, that the stones had been made and generated of liquid materials and distilled like water.[69]

Thus, "when we were in the quarries of Paris [Faubourg Saint-Marcel], we saw the distilling of water, which froze in our presence." And, he adds, it is these same stalactites that Catherine de Médicis had brought from the Marseilles region for her grotto at the Tuileries, stalactites that one saw in equal quantity in the very famous grotto at Meudon, executed by Primaticcio for the Cardinal of Lorraine.[70]

The Theatricalization of Nature's Alchemy

The borrowing on nature, then, is manifestly of two orders: a reutilization of stalactites and stalagmites, and an imitation of their process of formation. The theory of congelative salt is more impressionistic and imprecise, but no less pertinent as far as observation goes than the theory of the *sugo congelato atto a diventare pietra*. The symbiosis of earth and water, solidified mud, "congelations" of petrified water that partially cover the oozing walls of grottos, the water that drips from stalactites at the artist's will: all of this functions as a veritable staging

127

of mineral nature's generation. In this "womb of the earth" that the grotto represents, *natura naturans* exhibits itself in a full state of gestation.

The vocabulary used to describe the natural fabrication of stones ("congelation," "distillation," "filtering," "evaporation," "cooking," "concoction") is close to alchemical knowledge or derives from it. Such is the case with the concept of congelation, which had already appeared in Aristotle, but which was taken over by Avicenna in an argument clearly inspired by alchemical topics (Avicenna himself was considered to be an authority in this area, and his *De congelatione* was published in the fourth volume of the *Theatrum chimicum*). It is true that Palissy, like Agricola, is openly hostile to alchemy, which tries, according to him, to construct by means of a destroyer – fire – when all is actually born from liquid materials.[71] To the alchemists' credit, though, he retains the importance that they attribute to salts: "salt makes some marvelous congelations. The alchemists perceived something of this, for they worried terribly over these prepared salts."[72] But their ambition is totally out of proportion, since they "want to undertake a work [the generation of metals through transformation and augmentation] that is done occultly in the earth."[73] True alchemists, in fact – those who truly succeed in their creation – are nothing other than the artist-authors of these marvelous grottos, in which they know how to reconstitute the womb of the earth and to imitate its generative process, thus realizing a veritable theatricalization of nature's alchemy.

My intention, I think it worth emphasizing, is not to suggest that the scientific writings known in the sixteenth century, treating the origin and the formation of stones, could somehow have directly influenced the working out of such and such a grotto, constituting the material for its "program," as we think, in the case of painting, of a mythological, historical, or literary source. I do not mean to offer a parascientific iconography of grottos. My intention has to do rather with seeing within what cultural patrimony and within what epistemic conditions of appearance the Mannerist grotto spread and evolved, developing that characteristic trait that we, as a shorthand, qualify as "naturalist" (a term that one must of course immediately reconnect with the current natural philosophies, notably alchemy). It would be vain to imagine that some opinion or some thesis would have seen itself translated precisely and rigorously into the grotto's constituent decorative material. These debates over ideas, though – that which returns for a less specialized audience, the dross from the most detailed scientific speculations and observation and, in a much more general fashion, that vast rebirth of knowledge about nature – cannot be foreign to the evolution that grottos underwent in the course of the sixteenth century. These ideas constitute their epistemological compost, and the grottos, inversely – like *naturalia* and *mirabilia* collections – are the place for experimentation with and projection of these scientific preoccupations, the place where their mythic counterpart and their fantasmatic reverse simultaneously surface.

Coral, Mother-of-pearl, Shells

To conclude, I will examine the case of three other frequently used materials: coral, shells, and mother-of-pearl. All three seem to have a synthetic function, and to occupy a nodal position: they are associated with revetment made from calcareous concretions; they manifest a double character of preciousness and *meraviglia*; and they pertain to questions concerning the petrifaction, fossilization, and transmutation of elements.

Where and how did coral and mother-of-pearl appear in artificial grottos? Let us take, as an example, the grottos of the Villa Medici at Pratolino. The Grotto of Galatea, above all, is "entirely of mother-of-pearl, with a great basin of water ornamented with rocks, corals and shells," and two nymphs "hold branches of coral from which water springs" (De' Vieri[74]). This association is found again in the grotto nearby, called the Grotto of the Stufa, the center of which was occupied by a *monte di spugne* "decorated with mother-of-pearl, shells and coral" (Sgrilli[75]). The proximity to the calcareous concretions is yet more appreciable in the Grotto of the Spugna, in which the great stalagmite is "surrounded by small white *spugne*, coral branches and shells" (Sgrilli[76]), as it appears in a drawing by Giovanni Guerra. In the figure of the giant Appenine, sculpted by Giambologna, are arranged some chambers: that of Thetis is "full of corals and other very noble stones" (Codex Barberini[77]); the statue of the nymph herself is entirely covered in shells, and the great octagonal basin on which she stands is ornamented with mother-of-pearl bats and snails. On the upper level, disposed within the body of the giant, could be seen a "jasper vase [. . .] with a coral flower brought from the Red Sea at its center, from which the water flows" (De' Vieri[78]). We might add that, in what was to have been the *stanza segreta del Narcisso* (the "secret room of Narcissus") on the east side of the villa, there could be found a small fountain "the material of which could not have been more precious, being formed of mother-of-pearl and of small, very noble stones."[79]

The relation of *convenientia* between these elements and the *spugne* clearly indicates a family tie. Of the great stalagmite, brought from Corsica and installed in 1584 at the center of the labyrinth in Pratolino's Parco Vecchio, a chronicler from the period writes: "it is entirely polished with water, such that it seems to be made of marble, and, in other spots, of salt, or mother-of-pearl. Time and water have rendered it with such beauty that it is a marvel."[80] As Cristina Acidini observes,[81] Aldrovandi thought that shells had the nature of stones. Yet as curious as that seems, it is coral that is most closely associated with *spugne*, and this on account of the means of its formation. Writing of the *sugo atto a diventare pietra*, which is the material cause of calcareous formations, Agricola declares that coral "is produced by the congelation of this substance."[82] In a passage from his treatise *De la natura delle cose fossili*, he continues:

Yellow amber is generated from a thick substance found in the sea; dead man's fingers is born from a saline substance, proper to the sea; similarly, coral is the product of such a substance converted into stone. [. . .] Following the example of other stones that come from the subterranean congelation of this type of substance, coral displays several colors.[83]

The relation *spugna*–coral, then, is interdependent with the theme of *natura naturans*, and it contributes to making the grotto into a staging of nature surprised in full gestation. Playing out here as well is a *transfusio elementorum* between earth and water. For Riccio, the coral branch is a "tiny soft green tree that is born at the bottom of the sea" and transformed into stone once it comes out of the water. At Pratolino, its aquatic origin is recalled by the water that springs from the branches held by the nymphs in the Grotto of Galatea.

There are other traits common to *spugne*, coral and mother-of-pearl: all three are precious and all three, falling within the category of marvelous, call up mythic interpretations. Thus, coral originates from the petrifying power of the Gorgon vanquished by Perseus. The multiple magical and apotropaic virtues it was recognized to hold made it a prized amulet, which one would fix to the neck or wrist of children,[84] and beautiful branches of coral (preferably black or white) were an obligatory component of wonder cabinets. Stalactites, too, were submitted to such a mythification – their scenographic qualities were extensively exploited in some artificial grottos, like the Grotto Pavese in Genoa (fig. 6.1) – but it is more difficult to recognize that they could be classified among prodigies, as Agricola points out in an ironic manner, apropos of the colors of the *sugo atto a diventare pietra*:

> Not knowing the causes and the natures of things, one takes them for prodigies, and the authors of works on the latter have spoken in these terms: if the substance that comes out is white, they associate it with streams of milk; if it is red they are rivers of blood; if it is green, turning more fair, it originates from rivers of oil.[85]

Notes

1   D. Heikamp, "La Grotta Grande del giardino di Boboli," *FMR*, 1985, 35, p. 105.

2   See C. Acidini Luchinat, "Rappresentazione della natura e indagine scientifica nelle grotte cinquecentesche," in M. Fagiolo (ed.), *Natura e artificio*, Rome, 1979, pp. 144–153. See also L. Magnani, *Tra magia, scienza e "meraviglia": Le Grotte artificiali dei giardini genovesi nei secoli XVI e XVII* (exh. cat.), Genoa, 1984, pp. 39–44.

3   *Antris et criptis assuevere crustam veteres adigere asperam ex industria adpactis minutis glebis ex pumice aut spuma lapidis Tiburtini, quam Ovidius vivum appellat pumicem* (L. B. Alberti, *De re aedificatoria*, Florence, 1984, IX, IV, Italian trans. *L'Architettura*, Milan, 1966, vol. II, p. 804).

4   Ovid, *Les Métamorphoses*, III, 157–160 (trans. J. Chamonard, Paris, Garnier-Flammarion, 1966, p. 93).

5   Idem, *Les Fastes*, II, 315 (trans. H. Le Bonniec, Paris, Les Belles Lettres, 1990, p. 52).

6   Pliny, *Histoire naturelle*, XXXVI, 154–155 (trans. R. Bloch, Paris, Les Belles Lettres, 1981).

7   See Theophrastus, *De lapidibus*, III, 19 (Latin trans. F. Wimmer, Paris, 1856; Eng. trans. D. E. Eichholz, Oxford, 1965).

8   See Vitruvius, *De architectura*, II, 6 (trans. C. Perrault, Paris, 1673).

9   G. Agricola, *De natura fossilium*, in *De ortu et causis subterraneorum, De natura eorum quae effluent ex terra, De natura fossilium, De veteribus et novis metallis, Bermannus, sive de re metallica dialogus*, Basel, 1546 (Italian trans. Venice, 1550, pp. 272–273). On the *pumex* in the treatises of the 16th century, see C. Gessner, *De rerum fossilium, lapidum et gemmarum [. . .]*, Tiguri, 1565, p. 31ff.; A. Cesalpino, *De metallicis libri tres*, Rome, 1596; F. Imperato, *Dell'historia naturale [. . .]*, Naples, 1599, XXII, 1–2, pp. 584–589; U. Aldrovandi, *Musaeum metallicum*, Bologna, 1648, pp. 696ff.; M. Mercati, *Metallotheca Vaticana*, Rome, 1719, pp. 150–152 (for the *pumex spumosus*, of marine origin, see pp. 140–141). The treatises of Aldrovandi and Mercati were elaborated at the end of the 16th century.

10   A. Del Riccio, *Istoria delle pietre*, 1597, chap. XLVIII (ed. P. Barocchi, Florence, 1979).

11   See F. Sear, "Roman Wall and Vault Mosaics," *Mitteilungen des Deutschen Archaelogischen Instituts, Romische Abteilung*, suppl. 23, Heidelberg, 1977, pp. 37ff., and F. Rakab, "Ein Grottentriklinium in Pompeji," ibid., LXXI, 1964, p. 189.

12   As Mariette De Vos thinks, on the basis of examples preserved in Rome, notably on the Palatine. See above all the corrective remarks in H. Lavagne, *"Operosa antra." Recherches sur la grotte à Rome de Sylla à Hadrien*, École française de Rome, 1988, pp. 411–418.

13   Letter of July 13, 1538, addressed to monsignore Guidiccione (A. Caro, *Lettere familiari*, Florence, 1957, no. 61; reprinted in E. MacDougall (ed.), *Fons Sapientiae. Renaissance Garden Fountains*, Washington, 1978, p. 109): *un muro rozzo di certa pietra che a Roma si dice asprone, specie di tufo nero e spugnoso*.

14   For the written documentation, see, as well as the texts already cited, the passages mentioned in P. Grimal, *Les Jardins romains* (1944), Paris, Librairie Arthème Fayard, 1984.

15   See F. Sear, "Roman Wall and Vault Mosaics," p. 37, and, above all, H. Lavagne, *"Operosa antra,"* passim.

16   See E. MacDougall, "The Sleeping Nymph: Origins of a Humanist Fountain Type," *Art Bulletin*, LVII, 1975, pp. 357–365.

17   G. Vasari, *Le Vite de' più eccellenti pittori, scultori ed architetti [. . .]*, Florence, 1568 (reedited in G. Vasari, *Le Opere*, ed. G. Milanesi, 2nd ed., Florence, 1906, vol. VI, p. 556).

18   See idem, *Le Opere*, vol. I, p. 140.

19   Letter of July 26, 1543, to G. B. Grimaldi (C. Tolomei, *Lettere*, Venice, 1550, I, pp. 41–43; cited in E. MacDougall (ed.), *Fons Sapientiae*, pp. 12–14).

20   Idem, ibid. (E. MacDougall (ed.), *Fons Sapientiae*, p. 13).

21   A. Del Riccio, *Istoria delle pietre*, chap. CII. The author makes such an observation only for the *spugne*, and not for the *pomice* (see fol. 110r–v).

22   Idem, ibid., fol. 40r–v.

23 P. F. Giambullari, *Apparato e feste nelle nozze dello illustrissimo Signor Duca di Firenze [. . .]*, Florence, 1539, pp. 52–53.

24 A. Del Riccio, *Istoria delle pietre*, fol. 40v.

25 Idem, ibid.

26 See P. F. Giambullari, *Apparato e feste [. . .]*, and L. Zangheri, *Pratolino. Il Giardino delle meraviglie*, Florence, 1979, vol. I, pp. 118–119.

27 See L. Zangheri, *Pratolino*, vol. I, pp. 114–115, and L. Magnani, *Tra magia, scienza e "meraviglia."*

28 B. S. Sgrilli (1742), cited in L. Zangheri, *Pratolino*, vol. I, p. 119.

29 See L. Zangheri, *Pratolino*, vol. I, pp. 143–144.

30 See A. Del Riccio, *Istoria delle pietre*, fols. 40v–41r. On stalagmites, see also C. Gessner, *De rerum fossilium [. . .]*, pp. 73ff.

31 C. Tolomei, *Lettere*, p. 13.

32 B. S. Sgrilli, cited in L. Zangheri, *Pratolino*, vol. I, p. 119.

33 See D. Heikamp, "La Grotta Grande [. . .]," p. 104.

34 *Par che l'acqua gemendo vi sia naturalmente ingrommata* (A. Caro, *Lettere familiari*, p. 110; ed. M. Menghini, Florence, 1968, p. 114).

35 G. Vasari, *Le Opere*, vol. I, p. 141 (ed. A. Chastel, *Les Vies des meilleurs peintres, sculpteurs et architectes*, Paris, Berger-Levrault, 1981, vol. I, p. 104).

36 See idem, ibid., vol. I, pp. 140–143.

37 See P. Grimal, *Les Jardins romains*, p. 401, and M. De Vos, "Nerone, Seneca, Fabullo e la Domus Transitoria al Palatino," in *Gli Orti farnesiani sul Palatino* (colloquium proceedings, Rome, 1985), Rome, 1990, pp. 167–186.

38 See Aristotle, *Météorologiques*, III, 6 (378 a–b), Paris, Les Belles Lettres, 1982, and F. Imperato, *Dell'historia naturale [. . .]*, XIII, 1, pp. 372–373, in addition to the same author's *De fossilibus opusculum*, Naples, 1610, pp. 10–11.

39 Plato, *Timaeus*, 59a–b.

40 See Theophrastus, *De lapidibus*, trans. F. Wimmer, pp. 340–341. See also the introduction by D. Eichholz to his English translation.

41 See Avicenna, *De congelatione et conglutinatione lapidum*, in *Theatrum chimicum*, IV, Argentorati, 1659, pp. 883–887 (there exists a more recent Latin edition, by Holmyard and Mandeville: Paris, 1927). This treatise was translated from Arabic into Latin around 1200.

42 See Albertus Magnus, *De mineralibus*, trans. D. Wyckoff, Oxford, 1967, I, I, 203. This work had at least six Latin editions between 1476 and 1569.

43 See idem, ibid., I, I, 5–8.

44 On the ancient and medieval texts treating precious stones and their medical or magical powers, see idem, ibid., trans. D. Wyckoff, appendix B, pp. 264–271.

45 G. Agricola, *De ortu et causis subterraneorum, De natura erorum quae effluent ex terra, De natura fossilium, De veteribus et novis metallis, Bermannus sive de re metallica dialogus*, Basel, 1546 (Italian trans. Venice, 1550). This collection having primarily been known, in the 16th century, in its Italian version, it's this that I quote (as already above, p. 114).

46 Idem, ibid., fols. 38r and 40r–v.

47 See idem, ibid., fols. 49r–50v.

48 *Quelle pietre, che l'acqua con humettarle, le dissolve, ci mostrano, che il calore deseccandole le habbia conglutinate e fatte: quelle altre poi al contrario, che co'l calore del fuoco si liquefanno, come sono le selici; ci accennano essersi per mezzo del freddo*

unite et generate per che il conglutinarsi et unirsi insieme; e le sue contrarie qualità, che sono il risolversi, et il liquefarsi, da cause tra se contrarie derivano e nascono. Il calore con cavare l'humore da la materia, le viene à fare dura: il freddo à l'incontro con escluderne per la maggior parte l'aere unisce e stringe fortissimemente questo humore istesso (idem, ibid., fol. 58r).

49 See L. Thorndike, *History of Magic and Experimental Science*, New York, 1923–1958, vol. 6, ch. XXXVIII, p. 291.

50 *Non è ne la materia de le pietre la virtù, che le da la forma, come è nel seme ne ancho è nel luogo altra virtù, che quella de le qualità* (G. Agricola, *De ortu [. . .]*, fols. 55v–57v).

51 On Cardanus's and others' points of view, see G. Fallopio, *De medicatis aquis, atque de fossilibus tractatus*, Venice, 1564, chap. VIII, pp. 102–110. See also U. Aldrovandi, *Musaeum metallicum*, pp. 437–440.

52 G. Agricola, *De ortu [. . .]*, fols. 10r and 58r, and *De natura eorum [. . .]*, ibid., fol. 109vff.

53 See idem, *De natura eorum [. . .]*, ibid., fol. 98r–v, and *De natura fossilium*, ibid., fol. 204r.

54 *Il sugo atto à diventare pietra, ò gocciando ne le spelonche da le sue commissure, e fibre, e vene; prima che cada giu, s'indura e fa pietra; e restano su attaccate le sue goccie e appese; [. . .] ò s'impetrano le sue goccie, stillate e cadute che sono giu à terra come ne le grotte Coricie si vede: ò pure nel'un modo e nel'altro aviene; come in quella famosa speloncha si vede, che è presso Amberga; dove per questa via si generano candide colonne: ò pure di diverse colore, come scrive Plinio vedersi in una gran grotta in Phausia Chersonese di Rodi: si veggono ancho colonne per questa via nate in Demoneso isola di Cartaginesi: in una certa spelonca, che la chiamano Polita* (idem, *De natura eorum [. . .]*, ibid., fols. 109v–110r). See also U. Aldrovandi, *Musaeum metallicum*, p. 630.

55 See G. V. Soderini, *Trattato di agricoltura*, Florence, 1811. Soderini (1526–1596) is also the author of treatises on viticulture (Florence, 1600), on gardens and vegetables (Florence, 1814), as well as on trees and domestic animals. The ensemble was published or republished by A. Bacchi Della Lega (Bologna, 1902–1903). For the original passage, see G. V. Soderini, *I due trattati dell'agricoltura e della coltivazione delle viti*, Bologna, 1902, pp. 192–193 (also cited in M. Fagiolo (ed.), *Natura e artificio*, pp. 234–235). We should note that Soderini also edited a *Breve descrizione della pompa funerale fatta nelle essequie del ser.mo D. Francesco Medici [. . .]* (Florence, 1587).

56 B. Palissy, *Recette véritable*, Paris, Macula, 1996. For the grottos of Écouen (finished around 1563) and of the Tuileries (around 1565), see idem, *Architecture et Ordonnance de la grotte rustique de Monseigneur le Duc de Montmorancy [. . .]*, La Rochelle, 1563 (reissued Paris, 1919, and as an appendix to the *Recette véritable*, pp. 243–272). See also *Revue de l'art*, 1987, 78 (issue dedicated in part to Bernard Palissy), pp. 84–85, where it is demonstrated that the *Devis d'une grotte pour la royne mère du roy* (see *Les Oeuvres de Bernard Palissy*, ed. A. France, Paris, 1880, pp. 465–471) is a forgery made around 1860. See also L. N. Amico, *Bernard Palissy et ses continuateurs*, Paris, Flammarion, 1996, ch. II.

57 B. Palissy, *Discours admirable de la nature des eaux et fontaines tant naturelles qu'artificielles, des métaux, des sels et salines, des pierres, des terres, du feu et des émaux*, Paris, 1580 (reprinted in *Les Oeuvres de Bernard Palissy*, pp. 161–461).

58 Idem, ibid., in *Les Oeuvres [. . .]*, p. 164.

59 See idem, ibid., pp. 240–255 and 266.

60 See idem, ibid., p. 295.

61 See idem, ibid., pp. 338 and 446.

62 Idem, ibid., p. 267.

63 Idem, ibid., p. 446.

64 Idem, ibid., p. 435.

65 See idem, ibid., pp. 350 and 358.

66 See idem, ibid., p. 319.

67 Idem, ibid., p. 320.

68 Idem, *Recette* véritable, p. 111.

69 Idem, *Discours admirable [. . .]*, in *Les Oeuvres [. . .]*, p. 321.

70 See idem, ibid., p. 324. On the grotto of Meudon and on grottos in France in the 16th century, see N. Miller, *French Renaissance Fountains*, New York University, Ph.D. dissertation, 1966, Ann Arbor, 1968, ch. VII. See also, by the same author, "Domain of Illusion: the Grotto in France," in E. MacDougall (ed.), *Fons Sapientiae*, pp. 175–205, and *Heavenly Caves: Reflections on the Garden Grotto*, London, 1982, pp. 51f. On the only grotto on the Meudon, see P. de Ronsard, *Chant pastoral sur les nopces de Monseigneur Charles Duc de Lorraine, et Madame Claude Fille II du Roy*, Paris, 1559 (reprinted in *Oeuvres complètes*, ed. P. Laumonier, I. Silver, and R. Lebègue, Paris, vol. IX, 1937, pp. 73ff., and in *Oeuvres complètes*, ed. J. Céard, D. Ménager, and M. Simonin, Paris, Gallimard, "Bibliothèque de la Pléiade," 2 vols., 1993–1994), a poem where Ronsard exalts the esoteric, religious, and initiatory value of the grotto; see also R. Biver, *Histoire du château de Meudon*, Paris, 1923, pp. 28–35.

71 See B. Palissy, *Discours admirable*, in *Les Oeuvres [. . .]*, pp. 240 and 440.

72 Idem, *Recette véritable*, p. 115.

73 Idem, *Discours admirable*, in *Les Oeuvres [. . .]*, p. 258.

74 De' Vieri, cited in L. Zangheri, *Pratolino*, vol. I, pp. 114ff.

75 B. S. Sgrilli, cited in idem, ibid., p. 118.

76 Idem, ibid., p. 119.

77 Codex Barberini, cited in idem, ibid., p. 148.

78 De Vieri, cited in idem, ibid., p. 146.

79 Codex Barberini, cited in idem, ibid., p. 152.

80 Cited in D. Heikamp, "Les merveilles de Pratolino," *L'Oeil*, 1969, 171, p. 21.

81 See above, n. 2.

82 G. Agricola, *De natura eorum [. . .]*, in *De ortu [. . .]*, fol. 99v.

83 Idem, *De natura fossilium*, ibid., fol. 246v. On coral, see also U. Aldrovandi, *Musaeum metallicum*, pp. 284ff., and M. Mercati, *Metallotheca Vaticana*, pp. 114–121.

84 See A. Del Riccio, *Istoria delle pietre*, ch. CXXIII. On the magical virtues and symbolic values of coral, see U. Aldrovandi, *Musaeum metallicum*, p. 296.

85 G. Agricola, *De natura eorum [. . .]*, in *De ortu [. . .]*, fol. 99v.

7

Imitation, Innovation, and Renovation in the Counter-Reformation: Landscapes *all'antica* in the Vatican Tower of the Winds

Nicola Courtright

The nature of art produced during the Counter-Reformation in Italy presents a vexed problem that is filled with contradictions. It is clear that many of the canonical principles underlying Renaissance style – including the imitation of antiquity and the search for artistic novelty that revealed the artist's genius – came into question at that time. For artists working after the upheavals in the Catholic Church that were provoked by the Reformation, the issue of classical art as the basis for style and subsequent pictorial innovation was particularly charged, because both were connected in the minds of many reformers with the notion of dangerous licentiousness that would convey the wrong message to the wavering faithful. The most famous example is found in Gilio's *Dialogo nel quale si ragiona degli errori e degli abusi de' pittori circa l'istorie*, published in 1564. In the text, the discussants criticize Michelangelo's treatment of the Last Judgment in the Sistine Chapel both for the artist's return to antique practices to describe sacred history and for his preference for demonstrating the excellence of his *ingegno* and artistry – the bases of pictorial innovation – over historical verisimilitude.[1]

But no single solution emerged from this kind of critique. At the Council of Trent, the framers of the decree concerning art still did not legislate how and what artists were to paint. Above all, they wished to prevent an idolatrous response to art and to reinforce art's valuable instructive nature in moving the faithful to piety and in teaching correct doctrine. The decree thus primarily concerned not the creation but the veneration of art.[2] Even though treatises written subsequently by church reformers outlined more specifically the directions that artists should take, none can be seen as dictating a specific or uniform appearance for works of art. And though modern iconographical studies have successfully related themes in art of the later sixteenth century to doctrines promulgated at the Council of Trent, to church reforms, to devotional literature, and to artistic treatises, nonetheless positing a monolithic approach to Counter-Reformation art has proven unfruitful.[3] Further, the existence of a single, Counter-Reformation style is at best improbable, not least of all because of regional and personal artistic differences.[4]

Yet variety does not negate the possibility that a certain manner or attitude toward art may have been regarded as the embodiment of universally understood principles, that some art was crafted purposefully to create a pictorial model for such reforming precepts, and that this art would become an influential prototype for a later body of work. The character of the paintings in one late-sixteenth-century monument in the Vatican suggests that ideas current during the Counter-Reformation may well have provided a rationale for a favorable attitude toward the innovative transformation of past art. Although this attitude is related in some important ways to Renaissance precepts, it was colored deeply by specifically Counter-Reformation issues and led in turn to a commonly shared visual language that has been considered the hallmark of much seventeenth-century art.

Around 1580, Pope Gregory XIII (1572–85) commissioned the Dominican papal cosmographer Egnatio Danti to lead a team of artists to decorate a newly built suite in the Vatican Palace.[5] The apartment, known from its inception as the Tower of the Winds, surmounts the western wing of the great courtyard Bramante planned early in the century to the north of the old Vatican Palace. The Tower's most overt reference was to a famous monument of antiquity. Danti revealed in a manuscript explaining his contributions to the program that the term *turricula ventorum* alluded to the classical building known as the Tower of the Winds in the Athenian Agora. Built, according to recent scholarship, before 65/4 B.C.E., the ancient structure contained a wind vane and featured a personification of a wind in relief on each of the eight sides of its exterior. By Gregory's pontificate, knowledge of the ancient Tower of the Winds had reached Rome in several ways: a passage in Vitruvius' *De architectura* (1.6.4), Varro's description in *Rerum rusticarum* (3.5.17), and sketches by Ciriaco d'Ancona, who traveled to Athens in 1436 and 1444.[6] Danti wrote in his treatise, "Anemographia," which expanded upon the origins and structure of the wind vane he placed in the vault of the suite's largest room, that he had used the one designed by Andronicus Cyrrestes in the ancient marble tower as a model.[7]

Danti's allusion to antiquity is more profound than the author reveals in his manuscript. The Athenian and Vatican towers measured not only winds, but time. Two separate devices, sundials on the exterior and an elaborate clock run by water on the inside, marked the passage of the hours in the ancient monument and earned it the nickname *Horologion.*[8] Danti's Vatican tower likewise measured time, although the instrument he invented to do so charted the passage of the year. A ray of light, admitted through a small opening in the wall of the largest room, moved across a meridian laid along the floor, accurately tracking the course of the seasons. On the spring equinox, the beam of light fell in the exact center of the meridian.[9] Because of the meridian, the project as a whole has long been recognized as a tribute to Gregory XIII's renowned reform of Julius Caesar's calendar, one of the major achievements of his papacy. Through the recollection of both Greek and Roman measurements of time, Danti may well have wished to carry on the Renaissance topos of contemporary Rome as a new Athens, now governed by the papacy as it had once been governed by a ruler who claimed the Greek inheritance, Caesar.[10]

As much as this seeming tribute to the Athenian monument and the classical worlds asserted the continuing debt of post-Renaissance culture to antiquity, however, Gregory's tower also gave the appearance of having permanently transformed the ancient legacy. Danti describes the painted program of the chamber containing the instruments, the Meridian Room, in undisguised Counter-Reformatory, rather than classical, terms. The author intended the representation of winds there to be understood not just as an allusion to the ancient tower but as a contemporary allegory for schismatic attacks against the church.[11] The biblical subjects, including Christ in Peter's ship battered by winds (Matthew 8:23ff.) and the apostle Paul shipwrecked in a storm at Malta (Acts 17:13ff.) indicated that the Gregorian Tower of the Winds served unmistakably Christian ends.

This transformation parallels the way that the papal calendar in fact replaced the classical one in much of the Western world. The new calendar was not only more accurate than Caesar's, but its primary purpose was to correct the date of Easter, the feast commemorating the fundamental event of Christian faith, Christ's resurrection.[12] The Gregorian reform took the efforts of another Roman leader as its model: it explicitly intended to restore Easter to the date determined by the fourth-century Council of Nicaea, convened by the emperor Constantine to arrive at a communal celebration of the feast. The calendar therefore acted, not as what opinion commonly assumes was a scientific corrective, but as a vehicle of reinforcing Christian faith. The fact that Pope Gregory XIII sponsored this reworking of the ancient scientific legacy to benefit Christianity was also significant, for he thereby allied himself with the deeds of Constantine, who, the church maintained, had transformed the Roman Empire into a Christian one.[13] In reforming time to serve a salvific Christian purpose, Gregory likewise claimed to surpass his ancient, pagan predecessors in the metaphysical domain, in addition to the temporal one.

The other rooms in the Tower also visibly transform an ancient heritage. The Flemish origins of the decoration of two chambers painted by Matthijs Bril are easily recognizable in the landscapes' division into zones, the frequent rise in the center of the composition crowned by trees, and above all, the bright, almost acidic blues and greens of the palette.[14] But three aspects of the decoration ultimately derive from ancient prototypes and Renaissance amplifications upon

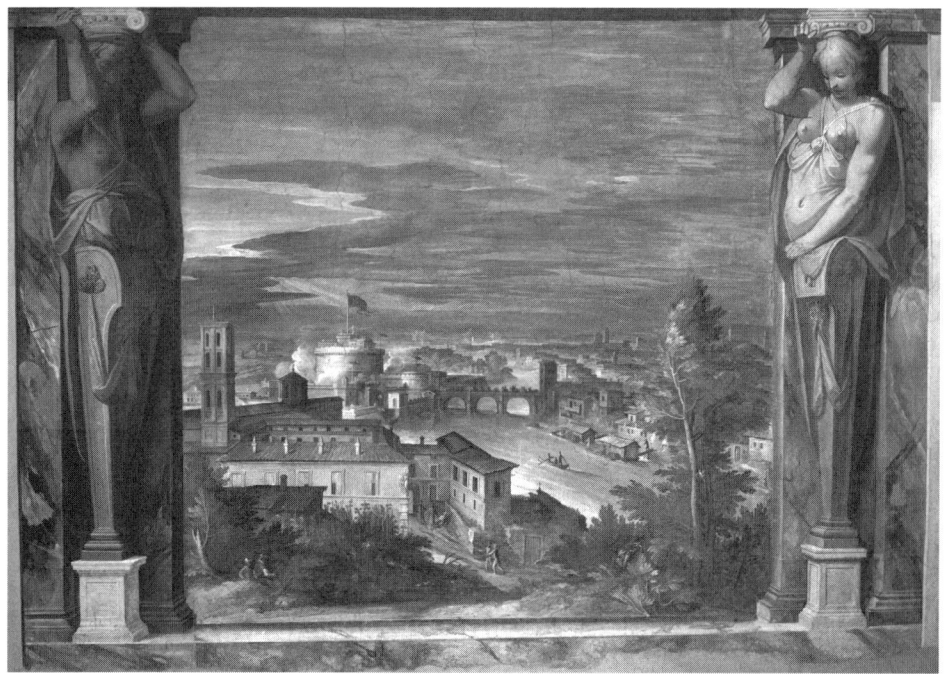

Figure 7.1   Paul Bril, *View of Rome from the Janiculum Hill*, Room with Topographical Views (east wall), Tower of the Winds, Vatican Palace. Photo: Musei Vaticani, Archivio fotografico, III.28.8.

them: the use of landscape views; the illusionistic architectonic framework flanking the views; and the kind of staffage populating the countryside.

Following the spirit of Vitruvius' advice to find "subjects in the characteristics of particular places," the artist painted topographical views of Rome in one of the rooms.[15] Two of the floor-to-ceiling frescoes depict the city from different viewpoints. On one wall Bril painted Rome seen from the direction of the Vatican (fig. 7.1). In the foreground we see the Borgo, featuring the hospital and church of Santo Spirito and the papal fortress, the Castel Sant'Angelo, separated from the city of Rome to the right by the Tiber River. The bridge, the Ponte Sant'Angelo, links the city proper to the papal precinct. In another fresco, the ruined medieval Torre delle Milizie dominates the foreground of a view from the Viminal Hill. The round dome of the Pantheon appears in the center of the scene. In the background is the Vatican, visible to all of Rome: the basilica of Saint Peter's, recognizable by its unfinished dome to the left, and to the right the papal palace, culminating in the Tower of the Winds above the long corridor of the Belvedere.

These portraits of Rome are remarkable for their verism. The city, seen from a low viewpoint, recedes perspectively and fades into the hazy distance. In contrast with another familiar genre of city portrait that renders the entire town from a bird's-eye perspective or incorporates all key topographical details like a map – the view of Parma in the Palazzo Farnese in Caprarola is one possible response in the Renaissance to the Vitruvian dictum to paint particular places – the artist in the Tower represented a partial view of the city and employed a more naturalistic perspective.

Among the first monumental paintings to represent towns with a factual specificity or verism combined with a low, naturalistic viewpoint that anticipated the style of those in the Tower were the cityscapes or *vedute* in Venetian *scuole* representing historical events and rituals. Bril surely knew them, for he had modeled a series depicting a religious procession, the translation of Gregory of Nazianzus' remains to Saint Peter's with Roman neighborhoods as the backdrop, upon this type in another part of the Vatican Palace.[16] What primarily distinguishes Bril's fresco in the Tower of the Winds from the veristic Venetian type of city view is its illusionistic architectural framework. The monumental landscapes, flanked by fictive herms resting on a parapet and supporting a cornice, were depicted as though they were observed through openings in the wall, a decorative type originating in ancient decoration of loggias and galleries. Pliny the Elder, who wrote that the Augustan artist Studius (or Ludius) introduced the genre of painting seaside towns on the walls of open galleries or terraces (*subdialibus*), and Vitruvius, who also mentions the decoration of galleries, corridors, or open porticoes (*ambulationibus*) with landscapes, both suggest that the real view of landscape framed by a colonnade was mirrored by a fictive one on the opposite wall.[17] Preserved ancient wall-painting and Renaissance versions of this type, however, demonstrate that the eye-deceiving techniques common to the *veduta* were only employed for topographical views in which an illusion of reality was otherwise denied. For example, in Venetian *scuole* the paintings were placed high on the wall, preventing the viewer from considering the art an extension of his or her own space. And topographical views inserted into an illusionistic architectural framework like those in the Tower generally were painted so as to avoid the illusion of reality. The stylized bird's-eye view of the Villa Farnese at Caprarola framed by herms in the loggia of the Villa Lante at Bagnaia is but one example.[18] In the Tower, Bril combined the veristic *veduta* with a framework that ummistakably placed the viewer within the fictive reality.

The paintings in the Tower carry the sense of illusion to a new level by making reference to the actual location of the viewer. Two important aspects deserve mention. First, the overall impression of the landscape in both rooms is that of a prospect from a high belvedere open on all sides: the vantage point is elevated, views of landscape cover all of the walls, and the fictive marble parapet running around the rooms acts as a barrier to prevent the viewer from stepping out into nature. These features allude to the elevated, freestanding physical situation of the papal suite. Second, the composition with the Borgo complements the actual view from the Tower. There are no real precedents for representing Rome from the perspective in this view: artists had previously sketched the individual monuments found here, such as the Castel Sant'Angelo, or had drawn panoramas of Rome from a related site, but this exact viewpoint had never been documented.[19] Although the artist shifted the vantage point slightly southward toward the adjacent Janiculum, the city still is regarded from the direction of the Vatican. As we have seen, the Tower of the Winds, rising above the body of the Vatican Palace, faces the city of Rome. In this fresco, the sensation of reality inherent in *vedute* was underscored by the choice of a viewpoint that resembled the observer's actual position.

Contributing to the impression of an actual view is the way in which imaginary landscapes are blended with the topographical views, another of the Tower's innovations. This second type of landscape shares the same viewpoints, perspectival recession, and horizon lines. Illusionistic decoration in which the paintings seem connected by means of compatible horizons and viewpoints was not uncommon in antiquity and the Renaissance, but all previous continuous views were largely fantasy. An important predecessor of this type for the Tower is the Sala delle Prospettive in the Villa Farnesina, where Roman monuments visible from the site are depicted, but on the whole the room gently evokes the setting rather than replicating Rome's physical appearance as concretely as the Tower.[20] Also, topographical and imaginary landscapes were in fact often combined in the same decorative scheme in villas painted a few decades before the Tower. Yet these remained essentially unrelated visually when forced into a unified structure: witness the colonnade of pilasters in the loggia at Caprarola.[21] The two categories of landscape maintain discrete perspectives appropriate to their separate genres. In the Tower, by contrast, the viewer perceives a continuous, harmonious view.

Further, each genre – topographical and imaginary – takes on additional characteristics of the other in order to contribute a new sensation of illusionism to the space. Before the Tower, monumental imaginary landscapes typically included human activities appropriate to a rural setting, such as those in the Villa Barbaro, while views of actual localities within an illusionistic framework are either not populated or the staffage is not integrated with the city itself.[22] Additionally, topographical landscapes by definition feature relatively large, detailed renderings of buildings that characterize the location, whereas imaginary landscapes in villas generally contain buildings in smaller scale that are articulated with less precision. In the Tower, the topographical landscapes are peopled with men walking, returning from the hunt, or boating, in the same manner as the imaginary ones. And in one view of an imaginary town in the Tower, the architecture is depicted with the same grandeur, solidity, and detail as the real structures in the views of Rome (fig. 7.2).

Once the observer analyzes the picturesque staffage familiar from much Flemish landscape painting, it becomes clear that the artist revived ancient prototypes by including almost every motif mentioned by Vitruvius and Pliny as characterizing the ancient sacro-idyllic landscape.[23] Hunters emerge from the woods in the foreground of an imaginary landscape; fowlers catch birds in a net with an owl decoy in the underbrush behind the Ospedale di Santo Spirito on the Tiber (fig. 7.1); "figures of people on foot," noted by Pliny walk on wooded paths

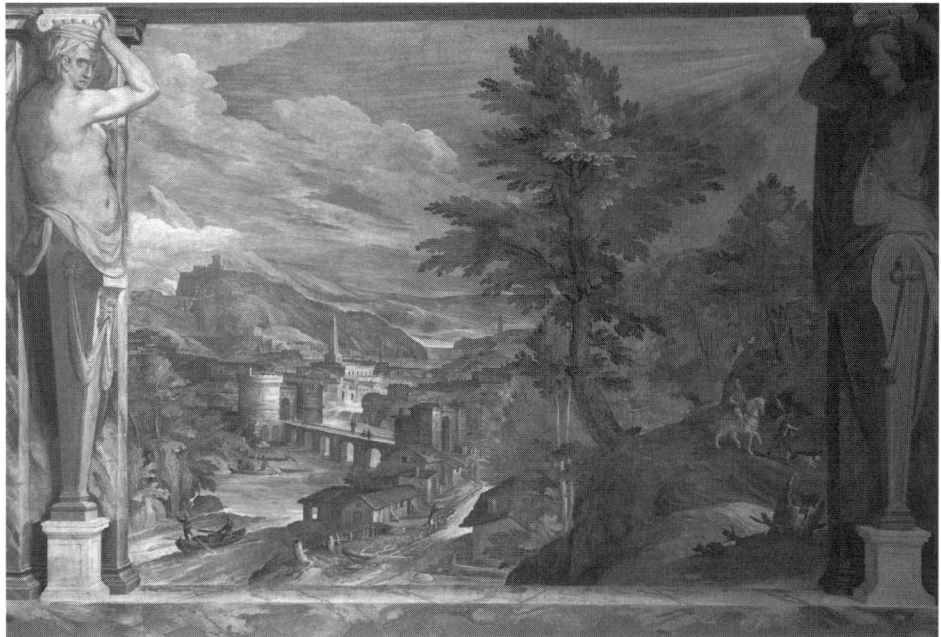

Figure 7.2 Paul Bril, *View from a Hillside toward an Imaginary Town*, Room with Topographical Views (west wall), Tower of the Winds, Vatican Palace. Photo: Musei Vaticani, Archivio fotografico, III.28.9.

and cross bridges in various scenes. Even a man in a carriage, like the one described by the same author, can be found on his way to Rome in the other view of the city.[24]

All of these elements have a metaphorical component, present already in antiquity, that propels the monumental murals into a determinedly ideal realm. The visual emphasis in all of the landscapes upon untamed nature in the form of Pliny's "sacred groves, woods, and hills," and upon hallowed pagan temples or columns present there, reflects an underlying spiritual component that, in a general way, informed the ancient genre of the sacro-idyllic landscape painted in villas.[25] The abundance of rustic motifs, water, and isolated towers not only augments the viewer's sense of removal from city life into a sanctified realm, but also changes topographical reality. To emphasize this natural, ideal character in the portraits of Rome, the artist extended both actual views by painting imaginary, wild landscapes to the side, an effect that heightens the impression of the viewer's removal into nature above the urban setting. Bril accompanied this visual relationship with subtly altering the topography itself. Contemporary panoramas reveal that the Janiculum Hill, for example, did not rise as precipitously nor was as wooded as the fresco suggests.[26]

Upon closer observation, it becomes clear that the artist has translated the general sacro-idyllic vocabulary of the imaginary landscapes into an unmistakably

141

spiritualizing Christian tongue. The theme sounded here is pastoral and, ultimately, idyllic. On one wall, the prominent lyre-playing shepherd who surveys the scene from the left evokes the Golden Age described by ancient authors, for he appears to be composing the poetry of Arcadia that lauds the ideal setting.[27] As is well known, the perfection that Arcadia represented also implied an ideal period in history that had particular resonance for Christians. It was Christ's own characterization of himself as the Good Shepherd (John 10:11) that caused rustic and pastoral themes to become the dominating feature of much early Christian art and exegesis. Using classical pastoral vocabulary, early Christian writers equated the Virgilian and Ovidian Golden Age with the Christian earthly paradise.[28] Indeed, the imagery employed here was a prominent feature of sacred art, for early Christian catacombs and mosaics were replete with shepherds, herdsmen, farmers, sheep, and fowl. One rustic vignette in the Tower's landscape, the woman feeding a flock of geese, was evidently adapted from the late medieval apse of San Clemente in Rome. This composition of curling vines and rustic motifs is itself a revival of early Christian paradisiacal mosaics. To the Counter-Reformation papacy, the peerless faith and personal sacrifice of the first followers of Christ made the early Christian period the touchstone of contemporary reform.[29] Recreating its idyllic imagery on the walls of the papal apartment transposed that perfect era to the present.

The imaginary frescoes as a whole help to define a related spiritual ideal that was an important legacy of early Christian art and thought to the late sixteenth century: humility. In addition to the common folk peopling the landscapes, the wooden shacks and other rustic dwellings in the foreground of each imaginary view are unusually prominent, a striking augmentation of the usual vocabulary of Renaissance villa decoration. The emphasis upon modest dwellings and their inhabitants, often within the setting of classical ruins, was a familiar feature of Flemish painting and became a fundamental characteristic of the Bril brothers' art.[30] This juxtaposition becomes even more significant when made within a papal domicile because of its connection with a tradition that transcended mere picturesque or rustic associations. Literary theorists glossing Virgil's *Eclogues* maintained that pastoral poetry, owing to its depiction of herdsmen and shepherds rather than heroes, was characterized as the lowest style, or *stilus humilis*.[31] The shepherds, herdsmen, farmers, sheep, and fowl of pastoral poetry that became allied with Christian imagery in exegesis thus often signified a lowly counterpoint to noble or high imagery. Once early Christian writers such as Augustine linked the lowest style to the humility embodied by Christ, humble imagery embedded in the lowest of styles partook of the authority inherent in the grander *genera*.[32]

Thus, when Bril set off rickety structures against monumental classical architecture, the visual contrast suggested the opposition of a humble era to the epoch of pagan grandeur. Further, by infusing the staffage with recollections of early Christian art, Bril evoked the modest beginnings of Christian civilization in particular. The dominating presence of such humble imagery replete with

Christian associations in the imaginary views intimated the supersession of the old by the new culture. As the representation of the modest domiciles of ordinary folk and simple structures such as wooden skiffs and floating mills, as well as of the impoverished citizens themselves, assumes great prominence in the portraits of Rome, the laudable humility fundamental to the sixteenth-century image of the primitive church visibly embraces the contemporary capital.

The Tower's topographical *vedute* extend the spiritualizing Christian tenor of the imaginary views and attribute it to a particular time and place: Gregory's papacy and its heart, the Vatican. The staffage engages in devotional acts that demonstrate to what degree all the noted monuments of the city – be they ancient, like the former Tomb of Hadrian transformed into a papal domain and the Pantheon into a Christian church, or medieval, like the basilica Constantine built to honor Saint Peter's remains – serve the Christian religion and its head, the pope.[33] In the fresco depicting the Torre delle Milizie, the man in the carriage performs an act of charity: he has instructed his servant to give alms to the crippled beggar seated by the side of the road. In the other view of Rome, men perform an act of charity behind the hospital of Santo Spirito, where they aid a sick man (fig. 7.1). The people on foot in the background of the Borgo view also have devotional significance: a pair of ecclesiastical figures, accompanied by a retinue, take the processional route to Saint Peter's Basilica and the Vatican Palace over the Ponte Sant'Angelo. They are welcomed by blasts from the cannons of the medieval fortress, a custom reserved for important visitors who were then habitually received by the pope in the palace.[34]

The combination of charity and a devotional procession to the Vatican in the same scene had special meaning for the Gregorian pontificate. One of the major events of Gregory's papacy was the Holy Year that he sponsored in 1575. The perennial imagery of Holy Years, celebrated once every twenty-five years, was that heaven had descended and salvation was at hand; Rome becomes Heavenly Jerusalem.[35] Because the prototypical act of charity was Christ's sacrifice of his life for the sake of humankind's salvation, the practice of charity marked the arrival of the Celestial City on earth. Literature and prints issued for the Holy Year laud the chief Christian virtue of charity above all else. One print representing the personification of *Sancta Roma* amid charitable acts is accompanied by an inscription describing the apocalyptic descent of Heavenly Jerusalem.[36] The image implies in visual terms that these acts bring about the transformation of Rome into the salvational city.

The procession to the Vatican imbues a ritual practice of Gregory's pontificate with equally metaphysical significance. Earthly pilgrimage had long been associated with the spiritual path to heaven, and this traditional relationship was exploited during Gregory's Holy Year, when the pontiff built a road and repaired bridges to open a direct devotional route between basilicas for worshipers.[37] An emblem depicting one of the renovated bridges on the processional way has a verse explaining that the bridge now offers safe passage to heaven.[38] The destination of this pilgrimage is significant, for it was at Saint Peter's where, beginning in 1500, the pope himself in the inaugural celebration opened the walled-up Porta Santa, called the entryway to heaven and likened to the Golden Gate at Jerusalem.[39] Following bitter Protestant criticism of the papacy, the basilica and the papal residence itself became visible proof that a new reforming zeal and hyperspirituality issued from the pontiff personally. Counter-Reformation popes, having initiated the theme of Rome as the unblemished moral center of the Christian universe, linked the acts of the pope himself from his seat in Rome to the moral rebirth of the Christian commonwealth.[40] Thus, combining the act of pilgrimage to the papal precinct with the Christian virtue most closely associated with salvation in Bril's *vedute* suggests, first, that reformed Rome demonstrated the kind of sanctity that equated it with the Celestial City and, second, that the Vatican was its epicenter.

It is the illusionistic system that integrates contemporary Rome with the exemplary world portrayed in the imaginary landscapes. Because of the visual harmony between the imaginary and topographical scenes, the suggestion of the idyllic Golden Age in the fantasy landscapes carries over to the *vedute* of Rome. This seamless union of real and ideal worlds makes possible the representation of traditional allegorical associations of Rome, in, for its time, a breathtakingly naturalistic mode. The frescoes in the papal apartment inextricably knit the idealized, transcendent concept of Rome with its everyday physical appearance.

Bril's innovative picture of Rome anticipated great changes in the following century. Some decades later, in Bernini's design for the crossing of Saint Peter's, where the Baldacchino's twisted columns represented in colossal form the relics believed to have been transported from Solomon's Temple in Jerusalem to the Eternal City, Rome proclaimed its identity as the second Jerusalem, not only during Holy Years, but as a permanent, ongoing celebration. As Irving Lavin has shown, the statues in the piers respond across the space to the descent of the Heavenly City and demand the worshiper's visceral participation in the sacred event.[41] An adumbration of the concept underlying Bernini's invention, realized for a different function and with radically different means, can nevertheless be glimpsed in the Tower of the Winds: the views of Rome painted on the walls of Gregory's apartment had portrayed the city as a perpetual paradise and the Vatican as its fulcrum, and likewise had involved the patron in their construction of reality.

The nature of the transformation of the Tower of the Winds' decoration from ancient and Renaissance models deserves attention as well. It is not subtle: rustic, pastoral, and idyllic motifs become explicitly Christian and contemporaneous; the illusion of a view is insistently naturalistic, likewise catapulting the spectator into the present instead of allowing him merely to recollect the past. Further, the innovations do not boldly declare the personality of the artist, but rather sublimate the appearance of personal virtuosity in favor of the illusion of perfected nature truthfully depicted. Indeed, these departures from tradition are so marked that, in my view, they indicate a visible change from Renaissance attitudes toward the imitation of past art and antiquity in particular. The notion that dominated much Renaissance theory – artists selectively imitating past art in a fashion that nevertheless allowed for originality and progress – yields here to such a transformation of the past that it appears to mark a new beginning.[42] To be sure, it is a commonplace to note an intensive preoccupation with nature and a pointed involvement of the viewer as the hallmark of an artistic break from Mannerism that announces the onset of the Baroque period.[43] But here these pictorial innovations appear to be so connected to Christian reform as to be inseparable from it.

This observation has two ramifications. First, it countermands the generally held view that Counter-Reformation art was conservative and intentionally unoriginal in order to assert church orthodoxy.[44] Second, it demonstrates a parallel between artistic innovation and a Christian ideology of reform. The early Christian idea of *renovatio* was distinct from previous pagan and Old Testament concepts about renewal or the return to a perfected era, as Gerhart Ladner has shown, because inherent in it was the notion of an intentional departure from the past.[45] The apostle Paul best expressed the most radical consequence of this idea in his second letter to the Corinthians, where he wrote: "if anyone is in Christ, he is a new creation; the old has passed away, behold, the new has come" (2 Corinthians 17). As it had frequently done in the past, Christian reform ideology once again provided the license for a new artistic expression of ideas that might incorporate ancient imagery for its own purposes but need not pay homage to the "pagan" tradition, which had proved problematic for much Counter-Reformation thought. The art in the Tower of the Winds, by uniting an iconographical program demonstrating Christian renewal with innovative artistic forms that downplayed the personality of the artist, provided a concrete example of a path diverging from Renaissance syncretistic attitudes toward antiquity. Linking the notion of innovation inseparably to a Christian conscious-ness of reform, I propose, provided an alternative to the imitation of antiquity that was vaunted again in the early seventeenth century. For a time, artistic innovation could be explicitly connected with the expression of religious renewal rather than with artistic genius or the emulation of antiquity. For a time, antiquity was not necessarily privileged as the foremost wellspring of ideas.

Notes

This article is an expansion of the paper I gave at the conference on Antiquity and Antiquity Transumed, March 1994, which was initially published as "The Transforma-tion of Ancient Landscape through the Ideology of Christian Reform in Gregory XIII's Tower of the Winds," *Zeitschrift für Kunstgeschichte* 58 (1995): 526–41. I am grateful to Irving Lavin, who fundamentally aided the formulation of my ideas on the issues raised here. I am further indebted to David A. Levine, Ann Kuttner, and Alina Payne for reading and commenting thoughtfully on the text. My thanks also go to Jack Freiberg for his invaluable assistance.

1 In Paola Barocchi, ed., *Trattati d'arte del Cinquecento fra Manierismo e Controriforma* (Bari: Gius. Laterza & Figli, 1961), 2: 1–115. M. Ruggiero (77–80) objects to the sacred figures rendered in the nude, in the fashion of ancient masters. Concerning innovation, the author's M. Pulidoro (55) opines, "Non penso che sia niuno, quanto si voglia goffo pittore, che non sappia o non pensi che Michelagnolo più tosto compiacer voluto si sia de l'arte, che de la verità istorica, e quello che egli non ha fatto non sia da ignoranza proceduto, ma dal voler mostrare ai posteri l'eccellenza del suo ingegno e la eccellenza de l'arte che è in lui." Gabriele Paleotti, *Discorso intorno alle imagini sacre e profane* (1582), in Barocchi, ed., *Trattati*, 2: 117–509, also addressed these issues. His ch. 32 in Book 2 (398–407), for example, reveals his caution about *novità* in works of art.

    These crucial concepts were discussed by Charles Dempsey, "Mythic Inventions in Counter-Reformation Painting," in P. A. Ramsey, ed., *Rome in the Renaissance: The City and the Myth, Papers of the Thirteenth Annual Conference of the Center for Medieval and Early Renaissance Studies* (Binghamton, N.Y.: Center for Medieval and Early Renaissance Studies, 1982), esp. 65–66. See also the fundamental essay by Paolo Prodi, *Ricerca sulla teorica delle arti figurative nella Riforma Cattolica* (1962), rev. ed. (Bologna: Nuova Alfa Editoriale, 1984), and a review focusing on the issue of a Counter-Reformation style by Hubert Jedin, "Das Tridentinum und die bildenden Künste. Bemerkungen zu Paolo Prodi, Ricerche sulla teorica delle arti figurative nella Riforma Cattolica (1962)," *Zeitschrift für Kirchengeschichte* 74 (1963): 321–39. One might posit that suspicion of novelty, at least in religious imagery, is one issue already present in the decree issued at the Council of Trent on 3 and 4 December, 1563, for it bars "any unusual image unless it has been approved by the bishop"; translated in Elizabeth Gilmore Holt, ed., *A Documentary History of Art*: vol. 2, *Michelangelo and the Mannerists: The Baroque and the Eighteenth Century* (Princeton, N.J.: Princeton University Press, 1982), 65. Paleotti treats this aspect of the Tridentine decree in his *Discorso*, Barocchi, ed., *Trattati*, 402.

2 Holt, ed., *Documentary History*, 2: 63–65.

3 Authors of treatises include Gilio (1564) and Paleotti (1582), both in Barocchi, ed., *Trattati*, vol. 2 (see n. 1). Authors who address Gilio's and Paleotti's interpretations of Tridentine thought and its relationship to art of the time are A. W. A. Boschloo, *Annibale Carracci in Bologna: Visible Reality in Art after the Council of Trent* (The Hague: Government Public Office, 1974); and Dempsey, "Mythic Inventions." Major treatments of Counter-Reformation iconography are Emile Mâle, *L'Art religieux après le Concile de Trente: Etude sur l'iconographie de la fin du XVIe siècle* . . . (Paris: A. Colin, 1932), and J. B. Knipping, *Iconography of the Counter Reformation in the Netherlands: Heaven on Earth*, 2 vols. (Nieuwkoop and Leiden: De Graff, 1974).

4 For the initial debate centering around the question of whether it was a Mannerist or Baroque style that best reflected church reforms, see Werner Weisbach, *Der Barock als Kunst der Gegenreformation* (Berlin: P. Cassirer, 1921); Nikolaus Pevsner, "The Counter Reformation and Mannerism," in idem, *Studies in Art, Architecture, and Design* (London: Thames and Hudson, 1968), 1: 11–34; and Weisbach, "Gegenreformation—Manierismus—Barock," *Repertorium für Kunstwissenschaft* 49 (1928): 16–28. For an evaluation of this debate and later literature, cf. Jedin, "Das Tridentinum und die bildenden Künste"; Boschloo, *Carracci*, 142–44; and

Maria Calí, *Da Michelangelo all'Escorial: Momenti del dibattito religioso dell'arte del Cinquecento* (Turin: Giulio Einaudi, 1980), 1–48.

Federico Zeri, *Pittura e Controriforma: "L'arte senza tempo" di Scipione da Gaeta*, 2nd ed. (Turin: Giulio Einaudi, 1957), outlines characteristics of a separate Counter-Reformation style defined by its devotional value. Numerous authors, notably Jedin, "Das Tridentinum und die bildenden Künste"; Prodi, *Ricerca*, 117–22; Boschloo, *Carracci*, 142–44; and Claudio Strinati, "Roma nell'anno 1600: Studio di pittura," in *Roma nell'anno 1600*, vol. 10 of *Ricerche di storia dell'arte* (Rome: La Nuova Italia Scientifica, 1980), 15–43, reject the idea of a single Counter-Reformation style, owing to their objections to a monolithic definition of the post-Tridentine period. They make a case for stylistic divisions determined by geography and by bishoprics. Charles Dempsey, in "The Carracci and the Devout Style in Emilia," in H. A. Millon, ed., *Emilian Painting of the 16th and 17th Centuries: A Symposium* (Bologna: Nuova Alfa, 1987), 75–87, outlines the history of a regional reform style that had widespread ramifications. Jack J. Spalding, "Santi di Tito and the Reform of Florentine Mannerism," *Storia dell'arte* 42 (1983): 41–52, defines a reform style in the work of one artist.

5   See Nicola Courtright, "The Vatican Tower of the Winds and the Architectural Legacy of the Counter Reformation," in *IL60: Essays Honoring Irving Lavin on his Sixtieth Birthday* (New York: Italica Press, 1990), 117–31; Fabrizio Mancinelli and Juan Casanovas, *La Torre dei Venti in Vaticano* (Vatican City: Libreria Editrice Vaticana, 1980); and Antonio Pinelli, "Il 'bellissimo spasseggio' di papa Gregorio XIII Boncompagni," in Lucio Gambi and Antonio Pinelli, eds., *La Galleria delle Carte geografiche in Vaticano* (Modena: Franco Cosimo Panini, 1994), 9–71.

6   Edward W. Bodnar, *Cyriacus of Ancona and Athens* (Brussels/Berchem: Latomus, 1960), 35ff. and 50ff., discusses the dates of Ciriaco d'Ancona's trips to Athens. Cf. Beverly Louise Brown and Diana E. E. Kleiner, "Giuliano da Sangallo's Drawings after Ciriaco d'Ancona: Transformations of Greek and Roman Antiquities in Athens," *Journal of the Society of Architectural Historians* 42 (1983): 328–31. For examples of imaginative reconstructions of the Tower in illustrated editions of Vitruvius, beginning with that published in 1511 by Fra Giocondo, see Carol Krinsky, ed., *Vitruvius. De architectura comm. Cesare Cesariano* (Como, 1521 ed.; Munich, 1969), 127–28.

A print allusive of the ancient structure also appears on the title page of Danti's treatise *Anemographia* (Rome, 1578). Below it is the inscription "Andronica Turris mar." A copy of this image is also represented, without the inscription, in the Italian translation of the *Anemographia: Dell'uso et fabbrica dell'astrolabio et del planisferio con l'aggiunta dell'uso, & fabbrica di novi altri istromenti astronomici* . . . (Florence, 1578), 251.

7   In "Anemographia F. Egnatij Dantis O.S.D.: In Anemoscopium Vaticanum Horizontale, ac Verticale instrume(n)tum ostensorem Ventorum," dated 24 January 1581 (Bibl. Vat. 5647), fol. 13v.

8   Varro, *Rerum rusticarum* 3.5.17. J. V. Noble and D. J. de Solla Price, "The Waterclock in the Tower of the Winds," *American Journal of Archaeology* 72 (1968): 345–55, discuss the time mechanism.

9   Danti had built meridians and other measuring devices earlier as court cosmographer in Florence under Cosimo I. For the meridian and other instruments in Santa Maria

Novella, see Maria Luisa Righini and Thomas B. Settle, "Egnatio Danti's Great Astronomical Quadrant," *Annali dell'Istituto e Museo di Storia della Scienza di Firenze* 4 (1979): 3–13; Leonardo Ximines, *Del vecchio e nuovo gnomone fiorentino e delle osservazioni astronomiche fisiche ed architettoniche fatte nel verificarne la costruzion* (Florence, 1757), xlv–xlvi; and Juan Casanovas, "The Vatican Tower of the Winds and the Calendar Reform," in *Gregorian Reform of the Calendar: Proceedings of the Vatican Conference to Commemorate its 400th Anniversary 1582–1982*, ed. G. V. Coyne et al. (Vatican City: Specola Vaticana, 1983), 193. For the gnomon Danti placed in the cathedral of San Petronio, Bologna, see his treatise, *Usus et tractatio gnomonis magni quem Bononiae ipse in Divi Petronii templo . . .* (Bologna, 1576).

10   For the idea of Rome as the New Athens, promulgated by Renaissance popes, see Charles L. Stinger, *The Renaissance in Rome* (Bloomington, Ind.: University of Indiana Press, 1985), 287. I am grateful to the anonymous reader of the manuscript of my book, *The Papacy and the Art of Reform: Gregory XIII's Tower of the Winds in the Vatican*, Cambridge: Cambridge University Press, 2003, for this connection.

11   Danti, "Anemographia," Biblioteca Apostolica Vaticana, Vat. lat. 5647, fol. 15r.

12   For the history of the association of the Tower with the calendar reform, see Courtright, "The Vatican Tower," 124–26; and Casanovas, "The Vatican Tower," 189–96. Literature focusing on this aspect of the Gregorian reform of the calendar includes Ferdinand Kaltenbrunner, "Die Polemik über die gregorianische Kalender-Reform," *Sitzungsberichte der philosophisch-historischen Classe der Kaiserlichen Akademie der Wissenschaften, Wien* 87 (1877): 485–586; idem, "Beiträge zur Geschichte der gregorianischen Kalenderreform," *Sitzungsberichte der philosophisch-historischen Classe der kaiserlichen Akademie der Wissenschaften, Wien* 97 (1880): 7–54; Vittorio Peri, *Due date, un'unica Pasqua: Le origini della moderna disparità liturgica in una trattativa ecumenica tra Roma e Costantinopoli (1582–84)* (Milan: Editrice Vita e Pensiero, 1967); and *Gregorian Reform of the Calendar*, passim (as above).

13   For the late sixteenth-century papal preoccupation with Constantine, see Jack Freiberg, "In the Sign of the Cross: The Image of Constantine in the Art of Counter-Reformation Rome," in *Piero della Francesca and His Legacy*, ed. Marilyn Aronberg Lavin, Studies in the History of Art, 48, Center for Advanced Study in the Visual Arts, Symposium Papers 28, National Gallery of Art, Washington, D.C., 67–87; idem, *The Lateran in 1600: Christian Concord in Counter-Reformation Rome* (Cambridge: Cambridge University Press, 1995); and Nicola Courtright, review, Lucio Gambi and Antonio Pinelli, eds., *La Galleria delle Carte geografiche in Vaticano . . .*, and Margret Schütte, *Die Galleria delle Carte Geografiche im Vatikan*, *The Art Bulletin* 79 (1997): 156–60.

14   A document written shortly after Gregory's death attributes the landscape decoration to Matthijs Bril and not to his better-known brother, Paul; Bibl. Vat., Boncompagni D 5, fol. 240v, published in Ludwig von Pastor, *The History of the Popes from the Close of the Middle Ages*, ed. Ralph Francis Kerr, 40 vols. (London: Kegan Paul, Trench, Trubner & Co., 1923–53), vol. 20, p. 651, app. 11. Because Matthijs' reputation was built on his mastery of topographical landscapes – there are two among the monumental views in the Tower – and the decoration was almost certainly completed before Matthijs' death in 1583, there appears to be no reason

to attribute any of the paintings to Paul. I am grateful to Egbert Haverkamp-Begemann for his contribution to my thinking on this point.

15 Vitruvius, *De architectura* 7.5.2. Juergen Schulz, "Pinturicchio and the Revival of Antiquity," *Journal of the Warburg and Courtauld Institutes* 25 (1962): 35–55, treats early Renaissance responses to the Vitruvian dictum. Idem, "Jacopo de' Barbari's View of Venice: Mapmaking, City Views, and Moralized Geography before the Year 1500," *The Art Bulletin* 60 (1978): 425–74; Uta Feldges, *Landschaft als topographisches Porträt: Der Wiederbeginn der europäischen Landschaftsmalerei in Siena* (Bern: Benteli, 1980); and *The Origins of the Italian Veduta*, exh. cat. (Bell Gallery, Brown University, Providence, R.I., 1978), discuss early modern topographical landscapes in general.

16 Patricia Fortini Brown, *Venetian Narrative Painting in the Age of Carpaccio* (New Haven and London: Yale University Press, 1988). Bril's ten scenes depicting the translation are in the uppermost (fourth) story of the Vatican Logge, termed "la Terza Loggia." Executed after the ceremony took place on 11 June 1580, the commission is treated by Roberto Almagià, *Le pitture geografiche murali della Terza Loggia e di altre sale vaticane* (Monumenta cartographica vaticana, IV) (Vatican City: Biblioteca apostolica vaticana, 1955). Bril's contribution is discussed by Maurice Vaes, "Mathieu Bril: 1550–1583," *Bulletin de l'Institut Historique Belge de Rome*, 8 (1928): 311–31; and F. Sricchia Santoro, "Antonio Tempesta fra Stradano e Matteo Bril," in *Relations artistiques entre les Pays-Bas et l'Italie à la Renaissance: Etudes dédiées à Suzanne Sulzberger* (Etudes d'histoire de l'art publiées par l'Institut Historique Belge de Rome, 4) (Brussels: Institut Historique Belge de Rome, 1980), 227–37.

17 Pliny the Elder, *Historia naturalis* 35.37.116–17; Vitruvius, *De architectura* 7.5.2, and 6.7.6, where he describes *telamones* or *atlantes* supporting cornices on either side of landscape views. See Roger Ling, "Studius and the Beginnings of Landscape Painting," *The Journal of Roman Studies* 67 (1977): 1–16, for the ancient tradition of landscape representation on walls. For the Renaissance revival of landscape in illusionistic architectural framing, see Schulz, "Pinturicchio," 37–42; and Eva Börsch-Supan, *Garten- Landschafts- und Paradiesmotive im Innenraum: Eine ikonographische Untersuchung* (Berlin: Bruno Hessling, 1967), 240–73.

18 David R. Coffin, *The Villa in the Life of Renaissance Rome* (Princeton, N.J.: Princeton University Press, 1979), 343–46, discusses the loggia at Bagnaia, completed in 1578.

19 See, for example, the view of the Castel Sant'Angelo and a procession over the bridge in the copy of a drawing after Domenico Ghirlandaio executed around 1491 in Hermann Egger, *Römische Veduten. Handzeichnungen aus dem XV. bis XVIII. Jahrhundert zur Topographie der Stadt Rom* (Vienna and Leipzig: Friedrich Wolfrum & Co., 1911), pl. 8. For other examples of views of the Castel Sant'Angelo from different perspectives, see Egger, pls. 9–12, and vol. 2, 2nd rev. ed. (Vienna: Anton Schroll & Co., 1932), pls. 111–13, 117; and Brown University, *Origins of the Italian Veduta*, exh. cat. (Providence: Brown University, 1978), 36–37, figs. 16–17.

20 For the Villa Farnesina landscapes in the Sala delle Prospettive, executed c. 1517–18 by Baldassare Peruzzi, see Christoph Luitpold Frommel, *Baldassare Peruzzi als Maler und Zeichner* (Beiheft zum Römischen Jahrbuch für Kunstgeschichte, 11) (Vienna and Munich: Anton Schroll & Co., 1967/68), 87–91; and S. J. Freedberg,

Painting of the High Renaissance in Rome and Florence (New York: Harper & Row, 1972), 402–3.

21 The landscapes in the loggia (Sala d'Ercole) at Caprarola were painted in 1572; see Loren W. Partridge, "The Sala d'Ercole in the Villa Farnese at Caprarola, Part I," *The Art Bulletin* 53 (1971): 467–86, and esp. 476–77; and idem, "The Sala d'Ercole in the Villa Farnese at Caprarola, Part II," *The Art Bulletin* 54 (1972): 50–62. For the earlier Salotto of the Villa d'Este, Tivoli, c. 1568, which also juxtaposes a topographical view with imaginary ones, see David R. Coffin, *The Villa d'Este at Tivoli* (Princeton, N.J.: Princeton University Press, 1960), 50–54.

22 For the Villa Barbaro frescoes, dated c. 1560, see Konrad Oberhuber, "Hieronymus Cock, Battista Pittoni und Paolo Veronese in Villa Maser," in Tilmann Buddensieg and Matthias Winner, eds., *Munuscula Discipulorum: Kunsthistorische Studien, Hans Kauffmann zum 70. Geburtstag 1966* (Berlin: Bruno Hessling, 1968), 207–24.

23 Hiring a Flemish landscape painter and simultaneously retaining the Flemish character of the landscapes may have been ideological, for it suggests the power of the church for artists precisely from lands most threatened by Protestantism.

24 Pliny, *Historia naturalis* 35.37.116–17.

25 Cf. M. Rostowzew, "Die hellenistisch-römische Architekturlandschaft," *Mitteilungen des kaiserlichen deutschen archäologischen Instituts. Römische Abteilung* 16 (1911): 12ff. and passim; Pierre Grimal, "Les Maisons à tour hellénistiques et romaines," *Mélanges d'archéologie et d'histoire. Ecole française de Rome* 56 (1939): 28–59; and Ling, "Studius," 8. On the sacro-idyllic landscape, see Peter Heinrich von Blanckenhagen and Christine Alexander, *The Paintings from Boscotrecase*, Mitteilungen des deutschen archäologischen Instituts. Römische Abteilung, 6. Ergänzungsheft (Heidelberg, 1962), 60, n. 111; Peter Heinrich von Blanckenhagen, "The Odyssey Frieze," *Mitteilungen des Deutschen Archäologischen Instituts. Römische Abteilung* 70 (1963): 134; and Ling, "Studius," passim.

26 Cf. Anton van Wyngaerde's mid-sixteenth-century panorama from the Janiculum; Herrmann Egger, *Römische Veduten*, 2: 45 and pl. 112.

27 See Luba Freedman, *The Classical Pastoral in the Visual Arts* (New York: Peter Lang, 1989), 103–52.

28 A. Bartlett Giamatti, *The Earthly Paradise and the Renaissance Epic* (Princeton, N.J.: Princeton University Press, 1966), 30–33; and Ernst Robert Curtius, *European Literature and the Latin Middle Ages*, trans. Willard R. Trask (Princeton, N.J.: Princeton University Press, 1973), 195–200.

29 For the imagery in San Clemente, see Hélène Toubert, "Le Renouveau paléochrétien à Rome au debut du XIIe siècle," *Cahiers archéologiques* 20 (1970): 122–54. Literature on the revival of Early Christianity in the Counter-Reformation includes Gisella Wataghin Cantino, "Roma sotterranea. Appunti sulle origini dell'archeologia cristiana," in *Roma nell'anno 1600, Ricerche di Storia dell'arte* 10 (1984): 5–14; and Alessandro Zuccari, *Arte e Committenza nella Roma di Caravaggio* (Turin: ERI/Edizioni Rai Radiotelevisione Italiana, 1984).

30 Joachim Patinir is but one of the Flemish artists who emphasized humble dwellings within his landscapes. The Brils' interest in the *all'antica* landscape, which they merged with the traditional focus upon ordinary architecture, was anticipated by Northern artists who went to Italy. Van Mander noted that the first of these, who had then executed landscapes in the manner of the antique ("antikijcksche wijse"),

was Matthijs Cock; *Schilder-boeck*, 232r, translated in *The Lives of the Illustrious Netherlandish and German Painters*, ed. Hessel Miedema, 2 vols. (Doornspijk: Davaco, 1994), 1: 186–87. The *all'antica* style that he and his brother Hieronymus developed was characterized by a looser brushstroke and the inclusion of classical buildings or ruins, and in drawings, rapid penstrokes, and white highlights; see Heinrich Gerhard Franz, *Niederländische Landschaftsmalerei im Zeitalter des Manierismus* (Graz: Akademische Druck- und Verlagsanstalt, 1969), 140–53. For this style in the Brils' contemporaries Pauwels Franck (Paolo Fiammingho) and Lodowijk Toeput (Pozzoserrato), see Franz, *Niederländische Landschaftsmalerei*, 300–08; and R. A. Peltzer, "Niederländisch-venezianische Landschaftsmalerei," *Münchner Jahrbuch der bildenden Kunst*, n.s. 1 (1924): 126–53.

31 Helen Cooper, *Pastoral: Mediaeval into Renaissance* (Ipswich, Eng.: D. S. Brewer et al., and Totowa, N.J.: Rowman & Littlefield, 1977), 127. *The "Parisiana Poetria" of John of Garland*, ed. and trans. Traugott Lawler, Yale Studies in English, 182 (New Haven and London: Yale University Press, 1974), 38–39 and 86–87, describes the related medieval literary division based upon Virgil. Representing the pastoral mode in literature was not just limited to shepherds; Sannazaro wrote eclogues called "piscatorials" from the point of view of fishermen, who are represented in the Tower's friezes; see Jacopo Sannazaro, *Arcadia and Piscatorial Eclogues*, trans. Ralph Nash (Detroit: Wayne State University Press, 1966); cf. Cooper, *Pastoral*, 108.

32 Augustine, *De doctrina christiana* 4.17.34–19.38, vol. 32 of *Corpus christianorum, series latina*, ed. Joseph Martin (Turnholti: Brepols, 1962), 141–44. Erich Auerbach, "Sermo humilis," in *Literary Language and Its Public in Late Latin Antiquity and in the Middle Ages* (Bollingen Series 74), trans. Ralph Manheim (New York: Pantheon, 1965), 27–66, develops this idea in patristic thought.

33 The ancient Roman practice of representing or describing urban Roman topography to offer, in effect, a tour of the capital's sacred sites may be revived here in general terms; see Eleanor Leach, *The Rhetoric of Space: Literary and Artistic Representation of Space in Republican and Augustan Rome* (Princeton, N.J.: Princeton University Press, 1988). I would like to thank Ann Kuttner for this idea.

34 The diary of the Master of Ceremonies, Francisco Mucantius, preserved in the Biblioteca Vaticana, cites many examples of cannon shots fired to honor visitors entering Rome, e.g., Bolognese envoys received in 1572 (Boncompagni C 5, fols. 32v–33r); and Japanese envoys in 1585 (Boncompagni C 6, fol. 317r).

35 Herbert Thurston, *The Holy Year of Jubilee* (St. Louis, Mo.: B. Herder, 1900); and Marcello Fagiolo and Maria Luisa Madonna, *Roma Sancta: La città delle basiliche* (Rome: Gangemi Editore, 1985).

36 Thurston, *Holy Year*, 260–62.

37 Gregory XIII's restorations of Rome for the Holy Year are discussed in the biography written from 1589 to 1597 by Giovanni Pietro Maffei, *Degli Annali di Gregorio XIII. Pontefice Massimo* (Rome: Stamperia di Girolamo Mainardi, 1742), 1: 106–8. See also M. Teresa Russo, "1575: Organizzazione e cronaca di un giubileo," *Strenna dei Romanisti* 36 (1975): 371–85; Marcello Fagiolo and Maria Luisa Madonna, eds., *Roma 1300–1875: La città degli Anni Santi* (Milan: Arnaldo Mondadori Editore, 1985), 178–96; and Philip Jacks, "A Sacred Meta for Pilgrims in the Holy Year 1575," *Architectura* 19 (1989): 137–65.

38 The verse in Principio Fabrizi, *Delle allusioni, imprese, et emblemi del sig. Principio Fabricii da Teramo sopra la vita, opere, et attioni di Gregorio XIII pontefice massimo libri VI*...(Rome: Bartolomeo Grassi, 1588), 103: 157, lauds the repair of the Pons Senatori, dedicated to the Virgin, by Gregory (whose personal emblem was the dragon) for the Jubilee Year:

> Però l'anno, che'l Ciel'apre, e diffonde
> L'ampio Tesor, che dal Costato uscio
> del gran secondo, & innocente Adamo:
> Drizza d'Eua seconda il Ponte à l'onde
> Questo gran DRAGO à le nostr'Alme pio
> Acciò sicuri al Ciel di quì passiamo.

39 Eva-Maria Jung-Inglessis, "La Porta Santa," *Studi Romani* 23 (1975): 473–85. See also Thurston, *Holy Year*, 28–54; and Marcello Fagiolo and Maria Luisa Madonna, eds., *Roma 1300–1875: L'arte degli Anni Santi* (Milan: Arnoldo Mondadori Editore, 1984), 58–88.

40 Frederick J. McGinness, "The Rhetoric of Praise and the New Rome of the Counter Reformation," in P. A. Ramsey, ed., *Rome in the Renaissance: The City and the Myth*, Papers of the Thirteenth Annual Conference of the Center for Medieval and Early Renaissance Studies (Binghamton, N.Y.: Center for Medieval and Early Renaissance Studies, 1982), 355–70.

41 Irving Lavin, *Bernini and the Crossing of Saint Peter's* (New York: New York University Press, 1968).

42 The vast literature on Renaissance theories of imitation in art includes: Jeffrey Muller, "Rubens's Theory and Practice of the Imitation of Art," *The Art Bulletin* 64 (1982): 229–47; E. H. Gombrich, "The Style *all'antica*: Imitation and Assimilation," in his *Norm and Form: Studies in the Art of the Renaissance* (London: Phaidon, 1966), 122–28; Jan Bialostocki, "The Renaissance Concept of Nature and Antiquity," in *Acts of the XX. International Congress of the History of Art*: vol. 2, *The Renaissance and Mannerism: Studies in Western Art* (Princeton, N.J.: Princeton University Press, 1963), 19–30; and Eugenio Battisti, "Il concetto d'imitazione nel Cinquecento italiano," reprinted in his *Rinascimento e Barocco* (Turin: Giulio Einaudi, 1960), 175–215.

43 Analyzed by John Rupert Martin, "The Baroque from the Point of View of the Art Historian," *Journal of Aesthetics and Art Criticism* 14 (1955): 164–71; and idem, *Baroque* (Princeton, N.J.: Princeton University Press, 1977).

44 Cf. Zeri, *Pittura e Controriforma*.

45 Gerhart B. Ladner, *The Idea of Reform: Its Impact on Christian Thought and Action in the Age of the Fathers*, rev. ed. (New York: Harper & Row, 1967).

8

Landscapes and Still Lifes

Pamela M. Jones

According to the optimistic view of the world that Borromeo held, all created things, animate and inanimate, had positive value. They were not to be despised, but rather appreciated as gifts from God, which manifested his wisdom, generosity, and his divine plan. To Borromeo, created things had essentially two main purposes: to keep human beings alive by providing them with food, drink, and shelter, and to attract contemplative minds by appealing to human beings' senses.[1]

The Archbishop understandably also devised meditative prayers on this aspect of God's world. His *Modo*, for example, provided priests with guidelines for administering an exercise on "The Glory of God," an exercise that recalls Ignatius's "Contemplation to Attain Love of God" as well as his "First Principle and Foundation."[2] In the prelude to Borromeo's prayer, the exercitant was first to imagine seeing all celestial and terrestrial creatures contributing to God's glory, each according to its own capacity. He or she was then to entreat the Lord for grace in performing the exercise effectively.

The exercise itself centered upon six points, each, of course, only briefly summarized because it was the priest's role to elaborate on them according to the exercitant's needs. Beginning at the bottom of the ladder, the exercitant was to consider how each creature manifested God's glory and helped to fulfill his will in doing merely that for which it was created.[3] The second point concerned the greatness of God, who was able to extract glory from everything – from the devil, hell, and sin, as well as from mute creatures and inanimate things. Borromeo also noted that God derived glory from natural phenomena, the movements and influences of the heavens, the four elements, and, indeed, from the entire mechanism of the world. In ascending the ladder according to point three, the exercitant was to meditate on humankind's superiority over the other creatures. The elevated nature of the human being was due to an ability to act, express him or herself, and understand God's plan. Furthermore, nearly all the actions of inferior beings were performed for human beings' use; this demonstrated that humankind was created to give more glory to God. Under point four, the exercitant grew to understand his or her responsibility according to the divine plan: because God's will was his greatest glory, the human being, who alone among all the creatures was truly active, was obligated to fulfill it. Point five allowed the exercitant to further distinguish human nature from that of inferior creatures. Because only human beings were able to articulate praise of the Creator, it was essential for them to do so to their utmost capacity. That meant praising all created things, praising God when eating his creatures, when experiencing natural phenomena, and so on. Finally, the sixth point reinforced the exercitant's understanding of divine will by proposing that he or she consider how humankind both served the glory of God and benefited from it.[4]

Although his guidelines in the *Modo* and comments in *Le Piaceri* and *Le Laudi* reveal that Borromeo regarded the ultimate value of created things as being steps on the hierarchical ladder of God's world, and therefore as worthy subjects for contemplation, it is important not to overlook the joyous, delightful, inspirational aspect of his feeling for nature. From his earliest years, Federico had particularly enjoyed and profited from study and prayer outdoors in nature. He was seriously discontented in Rome when his active life began to encroach upon his contemplative life. Upon seeking spiritual guidance from Filippo Neri, young Federico became involved in the Oratorians' *ragionamenti spirituali*, collective meditations in which men discussed their own individual paths to spiritual equilibrium. Agostino Valier, one of Borromeo's advisors in Rome, captured the spirit of these meditations in his imaginary dialogue of around 1591 entitled *Philippus, sive de laetitia Christiana*. The dialogue's interlocutors included a group of prominent Church reformers, with Filippo Neri, true to form, as leader of their discussions. In treating the subject of how to attain Christian joy, Valier had each man present his own individual method; Borromeo's method, as Valier expressed it, involved contemplating the wisdom and power of God through his created world.[5] Borromeo's method of attaining Christian joy, therefore, was fundamentally Christocentric, for according to I Corinthians 1: 24, Christ himself is the wisdom and power of God. Christocentric spirituality involves the distinction between the supernatural and natural worlds, which are linked through Christ. Thus, in seeking Christian joy through contemplation of the created world, Borromeo of course believed that although nature was in itself good, grace was needed in order to bring it to perfection.

When in the 1590s Borromeo began consistently to collect paintings, he concentrated almost exclusively on acquiring landscapes.[6] At that time, other genres had little appeal for him. Borromeo's initial patronage of landscapes – and one still life – seems to have been motivated by a sudden inability to spend time in prayer out of doors, which suggests that these paintings had a special role in his spiritual life during his Roman years.

Because Flemings had a virtual monopoly on landscape painting as an independent genre when Borromeo began collecting landscapes in Rome, it was inevitable that he turned to his friends Jan Brueghel the Elder and Paul Bril when commissioning such works.[7] Thus, there are personal and historical reasons for Borromeo's early patronage of Flemish landscapists. Moreover, Borromeo's preference for the Flemish style of landscape and also still-life painting was informed by his spirituality, as an examination of his devotional treatises will show, and Italian landscapes – when they were produced – tended not to meet Borromeo's spiritual criteria. This partly explains why long after 1600 Borromeo continued to acquire Flemish works of these genres.

Several of the first Flemish landscapes that Borromeo commissioned depicted hermits or monks studying or praying. It is worth stating now that although Borromeo's appreciation of such paintings was partly rooted in his belief in the usefulness of contemplating nature, a central topic here, it was equally rooted in his appreciation of the ultimate subject of monastic themes themselves, that is, the subject of how to live as a natural man. At present, we are concerned with the former layer of Borromeo's interest in nature themes: his use of such works in devotional prayer.

In painting hermits and monks in landscapes for Borromeo, Brueghel adapted engraved sources to fit his patron's particular spiritual beliefs. Although both Brueghel's *Landscape with a Hermit Reading and Ruins* of 1596 and *Mountain Landscape with a Hermit* of 1597, for example, were based on engravings by Jan and Raphael Sadeler after drawings by Marten de Vos, in each case, Brueghel omitted the very details that identified the engraved figures as specific men.[8] In departicularizing his engraved sources that Borromeo seems to have provided, Brueghel sought to emphasize the universal themes of solitary life and contemplation of nature. Hence, Borromeo's comment in *Le Piaceri*, in which he admonished humankind for living apart from nature, although not quoted from any one particular patristic authority, bespoke an ancient Christian tradition derived from patristic literature:

> Solitary life preserves and nurtures a high peace. . . . O you mortals, you very soon forgot your old and paternal soil! What was the first thing to greet your eyes when they were opened by God's fingers? Were they not the trees and greenery? Were you not created in the midst of this? Miserable, then, and tearful will be the condition of them who will not render any profit from, or give any sign of living in solitude. . . .[9]

In *Le Piaceri* and *Le Laudi*, Borromeo frequently cited ideas of Gregory Nazianzus and John Chrysostom; the former attributed to nature a soothing quality that mitigated pain, and both regarded natural things as partaking of divine philosophy and wisdom, which invited men to virtue.[10] In addition to Christian literature, the Archbishop was probably also aware of Alberti's description in *De Re Aedificatoria* of how looking at paintings of fountains and brooks could relax the mind just as when unable to sleep imagining flowing waters or lakes relieved the spirit and caused one to feel drowsy.[11] Borromeo's attitude reveals that he felt that paintings of nature had to operate in the same way as nature itself in order to simulate metaphysical reality.

Although depicting hermits and monks in landscapes was the most obvious way of visualizing these ideas, only one logical step was required in order to get to the very crux of the matter: nature itself. Brueghel's *Forest Landscape with a Brook* and Paul Bril's *Forest Landscape with a Marsh*, also datable to the mid-1590s, express well the Archbishop's belief in nature as redolent of God's wisdom, creativity, and generosity to humankind. Thus, Borromeo's appreciation of nature themes was not contingent on their containing religious figures or stories, as also indicated by his praise in *Musaeum* of Bril's *Seascape*, which shows ordinary persons engaged in everyday activities. In *Musaeum*, Borromeo lauded the calm and beauty of *Seascape* and delighted in the sense that he could move endlessly through it. Indeed, *Seascape* shared with Brueghel's and Bril's forest scenes the intimate scale and low viewpoint that made them ideally suited to contemplation according to the exercises that Archbishop Federico discussed in the *Modo* and the *Viaggio spirituale*. It is easy to imagine Borromeo contemplating landscapes from inside his study in the Archiepiscopal Palace in Milan, a practice he mentioned in *Pro suis studiis* of 1628.

Among Borromeo's most cherished paintings was the series of the *Four Elements*, which he commissioned from Brueghel between 1608 and 1621. In this case, the Archbishop's writings not only provide additional information regarding his spiritual conception of nature, but shed light on his particular enthusiasm for Brueghel's characteristically Flemish style.

Brueghel's *Four Elements* were nominally secular scenes representing elemental nature, although, of course, elemental nature itself had spiritual significance to Borromeo. The pictures had various levels of meaning, which delighted him. For example, *Fire*, which contains demons confronting humans near caves, also represented hell, and was counterbalanced by *Earth*, which, in depicting figures of Adam and Eve with God in the background, also represented earthly paradise. In his chapter on divine providence in *Le Laudi*, Archbishop Federico touched upon such contrasts of nature:

> Now this nature, is she not perhaps the very humble servant and obedient handmaiden of God, who joins the extreme parts of created things by the knot of many *convenevoli e proportionati mezzi* [suitable and proportioned means]? Hence, the pleasantness of the air does much to diminish and moderate the pride of fire. And the harshness and hardness of the earth are sweetened and softened by the softness of the waters, and by their pliant quality and substance. And from hills one ascends yet to mountains, and from the plains to hills, and from the rivers to lakes, and then one crosses seas, navigating. Similarly, this nature, minister of God, mitigates . . . bitternesses with pleasantnesses, darkness with light, misshapen things with the stalwart, disasters with happinesses, and sorrows with delights, so that everyone understands Him to be the pious, and meek, and sweetest God. . . .[12]

A recurring theme of Borromeo's treatise was praise of God's marvelous ability to create an orderly, harmonious world in this way.

In *Musaeum*, Borromeo enthusiastically praised Brueghel's treatment of natural elements in the Passion series in the *Holy Water Stoup*, noting that in them the artist had succeeded in squeezing into small formats trees, mountains, rocks, valleys, rivers, seas, and natural things that in reality were separated by great distances. In this way, Borromeo wrote, Brueghel imitated "nature itself not only in color, but also in talent, which is the highest quality of nature and of art."[13] Remarks like this recall his notion of "*convenevoli mezzi.*" Borromeo also lauded the same qualities in Brueghel's *Four Elements* series. For example, in the guidebook, he wrote of the *Element of Water*: "Thus in the representation of the element of water, he [Brueghel] has introduced so many and such varied kinds of fish as to make one believe him no less skilled at fishing than at painting. And there he has collected and disposed in beautiful display every sort of those freaks of nature and refuse of the sea that are the seashells."[14] How closely these remarks resemble passages in his devotional treatises is demonstrated by comparing them with comments in his chapter on animals in *Le Laudi*: "After which consideration [the habits of birds], entering thoughtfully into the most ample fields of the sea, then we will find schools of fish, which, in addition to their number, with enormous greatness of types, provide us testimony of the generosity of that Lord who produced them...."[15] Among created things, it was the small, weak, and miserable ones – the meek – that manifested God's wisdom and creativity most highly, as Borromeo, following John Chrysostom, continually asserted in both devotional treatises.[16] Thus, the salient features of Brueghel's Flemish style – very realistically rendered animate and inanimate things painted on a miniaturistic scale and placed within additive compositions featuring a variety of natural formations juxtaposed in an improbable way – were particularly suited to expressing Borromeo's conception of God's world. Borromeo did not create Brueghel's artistic style: he encountered it. Certainly no Italian landscape painter of Borromeo's day could have competed with Brueghel on these very important terms.[17]

To Borromeo, the spiritual significance of landscape paintings was imbedded in the very creatures, objects, formations, and natural phenomena themselves rather than being dependent upon the works' containing religious figures or narratives.[18] Also linked to Borromeo's metaphysics was his appreciation of still lifes. After having described in *Pro suis studiis* how he contemplated landscape paintings, the Archbishop went on to mention his similar use of still-life paintings:

> [When I am in my study and] it is hot, flowers are pleasing to me, and some fruit on the tables. And I have enjoyed most of all having the fruits of spring, and the flowers of it, and still in the summer – according to the diversities of the weather – [I have enjoyed] having various vases in the room, and varying those according to opportunity, and according to my pleasure. Then when winter encumbers and restricts everything with ice, I have enjoyed from sight – and even imagined odor, if not real – artificial flowers ... expressed in painting ... and in these flowers I have wanted to see the variety of colors, not fleeting, as some of the flowers that are found [in nature], but stable and very endurable.[19]

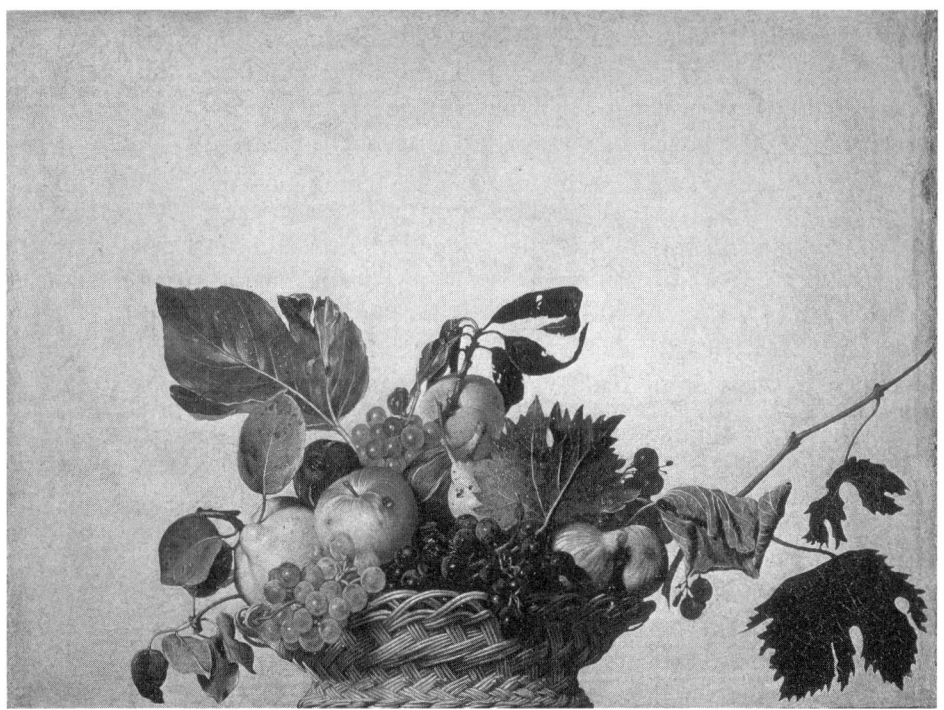

Figure 8.1 Michelangelo Merisi, called Caravaggio, *Basket of Fruit*, 1598. Oil on canvas. AKG-images / Nimatallah.

Because he regarded painted still lifes as acceptable substitutes when the real objects were unavailable, Borromeo suggested that in rendering their beauties, permanent paintings could even surpass actual created things. Thus, he regarded Brueghel's ability to reproduce the colors of created things with great accuracy as one of his highest achievements. Predictably enough, all but one of the paintings of this genre that Borromeo acquired were by his favorite Flemish artist. The great exception was Caravaggio's *Basket of Fruit* (figure 8.1).

Caravaggio's *Basket of Fruit*, which Borromeo probably commissioned directly from the artist in Rome sometime between 1595 and 1601, was perhaps the first still life to enter his collection. Borromeo must have been quite familiar with the artist's works in Rome, because Caravaggio's early patrons were his friends and colleagues. Although Francesco Maria Del Monte owned a now lost *Carafe* of unknown date by him, most of Caravaggio's still-life painting seems to have been limited to details within larger compositions.[20] The Ambrosian *Basket of Fruit* is his only surviving work of its kind.

The monumental basket, which projects over a ledge toward the viewer, contains fruits and leaves noteworthy for their detail and insistent physicality. In *Musaeum*, Borromeo praised the beauty and excellence of the work. He presumably appreciated the confrontational character of Caravaggio's still life,

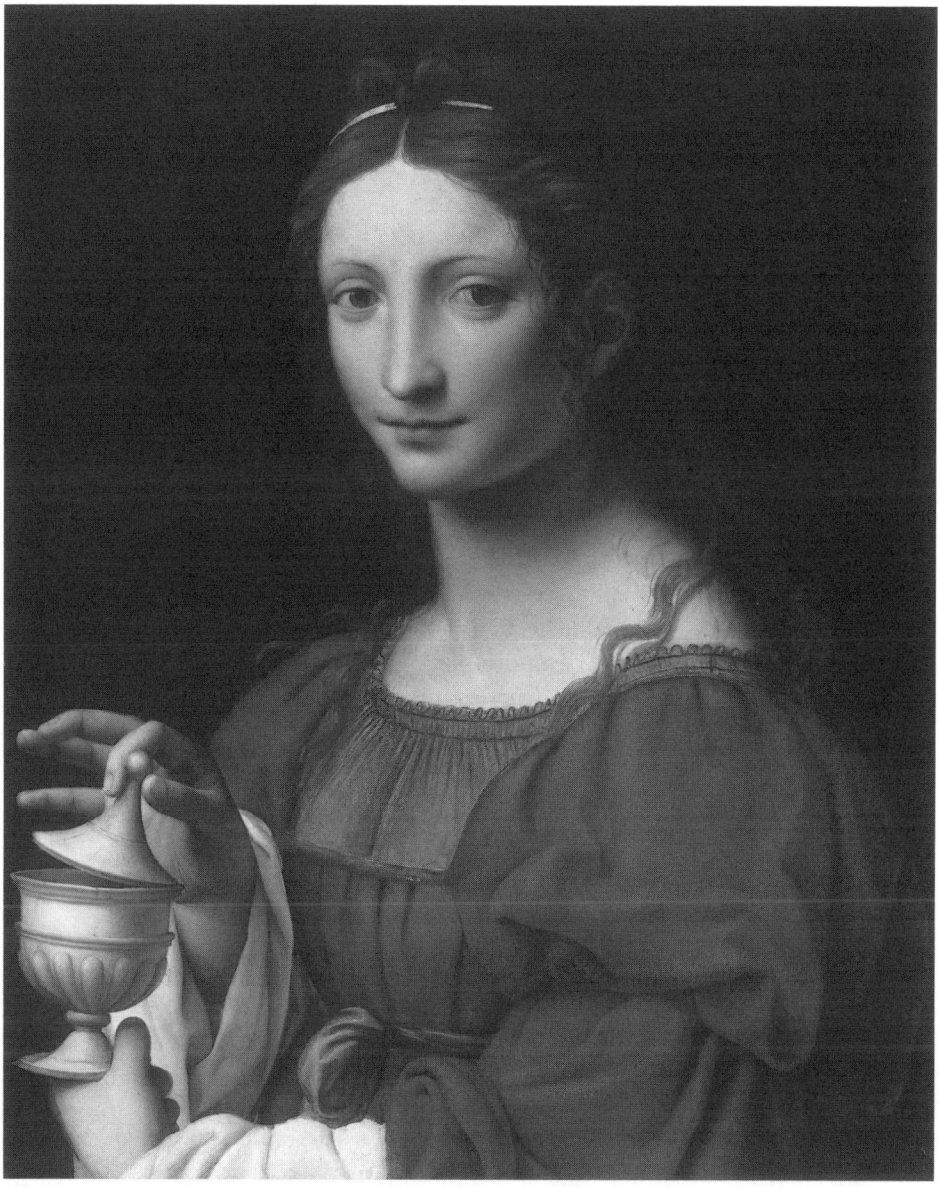

Figure 8.2 Bernardino Luini, *The Magdalene*, ca. 1525. Samuel H. Kress Collection, Image © 2005 Board of Trustees, National Gallery of Art, Washington.

because it was this feature of Luini's *Magdalene* (figure 8.2) – her direct gaze at the beholder – that he explicitly praised in *Musaeum*. Moreover in the *Basket of Fruit* as well as in several of his religious paintings of around 1595 to 1601, which Borromeo knew, Caravaggio followed the Lombard tradition of focusing on the subject itself by avoiding particularizing settings.[21] Caravaggio's vigorous still life, cut off from any context and lit independently from its pale, flat background, must have appealed to Borromeo as a discrete vision of meditational prayer. Moreover, Archbishop Federico presumably interpreted the worm-eaten fruit and desiccated leaves in the basket as allusions to the transitory character of God's earthly gifts.

Caravaggio left Rome in 1606, five years after Borromeo, and it was perhaps only in that year that Borromeo began to acquire more still-life paintings, all of them by Brueghel.[22] The largest and most ornate still life that Brueghel painted for Borromeo was the *Vase of Flowers with a Gem, Coins, and Shells* of 1606 (IA: 25). Despite the popularity of the genre in Flanders, it may have been the first flower piece that the thirty-six-year-old Brueghel had ever painted.[23] In a letter to Borromeo of April 14, 1606, the artist wrote: "I have begun and destined for Your Illustrious Lordship a bunch of flowers that is found to be very beautiful, as much for their naturalness as also for the beauty and rarity of the various flowers, [of which] a few are unknown and little seen in this area; for that [reason] I have been to Brussels in order to depict from nature some flowers that are not found in Antwerp."[24] In June, Brueghel wrote that he would paint the flowers life-size and that there would be over 100 varieties represented. A further remark that Brueghel made to Borromeo about this painting, although seemingly casual, is of utmost importance: "I believe that so rare and varied flowers never have been finished with similar diligence; in winter this painting will make a beautiful sight. A few of the colors are very close to nature. . . ."[25] It is evident that Borromeo believed that the great variety in nature – so magnificently depicted in the *Vase of Flowers* – reflected God's goodness. Brueghel's correspondence suggests that he realized how the Archbishop would use the flower painting (which seems to have been unsolicited rather than commissioned) and it is thus possible that Brueghel first began painting works of this genre as a response to Borromeo's own particular interest in nature.

Borromeo's appreciation of the variety and rarity of natural things is evident as well in his brief, undated notes entitled *Lista di varij fiori*, in which he catalogued twenty-five varieties of rare flowers that Grand Duke Ferdinando I de' Medici had in his gardens in Florence.[26] In Borromeo's era, an interest in unusual species of flowers was shared among many Italian aristocrats, who often exchanged images or even actual pieces of rare flowers.[27] Whether or not Borromeo ever planted rare flowers is unknown, but certainly he was an enthusiast. This is important, for it would be absurd to imply that he collected paintings of natural and manmade things exclusively as devotional or even didactic aids. Notwithstanding his profound concern for the roles of art in Christian society, Borromeo's writings also reveal his sheer enjoyment of visual beauty in both nature and art.

Borromeo's acknowledgment of the striking differences between the styles of Caravaggio and Brueghel is implicit in his statement in *Musaeum* about Caravaggio's *Basket of Fruit* (figure 8.1): "I would have liked to place another similar basket nearby, but no other having attained the beauty and incomparable excellence of this one, it remained alone." Although Borromeo highly valued Brueghel's two flower paintings, they themselves were displayed as pendants, and, as vertical works, perhaps were not ideally suited to hang beside Caravaggio's still life. Yet Borromeo, who could have commissioned from Brueghel a horizontal still life with a basket, can only have failed to do so precisely because of the incompatibility of the two virtuoso styles that he so admired.[28]

Borromeo must have recognized in Caravaggio's and Brueghel's styles two different ways of looking at the natural world. In the *Basket of Fruit*, Caravaggio presented a discrete view of created things just as Borromeo would have experienced them when looking at a real basket placed on a table in his study. Yet the inability to reach out and take hold of the incomparably tangible objects in Caravaggio's painting must have called to Borromeo's mind what he believed to be the ultimately specious reality of natural and artificial things. On the contrary, Brueghel's still lifes, as Borromeo knew well from the artist's correspondence, did not present discrete views of nature, for he depicted natural things from various different regions within single paintings. Brueghel emphasized the infinite numbers, varieties, and microscopic sizes of created things scattered throughout the world.

Borromeo's appreciation of Brueghel's panoramic or composite views of small created things seems to have been informed by his familiarity with religious writings and scientific discoveries. On the one hand, Borromeo, as made manifest in his devotional tracts, shared St. Augustine's tendency, evident in *The City of God*, to catalogue the praises of God's world. On the other hand, Borromeo was aware of the scientific discoveries in his own era of unimagined natural things so far away or so small that they had been invisible before the invention of the telescope and microscope.[29] Indeed, in *Pro suis studiis*, Borromeo recounted his pleasurable use of all sorts of optical devices, including prisms, mirrors, the camera obscura, and the telescope and microscope. Concerning the latter two, he wrote:

> [T]he telescope [*cannochiale*] . . . deserves esteem, because it has allowed us to see much better half the world which we did not see [before]; indeed it has discovered for us new worlds. . . . There are also those microscopes [*occhiali picoli*] which help one to see minute things, but in such great size that it is a marvelous thing. In [looking through] these I have enjoyed making the acquaintance of just as many very distinct, very small little animals as exist. . . . I have understood [from this experience] that little animals that are much smaller than an eye of a needle are of the very same species – even if they do not appear to be, they truly can be! – as the larger animals that are visible with the naked eye. All of which demonstrates the supreme Workmanship of nature, that is, that small things are not made with less industry and diligence and toil and care and artifice than the large. . . . And I speculate to myself [about] how many of the marvels of nature and of God still remain [to be discovered] . . . that are not known, and perhaps will never be known.[30]

161

Borromeo's discovery of these newly visible worlds, which could not be seen at once, but only in a fragmentary way, by repositioning and refocusing a telescope or by placing specimens one by one under the lenses of the compound microscope, inevitably must have reinforced the cataloguing inclination so closely linked with his love of God's world and of Brueghel's paintings. But his eye lingered at least as long on Caravaggio's *Basket of Fruit*, in which meticulous rendering of details and textures created an utterly different, bold effect. Thus, however differently we today assess the styles of Brueghel and Caravaggio (one as displaying Mannerist characteristics, the other Baroque), in Borromeo's opinion, each artist's style was natural, for Brueghel captured the physical appearance and metaphysical significance of nature broadly or in panorama, Caravaggio the same qualities of nature discretely or in tangible proximity. To Borromeo, nature seen from either vantage point was beautiful and joyous, and it attracted not merely his contemplative mind, but also his delighted eyes.

Notes

1 F. Borromeo, *I Tre piaceri della menta christiana* (Milan, 1625), throughout, esp. pp. 83–4, for attracting contemplative minds through sensory appeal. Also F. Borromeo, *I Tre libri della Laudi divine* (Milan, 1632), throughout. See the Introduction to P. M. Jones, *Federico Borromeo and the Ambrosiana: Art and Patronage in Seventeenth-Century Milan* (Cambridge: Cambridge University Press, 1993) for a definition of Christian optimism.

2 F. Borromeo, *Del Modo di dare gli esercitii a persone capaci*, Ambros. Ms. G25inf, no. 3, n.d., fols. 27r–8r; Ignatius's "Contemplation to Attain Love of God" (pp. 99–103) and "First Principle and Foundation" (p. 12) in St. Ignatius of Loyola, *The Spiritual Exercises of St. Ignatius*, ed. L. J. Puhl, S. J. (Chicago, 1951). Man's duty to glorify God is a theme of Ignatius's *Spiritual Exercises* and also had a role in Calvin's thought, on which see W. Bouwsma, *Venice and the Defense of Republican Liberty: Renaissance Values in the Age of the Counter Reformation* (Berkeley and Los Angeles, 1988), p. 107.

3 Borromeo's exercise on "The Glory of God" illustrates the impact of Pythagoreanism and Neo-Stoicism on his cosmology and of Augustinianism on his conception of the role of the human will and heart. See Jones, *Federico Borromeo*, Chap. 1, for discussion of these ideas in connection with Borromeo's *Le Laudi*, and for a bibliography.

4 For a related meditation, see Borromeo's "Vedere Dio Rilucere nelle cose creati," in F. Borromeo, *Il Mio viaggio spirituale, cioè modi per Caminare alla perfezzione christiana*, Ambros. Ms. A. 163 Sussidio, n.d., fols. 27–9.

5 See A. Valier, *Filippo, ossia dialogo della letizia christiana* [anon. transl. of *Philippus, sive de laetitia Christiana*, 1591] (Rome, 1817), pp. 27–30; for more detail see P. M. Jones, "Federico Borromeo as a Patron of Landscapes and Still Lifes: Christian Optimism in Italy ca. 1600," *Art Bulletin* 70 (1988), p. 270.

6 The Introduction to Catalogue I in Jones, *Federico Borromeo* outlines the chronology of Borromeo's acquisitions.

7   See L. Salerno, *I Pittori di paesaggio del Seicento a Roma*, bilingual ed. with Eng. transl. C. Whitfield and C. Enggass, 3 vols. (Rome, 1977–8), col. I, pp. 60–111, and, on patrons, pp. lx–lxii. The Carracci were painting landscapes in Bologna well before 1600, but in the 1690s, Flemish ones were more commonly available in Rome. The fact that after 1618, Borromeo collected works of art (such as casts of antique sculptures and copies of sixteenth-century frescoes in Rome) almost exclusively to fill lacunae in his museum's canon also partially accounts for his failure to commission landscapes from Italian painters. See Jones, *Federico Borromeo*, Chap. 3, on Borromeo's canon.

8   For Brueghel's sources, see the entries in Jones, *Federico Borromeo*, Catalogue IA; also Jones, "Federico Borromeo as a Patron," pp. 263–5. On Bril's less creative use of the same engraved series, see P. M. Jones, "Two Newly-Discovered Hermit Landscapes by Paul Bril," *Burlington Magazine* 130 (1988), pp. 32–4.

9   Borromeo, *Le Piaceri*, pp. 117–20. Borromeo was referring to the Garden of Eden, where humankind first lived.

10 See citations throughout the texts. Also A. Martini, "*I Tre Libri delle laudi divine*" *di Federico Borromeo, Ricerca Storica-Stilistica* (Padua, 1975), esp. pp. 28, 194–5.

11 L. B. Alberti, *L'Architettura* (*De Re Aedificatoria*), ed. and trans. G. Orlandi (Milan, 1966), vol. I, pp. 804–6. Alberti, in turn, depended upon Vitruvius. See discussion in E. Gombrich, "The Renaissance Theory of Art and the Rise of Landscape," in *Norm and Form: Studies in the Art of the Renaissance I* (London and New York, 1978), pp. 107–21. Gombrich's important study is a good example of the classicist bias in art-historical inquiry concerning the sixteenth and seventeenth centuries in Italy.

12 Borromeo, *Le Laudi*, pp. 15–16. This belief in harmony established through antitheses is Augustinian. See P. Schaff, ed., *St. Augustine's City of God. Vol. II, a Select Library of the Nicene and Post-Nicene Fathers of the Christian Church* (Grand Rapids, MI, 1956), pp. 214–15; J. P. Migne, ed., *Patrologia Latina* (Paris, 1844–64), vol. 41, col. 332.

13 Borromeo, *Musaeum Bibliothecae Ambrosianae* (Milan, 1625), p. 16.

14 Ibid., p. 17.

15 Borromeo, *Le Laudi*, p. 144.

16 Borromeo, *Le Piaceri* and *Le Laudi*, throughout; Martini, "*I Tre Libri*," pp. 26–30.

17 According to Borromeo, even Bril – whose tendency to repeat motives in paintings for him Borromeo criticized in *Musaeum* (pp. 23–4) – had difficulty in competing with Brueghel in this respect. Borromeo did greatly appreciate the most Italianate of his pictures by Bril, the *Seascape* of 1611 (Jones, *Federico Borromeo*, Cat. IA: 24): this was due to its spaciousness. Yet even it was more detailed than most Italian paintings of that date.

18 In *Musaeum*, Borromeo did not mention the Christian subject matter in Brueghel's *Four Elements* series, for example.

19 Borromeo, *Pro suis studiis*, Ambros. Ms. G130inf, no. 8, 1628, fols. 254v–5r. Later in the same passage, Borromeo added that he also appreciated still lifes rendered in silk threads.

20 For Caravaggio as a painter of still lifes, see H. Hibbard, *Caravaggio* (New York, 1983), pp. 80–5 and cat. no. 75 on pp. 262–5; L. Salerno, *La Natura Morta italiana 1560–1805*, bilingual ed. with Eng. transl. R. E. Wolf (Rome, 1984, pp. 46–50); *The Age of Caravaggio* (1985, pp. 206–11). On the development of Italian

still-life painting, see Salerno (1984) and also J. T. Spike, *Italian Still Life Painting from Three Centuries*, exhibition catalogue (New York, 1983).

    The *Carafe* is listed in Del Monte's inventory of 1627: C. Frommel, "Caravaggios Frühwerk und der Kardinal Francesco Maria Del Monte," *Storia dell'Arte*, 9/10 (1971), pp. 5–52, p. 31.

21   Relevant religious pictures of the time by Caravaggio include *The Repentant Magdalene, St. Catherine of Alexandria, Judith Beheading Holofernes*, and the London *Supper at Emmaus*. For illustrations, see literature cited in n. 20 above. For Caravaggio's North Italian predecessors, see *The Age of Caravaggio*, exhibition catalogue (New York, 1985), pp. 49–88.

22   Caravaggio left Rome in 1606. See bibliography cited in Jones, *Federico Borromeo*, Cat. IA: 42 and in *The Age of Caravaggio* for details on Caravaggio's whereabouts. Brueghel's *Mouse and a Rose* (ibid., Cat. IA: 33) might have entered Borromeo's collection in 1596; precisely when Caravaggio's *Basket of Fruit* entered his collection is indeterminable.

23   For the development of Brueghel's flower paintings, see K. Ertz, *Jan Brueghel der Ältere (1568–1625), Die Gemälde mit Kritischer Oeuvre-katalog* (Cologne, 1979), pp. 252–325; M.-L. Hairs, "A propos d'un tableautin attribué à Georges Hoefnagel," *Bulletin des Musées Royaux des Beaux-Arts de Belgique* 14 (1985), pp. 37, 47, 52.

24   Crivelli's groundbreaking publication of the correspondence is indispensable; see G. Crivelli, *Giovanni Brueghel, pittore fiammingo, ò sue lettere e quadretti esistenti presso l'Ambrosiana* (Milan, 1868), p. 63.

25   Ibid. (pp. 74–5). The letter is dated August 25, 1606.

26   The *Lista* bears the heading "Cipolle di pice sorti et fiori non pice veduti havuti da Gicopo Giardinieri del Gran Duca." The flowers are recorded as having come from France, Flanders, and Constantinople.

    C. Coope, "Federico Borromeo's *Musaeum*," M. A. thesis, Courtauld Institute of Art, 1977, p. 29. Called F. Borromeo, *Lista di varij fiori*, Ambros. Ms. G310inf: 28, n.d. a book, but it is simply a little list.

27   G. Masson, "Italian Flower Collectors' Gardens," in D. Coffin, ed., *The Italian Garden* (Washington, DC, 1972), pp. 63–80. What, if any, use Borromeo made of this list is unknown.

28   In 1617, Brueghel painted such a work (but not for Borromeo): *Basket and a Glass of Flowers*. See Ertz, *Jan Brueghel*, cat. no. 322 and fig. 371. Ertz listed the painting as in De Boer's gallery, Amsterdam.

29   See P. Schaff, ed., *St. Augustine's City of God. Vol. II, A Select Library of the Nicene and Post-Nicene Fathers of the Christian Church* (Grand Rapids, MI, 1956), Bk. 22, pp. 479–511; J. P. Migne, ed., *Patrologia Latina*, 221 vols. (Paris, 1844–64), vol. 41, cols. 751–804.

    Without more comparative studies, it would be premature to try to evaluate conclusively Borromeo's interest in the telescope and microscope in light of Alpers's assessment of the fundamental differences between Dutch "descriptive" and Italian "literary" art. But it is undeniable – as Elizabeth Cropper and Charles Demsey noted – that in the seventeenth century, Italians shared Dutchmen's interest in optical devices and close attention to observation of nature. Borromeo knew *both* Northerners and Italians interested in astronomy, and he collected mainly Flemish but also Italian art that reflected concern with the details of nature. The phenomenon seems to have been pan-European. Nevertheless, it was mainly his works by

Flemings that seem most closely related to Borromeo's cataloguing and observationist tendencies.

See S. Alpers, *The Art of Describing: Dutch Art in the Seventeenth Century* (Chicago, 1983); E. Cropper and C. Dempsey, "The State of Research in Italian 17th-Century Painting," *Art Bulletin*, 69 (1987), pp. 494–509, p. 507.

30   Borromeo, *Pro suis studiis*, fols. 256r–8v.

Borromeo corresponded with Galileo about astronomy from at least 1613 until 1627. The Jesuit Bonaventura Cavalieri told Galileo that Borromeo did not understand the telescope, for to him the stars seemed smaller with it than without it. Galileo wrote to Borromeo that rather than trying to explain its use in a letter, he would visit Borromeo to demonstrate it.

There is no evidence that Borromeo espoused the ideas that placed Galileo in trouble with the Church.

On the correspondence, see A. Favaro, "Federico Borromeo e Galileo Galilei," in *Miscellanea Ceriani. Raccolta di Scritti per onorare la memoria di Monsignor Antonio Maria Ceriani*, ed A. Ratti (Milan, 1910), pp. 308–28.

It is unknown precisely how Borromeo became aware of the microscope, but he had many contacts with scientists and scholars interested in it, including Galileo, Cristoforo Scheiner, Marcus Welser (who sent Borromeo Scheiner's *Tres epistolae de maculis solaribus* in 1612), and Johann Faber (all discussed by Favaro).

Borromeo's passage is close in spirit to that in Constantijn Huygen's autobiography, which Alpers (1983), quoted on p. 9. Huygens lived from 1596–1687.

Part III
Figures and Bodies

Introduction

That central Italian patrons and artists alike were, by the late sixteenth century, interested not only in incorporating landscape and still-life elements in their paintings, but also in making those elements a central pictorial subject, marks a dramatic departure from the principles that guided Italian art just a few decades before. The words placed in the mouth of Michelangelo in a dialogue written by Francisco de Hollanda at mid-century, to the effect that the depiction of landscapes was fine for northern painters, and for those who would appeal to women, but not for Italian men with *disegno* – these words may not really have been Michelangelo's own, but anyone looking at his painting could conclude that his own views were not far different.

It is not so surprising that sixteenth-century sculptors, particularly those who worked in the round, should so religiously have taken the body, specific or generic, nude or draped, as their central subject. What seems more remarkable is that the same is true for painters, for other craftsmen, and, occasionally, even for architects. In the previous century, the writer Leon Battista Alberti had famously formulated the notion of the pictorial *istoria*, a format keyed to the human figure. The Quattrocento also saw the popularization of the "Vitruvian man" as a gloss on ancient architectural theory; thereafter, any architect who could read would have added impetus, should any have been needed, to think about buildings in corporeal terms. By the sixteenth century, bodies came to be basic constituents of ornamental composition, and anatomy to play a central role in academic training. An artist like Michelangelo might seem to reject the path Leonardo blazed, devoting little attention to the pictorial environments his characters occupied, but in doing so, he was only suppressing distractions from the bodies that were *already* foregrounded in his rival's paintings.

This part, consequently, juxtaposes approaches to figuration in sixteenth-century art. The first essay, a short piece by Elizabeth Cropper, brings out the increasingly complex relationship that developed between the strongly figural mural painting of the period, and a pictorial genre in which the figure was a

169

sine qua non: portraiture. If we are to think of the art of Pontormo and his pupil Bronzino as a strikingly anthropocentric one, we should, to follow Cropper, attend to the way the artists built up compositions large and small, isolating, arranging, and rearranging single figures. In the two artists' paintings, figures are repeated, sometimes in reverse, in a way that suggests the reuse of drawings. In portraits, too, a particularly powerful figural invention could serve as a template for subsequent works, even when the sitters came from notably different cultural milieus. Recognizing these templates, Cropper demonstrates, allows one to evaluate the continuities within the workshop. They allow one to discern the standard forms that the painters associated with masculine elegance, apart from the attributes that individualized persons and pictures, linking them to a specific place and moment.

Nancy Vickers's essay, "The Mistress in the Masterpiece," is equally concerned with workshop practice, this time a sculptor's workshop. What Vickers highlights, however, is the importance of the model, and of the creative scene in which an unclothed assistant poses, or is posed, for the piece that results. Keying her discussion to the *Nymph of Fontainebleau*, a large bronze relief that Benvenuto Cellini made during a sojourn in France, Vickers focuses on the fact that the same artist's autobiography later treats that work as a visual record of the abusive relationship he had had with the woman who had modeled for the work. Compelling an economic dependent both to submit to sexual degradation and to maintain painful physical postures for the benefit of the master's art, Vickers argues, entwines the artist in a series of rivalries both at the court and within the studio. If Cropper would have us look for the formal dependence of one design on another, Vickers would ultimately have us attempt to excavate the artist's model, and the workshop environment generally, from paintings or sculptures that leave them only partially visible.

Leo Steinberg gives us yet a third way of thinking about the bodies in a composition: not in terms of the templates that structure sequences of design, nor in terms of poses that record the scene of the artwork's making, but rather as corporeal *motifs*, in this case a motif Steinberg terms the "slung leg." Framing Michelangelo's Florence *Pietà* within a history in which the overriding connotations of the slung leg gradually shifted from the heroic to the erotic, Steinberg suggests how the search for a metaphoric visual language that might simultaneously convey the nobility of the Christocentric subject and the intimate bond between Christ and his mother brought Michelangelo to, and then beyond, the threshold of the vulgar. Steinberg's provocative essay demonstrates the attraction profane imagery held for artists seeking to push sacred subjects to increasingly expressive ends; it also shows how certain configurations of the nude, the sign par excellence of the high style, could become not only controversial to more conservative religious critics, but even distasteful to artists themselves.

The final piece in the section, Alina Payne's "Reclining Bodies," tackles the use of bodies as ornaments, now with special attention to the theory and practice of architecture. Payne's essay poses a series of related questions about the role of the "figure" in Cinquecento decoration – why, for example, sixteenth-century writings on architecture give such minimal attention to the figural sculptures that prominently decorated many buildings, and why, given the absence of this literary record, those sculptures seemed so necessary to the builders. Payne's discussion, which leads her through a consideration of the reception of Vitruvius, of the relation of Cinquecento architectural theory to poetics and rhetoric, and of the blurring of boundaries between architecture and its sister arts, illuminates the place of anthropomorphism in Cinquecento architecture more broadly.

9

Preparing to Finish: Portraits by Pontormo and Bronzino around 1530

Elizabeth Cropper

Vasari writes, in a statement that has become a commonplace, that Bronzino, having studied with Jacopo Pontormo for many years, adopted his master's manner to such an extent, and imitated his works in such a way that for a while the works of the one were mistaken for those of the other.[1] Such confusion was all the more remarkable, according to Vasari, because Pontormo behaved strangely towards even his favorite students, not letting anyone see his work until it was completely finished. Bronzino's patience and his affection for Pontormo allowed him to penetrate this obsessive secrecy, so that he became not only a true disciple, but also like a son to his reclusive master. Nonetheless, still following Vasari's account, Pontormo's manner of teaching even his favorite pupil was unusual. Although he let Bronzino watch him paint, Pontormo neither allowed his *giovani* to touch what he was doing, nor did he help them in their work. Vasari's account has not gone unchallenged, and we now have a much clearer sense of how Pontormo helped Bronzino in particular by providing drawings at the early stages of preparation.[2] But, unlike artists who trained the *giovani* in their shop more conventionally by letting them participate in the preparation of larger projects in small ways, Pontormo does seem to have expected Bronzino to learn from executing a whole piece of work from beginning to end. Vasari records how the pupil first painted two lunettes above the door of the cloister at the Certosa at Galluzzo, one a *Dead Christ with Angels* in fresco, and the other a *Martyrdom of St. Lawrence* in oil.[3] Although he had watched Pontormo paint the frescoes in the cloister at close hand, Bronzino had no previous experience with the use of oil for this purpose. In a similarly independent way, and at Pontormo's bidding, Bronzino painted at least one of the Evangelists in the *tondi* of the Capponi Chapel, «tutto da sé», as Vasari puts it.[4] Two unusual and potentially conflicting aspects of Pontormo's, and thus Bronzino's working procedures emerge when the material evidence is considered together with Vasari's account. One is that a concern for a high degree of finish is combined with a determination that the work should not be seen until it acquires that degree of finish, or is «finished». A second practice, especially characteristic of Bronzino, involves making quite striking compositional changes, sometimes even after a work has been brought to a high level of completion. Recent technical analysis of the *Allegory* in the National Gallery, London, confirms this, but significant changes have long been noted in such works as Bronzino's *Portrait of a Young Man* in the Metropolitan Museum, New York, and the *Portrait of a Young Woman with her Little Boy* in the National Gallery of Art, Washington.[5] Closely related to both of these unusual practices is the process by which Pontormo and Bronzino built up their compositions. In Pontormo's case we have a large number of drawings from the nude model. The pose is often extraordinarily original, but the contours of these chalk drawings, however loaded with *sfumato*, are closed; where several figures are juxtaposed, each is conceived as a separate body, not as part of a dynamic composition.[6] Pontormo also made highly finished drawings for compositions, and among those surviving are studies for the figures of Mary and the Angel for the Capponi *Annunciation* fresco, for the Poggio a Caiano lunette, and for the Pinadori *Visitation*. Some drawings from the model are for individual figures in compositions, such as that for the young man at the upper right of the Capponi *Deposition*. Very few drawings by Bronzino exist by comparison, but what we know of them suggests a similar approach: Bronzino made careful studies of single figures that could be rearranged entirely quite late in the finishing of the work.

The isolation of single figures, their juxtaposition, and even replacement through insertion, is then typical of both Pontormo's and Bronzino's working procedure.[7] Such a way of working does not follow Quattrocento practice, nor does it involve the sort of compositional drawing that Leonardo invented, in which whole compositional ideas are worked out freely on paper before more detailed studies are made.[8] In the Certosa frescoes, where complex compositions were called for, Pontormo elected to deploy superimposed layers of figures in a compositional mode derived from Dürer, rather than adopt the dramatic spaces and integrated compositional devices Leonardo and Raphael had established.[9] Pontormo's insertion of single figures into a composition, almost as cut-outs or appliqués, may be explained in part by his early experience with fresco painting, where the use of cartoons for single figures was standard practice. In Pontormo's lunette at Poggio a Caiano, to turn to the most conspicuous example, the traditional device of the inversion and repetition of cartoons for individual figures is raised to a principle of design: elegant *contrapposto* and rhythmic variety signify a level of sophisticated *disinvoltura* that deconstructs narrative.[10] Yet Pontormo did not limit this practice to fresco: the contrapuntal arrangement of figures in the Pinadori *Visitation*, for example, evokes a recognition of such patterning just as self-consciously. That Pontormo was working in this way around 1529/30, when Bronzino was closest to him, helps to explain the relationship between two of Bronzino's most remarkable early portraits – the *Portrait of a*

Youth in the Metropolitan Museum, New York, and the *Portrait of Guidobaldo della Rovere* in Palazzo Pitti, Florence – and Pontormo's own extraordinary *Portrait of a Halberdier* (*Francesco Guardi*), now in the J. Paul Getty Museum, Los Angeles.[11] Understanding that this relationship may involve the use of some kind of a template also has implications for the chronology of these works. Of the three portraits in question only the portrait of Guidobaldo della Rovere can be dated securely. The inscription indicates that the sitter is eighteen years old, and the portrait must therefore have been painted by Bronzino in Urbino or Pesaro some time between 2 April 1531 and 2 April 1532.[12] The *Portrait of a Young Man* in New York, on the other hand, has been assigned widely varying dates. The X-ray evidence makes it indisputable, however, that the portrait was painted in two campaigns (and some of the changes are even visible to the naked eye). The first version, with its simpler architectural background and less mask-like face, is usually placed before 1535. Smyth proposed a beginning date in the late 1520s, close to the *Halberdier*, whereas Cox-Rearick argued that the portrait could not have been started before Bronzino left for Pesaro in 1530, and that it was finished closer to 1540, presumably in Florence.[13] Smyth, on the other hand, proposed that the portrait, begun in Florence, was reworked when Bronzino went to Pesaro. To explain how such a reworking was possible he suggested that this is a self-portrait, but the idea has not met with general acceptance and the sitter remains unknown. Moreover, the Urbino connection, which even led to the illustration of the portrait on the cover of a modern English translation of *The Book of the Courtier*, no longer holds water.[14]

In 1989, in the catalogue for the sale of Pontormo's *Halberdier*, Cox-Rearick dated the Metropolitan portrait to 1540–1545, dropping her original support for the idea that it could have been started earlier in the 1530s.[15] This followed her determination that the *Halberdier* is a portrait of Cosimo 1 and could not, therefore, date earlier than 1537 when the sitter was eighteen. She still saw a connection between the two portraits of young men, but now redated both. Obviously such a redating of the *Halberdier* to 1537 would have important consequences for the chronology of Bronzino's portraiture as a whole, not to mention Pontormo's. In my recent study of Pontormo's *Halberdier*, I argued instead that the evidence of costume, identity, chronology and provenance all confirmed the traditional dating of the work to the late 1520s, and that the sitter was Francesco Guardi, a young supporter of the Florentine republic, who was born in 1514.

Comparison of the three portraits in question leads to the conclusion that the extraordinarily close relationship among them goes well beyond superficial appearance (splendidly dressed young men, looking directly outwards, and so on). A photograph, taken in 1970, showing the *Halberdier* hanging beside the Bronzino *Portrait of a Young Man* in the Metropolitan Museum (fig. 9.1), documents the intuitions of Smyth and others about the similarities between the two.[16] The panels were almost exactly the same size (92 × 72 cm, for the *Halberdier*, and 95.5 × 74.9 cm, for the *Portrait of a Young Man*), which led

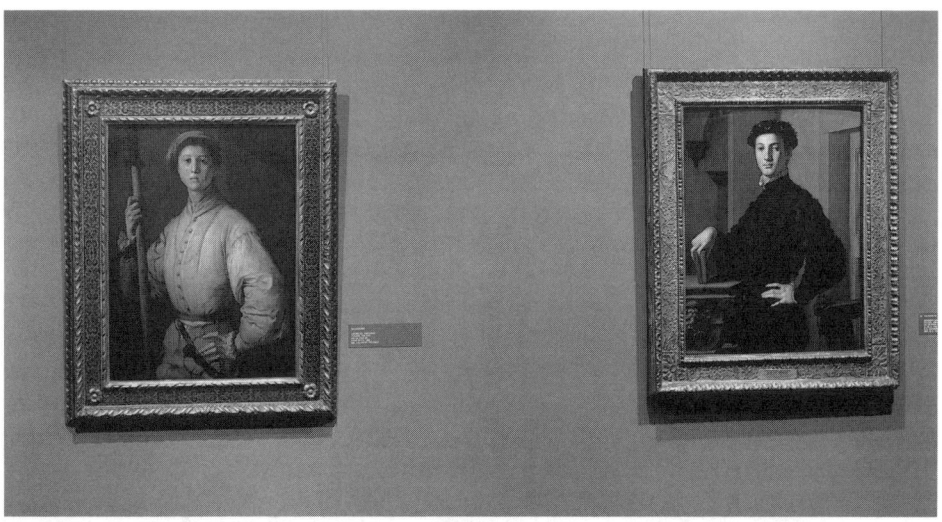

Figure 9.1 Gallery view of Pontormo, *Halberdier*, and Bronzino, *Portrait of a Young Man* (29.100.16) hanging next to each other, 1970. The Metropolitan Museum of Art. Photograph, all rights reserved, The Metropolitan Museum of Art.

Smyth to suggest that they may even have been acquired in the same way and at the same time.[17] The identical presentation of the figures within that format, however, provides the true link: panels of the same size would look very different if painted with figures of different scales and poses. When a tracing of the main outlines of Pontormo's figure is laid over an illuminated X-ray of Bronzino's young man, the results are impressive.[18] The contours of the head, neck, shoulders and upper arms of Bronzino's youth follow those of Pontormo's figure closely, though not exactly (the proper right cheek and jaw, for example, in Bronzino's portrait cut a narrower silhouette). More surprising is the congruence between the contours of the head, face, and central line of the chest of Bronzino's *Portrait of Guidobaldo della Rovere* and those of the *Halberdier*. The figures look very different, and the more vertical format makes the comparison harder to see (the panel measures 114 × 86 cm), but when the tracing of Pontormo's figure is superimposed on an illuminated, full-size X-ray of Bronzino's portrait the relationship again becomes clear (fig. 9.2).[19]

Bronzino did not adopt a format provided by his teacher because of any lack of experience on his part. Vasari reports that the artist had painted many portraits before going to Pesaro, and Cecchi's recent identification of the sitter in the Castello Sforzesco portrait (98 × 73 cm) as Lorenzo Lenzi means that the latter, at least, might date before that visit.[20] Moreover, this would not be a unique instance of Bronzino following a design by his teacher around this time. In the *Pygmalion and Galatea*, for example, painted either soon before the Pesaro trip or very soon thereafter as a cover for Pontormo's portrait of Francesco

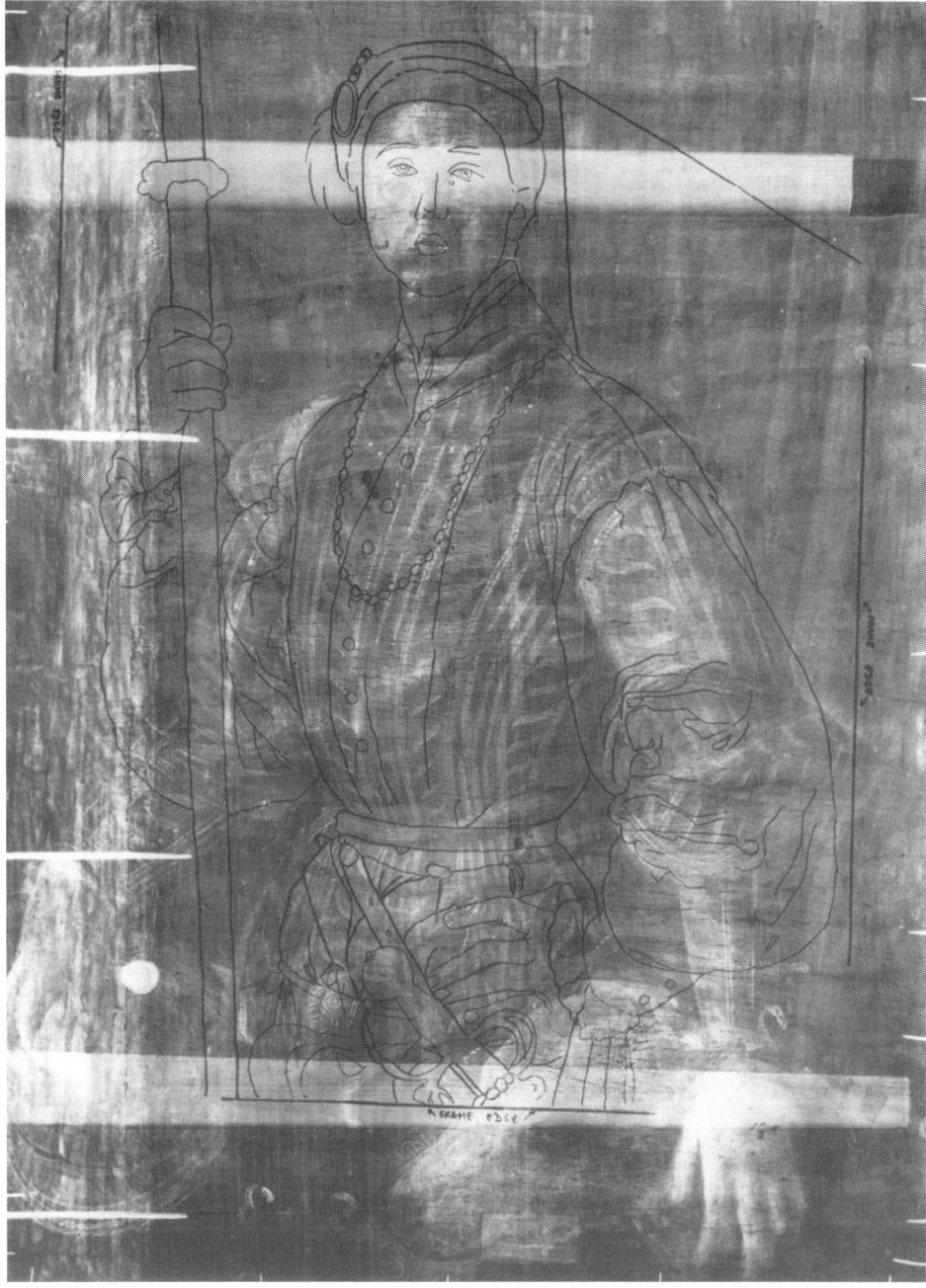

Figure 9.2 X-ray photograph of Bronzino, *Portrait of Guidobaldo della Rovere*, with mylar overlay tracing of Pontormo, *Halberdier*, tracing of head. Photo courtesy of Elizabeth Cropper.

Guardi, Bronzino reutilized drawings by Pontormo for the two main figures.[21] That he chose to repeat Pontormo's format for these two portraits suggests instead that there was something strikingly original about the *Halberdier*.

After Bronzino returned from Pesaro he quickly engaged in an intense analysis of Michelangelo's statue of Giuliano de' Medici for the Medici Chapel in San Lorenzo. With his search for a critical definition of a Florentine style came a parallel study of Michelangelo's architecture.[22] In the Uffizi *Young Man with a Lute*, the pose is close to that of the Giuliano figure. The architecture, on the other hand, including the high-backed wooden *lettuccio* behind the as yet unidentified lyric poet, remains simple; the *pietra serena* door frame, and the molding at the top of the seat link this interior to the first version of the Metropolitan portrait, with its simple door and similar molding. In the *Portrait of Ugolino Martelli* the Giuliano figure is reversed, but instantly recognizable nonetheless. Architecture plays a more significant role here, for the elaborate *pietra serena* articulation bespeaks a Florentine style in a more precise way; the scrolling consol under the window to the right, a clear reference to the *finestre inginocchiate* of neighboring Palazzo Medici, just as instantly identifies Michelangelo as master of this style. Less complex, but now closer to the setting of the Martelli portrait, is the architectural background in the final version of the *Portrait of a Young Man* in New York.[23] Even in the Martelli portrait, however, the juxtaposition of the head of the sitter to the projecting corner of the building behind him is an echo of the *Halberdier*. This echo persists in the most complex of the group, the *Portrait of Bartolomeo Panciatichi*, in which the torsion of the Giuliano figure is abandoned and the figure again faces us directly, even as the architecture becomes more imaginatively Michelangelesque.

The closeness of their main contours brings the relationship between the *Halberdier* and the *Portrait of a Youth* into much sharper focus. Bronzino's simpler, first version of the portrait derives more directly from Pontormo's image; in the second phase, perhaps close to the execution of the *Young Man with a Lute*, Bronzino seems to have decided to bring the portrait up-to-date, to conform with his own meditations on Michelangelo's work in San Lorenzo as a source for a new style that could signify Florentine values after the imperial imposition of Medici rule. This sequence makes it even less likely that Bronzino would have initiated the *Portrait of a Youth* following Pontormo's example if the *Halberdier* had been painted only in 1537. By then the model of Pontormo had been overlaid by that of Michelangelo. And the relationship between Pontormo's invention and the basic outlines of Bronzino's firmly datable *Portrait of Guidobaldo della Rovere*, brings more conclusive support to this position. In Urbino Bronzino was indeed, as Smyth and others have noted, experimenting with the chiaroscuro of north Italian painting, vying with Titian and Dosso; but the evidence of the common format makes it easier to understand why the portrait of Guidobaldo was at one time attributed to Pontormo.[24]

A vast social and political distance separated the heir to the Duchy of Urbino (and regent at the time of the portrait) from Francesco Guardi, the young man painted by Pontormo in defense of his republic against the army of Charles V. We do not know the name of Bronzino's other sitter.[25] His palace, especially in the second version, establishes that he is a Florentine; but, in contrast to Guardi's bright republican colors and steady gaze, the black silks of this young man are appropriate for a civic world of courtly elegance. The grotesque ornaments of his furniture, his book cracked open but with its spine turned away, suggest simultaneously self-presentation and ironic concealment. Yet, however different the station, age, and outlook of these three young men, each of their portraits (all painted, I believe, within a three or four year period) is an exploration of a new kind of manhood that had to negotiate the values of the city, of the court and of the battlefield; each image is nothing less than a transformation of human relations.[26] Bronzino, trained to think in terms of models for single figures rather than the analysis of groups of figures in space, began both of his portraits with a form, to which he added the attributes that made a man powerful and elegant, with arms dominating in the one, letters in the other. Underlying all three, however, is the same virtuous *civiltà* that Pontormo established in his model, through the juxtaposition of the curve of a cheek and neck, the slope of neck, shoulder and arm, the turn of the body, and the strong curving line running from chin to waist. This is an anatomy of beauty and grace as precise as any contemporary anatomy of the female form.[27]

Vasari considered Bronzino's portraits to be most natural, to have been made with «incredible diligence» and to have been finished in such a way that they left nothing to be desired. The photographs presented here provide some new evidence concerning Bronzino's preparatory steps towards those astonishing finishes. The beginnings of Bronzino's portraits around 1530 were remarkably singular in their adoption of Pontormo's model.

Notes

1 G. Vasari, *Le Vite de' più eccellenti pittori, scultori et architettori*, ed. G. Milanesi, vol. VII, Firenze 1906, pp. 593–594. See also C. H. Smyth, «The Earliest Works of Bronzino», in: *The Art Bulletin*, XXXI, 1949, pp. 184–210, esp. Appendix 1, «Bronzino's Apprenticeship to Pontormo», pp. 207–210. Citations of the standard literature on Pontormo and Bronzino will be kept to a minimum here.

2 Countering Vasari's statement, Smyth, 1949 (as in n. 1), p. 199, for example, argues that Pontormo reworked the head of St. John in Bronzino's *Holy Family* in Washington. Most recently, Elizabeth Pilliod has undertaken a close examination of the early relations between the two painters. See her ground-breaking «Pontormo and Bronzino at the Certosa», in: *The J. Paul Getty Museum Journal*, XX, 1992, pp. 77–86, and «The Earliest Collaborations of Pontormo and Bronzino: The Certosa, the Capponi Chapel, and the *Dead Christ with the Virgin and Magdalen*», in: *The Craft of Art: Originality and Industry in the Italian Renaissance and Baroque Workshop*, ed. by A. W. Ladis and C. Wood, Athens, Ga., and London 1995, pp. 134–164. In the latter (pp. 153–156) she proposes, with great insight,

that the *Study of Two Pairs of Legs and a Hand* in the Uffizi is by Pontormo and that it was then utilized by Bronzino in his *Pietà* for S. Trinita.

3   Vasari, ed. Milanesi, 1906 (as in n. 1), vol. VII, p. 594. Pilliod, 1995 (as in n. 2), pp. 138–141, also presents important new evidence for Pontormo's having produced drawings for Bronzino at the Certosa. In which case, as she suggests, Bronzino seems to have been on his own only from that point on, adapting these studies to the format and executing the colors.

4   Vasari, ed. Milanesi, 1906 (as in n. 1), vol. VII, pp. 270–271. In the *Life of Bronzino* (p. 594), in a famous inconsistency, Vasari states that Bronzino painted two Evangelists and colored some of the vault. For the consensus that he painted the *Saint Mark* and the *Saint Luke*, see: Pilliod, 1992 (as in n. 2), p. 148, and p. 163, n. 44. Pilliod (p. 150) also establishes that Bronzino's *St. Luke* is derived from a reversal of the general contours of a *Study of a Patriarch* by Pontormo. This is just the kind of practice my current proposal also implies.

5   For the London picture, see: C. Plazzotta & L. Keith, «Bronzino's *Allegory*: New Evidence of the Artist's Revisions», in: *The Burlington Magazine*, CXLI, 1999, pp. 89–99. On the Metropolitan portrait, see: A. Burroughs, «Bronzino x-Rayed», in: *Creative Art*, VII, 1930, pp. 222–224, and idem, *Art Criticism from a Laboratory*, Boston 1938, pp. 89–92. For the Washington portrait, see: J. Cox-Rearick, «Bronzino's *Young Woman with Her Little Boy*», in: *Studies in the History of Art*, XII, National Gallery of Art Washington, 1982, pp. 67–79.

6   The best discussion remains J. Cox-Rearick, *The Drawings of Pontormo*, 2 vols., Cambridge, Mass., 1964. See esp. vol. 1, pp. 3–94, for her illuminating Introduction, in which Pontormo's drawings are categorized in relation to his unusual compositional practices.

7   See Smyth, 1949 (as in n. 1), p. 206, on Bronzino's «additive practice», his «piece-by-piece juxtaposition» in the London *Allegory*, «as if the outcome were the result of the skillful insertion and final adjustment of the separate parts, rather than of organic growth». The new technical evidence supports this view.

8   See Cox-Rearick, 1964 (as in n. 6), vol. 1, pp. 17–22, for further discussion.

9   Smyth, 1949 (as in n. 1), p. 204, considers the impact of the fact that «Bronzino had been deprived as a youth of the artistic benefits of his own century and faced Pontormo's innovations without grounding in the fluent idiom of the full Cinquecento, which Pontormo's flights presupposed».

10   Cox-Rearick, 1964 (as in n. 6), vol. 1, pp. 44–45, identifies this moment with the appearance of a new way of preparing compositions in which the whole is equated with the sum of individual parts. Cox-Rearick also sees that this involved an embrace of personal style and a rupture with what she calls «the classical dialectic system». See further (p. 46) on Pontormo's «erratic and unpredictable manner of preparing for a painting». The corollary of this is that Pontormo could not teach in the familiar way.

11   For a preliminary suggestion of this relationship, see: E. Cropper, *Portrait of a Halberdier* (Getty Museum Studies on Art), Los Angeles 1997, pp. 100–106. Bronzino was, of course, already an independent painter at this moment. The firm dating of the *Pietà* to 1529, together with Pilliod's observation concerning Bronzino's use of a drawing by Pontormo for the legs of Christ in that work (see n. 2 above) is significant here. See L. A. Waldman, «Bronzino's Uffizi *Pietà* and the Cambi Chapel in S. Trinita, Florence», in: *The Burlington Magazine*, CXXXIX, 1997, pp. 94–102.

12 C. H. Smyth, *Bronzino Studies*, Ph.D.diss., Princeton University, 1955, pp. 130–135, following C. Justi's identification of the portrait as Guidobaldo in: «Die Bildnisse des Kardinals Hippolyt von Medici in Florenz», in: *Zeitschrift für Bildende Kunst*, VIII, 1897, pp. 34–40.

13 Cox-Rearick, 1982 (as in n. 5), pp. 67–70, where it is also proposed that the identity of the sitter may have changed between the two versions.

14 The persistent belief that the portrait has some connection with Urbino is based on two errors. One is the inscription on the engraving included in the *Choix de gravures [. . .] d'après les peintures [. . .] de la galerie de Lucien Bonaparte*, which identifies it as «A Duke of Urbino by Sebastiano del Piombo». The second, less widely recognized, is the identification of the engraver as Prospero Fontana. See F. Zeri & E. Gardner, *Italian Paintings. A Catalogue of the Collection of The Metropolitan Museum of Art: Florentine School*, New York 1971, pp. 201–202, for the identification of the engraver as Pietro Fontana (1762–1837). The portrait appears on the cover of B. Castiglione, *The Book of the Courtier*, trans. C. S. Singleton, Doubleday, New York 1959. The Penguin Classic edition (1967) adopts, more appropriately, Raphael's portrait of the author.

15 J. Cox-Rearick, in: *An Important Painting by Pontormo from the Collection of Chauncey D. Stillman*, sale cat., Christie's, New York, Wednesday May 31, 1989, p. 38.

16 I thank Keith Christiansen of the Metropolitan Museum for his generosity in giving me access to the curatorial files. I first published this photograph from those files in: «Pontormo's *Halberdier*», in: *Center 16: Record of Activities and Research Reports*, June 1995–May 1996 (National Gallery of Art, Center for Advanced Study in the Visual Arts), Washington, DC, 1996, pp. 75–78. I owe Dr. Christiansen yet more thanks for arranging to photograph the X-ray with the tracing overlaid discussed below.

17 Smyth, 1955 (as in n. 12), p. 118.

18 I want to thank Dawson Carr of the J. Paul Getty Museum for having this tracing made on a mylar sheet.

19 My sincerest thanks are due to Dr. Serena Padovani of the Galleria Palatina for letting me examine the portrait closely and for arranging for me to borrow the X-ray of the recently restored painting in order to make these photographs with the tracing superimposed.

20 A. Cecchi, «*Famose Frondi de cui santi honori [. . .]*; un sonetto del Varchi e il ritratto di Lorenzo Lenzi dipinto dal Bronzino», in: *Artista*, 11, 1990, pp. 8–19, and idem, «Il Bronzino, Benedetto Varchi e l'Accademia Fiorentina: ritratti di poeti, letterati e personaggi illustri della corte medicea», in: *Antichità viva*, XXX, 1–2, 1991, pp. 17–28. Lenzi was born on 23 October 1516. Cecchi insists that the sitter could not be older than 12 and so dates the portrait no later than 1528, but I see no reason why it could not have been completed as late as 1532 [see now C. B. Strehlke, *Pontormo, Bronzino, and the Medici*, exhibition catalogue, Philadelphia Museum of Art, Philadelphia, 2004, pp. 100–103].

21 See Cropper, 1997 (as in n. 11), p. 95.

22 For preliminary discussion of this important question, see: E. Cropper, «Prolegomena to a New Interpretation of Bronzino's Florentine Portraits», in: *Renaissance Studies in Honor of Craig Hugh Smyth* (I Tatti Monographs, 7), ed. by A. Murrogh, F. Superbi Gioffredi et al., vol. 11, Florence 1985, pp. 149–162, esp. p. 157.

23 The furniture is also embellished with grotesque carvings (probably a reference to the work of Bronzino's friend Battista del Tasso) in both portraits. Such carving already appears in the first version of the Metropolitan portrait, however, providing another reason to see this as an entirely Florentine work.

24 See C. H. Smyth, «On Non-Florentine Sources of Bronzino's Portraits», in: *Bronzino as Draughtsman: An Introduction (with Notes on his Portraits and Tapestries)*, Locust Valley, NY, Appendix 1, pp. 80–86, for suggestions that Bronzino was also looking at Lotto and Piero della Francesca, in addition to Sebastiano and Titian. My point is that whatever else Bronzino was looking at, his primary model derived from Pontormo.

25 My work on the Guardi portrait makes me especially cautious about identifying sitters. Yet, even as he states that Bronzino made more portraits than he could list, Vasari provides the names of several notable subjects. Now that Cecchi has identified the Lenzi and Sofferoni portraits (see above, n. 19), only the names of Bonaccorso Pinadori and Pier Antonio Bandini and his wife remain unattached. Without exploring the probable association of the pair of portraits now in Ottawa and Turin with the latter two, I would like to suggest that the Metropolitan portrait might represent Bonaccorso Pinadori, son of Bartolomea Pinadori, the widow who commissioned the Carmignano *Visitation* from Pontormo. For Bonaccorso's genealogy, see: M. G. Trenti Antonelli, «La Visitazione di Carmignano», in: *La Maniera moderna in Toscana. Il Pontormo: le opere di Empoli Carmignano e Poggio a Caiano*, Venezia 1994, pp. 30–49, esp. pp. 32–35. On 13 April 1528, Bonaccorso di Pietro Pinadori (b. 31 December 1502) undertook the guardianship of his younger brothers Jacopo and Filippo, his father having died in 1526. The inventory taken at that time includes cassoni, beds, tables and linens. See ASF Not. antecos. 20480, 227–229v. Bonaccorso was one year younger than Bronzino, whom Smyth once proposed as the sitter. Here the issue of the date is probably more important than the matter of age. Interestingly, the Piasecka Johnson portrait (another work closely related in format to Pontormo's *Halberdier*), for which see: Cropper, 1997 (as in n. 11), pp. 100–106, most likely shows a rather younger man, Carlo Neroni, whose father had also died in 1526, and who is, therefore, also shown as the new head of a Florentine household. The changes in the position of the hand holding the book, revealed in the X-ray, and new placement of the index finger within the pages, suggest that Bronzino was responding to Pontormo's example when he reworked the image. That there is a relationship to the hand of Guidobaldo, resting on his helmet, also seems likely.

26 The Greek inscription on Guidobaldo's helmet becomes especially significant here, though its source has yet to be determined. For the identification of Guidobaldo's costume armor as a harness for use in the hunt, see: M. Scalini, «Il "giubbotto di ferro cesellato a foggia di colletto trinciato con scarselle" di Guidobaldo della Rovere (1514/1538/1574) e altri resti rovereschi», in: *Waffen- und Kostümkunde*, XXXIX, 1997, pp. 38–50. See, however, the note by S. W. Pyhrr & J.-A. Godoy, in: *Heroic Armor of the Italian Renaissance: Filippo Negroli and his Contemporaries*, exhibition catalogue (Metropolitan Museum of Art), 1998, New York 1998, p. 24, n. 55, taking issue with the attribution of the set to the Negroli atelier. If Guidobaldo is shown dressed for a ceremonial hunt (and hence the dog), then the presentation of a courtly "mixed" character – warrior and gentleman – becomes all the more

181

intriguing. Faced with such a challenge, Bronzino had the example of the similarly "mixed" character of the figure of the armed civilian Francesco Guardi to hand.

27　And one that Pontormo created in part, as I have suggested, out of his analysis of the youthful beauty of Donatello's marble *David*. See Cropper, 1997 (as in n. 11), pp. 84–89.

10

The Mistress in the Masterpiece

Nancy J. Vickers

When Virginia Woolf argued that "masterpieces are not single and solitary births" but rather "the outcome of many years of thinking in common, of thinking by the body of the people," she stressed the illusory nature of the old dream of artistic autonomy (68–69). Indeed her usage places the term "masterpiece" in contradiction with its origins – the piece by which one proves one is a master, the single part of a whole (a genre, an author's *corpus*) that silences, by the strength of its voice, all other parts. In the sixteenth century – that period of aggressive/defensive individualism – it was the elusive masterpiece that constituted the obsessive project of self-fashioning patron and self-fashioning artist alike. This essay examines one attempt at mastery, Benvenuto Cellini's bronze relief entitled "The Nymph of Fontainebleau," in order to locate the position of "the body of the people," here a specifically female body, within it. I turn to this "text," on the one hand, because it is characteristic of Fontainebleau – that is to say, French mannerist – style, and, on the other, because "The Nymph of Fontainebleau" took multiple discursive forms. We have, and this is unusual in the world of Renaissance texts, a narrative of its making in the autobiographical mode, two highly detailed descriptions in the ecphrastic mode, and, of course, the relief itself – all by the same hand. Consequently, the analysis of the production and consumption of this "masterpiece," not as isolated product but as process in context, is enhanced by the identifiability of telling gaps, repetitions, and points of convergence between multiple rhetorics.

The "Nymph of Fontainebleau" was commissioned by Francis I to represent a place: "Il Re desiderava d'averci una figura, che figurassi Fontana Beliò" (371).[1] Cellini's figure to figure Fontainebleau was destined to articulate a privileged site, to introduce courtier-spectators into the text that was Fontainebleau, to crown the main entrance of a palace that was at once a preferred royal playground and a preferred sign of royal authority. For Francis, the trapping of extravagant pleasure marked extravagant prerogative and power. Begun upon his return from a humiliating military defeat at Pavia and a humiliating captivity in

Spain, Fontainebleau – the birthplace of French mannerism – emerged, André Chastel maintains, from "the need for prestige" and the "need for caprice" (xiii, translation mine): the failures of the warrior would be supplanted by the successes of the patron. "Having lost Italy," Michelet noted, "Francis created Italy in France" (354, translation mine). Cellini, a Florentine goldsmith turned sculptor, expatriated in 1540, and was charged with conferring upon Francis's place its *genius loci*; he chose to represent a water nymph, for the source of the name – Fontainebleau – was the name of a source in the forest that surrounded the palace.[2]

The narrative of the nymph begins, however, at a point that predates Francis's commission, at a moment in Cellini's career when he was most actively operating the all important conversion from artisan to artist, from craftsman to sculptor. Such a radical professional move required the mastery of new and consecrated media – first casting in bronze and later sculpting in marble. Cellini's first commission from Francis had been the creation of a dozen silver candlesticks, each to be a god or goddess, and each, following royal specification, cut to "exactly the same height as his Majesty himself" (256). Cellini wisely began with the subject that most nearly reflected the King's public self-image, a six-foot Jupiter: "I also felt inclined," he writes in what is arguably the most transitional sentence in the *Vita*, "to cast in bronze the large model I had made for the silver statue of Jupiter. It was the sort of work I had never tackled before" (264). Indeed no matter how monumental, work in silver was still artisan's work: Cellini's chapter on the fashioning of the candlestick appears in his "Treatise on Goldsmithing" not in his "Treatise on Sculpture." In "setting his hand" ("messo mano") to new matter, Cellini sought the help of Parisian master founders, but no sooner had the masters begun than Cellini proposed a contest to be won by the novice:

> They set their hands ("messon mano") to the project, and when I noticed that they were not going about it in the right way, I hurriedly began work on a head of Julius Caesar, a bust in armor, much larger than life size. I copied it from a little model that I had brought from Rome, that was copied from a splendid ancient head. I also set my hand ("messi mano") to another head of the same size that I copied from a beautiful girl that I kept around for my sexual pleasure ("per mio diletto carnale"). To it/her ("a questa") I gave the name Fontainebleau, which was the place that the King had chosen for his own pleasure ("per sua propria dilettazione"). (365; 264–65)

From this context of artistic rivalry, a first *figura* of Fontainebleau emerges. Cellini's initial bronzes – the pieces with which he outdoes two old masters – form a couple: on the one hand, an armed warrior-ruler imitated from art (the antique model) and, on the other, "Fontainebleau," the head of a woman imitated from nature (the living model). In "Fontainebleau" Francis, the warrior ruler, takes his pleasure ("sua propria dilettazione") and in "Fontainebleau," Cellini, the artist-subject, also takes his ("mio diletto"). This fusing of statue, place, and woman under the name Fontainebleau signals still another rivalry, one that transcends the contest between artists, to reveal a tension between patron and subject that is cast in unavoidably sexual terms.[3] Each is the prideful possessor of Fontainebleau.

But to move from the head of Fontainebleau to the full-bodied nymph, the narrative must continue. Invited with his apprentices to leave Paris for the day, Cellini asks his most trusted employee, Pagolo Miccieri, to stay behind and keep watch over first, his property, and second, that same "beautiful girl," whom, he adds, "I keep around principally for the use of my art" ("per servizio de l'arte mia") "and without whom I could not do it" (384; 279). He goes on to explain that "because he is a man," he has used her for sexual pleasure ("me ne son servito a i mia piaceri carnali") and that he suspects (hopes?) she will give him a son (384; 279). Once out of town, Cellini becomes suspicious, returns home unannounced, and virtually catches Pagolo and the girl, Caterina, in the act. Both are chased from the workshop; there are lawsuits and altercations; and finally Cellini, threatening murder, forces them to marry; this step is but the prerequisite to a carefully plotted and amply described revenge:

> Not satisfied with having made Pagolo take such a shameless little whore as his wife, in addition – to round off my revenge – I used to copy from her . . . I made her pose in the nude . . . and then I had my revenge by using her sexually, mocking her and her husband for the various horns ("le diverse corna") I was giving him. I also made her pose in great discomfort for hours at a stretch. Her discomfort annoyed her as much as it pleased me ("me dilettava"), since she was very beautifully made and won me great honor. . . . So, I said to myself, I get two kinds of revenge out of this. First, she's now married, so these are not empty horns ("corna vane") like the horns she gave me when she played the whore with me. Thus I'm taking an excellent revenge against him, and also against her, by making her pose in such discomfort which, beyond the pleasure, wins me credit and profit. What more could I want?
>
> While I was weighing these matters, the slut redoubled her insults, talking about her husband. What she said and did nearly drove me out of my mind, and giving in to my rage, I seized her by the hair and dragged her up and down the room, beating and kicking her until I was exhausted. . . . When I had given her a good pummelling, she swore she would never return; so for the first time I realized what a mistake I had made, since I was losing a splendid opportunity to win honor. Besides this, I saw her all torn, bruised, and swollen, and I realized that even if she did come back it would be necessary to have her treated for two weeks before I could use her ("me ne potessi servire"). (396–97; 288–89)

Once Caterina has left, Cellini consults his servant, Ruberta, who scolds him for being so cruel to such a beauty. He excuses himself by recounting the story of her infidelity, which Ruberta dismisses, explaining that infidelity is a French custom, and that in France there is not a husband without his horns ("le sue cornetta") (398; 289). He asks Ruberta to intercede with Caterina, because he "would be pleased to finish his work by using her" ("perché io arei auto a piacere di poter finire quella mia opera, servendomi di lei") (398; 289). Ruberta tells him that he is naive, that the best strategy is to do nothing at all. Caterina will return even sooner if left on her own. And when, for reasons about which we can only speculate – money, the protection of her husband's position, her desire to be the Nymph of Fontainebleau – she does, Cellini adds:

> Then I began to copy her, and in between times we enjoyed sexual pleasures ("le piaccevolezze carnali") and then, at the same hour as the day before, she provoked me so much that I had to give her the same beating; and this went on for several days, always in the same pattern, with little variation. Meanwhile I, who had won myself great honor and finished my figure, gave the orders to cast it in bronze. . . . My figure came out beautifully, and was as finely cast as anything has ever been. (398–99; 290)

The narrative of the making of Fontainebleau stands out in Cellini's 550-page autobiography – by its exceptional length, which I have significantly abbreviated, by the nature of its subject, by its granting of the only detailed representation we are ever given of modeling (in both senses of the term) in Cellini's workshop, and – in an autobiography that confesses murders, betrayals, thefts, and emprisonments – by the fact that it is the only narrative prefaced by an apology. Here, for once, Cellini acknowledges that he has done something wrong – although to Pagolo not to Caterina: "If when telling the events of my life I never admitted to being wrong, I would not be believed when telling of events in which I know that I was right. I know I made a mistake in wanting to take such a strange revenge against Pagolo Miccieri" (288). Caterina's body, then, stands not primarily as the instrument of direct revenge against her – through the discomfort the artist takes pleasure in inflicting upon her – but, more important, as the medium of revenge against her husband. Indeed she is not beaten until she speaks his name. Her flesh becomes simultaneously the medium of Cellini's artistic accomplishment and the shield that absorbs the blows in a battle between male sexual rivals. "'To cuckold,'" notes Eve Kosofsky Sedgwick, "is by definition a sexual act, performed on a man, by another man" (49). Even Cellini's desire to win favor is at times obscured by his desire to cuckold Pagolo, to confer horns upon him (the repeated *corna* and *cornetta*) that will not only equal but surpass the horns Pagolo conferred upon Cellini. What is most intriguing is the telling coincidence of still another tale of sexual rivalry, here immeasurably more explicit, with still another figuring of Fontainebleau. Out of daily domestic violence emerges a work of art, and the vocabulary of investment in the violence tellingly repeats the vocabulary of investment in the art. Caterina's flesh is positioned to serve (*servire*) both sexual and artistic needs; she provides not only bodily but also visual pleasure (*piacere*) through the "delightful" spectacle of beauty under pressure.

The Nymph was intended to decorate the Porte Dorée of the palace. Above that doorway was a half circle for which the King ordered his figure to represent Fontainebleau. In the $13\frac{1}{2}$ foot lunette Cellini placed an $11\frac{1}{2}$ foot woman ("una femmina" not "una ninfa") reclining in what he calls a beautiful attitude

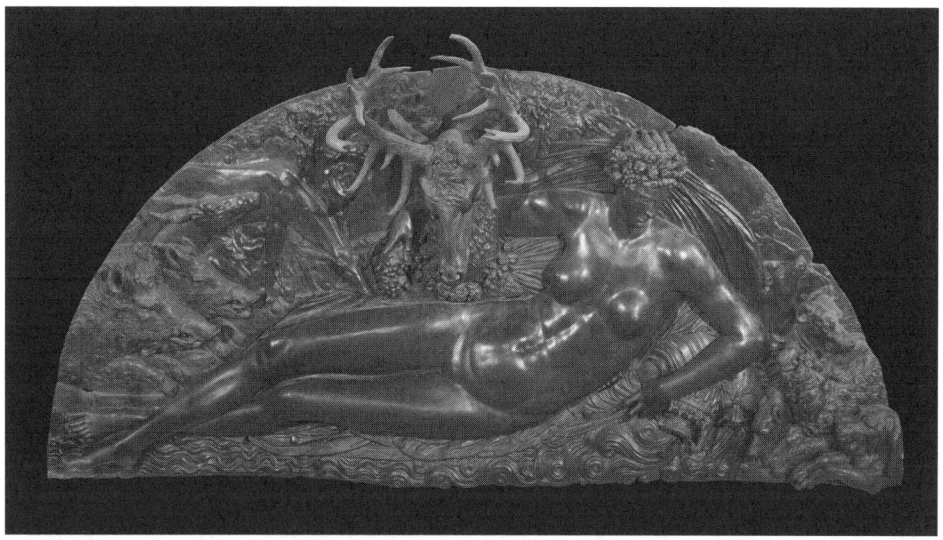

Figure 10.1 Benvenuto Cellini, *The Nymph of Fontainebleau.* akg-images / Erich Lessing.

("in bella attitudine") (372; 270). Her right hand rests on a stag, "one of the King's emblems" (270);[4] her left hand rests on vases from which water seems to flow (see figure 10.1). On the left there are fauns and boars and on the right, hunting dogs of various kinds. At the sides Cellini designed matching bases and cornices and between them, instead of columns, he placed two 11½ foot satyrs. Each held up the doorway with one arm while in the other he held a weapon – a club or a ball and chains; each looked "fierce" and "aggressive" and was meant "to terrorize" the spectator (270). Although Cellini calls these figures satyrs, he notes that they have nothing of the satyr about them, except for their little horns ("certe piccole cornetta") and their goaty heads; all the rest is in human form (372; 270). Cellini enclosed the whole work in an oblong and for each of the upper angles he designed an angel with a torch in her hand signifying victory. Above them was a salamander, the King's device.

Cellini's never-assembled project, then, was an exceptional full-bronze doorway, an enterprise of virtuoso originality and ambition.[5] Of the scattered, extant fragments of his monumental projects, the nymph is indeed the most monumental; she is, for example, over a foot taller than the Perseus that dominates Florence's Piazza della Signoria. This doorway, moreover, was not understood either by Francis or by Cellini to be empty, albeit impressive, decoration; it communicated meaning[6] both to artist and to patron:

> The King began by asking me what was the idea behind the beautiful design [for yet another project], saying that without a word from me he had understood all I had done as regards the doorway. . . . He was well aware that I didn't work like

the kind of fool whose art has a certain amount of grace but is completely devoid of significance. (271)

Indeed the door lends itself to ready interpretation. It is clearly a celebration of the Château, that is to say, a celebration of Francis. As a classicizing rendering of woods and waters, the spaces Renaissance reality populated with stags, boars, and hounds, and Renaissance fantasy with nymphs and satyrs, it underlines not only the principal natural features of the forest surrounding Fontainebleau, but also the principal pastimes, hunting and bathing, of the court that frequented it. The stag-king predictably dominates the scene; he is at once possessor of and possessed by Fontainebleau; he is regally crowned by two angels bearing torches to light up his identifying symbol, his salamander amid the flames.

But what, indeed, is the rhetoric of this image? Male figures are vertical; females, horizontal or diagonal. The line that centers the image, its center of power, moves through the nymph's body – note what part of her body – to the stag, and then to the crowning and perhaps crowned salamander. In the imagistic discourses of Francis's power, centering often signals not only dominance, but dominance articulated in sexual terms. Here a lateral, diagonal female gesture serves to underline that centering; the coronation accomplished by the female victories only highlights the central axis. The drama of the lunette thus resides primarily in the stag and the nymph, and secondarily, in the satyrs.[7] For although the latter are fiercely monumental, they are also side-lined. The nymph, none the less, is displayed between two categories of armed male figures: since she traverses the space that separates the horns of the stag from the club or ball and chains of the satyrs, her displayed nakedness constitutes a locus of seemingly inevitable conflict between enemies whose tense opposition is masked only by a strategy of representation that places them momentarily "at rest." Similarly, the low relief on either side of her underlines her median status: on one side, the beasts of the forest and on the other hunting hounds, in short, the opponents of the hunt who, if they are to engage one another, must do so across her body.

Status in the spatial hierarchy, moreover, is reflected in the hierarchy of relief: the angels and the animals are, for the most part, in low relief ("di basso rilievo"); some fauns and boars are in half relief ("di mezzo rilievo"); the satyrs are in more than half relief ("piú che di mezzo rilievo"); the nymph, described initially like the satyrs as in "more than half relief" is later particularized – her head and selected parts of her body stand out in full, while others remain in half; and finally "a great part of the stag's neck" is brought out in "full relief" ("di tutto relievo") (372; 270; see also *Trattato*, 655).[8] The stag's horns, moreover – tellingly unmentioned in either of the descriptive texts – constitute the lunette's most outstanding and indeed upstanding feature. These horns are so foregrounded as to break out of the architectural frame; they extend above the half-circle and thus isolate themselves as the stag's crowning glory. Sixteenth-century hunting treatises indeed term certain stag horns a "couronne" (Du Fouilloux, 20v); here isolation directly under Francis's device underlines a specifically majestic function.

Indeed all of the male figures in the doorway program, like all of the male figures in the narrative of its creation, have horns. The "certe piccole cornetta" (372) of the satyrs – the detail that identifies them as satyrs – points us back to Ruberta's characterization of *every* French husband (she includes, I presume, royal ones): "In Francia non era marito che non avessi le sue cornetta" (398). The repeated horns of Cellini's narrative – he gives Pagolo a variety of horns ("diverse corna"), those horns are real horns not empty horns ("corna vane") like the horns Pagolo had given him – repeat themselves in the doorway (396–97). Nowhere else in Cellini's texts are horns even mentioned; nowhere else in his plastic works do we find such a virtuoso display of the artist's ability to horn his subject. A crown of horns, moreover, is an ambivalent signifier: horns speak contradiction. They confer both respect and humiliation; they assert potency and impotence; they convey armed courage as well as flight before the enemy; and they identify the majestic king of the forest as well as the pathetic victim of the hunter, the victim whose horns are mounted as a sign of his having been mastered, whose body is ritually torn to bits and thrown to the dogs. In short, the language of horns is double: it may readily voice the opposite of what it seems to say. The subject-artist's glorification of his King simultaneously speaks an insult – *cornuto* – the insult imposed upon the heads of men when they cannot master women.

The fate of becoming first a *cornuto*, a horned man, and ultimately a stag is, of course, the fate imposed upon Actaeon by Diana. While hunting he stumbles upon the goddess and her nymphs bathing in a forest source. Diana, upon seeing him see her (the forbidden nakedness of the divine, but of a female divine) scatters him with drops of water that initiate his metamorphosis. His staglike flight into the woods carries him only to death, to dismemberment by his own hounds, as he pathetically attempts to articulate his identity; the words "Know your master" are, according to Ovid, the words he cannot utter (*Metamorphoses*, 3.230, translation mine). This tale of the hunter hunted, of the master mastered by a woman he cannot control, is clearly inscribed by Cellini in his personification of Fontainebleau. A female nude in a source accompanied by a stag would connote Diana to any sixteenth-century spectator-reader. Indeed, after Francis's death, Henri II gave Cellini's lunette to his mistress, Diane de Poitiers, to decorate her château at Anet.[9] When, in the nineteenth century, the original was moved to the Louvre, catalogues referred to it as "the Diana."[10] Rosso's "Nymph of Fontainebleau," a strikingly similar image, which – if indeed by Rosso – must predate that of Cellini, notably does not include a stag; it is Cellini who inscribes the stag within the embrace of the figure that figures Fontainebleau.

A stag's head in this position – that is to say viewed full front – is called in the heraldic code "a stag at gaze," and I would like to take my cue from that heraldic notation in analyzing what this stag's gaze accomplishes. It is, in the doorway complex, an isolated gaze: the victories look up to the salamander; the animals look horizontally into and out of the frame; the nymph looks down and to the side, perhaps at one of the hounds;[11] the satyrs, it seems, turn slightly up and toward the center, in the direction of the nymph and the stag they are supporting. The stag, however, looks straight ahead; his stare directly engages his spectator. The nymph was, of course, created to be viewed by any number of people – in short an entire court, men and women, as well as its visitors – but its lesson to them was, I would argue, the privileged status of its principal, its inscribed, viewer. In the stag's gaze, the King as viewer mirrors himself. He, as well as everyone else, reads his control of his possession, his mastery of a graciously consenting Fontainebleau.

Representations of the Diana–Actaeon story play a special role in the visual arts in that they dramatize the act of seeing, they self-reflexively figure the voyeuristic pleasure of a male gaze riveted on female nakedness.[12] The casting of the royal gaze in these terms communicates once again a double message: on the one hand, the stag-king is an Actaeon who, for the duration of this representation, is not dismembered; he is a voyeur embraced by the object of a previous, forbidden gaze, a voyeur permitted the pleasure of viewing a Diana whose threat has obviously been neutralized. On the other, the freeze frame represented is a moment lifted out of a narrative, leaving its viewer to wonder if plot has been permanently halted by royal prerogative or whether it is to be resumed. Let me compare two Fontainebleau images, clearly done in the 1540s, as elaboration: the first, attributed to Claude Badoyn and most probably a tapestry design, is entitled "Francis I and the Nymphs of Fontainebleau," (Musée du Louvre). In the background we see the Château and in the foreground the fountain itself populated by naked nymphs striking a variety of poses. The "bathers' convention" is, of course, a traditional test of artistic virtuosity, a proof of mastery of that ultimate challenge to the figurative artist, the human body. Display of multiple nudes viewed from multiple perspectives is, first and foremost, ostentatious display of the master's control of his medium. To the left, Francis and his court stand at the edge of the spectacle, and yet no one but Francis looks at it. The gazes of his courtiers all turn in upon each other; only he enjoys the privilege, the pleasure of looking. It is his gaze, a royal gaze – and in a nation under Salic law – a male gaze, that dominates the scene.

Turning next to an engraving by Jean Mignon after Luca Penni (Graphische Sammlung Albertina, Vienna), the Diana–Actaeon story is transposed into a typically bellifontaine setting; the natural pool has become a classicizing bath. From it, Diana, protected by her nymphs, scatters water on a hunter who has already assumed his stag head. His pose, moreover, virtually repeats that of the King in the previous sketch: the turn of the head, the disposition of the *contrapposto*; the angle of the armed arm; the movement of the hand toward the naked woman; even the cut of the garment. Centered above the engraving is the previously cited imperative from Ovid's *Metamorphoses*: "Dominum Cognoscite Vestrum," "Know your (masculine) master." The citation, tellingly, is from the scene that this engraving has specifically written out of the story; in the background we see Actaeon in flight but nowhere do we see him torn to bits by his dogs, nowhere do we see him attempt to speak his mastery of them. What then does "Know your master" mean? Who speaks it? Does Diana assert, in the masculine, a control that has been neutralized by the engraving's erasure, or rather is the revised master a regally posed Actaeon? For in any neutralizing representation of Diana with a stag, either the stag tames Diana or Diana tames the stag.

To carry neutralization one step further we need only return to Cellini's lunette, to a Diana who embraces her Actaeon. However, this Actaeon does not encounter Diana's gaze; he – as a mark of possession – displays her to view: "The very act of rendering visible," writes Sharon Willis, "expresses a capture, and a power relation" (96). I would like to dwell momentarily on the notion of "display" since it reveals, I think, one of the defining strategies of this image. "To display" – from the Latin *displicare*, "to scatter, to disperse, and, in late Latin, to unfold – as in unfolding a banner to view" – is "to spread something out, to open it up, to exhibit it to be seen, and, by extension, to exhibit it ostentatiously."[13] In the "Display of Heraldry" it signifies "to lay or place a human or animal form with the limbs extended"; in the "display of rhetoric," "to set forth in representation, to depict, to describe." Consider, for example, the "Nymph of Fontainebleau" attributed to Rosso (Bibliothèque Nationale, Paris), who is posed so much like Cellini's and yet with a difference. As veil, her legs bend up and turn sideways; her right arm crosses her body; her head is only seen in profile. When we shift to Cellini (figure 10.1), the entire body is tipped forward to a point of precarious imbalance; the front leg drops and both legs are elongated; both shoulders (not just the left) are thrown back to open up the chest, both arms extend; and the head twists away from the center to permit a mixed profile and frontal view. The left leg, for example, strikes an impossible pose, flatly frontal at the foot while in profile at the knee. Even the mannered gesture that ostensibly asserts the nymph's power, her possessive embrace of a subdued stag/king, reveals through the discomfort implicit in its taut flatness the uneasiness provoked by such an assertion. Cellini's staging of gracious consent and control through easy repose reveals on close examination a calculated contortion aimed at enhancing voyeuristic pleasure: "I made her pose in great discomfort" ("con gran disagio") "for hours at a stretch. And in that discomfort" ("questo disagio") "she was as much annoyed as I was delighted" ("me dilettava"), "since she was very beautiful and won me great honor"; and again, "so I'm also taking revenge against her . . . by making her pose in such discomfort" ("con tanto disagio") "which, beyond the pleasure" ("oltra al piacere"), "wins me credit and profit" (396–97; 288–89). It is, in this exchange between male artist and female model, her *disagio* which permits his *piacere*, his *diletazzione*. It should be noted that Cellini virtually never describes working from an adult male model and that his female models are typically bound to him through a triple power relation: they are servants within his household; they serve his sexual needs; and they serve the requirements of his art. The very vocabulary of heterosexual hierarchies that unites male artist, male patron, and male viewer, then, in sexual/aesthetic pleasure articulates, as its corollary, the

191

discomfort of its female subject. A female viewer's response, determined as it is by a displacement of the structuring identification away from the seer and onto the object seen, then reenacts *disagio*. This response, too, as Lillian Robinson and Lise Vogel have argued in a related context, is part of what the image means.[14]

The label "mannerist" as applied to works of art derives from the Italian *maniera* ("style"), which derives in turn from the Latin *manus* (hand). It is commonly held that mannerist art is about style. As such it places subject matter (*materia*) in the background in order to highlight skill (*maniera*), to call attention to the original touch of the individual who manipulates the subject. "Manner," writes Claude-Gilbert Dubois, "is the opposite of matter. One would have to invent 'matterism' to stand as complement to 'mannerism.' The matterist would have something substantial to say, for the mannerist there is no substance. The mannerist has nothing to say, except the manner of saying nothing" (15, translation mine). Dubois goes on to argue that in the relationship between the mannerist artist and the figure his art would ostensibly represent, it is the mark of the hand of the artist rather than the mimetic representation of the model that is structured to command attention. It is only logical, then, that mannerist art has prompted stylistic analysis, analysis of manner at the expense of analysis of matter. But the rhetoric of mannerist art does indeed say something, at the very least something about the ability of certain matter to move to the background while being positioned in the foreground.[15] What matter – if we can postulate a subject matter, a matter not subjected but acting as subject – would in fact lend itself to (consent to? submit to?) its own neutralization, would offer up its body to serve (*servire*) the "profit and credit" of the master mannerist. When Cellini sets his hand to his matter, that application takes three forms: the caressing of the "piacevolezze carnali," the pummeling of the rage, and the modeling of the masterpiece. And each manipulation is to leave *his* mark: he would, after all, give himself a son through Caterina, that is, imprint male form on formless female matter through the gesture of insemination; he would beat her to vent his rage against Pagolo, to take revenge in the tears and bruises of her flesh; and finally, he would win favor from Francis by privileging royal pleasure, by displaying Fontainebleau to view at the cost of (indeed because of) Caterina's bodily discomfort. In each case, Caterina's flesh is positioned as medium in the articulation of a relationship between men. Between the horned satyrs and the horned stag – potent or impotent, but in either case marked as male – lies Fontainebleau. Through her a complex hierarchy of male rivalries is played out: through the ostentatious display of Fontainebleau, Francis outdoes his rival sovereigns; through the subversive possession of Fontainebleau, the subject rivals the monarch; through the artistic mastery displayed in Fontainebleau, Cellini not only equals but surpasses rival masters; through intercourse with and abuse of Fontainebleau, Cellini makes clear who is master of the house.[16]

But the story of Fontainebleau is not quite this straightforward: there is indeed another woman in this text and she, too, at some level, is its source. Cellini recounts as follows one of the King's visits to his workshop:

> And because he had with him *his* Madame d'Etampes [his mistress], they began to talk about Fontainebleau. Madame d'Etampes said to his Majesty that he ought to have me make something beautiful to decorate *his* Fontainebleau. (268, italics mine)

"His Fontainebleau" can, of course, be read two ways in Madame d'Etampes's mediating sentence: *his* palace or *his* source. Francis opted for the second, enthusiastically turning to Cellini, to ask him how he would go about making a fountain, how he would convert a natural source into a work of art. So Cellini set his hand ("messi mano") to a model of Fontainebleau (371; 268). A month and a half later, when Francis returned, the master craftsman had produced *two* models: on seeing the first, that of "The Nymph of Fontainebleau," the King was delighted; on seeing the second, that of the fountain itself, the King's pleasure became even greater. Cellini's fountain was a square and in each of its four corners sat a female figure, each figuring one of those *virtù* which the King protected and in which he took delight ("si diletta") (374): one figured literature, another figured the arts of design (sculpture, painting, architecture); still another, music; and the last liberality – that is, patronly support, money – which made possible the existence of all of the *virtù*. For Cellini, Francis's "fathering of the arts" was literal; Jupiterlike, he inseminated them with a shower of gold. Through them he took his pleasure; through them he left his mark on French culture. In the center of Fontainebleau, Cellini planned a pedestal taller than the basin of the fountain itself, upon which a fifty-four-foot nude figure to represent Francis, a Mars, was to be constructed: "In very truth," said the King, calling his treasurers, "I've found a man after my own heart" (271).

Fontainebleau may well be a place where, as Malherbe later wrote, "Nature submitted to the miracle of Art" (82, translation mine),[17] but it is also a place where art submitted to the early modern monarch. And yet irony, here, belongs to the realm of individual history and not official image making. For it was, Cellini maintains, that aristocratic mistress who outmaneuvered the master artist by outsmarting, and ultimately outliving, the master monarch. Indeed the risk of medium turned unruly, of matter turned subject, is the constitution of an obstacle. Moving in the space between the King and the "man after his own heart" – acting as woman and as aristocrat – this mistress it seems horned them both by finding sexual/political pleasure in bodies other than that of her master and by plotting to scatter the frustrated, consumed, fragmented *corpus* of a Renaissance Actaeon named Cellini.

Notes

1   Quotations from Cellini's *Vita* in Italian are from the Bruno Maier edition; English translations are my adaptations of the George Bull translation. My modifications of Bull are generally directed at achieving a more literal rendering of Cellini's prose. All references are in parentheses in the text: if only Italian appears, the page reference is to Maier's edition; if only English appears, the page reference is to Bull's translation; if both Italian and English appear, the first reference is to Maier and the second to Bull.
2   On the origins of the myth of a "Nymph of Fontainebleau" and on her various representations, see Pressouyre (88–89).
3   On Cellini's awareness of the type of patrons for whom he worked and of their uses of his art, see Avery (206–8).
4   On Cellini's identification of the stag as an emblem of the King, see Pressouyre (88).
5   See Grodecki (62); and Pope-Hennessy (409 and 411).
6   See Pope-Hennessy (411); and Pressouyre (89).
7   My reading here differs from that of Pope-Hennessy, who considers the two monumental satyrs the "dominant feature" of the doorway (406).
8   Laura Mulvey's distinction between the flat spatial disposition of the "woman as icon" in film and the "three dimensional space" of the "active male figure" may be suggestively related to the generally heightened relief of the stag and satyrs in contrast to the generally imbedded relief of the nymph. See Mulvey (12–13).
9   On the history of the identification of the "Nymph of Fontainebleau" with Diana, see Pressouyre (89–90).
10 See Pressouyre (89–90).
11 See Pressouyre (88).
12 See my "Diana Described." Bardon characterizes Cellini's stag as a prisoner of beauty and virtue, as an "Actéon royal figé dans sa profanatoire admiration" (56).
13 Definitions are adapted from the *Oxford English Dictionary.*
14 The analysis of Robinson and Vogel emerges from an anecdote recounting a female spectator's reactions to Boucher's *Reclining Girl*, a portrait of a mistress of Louis XV (280 and 298). See also Mulvey on male visual pleasure.
15 On the ways in which the privileging of "manner" tends to neutralize "matter," see Suleiman.
16 My theoretical framework clearly suggests the triangulated construct of mimetic desire outlined by René Girard, but as recast in the work of such feminist critics as Mary Jacobus, Patricia Klindienst Joplin, and Eve Kosofsky Sedgwick, whose analyses are attentive to the role played by gender in the positioning of individuals upon that triangle.
17 Cited by Cahn (78).

Works cited

Avery, Charles. *Florentine Renaissance Sculpture.* New York: Harper and Row, 1970.
Bardon, François. *Diane de Poitiers et le mythe de Diane.* Paris: Presses Universitaires de France, 1963.

Cahn, Walter. *Masterpieces: Chapters in the History of an Idea*. Princeton: Princeton University Press, 1979.

Cellini, Benvenuto. *The Autobiography of Benvenuto Cellini*. Trans. George Bull. Harmondsworth and New York: Penguin, 1956.

——— *Trattato della scultura*. In *La Vita, con l'aggiunta di: trattato dell'oreficeria, trattato della scultura, discorsi sopra l'arte, lettere e suppliche, poesie*. Milano: Longanesi, 1958.

——— *La Vita*. Ed. Bruno Maier. Novara: Istituto geografico de Agostini, 1962.

Chastel, André. "Fontainebleau, formes et symboles." *L'Ecole de Fontainebleau*. Paris: Editions des Musées Nationaux, 1972; pp. xiii–xxviii.

Dubois, Claude-Gilbert. *Le Maniérisme*. Paris: Presses Universitaires de France, 1979.

Du Fouilloux, Jacques. *La Vénerie*. 1585; repr. Angers: Charles Lebosse, 1849.

Grodecki, Catherine. "Le Séjour de Benvenuto Cellini à L'Hôtel de Nesle et la fonte de la Nymphe de Fontainebleau d'après les actes des notaires parisiens." *Bulletin de la Société de l'Histoire de Paris et de l'Ile-de-France* (1971); 98:45–80.

Jacobus, Mary. "Is There a Woman in This Text?" *New Literary History* (1982); 14:117–41.

Joplin, Patricia Klindienst. "The Voice of the Shuttle is Ours." *Stanford Literature Review* (1984); 1:25–53.

Malherbe, François. *Oeuvres*. Ed. Antoine Adam. Paris: Gallimard, 1971.

Michelet, Jules. *Histoire de France*. Paris: Bonnot, 1978. Vol. 10.

Mulvey, Laura. "Visual Pleasure and Narrative Cinema." *Screen* (1975), 16(3):6–18.

Ovid. *Metamorphoses*. Trans. and ed. Frank J. Miller. 2 vols. London: Heinemann, 1916. Vol. 1.

Pope-Hennessy, John. "A Bronze Satyr by Cellini." *The Burlington Magazine* (1982), 124:406–12.

Pressouyre, Sylvia. "Note additionnelle sur la Nymphe de Fontainebleau." *Bulletin de la Société de l'Histoire de Paris et de l'Ile-de-France* (1971), 98:81–92.

Robinson, Lillian S., and Lise Vogel. "Modernism and History." *New Literary History* (1971), 3:177–97. Repr. in *Images of Women in Fiction: Feminist Perspectives*. Ed. Susan Koppelman Cornillon. Bowling Green: Bowling Green University Popular Press, 1972; pp. 278–307.

Sedgwick, Eve Kosofsky. "Homophobia, Misogyny, and Capital: The Example of *Our Mutual Friend*." *Raritan* (1983), 2(3):126–51. Repr. in *Between Men: English Literature and Male Homosocial Desire*. New York: Columbia University Press, 1985.

——— "Sexualism and the Citizen of the World: Wycherley, Sterne, and Male Homosocial Desire." *Critical Inquiry* (1984), 11:226–45.

Suleiman, Susan. "Reading Robbe-Grillet: Sadism and Text in *Projet pour une révolution à New York*." *Romanic Review* (1977), 68:43–62.

Vickers, Nancy J. "Diana Described: Scattered Woman and Scattered Rhyme." *Critical Inquiry* (1981), 8:265–79. Repr. in *Writing and Sexual Difference*. Ed. Elizabeth Abel. Chicago: University of Chicago Press, 1982; pp. 95–109.

Willis, Sharon. "Lettre sur des taches aveugles: A l'usage de celles qui voient." *L'Esprit créateur* (1984), 24:85–98.

Woolf, Virginia. *A Room of One's Own*. New York and Burlingame: Harcourt, Brace & World, 1929.

11

Michelangelo's Florentine *Pietà*: The Missing Leg

Leo Steinberg

The Christ in Michelangelo's Florentine *Pietà* (fig. 11.1) is short one leg, and yet the missing limb is rarely missed, so well does the figure in its truncated state seem to work. Some even regard the lack of the other leg as an aesthetic gain.[1] It is to those who take this position or who for any reason whatever deplore the attempt to put back what Michelangelo had removed that I offer this consideration: Michelangelo certainly did not conceive a Christ with amputations. He planned a whole, and whatever that whole was meant to embody he lived with for some eight years until the mid-1550s when he destroyed the work. And any thought that Michelangelo entertained for nearly a decade is worth thinking again. Hence we may well ask how the missing member completes Michelangelo's group.

There is only one action possible for the missing leg. The left groin still shows a slot or socket for its insertion, presumably for a replacement to be cut from a separate block. And a hollow place on the Virgin's thigh shows where it lay. It is indeed in this only possible pose that the leg appears in a number of painted and engraved reconstructions dating from the late sixteenth century.[2] The left leg of Christ is slung over the Virgin's thigh. It forms a connection which in later sixteenth- and seventeenth-century art becomes a common and unmistakable symbol of sexual union.

The word *symbol* is crucial. Looking at a seventeenth-century genre scene of lovers linked in this pose, one might mistake it for something "taken from nature." But in fact, the scheme of two figures of opposite sex seated side by side, with the leg of one bridging the thigh (or both thighs) of the other, is a received convention. It is as a symbolic form that an artist such as Govaert Flinck or Jacques de Gheyn naturalizes it into his style.

During the seventeenth century this token gesture was finally vulgarized. By the mid-1600s it had come to seem no less appropriate to bourgeois than to divine lovers. Then, not before, does one find it performed by common soldiers and unbuttoned wenches besieging the Prodigal Son. But in the decades that more closely concern us, one discovers – tracing the motif backward in time –

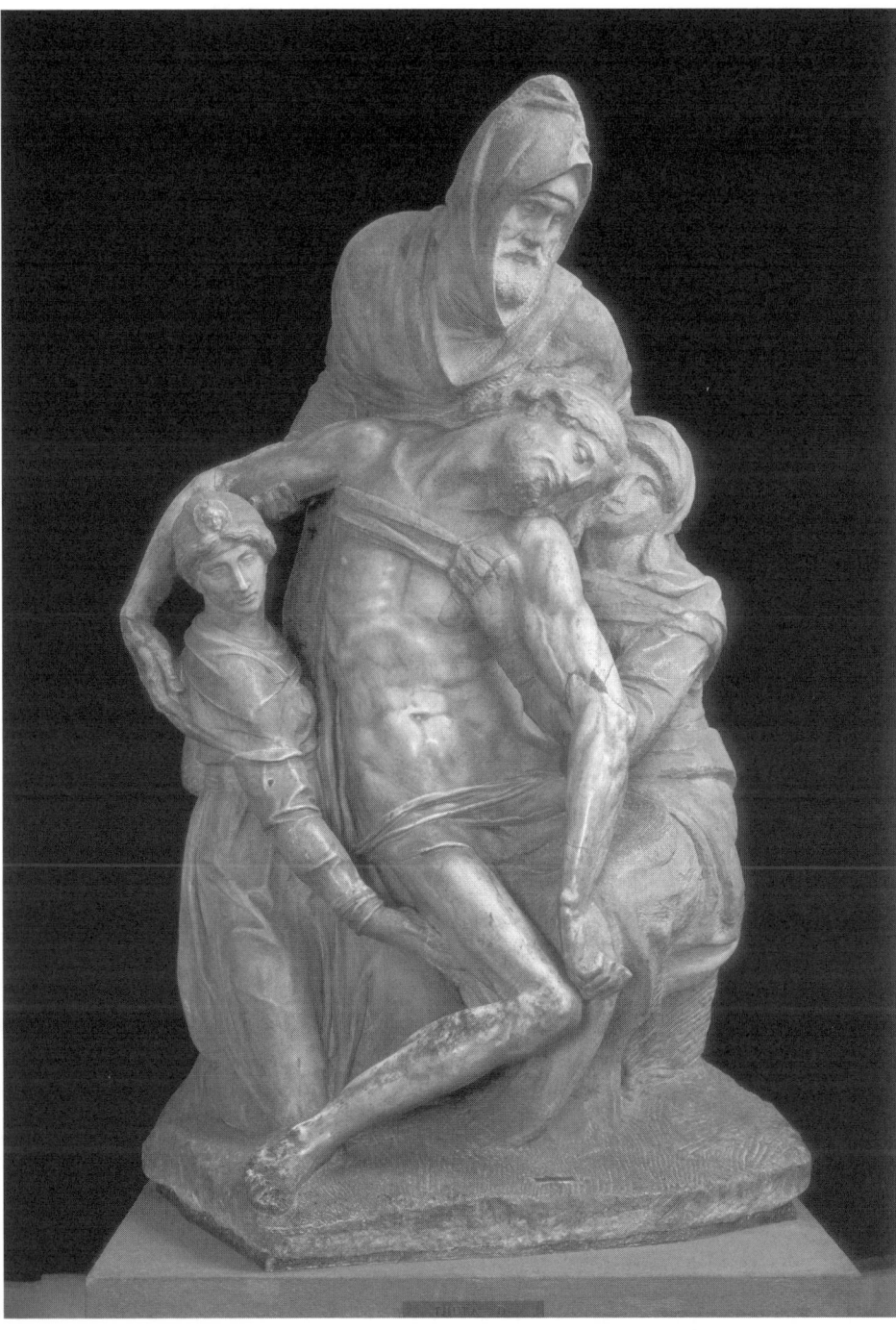

Figure 11.1   Michelangelo, *Pietà*. Florence, Duomo Museum. Bridgeman / Alinari
Archives-Florence.

that the slung leg (its sex interchangeable and in Italy usually assigned to the woman) becomes progressively less profane, almost solemn in context. In the quarter-century that immediately follows Michelangelo's abandonment of the *Pietà*, i.e., before 1580, the slung leg occurs only in allegories, or in Biblical and mythological scenes. By 1550 the motif is assimilated to scenes of Lot and his daughters – perhaps because the sexual act represented is at the opposite pole from trivial or private lust, being rather a desperate if misguided attempt to save the human race from extinction. In a very few instances the slung leg motif occurs in Lesbian situations – once in a drawing by Giulio Campi where Jupiter, in Diana's person, seduces Callisto; and once in a Fontainebleau print of *Women Bathing*, attributed to Jean Mignon after Luca Penni. This engraving of the mid-1540s may well be unique in exhibiting the slung leg motif without a mythological pretext.

The slung leg in sixteenth-century art is invariably a token of marital or sexual union, of sexual aggression or compliance. As a conventional sign it is so unambiguous and legible, that when a given story calls for the awkward depiction of a nymph loved by a horse (as happens in the rare myth of Philyra and Saturn in equine disguise), it is the slung leg that conveys the message.

Most relevant to this inquiry is the incidence of the motif from its first emergence before 1520 to about 1547 when Michelangelo's *Pietà* was begun. During this quarter-century the motif is extremely rare, confined to a few prints, drawings, and small cabinet pictures; and not only is it reserved for divine and heroic lovers but it tends to remain within a context of marriage.

The currency of the motif is established in the late 1520s and 1530s by engravings after Perino del Vaga and others of Raphael's circle, the subjects being the loves and nuptials of divine couples: Mars and Venus, Bacchus and Ariadne, Neptune (as suitor) and Thetis (fig. 11.2). And finally, as the earliest significant occurrence of the motif *in its canonic form*, it appears in the *Isaac and Rebekah* fresco in Raphael's Vatican Logge: "Abimelech, King of the Philistines, looked out at a window and behold, Isaac was sporting with Rebekah, his wife" (Gen. 26:8). We need hardly remind ourselves that the Old Testament scenes in "Raphael's Bible" refer by anticipation to Christ. So too Isaac's "sport with Rebekah" is a link in the chain of Christ's ancestry – which may explain such of the fresco's features as the fountain, the benediction of the great sun, and the brightness at the young patriarch's loins.

Variant forms of the motif appear shortly before 1520.[3] Not all can be traced to Rome, nor to a single milieu. And this emergence of a purely symbolic gesture over a period of some ten years in various artistic circles suggests that one or several antique models had come to be known – by hearsay perhaps to some, by actual acquaintance to Raphael and his school. The presumed model, however, turns out to be strangely elusive. It is not found in antique *symplegmata*, the ancient name for groups of figures interlocked in combat or love. It does not appear among the countless vase and wall paintings of antiquity that depict sexual relations. I have located only one instance of it, and this a recent archeological

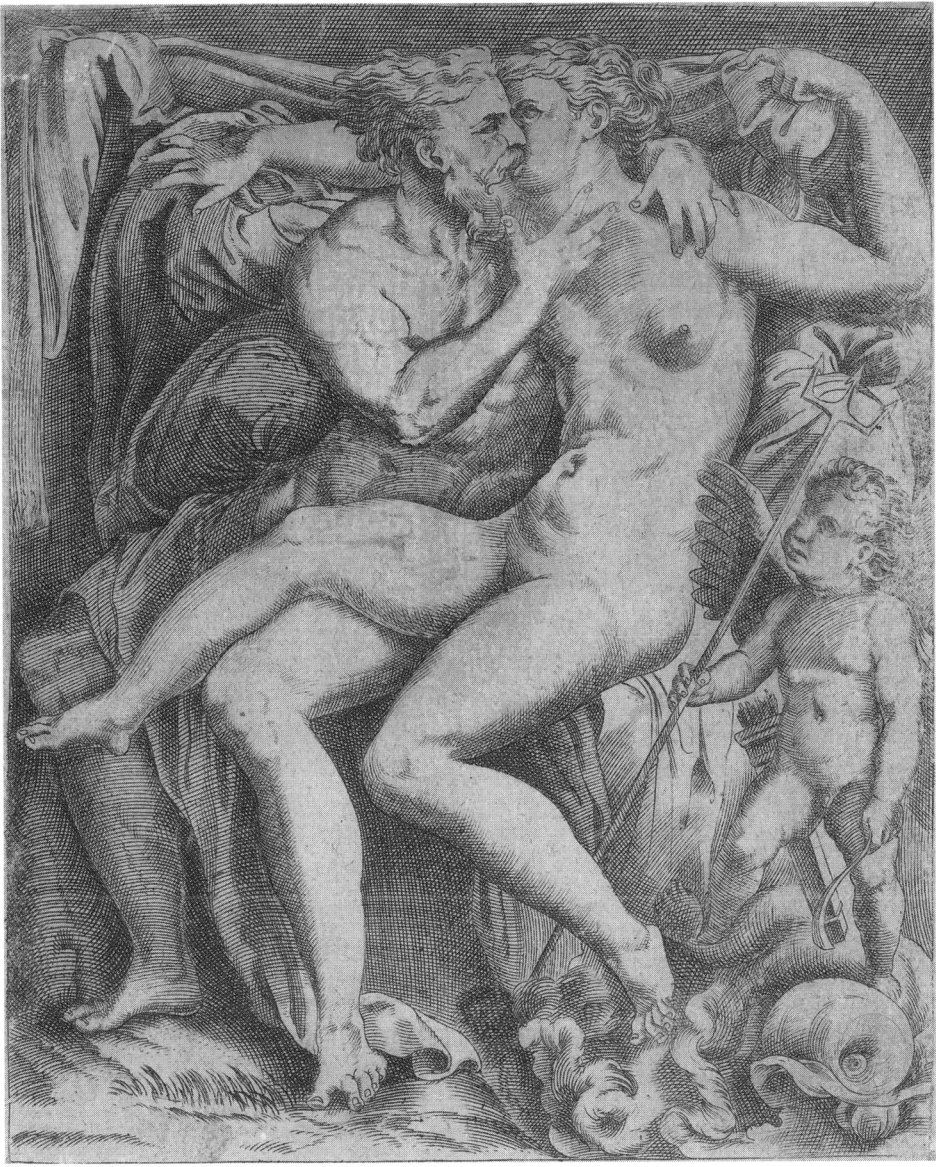

Figure 11.2 Jacopo Caraglio, after Pierino dal Vaga, *Neptune and Thetis*. © The Trustees of the British Museum.

find. It came to light in 1962 at Dherveni near Salonika in northern Greece, where six tombs of the fourth century B.C. were excavated.[4] Their most spectacular yield was a splendid gilt bronze krater, containing cremated ashes. It stands three feet high and displays continuous relief decoration of satyrs and maenads dancing. The dance centers upon a ritual action – the uncommon scene of the marriage of Bacchus and Ariadne. The scene is so rare, yet in this representation

199

so precise and perfected, that it suggests the possibility that we are privy to a mimetic ritual such as may have formed part of the mysteries of Dionysus. The bride is seated and draped, her veil held out in the traditional bridal gesture. She turns towards her divine spouse, a naked god, his leg flung over her thigh.

Let me assume that some comparable image had become known in Rome before 1520. This would account for the multiple emergence of a purely symbolic action and for the close resemblance of the slung leg in Renaissance works to that of Dionysus on the Dherveni krater. The model need have been no more than a small gem or cameo seen and understood by a handful of men. Present evidence indicates that a few Roman artists of the second and third decades of the Cinquecento knowingly adopted the slung leg as an antique symbolic form, implying a context of heroic or sacred love, or more exactly, of divine marriage.

The antique derivation alone may have lent the slung leg motif a dignity not normally associated with sexual sport. But only Michelangelo could reconceive this same pose as a consecration. As he meditates on the ancient gesture, death and love coalesce in it and the slung leg unites Mary and the crucified Christ in mystic marriage.[5]

I know of only one later artist who followed Michelangelo in making love and death converge in the slung leg motif. He is the Dutch sculptor Hubert Gerhard, who had studied in Florence in the 1580s. In his bronze *Tarquin and Lucrece* at the Metropolitan Museum, New York, the rising leg of the ravisher is at once amorous and murderous. In Michelangelo's marble group the themes of love, death, and communion are more intimately interfused. There can be no question that he conceived the action of the left leg in perfect awareness of what it meant and what it contributed. Tolnay spoke with precision when he suggested that the Virgin's face was "transfigured by supernatural bliss," and that the essence of the *concetto* was "a kind of ultimate sposalizio."[6]

Three things follow from the interpretation of the missing leg of the Christ: first, a closer pattern of symbolic and formal coherence for the entire group; second, a new way of thinking about Michelangelo's reasons for destroying the group; third, the possibility of identifying the slung leg motif in other classes of monuments. I shall treat each in turn.

1. Does the marital symbolism of the missing leg enhance the coherence of the whole group?

The Virgin is not alone in being the Spouse of Christ. In Christian tradition, Christ as bridegroom is as multipresent as is his body in the Host of the altar. The Church is his Bride. The human soul is his bride. The nun who has taken the veil is his bride. So is St. Catherine, whom he espouses with the same words from Canticles – "Come unto me, my fair love and my spouse" – which also welcome the soul of the Virgin. And so, for Savonarola, is Mary Magdalene, whom, in his fervent evocation of the Passion story he exhorts to weep ever more copiously for her "Sweet Spouse."[7]

This introduces the other woman, the Magdalene figure on our left. We do not much like looking at her because, after Michelangelo's destruction of the unfinished group and its subsequent restoration by Tiberio Calcagni, it was this figure that was most overworked, scaled down, pettified. Nevertheless, in the role he has made her play, as Magdalene and as counterpart of the Virgin, she is all Michelangelo's.

She is embraced. That she is truly embraced, not merely caught in the peripheral sweep of a circuiting rhythm, is confirmed by one small nuance. The drapery fold between the Magdalene's breasts that flows down her abdomen is not her own garment but the loose end of Christ's winding sheet. Released from his chest it presses gently against her body. The delegated caress of the shroud confirms the Magdalene as an object of love.

At this point a vast medieval tradition concerning the erotic association of Christ and the Magdalene becomes relevant.[8] Thus Rabanus Maurus in the ninth century: "Mary Magdalene suffered as lovers are accustomed to suffer, and mourned inestimably concerning the corporeal absence of her beloved lover." Passion plays kept the tradition alive. In the *Noli me tangere* scene of a late fifteenth-century English play Mary exclaims: "O mine heart, where hast thou bee. / Come home again and live with me!" And in the anonymous fourteenth-century Italian Life of St. Mary Magdalene she cries out: "Oh, most blessed Cross! Would I had been in Thy stead, and that my Lord had been crucified in mine arms, my hands nailed against His, . . . so that I had died with Him, and thus neither in life nor death ever departed from Him."[9]

An erotic energy derived from these un-Biblical fantasies invests Michelangelo's group. The Magdalene's approach to Christ's body betrays a sexual intimacy either uninterrupted or generated by death.[10]

But the Magdalene is not simply a paramour. She is here what she is to the whole patristic tradition – the sinner in the flesh, the forgiven harlot, repentant. And it is in this dual role, as lover and penitent, that she too inhabits what Tolnay called "the essential *concetto*." She is the counterpart of the Virgin in a bilateral scheme. "It is she whom he loved more than any other woman in the world, save the Virgin Mary," says the fourteenth-century Life. The two Marys are continually paralleled in the sermons. Both stand for the Church – the sinner turned, and the one without sin, personifications of Penitence and Immaculacy. Together, bracing and being embraced, they sustain the dead body like the heraldic supporters of an escutcheon. Both are, or were meant to be, folded within the limbs of Christ's body.

Finally, the secret intimacies that connect the two Marys and Christ help to define the unity of the entire group. Since the sculptor had planned to erect this image of Christ at his tomb, it is appropriate that he should have projected his likeness upon the Joseph of Arimathea, who, after the Descent from the Cross, received Christ in his sepulchre.[11] Between Joseph's unused tomb and Mary's unopened womb elaborate analogies had been drawn since St. Ambrose.[12] And St. Augustine closes his Sermon 248, "De sepultura Domini," with words that work like a commentary upon Michelangelo's group: "If indeed she received the Lord deep in her womb, he received him deep in his heart." They are at one, therefore, in the communion of grief. But the contrast is no less poignant, for the women serve – in a given visual corollary – to isolate the hooded mourner who bears Michelangelo's face. His only contact with Christ's body is with the arm that embraces the sinner, and his towering solitude contrasts with the communion of lovers under his hands.

2. Is it likely that the outright carnality of the symbolic slung leg helped to motivate the destruction of the *Pietà*?

Let us hear Michelangelo, as Vasari reports him, speak of this work. Since it was uncommissioned, it was, we are told, done as a pastime, for recreation, and "because the use of the mallet kept him [he was then seventy-five!] in good health."[13] As an apology for an intended tomb monument such remarks seem evasive almost to the point of flippancy. We then learn that the work was destroyed. And Vasari, because he cannot imagine why, offers three reasons: The marble, he says, was marred by many flaws. (But Michelangelo himself speaks of only one troublesome vein in the stone, and furthermore this is not convincing ground for destroying a work nearly completed.) Second, says Vasari, the marble was hard, making the sparks fly from the chisel. (But though this might be reason for abandoning the work, it hardly explains the added labor of breaking it up; and furthermore, what remains of the stone shows Michelangelo equal to it.) Third and last, says Vasari, "the artist's standards were so high that he could never be content with what he had done." (But how should such general discontent explain a unique instance of mutilation? Though the Florentine *Pietà* is not the poorest of Michelangelo's works, it is the only one he took the trouble to smash.)

Elsewhere in Vasari's account, the sculptor himself being pressed to explain "why he had ruined such a marvelous work," he responds with a tangle of incongruous motives: "It was because of the importunity of his servant Urbino who nagged at him daily that he should finish it; and that among other things a piece of the Virgin's elbow got broken off, and that even before that he had come to hate it, and he had had many mishaps because of a vein in the stone; so that losing patience he broke it, and would have smashed it completely had not his servant Antonio asked that he give it to him just as it was."

The story ends with Michelangelo consenting to let a young pupil, Tiberio Calcagni, reassemble the group on behalf of a wealthy admirer who promises to pay two hundred ducats in gold to the servant Antonio, who now owns the pieces.

Here again are some patent evasions. Michelangelo says he has come to hate the work to the point of wanting it utterly smashed; but he attacked only that corner of the block which involved Christ's left leg and arm. He then allows the group, including the arm, to be restored – but not the leg. And there is indication that he had broken this leg into fragments. For the inventory of his house taken in 1566 (after the death of Daniele da Volterra who had taken it over) includes "un ginocchio di marmo della Pietà di Michelangelo" – presumably from this work. A knee only was allowed to survive.[14]

One other incident points to the leg as the focus of special concern. It is a short anecdote which Vasari, at the end of his Michelangelo *Vita*, tells to illustrate an interesting character trait:

> One night Vasari was sent by Pope Julius III to Michelangelo's house for a drawing. He found the master working on the marble Pietà which he broke. Recognizing the knock, Michelangelo rose and took a lantern. When Vasari had explained his errand, he sent Urbino [his servant] for the design and began to speak of other things. Vasari meanwhile cast his eyes upon a leg of the Christ which Michelangelo was working on and was trying to alter, and in order that Vasari might not see it, he let the lantern fall, and being now in the dark, called Urbino to bring a light; in the meantime, stepping out of the room where he had been, he said, I am so old that death frequently drags at my cloak to take me, and one day I myself will fall like this lantern and so the light of my life will go out.

A dark story, not the kind that yields real evidence. It contributes nothing to our purpose if we assume that Michelangelo kept open house in his studio, and that the *Pietà* was normally left exposed, so that Vasari would have known the *concetto* from previous visits. On the other hand, if Michelangelo was normally secretive about all or any of his unfinished works, and if, carving the *Pietà* by night, he normally kept it covered by day, then Vasari's story gains interest. The question cannot be wholly resolved.[15] But it is worth recalling that Michelangelo's secretiveness was proverbial. Forty years after his death, Van Mander writes in his *Schilderboek* that Hendrik Goltzius never allowed unfinished works to be seen and that "in this as in many other things, he resembled the great Michelangelo." In the first (open house) alternative, assuming Michelangelo's friends to be familiar with the work he had in hand, the sculptor's embarrassment on the occasion of Vasari's nocturnal call would be due to some fresh mishap in the carving, caused perhaps by the emery vein. In this hypothesis it is mere coincidence that the location of this vein coincides with that of the slung leg (whose eroticism, being merely symbolic, would hardly have caused the sculptor anxiety). A flaw in the marble becomes the sufficient reason for the destruction of the *Pietà*. Michelangelo would have been moved to destroy his work by a succession of accidents to the stone and the vexation that followed. The destructive act tells us nothing that is not technical about the work, nor about the artist beyond proving his irascible temper.

There is now another way of posing the problem. The Florentine *Pietà* employs a direct sexual metaphor on a scale unprecedented in Christian devotional art. Michelangelo's figurative use of the human figure recalls the poetic idiom of those earlier mystics and preachers who described the ultimate religious experience in figures of physical love. St. Bernardino of Siena for instance says sexual ecstasy when he means mystic transport, and there is nothing uncommon in this kind of *wording*.[16] But poets and mystics had the freedom of figurative speech as an ancient charter. It was another matter to claim such poetic license in the concretions of palpable sculpture. Now, with the reformist atmosphere settling on Rome, Michelangelo may have felt certain resources of confidence failing: confidence that his intent would not be pruriently misunderstood, and confidence in the transcendent eloquence of the body – in the possibility of infinitely spiritualizing its anatomic machinery while still respecting its norms. Perhaps it was simply the vulgarization of his metaphorical idiom in the work of others that crowded and threatened his confidence. Or, more specifically, that the accelerating diffusion and coarsening of the slung leg motif during the very years of his work on the *Pietà* rendered the pose increasingly unacceptable. Such musings – for there seems no way to move them beyond conjecture – suggest alternative or additional motives for Michelangelo's destructive act. They keep open the possibility that he shattered his work not because he was vexed by a servant's nagging, and not because part of the Virgin's elbow had splintered off, but that he destroyed it in despair: that he saw himself pushing the rhetoric of carnal gesture to a point where its metaphorical status passed out of control; that he felt himself crossing the limit of what seemed expressible in his art. His demolition then would be a renunciation, comparable to that which sounds again in the final lines of his sonnet:

> To paint or carve no longer calms
> the soul turned to that Love divine
> Who to embrace us on the cross opens his arms.[17]

The date of the sonnet falls within the year of the destruction of the *Pietà*.

3. Does the interpretation of the slung leg motif carry over to other classes of monuments?

There can be no doubt that the motif is sexual when it couples adults. The question arises whether we are to recognize the same symbolic charge in images of the Virgin and Child. In the early sixteenth century (in pictures by Raphael, Puligo, Andrea del Sarto; some half-dozen Michelangelo drawings, etc.) the motif of the infant's leg arched over the mother's thigh is so common as to suggest either that it is wholly innocent or that, being thoroughly understood, it was felt to be more safely assigned to the lively Child than to the Man. In Michelangelo's early marble tondo, the *Madonna Taddei*, as in Andrea del Sarto's *Madonna del Sacco* (1526), the Child's leg scaling the Virgin's thigh is presumably innocent; doubt on this score may even meet with resentment. On the other hand, the infant's pose may have been at first playful, athletic, striding forth, to become erotic only by a subsequent adaptation to the slung leg motif. One's faith in the abiding innocence of the motif is shaken on comparing certain works of slightly later date in which the Child seems cast in a similar role. Thus a remarkably similar pose is struck by the Christ Child in a Parmigianino design preserved in a seventeenth-century engraving by Schelte à Bolswert.[18] Here the "innocence" of the pose can no longer be argued, particularly when it is found, by comparing Giulio Romano's *Cupid and Psyche*,[19] that regardless of the boy's age this bestriding a woman's thigh is an unmistakable gesture of male appropriation. In Parmigianino's design the erotic tenor is further emphasized by the riper age of the Child: not a babe, but the young Saviour embracing with one hand the urn of his Passion while his other hand grasps Mary's shoulder. And this seizing a shoulder is another ceremonial gesture of possession-taking, whether it be Death laying hold of a youth, or Mars claiming Venus.[20]

There is a wide frame of reference for these sixteenth-century images in which the nuptials of the heavenly spouse are prefigured in the approach of the Child. The emotions projected into such pictures may not always have been formal doctrine, but their part in the religious imagination of Mediterranean Europe was vital. A millennial procession of symbolic equations had left thought and feeling caught in a constellation of metaphors. Within it, subtle theological formulas and secret fantasies could equally find accommodation. The Old Testament's Song of Songs, which in the Rabbinical exegesis declared God's love for Israel, became, in the Christian translation, Christ's love for his Church. "It can be said frankly and safely," writes St. Gregory the Great, "that when in the mystery of the Incarnation the Father celebrated the wedding of his royal son, he gave him the Holy Church as his companion. The womb of the Virgin Mother was the nuptial couch of this bridegroom."[21]

But from the second century onward Mary herself becomes a type of the Church. Before long, the Church is figured in Mary as Mary is in the Church. Christ is the bridegroom of the one as of the other. By the twelfth century, *Ecclesia*, herself Virgin and Mother and Beloved of Christ, has become in every respect interchangeable with the Virgin. As in the doctrine of Perichoresis, which describes the two natures of Christ, Mary and Church wholly inhere in each other. "Everything that is said of the Church," writes Honorius of Autun in his authoritative commentary on Canticles, "can also be understood as being said of the Virgin herself, the bride and mother of the bridegroom."[22]

In the reading of Canticles, and in its pictorial complement, the Beloved embraced by Christ became and remained an ambivalent symbol. In illuminated twelfth-century Bibles, or in manuscript commentaries on Canticles, the initial *O* of the opening "Osculetur me oscula oris sui" may enclose lovers who share even their single halo; but the lady's identity, whether Virgin or Church, is undefined.[23]

But another type exists which seems to demand a simple Marian interpretation. It occurs when the bridegroom of Canticles takes form as the newborn Christ – as in the Lyons Bible.[24] Here the historiated initial which opens the "Let him kiss me with the kisses of his mouth" contains a Madonna and Child, the Child coming as bridegroom, as lover, as man, striding toward her, embracing, their cheeks sharing one contour so that their eyes touch and their coupled lips align as in a kiss folded out.

There is a tradition here which reaches both forward and backward. An engraving by Abraham van Merlen, a Jesuit illustrator of about 1600, shows

205

the Madonna and Child over the legend "My beloved is mine, and I am his. . . . He shall lie all night betwixt my breasts" (Cant. 2:16, and 1:12). On the other hand, the Lyons Bible initial, painted by an unknown Byzantinizing illuminator, points back to the byzantine Madonna of "sweet love," the *Glykophilousa*. It is here and in its derivatives that one finds, in the tender contact between the Mother and Child, the first veiled erotic allusions to their mystic marriage.[25] The intent of countless later Madonna and Child confrontations in art is to reveal the Child Jesus as fully the Christ and fully man who, having chosen his mother, now chooses her for his Virgin bride.

Nowhere were such thoughts more compellingly realized than in the preaching of Savonarola, which Michelangelo heard in his youth. In Savonarola's remarkable expostulation for the pregnant Virgin, his "Sponsa Jesu," Mary yields dramatically as mother and bride to the awaited Bridegroom. Addressing herself to the Father, she pleads that he vouchsafe her a delivery as hurtless as the conception had been: ". . . così come io lo ho conceputo senza pudore e senza violamento della mia verginità, così ora per tua grazia lo partorisca senza dolore perseverando vergine e illibata."[26]

So far we are on traditional ground. Savonarola merely presents as dramatic monologue what earlier Fathers, such as Andrew of Crete (ca. 700) had expressed by apostrophe: "Your chastity, O Virgin, has remained as it was at the beginning, inviolate. For Christ the sun, like a bridegroom from the bridal chamber, has come forth from you."[27] But the traditional evocations of sun and bridegroom, derived from the Psalms, grow strangely sensual in Savonarola's lines for the Virgin as they turn into direct address: "Come forth then, my Son, even as the bridegroom from his bridal chamber. Issue forth from my womb, . . . Gladden your handmaid's soul, fulfill at last your mother's desire, my soul has desired you and desires you continually, Jesus mine, I can wait no more, I am consumed, I melt, I languish in love. . . ."[28]

For Savonarola the delivery of the Christ Child was not only, as it had seemed to earlier visionaries, quick, painless, and without lesion; it was pleasurable, and the pleasure ecstatic. And the Infant Bridegroom who came forth in such sheer virility must be tremendous and ardent.

In sheer virility he appears in Michelangelo's *Madonna Medici*, ca. 1525–1531 (fig. 11.3). The Christ Child is an infant Hercules, sitting forward, straddling his Mother's thigh. His upper body swerves through an astonishing 180 degrees, and he appears to be nursing. But his left hand, grasping the Virgin's shoulder, leaves infancy as far behind as does the precocious athleticism of his physique.

Why the crossed legs of the Virgin? Perhaps Michelangelo was alluding to an old Medicean image. In the cortile of the Medici Palace, the frieze decoration consists of relief tondi in which ancient gems from the Medici collection are monumentalized. One of these shows a nude child turning toward a seated woman, draped, her legs crossed; it represents the wedding procession of Eros and Psyche: divine love and the human soul about to be married in heaven.

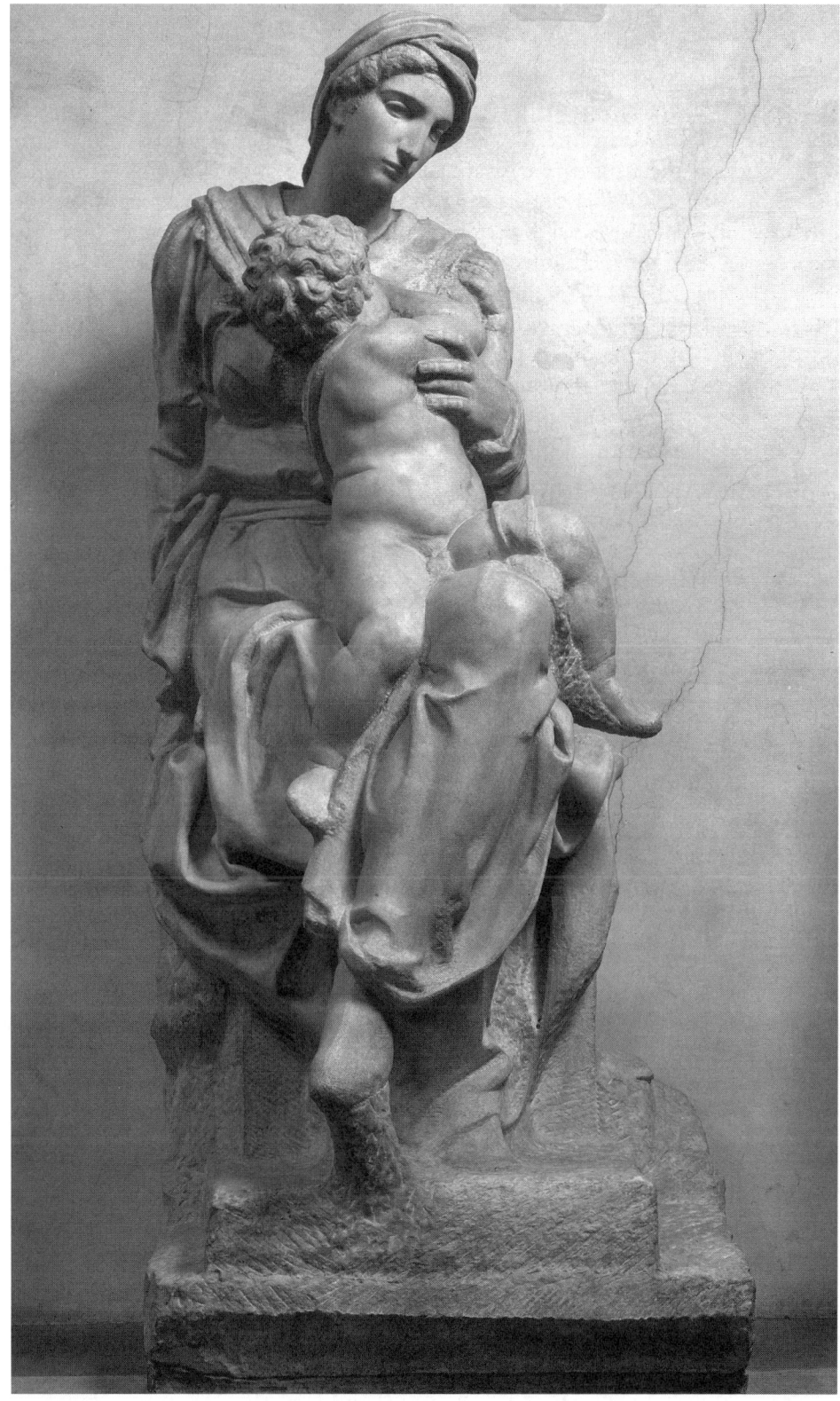

Figure 11.3 Michelangelo, *Medici Madonna*. Florence, Medici Chapel, San Lorenzo. Bridgeman / Alinari Archives-Florence.

Tolnay suggested that the Madonna's legs were crossed so as to elevate the Child "to bring it closer to the bosom." But in three surviving Michelangelo drawings that anticipate the *Madonna Medici*[29] the Child is already fast at the breast though the Mother's legs are uncrossed; it is rather her lofty shoulder that is out of reach. What the crossing of the Madonna's legs accomplishes is to lift the Child far above her breast level; evidently the literal contact here was dispensable since the mere direction of the Child's turn would suffice to suggest suckling. But with the Madonna's legs crossed, the Child rides the high crest of her thigh.[30] Now all his body, his straddling seat and his grip on her shoulder, reveal in the Child the divine lover electing his spouse.

Anatomy, said Freud, is destiny. In Michelangelo's hands it became theology.*

Appendix A: The Slung Leg

The attempt to construct a "history" of the slung leg motif is somewhat foolhardy, since a single find may modify or even upset the structure, and examples are bound to keep turning up. But to forestall an undue expansion of the inventory, let me redefine what I consider the chief limiting feature of the motif. Pairs of lovers of whom one sits on the lap of the other, or on one thigh within his lap, are ruled out. The "canonic form" requires that each partner maintain his own seat, so that the leg that is thrown across becomes a gesture toward the other, a wooing or claiming, an action that visibly changes a relationship or establishes a condition. Whereas the settled intimacy of the lap-sitting pose, even though it include a slung leg, suggests the condition itself. (E.g., the Michelangelesque *Adam and Eve* drawing at the Musée Bonnat, Bayonne; see Jacob Bean, *Catalogue of Italian Drawings*, 1966, No. 66.)

Ruled out on another count are seated couples with elaborately intertwined legs, as in Robetta's *Allegory of Envy* engraving of ca. 1520 (B. xiii, 24; A. M. Hind, *Early Italian Engraving*, London 1938–1948, D.II,31 and pl. 294) or as in Mabuse's picture *Hercules and Dejanira*, 1517, in the Barber Institute, Birmingham. (See H. Pauwels, *Jan Gossaert, genaamd Mabuse*, Rotterdam Exhibition Catalogue, 1965, pl. iv.) I would call these the "hearsay type," since they suggest a knowledge of the symbol but not of its authentic form. In the work of Mabuse, who sojourned in Rome during 1508–1509, the motif appears twice more in similarly unorthodox fashion: in a drawing of Adam and Eve at the Albertina, dated 1525 (Rotterdam Catalogue, 61), and most significantly in his early woodcut of ca. 1515, *Hercules and Dejanira*. In both of these it is the husband's leg that crosses the wife's. The woodcut has further importance as a likely source for Rubens's *Shepherd and Shepherdess* in Munich.

The two earliest instances of the motif in its canonic form both occur in rare Italian engravings with obscure subjects. First, the *Faun Family* by the still unidentified Bolognese Master I.B. with the Bird (B. xiii, 248, No. 7; Hind, v,

256, No. 6, and pl. 837). The Master I.B.'s activity is documented from 1500 to 1506 but probably extends for two decades longer. In the *Faun Family* a Leonardesque nymph lays her leg over the thigh of a laurel-crowned wildman.

Next comes an Agostino Veneziano engraving of 1516 (Fig. 15; B. xiv, 241) – after a Bandinelli design, according to Bartsch. Bartsch's title, "The News Brought to Olympus" (retained in Passavant, *Peintre-Graveur*, vi, 57, No. 60) is a confession that the subject is unidentified. The pattern of the amorous group in the sky seems to anticipate both Raphael's Isaac fresco and some of the action of Michelangelo's Christ.

Raphael's fresco of 1520 (probably executed by Perino del Vaga) is followed in 1527 by the Caraglio engravings after Perino's designs (B. xv, 11 and 14), and by one undescribed and undated engraving of Venus and Mars, attributed to Giorgio Ghisi after Giulio Romano (illustrated Bartsch, vol. 15a, unpublished; Institute of Fine Arts library, New York University). That these prints were chiefly responsible for the diffusion of the motif is confirmed by a majolica dish at the Metropolitan Museum, New York, dated Urbino 1542, and attributed to the shop of Orazio Fontana. Here the Caraglio–Perino *Neptune and Thetis* (B. 11) is adapted to a *Story of Venus and Mars*. The dispersion of prints may also account for the occurrence of the motif in two Venetian pictures of the 1530s: Bonifazio's *Lot and His Daughters* in the Walter P. Chrysler Collection, New York, and the *Mythological Scene* in the London National Gallery (No. 1123), formerly given to Bonifazio, now catalogued as "Venetian School." The set of engravings by Bonasone entitled *Loves of the Gods* (especially B. 151 and 155) again displays our motif, but cannot be dated with certainty before the mid-century. The earliest Italian sculpture to display the motif may be Riccio's small bronze *Satyr and Satyress* in the Victoria and Albert Museum, London.

If the above listing reads like a random sampling from a great store, I have defeated my purpose. I have cited every instance of the motif before about 1540 that I, with the help of friends, have been able to find.

Appendix B: Vigenère's Credibility

The chief witness for the "open house" theory is the French *littérateur* Blaise de Vigenère (1523–1598), who visited Rome in 1550. In his annotated translation of Philostratus, Vigenère claims to have known Michelangelo and to have watched him work. His description of the aged sculptor plying hammer and chisel is significant on three counts. First, it describes Michelangelo's attack on a marble block as all fury and impetuosity – sufficient to explain any subsequent accident, mutilation, or failure. Second, it challenges as a romantic legend the tradition of Michelangelo's secretiveness; if a young visiting foreigner had such easy access to Michelangelo's atelier that he could stand by for a quarter-hour while the master worked, then the traditional view needs drastic modification. Third, Vigenère's testimony seems to furnish the *terminus ante quem* for the inception of the Florentine *Pietà*, for it is with this work that the marble observed by Vigenère has been identified. (H. Thode, *Michelangelo und das Ende der Renaissance*, Berlin, 1912, II, 690: "Den Beginn der Arbeit, . . . lernen wir durch Blaise de Vigenère kennen: mit ungestümen, leidenschaftlichen Hammerschlägen sucht der Meister dem Block, ihn formend, sein stürmisches Seelenleben aufzuzwingen." Denyse Métral, author of *Blaise de Vigenère: Archéologue et critique d'art*, Paris, 1939, 93, concludes, on mistaken grounds, that the marble block observed by Vigenère "est la Pieta du Dôme de Florence, seul groupe que Michel-Ange ait sculpté dans sa vieillesse." And so Herbert von Einem, "Bemerkungen zur Florentiner Pieta Michelangelos," *Jahrbuch der preussischen Kunstsammlungen*, 61, Berlin, 1940, 77: "1550 hat der Franzose Blaise de Vigenère Michelangelo an einer Gruppe mit solchem Ungestüm arbeiten sehen, dass er in Angst war, sie würde in die Büche gehen, vermutlich handelt es sich hier um die florentiner Pieta.")

The importance of Vigenère to Michelangelo studies derives above all from the personal contact he claims to have had with the master. It is because he twice reports opinions heard directly from Michelangelo's lips that his recollections are ranked as primary sources. "Vigenère a personellement connu Michel-Ange, il en parle . . . en évoquant ses propres souvenirs. Ce qu'il dit a la valeur d'une source" (Métral, 238). Against this prevailing opinion, I maintain that Vigenère speaking on art is not a credible witness and that his references to Michelangelo are practically worthless.

Before citing the texts, a few words about the author in general. He is an enthusiastic student of antiquity, including Hebrew and Greek, and a prolific translator and annotator of the Latin historians. His interests range remarkably wide, from a history of Poland (1573) to a treatise on occult signs (1586). The very year 1578 in which he published *Les Images . . . des deux Philostrates*, also saw the publication of his treatise on comets and of his Lamentations of Jeremiah in verse. His literary manner, however, tends to be rambling and uncritical, and his memory is cavalier: "Les souvenirs de Vigenère ne sont pas très précis," says his devoted biographer (Métral, 90). As for his reliability, the best she can adduce in his defense is that he never misleads the reader on purpose: "Lorsqu'il trompe le lecteur c'est qu'il se trompe lui-même" (Métral, 81).

Nowhere does Vigenère sound more remote and naïve than in discussions of art. Clearly, he entered the field only because Philostratus's descriptions of pictures had become a literary monument. When dealing with the art of his own period, he records remembered hearsay and makes it his own by exaggeration. Thus, for example, his earliest reference to Michelangelo declares the *Torso Belvedere* to have been "l'escolle principalle de Michel l'Ange, où il se façonna tel qu'on l'a veu depuis en ses ouvrages de relief et de platte peinture." (See Vigenère's translation from the Latin version of 1556 of Chalkondylas's Turkish history: *L'Histoire de la Décadence de l'Empire Grec et establissement de celuy des Turcs, . . . par Nicolas Chalcondyle*, Athénien, Paris, 1577, fol. F.III v.)

Following are Vigenère's two recollections of Michelangelo's sayings. (Note that in both of them Michelangelo is made to speak in unison with another party.)

The first occurs in Vigenère's translation of *Les Décades de Tite-Live*, 1583. The Capitoline Hill is under discussion and Vigenère remarks: "Là est encore pour le jourd'huy un petit satyre de marbre tout rompu et repiecé, mais l'un des plus belles excellents chefs d'oeuvre qui se puisse voir, comme mesme je l'ay ouy autrefois de la bouche propre de Michel Lange et d'un maistre Jacques natif d'Angoulême qui l'esgalloit en la statuaire. . . ." Of this mysterious Jacques, whom Vigenère believed to be Michelangelo's equal, no trace has been found. Vigenère must have been his loyal friend, for he speaks of him at greater length in the *Philostratus* (ed. 1614, p. 855), where we hear that in 1550 the young sculptor Jacques d'Angoulême prevailed over Michelangelo in a competition "for the model of an image of St. Peter."

This memoir was published thirty-three years after the alleged event. Fourteen years later the second edition of *Les Images des Philostrates* (ed. 1597, p. 951) introduces Michelangelo as *paysagiste*: "L'escholle pythagoricienne . . . reduisoit les genres de couleurs à ces quatres: le noir et le blanc; le jaune et le rouge. Néanmoins j'ay ouy dire plusieurs fois à Michel l'Ange et à Daniel de Volterre qu'ils aimeroient mieux se passer du jaulne que du bleu à cause du ciel qui intervient en tous ouvrages presque. . . ."

The two longest references to Michelangelo are found again in the *Philostratus* (pp. 853–55), not however in the original 1578 publication, but only in the augmented edition of 1597, that is to say, one year before the author's death at seventy-five, and forty-seven years after the events recalled. We are given a conventional *paragone* dispute. Sculpture is more difficult than painting, rules Vigenère, witness the fact that Michelangelo, who excelled in both arts, could carve only one figure for every hundred he painted. We then hear of a Michelangelo undertaking of which no other rumor has reached us: "L'entreprise de Michel l'Ange estoit hautaine et fort hardie, sentent bien sa main asseurée, lequel commança l'an 1550, que j'estois à Rome, un crucifiement où il y avoit de dix à douze personnages, non pas moindres que le naturel, le tout d'une seule pièce de marbre, qui estoit un chapiteau de l'une de ces huict grandes colonnes du temple de la paix de Vespasian . . . mais la mort qui le prevint empescha la perfection de ce bel ouvrage, selon sa coustume ordinaire. . . ."

There are two ways to read this account. Taken literally it is wild enough to be dismissed out of hand. No capital accommodates a lifesize Crucifixion, and no twelve-figure project begun by Michelangelo passes unnoticed. The alternative is to understand that Vigenère was again writing from hearsay, and that the inaccuracies in his story are slight, venial, and in character. His "Temple of Peace of Vespasian" is presumably the Basilica of Constantine. His "ten to twelve lifesize figures" is a hyperbolic expression for "many," and his "Crucifixion" is our *Pietà*, a complex group of many figures which the sculptor was then carving from a single block and never completed. If Vigenère's "Crucifixion" refers to anything real at all, then it must be to the Duomo *Pietà*. But then it is also apparent that he never laid eyes on it, nor ever claimed to have seen it.

What he did claim to have seen he describes as follows: "Je puis dire avoir veu Michel l'Ange bien que aagé de plus de 60 ans, & encore non des plus robustes, abattre plus d'escailles d'un très dur marbre en un quart d'heure, que trois ieunes tailleurs de pierre n'eussant peu faire en trois ou quatre, chose presqu'incroyable qui ne le verroit: & y alloit d'une telle impétuosité & furie, que je pensois que tout l'ouvrage deust aller en pièces, abattant par terre d'un seul coup de gros morceaux de trois ou quatre doigts d'espoisseur, si ric à ric de sa marque que s'il eust passé outre tant soit peu plus qu'il ne falloit, il y avoit danger de perdre tout . . ." (p. 855).

What should one make of this oft-quoted passage, coming as it does from a garrulous *littérateur* who understands nothing of the sculptor's métier, remembers little, and exaggerates by routine? Every Michelangelo marble tells of the master's sense of its grain and density, of the responsive intuition of depth with which he cut every surface. It seems preposterous to impute frenzy and expressionist recklessness to Michelangelo's working process on the strength of Vigenère's naïve observation. If Vigenère did indeed watch Michelangelo carve for a quarter-hour, then what he saw was a block so rough-hewn that its figural composition was not yet discernible, at least not to him. This roughness and the boulder size of the chips being cut away suggest a preliminary operation which in sixteenth-century Rome would normally take place in the courtyard outdoors. And this indicates once again that Vigenère was not in Michelangelo's studio but was watching from some distance away, perhaps from a window. He was at any rate recording his recollection at a remove of forty-seven years.

To identify Vigenère's "manhandled marble" with his "Crucifixion," as Métral proposes to do, is unsound. When Vigenère speaks of the "Crucifixion," he does not claim to have seen it in progress; nor, when he comes to speak of the marble he saw, does he indicate any subject, origin, or destination for it. Though he describes the "Crucifixion" and the "manhandled block" on adjacent pages, he makes no connection between the two, and it is wholly unwarranted for the reader to make them the same.

But suppose we forget Vigenère's fabulous "Crucifixion" and simply identify the "manhandled marble" he saw with the Florentine *Pietà*, as Thode and Von Einem have done? This again seems arbitrary, since there are several other Michelangelo marbles that Vigenère might have seen in 1550. There was the large marble group which was eventually cut down to become the *Pietà Rondanini*. Vasari mentions yet another *Pietà* (". . . un altro pezzo di marmo dove era stato già abbozzato un'altra Pietà, molto minore" – Vasari–Milanesi, VII, 245), of which however nothing further is known. The location in 1550 of the architectural fragment from which the disputed *Pietà Palestrina* was carved is not known. But Michelangelo certainly had other marble blocks standing about, including an unfinished seated pope (St. Peter or Julius?), mentioned in the 1564 inventory of his estate, but of whose earlier history nothing is known (Thode, *Kritische Untersuchungen*, Berlin, 1908–1913, II, 283–84).

It is arguable that of all these candidates the Florentine *Pietà* is the least likely to have been seen by Vigenère. For Vigenère is not, as Métral believes, the essential source "faute duquel on ignorerait la date à laquelle le maître a commencé cette dernière sculpture" (p. 93). That date emerges more unequivocally from the first 1550 edition of Vasari's *Lives*: "E bozzato ancora in casa sua, quattro figure in un marmo nelle quali è un Christo, deposto di croce: la quale opera può pensarsi, che se da lui finita al mondo restasse, ogni altra opra sua da quella superata sarebbe per la difficultá del cavar di quel sasso tante cose perfette."

Since Vasari's manuscript was finished by 1546–47, both Tolnay and Von Einem argue that the *Pietà* must have been under way by that time. And if begun before 1547, it is unlikely that after three or four years of constant labor ("lavorava Michelagnolo quasi ogni giorno per suo passatempo, intorno a quella Pietà . . ." Vasari–Milanesi, VII, 242–43) he would still be at a roughing-out stage in 1550.

Unfortunately the date for the beginning of the *Pietà* cannot be so precisely fixed. While it is true that Vasari's manuscript was written by 1546–47, the documents assembled by Wolfgang Kallab (*Vasari-Studien*, Vienna, 1908, 83) indicate that additions and changes were continually made until October 1549, when Duke Cosimo finally ordered the manuscript to go to press. Let us suppose that the *Pietà* was begun as late as, say, 1548; a "stop-press" reference to it may have been exactly what Vasari wanted. Since he was concerned to keep the *Lives* up to date, adding biographies of four artists who had died during 1546 and 1547, and since the entire historical structure he had devised culminated in Michelangelo, it is quite possible that he might have made the effort to mention that latest work of the supreme master which, surpassing all his earlier productions, promised to become the absolute pinnacle of world art.

Vasari had left Rome in the fall of 1546. And here again we face a dilemma. If we accept his reference to the roughed-out *Pietà* as the account of a personal visit, then the Florentine *Pietà* was indeed begun in 1546. But Vasari's description seems rather to be based on a verbal or written report, supported perhaps by a sketch. And in that case both the work's beginning and the (inserted?) mention of it in Vasari's manuscript may fall anywhere before the autumn of 1549. Later it cannot have been. In February 1550 Vasari arrived once again in Rome, but in the following month, March 1550, his *Lives* was delivered complete by the ducal printer in Florence.

The following conclusions seem justified: the Vasari material does not permit closer dating for the inception of the *Pietà* than 1546–1549. Nevertheless, there is no ground for believing that this was the work which the visiting Vigenère saw as a roughed-out block in 1550. If Vigenère's story of a Michelangelo "Crucifixion" carved from an antique capital is a garbled reference to the *Pietà*, than it is certain that he never saw it. And there is no reason whatsoever to think that Vigenère ever saw the inside of Michelangelo's house.

213

Notes

1 Thus Henry Thode, *Michelangelo, Kritische Untersuchungen*, Berlin, 1908–1913,
   II, 278: "Für das linke Bein Christi ist gar kein Platz vorhanden. . . . Die einzige
   Möglichkeit es anzubringen wäre die gewesen es vorne über Marias Bein herabhängen
   zu lassen. . . . Dies aber hätte eine nicht nur unschöne, sondern unmögliche Stellung
   ergeben." Thode is followed by Herbert von Einem, *Michelangelo: Die Pieta im
   Dom zu Florenz*, Stuttgart, 1956, 6: "Rätselhaft ist das Fehlen des linken Beines
   Christi. Wir wissen dass es vorhanden gewesen ist . . . Aber es ist keine Frage, dass
   sein Fehlen ein künstlerischer Vorzug ist. Sollten wir hier den Grund fassen können,
   warum Michelangelo das Werk aufgegeben hat?"

2 Engraving attributed to Cherubino Alberti, ca. 1580, Bartsch, VII, 23; Sabbatini,
   before 1576, altarpiece in the sacristy of Saint Peter's, Rome; a free copy of it by
   Antonio Viviani in Santa Maria dei Monti, Rome. Both described in Baglione's
   Vite . . . , Rome, 1642, 18 and 103.

3 See Appendix A dealing with the slung leg motif.

4 See J. Makaranos in *Archaiologikon Deltion*, 18 (1963), Athens, 1965. Summaries
   in German and English respectively appeared in *Du*, Oct. 1965, and in *Horizon*,
   Fall 1966. Most recent discussion in T. B. L. Webster, *The Art of Greece: The Age of
   Hellenism*, New York, 1965, 20–23.

5 Summaries of orthodox doctrine and poetry describing the Virgin as *Sponsa Dei*,
   and specifically as Bride of Christ, are contained in Yrjo Hirn, *The Sacred Shrine*
   (1909), Beacon Press edition, Boston, 1957, especially pp. 291ff. and the chapters
   "Annunciation" and "Incarnation." See also Henri de Lubac, *Méditations sur l'Église*,
   Paris, 1953, ch. IX, in English as *The Splendour of the Church*, Deus Books, Paulist
   Press, Glen Rock, N.J., 1963, 198ff.

6 *Michelangelo: The Final Period*, Princeton, 1960, 87.

7 Savonarola, *Tractato dello Amore di Jesu Christo*, Florence, 1492, unpaginated.

8 The medieval sources adduced in this and the following paragraphs are cited in
   Helen M. Garth's exemplary study, *St. Mary Magdalene in Medieval Literature*,
   Johns Hopkins, 1950.

9 The eroticism of the Magdalene's exclamation is implicit in its very form, which is
   a commonplace of love poetry. The lover envies whatever object is in contact with
   the beloved. Thus in Longus's *Daphnis and Chloe* (3rd cent. A.D., trans. Moses
   Hadas, New York, 1953, 25): "Would that I could become a pipe, so that he might
   breathe upon me!" Or Romeo in the Balcony Scene (Act II, sc. ii): "Oh, that I were
   a glove upon that hand, that I might touch that cheek!" But we may add to these
   Mary's farewell at the Entombment: "Oh most happy stone that dost now enclose
   the holy body which for nine months was hidden in my womb. I bless thee and
   envy thee . . ." (quoted in Hirn, *Sacred Shrine*, 338).

10 Compare Michelangelo's other attacks on the subject, notably in the reworked
   drawing for a Descent from the Cross, ca. 1545–1555, at the Ashmolean Museum,
   Oxford (see K. T. Parker, *Catalogue of the Collection of Drawings*, Oxford, 1956, II,
   342, pl. xcii). Michelangelo here participates in one of the great minor themes of
   16th-century art: the insinuated attachment of the Magdalene to Christ in scenes of
   Pietà and Entombment. Few subjects offered such challenge to ardor and ingenuity,
   indiscretion and tact.

11 The identity of the topmost figure is discussed by Wolfgang Stechow in "Joseph of Arimathea or Nicodemus," in *Studien zur Toskanischen Kunst*, Festschrift Heydenreich, Munich, 1964, 289–302. After an impressive accumulation of scholarly argument on both sides, the question remains undecided. But it appears to me, as I think it does to Prof. Stechow, that the weight of probability continues in Joseph's favor.

12 See Hirn, *Sacred Shrine*, ch. vii, esp. 337ff. Hirn quotes the Ambrosian Easter Hymn: "Thou who wast before born of a Virgin, art born now of the grave"; and from Ephraim Syrus (ca. 306–378), who compares Christ's emergence from the sealed grave to the fact of Mary's anatomical virginity: "Thus didst thou show, O Lord, by thy resurrection from the grave, the miracle of thy birth, for each was closed and each was sealed, both the grave and the womb. Thou wast pure in the womb and living in the grave, and Mary's womb, like the grave, bore an unbroken seal." See also St. Augustine (Sermon 248, "De sepultura Domini, *PL*, XXXIX, col. 2204): ". . . No less honor is due to the tomb which raised the Lord than to the womb of Holy Mary which brought him forth."

   In the verse from Crashaw's "Steps to the Temple," with which Hirn opens his chapter, Joseph of Arimathea is to Joseph of Nazareth as the sepulchre is to the womb: "How life and death in Thee / Agree! / Thou hast a virgin womb, / And tomb. / A Joseph did betroth / Them both."

13 Vasari–Milanesi, VII, 217: ". . . per dilettazione e passar tempo, e, come egli diceva, perchè l'esercitarsi col mazzuolo lo teneva sano del corpo." References to the work's destination as a tomb monument are on p. 218 – ". . . egli avessi avuto animo che la dovessi servire per la sepoltura di lui" – and again in vol. VIII, 377, in Vasari's letter of March 18, 1564, to Michelangelo's nephew: ". . . la faceva per la sepoltura sua." The same letter refers to the Joseph of Arimathea figure as an intended self-portrait.

   For further references to the *Pietà* in Vasari see pp. 242ff. and 281f.

14 See E. Steinmann and R. Wittkower, *Michelangelo Bibliographie*, Leipzig, 1927, No. 778: *Il Buonarroti*, ed. Benvenuto Gasparoni, I, Rome, 1866, 178.

15 See Appendix B for the supposed eyewitness testimony of Blaise de Vigenère.

16 "Sometimes the soul, through the penetrating alterations of love, enters the marriage bed of heavenly mysteries; . . . in which the soul tastes what it is to be almost translated into the profound and infinite abyss of God. It happens also that, in some unthinkable and most fervid act of love [*ferventissimo actu amoris*] in one glorious moment, a spiritual marriage with Christ is consummated." St. Bernardino of Siena, *Opera omnia*, Florence, IV, 1956, Sermo LI, "De admirandis gratiis beatae Virginis," 549.

   An Early Christian example of sexual metaphor relevant to the Pietà theme occurs in the *Symposium* of Methodius of Olympus (summarized in Herbert A. Musurillo, *The Fathers of the Primitive Church*, Mentor-Omega Books, 1966, 213): "Christ's final act was to sleep in the ecstasy of his Passion, during which he procreated through the virgin Mother Church all those who would be baptized in his blood."

17 Sonnet CXLVII – "Giunto è già 'l corso della vita mia"; sent to Vasari on Sept. 19, 1554.

18 Catalogued under Bolswert in Hollstein, III, 77, 170, as "The Virgin with the Child on her lap, after Franc. Mazzuoli"; more accurately in Le Blanc, *Manuel de l'amateur d'estampes*, I, 15: "La S. Vierge adorant l'enfant Jésus qui monte sur ses genoux en s'appuyant sur un vase."

19 See Frederick Hartt, *Giulio Romano*, New Haven, 1958, I, Catalogue of Drawings, No. 139, and 88–89; and II, fig. 149. Hartt dates the drawing (Louvre 3497), which he connects with Giulio's first Mantuan period, 1526.

20 With hand laid on shoulder Eros takes hold of Paris (Hellenistic relief, Naples), Hercules reclaims Alceste from Hades (Pompeian fresco and Christian catacomb painting, Rome, Via Latina), Death claims a youth (etching by the Housebook Master, Lehrs, 53), Mars seizes Venus (Marcantonio Raimondi engraving, B. 325), and Eve appropriates Adam (Ludwig Krug relief, 1514, Berlin-Dahlem). "And as I said this, I placed my hand on the shoulder of my man," boasts Aretino's courtesan Nanna. As a token of marital status, from Roman and Early Christian times onward the gesture is as common as it is self-explanatory.

 In a drawing of the Lamentation at the British Museum, catalogued as by Michelangelo and datable in the late 1530s, the dead Christ, cradled in Mary's lap, lays his left hand on her shoulder (J. Wilde, *Italian Drawings in the British Museum: Michelangelo*, London, 1953, No. 64r).

21 Quoted in De Lubac, *Splendour*, 209, from St. Gregory, "Hom. XXXVIII in Evangelia," No. 3, *PL*, 76, 1283.

22 ". . . Ipsa [Maria] gessit typum Ecclesiae, quia virgo est et mater. Virgo, quia ad omni haeresi incorrupta; mater, quia parit semper spirituales filios ex gratia. Et ideo omnia, quae de Ecclesia dicta sunt, possunt etiam de ipsa Virgine, sponsa et mater sponsi, intelligi" (*PL*, 172, 494).

23 See, for example, St. Jerome, *Expositio in Canticum canticorum*; MS of the latter 12th century, Abbaye de Saint-Amand, Lat. 1808, fol. lv.

24 Lyons, MS 410, fol. 207v, second half of the 12th century; see *Bibliothèque nationale, les manuscrits à peintures en France du VIIe au XIIe siècle*, Paris, 1954, No. 330.

25 The Child touching the Virgin's chin is a common feature of the *Glykophilousa* type. As a tender gesture, expressing a love at once childlike and faintly precocious, it passes into the Italian Trecento. But the motif had been known since Greek vase painting, where the suitor would caress the chin of the *eromenos*, the beloved. With this charge of adult eroticism the motif appears in French Gothic art and reappears in the Renaissance (e.g., Giulio Romano's *Jupiter and Olympias* at the Palazzo del Te; Hartt, *Giulio Romano*, fig. 263). Thereafter, a 16th-century Virgin whose chin is held or chucked by the Child is unmistakably the object of fullblown masculine devotion (e.g., Cornelis van Cleve's *Madonna*, Detroit; Burgkmair's *Madonna and Child* woodcut, B.VII, 8; Giovanni Francesco Rusticci, *Virgin and Child with St. John*, marble tondo, Bargello). Is this eroticizing of the chin-chucking motif an effect of Gothic and Renaissance gallantry, or was the erotic meaning, even though veiled by the hieratic manner, always implied?

26 *Sermoni e prediche di F. Girolamo Savonarola*, Prato, 1846, I, Sermo XIX, "Della nativita di Cristo," 485.

27 Andreas Cretensis, *Canon in Beatae Mariae natalem, PG*, 97, 1323.

28 "Egredere igitur, fili mi, tanquam sponsus de thalamo suo. Esci del ventre mio, . . . Letifica l'anima dell'ancilla tua, adempe oromai il desiderio della madre tua, l'anima mia t'ha desiderato e desidera continuamente, Gesù mio, io non posso più aspettare, io mi consumo, io mi sento tutta liquefare, io languisco d'amore."

29 The three drawings – in the Louvre, the Albertina, and the British Museum – are reproduced in Tolnay, *Michelangelo*, V, figs. 98, 99, 101.

30   Michelangelo may be invoking yet another Medicean image, Mantegna's little *Madonna delle Cave* in the Uffizi, mentioned by Vasari among the pictures of Don Francesco de' Medici (*Andrea Mantegna: Catalogo della mostra*, Mantua, 1961, No. 24). It has not so far been possible to establish the date of the picture, nor how early it entered the Medici Collection. In this small masterpiece certain features seem to anticipate the *Madonna Medici*: the Child's straddling seat; the Virgin's projecting foot with its tip hovering in mid-air; and the placement of her hand as if to protect the place which will receive the thrust of the lance.

*   The conclusions of this article were initially presented in somewhat different form in a longer paper entitled "The Metaphors of Love and Birth in Michelangelo's Pietàs," which was read in April 1967 at the Institute for Sex Research, Indiana University, and which is to be published during 1969 by Basic Books, Inc., in a collection of papers on erotic elements in art commissioned and edited by the Institute. To the indefatigable Cornelia V. Christenson, who conceived and organized the project, I extend my warm appreciation. My many thanks are due to Professor Kathleen Weil-Garris Posner, Professor Irving Lavin, Professor David Kunzle, Mrs. Marie Tanner, Miss Ruth Campbell, and more of my colleagues and students who have helped inestimably with criticisms and suggestions. A small timely reference sent by a friend – beyond enriching or correcting what one has in hand – can change one's day as the poet said music did: "Who hears music feels his solitude peopled at once."

12

Reclining Bodies: Figural Ornament in Renaissance Architecture

Alina Payne

Criticism and Historiography

It is commonly acknowledged that the appropriation of classical ornament con-stituted a defining feature of Renaissance architecture. Indeed, its deployment and design elicited a rich body of theory that is preserved in the numerous treatises of the period.[1] Yet despite this considerable act of attention, neither definitions nor a general theory of ornament was ever explicitly formulated. The orders claimed exclusive prominence in the literature, while the human figure that so often accompanied them – the masks, herms and terms, caryatids, figural bas-reliefs, reclining bodies on window and door pediments, and upright ones on roof parapets and stair balustrades – received no commentary. Why they were there, whose province this sculpted matter belonged to, and how they were thought to interact with the columns and pilasters, cornices and entabla-tures, remain open questions.

Occasional insights can be gleaned from the literature of the period. For example, in the fourth book of the *Quattro libri* (1570), Palladio presents his reconstructions of the various Roman and foreign antiquities best known to his contemporaries. As we know, much of this was an exercise in imagination, for although some of the ruins now lost to us were still standing, many of the temples he illustrates were in bad repair and, worse, obscured by *tumuli* and medieval construction. A far greater figment of his imagination, however, was the figural sculpture with which he completes, and evidently believes he has embellished, parapets, pediments, colonnades, and niches. In fact, he admits as much when he describes the temples of Mars Ultor in the Forum Augusteum and the Temple of Minerva in the Forum Transitorium (or Forum of Nerva): "I have shown tabernacles with statues since the ruins *seem* to suggest this."[2]

218

And as if to ensure that his readers do not think him entirely fanciful, he adds, "No one should marvel that I have shown such a wealth of statues in this building, because we read that in Rome there were so many that they seemed to constitute another people."[3] The image, which belonged to Cassiodorus, was apparently as well known as Augustus's quip that he had found Rome brick and left it marble.[4]

But this is as far as Palladio will go with his comments on the sculptural matter attached to or placed on Roman buildings. Curiously enough he is even less forthcoming when he describes his own buildings. Although they too are inhabited by petrified bodies – parapet figures, reclining nudes on window pediments, caryatids or modified caryatids, figures on balustrades standing sentinel at entrances, not to mention varied figural bas-reliefs embedded in walls – none is mentioned even in passing. It could be argued that as they were conceived and carved by others – such as Vittoria, Rubini, Zelotti, and India and their teams of sculptors, *scalpellini*, and *stuccatori* – they did not belong to the architect's province. Sketched into the façade by him, they awaited the input of others. Still, it seems difficult to believe that such an important component of a façade – one, moreover, that would affect its reception just as much as the columns and pilasters, and one that in some of Palladio's buildings takes on significant proportions – should be brushed off as if of no architectural consequence at all.

Although Palladio may be a good example to illustrate how often such sculptural devices were used, he may not be as instructive with respect to theory. His texts are very concise and factual, and his silence on the sculpture of his façades may not in itself be that singular. However, *not one* Renaissance author comments on the sculptural programs of his buildings and projects: not Francesco di Giorgio, sculptor though he was; not Alberti, who may well be expected to have done so since he wrote authoritatively on all the visual arts; not Serlio, despite his evident interest in the representation of personality types and character through architectural detailing; not Scamozzi; and certainly not Vignola.[5] And this silence extends beyond the architectural treatise. Even Vasari, who had explicitly set out to explicate art with categories that crossed mediums left architectural sculpture outside his purview.[6] The architects' and critics' collective gaze was firmly trained on the orders, and the sculpture they routinely included on the façades they designed was passed over in silence. Thus, we do not know how these figures were proportioned, if their dimensions were part of the larger network that embraced the whole façade, how their gestures were selected and how they were positioned, why some were languidly hugging pediments while others lined the roofs in *contrapposto*.[7]

Occasionally an author offers faint hints. In Book VII of *De re aedificatoria*, for example, Alberti assures his readers that in antiquity, "the use of statues was splendid (*egregius fuit usus statuarum*)," and he defines them as the ornament of public and private buildings alike.[8] Yet as promising as this may sound, it is only moderately relevant. In this section he describes everything as ornament (not only columns and cornices but also roofs and vaults, gates, streets, arches, and so forth). Moreover, this statement occurs in a passage focused on commemorative monuments and effigies, and thus does not directly concern architecture.

Gherardo Spini, a Florentine *letterato* who wrote a treatise on ornament in the 1560s, makes a more pertinent statement.[9] Unlike his predecessors he includes a short commentary on the acroteria in his systematic survey of all architectural ornament. For him, this device is the final touch in the sequence that starts with the column base and reaches all the way to the roof. And with great acuity, he declares it to be most successfully used when representing winged deities such as Fame and Victory.[10] It is clear from the context of his overall argument that Spini sees such figures, frozen in the act of taking flight and suggesting unfettered movement, levity, and weightlessness, as a necessary counterpoint to the load-versus-support dialectic that the columns and beams set up. Yet despite the perceptiveness of these observations, Spini remains unique among his contemporaries in discussing acroteria as a formal device of the façade and as sculptural ornament.

Given that such a blind spot affects commentaries of their own work, perhaps it is not surprising to see how few Renaissance architects analyze triumphal arches critically. This is not to say that they pass unnoticed, for the *taccuini* from the period are bursting with sketches that demonstrate how attentively their details were studied.[11] Palladio, for example, planned a separate book on triumphal arches and many of his preparatory drawings have been preserved.[12] What he would have said about them is hard to speculate on, though from scattered remarks we know that he admired their form and details. He specifically praises the *intagli* of the Arch of Titus as an example of "*edifici che furono fatti ai buoni tempi*" and describes the Arch of Constantine as "very beautiful."[13] Such an attentive examination of triumphal arches can be traced back to Alberti, who was the first to include them in his treatise on architecture and comment on their figural ornament. Thus, he recommended that "statues may be best set up on the ends of the beams where they project from the work to embrace the columns" (VIII, 6), yet he offered no comment on the visual function that such a gesture performs. Moreover, the passage is so brief, and had so little resonance even within Alberti's own treatise, that it did not generate a tradition of critical attention.[14]

An exception among his contemporaries, Serlio discusses triumphal arches in his Book III (1540) on antiquities at great length. Yet, like Alberti, he omits figural ornament from the discussion. Instead, he focuses on the agglomeration of profiles and the rich carvings that characterize these later products of Roman art. Although evidently drawn to them, he finds them licentious and confused, and he dismisses all triumphal arches one by one, with the exception of the least interesting of all, the Arch at Ancona.[15] His illustrations are no less biased, for he edits out all traces of extraneous ornament, figural sculpture in particular. It may be that early criticism of the sculptures on the Arch of Constantine had set a precedent for such treatment; after all Raphael had dismissed them as the products of a "late" and exhausted style producing *figure sciochissime* (foolish figures), and Serlio may very well have been familiar with such a view from his days in the ambience of the Raphael and Peruzzi circles in Rome.[16] But even if true, such shortcomings in the execution of specific sculptural forms do not adequately explain why he should entirely neglect a whole class of ornament.

The absence of a discussion of figural ornament in architectural discourse has been accentuated by our own disciplinary biases and a scholarly tradition that came of age at the end of the nineteenth century. Such neglect is hardly surprising in an intellectual climate in which both representation and ornament were under attack.[17] Indeed, whether focused on tectonics or abstraction, on materials and building technique or empathy theories, definitions of ornament that went back to Schinkel and Riegl, Wagner and Worringer did not include the human body.[18]

It is certainly true that Jakob Burckhardt devoted a fair amount of space to architectural decoration in his *Die Geschichte der Renaissance* (1867, 1878) as he drew attention to now frequently neglected items such as door surrounds, candelabra mullions, interior decoration, fireplaces, infilling of pilasters, friezes and window surrounds, altars and pulpits.[19] Yet he was also quick to distinguish between figural sculpture focused on the human body and decorative carving that drew on vegetal motifs. The former was excluded from this survey; even the latter received only an ambiguous accolade. Thus, he stated that "the great architects almost all loved ornamental work, and, if nonetheless they designed their buildings to be simple and grand, for them this factor has to be taken all the more deeply into consideration."[20] The emphasis on "simple and grand" as the business of architecture resurfaces later when he declares that "architecture, more than once threatened by the dominance of a decorative style, held to the course of its high destiny thanks to the activities of the great Florentines."[21] Even Wölfflin, who liked sculpture and was himself a great supporter of Adolf von Hildebrand, concentrated on the orders and the proportional relationships they set up on façades when he dealt with Renaissance architecture.[22] In his *Prolegomena zu einer Psychologie der Architektur* (1886), Wölfflin argued that "ornament is an expression of an excess of force to form. The heavy mass produces no flowers. . . . Weight is overcome, the excess of striving force manifests itself in the rise of the gable and celebrates its greatest triumph in the plastic figures that, freed from pressure, unfold freely."[23] Yet when he talked about liveliness of surface or movement and excitement, he referred only to niches and pilasters, and sculpture receded into the background.[24]

That half a century later Wittkower should similarly ignore ornament, particularly figural ornament, need not surprise us.[25] For his generation, truth and honesty of structure were the ultimate goals of architecture, and so Alberti's adage that "the work ought to be constructed naked, and clothed later; let the ornament come last" (IX, 8) rang a familiar note.[26] That Alberti meant no value judgment, but simply advised on a sequence of building operations so as not to damage finished parts if set up too soon, naturally escaped notice. Finally, in what became the principal reference work for modern scholarship, Heydenreich and Lotz attended little to ornament, figural or otherwise. On the few occasions when they did, as in the case of Alessi, they labeled his façades "pictorial" (*malerisch*). In a world focused on structure and its expression, on "space-time" and essential form, this was not altogether a compliment.[27]

Sculpture scholars have been equally disinterested in architecture with the exception of those working on Donatello and Michelangelo.[28] Around the turn of the century, some scholars brought architecture and sculpture together in the same work, as did Pietro Paoletti and Julius Baum.[29] Yet the echoes of these works remained weak. The treatment of the oeuvre of sculptor-architects like Ammannati and Sansovino is particularly revealing in this instance. Though we have exemplary studies on both, they tend to act out the prejudices of the field: some study their sculpture, others their architecture. Consequently, the two parts of one artistic personality remain essentially isolated.[30] Although there have been occasional efforts to redress the imbalance, such as Wolfgang Lotz's short but powerful formal analysis of Sansovino's sculpted frieze for the Marciana or the work on the sculptors associated with Palladio, this has not materially affected the interests, questions, and research among historians.[31]

For a world focused on abstraction and technology, neglecting figural ornament was perhaps inevitable. However, it is more difficult to explain why Renaissance authors should have done so too. And it is precisely because this omission is so baffling that it deserves attention. Located at the point where architecture and sculpture meet (or part), figural ornament, as dealt with at both the level of theory and practice, allows us unique opportunities to investigate how Renaissance architects defined ornament and construed the relationship between the visual arts.

Ornatus

What caused this gap between the practice of architecture and its commentators? One evident reason for the absence of a discourse on figural ornament has to be sought at the fountainhead of all architectural theory: Vitruvius's *De architectura*. His treatise, the blueprint for all those that followed from the Renaissance onward, entirely neglected this aspect. For Vitruvius, architecture precedes the other arts and supplies them with their context; paintings, mosaics, and sculpture are added later by other craftsmen, attached, embedded, and mortared into walls, roofs, and porticoes. As such, architecture is isolated away from this *Gesamtkunstwerk*; it precedes it and sets its parameters.[32] Implicitly, how the arts communicate with architecture is the sculptors' and painters' problem. Vitruvius's well-known vituperation against the irrational painted architecture of the second Pompeian style is only one example that confirms this bias: the painter fails to attend to the architectural narrative, and the whole is an unmitigated disaster.[33]

These structural characteristics of *De architectura* had a direct impact on the treatise writers of the Renaissance: Vitruvius excluded sculpture, and so did his readers. However, three other moves Vitruvius made affected decisively, if more subtly, the way in which a theory of architectural ornament was formulated. First, he suggests that the *ornamenta* might be isolated as a concern unto itself.[34] This is evident in Book IV, 2 where he discusses the elements above the column and supplies origins and prescriptions for their correct use. When he defines the *ornamenta* as *imago* (triglyphs and dentils as representations of beam-ends and purlins) in a subsequent passage, he reinforces the separation between building and ornament. Nevertheless, Vitruvius was ambiguous on this point. In Book III, for example, the orders are embedded in and indistinguishable from the building type itself. Yet his Renaissance readers privileged the notion of an applied ornamental screen that starts with pedestals, runs through columns and entablatures, and ends with acroteria.[35] Such a reading began to gain currency with Alberti, who declared the column to be "the principal ornament without any doubt" and became so established that the fact that Vitruvius had never stated as much was completely lost from view.[36]

If Vitruvius's first prophetic move was to suggest that ornament could be isolated as a concern, his second was to compare his endeavor in setting down the theory of architecture with that of Cicero, Lucretius, and Varro.[37] However, Cicero wrote on rhetoric, Varro wrote on the Latin language, and Lucretius wrote on the origin of things. These terms of comparison, though perhaps innocent enough for Vitruvius to use, were nevertheless not innocent of innuendo, particularly for Renaissance readers whose entire culture was so language driven and dependent on texts. For them, the subtle association of architecture, language, and rhetoric would have been implicit, whether Vitruvius had intended it or not.

Finally, Vitruvius made one other interesting opening in his treatment of ornament: his aesthetic category *decor* seemed to be of one family with the *decorum* of poetics and rhetoric.[38] And since *decor* particularly affected the appropriate deployment of ornament – which orders and decorative motifs were appropriate for which deity – and its definition came so close to that of *decorum*, the two virtually merged in the Renaissance reception of *De architectura*.[39]

These three aspects of Vitruvius's treatise may not seem significant in the context of the whole work, yet small gestures though they were, isolating ornament as a category, implying a *paragone* between architecture and the literary arts, and opening up ornament to the theory of *decorum* did not pass unnoticed by the reception. To be sure, ornament was already on the way to acquiring independent status in the Renaissance, as the contemporary *taccuini* with their endless records of carved details and measurements amply testify. Perhaps with the sole exception of the temple pediment, ornament produced the most powerful visual impact and gained an almost iconic currency as the most obvious way of declaring the appropriation of antiquity. No other aspect of ancient architecture had the same associative power when used as quotations; without its grid of classicizing pilasters, the Rucellai palace would have been just another Florentine block.

Once isolated, ornament could enjoy a semiautonomous existence. Separated from the main trunk of architecture, it could feed off other disciplines, especially those where ornament was a distinct category and claimed its own body of theory and critical vocabulary. Thus, when it came to a theory of ornament, it was difficult to resist the *paragone* that Vitruvius had so subtly proposed and not rely on the models provided by the literary arts. As his readers learned all too soon, the theoretical apparatus provided by *De architectura* was thin, at least when compared to that of rhetoric and poetics, where *ornatus* was part of a highly complex and developed analytical vocabulary and theoretical framework. Inevitably they turned to Cicero, Quintilian, and Horace for guidance to fill in the gaps.[40]

This process of appropriation of a theoretical apparatus from another discipline did not happen overnight. At first, architects were more concerned with identifying the forms that Vitruvius named, connecting and reconnecting signified and signifiers. From Alberti through Francesco di Giorgio to Bramante, Raphael, and Peruzzi, architects were preoccupied with little else. But as archaeological expertise sharpened and ever more authoritative translations and commentaries of Vitruvius's text became available, the interest in a theory of ornament formation and use increased, as did the isolation of ornament into a self-contained category. Already Alberti had intended the second half of his treatise to focus on ornament, even if he ended up broadening this topic; Francesco di Giorgio also focused on *colonne* separately and gave the orders their own chapter. Nevertheless, it is Serlio who consecrated the primacy and internal cohesiveness of ornament as an independent category by using it as the lens through which he looked on architecture. In Book IV, *Regole generali d'architettura sopra le cinque maniere degli edifici* (1537), columns, entablatures, and cornices combine and recombine into ever more complex systems, from door frames, through gates and fireplaces, until they become entire façade arrangements for town houses, villas, and palaces. Though he never made the connection himself, Serlio's Book IV may be seen as the complement to the *ornatus* section of any treatise on rhetoric or poetics. The gradual buildup from simple to complex forms, complete with their definitions, parameters for use, examples, warnings against abuses, and possible effects, constitutes the architectural equivalent of the structured presentation of literary *figure*.

Perhaps the consequence of isolating ornament into a self-contained category is nowhere more evident than in Gherardo Spini's *Trattato intorno all'ornamento* (ca. 1569). An author of poetry and scientific treatises, a member of the Accademia Fiorentina, involved with various literary and scientific circles, Spini was also in close contact with artists, among them Vincenzo and Ignazio Danti, Ammannati, Cellini, Dossio, and Bernardo Gamucci.[41] Perhaps, given his literary formation, treating ornament as an independent concern was a self-understood strategy for Spini, and it may be that his work illustrates the prejudices of his own discipline.

Yet the very fact that he enters the architectural arena, focuses on ornament, and structures his text with the rigor of a treatise on rhetoric indicates that such trespasses were possible, latent in the discourse, and that he simply enacts links that were already there. Most important, he demonstrates that these links were associated with ornament.

For Spini, the cardinal points of his theory of ornament are *imitatione, corrispondenza, invenzione,* and *decoro,* categories customarily associated with the composition of a poem or tragedy.[42] Indeed, he says so outright when he concludes that "from here derives the similitude between the architect and the poet[,] for both delight with the same means in general."[43] Once he establishes this simile, Spini sets out to develop a rigorous theory of architectural *imitatio.* And he bases it on the treatises on poetics by Aristotle and Horace. To be sure, his efforts to derive every piece of the ornamental ensemble from construction is not new, though he is more consistent than most others. What is new is the reason he offers for this procedure: "Imitation is the representation and similitude of something that has been first produced by Nature or by Art," and he continues,

> Indeed imitation has great force to move man to pleasure and delight, given that his nature is intellectual; because while he recognizes through the means of the work which is being represented the intention of the artist, he feels delight above anything else, as there is no pleasure that equals that of the intellect and of learning . . . it will suffice that in imitating something the architect gives another the opportunity to recognize it, and who recognizes learns and concludes what everything is, as human beings naturally find pleasure in recognizing the things that they see.[44]

Clearly the shadow of Aristotle looms in the background and shows how, by way of ornament, architecture can enter the discourse on *imitatio* that united the figural and literary arts.[45]

That architectural ornament could be conceived of in this manner by the 1570s was not only a direct result of the gradual isolation of ornament as category but owed much to three other phenomena. First, the reception of *De architectura* was largely left in the hands of *letterati* and historians, who routinely imported literary theory to fill in its gaps. Second, the developing language of architectural criticism had borrowed heavily from literary criticism and so invited transference from one to the other. Third, the debate on the *questione della lingua* that shaped Italian culture in the sixteenth century offered striking parallels to what may be termed the *questione dell'ornamento,* that is, the debates on the correct use of architectural ornament.[46]

As far as the reception of *De architectura* was concerned, it had been in the hands of humanists since the time of Sulpitius and Pomponio Leto's Accademia Romana. Its language, already a hindrance to Vitruvius himself, who complained that he had to resort to Greek all too often due to a lack of appropriate Latin terms, was difficult to translate into an even less shaped Italian. As result it was in a "receiving mode": notions, concepts, and categories had to be named and, more often than not, were imported from the literary arts in which the translators were expert. When Barbaro, for example, translated *decor* with *decoro*, when he compared the *maniere del dire* with the *maniere del edificare*, when he talked of the *stile misto*, he both enriched the vocabulary of architectural theory and provided opportunities for a whole theoretical apparatus from the literary arts to seep through the porous wall of language.[47]

In some cases, more was at stake than the translation of terms. Criticism demanded its own vocabulary. To be sure, literary critics drew their most powerful similes and delivered the most incisive observations when using a vocabulary rich in images. Yet the attentive reading of detail, such as Serlio initiates and Scamozzi later fully articulates, depended in large measure on the practices of literary critics. The *questione della lingua* had prompted ever closer analyses of language, and works such as Carlo Lenzoni's *In difesa della lingua fiorentina e di Dante* (1556), where he sought to pinpoint the effects of consonants, vowels, and their combinations on the sound of words, were the natural outcomes of such attention. For him few consonants produced "weakness, lowness and sweetness," many produced "gravity and grandeur," and excessive use caused "inflation and difficulty."[48] Scamozzi's description of the effects of individual profiles, such as cymas, egg and dart, *cavetti*, and crown molds, on the work as a whole owed not a little to this tradition of analysis:

> It is a certain thing that the soft (*morbide*) profiles make buildings turn out well, in such a way that they have firmness and beauty: and as the manners that are too solid, and too swollen make them seem deformed, squat, and without grace; thus, to the contrary, styles that are not fleshy enough (*scarnate*), or too sharp as some use, make the work appear weak and dry: in such a way that the marble and any other noble stone becomes like wood, completely dry and without pulp (*spolpato*).[49]

Indeed, the parallelism between sixteenth-century projects to consolidate the Italian language and develop a systematic ornamental vocabulary for architecture is striking. Both architects and humanists were engaged in sifting through a thesaurus of forms and words and striving to identify criteria for their selection. The concern with setting up grammars on the one hand, and books of *regole* on the other, was only one of a series of similar responses to what were in effect similar conditions. When Vignola wrote his virtually textless *Regola deli cinque ordini* (1562) and Guillaume Philandrier his virtually imageless *Vitruvii Pollionis De Architectura Annotationes* (1544), both were reacting to the impact of the exegetical methods current in the literary circles of the Accademia della Virtù in whose great archaeological project they had both participated.[50]

In all these instances, theoreticians and critics acted in their own ways on that which Vitruvius had offered. And in so doing, they demonstrated that he had been too strong for his reception. What they talk about was what he talked about and in a world in which language and its formation took on such prominence they leaned toward the most rapidly expanding and most heavily used critical and theoretical apparatus available, that is, the apparatus provided by the language arts. Vitruvius had hinted that such a rapprochement was possible, and so it was.

Figura

The theory of the literary arts was not alone responsible for the architects' failure to include figural sculpture in their definitions of ornament and its functions. Yet this phenomenon of borrowing affected decisively the direction in which their attention was channeled, the issues they favored, and the problems they privileged. The remarkable *fortuna* of the *decorum* concept in architecture is one such consequence; so is the *vocabolario* mentality that invaded its treatise industry and caused a growing interest in *regole* and encyclopedias of parts; so is ultimately also the focus on the orders. Once conceived in terms of *maniere del parlare*, they necessarily took over the center stage of ornament theory, as the *genera dicendi* had taken over center stage in any treatise on rhetoric and poetics. In conjunction with Vitruvius, this set up the *forma mentis* with which ornament was approached.

It would therefore seem that we witness a parting of the ways between practice and theory, visual and verbal. The sculptural ornament so central to Renaissance architecture escapes theory and disappears into some form of collective blind spot. Yet is this cleavage one that separates the two on the surface, or are these truly noncommunicating vessels? Does the theory associated with the orders suggest nothing when considering figural devices?

The presence of the human body on a façade is no novelty in the Renaissance. If the Roman remains did not afford any other examples but the triumphal arches and written documents, that was certainly enough. But there was more, for free-standing sculpture was also a feature of Gothic architecture, and despite the shift in taste toward a classical vocabulary, it survived in the context of religious art, especially in the design of chapels, funerary monuments, and, most important, church façades. In all these cases, the religious origin of the device and its connotations remained strong: the figures are placed in niches as if in the consecrated space of the church. From the cathedral at Cremona to Donatello's *St. George* at Orsanmichele and *Annunciation* at St. Croce, the examples illustrating this type are legion. The same survival path is also true of acroteria figures. If they were missing from ancient temples, and architects knew of them only from Vitruvius, the Gothic figures on pinnacles certainly carried forward the notion of a petrified *gens*, negotiating the delicate transition between building and sky as a diaphanous intermediary.

A dialogue between figure and frame – that is, an exchange between sculpture and architecture – was certainly developing in this religious context. Tomb sculpture offered another powerful point of intersection for the two media.

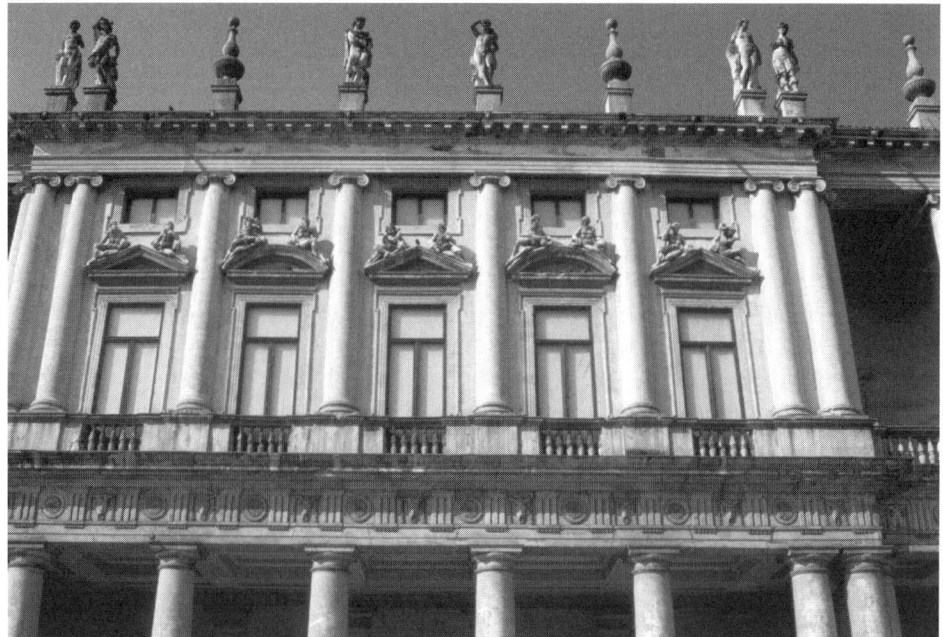

Figure 12.1   Andrea Palladio, detail, Palazzo Chiericati, Vicenza. © Carmen Redondo / CORBIS.

Still, rich though this tradition was, there were no examples of reclining, free-standing nudes on a pediment such as are most conspicuously evident in Palladio's palace façades (figure 12.1). In fact these architectural "*gisants*" seem to be a device newly invented in the Renaissance, which makes it all the more interesting to ask, Why was it deemed necessary? What function did it perform? Why were the figures in niches and parapets, the *statue* that Palladio mentions, insufficient? One precedent was certainly the winged victories framing the central opening of Roman triumphal arches. Yet they were fully clothed, relatively flat reliefs, and contained within spandrels, not detached from the wall, literally reaching out into the viewer's space, without an evident inconographical function to elucidate their suspended position or their nudity.

Something approaching Palladio's device may be seen in the Loggia Cornaro by Falconetto; in Ammannati's Arco Benavides, in Sanmicheli's Veronese palaces, and in Sansovino's Marciana and Loggetta. As has been observed, all are indebted to some degree to Raphael's late work, to his façade of the Palazzo Branconio, where statues in niches traditionally associated with a religious type were brought into the domain of the profane, literally leaping from religious three-dimensional icons to a purely decorative device that allowed texture, light, shade, and movement to enhance the tactility of the architectural elements of the façade.[51] In Falconetto's case the theater-related context for the Loggia, the tight three-way relationship among himself, Ruzzante, and their patron Alvise

Cornaro, may suggest why detached "live" figures should suddenly inhabit the blank window spaces of a reconstructed *scaena frons*.[52] And in Sansovino's case as in Ammannati's, the origin of the winged victories in triumphal arches is still apparent, especially as they gracefully enhance similar arched openings. Yet although their figures are more outspokenly three-dimensional and nude than the Roman exemplars, there is still another leap from here to Palladio's pedimental figures.

It is possible to argue that the leap occurs in the wake of Michelangelo's Medici chapel at San Lorenzo and that his treatment of the sarcophagi with their reclining nudes, generically named Dawn, Night, and so on, is the missing link that connects Palladio's Palazzo Chiericati with medieval tomb sculpture and Roman victories (figure 12.2). An inhabitable sculpture or a sculpted piece of architecture, Michelangelo's chapel begged the kind of translation across media that I would like to suggest occurred here. The uniform use of marble for figures, furniture, and spatial container enhances the equivalence between them. Every dentil, volute, garland, and bead-and-reel appears to be of one family with the stone furniture, the sarcophagi, and the bodies placed on them. They are all seemingly carved by the same tools, the same hand; the architectural details belong to sculpture in the same way that the geometry of the bodies placed along pyramids and diagonals suggests that they belong to architecture. On the eve of the seventeenth century, Scamozzi suggested as much when he attempted to define architectural forms and was forced to resort to the Michelangelesque reclining bodies to reinforce the traditional image of the Vitruvian man.

But not only bodies enter the architectural structure of the whole. A close look at the sarcophagus shows clearly that its lid has much of the so-called *tetto spezzato* (broken pediment) that was to become such a disputed architectural feature in the later sixteenth and seventeenth centuries. Moreover, this practice was put at Michelangelo's door by many later critics like Pirro Ligorio and Teofilo Gallaccini, who were exasperated with the excesses of the *epigoni*.[53] The same convex curve, very slight yet taut, the same scrolls and interruption in the middle that we find in the Porta Pia, we also find in the Medici sarcophagi. Nor does this effect of telescoping one member into another across media end here. The curve and counter-curve of the sarcophagus lid echo the curve of the niche pediments and garlands; its supports respond to the pilasters framing them; the reclining nudes refer to the figure of Lorenzo contained in his architectural setting. And, the same profiles make up the sarcophagus lid as the niche and door frames, thus suggesting continuity between them. As a final gesture, the scroll placed directly below the knee joints of the seated figure, and replete with connotations of mobility, simultaneously carries architectural connotations by recalling the Ionic volute. Indeed, it is only by comparison with more traditional funerary monuments and with ancient sarcophagi that it becomes clear just how deliberately architectural the Medici ensemble is.

Michelangelo had already proposed the human figure as ornament with the *ignudi* of the Sistine ceiling and in the façade of San Lorenzo in Florence. And

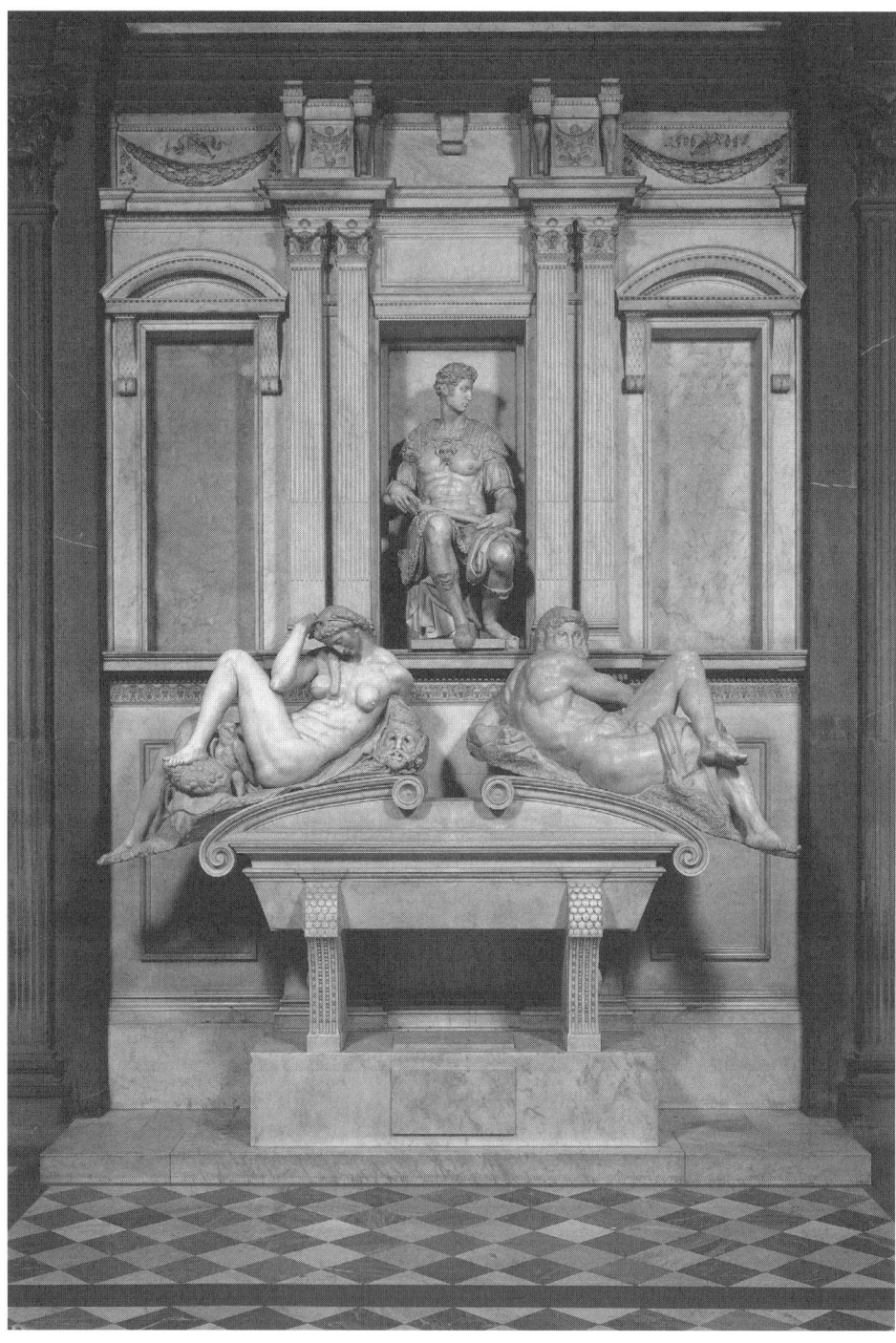

Figure 12.2   Michelangelo, tomb of Giuliano de' Medici. Florence, Medici Chapel, San Lorenzo. AKG-images / Rabatti-Domingie.

certainly Palladio would have known this work and its offspring in the painted work of others.[54] But the impact of the Sistine ceiling should not obscure the kind of transposition possible between two three-dimensional arts like architecture and sculpture – and one that could have reached the Veneto through the confluence of relationships between Sanmicheli, Sansovino, Ammannati, Falconetto, and Palladio, in which patrons like Trissino and Cornaro played their part.[55] Indeed, Vasari tells us that "everyone was astounded" at the sight of the Medici chapel and goes on to describe its extraordinary impact, particularly on architects.[56]

Seen in this context, Michelangelo's anonymous naked figures set into a classical interior and reclining on a classicizing sarcophagus enhance and modify the tradition of the detached figures set up on triumphal arches or winged victories in the spandrels of the arch itself. Like them, from being sculpture they become architectural ornament. Palladio may talk of *statue* when he describes ancient building complexes, but in fact they have ceased to be unique objects authored by one artistic personality. In his pedimental figures, we witness a recession of authorship, a recession of the object as artifact to be admired and apprehended in its uniqueness. His figures stop being one exceptional object offered to close-up view, to be walked around and almost touched; they become one of many. According to the illustrations in the *Quattro libri*, there were fourteen such figures intended for the Palazzi Barbaranno and Iseppo da Porto and ten for the Palazzo Chiericati (and, if we add the parapet figures, another eight in the case of the former). Just as a column is one of many, just as the Corinthian capital is one piece of sculpture in the round among many, these figures too are exactly repeatable objects. Lifted high off the ground (not even on the first story as in the case of the Marciana, but all on the *piano nobile*), an intermediary layer of deep carving between the column capitals and the ground floor rustication, they are not presented as a unique artifact to be appreciated as the "original." Alberti said as much: "But I would have the ornament that you apply be for the most part the work of many hands of moderate skill."[57] Walter Benjamin's mechanical reproduction is far in the future, but the aura is nevertheless the issue here. Between architectural ornament and sculpture lies multiple reproduction; the aura is missing.[58] Neither unique accomplishments deserving of commentary in their own right, nor precisely quantifiable (like the orders that can be described piece by piece for a reader), these figural sculptures inevitably disappear through a fissure between image and text.

We are witnessing here the translation of a sculptural motif into an architectural one, and this is happening purely at the formal level, for there are no iconographic implications associated with it as there are with the figure placed within a niche. Nor is this a preferred device for sculptor-architects like Sansovino or Sanmicheli. Palladio who crosses media less than others, is perhaps the most frequent user of the pedimental reclining nude in the sixteenth century, and his interest in this form is a testimony to its absorption into the professional architect's vocabulary.

Why do architects reach out for this device? Why add more sculptural incident to the façade? Certainly, when Renaissance architects wanted to signify a Gothic manner (as in the proposals for the completion of the façade of San Petronio in Bologna, for example), they covered the surfaces with figural sculpture. Why then skirt potential failure?[59] To say that they were necessary props for an *all'antica* appearance (as Palladio argued) is to stop short of the real issues. With this example I would like to argue that in a visual culture focused on *moti* and *istoria*, architecture seeks a point of contact. Palladio resists the humanization of the frame in the manner of Alessi, Serlio, and other north Italian architects, or indeed, that of the northern European tradition. Yet he uses it to explicate architecture more subtly and more effectively. From the late 1540s, Palladio begins to add figural sculpture to the *piano nobile*. The trend starts with the Palazzo Porto Festa; continues with the Palazzo Chiericati, the early drawings for the Rialto Bridge, and the Palazzo Valmarana; and reaches a climax with Palazzo Barbaranno and Loggia del Capitaniato. These devices accompany a growing sculpturalization of his architectural members that seems to require an intensification of visual incident at the middle story.[60] His choice is for organic forms that literally lie beside and accentuate the swelling of a column, and so enhance the carrying message of a pilaster or the heavy, inert weight of a pediment.

We know that Palladio conceived of the classical frame of column/entablature /pediment in gestural rather than strictly tectonic terms.[61] This is especially evident when he discusses junction points of the frame, such as bases and friezes, that is, the points where the columns meet the platform or where the roof beams meet columns: "Likewise, since it is most appropriate that those things upon which a great weight is placed are squeezed, they [the ancients] placed bases under the columns, which, with their torus and scotiae seem (*paiano*) to be crushed by the weight above. Thus, they also introduced triglyphs in the cornices, modillions and dentils, to represent the ends of those beams in the attic which are placed to support the roof."[62] Clearly, for Palladio, bases and triglyphs exist no less in a world of representation and fiction than in one of loads and structure. For him, "abuses" in the use of ornament are those instances that violate this fiction. These are the *cartocci*, a manner of brackets or scrolls that occasionally supported columns but most often appeared in entablatures as *mensole triglifate* (brackets as triglyphs). Palladio's target is clear:

> For this reason instead of columns or pilasters which have to carry some weight one should never place *cartelle*, also called *cartocci*, which is a sort of involuted form which strikes the intelligent as extremely ugly, and to those who are not knowledgeable brings confusion rather than pleasure, and produce no other effect except to raise the expense. Similarly these *cartocci* will not be made to project out of entablatures; since it is necessary that all the parts of the cornice be made towards some effect, and display that which would be visible if the work were made of wood, and in addition, since it is appropriate that in order to support a weight something hard and able to resist is required, there is no doubt that these *cartocci* are entirely superfluous, since it is impossible that a beam or any other member

produce the effect they represent, and feigning to be soft and tender, I don't know with what reason they can be placed under something hard and heavy.[63]

This concern for expressive tectonics is not without precedent, though it builds up gradually over the course of two centuries. Alberti likened columns, beams, and arches with bones and ligaments, the wall with flesh (III, 14);[64] Francesco di Giorgio described the *fregio pulvinato* (curved frieze) as "little squashed pillows (*piumacetti*)";[65] Gherardo Spini described the entasis as *tumefazione* (bruising), found etymological grounds to suggest that the torus represented a muscle under stress, like the chest of a straining horse, and described the egg-and-dart motif as gravel squeezing through mortar under the pressure of the floor beams.[66] But none of these authors associated this organismic reading of ornament with the structural frame as consistently as did Palladio. Nor was their reference to *imitatio* as unequivocal. Of course, not being a *letterato* like Spini, Palladio does not resort to Aristotle to ground his argument. But his terms of expression – *fingere* (to seem), *dimostrare* (to demonstrate), *pare* (to appear), and *piacere* (pleasure aroused in the viewer) – testify to the assimilation of the theory of literary *imitatio* and its almost unself-conscious application to architecture.

What do the two strands of this argument – about figural sculpture and the exchanges with literary theory – reveal about the definition of ornament in Renaissance architecture? As the discourse on *imitatio* developed in the literary and figural arts slides imperceptibly into the reading of Vitruvius, ornament increasingly blends structural and corporeal references. By Palladio's time, the ornamental screen is understood to swell and contract as if it were a muscle. In this scenario, the human figure completes the story – the architectural *istoria* – of load carried by support. As figural ornament takes up the space halfway between the inert wall of the building and the street of moving bodies, it gestures the structure. In so doing, it beckons the viewer "in" as seductively and effectively as the strategically placed *figura* that Alberti recommended painters include in a well-structured painted *istoria*.[67] Located at the intersection of literary theory, figural *imitatio*, and architecture, ornament could and did slide between the artificial barriers with which scholarship so often separates disciplines. Yet it is precisely from its location on this edge that ornament facilitated dialogue and exchange between the arts and tied Renaissance architecture into the fabric of its culture.

Notes

I am grateful for the support of the Graham Foundation in preparing this chapter.

1 Payne 1999, 1–10.
2 Palladio 1980, 276: "Io ho posto de' tabernacoli con statue, come per le ruine *pare* che vi fossero."
3 Palladio 1980, 277.

4   Palladio 1980, 523, n. 5. Alberti mentions the story too (VII, 16). Alberti 1988, 240.

5   Alberti 1988; Francesco Di Giorgio 1967; Scamozzi 1964; Serlio 1964; Vignola 1985.

6   Vasari 1986. Vasari's 1568 edition of the *Vite* shows the same bias.

7   Payne 1999.

8   Alberti *Faksimile*, VII, 16, 134.

9   Spini 1980, 30–201.

10   Spini 1980, 179.

11   See especially Günther 1988.

12   Puppi 1990.

13   Palladio (1988, 18) comments on the Arch of Constantine in his *L'antichita di Roma* when he reviews the triumphal arches in Rome; it is the only arch that receives such an accolade. For Palladio's use of arches as authority to justify his use of bas-reliefs on the façade of San Petronio see Palladio 1988, 133. Palladio specifically praises the *intagli* of the Arch of Titus as an example of "edifici che furono fatti ai buoni tempi" unlike the Temple of Peace (Basilica of Maxentius) that he illustrates: Palladio 1980, 262.

14   Alberti 1988, 266.

15   Serlio 1619, 109v. For his criticism, see, for example, comments on the Arco dei Argentieri, which shows members that are *vitiose, confusione*, same profiles one on top of the other (100–101r); on the Arch of Constantine, which has *mensole e dentelli* and *confusione di intagli* (106v); and on the Arch at Benevento, which has too many *intagli* and caters to the *piacere del vulgo* (104v).

16   Rowland 1994, 104; Frommel 1989, 39–49.

17   The seminal text that best illustrates this position is without a doubt Adolf Loos's "Ornament und Verbrechen." Although traditionally dated 1908, more recent research shows that Loos wrote it as a lecture in late 1909 or 1910 (Rukschcio 1985, 57–68). Le Corbusier published the essay in 1920 in *L'Esprit Nouveau*. His own *L'Art décoratif d'aujourd'hui* (1925) and *Après le cubisme* (1918, with Amédée Ozenfant) constituted equally influential (if somewhat differently oriented) statements on the subject. On the larger issue of imbrication between architectural history writing and contemporary discourse, see Payne 1994, 322–342.

18   The tectonics discussion owed much to Friedrich Schinkel, whose well-known position ("Architektur ist eine Fortsetzung der Natur in ihrer konstruktiven Tätigkeit") was developed by Bötticher 1852 and others. On Schinkel, see Börsch-Soupan 1976, 161. The discussion, focused on materials and building technique as determinants for architectural form initiated by Gottfried Semper, found an enthusiastic reception in the written work of Otto Wagner. See his influential *Moderne Architektur* (Vienna 1896, 1898, 1902). For the abstraction-empathy lineage of the ornament discussion, see especially Riegl, *Stilfragen* (1893) and Worringer, *Formprobleme der Gotik* (1910) and *Abstraktion und Einfühlung* (1907).

19   Burckhardt 1987.

20   Burckhardt 1987, 192.

21   Burckhardt 1987, 191.

22   See, for example, the 1893 article on Adolf von Hildebrand: Wölfflin 1946a, 84–106.

23   "Das Ornament ist Ausdruck überschüssiger Formkraft. Die schwere Masse treibt keine Blüten"; "die Schwere ist überwunden, der Überschuss der strebenden Kraft

erscheint in der Hebung des Giebels und feiert den höchsten Triumph in den plastischen Figuren, die, dem Druck enthoben, hier frei sich entfalten können." Wölfflin 1946b, 41.

24 Geoffrey Scott, the champion of Einfühlung for the English-speaking world, also ignored the place of figural ornament in classical architecture and, like Wölfflin, concentrated on the orders, proportion, mass, and space. Scott 1965.

25 Wittkower 1949. The tradition leading up to Wittkower included Willich and Zucker's influential *Baukunst der Renaissance in Italien* (1914–1926). Following in the steps of Schmarsow, they focused on the spatial characteristics of Renaissance architecture and described ornament as "devoid of content" and "the architectural furnishing of the façade as unimportant." Willich and Zucker 1914, vol. 1, 1926, 2: 257, 266.

26 Alberti 1988, 312.

27 Lotz defines Alessi's treatment of the Villa Cambiaso as a case of "ornament drowning structure" and his style more generally as "pictorial." Heydenreich and Lotz 1974, 290–291. On the association of *malerisch* (pictorial) with ornament in modernist architectural criticism and theory, see Payne 2001. On structure/ornament, see Sankovitch 1998, 686–717.

28 von Bode 1902; Summers 1981.

29 See Paoletti 1897–1898.

30 See, for example, Boucher 1991; Howard 1975; Kiene 1995.

31 See Lotz 1977, 140–151. Among exceptions, see also Wolters 1992–1993, 102–110; Del Turco and Salvi 1995; Shell and Castelfranchi 1993; and Brandt 1994.

32 Vitruvius I, 1; II, 1, 7; 1983, 9–21 and 85.

33 Vitruvius VII, 5, 5; 1983, 107.

34 Vitruvius distinguishes the *ornamenta* from the columns and uses the term for the elements above the column that he discusses separately under this rubric. See Vitruvius, I, 1, 6 and IV, 2, 1.

35 Vitruvius, IV, 3.

36 Alberti 1988, VI, 13. Thoenes and Günther 1985, 261–271.

37 Vitruvius, IX, praef.

38 "*Decor* demands the faultless ensemble of a work composed, in accordance with precedent, of approved details. [*Décor autem est emendatus operis aspectus probatis rebus compositi cum auctoritate.*] It obeys convention (*statio*), which in Greek is called *thematismos*, or custom (*consuetudo*) or nature (*natura*)." Vitruvius, I, 2, 5.

39 On the aesthetic implications of *décor* and its reception in the Renaissance see Payne 1999, chaps. 1, 3; on its implications for the representation of a socioeconomic hierarchy through architectural means, see Onians 1988.

40 On the impact of literary theory on architecture, see Payne 1999.

41 On Spini's contribution to the theory of architecture, see Payne 2000b, 143–156.

42 Spini 1980, 68. For similar categories used in poetics, see Minturno 1563.

43 Spini 1980, 68.

44 Spini 1980, 68–69.

45 See Aristotle 1982, III, 4: "Speaking generally, poetry seems to owe its origin to two particular causes, both natural. From childhood men have an instinct for representation, and in this respect man differs from the other animals that he is far more imitative and learns his first lessons by representations. What happens in actual experience proves this, for we enjoy looking at accurate likenesses of things which

are themselves painful to see, obscene beasts, for instance, and corpses. The reason is this. Learning things gives great pleasure not only to philosophers but also in the same way to all other men, though they share this pleasure only to a small degree. The reason why we enjoy seeing likenesses is that, as we look, we learn and infer what each is, for instance, that is so and so." On the tradition of imbrication between the literary and figural arts, the seminal work remains Rensselaer W. Lee, *Ut pictura poesis: The Humanistic Theory of Painting* (New York: Norton, 1967).

46 On the relationship between the debates on language and architectural ornament, see Payne 2000c.

47 Barbaro 1567, 115.

48 Lenzoni 1556, 129.

49 Scamozzi 1615, II, 140.

50 For the archaeological and exegetical program of the academy, see especially Tolomei 1985, 31–61.

51 Howard 1975, 27.

52 On Cornaro's relationships with Ruzzante and Falconetto, see Fiocco 1965; *Alvise Cornaro e il suo tempo*, ed. L. Puppi (Padova: Comune di Padova and Assessorato ai Beni Culturali, 1980).

53 Coffin 1964, 191–211; Gallaccini MS, f. 78v.

54 Burns and Tafuri 1998.

55 Perino del Vaga's drawing of a project for the façade of the palace of Andrea Doria in Genoa (Amsterdam, Rijksmuseum, 1948/133) shows similar devices and may suggest another possible filiation. See Burns and Tafuri 1989, 1998, 307.

56 Vasari 1986, 901.

57 Alberti 1988, IX, 8, 312.

58 Benjamin 1968, 217–252.

59 See, for example, Vasari's criticism of the Gothic manner, in particular of the "maledizzione" of agglomerated sculptural incident in his introduction to architecture. Vasari 1986, 35.

60 The trend toward increased sculpturalization in Palladio's work has been noted and variously assessed; see Ackerman 1977. Puppi finds the late work problematic for this reason and describes his manner as "exaggerated pictorialism"; see Puppi 1986, 236. In an earlier article, Wolters (who focuses mostly on interior decoration but also assesses the Loggia del Capitaniato) also sees Palladio's "decorated" style as attributable to outside factors (whims of the client or professional *stuccatori* to whom he would have given no design guidance). Wolters 1968, 255–267.

61 On Palladio's tectonics, see Payne 1999, ch. 8.

62 Palladio 1980, 67.

63 Palladio 1980, 67.

64 Alberti 1988, 385.

65 Francesco di Giorgio Martini 1967, II, 385.

66 Spini 1980, 84.

67 "In an *istoria* I like to see someone who admonishes and points out to us what is happening there; or beckons with his hand to see; or menaces with an angry face and with flashing eyes, so that no one should come near; or shows some danger or marvellous thing there; or invites us to weep or to laugh together with them." Alberti 1966, 78.

Works cited

Ackerman, J. S. 1977. *Palladio*. Harmondsworth.

Alberti, L. B. 1966. *On Painting*, trans. J. Spencer. New Haven, CT.

——. 1988. *On the Art of Building*, ed. and trans. J. Rykwert, N. Leach, and R. Tavernor. Cambridge, MA.

Alberti Index. [1975]. *Leon Battista Alberti. De re aedificatoria. Florenz 1485. Index verborum und Faksimile*, ed. H.-K. Lücke. Munich.

Aristotle. 1982. *The Poetics*, ed. and trans. W. Hamilton Fyfe. London.

Barbaro, D. 1567. *I dieci libri dell'architettura di M. Vitruvio tradotti et commentati da Mons. Daniel Barbaro eletto Patriarca d'Aquileia da lui riveduti et ampliati*. Venice.

Benjamin, W. 1968. "The Work of Art in the Age of Mechanical Reproduction," in W. Benjamin, *Illuminations*. New York.

Bode, W. von. 1902. *Florentiner Bildhauer der Renaissance*. Berlin.

Börsch-Soupan, E. 1976. "Der Renaissance Begriff der Berliner Schule im Vergleich zu Semper," in *Gottfried Semper und die Mitte des 19. Jahrhunderts*, ed. E. Börsch-Soupan. Basel.

Boucher, B. 1991. *The Sculpture of Jacopo Sansovino*. New Haven, CT.

Garris Brandt, K. W. 1994. "The Relation of Sculpture and Architecture in the Renaissance," in *From Brunelleschi to Michelangelo: The Representation of Architecture. Palazzo Grassi, April–November 1994*, ed. H. Millon and v. Lampugnani. Milan.

Burckhardt, J. 1987. *Architecture of the Italian Renaissance*. Chicago, 1st ed. Stuttgart, 1867.

Burns, H., and M. Tafuri, 1998. "From Serlio to the Escorial." *Guilio Romano*.

Coffin, D. 1964. "Pirro Ligorio and the Nobility of the Arts." *Journal of the Warburg and Courtauld Institutes*, 27, 191–211.

Coulton, J. J. 1977. *Ancient Greek Architects at Work: Problems of Structure and Design*. Ithaca, NY.

Del Turco, N. R., and F. Salvi. 1995. *Bartolomeo Ammannati. Scultore ed architetto, 1511–1592*. Florence.

Fiocco, G. 1965. *Alvise Cornaro; il suo tempo e le sue opere*. Vicenza.

Francesco Di Giorgio Martini. 1967. *Francesco di Giorgio Martini. Trattati di architettura ingegneria e arte militare*, ed. C. Maltese and L. Degrassi Maltese. Milan.

Frommel, C. L. 1989. "Serlio e la scuola Romana," in *Sebastiano Serlio*, ed. C. Thoenes, 39–49. Milan.

Gallaccini, T. (n.d.). [*Trattato sopra gli errori degli architetti*], Ms. King's 281, British Library, London.

Günther, H. 1988. *Das Studium der antiken Architektur in den Zeichnungen der Hochrenaissance*. Tübingen.

Heydenreich, L. H., and W. Lotz, 1974. *Architecture in Italy, 1400–1600*. Harmondsworth.

Howard, D. 1975. *Jacopo Sansovino. Architecture and Patronage in Renaissance Venice*. New Haven, CT.

Kiene, M. 1995. *Bartolomeo Ammannati*. Milan.

Lee, R. W. 1967. *Ut pictura poesis: The Humanistic Theory of Painting*. New York.

Lenzoni, C. 1556. *In difesa della lingua fiorentina et di Dante*. Florence.

Lotz, W. 1977. "The Roman Legacy in Sansovino's Venetian Buildings," in W. Lotz, *Studies in Italian Architecture*, 140–151. Cambridge, MA.

Minturno, A. 1563. *L'arte poetica*. Venice.

Onians, J. 1988. *Bearers of Meaning.* Princeton, NJ.

Palladio, A. 1980. *I quattro libri dell'architettura*, ed. L. Magagnato and P. Marini. Milan.

——. 1988. *Andrea Palladio. Scritti sull'architettura (1554–1579)*, ed. L. Puppi. Vicenza.

Paoletti, P. 1897–1898. *L'architecture et la Sculpture de la Renaissance à Venise*. Venice.

Payne, A. 1994. "Rudolf Wittkower and Architectural Principles in the Age of Modernism." *Journal of the Society of Architectural Historians*, 53, 322–342.

——. 1999. *The Architectural Treatise in the Italian Renaissance*. New York.

——. 2001. "Architecture, Ornament and Pictorialism: Notes on the History of an Idea," in *Architecture and Painting*, ed. K. Koehler. London.

——. 2000a. "*Ut poesis architectura*: Poetics and Tectonics in Architectural Criticism c. 1570," in *Antiquity and Its Interpreters*, ed. A. Payne et al. 143–156. New York.

——. 2000b. "Architects and Academies: Architectural Theories of *Imitatio* and the Literary Debates on Language and Style," in *Architecture and Language*, ed. G. Clarke and D. Crossley. New York.

Puppi, L. (ed.). 1980. *Alvise Cornaro e il suo tempo*. Padua.

——. 1986. *Andrea Palladio: The Complete Works*. New York.

——. 1990. *Palladio Drawings*. New York.

Rowland, I. 1994. "Raphael, Colocci and the Orders." *Art Bulletin, 76*.

Rukschcio, B. 1985. "Ornament und Mythos," in *Ornament und Askese im Zeitgeist des Wien der Jahrhundertwende*, ed. A. Pfabigan, 57–68. Vienna.

Scamozzi, V. 1615. *L'idea della architettura universale*. Ridgewood, NJ, 1964; facs. ed., Venice: by the author.

Schmarsow, A. 1903. *Unser Verhältnis zu den bildenden Künsten*. Leipzig.

Scott, G. 1965. *The Architecture of Humanism*. Gloucester, MA.

Serlio, S. 1619. *Tutte l'opera d'architettura et prospettiva di Sebastiano Serlio Bolognese*. Ridgewood, NJ, 1964; facs. ed. Venice; Giacomo de Franceschi.

Shell, J., and L. Castelfranchi (eds.). 1993. *Giovanni Antonio Amadeo. Scultura e architettura del suo tempo*. Milan.

Spini, G. (n.d.). [Degli'ornamenti dell'architettura di Gherardo Spini]. Ms. It, IV, 38 Biblioteca Nazionale Marciana, Venice.

——. 1980. "I tre primi libri sopra l'istituzioni intorno agl'ornamenti," in *Il disegno interotto. Trattati medicei d'architettura*, ed. F. Borsi et al., 300–201. Florence.

Summers, D. 1981. *Michelangelo and the Language of Art*. Princeton, NJ.

Thoenes, C., and H. Günther, 1985. "Gli ordini architettonici: rinascitá o invenzione?" in *Roma e l'antico nell'arte e nella cultura del Cinquecento*, ed. M. Fagiolo, 261–271. Rome.

Tolomei, C. 1985. "Lettera al conte Agostino Landi," in *Trattati. Con l'aggiunta degli scritti di architettura di Alvise Cornaro, Francesco Giorgi, Claudio Tolomei, Giangiorgio Trissino, Giorgio Vasari*, ed. E. Bassi and M. Walcher Casotti, 31–61. Milan.

Vasari, G. 1986. *Le vite de'piu eccellenti architetti, pittori, et scultori italiani, da Cimabue insino a' tempi nostri. Nell'edizione per i tipi di Lorenzo Torrentino Firenze 1550*, ed. L. Bellosi and A. Rossi. Turin.

Vignola, G. B. da. 1985. "La regola delli cinque ordini," in Pietro Cattaneo and Giacomo Barozzi da Vignola, *Trattati. Con l'aggiunta degli scritti di architettura di Alvise Cornaro,*

Francesco Giorgi, Claudio Tolomei, Giangiorgio Trissino, Vasari, ed. E. Bassi and M. Walcher Casotti. Milan.

Vitruvius, M. P. 1983. *De architectura. On Architecture*, ed. and trans. F. Granger. London.

Willich, H., and P. Zucker, 1914–1926. *Baukunst der Renaissance in Italien*. Wildpark-Potsdam.

Wittkower, R. 1949. *Architectural Principles in the Age of Humanism*. London.

Wölfflin, H. 1946a. "Ein Künstler über Kunst," in *Kleine Schriften*, ed. J. Gantner, 84–106. Basel.

——. 1946b. "Prolegomena zu einer Psychologie der Architektur," in *Kleine Schriften*, ed. J. Gantner, 13–47. Basel.

Wolters, W. 1968. "Andrea Palladio e la decorazione dei suoi edifici." *Bollettino del centro internazionale di studi Andrea Palladio, 10*, 255–267.

——. 1992–1993. "Architettura e decorazione nel cinquecento veneto." *Annali di architettura, 4–5*, 102–110.

Part IV
The Artist

Introduction

Accustomed as we are to associating sixteenth-century artworks with named individuals, we easily forget that this practice, in the period itself, was something relatively new. Before 1500, few buildings in Italy, and probably few paintings, would have been widely recognized as being "by" a specific person. Among the most significant changes in the visual arts in the period was the increasing dominance of the idea that the makers of certain kinds of crafted objects had a status comparable to that of an "author."

The process had begun much earlier: There was, from early in the fifteenth century, a growing sense that artists had individual styles, and that art was a product of the imagination; writers began to reiterate and respond to the Horatian doctrine of *ut pictura poesis* ("as in painting, so in poetry"), and artists began to work in places that they and others likened to scholars' studies. By 1500, Italy had seen both the individualization and the elevation of the craftsman, or at least of certain kinds of craftsman, a process that would only be reinforced by the subsequent popularization of artist's biographies, by the emerging interest of artists in writing about their own works, and by the public critical response that such works began to garner. We can fairly talk about the era as the one that saw the emergence of "the artist" in a form we would largely recognize today.

Such a change in the status of the makers of certain objects brought with it a reconfiguration of what Paul Kristeller famously termed the "system of the arts." To say that the painter, or the architect, was like a poet, was to imply that the same figure was in some significant way unlike other kinds of makers – tapestry weavers, for example, or woodworkers. The sixteenth century saw real changes in the way professions were organized: one thinks, for example, of the enormous workshop Raphael established in Rome, which provided a model for how to orchestrate large-scale multi-media projects. Corresponding to these organization shifts, moreover, were new kinds of practices – the increasing use of drawn designs for buildings, and of wax and clay models for sculptures. There were also changes, however, in how observers and participants thought about individual artistic fields and the relationship between them. These changes could be no less consequential than the more practical ones: they affected the wealth and prestige of the craftsmen involved (the "artist," in theory at least, might socialize with his patrons; his counterpart remained a laborer). More concretely, they affected the kinds of materials with which an artist might choose to work, the level at which the artist might participate in a given project, and even the kinds of assignments artists might agree to undertake.

The essays in this part look at the changing shape of three particular fields. The first piece, by Catherine Wilkinson, considers the invention of the "architect," primarily in Italy, but also in France and Spain, in the fifteenth and sixteenth centuries. As a role, the architect emerged from the traditional position of the master mason, and Wilkinson points both to the circumstances that allowed this and to their importance for the real structures that went up. The "architect," as Wilkinson presents him, was a figure who combined practical experience with book learning – embodying a new kind of expertise that already allows the architect to be compared to the new kinds of artists in other fields. And as painters and sculptors, too, began presenting themselves above all as "designers" (the masterminds behind a work who might leave practical execution to others) so too did the possibility of the architect require a certain distance from actual building. Architects were frequently amateurs of one sort or another – painters, sculptors, and even patrons, none of them with formal training, might become architects. As Wilkinson shows, the new artistic formats associated with architec-ture in the sixteenth century (measured drawings of plans, elevations, and sec-tions) reflect this distance, as well as the need architects discovered to communicate their conceptions to workers. The same new architectural "products," moreover, also cemented the shift in status such professionals enjoyed, as the drawings themselves came to be collected and published, further associating the architect with a community of readers and writers.

If Wilkinson's architects gradually became like authors, then the world of prints, the field that Michael Bury treats, might seem to offer a complementary scenario. The new prestige of the artist depended on his or her role as an inventor, a role that could remove him or her from the actual execution of works, and on this model, no field would seem to have been more *dis*advant-ageously positioned than that of reproductive printmaking. Printmaking itself was every bit as modern as "architecture," the practice having been invented only in the fifteenth century. Yet as artists saw the advantages to using print media, the artisans they employed to actually carry out the works risked looking like the masons that the architects had transcended. At least from the early nineteenth century, when Adam von Bartsch insisted that reproductive engravers could *not* be counted as "authors," Renaissance printmaking as a whole has fared less well in the literature than the "arts of design." Bury's essay sets out to challenge this notion from the ground up, starting with the idea that the prints we know to be connected to another artist's invention can fairly be called reproductions, or even translations. Drawing attention to the proof states of, preliminary drawings for, and inscriptions on a group of engravings by the mid-sixteenth-century Mantuan printmaker Giorgio Ghisi, Bury points out that there are reasons to doubt whether even the prints that look most like known paintings (and that we are thus most tempted to understand on analogy to modern photographs) were truly intended or understood as attempts to disseminate knowledge of the originals. Highlighting points of inconsistency in subject matter between the original and the "copy," and suggesting even that the reproductive author may not always have *known* the originals his works have long been thought to reproduce, Bury instead treats these sheets as "self-contained subject prints." His argument raises questions about the relationship that obtained between professional printmakers and their newly ennobled artistic brethren: On the one hand, "invention" itself becomes a slippery category; as it becomes difficult to attach this to or detach it from an individual maker, the artist–author analogy becomes cloudier. On the other, prints that seem to show paintings begin to look less like, for example, the printed design books that architects were authoring, complicating the role we imagine print to play in the promotion of non-engravers.

Both Wilkinson and Bury take the actual practices of specific individuals or groups of professionals as their point of departure. Marco Collareta's essay looks at such a group as well, but its primary focus is the writer who did more than other to shape historical perceptions of the artistic profession in the Renaissance, Giorgio Vasari. In particular, Collareta is interested in Vasari's treatment of goldsmithery, a historically fundamental profession to which the painter-historian was surprisingly hostile. What Collareta shows is that, especially in his accounts of Quattrocento goldsmiths like Brunelleschi and Luca Della Robbia, Vasari wrote his biographies in such a way as to imply a hierarchy of activities, one that rejected the values that fifteenth-century artists themselves would have appreciated, and accorded with the exclusionary thinking that guided Vasari's thinking on the arts after the founding of Florence's Accademia del Disegno. Writing in a biographical mode, Collareta shows, allowed Vasari willfully to manipulate his stories of the careers early artists followed. Vasari's rhetorical subordination of technique to "art" or "design" distorted history, but it also coincided with a rethinking on the part of Vasari's contemporaries of just how they might present their own formation and practice.

13

The New Professionalism in the Renaissance

Catherine Wilkinson

If the fifteenth century saw the emergence of a new conception of architecture, it took another century for the architect to find, claim, and establish his place in the variegated and rapidly changing social structures of the Renaissance. Alberti had a clear idea of architecture as a vocation for a gentleman with a liberal education and a special knowledge of mathematics and geometry; but his view of architecture as a profession was indistinct. In *De re aedificatoria*, written about 1450, he expressed the modern view of an architect as the complete designer, capable of planning cities and designing everything from palaces and churches to a humble farmhouse; but he had nothing to say about the training of an architect or about building practice except in the vaguest terms. A century later, Philibert Delorme (1510–70), like Alberti a distinguished writer, was able to envisage a self-governing profession of specialists with accepted standards of training and clearly defined responsibilities and privileges. In his *Premier tome de l'architecture*, published in 1567, he defined the spheres appropriate to the patron, the architect, and the workman and set up guidelines for their working relation. His second book opens with a summary of the aims that inform his treatise:

> In the preceding book we have sufficiently advised the architect and the Seigneur, or whoever would like to build, of their positions and duties as the two principal heads of the building enterprise. It remains in this second book to turn our pen to the third class of persons, without whom no building can be perfect. These are the master masons, the stone cutters, and the workmen (whom the architect must always control) who as well must not be deprived of our labor and instruction here, since it has pleased God for us to give it. [*Premier tome de l'architecture*, Bk. II, Fol. 31]

What makes Philibert's view of the profession so much more focused than anything before is that he outspokenly contrasted his architect to those who designed buildings but were not, in his view, architects. Patrons, he said, should employ architects instead of turning to "some master mason or master carpenter as is the custom or to some painter, some notary or some other person who is supposed to be qualified but more often than not has no better judgment than the patron himself" (Bk. I, Fol. 6). Most of these would-be architects were really trained for manual work and had no knowledge of the principles of architecture. The others had stopped at book learning and, satisfied with their geometrical demonstrations, they could not apply their theory to the work. What they did was nothing but "a shadow of a real building" (Bk. I, Fol. 4, a paraphrase of Vitruvius).

The true architect was something different, a man who combined the practical experience of the master mason with the knowledge of the amateur, a man (as Philibert said) schooled not only in books but in long experience. What gave the architect as a professional man his definition was a set of relationships – both professional and social – with those he came in contact with: the patron, the workmen, and the administrator and officials of the building program. But Philibert's view was partly the consequence of his conflict with the building professionals, who considered themselves capable of devising a building and whose habits and privileges were undermined by the architect.

In separating himself from the mason and the carpenter, Philibert was making a social distinction. The architect was striving to present himself as the practitioner of a Liberal Art. This effort was relatively new in France but it was well established in Italy, where the emergence of the architect in the Renaissance parallels the rise of the painter and sculptor to the status of intellectual. In 1436, when Alberti wrote his dedication for the Italian version of his treatise on painting (*Della pittura*), he pointed to the renewal of the three arts of sculpture, painting, and architecture in Florence and made it clear that this achievement, culminating in the architect Brunelleschi's invention of perspective construction, was not a matter of manual skill but an intellectual feat, a discovery of new laws of art. For Alberti, the architect was an artist and an intellectual whose activity had nothing to do with that of a craftsman. But of the three arts, architecture was the most easily separated from the crafts. Traditionally founded upon geometry and mathematics, architecture was almost a Liberal Art. As we have seen, this idea was clear in Vitruvius' text and survived in late antiquity, but it was only latent in medieval building practice. The architect in Tuscany, since he did not belong to an architects' guild, was more easily distinguished from the craftsman than either the painter or the sculptor. In *De re aedificatoria* Alberti never mentioned the guilds, and his definition of an architect, which was based upon the authority of Vitruvius, was the first modern portrait of the artist-intellectual.

As Alberti had realized, the artist's striving for a higher social status depended upon a new style of patronage. The architect aspired to be educated like a courtier and to behave like one; and between him and his patron was the bond of a shared appreciation of the theory of architecture. *De re aedificatoria* was written to inform the humanist patron rather than the architect (Krautheimer, "Alberti and Vitruvius," p. 328). The distinguished patronage that every architect hoped for was the guarantee of his social status. In the middle of the sixteenth century, Giorgio Vasari was still extremely sensitive to the social position of artists, and he described the career of the Florentine architect Giuliano da Sangallo (1443–1516) as a progression from patron to patron. Giuliano enjoyed the protection and favor of Lorenzo de' Medici, who put him in touch with Alfonso of Naples. The project for Alfonso's palace of Poggio Reale apparently attracted the attention of Cardinal Giuliano della Rovere, later Pope Julius II, and Giuliano became his architect. The truly great patron could maintain an architect: Julius took Giuliano to France, presented him to the king, and called him to Rome when he was elected pope. Giuliano had every reason to expect a great future as papal architect, when Julius abruptly replaced him with Bramante (1444–1514). A patron like Julius with great means and an addiction to building was invaluable to artists, but he could be ruthless with them. Most distinguished architectural careers in the sixteenth century were built around such patrons: Julius II and Bramante, the Gonzaga and Giulio Romano, the Farnese and Antonio da Sangallo the Younger, Philip II and Juan de Herrera. Michelangelo (1475–1564) worked for a succession of great patrons including Julius II, the Medici, and the Farnese.

Philibert Delorme had been fortunate enough to find his first important patron in Cardinal Du Bellay, with whom he was closely associated in Rome and for whom he built the Château of St. Maur. Du Bellay passed him on to the French king Henry II, and Philibert's career would have been assured had not Henry's early death deprived him of his position at court. Philibert mourned his loss, but he was sufficiently aware of the vulnerability of an architect entirely at the whim of his patron to suggest some rules for their relationship. The patron's activity, he argued, ought to be confined to the preliminary stage of a project when he was free to request designs from a number of architects and, having selected one, to demand alternatives and revisions. He might go over the smallest details of the project but, once the plans were settled, he ought to withdraw and leave the architect alone.

In fact, this rarely happened, as one might suspect from Philibert's plea. There were few great patrons who did not demand changes, often at a very late stage in the building, and many felt free to torment the architect with their own ideas. Vasari complained that the Villa Giulia, where he himself had worked, could hardly be called anyone's design because Pope Julius III every day invented "some caprice of his own which the architects were obliged to carry out" (Milanesi ed., vol. 7, p. 694).

Most of the exchanges between patron and architect took place in person, and we have few accounts of them; but, occasionally, as when Michelangelo was in Florence designing the Laurentian Library, his negotiations with Pope Clement VII in Rome were conducted by mail. From the papal half of this correspondence that survives one can see that in the nine months between November

1523, when Michelangelo received the commission for the library in Rome, until the digging of the foundations in Florence the following August, the papal secretary wrote to Michelangelo at least once a month (often more), and every time he asked for drawings or responded to studies that had been sent to him – anything from technical studies of the foundations to "qualche nuova fantasia" for the library ceiling.

The behavior of Clement VII corresponds to Alberti's humanist ideal of the educated patron who is capable of discussing the fine points of design with his architect. Clement supervised the initial design of his building with great care, and he continued to follow its progress, approving subsequent designs as they were readied for construction. He was by no means an exception. Philip II of Spain represents this Renaissance patron in his extreme form. Not only did he demand a great number of designs, often from several architects, and have them worked up into synthetic perfect projects, but he went over the smallest details of construction in his administrator's and architects' accounts. I know of no other patron of his stature who would bother to decide with his architect whether a bit of construction should be contracted as a whole or executed by day-labor. Neither Clement VII nor Philip II would have taken such an active part in the design of the buildings they commissioned had they not considered architecture a suitable pastime for a prince, nor could they have involved themselves to this extent without close and constant communication with their architects.

The higher social standing for the architect that resulted from humanist patronage had its negative aspect. Without the protection of an established guild, the architect seems to have had few if any legal safeguards for his practice. A powerful patron might call in other architects at his pleasure or even cancel a project at an advanced stage. The history of Michelangelo's designs for the façade of the church of S. Lorenzo in Florence is almost impenetrable because so many architects seem to have been involved and so many changes made in the program within a relatively short period of time. Michelangelo won the commission and spent nearly two years supervising the quarrying of the marble blocks. But, in the end, Clement VII annulled the contract and the project came to nothing.

The patron might also reduce the building funds so that the architect would find himself in charge of a building he could not execute. This was a favorite device of Philip II when he had lost interest in an old-fashioned building, like the Alcázar in Toledo. It is also true, however, that patrons unwittingly overreached themselves. The vast unfinished pile of the La Pilota Palace in Parma and the fragment of another grandiose palace in Piacenza testify to the ambition of the Farnese, which exceeded their means. Aware of this danger, Philibert counseled architects as well as patrons to take a realistic view of their finances.

Incidentally, the financial side of architectural practice in the Renaissance is not always clear. Unless an architect was on salary for a large building program, as were the architects for St. Peter's in Rome, it is not always evident how he was paid. The documents of construction generally begin with the assembling of materials and the hiring of contractors and workmen. There are few financial records from the earlier phases. The cost of preparing drawings and models for presentation to the patron was considerable, and the architect may often have borne it himself. Philibert complained that he had spent a great deal of his own money on models. Architects who were attached to a single patron might be kept on retainer, however. Philibert was given the revenues of two abbeys by Henry II. One of them had stone quarries on its property, and he may have been given it so that he could exploit it directly. In general we know little about this sort of revenue, or about the practice of receiving a percentage from contractors.

Salaries for architects attached to major building programs or employed by city governments were good. Michelangelo was not impoverished by taking over as architect of St. Peter's, in spite of his complaints; and Sansovino did well as architect of the Procuracy of Venice. What we would like to know, however, is how much the designing services of an architect were worth apart from his duties as an official or as the responsible head of a building program. This is difficult to ascertain. Andrea Palladio (1508–80), who never held an official position or enjoyed the protection of a royal patron, never became a rich man. Apparently the designing and building of private palaces and villas was not very lucrative.

Not all of those who could afford to employ an architect could also afford to conduct themselves in a grand style. Patrician patrons were unlikely to require more than one palace or country house and a family chapel; occasionally they might finance a church. They could not keep an architect on retainer, and probably they could not expect to claim very much of his time unless they commissioned a monumental work. Through the sixteenth century, however, the smaller commissions became an increasingly significant part of some architects' practice. Antonio da Sangallo the Younger (1483–1546), who had an established practice in Rome in the 1530s and 1540s, was architect of St. Peter's and the Palazzo Farnese before Michelangelo, but apparently he was also known for more modest palace designs. The career of Palladio, the greatest architect of the later sixteenth century, was based almost entirely upon the Vicenzan and Venetian nobles for whom he designed palaces and country estates that were both elegant houses and practical centers for the farming investments of their owners. His reputation was seemingly established by his successful entry in the 1549 competition to remodel the city council hall in Vicenza – the so-called Basilica – but his numerous villa designs (over twenty are illustrated in his *Quattro libri*, published in Venice in 1570) and palace projects formed the bulk of his practice. The commissions for churches, which were more expensive as well as more prestigious, did not come until his later years.

In some cases, the architect so extended his practice that he had little to do with the execution of the building. Galeazzo Alessi (1512–72) designed the

Strada Nuova in Genoa, a new street with palaces for wealthy Genoese banking families. He also designed villas for the same patrons. But he may only have provided rough sketches for many of them, leaving the detailed designing and the supervision of construction to architects and decorators who were loosely associated with him. It would seem that he came to function as what Wolfgang Lotz has aptly called an "architect by remote control" (*Galeazzo Alessi*, p. 10).

The conduct of an architect's practice varied enormously in the sixteenth century, but it is clear from the records that architects like Palladio and Alessi had a larger number of commissions than their predecessors. Neither Palladio nor Alessi was attached to a court or to great patrons, and they were not obliged to supervise the construction of the buildings they designed, although they often did so. This is a notable change from the fifteenth century when, at the time Alberti wrote, there were only a handful of men who might be considered architects according to his definition of the term and only a few patrons with the intellectual pretensions to hire them. By the 1560s, this was no longer the case; and to judge from the number of surviving Roman palaces, it would seem that already in the 1540s it was customary for upper-class families to hire an architect. In France, Philibert Delorme recognized that without the relative security of the guild organization, an architect must support himself by smaller commissions, and he was proud to say that he had designed all kinds of buildings, from magnificent palaces to modest houses. By this time, the architect was well on his way to taking over the last preserve of the craftsman and master-builder.

A new working relationship with the building trades was as necessary to the sixteenth-century architect as was the new style of patronage. Alberti had quite consciously opened a gap between the architect and the craftsman, a gap so eagerly accepted by architects and, by the sixteenth century, already so firmly established in Italy that it was difficult to bridge from either side. It was responsible for the often bitter exchanges between men working as architects but placed on opposite sides of the division between the liberal and the mechanical arts. These debates usually concerned technical competence – the "craftsman-architect" accusing the "dilettante architect" of incompetence and the architect asserting his intellectual superiority over the craftsman. The craftsmen who were to execute the architect's designs were, in Alberti's words, just "an instrument to the architect" (*De re aedificatoria*, Preface). Philibert Delorme took much the same view when he spoke of the "third class of persons . . . the master masons, stone cutters, and workmen whom the architect must always control."

This view of the architect is so close to our own and so easily transposed into the modern relationship between the architect and the building contractor that we are likely to overlook the striking character of Philibert's assertion for its time. In France the situation was different from that in Italy. The masons and carpenters Philibert referred to had been but lately the masters of the royal works in France, men like Gilles Le Breton, the powerful Parisian master mason who had been employed under Francis I. Such men were organized in a closely knit system that effectively controlled construction and architectural design. As in the earlier medieval system, a man was trained through formal apprenticeship and, as he worked his way up in the system, each step increased his responsibilities until, as a qualified master mason, he could undertake the design and direction of a building himself. This profession did not acknowledge the distinction between designer and builder; nowhere did it recognize the separate function of an architect in Philibert's sense of the term. Buildings like the château of Azay-le-Rideau were designed and built by guild shops. Even as original a masterpiece as Chambord must, in the end, have been built this way, whatever the original involvement of Leonardo and Domenico da Cortona may have been.

In Spain, the building trades appear to have been more dependent upon large building programs and the shops less strictly organized than in France. Master-builders did not belong to a guild, and a man's training took place on the job. He rose in the hierarchy of workmen (usually beginning as a stone-cutter or as a mason if he aspired to become a master) to the position of supervisor or *aparejador*. As such he organized the workmen, estimated costs, and sometimes put up money for building materials. He was a master-builder in the last stage of his training. Then, as master of the works, he would finally be responsible for the design and for the proper execution of the building. The important appointments, for example the *maestro mayor* of any of the cathedrals, were the basis of a solid reputation, and, in principle, a man held only one such position at a time. By the early sixteenth century, however, the master was often absent on other projects, leaving the building in the hands of his supervisor – an indication of the weakening of the system as well as of a more varied practice. By this time, the master of the works was beginning to estrange himself from the rest of his trade and to become an architect in the full sense of the word.

The patron was represented at the works by a separate structure headed by the administrator at the building site and by the notaries and paymaster (if the program was a large one), who prepared the contracts for each major section of building or for expensive piecework like decorative carving, and paid the semi-skilled workmen by the day or week. They also paid the men on salary to the works – themselves, the master, and the contractor. These officials kept precise records of expenses, everything from the large cost for building stone to the price of renting a mule for the master to travel on to consult with the patron.

In Spain, as in France, this system ran smoothly as long as the designer remained the head of the organization of workmen. Obviously, it tolerated outsiders with difficulty, and we shall see that the transition to the new system was not accomplished without some open conflict.

In placing all responsibility for design upon the architect, Philibert removed the most cherished privilege of the master mason. The French guilds had only two means of defense: they could conspire against the architects who were placed over them (as they seem to have intrigued rather successfully against the Italian architect Serlio who had been brought to France by Francis I), or they could adopt the title of architect themselves, as Philibert suggested that they were doing. The use of this new title indicates that the integrity of the traditional system was lost. Henceforth, the position of master mason would no longer guarantee the right to design a building.

Something similar occurred in Spain when, in the reign of Philip II, the master-builders found themselves displaced first by architects imported from Italy and then by the king's courtier and amateur architect, Juan de Herrera (ca. 1530–1597). Herrera, who modeled his career on Alberti's image of the architect, was an accomplished mathematician and geometrician with an interest in Hermetic philosophy and some skill as a diplomat, but he had no practical training in building. That he was able to function as the royal architect was due entirely to the support of Philip II. Against the alliance of patron and architect, the building profession was relatively powerless. It fought back when outsiders were within its reach, but Philip II never placed Herrera in an official position as master of the works. The position remained vacant (as it did at the Escorial) or it was filled by a disciple of Herrera's who did have professional training but could be counted on to follow Herrera's plans (as happened at the Lonja in Seville). Thus the designing phase was removed from the control of the building trade, which without its former privilege and prestige nevertheless continued to function. Certainly, no building program as large as the Escorial could afford to dispense with an organization of craftsmen, and Philip II very sensibly retained the basic structure of organization. In fact, the traditional organization of a large building program was practical and, with certain modifications, it remained stable in western Europe through the seventeenth century. But one result of the appearance of the professional architect was that a stigma was now attached to practical training that prevented men apprenticed in the building trades from becoming architects without some compensating "liberal" education.

The situation is much clearer in France and Spain, where the architect confronted an established building profession, than it is in Italy. In areas where the building trades were well organized, as they appear to have been in Milan in the fifteenth century for example, there was resistance to the newfangled architect. Filarete was appointed by his patron Francesco Sforza to the cathedral works in the 1450s but was soon fired. When put in charge of the duke's vast project for a city hospital, he had great difficulty collaborating with the local builders who were active on the project. The conflict was not only between Filarete's Florentine style and that of the Milanese. As is amply documented in Filarete's *Trattato di architettura*, written about 1465, he took a lofty view of the architect's status and shared Alberti's view of workmen. This image of an architect deploying armies of workmen who toiled obediently under his commands did not sit well with the master-builders who were appointed to assist him. That he seems also to have had a lively contempt for the Milanese did not improve matters.

In provincial centers, the building trades may have been responsible for designing well into the sixteenth century. Palladio was apprenticed to a stonemason in Padua in 1521, and he worked as a builder in Vicenza until the 1530s.

253

But the building trades seem never to have dominated the practice of architecture in Italy as they did in France and Spain. Architects like Giulio Romano (1499–1546) in Mantua encountered no obstacles to their practice and, in Venice, the sculptor Jacopo Sansovino (1486–1570) was the leading architect.

As we have seen already, there was no architects' guild. Aspirants were obliged to take their training in another craft. Giuliano's father apprenticed him in wood sculpture. In some parts of Italy, as in France and Spain, the aspiring architect still apprenticed as a stone-mason or in stone sculpture as in the medieval period.

There were certainly architectural workshops in Italy, although we know very little about them. Filarete describes his shop, with its drafting table and his assistants busy about him. The Solari who were associated with him in Milan may have been something like a firm of master-builders. In Florence, Giuliano de Sangallo had a shop of workmen, including stone-carvers, whom he took with him to execute the palace at Savona for Julius II. Vasari mentions that Giuliano's confidence in his shop permitted him to leave the building in their hands and go to France. But these men were apparently not apprentices in architecture. Palladio's training (see below, p. 259) is exceptional for a Renaissance architect; few other Italian architects emerged from his background before the middle of the sixteenth century.

The absence of a powerful building profession in Italy in the Renaissance and the early prominence of architects are both related to the leading role taken by central Italy in architecture as well as the other arts. What was exceptional and precocious about central Italy, and Tuscany particularly, was its tradition of artist-architects. This tradition was founded on the belief (well rooted by the fifteenth century) that any artist could design a building since it was the conception of the work that mattered rather than the construction. This conviction derived from the custom of treating the three arts of painting, sculpture, and architecture as three branches of the same art of design, and it is probably very old in Tuscany. In the fourteenth century, Giotto the painter and Giovanni Pisano the sculptor received important architectural commissions. In fact, the majority of architects before the 1550s in Italy were trained as painters or sculptors; the career of Arnolfo di Cambio was exceptional. Vasari noted this phenomenon and ascribed it to the fact that artists were trained in *disegno* – "the father of our three arts" – which made it possible for them to extend their practice to another field. Developed by Vasari (and others) into a theory of artistic creativity, *disegno* was the foundation of the liberal status of the practice of art, without which it would not have been possible to distinguish painting, sculpture, and architecture from, say, silversmithing or furniture-making, and the artist from the craftsman.

The Florentine idea of *disegno* is discussed in Filarete's *Trattato*, and it was the basis of his image of the artist. Filarete trained himself as a sculptor and metalworker and came to Sforza's court as an architect but probably also as a complete artist. In his treatise, he described the architect as a courtier who devises entertainments for his prince, and designs fresco cycles and monumental sculpture as well as buildings. He imagined the artist in a position much like that which Leonardo da Vinci actually occupied at the Sforza court half a century later.

Practical experience in *disegno*, meaning essentially drawing and perspective, was the only feature of their formal training that Renaissance architects had in common. It was learned during their apprenticeship – as Leonardo certainly learned it in the shop of the sculptor and painter Andrea del Verrocchio. Intarsia workers were also trained in geometry and perspective; this may be why a number of architects, including Baccio d'Agnolo and Vignola, emerged from this craft. The only other shared experience was the architect's self-apprenticeship to the art of antiquity, which he normally served in Rome.

Equipped with a knowledge of perspective and mathematics and of the remains of Roman architecture, an artist could become an architect. This is apparently what Brunelleschi did or was believed to have done. It is probably the path that Filarete followed, because he became an architect only after a lengthy stay in Rome. This line of education is aptly brought out by Vasari in his life of Bramante. Drawn from the beginning to mathematics and geometry, Bramante took his training under a painter specializing in architectural perspective. Then, having decided to become an architect, he went to draw and measure the ancient monuments in Rome and there came to the attention of wealthy patrons. Vasari's picture of a great architect is no doubt distorted by his scheme of the development of the arts, his desire to play up the resemblance to the career of Brunelleschi, the prototypical Renaissance architect, and to play down the buildings of Bramante's first period in Milan. It is also in contrast to the career of a specialized architect like Giuliano da Sangallo, whom Vasari describes as a professional man, not an intellectual or an artist, who is elevated by great patrons. Vasari makes a negative example of Giuliano who, after his long service to Julius II, found himself idle and forced to beg permission to return to Florence while Bramante replaced him as architect in charge of the papal projects.

Vasari's biographies of the Sangallo architects are his only example of a continuing family tradition in central Italian architecture, but he is somewhat dubious about their standing. That he disliked Antonio da Sangallo the Younger and admired Michelangelo (who disliked the Sangallos even more) does not entirely explain his reservations. He emphasized the sound technique and the practical designs of both Giuliano and Antonio but he made it clear that, when it came to the greater projects, they were second-rate compared to geniuses in design like Bramante and Michelangelo. There is no doubt that Bramante and Michelangelo were indeed the greater architects, but Vasari's reluctance to praise the Sangallos as designers may be partly because they lacked a painter's or a sculptor's training, and were not artists in the true and noble sense.

The extent to which the *disegno* tradition and the image of the artist-architect dominated architectural practice in central Italy is remarkable. The architectural careers of Bramante, Raphael, Peruzzi, and Michelangelo all developed from their work as artists. Giulio Romano, who was raised in Raphael's painting studio and who was primarily a painter until 1523, could go to Mantua and become a distinguished architect. His work for the Gonzaga of Mantua shows no inexperience. Jacopo Sansovino, the Florentine sculptor, went to Venice a few years later and became architect to the Procuracy without much practical experience. Such designers seem to have enjoyed a freedom and acceptance that was rare in the fifteenth century. Alberti apparently chose to work closely with someone experienced in architecture, but there is no evidence that Giulio or Sansovino felt the need for such collaboration.

The technical inexperience of the artist-architects of the Renaissance should not be exaggerated. One cannot stand in front of Alberti's façade of San Andrea in Mantua and not recognize the control that the designer exercised over the smallest details of the decorative scheme even if, as in this case, we know very little about how it was done. Bramante, trained as a painter, was an experienced architect when he began to work for Julius II in 1505. In the 1490s, he had been consulted on the model for the crossing tower of Milan Cathedral, which was a technical problem of notorious difficulty. The view, expressed often, that Bramante was a magnificent designer with a poor notion of building technology is a little like saying that Shakespeare was more or less illiterate. The technical faults of Bramante's buildings for Julius II – the poor foundations in the Belvedere and the cracks in the piers of St. Peter's – were due to their unprecedented scale, the frenetic speed with which they were built, and to Bramante's experiments with a new building technique – the revival of Roman concrete construction which made possible, in the piers of new St. Peter's, the vast, molded forms that had not been seen since antiquity. Bramante's technical innovations were introduced in response to the artist's new conception of spatial organization, and even his admirers perceived his handling of structure as "bold rather than well-considered" (Serlio, Book 3).

The Italian artist-architect had no tie with the building trades; yet strictly speaking he was not an amateur, since his status as an artist qualified him as a designer. This image of the architect found its most complete expression in Michelangelo: sculptor, painter, and (as Vasari said) the model for a whole generation of architects. It survived in Italy well into the seventeenth century, when the sculptor and architect Gianlorenzo Bernini astonished his contemporaries with his versatility; but it was essentially a creation of the fifteenth century. One must remember that Bramante was over fifty when he began Saint Peter's in 1506 and that Michelangelo was trained before 1500.

In the sixteenth century, besides the amateur architect and the artist-architect, one also finds a third variety of architect: the specialist who considers himself both a gentleman like the amateur and a designer like the artist but who insists upon his independent status as a professional in his field. It is in this respect that Philibert Delorme's conception of the architect is avant-garde. At the opposite pole from the craftsman he placed "some painter or notary" (by whom he certainly meant Primaticcio, who had replaced him at Fontainebleau, and Pierre Lescot, who was involved at the Louvre). In his view, such a person was no better qualified to be an architect than was the mason. Philibert had no sympathy for those who dabbled in what he considered a serious profession. Confident of his own social status, he did not hesitate to affirm his close contact with the technical and craftsmanly side of architecture. He had been trained as a master mason himself in his father's shop in Lyons, and he was proud to say that he had been designing buildings since he was fifteen. As a man whose career had been made through his contacts with royal patrons in the highest intellectual circles of his day, he felt he could dispense with the trappings of a humanist. Philibert was concerned with designing buildings and with seeing them properly executed. He could see that the architect would have to be able to manage his workmen. Without proper supervision, he warned, the contractor might cheat the architect and build the walls so poorly that they would not support the roof. On the other hand, the architect himself must know what is feasible and not present plans for fantastic projects that could not be executed. Here Philibert was surely referring to Serlio's totally impractical scheme to vault the Salle de Bal at Fontainebleau. Philibert himself solved the problem by a magnificent wooden coffered ceiling designed on a system of his own invention (published in his own *Nouvelles inventions pour bien bastir* in 1561). Philibert had a specialist's admiration for ingenious structural solutions that is characteristically French and is not found in Italy to the same degree. It permitted him to admire Gothic vaulting – "la mode françoise" – which, "although it is out of fashion, is not to be despised," an attitude one does not find stated in Italy until Scamozzi's and Guarino Guarini's writing in the seventeenth century. Vasari, who was Philibert's Italian contemporary, could find no such redeeming virtue in Gothic architecture.

There are signs of the emergence of this kind of professional architect in central Italy, although here the emphases were reversed. Philibert's workshop training gave him professional authority over the master masons that Italian artist-architects like Serlio and Primaticcio lacked. But Antonio da Sangallo the Younger suffered because of his close tie to the trades. Cellini remarked spitefully that one shouldn't expect much from him since he was trained as a carpenter; and we have seen that his practical expertise, although admired by Vasari, did not entirely compensate for his lack of artistic training. It was this that Cellini really held against him: the fact that, as Ackerman has remarked, Antonio was "one of the few architects of his time who never wanted to be anything else" ("Architectural Practice," p. 149). He was a professional existing in an artistic environment that was in principle hostile to him. His own training (whether or not he was really an active carpenter) had come in Bramante's studio, where his uncle had arranged for him to work. He seems to have prepared drawings and supervised construction when Bramante was too infirm to do this himself. He is thus the first major Italian architect to have been professionally trained. He seems also to have been the first central Italian architect to develop a highly organized shop – the *setta sangallesca*, as Vasari called it, which was composed of assistants, draftsmen, and apprentices who owed their livelihood to Antonio's architectural practice.

From his position, Antonio could challenge the right of Michelangelo, a sculptor and a painter, to meddle in the design of the Vatican fortifications, to which Michelangelo is supposed to have replied that, although he didn't know much about painting and sculpture, he had had a lot of experience with fortifications. The joke was half true since Michelangelo had served the Florentine Republic as director of fortifications several years earlier. Without making too much of the anecdote itself (it is reported by Vasari), we do know from Francesco de Hollanda's *Dialogos*, written about this time, that Michelangelo was very much concerned with the Vatican project and, from other accounts, that he quarrelled with Sangallo over the plans. It is certainly characteristic that Antonio offered his challenge as a specialist to an amateur and that Michelangelo responded by asserting his own professional competence.

Nor is it surprising that their exchange concerned fortification design. According to Vasari, this was the area where the young Antonio first distinguished himself. Some years earlier, Pope Leo X had called together a team of military architects to plan the fortifications of Civitavecchia. After several days of discussion and the presentation of numerous schemes, no agreement could be reached until Antonio came up with a synthetic project that satisfied everyone, including the pope and the engineers. By the 1530s Antonio was the leading military architect of central Italy.

Military design, sometimes classed with architecture and sometimes with engineering, was practiced by nearly every major Renaissance architect except Palladio. In the fifteenth century, Filarete and Francisco di Giorgio included it in their treatises, and Leonardo recommended himself to Sforza as a military expert as well as painter, sculptor, and musician. In his brief discussion of the nobility of painting and of the artist in *The Courtier*, Baldassare Castiglione cited the application of drawing to the arts of war. War was a pastime, a serious concern of the nobility, and a fit and necessary object of study for a prince. Perhaps for this reason, a practitioner of military architecture in the Renaissance was a gentleman by consequence of his profession. In the sixteenth century, he was often an independent specialist. Military architecture had its own body of theory, and its practice involved precise calculations and drawings on the part of the designer; but only semi-skilled laborers were required for construction. Unlike medieval castles, Renaissance fortifications were of rough masonry or earth. Military architects dealt with the highest class of patron, with princes and city governments, and their expertise was highly valued. Many of the great military specialists of the period are no longer well known, but the reputations of a number of architects, including Michele Sanmichele in Verona and Galeazzo Alessi, who first appeared as a military architect in Perugia, were based on their military work. Vignola, Michelangelo, and Philibert Delorme could all claim to be experts in fortification design. Michelangelo may not have considered this as exalted a discipline as sculpture or painting but it was certainly a distinguished profession with no taint of association with the trades.

It is difficult today, when the artist's social standing is high and the profession of the craftsman is nearly atrophied, to appreciate the intense concern of the Italian Renaissance artist to establish his status. His efforts did not stop with learned discourses on the nobility of the arts or with his intimacy with the highest levels of society. In spite of his immense artistic reputation, Michelangelo always insisted upon the nobility of the Buonarroti family; and architects tried whenever they could to bring out the best in their ancestry. The practice of military design was perhaps the most obvious way for an artist to affirm a status on a par with the other professions such as medicine or law. Certainly, it was the first aspect of architectural practice to gain independent recognition.

Andrea Palladio was a professional architect and, of all the great Italians, his career most resembles that of Philibert Delorme in France. He was trained as a stone-mason and worked as a builder, and he advanced his career with the help of a humanist patron; but his career was nevertheless shaped by a characteristically Italian view of the architect. Andrea di Pietro della Gondola was discovered by the humanist Trissino, lifted out of his humble stone-mason's trade, re-educated, and re-christened to emerge as Palladio, the architect. His belated liberal education, as Ackerman has rightly stressed (*Palladio*, p. 21), was tailor-made for an architect – the study of geometry and proportion, Vitruvius, and Roman monuments. Palladio did not have Alberti's liberal education or an artist's training in *disegno*. He was, as Philibert said of his own training, more "educated in books and long experience." But unlike Philibert, Palladio never made a point of his earlier, humbler career. Although it undoubtedly influenced his approach to architecture, Palladio's apprenticeship as a stone-carver was politely passed over in silence when he became an architect and an associate of humanists and patricians (see his preface to the *Quattro Libri*, Venice, 1570).

It is no coincidence that the most advanced form of the architectural profession was to be found in France and in northern Italy – in provincial centers like Vicenza, where Palladio established his practice, in Genoa, where Alessi did much of his work, or in Verona, where Michele Sanmichele was the leading architect – and not in central Italy, where the artist-architect continued to dominate the scene. Yet even in Rome, there were signs that architecture was slowly becoming a specialist's field. Vasari, in spite of his belief in the unity of the arts of design, faulted the early artist-architects for their ignorance of building, often to the extent of not knowing the technical language. His own technical preface to the *Lives* is concerned with building technology – how to mount an architrave so that it will not crack – and only secondarily with the theory of architecture based upon the symmetry of the human body. In his second edition of the *Lives* (1568), Vasari added in the life of Antonio de Sangallo a story which probably happened later but which illustrates his own attitude. Pope Paul III had opened a competition for the design of the cornice of his palace and Vasari, as he told it, came to present Michelangelo's design with those of the other architects. After reviewing the various projects, the pope turned to Antonio and asked where Melighino's project was. Antonio, who was already humiliated by this competition for the design of part of his own building, had had enough: "Melighino?" he replied, "But really, Holy Father, he's a joke!" Emphatically, the pope reminded Antonio that he wished Melighino (who was a notary turned designer and courtier) to be taken seriously. The story shows that, although the pope might wish to encourage his favorite, an amateur was not taken seriously by professionals like Sangallo and Vasari.

Perhaps the clearest example of the new attitude is Michelangelo himself who, in spite of his own belief in the practice of *disegno*, protested that he was not an architect – by which surely he did not mean that he considered himself incapable of designing a building but that he lacked constructional expertise. From documentary evidence, even this was not quite true. Michelangelo was concerned with the technical aspects of building to a remarkable degree. This is not surprising, since he approached architecture as a sculptor famous for carving marble himself and for allowing only the smallest share of the work to his assistants. He took the execution of his buildings as personally as he took his sculpture, and his ornamental vocabulary was so complex and so idiosyncratic that it must have required both skillful workmen and the closest supervision. In his architectural practice, the result was a concern for building materials and building technology and a professional sense of responsibility for the construction. Although too old to supervise all the work at St. Peter's in person, he watched it carefully. When he was absent from Rome and a bit of unusual vaulting was improperly executed, he had it torn out and re-done, much to his personal "shame and vexation."

Michelangelo treated what we would call technical problems as design problems, and this brings him close to Philibert's view that the architect must concern himself as much with materials and techniques as with the design and ornament of architecture. In fact, this attitude brought them both closer to the craft of building than Alberti had envisioned for his humanist architect a century earlier, although it is merely an extension of the Classical ideal of the fusion of theory and practice. At any rate, by the 1560s, we may say that the architect had achieved full professional status and, like a doctor or a lawyer, he might take full responsibility for all aspects of his practice.

We must remember, however, that this still was not the profession in its modern form, which is a creation of the nineteenth century. As Ackerman has pointed out, the difference lies partly in the fact that in the sixteenth century, and indeed until the Industrial Revolution, every piece of a building was made to order. This created problems of communication. The new architect, who would not be working in the stone yard or be always present at the building site, needed to provide his workmen with precise instructions. An important part of this procedure, the more traditional way of communicating personally and verbally, escapes us today, so that at points we can be puzzled by how things were built at all. On the other hand, new devices were employed in the sixteenth century and old ones re-adjusted to establish communication with patrons and, more importantly, with the executants. The architect came to rely on models and increasingly on drawings to communicate his designs to the builders.

As we have seen, the medieval tradition of model-building in Italy continued in the Renaissance. The model was first of all made for the patron and occasionally for the public – a purpose it still serves. It was also used as a guide for the builders. In the sixteenth century, the character of architectural models seems to have varied considerably. Philibert complained of fancy models that were painted up to conceal a poor design; but models could be impressive. Michelangelo's ten-foot full-scale wooden model of the cornice for the Farnese Palace was hoisted into place so the pope could see how it would look. Such an elaborate and costly affair must also have been intended for the use of the workmen. Working models, usually of wood, were expensive. Sangallo's model for his design of St. Peter's is famous because it cost a fortune. Philibert, who complained of the expense of models, nevertheless advised the patron and the architect to invest in them because detailed models of all the major parts of the building would be justified in the long run. Michelangelo, who left a clay model of the staircase of the Laurentian Library for the workmen to follow when he left Florence, was using scale models for the workmen at St. Peter's many years later.

But, even in the fifteenth century, drawings were beginning to replace models in architectural practice. Filarete describes a type of drawing which he calls a "relief drawing," made on squared paper. From this master plan, further scale drawings of detailed plans could be made. The technique derived from the squaring of a panel for a perspective construction, as Alberti explained it in *Della pittura*, but Filarete seems to have been the first to apply the technique to architectural drawing. The close relation between perspective construction and methods of architectural drafting is essential to an understanding of the development of architectural drawings in the sixteenth century.

To judge from the copies of his treatise, Filarete's drawings were rather primitive, especially when compared with the beautiful architectural drawings that survive from the later Renaissance, when this branch of *disegno* came into its own. Unlike the fifteenth century, the sixteenth century is rich in architectural drawings of all sorts – studies after antiquity and contemporary buildings, sketches of an architect's ideas, and numerous plans and some elevations and sections, as well as perspectives and a great wealth of architectural details. From this collection of material we might expect to be able to read the progress of a building from the architect's first sketches to the final working drawings; but, in fact, the professional use that was made of these drawings is not clear. One problem is that there are seldom enough drawings from any one project to follow its evolution. But there are also consistent gaps in the evidence. As Ackerman has explained, finished drawings may be classed in two categories: first the large, carefully drawn, and attractively rendered projects that were made for the client; they are rare and they cannot have been much use for construction because they almost never include measurements or a scale. Moreover, they typically show the building that was to have been built rather than the one that was built. . . . The second type of finished drawing was intended for use in construction, but it is limited to details – a window, an entablature – and was intended only to guide masons and carvers. ["Architectural Practice," p. 161]

Where are the working drawings that might in some way correspond to the blueprints used in a modern office? One answer is that they are gone, used up on the job; another is that they never existed. Certainly a great number of drawings have perished, but it is puzzling that so few of the drawings that do survive can be identified as working drawings.

Many of the drawings we have were probably made for the patron. These include not only the presentation drawings from an initial phase of a project, but also the studies and sketches that were exchanged when the final plans were being negotiated and construction was actually under way. Such use of drawings is documented in the correspondence between Michelangelo and Pope Clement VII during the work on the Laurentian Library, already mentioned above. A number of drawings may also have been made during the meetings and consultations that were so often held between the patron and several architects. The numerous "ideal" plans of St. Peter's, which exist in a bewildering number of versions by different hands and which are often covered with notations and corrections, do not seem to relate to any identifiable stage of construction but may well be the product of group discussions with the patron. If we recall Vasari's account cited earlier of Sangallo's meeting with Pope Leo X and his military engineers, we realize that this group must have produced a number of drawings within a very few days.

Presumably, once the plans were settled, the approved design was passed on to the workmen for execution. A study for a fresco at the Farnese Palace at Caprarola shows the architect with some associates (perhaps intended to personify his liberal education) delivering his drawing to the contractor for execution while, in the background, the stone-cutters and masons are busy with the building. Certainly, by the mid-sixteenth century, it was possible to build a building without a model. Michelangelo's Laurentian Library must have been largely executed from drawings, since there is no record of a model until he left Florence. But what sort of drawings? The study for the fresco at Caprarola shows the architect holding a plan, and master plans were certainly made. The other type of working drawing is the architectural detail, and it may well be, as Ackerman has suggested, that when the architect was able to supervise construction, these were all that were needed.

There is, however, evidence of a different type of architectural drawing in the Renaissance – the perspective projection, the analytical section and elevation drawing – which is associated with the building of St. Peter's, specifically with the appointment of Raphael in 1514 as chief architect.

The appointment of Raphael (1483–1520) as architect of St. Peter's is the most striking example of the Italian confidence in the genius of the artist. St. Peter's was the most complex building program of the century, and Raphael had very little experience as an architect. His appointment came because of his status as a great painter and apparently on Bramante's recommendation. As Raphael realized himself, his other commitments, as well as his inexperience, made it impossible for him to work as Bramante had done, and we saw in the last chapter that he was given Giuliano da Sangallo and Fra Giocondo as architectural mentors. Raphael welcomed Fra Giocondo gratefully, but since Fra Giocondo was seventy-nine it was hardly to be expected that he would supervise construction for very long; and Giuliano was old and soon returned to Florence. Two years later (1516) Fra Giocondo died, and Raphael asked for another assistant. Antonio da Sangallo was given the job; thus was created the organized building operation at St. Peter's, with Antonio as chief supervisor until 1520 when, on Raphael's death, he became chief architect.

There is some reason to believe that Raphael may have shaped the assistants assigned to him into something resembling an architectural office, although how much of it was already established under Bramante before 1514 is still open to debate. One reason to favor Raphael, rather than Bramante, as the organizer of the work at St. Peter's is the character of Raphael's own painting atelier. Raphael's assistants worked as extensions of his own hand, preparing drawings and cartoons from his sketches and ideas as well as executing much of the work. Except perhaps for Giulio Romano, who was chief assistant and shop foreman, these artists were not independent personalities while they were in Raphael's shop, and they are identifiable only occasionally and only in the execution of works, not in their conception. Raphael's painting shop was a remarkable innovation. It is also closer to the modern architectural office than any architectural practice we know from the Renaissance.

Raphael was not a figurehead at St. Peter's; on the contrary, he was so preoccupied by his new responsibilities that contemporaries found him unlike his usual self. In spite of this, there are no drawings of St. Peter's that are certainly by his hand. A new plan of the building was drawn up during this period, and a model was begun. The plan, published by Serlio in 1540, and existing in other versions as well, is considered to be Raphael's design, but the many drawings from his period of office are certainly by others – chiefly Antonio da Sangallo. This suggests that he may have been using Antonio the way he used his painting assistants – to prepare studies from his ideas. He could then rework more finished plans.

If this is true, then Raphael's need for more precise kinds of architectural drawings is obvious. A building on the scale of St. Peter's could have been built from the few plans and details that would serve for a smaller building, but the spatial conception of St. Peter's was far more complex than that of previous buildings. It was too intricate to be held in the mind of the architect or conveyed to the patron and workmen by simple sketches and details. Perspective renderings made the project visible more cheaply and rapidly than a model. They could be revised, and measured sections and elevations could serve to prepare more detailed specifications – all of which could be done by assistants. As mentioned in the last chapter, the famous letter to Leo X concerning the projected "reconstruction drawings" of ancient Rome explained that the illustrations would be accurate and legible. They would show not only the foundations, which one could see from a plan, but also the character of the architecture in space – they would have been a complete application of *disegno* to architecture.

None of Raphael's drawings for this reconstruction project has been identified, and there is some question if any were made, but some of the new type of elevation and section drawings made for St. Peter's are preserved in a sketch-book belonging to Paul Mellon (figure 13.1). This type of drawing, however, cannot be associated with a new type of architectural practice. Raphael died in 1520, before his organization of the works was firmly established; and although

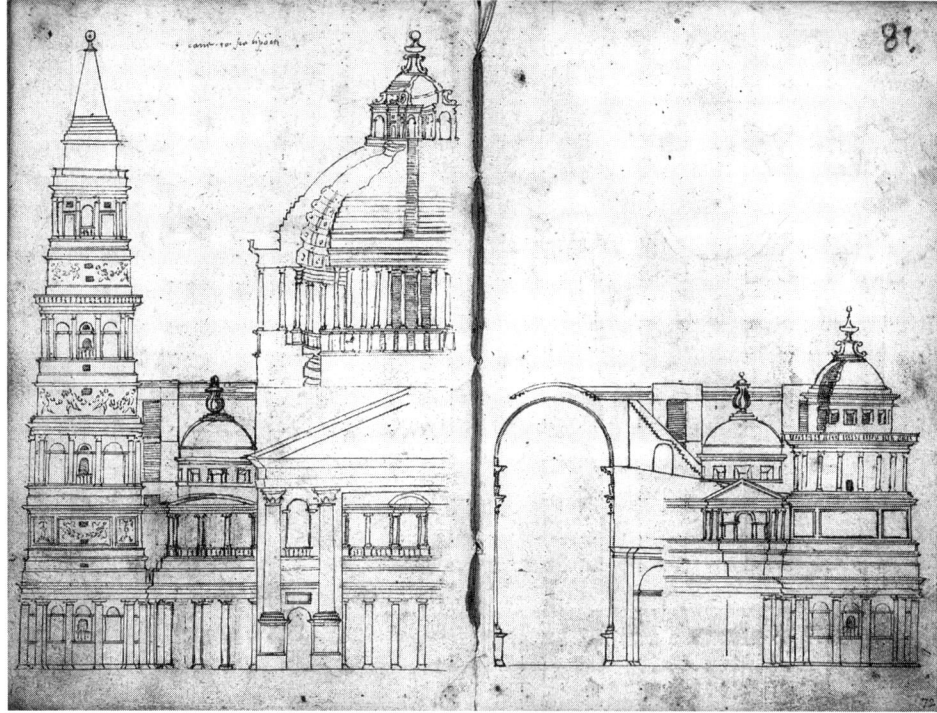

Figure 13.1 Menicantonio (?), combined elevation and section of an early project for St. Peter's, Rome; undated. The techniques of perspective projection, here applied to architecture, made it possible to represent the complex spaces of the new St. Peter's. Such drawings are the ancestors of the analytical drawings used in the modern office. The Pierpont Morgan Library, New York. 1978.44, f. 71v–72. Gift of Paul Mellon.

Antonio da Sangallo inherited his position and kept it until his own death in 1546, he seems to have invested most of his energy in the notorious wooden model and to have been satisfied with sketches for his own designing and with plans and details for working drawings. Nor did Michelangelo, who disliked delegating any design functions to others, choose to work as Raphael had. The measured elevation and section drawings which were later made from the model were apparently not used in the actual design process.

In the sixteenth century, however, the set of measured architectural drawings – plan, elevation, and section – did develop into the means of communication between architect and workmen. The Escorial, begun in the 1560s, was built largely from such drawings, although models were also made; a number of elevation and section drawings by Juan Bautista de Toledo and Juan de Herrera survive. Juan Bautista was Michelangelo's assistant at St. Peter's, so perhaps the analytical drawings were used in Italy more than surviving drawings would indicate. In France, Philibert Delorme was perfectly aware of Italian developments in architectural drafting after he returned from Rome in 1536. His copies of the elevation drawings for St. Peter's, which are preserved in Munich, are close to those in the Mellon sketchbook. Philibert, moreover, clearly saw the advantage to using drawings in building, although he was not prepared to give up model-building. He devoted the major part of his treatise to explaining the different types of drawing and illustrating the decorative vocabulary of Classical architecture. In his instructions to the masons, he states that he wishes to demonstrate "what instruments and methods the masons should use for measurement, as much as for the *orthographies* as for the *scenographies* – that is to say for the plans, elevations and façades of buildings – in order that they might have a sound knowledge before proceeding to any drawings or models" (Bk. II, Fol. 31).

Alberti had made it clear that architectural practice without theory was just a trade, not a discipline (*De re aedificatoria*, Bk. IX, Ch. x); but the actual relation between theory and practice in the Renaissance is a matter of debate. Wittkower (*Architectural Principles in the Age of Humanism*) identified humanist theories of proportion and geometry as a serious aspect of real buildings, particularly those by Alberti and Palladio. On the other hand, Krautheimer ("Alberti and Vitruvius") has shown that *De re aedificatoria* was not addressed to practitioners; and Ackerman ("Architectural Practice," p. 153) has observed that architects of the High Renaissance produced little theoretical writing of their own. Although I cannot agree with Ackerman's conclusion (p. 170) that High Renaissance architects were anti-theoretical in outlook, it is true that, in some of the later architectural treatises at least, the theoretical discussion often seems largely rhetorical and lacking in any direct relationship to design. The fact is that, like Vitruvius before them, Renaissance architects were anxious to unite theory with practice because the definition of their profession depended upon it. The development of a professional literature in the sixteenth century was largely the result of their coping with this problem.

Vitruvius' *Libri decem* was the only theoretical work on the fine arts to have survived from antiquity, and this accounts for the independent character of Renaissance architectural writing, which has no parallel in contemporary treatises on painting or sculpture. After *De re aedificatoria*, Vitruvius was the model and vehicle for discussions of architectural theory. Alberti's work was conceived as a modern answer to Vitruvius, but being written in Latin and having no illustrations, it could hardly have been of much use to the builder even after the first printed edition appeared in 1485. The sixteenth-century editions of Vitruvius, beginning with Fra Giocondo's Latin text in 1511, were still addressed to the same, but now more numerous, audience of humanist patrons and educated architects. The number and quality of these editions, both Latin and Italian, testify to the continuing fruitful bond among patrons, scholars, and architects. Daniele Barbaro's splendid edition (Venice, 1556) has an extensive scholarly commentary and illustrations by Palladio. By the end of the century, Vitruvius was accessible in other illustrated Italian editions and in French and German translations. In the commentaries upon Vitruvius' often obscure text, architects could keep abreast of current theories of proportion and composition, and they could study the Orders and reconstructions of some Classical buildings. But this did not make Vitruvius an architectural handbook, nor did the editors attempt to present the current state of architectural practice. Cesariano (edition of Vitruvius, Como, 1521) had used some contemporary buildings – notably the section of the cathedral of Milan and a schematic plan and elevation of Filarete's hospital – to illustrate Vitruvius' points and to assert a relationship between Milanese and Classical style; but he was chiefly interested in publishing his own, rather fanciful, reconstructions of ancient buildings.

The ambitious publications of the Bolognese architect Sebastiano Serlio (1475–1554) were the first to present architectural theory in the form of a professional manual. Serlio published his Book IV in Venice in 1537, the first to appear of seven projected books on architecture (he published five and a sixth appeared after his death). Serlio reduced the inheritance of humanist theory to a systematic presentation of perspective, the Classical Orders, and buildings of antiquity, with which he also included some modern buildings such as Bramante's Tempietto and the project for the dome of St. Peter's (Bk. III, Venice, 1540).

Serlio's theoretical commentary was perfunctory and revealed a certain divorce between a theoretical residue and the aims of a straightforward pattern book. In Book IV, for example, he presented each Vitruvian Order and then moved on to his own designs illustrating how it could be used. His Book V was a collection of his own designs for portals, from doorways to city gates, with no theoretical apparatus and no obvious relation to Vitruvian or Albertian theory. In other books, Serlio illustrated similiar series of variations on a theme such as the palace or private house, none of which is derived from Classical buildings. Serlio relied primarily upon his large woodcuts to demonstrate the principles of proportion and composition of Classical and modern buildings, and he included precise measurements and details. In his legible plans, elevations, and sections, architects could study classical reconstructions more easily than in any edition of Vitruvius, so that Barbaro's and Serlio's collections of designs amounted to a manual of the modern style.

The unprecedented success and enormous influence of Serlio's publications was due to the fact that they were, in large measure, a published version of the Renaissance architectural sketchbook where the architect kept his reference material: drawings after antique and contemporary buildings, and his own projects. As we have seen, the *Codex Escurialensis* is a fine fifteenth-century example, and a number of others survive from the sixteenth century. One can also find a precedent for Serlio's collection of building types in the fifteenth-century manuscripts of Francesco di Giorgio and, as Pedretti (*Leonardo*, p. 5) has observed, in Leonardo's medical illustrations. It would appear that many of Serlio's illustrations were based upon sketchbook drawings by his master Peruzzi.

Serlio's publications entirely superseded a modest little dialogue on the Classical Orders, *Las medidas del romano*, by the Spanish cleric Diego de Sagreda, published in Toledo in 1527 – a simple pattern book showing the Orders, ornamental columns and bases, a bit of entablature and a doorway, some of which appear to have been derived from contemporary Italian rather than Classical prototypes; and Serlio's works were the model for the architectural manuals of the later sixteenth century – the specialized treatises on the Orders, the collections of ideal building types, and the manuals of fortification design – all of which relied primarily upon their illustrations. In 1561, Philibert published his *Nouvelles inventions pour bien bastir*, which is an illustrated handbook on wooden construction. Vignola's famous *Regola delli cinque ordini d'architettura* appeared in 1562, and his *Due regole della prospettiva practica*, a manual of illustrations, was published in 1583, after his death, by the learned mathematician Ignazio Danti, who added a biography of Vignola and a theoretical commentary. Like Serlio's books, these works were meant for the widening market of practitioners who needed manuals of Classical and modern style for their own work. But Serlio was also the model and the license for such extraordinary publications as Wendel Dietterlin's *Architectura*, a collection of ideal projects published in 1593.

Two major theoretical treatises in the sixteenth century reintegrated theory with the professional approach to architecture found in the manuals. Philibert Delorme's *Premier tome de l'architecture* was a genuinely theoretical work, based upon Vitruvius but recast for contemporary needs and with a partly functionalist point of view. Following Serlio, Philibert published large and beautiful illustrations of the Orders, adding a theoretical commentary; but he also added a sixth "French Order" of his own invention. He justified his expansion of the Classical canon on theoretical grounds: the Orders had originally developed from local building traditions and available materials. Philibert reasoned that, like Corinth, which gave birth to the Corinthian Order, France should have her own national Order which would take into account the character of French building stone and employ decorated column drums rather than the single column shafts that were appropriate to marble. Philibert planned to devote another treatise to the problem of harmonic proportions – evidently to be a reconciliation of Classical theory and Christian number symbolism – but he never wrote it. The great reintegration of humanist theory with contemporary practice is the treatise published two years later: Andrea Palladio's *I quattro libri dell' architettura*, which appeared in Venice in 1570. Palladio demonstrated how theory and practice defined the architect's profession, in a manner so lucid and elegant that his book enjoyed a success that has never been equaled by any writer on architecture.

Like Philibert's, Palladio's theory is based upon Vitruvius, and he too followed Serlio's example and published his own work. But unlike Serlio, Palladio published his commissions. The *Quattro libri* included plans and elevations of twenty executed villas and seven more projects that Palladio did not expect would be built, and he named the place and patron of the executed works, so that, as he said, architects might visit them. As is well known, these buildings were not all built as he published them, and his plans are also ideal types in which the principles of Renaissance composition and theories of harmony are presented in measured plans and elevations. As an architectural theorist Palladio is a close relative of Alberti. But the practicing architect is as evident as the humanist scholar. Palladio presented in concise terms, and with splendid illustrations, the procedure for building – from choosing the site and materials to planning the heights of rooms and locating the staircase; and, to stress the Classical authority of this architecture, he followed his presentation of each building type with his reconstruction of its Classical model, based upon Vitruvius' text. Thus his illustration of an antique villa demonstrates the same principles as his own designs (figure 13.2).

The theoretician and the practitioner coexisted without friction in Palladio because he simply assumed the qualities in the architect that Philibert had insisted upon as separate, if reconcilable, aspects of the profession. Just as Palladio's architecture was a model of contemporary Classicism, so he himself was the model architect: well read in architectural theory, supremely knowledgeable about Roman antiquities, and personally responsible for sound and economical buildings for his clients. His ideas were not all new; many came from Alberti; but his self-portrait as an architect, and his illustrations incorporating the material of the manuals and his own practice in a Classical theoretical structure, defined the range of the architectural profession for years to come. One can follow Palladio's impact in editions, translations, and adaptations through the eighteenth century. The most immediate effect of the *Quattro libri*, however, was to focus the architect's view of his profession (as its delayed effect was to propagate a style). The fragment of Vincenzo Scamozzi's architectural treatise, published as *Idea dell' architettura universale* (Venice, 1615), is based upon Palladio's scheme and designs, although not upon his lovely style of writing. At the beginning, Scamozzi felt obliged to cite all the theoretical works of his predecessors that he could think of – Palladio, Philibert, Vignola, Alberti, and numerous others – before turning to his own exposition of Classical theory. The result is a somewhat undigested accumulation of two centuries of thinking about

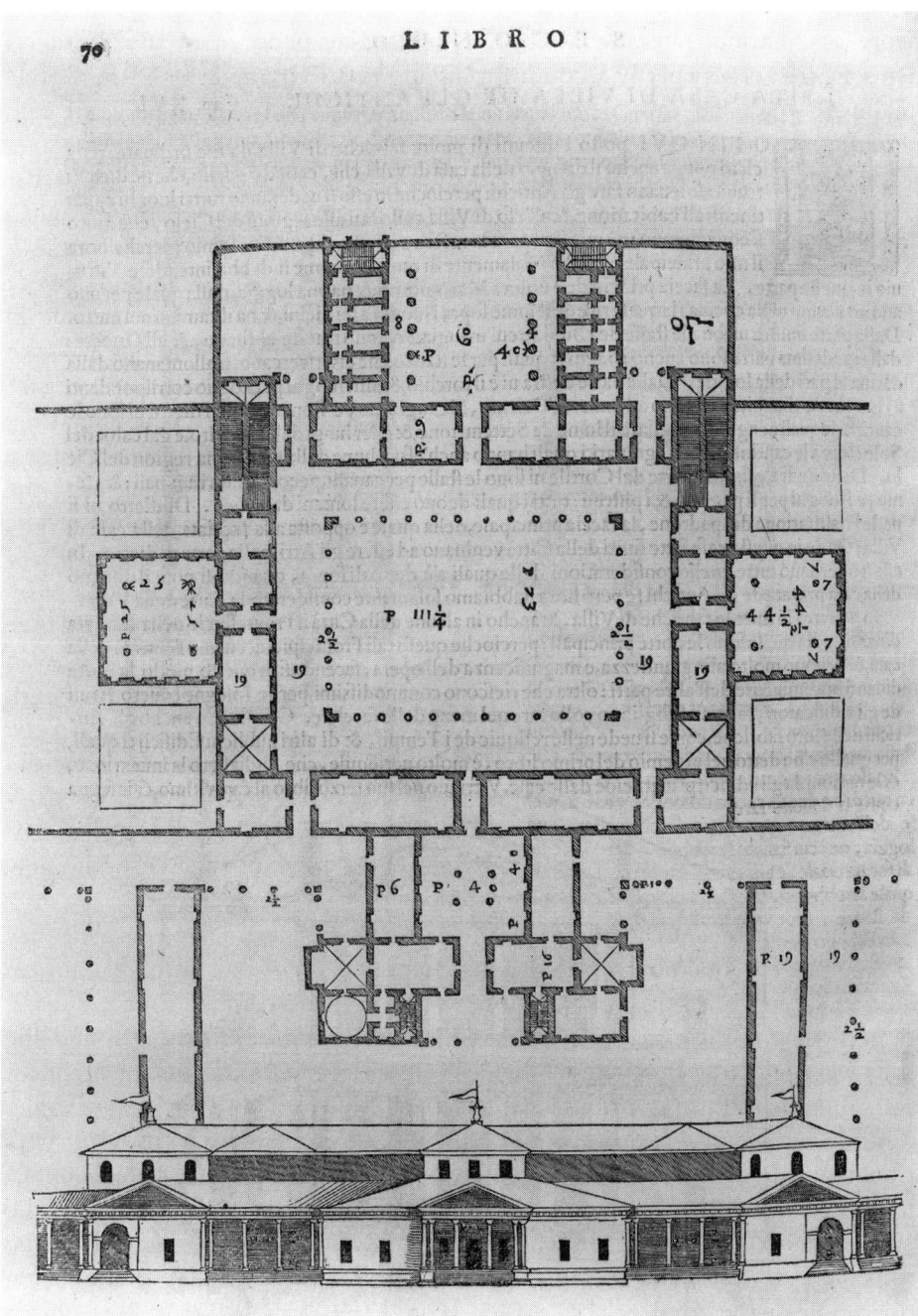

Figure 13.2 Palladio, reconstruction of a Classical villa, based upon Vitruvius, and a perfect statement of Palladio's own style, from his *Quattro libri*, 1570. The schematic plan and elevation are sufficient information for laying out a building and for determining the proportions of its major elements. Typ 525.70.671 (B) F, Department of Printing and Graphic Arts, Houghton Library, Harvard College Library. By permission of the Houghton Library, Harvard University.

architecture, but this was its innovative aspect. Scamozzi treated architectural theory as doctrine, but also as the accumulated experience of the architects themselves. This may partly account for his appreciative remarks on some Gothic buildings, which he viewed, not as models of style, but as architecture and therefore interesting.

The most modern aspect of the expanding architectural publication in the sixteenth century is the architectural print. The practice originated in the Roman print trade, which had developed from Raphael's innovative practice of publishing his own painted work in engravings by Marc Antonio Raimondi before 1520. It was anticipated in Serlio's woodcuts of some modern buildings and in the prints after Classical antiquities; but the publication of buildings was not really under way until the 1450s, when the Spaniard Antonio Salamanca organized the publishing of prints on a large scale in Rome. In 1546, he issued the engravings by Antonio Labacco (born 1495) after Antonio da Sangallo's famous model of St. Peter's – large plan, elevation, and section prints which were the first to be comparable to the earlier publication of Raphael's paintings. These were followed by other prints of modern buildings. An anonymous engraving of the hemicycle of St. Peter's appeared in 1564 and, in 1568–69, a famous series of engravings of the architecture of Michelangelo by the Frenchman Etienne Dupérac (1525–1604). Dupérac was both an architect and an expert on Roman topography, and his magnificent engravings of the elevation, section, and plan of Michelangelo's project for St. Peter's are of sufficient scale and accuracy to be essential for modern reconstructions of Michelangelo's ideas. But Dupérac did not work from elevations and sections by Michelangelo. He compiled his views from the wooden model and from detail drawings. His are essentially reconstructions and, in the case of St. Peter's, his engravings are apparently the only such views of the project that ever existed.

The Frenchman Lafreri published Dupérac's engravings of projects as if they were completed buildings. Like Labacco's prints, they were intended for an audience of specialists anxious to know what was being planned for St. Peter's; not surprisingly, the enterprise was largely in the hands of foreigners, and the prints were primarily for export. Single sheets soon developed into the architectural album – the most famous being Jacques Androuet du Cerceau's *Les plus excellents bastiments de France* (Paris, 1576–79), a vast series of plans and views of the major French châteaux. Adapting Dupérac's scheme to the publication of his own building, Juan de Herrera prepared an elaborate set of drawings of the Escorial which were issued in 1589 with a brief, separate text keyed to the prints. *Las estampas* and *El sumario* were, like Luigi Vanvitelli's monumental publication of the royal palace at Caserta in 1759, personal as well as official publications which aimed to place the buildings in the corpus of modern architecture. Dupérac's projects also suggested the notion of publishing an architect's complete oeuvre, first undertaken in the eighteenth century with the *Opus architectorum* of Francesco Borromini (Rome, 1735) and the *Architettura civile* of Guarino Guarini (Turin, 1737).

Such publications were designed for the specialist, whether amateur or professional. Patrons collected the treatises, manuals, and prints; but, by the end of the sixteenth century, most architects also had their own professional libraries. Juan de Herrera in Spain, for example, owned all the major works by sixteenth-century architects (except Palladio) as well as editions of Vitruvius and Alberti.

The change in architectural style which we saw taking place in the fifteenth century implied a new conception of architecture. Alberti's ideal of architectural harmony – the design to which nothing can be added and from which nothing can be taken away without spoiling it – required the architect to be responsible for every detail of his building; but, as a designer, he had no necessary role in the construction. The acceptance of Classical theory meant that architecture could not be learned on the job, it had to be studied. At the same time, the architect was free to design for any building material and to use any technical device that would make his building stand.

This view of architecture has characterized the profession until very recent times, when architects have begun to feel constrained by the image of the omnipotent designer; but, within the broad frame of post-medieval architecture, changes of style did imply some changes in practice. The radical alterations of a building during construction, which we have seen to be characteristic of the sixteenth century, would be inconceivable in a modern building. The modern building is a single form; the Renaissance building was conceived as a harmony of separate parts, each with its own identity. The long-term acceptance of this idea, and of the decorative vocabulary that was meant to express it, made it possible for a building to be designed in a series of stages. This was why Michelangelo could speak of returning to Bramante's forty-year-old plan for St. Peter's and could reshape the parts of the structure then standing – the remodeled fifteenth-century choir, Bramante's piers, and the hemicycle designed by Raphael and re-handled by Antonio da Sangallo the Younger – into his own conception. Michelangelo's modifications of the Palazzo Farnese must be understood in the same way; but his design of the Porta Pia (1561) already shows an eccentric relation among the individual elements, which denies them independence.

The complete submission of individual parts to the whole is, of course, a feature of Baroque architecture. Even as Classicizing a building as Bernini's Sant' Andrea al Quirinale (1658–70) depends upon the orchestration of elements, none of which makes sense without the others. In a façade by Francesco Borromini (1599–1667) the rhythm of the whole dominates to the extent that the Classical vocabulary is deformed or given up entirely.

A natural consequence of this new approach to architecture was an increased emphasis on the designing phase before construction. The number of studies required before a building was begun and the number and complexity of the drawings required to build it now increased. By the seventeenth century, this need was being met by the architectural office, where plans and working drawings were prepared by assistants. These men were not workmen, or even draftsmen, but junior architects, and they had to be capable of designing in the master's style. Borromini, who worked in this capacity for Bernini, deeply resented the subjugation of his own personality to another architect who would take the credit for his work and guide its style. One finds a similar situation in the French office of Jules Hardouin Mansart (1646–1708). The junior architects, who were responsible for detailed designing in an office, often later became independent architects. This did not mean, however, in the case of architects like Bernini or Mansart, that the master's building was not his own.

In 1665, Bernini (then sixty-seven years old) set off from Rome for Paris, where he was to prepare his final projects for the new Louvre of Louis XIV. Only two things need be noted here: first, that Bernini was not venturing – as Serlio had done more than a century ago – into unknown territory. French architects were there to meet him and, it soon appeared, to challenge his projects with their own. Second, although the personal style of Bernini differed quite profoundly from the French conceptions of Classicism, there is no doubt that Bernini's French colleagues shared his theoretical views on art. As Hibbard (*Bernini* [Baltimore, 1967], p. 174) has pointed out, Bernini's ideas were those of the sixteenth century: a belief in *disegno*, concern for order and proportion in architecture, a respect for antiquity; and these ideas exactly suited the taste of the young French Academy.

Bernini was not alone in stretching the Classical canons to include his own work. Throughout the seventeenth and eighteenth centuries, architects continued to study Vitruvius; to read the treatises of the sixteenth century; and, until the functionalist challenge of the eighteenth century, to conduct their discussions of architectural style in the terms framed by the architects of the Renaissance.

Bibliographical Notes

There is no general study of the architect's profession in the Renaissance. Perhaps because the greatest Renaissance architects are such familiar artistic personalities, scholars have not felt the need to investigate the profession in order to understand the buildings. The brilliant article by J. S. Ackerman, "Architectural Practice in the Italian Renaissance," *Journal of the Society of Architectural Historians* 13 (1954), 3–11, reprinted in *Renaissance Art*, ed. C. Gilbert (New York, 1970), was the first to demonstrate the importance of the subject; but his treatment is limited to the High Renaissance, primarily to the career of Antonio da Sangallo the Younger in Rome. The following works will serve as a guide to further study.

The best place to read about central Italian architects and their careers is Giorgio Vasari's *Vite de' più eccellenti pittori, scultori, ed architettori*, 2nd ed. (Florence, 1568), available in a number of modern editions and translations, the best of which is still G. Milanesi's of 1878. The most useful guide to the vast literature on Renaissance architecture is L. Heydenreich and W. Lotz, *Architecture in Italy 1500–1600* (Baltimore, 1973), which also contains the clearest and most recent discussion of the projects for

St. Peter's from Bramante to Sangallo. See also the comprehensive bibliography compiled by J. S. Ackerman and J. A. Pinto, *A Bibliography of Renaissance and Baroque Architecture* (Cambridge, Mass., 1974).

The career of the greatest of the artist-architects of the Renaissance, Michelangelo, can be studied in excellent modern scholarship. J. S. Ackerman's *The Architecture of Michelangelo*, 2 vols. (London, 1961), revised edition in one vol. (Baltimore, 1971), contains a wealth of information on architectural practice as well as a classic analysis of Michelangelo's architecture. The following are also well worth reading for what they reveal about Michelangelo's methods of design and the organization of the works at St. Peter's: H. A. Millon and C. H. Smyth, "Michelangelo and St. Peter's – I: Notes on a Plan of the Attic as Originally Built on the South Hemi-Cycle," *Burlington Magazine* 111 (1969), 484–501 (a new interpretation of Michelangelo's design for the attic); and H. Saalman, "Michelangelo: S. Maria del Fiore and St. Peter's," *Art Bulletin* 57 (1975), 374–409 (a study of the dome).

C. L. Frommel, *Der römische Palastbau der Hochrenaissance*, 3 vols. (Tübingen, 1973), is an invaluable source for architectural practice and patronage in Rome. H. Hibbard, *Carlo Maderno and Roman Architecture 1580–1630* (London, 1971), covers the later period. D. Howard, *Jacopo Sansovino: Architecture and Patronage in Renaissance Venice* (New Haven and London, 1975), is a carefully documented study of the Venetian situation. See also J. S. Ackerman, *Palladio* (Baltimore, 1966). C. Pedretti, *Leonardo da Vinci: The Royal Palace at Romorantin* (Cambridge, Mass., 1972), is a convenient study of Leonardo as an architect. I have not discussed Leonardo in this chapter because his career is atypical in so many ways; but, as Pedretti's monograph shows, it was full of implications for the future of architectural practice. Useful material on the many-sided career of Galeazzo Alessi may be found in the Acts of the International Congress in Genoa: *Galeazzo Alessi, e l'architettura del cinquecento* (Genoa, 1974), with an introduction by W. Lotz, pp. 9–12.

Any consideration of the theory of Renaissance architects must begin with R. Wittkower's classic study, *Architectural Principles in the Age of Humanism* (New York, 1965). J. von Schlosser's *La letteratura artistica*, revised edition by O. Kurz (Florence, 1964), is indispensable as a summary of the tradition of architectural writing; and it includes a comprehensive bibliography of architectural treatises. See also R. Krautheimer, "Alberti and Vitruvius," *Acts of the XXth International Congress of the History of Art* (Princeton, N. J., 1963), reprinted in the author's collected essays: *Studies in Early Christian, Medieval, and Renaissance Art* (New York, 1969), pp. 323–32.

No published Renaissance architectural treatise exists in an annotated modern edition, but later reprints and translations, if not the original editions, can be found in larger libraries. Philibert Delorme's *Premier tome de l'architecture* (Paris, 1567) was reprinted together with his *Nouvelles inventions de bien bastir* (Paris, 1561 and 1568) in Paris, 1892. See also A. Blunt, *Philibert Delorme* (London, 1958).

Andrea Palladio's *I quattro libri dell' architettura* (Venice, 1570) exists in numerous later editions and translations, the most accessible being the reprint of Isaac Ware's translation, *The Four Books of Architecture* (London, 1738), with an introduction by A. Placzek (New York, 1965).

Vignola's *Regola delli cinque ordini d'architettura* (Rome, 1562) exists in numerous later editions. His *Due regole della prospettiva practica*, edited by Ignazio Danti (Rome, 1583), was somewhat less popular.

Vincenzo Scamozzi's *Idea dell' architettura universale* (Venice, 1615) should be supplemented by his *Taccuino di viaggio da Parigi a Venezia*, edited by F. Barbieri (Venice and Rome, 1959).

On prints, see: C. Huelsen, "Das 'Speculum romanae magnificentiae' des Antonio Lafreri," in *Festschrift für Leo S. Olschki* (Munich, 1921); but there is no general survey of architectural prints, and they have not been studied in relation to architectural practice. On architectural drawings, W. Lotz's "Das Raumbild in der italienischen Architekturzeichnung der Renaissance," *Mitteilungen des Kunsthistorischen Instituts in Florenz* 7 (1956), 193–226, is fundamental.

For the seventeenth century, see also R. Wittkower's *Gothic Versus Classic: Architectural Projects in Seventeenth-Century Italy* (London, 1974), which contains much valuable information about practice.

I would like to thank James S. Ackerman and Henry Zerner for their helpful criticism.

14

On Some Engravings by Giorgio Ghisi Commonly Called "Reproductive"

Michael Bury

The purpose of this article is to extend our understanding of the reproductive printmaking of the sixteenth century. Following Wickhoff's article in the 1899 *Wiener Jahrbuch*,[1] with its characterization of Marcantonio's involvement with Peruzzi and Raphael, the major part of the engraving of this period came to be judged as mechanical rather than creative. Oberhuber has pointed out that the end of the nineteenth century, which was a time when mechanical methods of reproduction flourished, was also the moment of the rediscovery of original printmaking – the revival of etching and of the woodcut.[2] Looked at from the perspective of the original printmaker of the late nineteenth or early twentieth century, there were two reasons why most sixteenth-century engravings appeared to be rather inferior products. It could be seen how dependent the engravers had often been on the ideas of others, and that they had not invented their own compositions. It was also evident that the inventions depended on had often been developed in other media. In his still fundamental *History of Engraving and Etching*, A. M. Hind made evident his belief that a crucial element of any fine work of art was respect for the intrinsic qualities of its medium.[3] Such a sensibility was offended by the print that attempted to reproduce or translate an image created by another artist for a different medium. But if we no longer share these aesthetic attitudes, the term "reproductive" survives to characterize the major part of sixteenth-century engraving.

What value should be given to the term? As Evelina Borea has argued, it is unsuitable as a way of describing a print that records a painting: she proposed that the word "translation" should be used instead, while "reproduction" should be reserved for prints that replicate drawings or other prints.[4] This distinguishes two types of print, whose appearance was chronologically distinct: the print of translation came later than the print of reproduction. It also draws attention to the fact that the printmaker with a painting as his model faced a much more

275

demanding task in finding equivalents in his medium for what the painter had done in his, than a printmaker working from a graphic model. But to accept these distinctions is to accept that the central issue is the relationship of the print to its source. The fact that a printmaker utilized the work of another artist does not of itself mean that he was concerned either to reproduce or to translate that original. What I want to argue here is that in any particular case a primary task of the historian of prints should be to establish what the intentions of the printmaker were, and what functions the prints had.

In order to try to get to grips with this issue it seemed worth attempting to analyse certain engravings for which proof states have survived. Such impressions, taken by the engraver from the unfinished plate in order to check the progress of his work and better to judge what needed to be done, can provide important information about his choices and priorities. They have not come down to us in large numbers from the sixteenth century, and for many of the great engravers only one or two examples may exist. An exception is Giorgio Ghisi (ca. 1520–82): there are proof states of approximately a quarter of his plates, and therefore it is proposed to concentrate on some of those. Diane DeGrazia has speculated on the reason for the relative frequency of Ghisi's proofs, suggesting that the peculiar complexity of his images might have made regular checks on their progress essential for him.[5] David Landau tentatively proposed that Ghisi kept them with care and even gave them or sold them to collectors.[6] But it may simply be an accident of survival. Whatever the truth of the matter, the fact that it is possible to compare his working procedures on many different plates gives a reasonably firm foundation to the conclusions drawn from them.

There are two engravings by Ghisi that are particularly interesting to analyse in relation to the compositions from which they derive. These are the *Nativity* of 1553 and the *School of Athens* of 1550, which are both large, two-plate engravings.[7] The first is closely related to an oil painting by Agnolo Bronzino, and the second to Raphael's fresco in the Vatican. They were published in Antwerp and are among the most spectacular items issued by the engraver and entrepreneur Hieronymus Cock, soon after the establishment of his shop "*Aux Quatre Vents*".[8] Ghisi himself travelled north around this time, presumably to work for Cock; he is documented as resident in Antwerp in 1551. Cock published altogether five of his works between 1550 and 1555.

The *Nativity*, after Bronzino (fig. 14.1), was apparently engraved in 1553 and published in 1554. The oil painting to which it relates had, according to Vasari, been commissioned by Filippo di Averardo Salviati (1515–72), probably in the later 1530s, and remained in his private possession in Florence. It is now in Budapest. From Vasari's – and, later, Borghini's – comments it can be seen that it enjoyed some fame, but this was probably the result of Ghisi's engraving.[9] The proof state of the bottom half of the print, now in the British Museum, shows that in the first instance the figures taken directly from the Bronzino were set out and brought virtually to completion. But at this stage the landscape background was

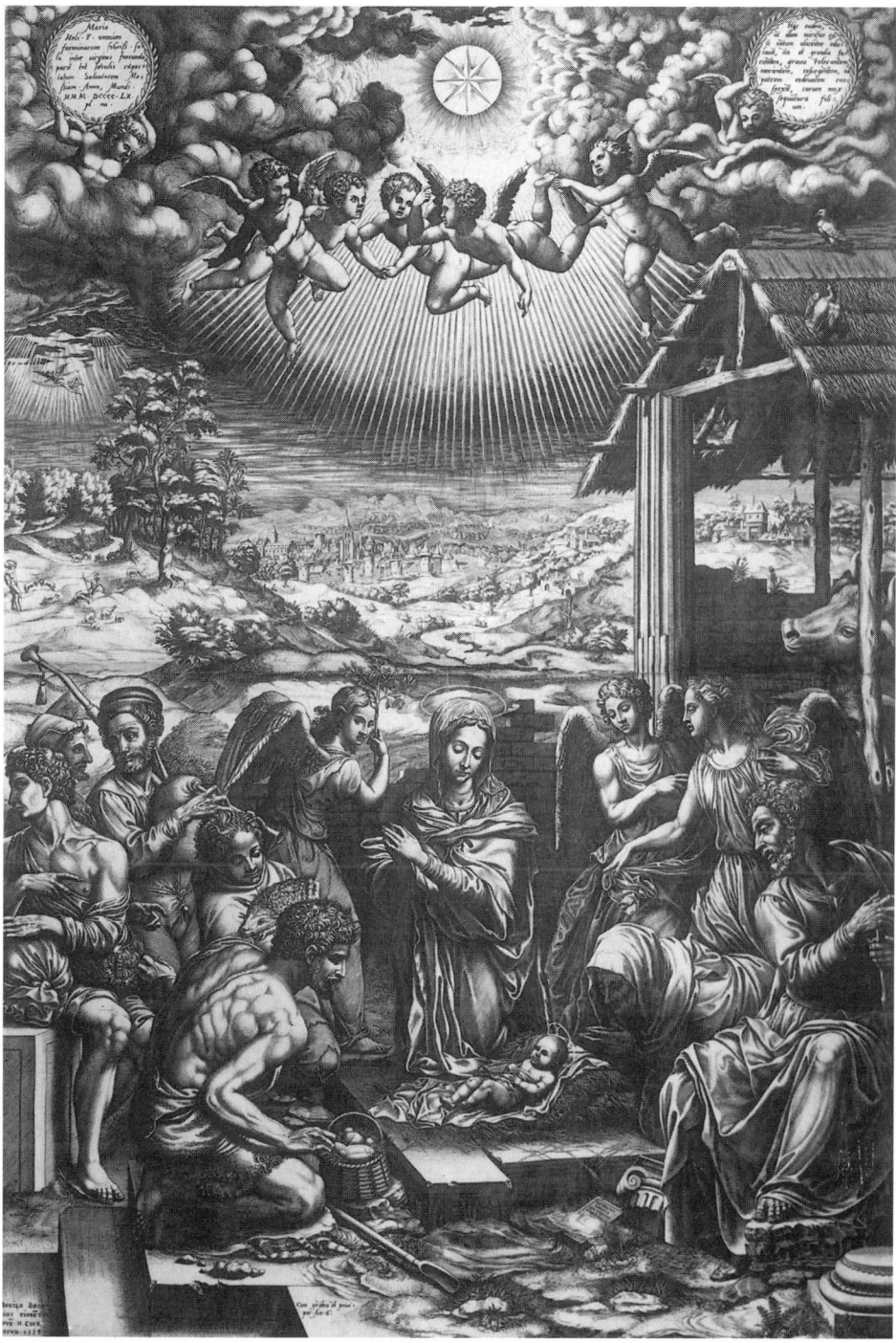

Figure 14.1 Giorgio Ghisi after Bronzino, *The Nativity*, 1553–54, engraving, 662 × 454 mm. Albertina, Wien.

not even indicated. The method of constructing the figures first may have been regularly used by engravers working from drawings. Caraglio, for example, appears to have worked up the figures in his *Challenge of the Pierides*, a proof impression of which is at Chatsworth, before planning the landscape.[10] In this case the designer, Rosso Fiorentino, perhaps provided him with no more than a composition of figures. Caraglio's reason for taking a proof impression was to plan a landscape appropriate to them, in the light of their appearance once engraved.

For Ghisi to complete the figures first, in an engraving after a painting, is intriguing. Apart from the fact that they are reversed and that haloes have been added to the Virgin and the Christ Child, the figures are meticulous records of Bronzino's.[11] The proof state draws attention, however, to the fact that Ghisi has enclosed the figure group more than Bronzino, heightening the wall behind the Virgin so as to provide a dark plane against which the principal actors could be given the strongest three-dimensional modelling. This may be connected with the decision to invent a completely new landscape of great mountains, trees, cities and houses, much more elaborately detailed than the one Bronzino had created. The landscape has a very Northern feeling to it, and relates well to the inventions of other artists working in Antwerp at the time. Peter Bruegel's finished drawing of a landscape with a walled town in the British Museum, dated 1553, can usefully be compared in terms of the intricate construction of the various elements.[12] The reason for the substitution might have been the need to appeal to local taste, if it was expected that the principal market would be found in the North. But equally Ghisi may have felt that the greater complexity of forms and contrasted tones were necessary for the visual success of a great engraving, for without the variety of textures and colours attainable using oil paint, the comparatively sparse landscape of Bronzino's painting would have looked bleak. These are not mutually exclusive motives, and both may have played a part. Whatever the reason, Ghisi achieved a compelling grandeur enhanced by remarkable light effects: the night scene brilliantly illuminated in the fore- and middle-ground, the city touched by light and the distant mountains darkly closing the prospect.

The radiant sky of Bronzino's composition was also transformed: Ghisi elaborated the heavenly vision of singing angels before an effulgence of divine light. He made the light less naturalistic, more evidently divine, a change that fits in with the decision to give haloes to the Virgin and Child. He also added extra angels, who carry inscriptions written in Latin celebrating Mary, the Mother of the Saviour. These are not titles, but devotional prompts to help the viewer meditate on the significance of the scene.[13] By this means the image was expanded and developed to become self-sufficient. The only indication of its dependency on another composition are the words *ANGILO BRON/SINI FIORE[N]TINO/INVE[N]* accompanying Cock's address as publisher. What was being communicated by that? There was no law that required it, and the decision to indicate Bronzino's responsibility for the invention must have been either Ghisi's or Cock's. There were presumably commercial motives for doing

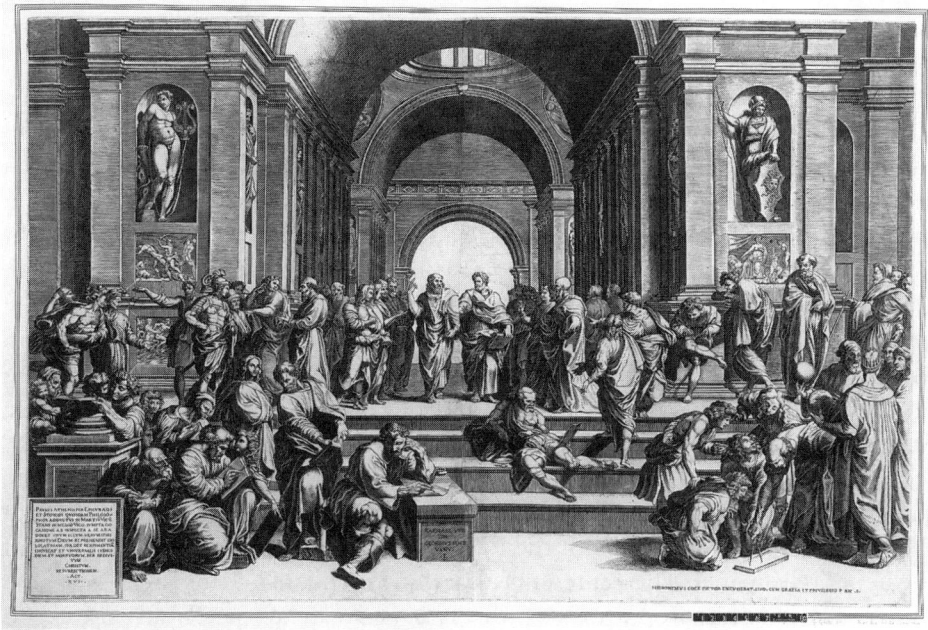

Figure 14.2   Giorgio Ghisi after Raphael, *The School of Athens*, 1550, engraving, 526 × 824 mm. © The Trustees of the British Museum.

so, for at least some of the potential buyers of the engraving might have been interested in the fact that this Florentine artist had been responsible. But responsible for what? The eventual purchaser, with no independent knowledge of the composition, would not have had the means of knowing what was Bronzino's and what was Ghisi's. What would the idea of "invention" have conveyed, what would it have been intended to convey?

The attempt to answer these questions must await a discussion of the second of the two engravings mentioned above: the *School of Athens*, after Raphael, published in 1550 (fig. 14.2). This was the first of Ghisi's works to be published by Cock. It is evidently derived from the fresco in the Stanza della Segnatura, but, as in the case of the *Nativity*, the relationship between the engraving and the fresco is not a straightforward one. The composition has been squared off in order to adjust the shape to the rectangularity of plate and paper. The decision to extend the image to fit the new format was a procedure frequently adopted at this time in engraved copies of frescoes. It was done in the *Incendio nel Borgo*, published by Salamanca in Rome in 1545, which has an inscription explicitly asserting that it was after Raphael's composition in the Vatican:[14] in a manner similar to Ghisi, the designer extended the buildings at the sides.[15] Another difference between the fresco of the *School of Athens* and the engraving is that the foreground figures in the latter have been set back from the forward edge. Raphael's *Incendio nel Borgo* underwent a similar alteration in the Salamanca

279

engraving, as did the *Galatea* at the hands of Marcantonio.[16] The architectural frames of the original frescoes acted as space-creating elements, and it may have been felt necessary to compensate for their absence.

But the most interesting differences are the changes to the relative sizes of the elements. For example the space given to the architecture is contracted; this can easily be seen from the way the niches with their statues of the Gods have been reduced in size. The proportion of the total height occupied by the disputing philosophers is thereby increased. In seeking an explanation for this, one might ask how accurate the drawing was from which the engraver must have worked. Could the drawing have been distorted by the actual visual experience of the fresco, the foreground figures being recorded by the draughtsman as larger than the background architecture because they were closer to him as he stood drawing on the floor of the room?[17] That seems unlikely, because of what appear to have been deliberate adjustments to the positions of the figures relative to the architecture behind them, especially on the left. In the engraving, the top of the turbaned head of the so-called Averroes is just below the base mouldings of the wall face, while the heads of the figures above him just reach the bottom of the upper relief panel. This represents a carefully graduated change relative to the fresco. The relative proportions of the two fictive relief panels are altered to accommodate it: the upper one in the engraving is rectangular rather than square, while the lower one is square rather than rectangular.

It is an open question as to who was responsible for the intermediary drawing from which the engraver worked. It could be argued that it was Hieronymus Cock, who described himself as *PICTOR* in the inscription, but it has also been suggested that it was Ghisi himself, who is recorded as having been in Rome during the pontificate of Paul III (1534–49).[18] It is evident that the drawing would have had to have recorded not only the forms, but also the distribution of light and shade, and who could better have done this than the engraver himself? He could at the same time have made a drawing of the *Disputa*, the subject of another engraving he made for Cock and which was published in 1552.[19]

However, there is one feature that argues against the idea that Ghisi made the drawing himself. It is evident that there was a desire to avoid an overlap of the heads of the figures with potentially confusing elements in the background. The positioning of several of the figures has been altered in order to ensure that they overlap flat planes of the architectural membering. But this has created a strange internal discrepancy. The upper figures on the left of the engraving are rather smaller, relative to the foreground figures, than they are in the fresco. Their heads are level with the bottom of the upper fictive relief panel, whereas in the fresco they overlap it. On the right side, below the statue of Minerva, the upper figures are considerably larger than their equivalents on the left: the principal standing figure there has been moved to the right to avoid overlap with the relief panel. It can, in fact, be seen that all the figures on the right side, relative to the architecture, are much closer to what is seen in the fresco than is the case in the left half of the engraving. It seems likely that if Ghisi had made the drawing he would have known how to deal with this discrepancy, and recreated a balanced composition for the purposes of his engraving. If, on the other hand, he had received a drawing from another, without having any knowledge of how to interpret and thus correct it, the observed oddities could be explained. However, it is impossible to be certain on this point; it is simply a question of balancing the probabilities. Whoever made it, one may deduce that the drawing was a very detailed one, but one that was conceived as an accurate and legible record of the elements, rather than of the precise structure of the fresco.

If some of the differences between fresco and engraving may have to be attributed to an anonymous draughtsman responsible for the intermediate drawing, then in any specific instance it becomes difficult to decide to whom the change should be attributed. However, the proof states that have survived reveal certain attitudes that can confidently be ascribed to the engraver himself, and which therefore allow one to make hypotheses (fig. 14.3). They show how the engraver started by building the principal groups of figures together in order to create a great architecture of forms continuing that of the spatial system of the vaulted hall above them. The central figures of Plato and Aristotle, and peripheral ones, such as the so-called Zeno and Epicurus and those immediately around them on the far left, were merely outlined.[20] Comparison with the finished state reveals that the connections between the groups on the two main levels are not yet fully established. For example, the dress of the standing man leaning on the architecture, supporting his head with his hand, is largely unmodelled; its completion will define the spatial relationship with the so-called Parmenides (or Xenocrates), who stands while resting on his knee a book at which he points in demonstrative argument. This is a key part of the composition, for on these and the neighbouring figures depends the connection of foreground and background.

This kind of procedure was not a standard one with Ghisi, as is shown by the so-called *Dream of Raphael*, where he worked systematically across the plate.[21] The proof state of the *Dream*, now in the British Museum, has the upper-left corner virtually blank, apart from the contours of the standing figure and the animals, while the rest is modelled in great detail. He evidently intended first to work over the whole, realizing all the elements in a middle range of tones. Once that was achieved he would then have gone back over the plate, intensifying the shadows and building up the richness of *chiaroscuro* that characterizes the finished engraving. Presumably this systematic method required a very detailed preparatory drawing. If Ghisi had made such a drawing in that case, why did he not do the same for the *School of Athens*? What may be inferred is that a primarily figural scene, with strong three-dimensional spatial qualities, needed an ordered procedure that would ensure that the tonal relationships had the required emphases. To have them worked out in a drawing would not have been sufficient; they had to be re-established in the special medium of the engraving.[22] In sum, the problems were quite different from those of the *Dream of Raphael*, which has an all-over quality because its figures are firmly incorporated into the dense *chiaroscuro* of the landscape.[23]

281

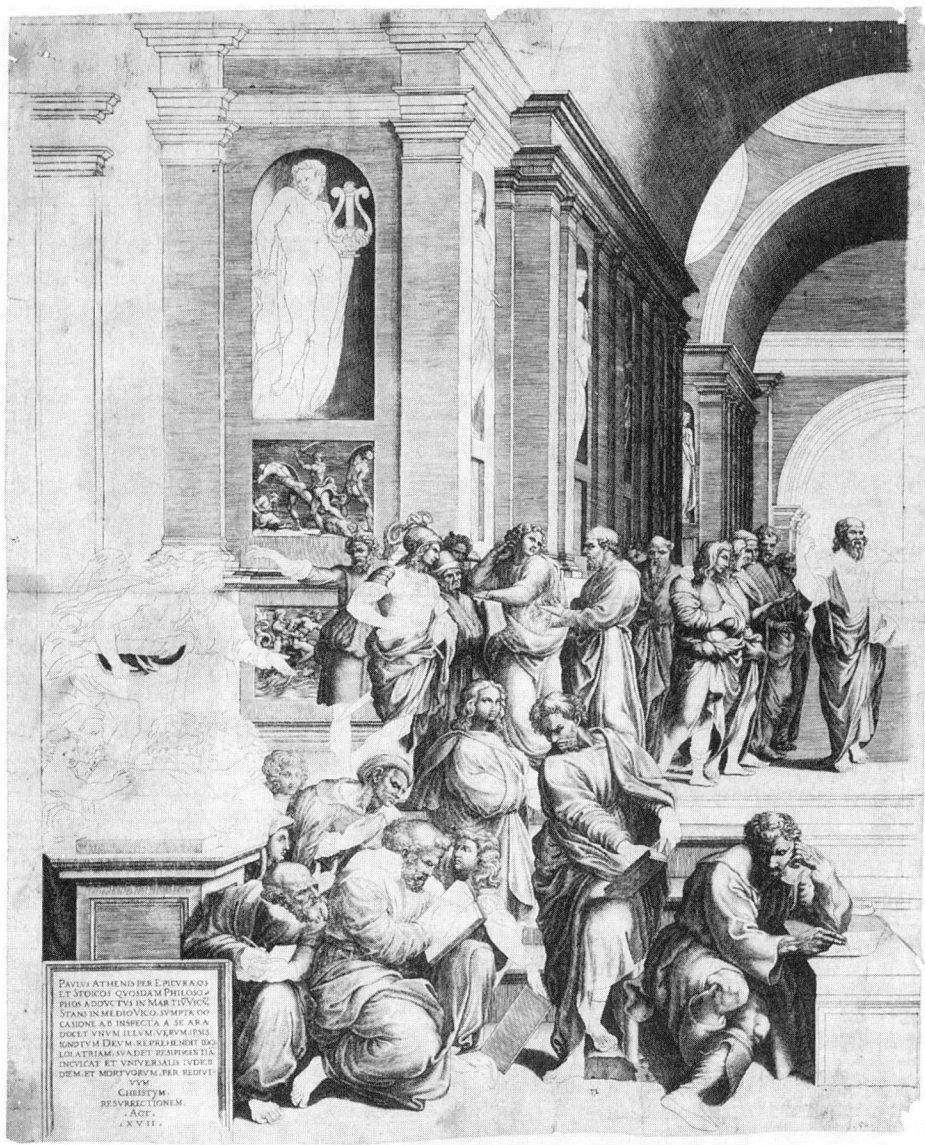

Figure 14.3   Giorgio Ghisi after Raphael, *The School of Athens*, proof state of left half, engraving, 263 × 412 mm. © The Trustees of the British Museum.

The method used by Ghisi in the *School of Athens* is very similar to the one used by Marco Dente in his *Massacre of the Innocents*, after Bandinelli.[24] The proof state of the *Massacre* in the British Museum shows how Marco established the principal groups around the central space, weaving them together into a complex chain of forms. The foreground group of mothers, desperately mourning their dead children, was considered separately, for in the proof their connection with the other figures is not yet established. Marco evidently also left to the last stage of work on the plate the peripheral figures with their crucial framing function. It is interesting that there is no trace in the proof of the architectural closure of the sides, which is an important feature of the finished engraving. It seems likely that Marco added the enclosing walls to achieve a better *chiaroscuro* effect, and this may have been his own idea. One recalls Vasari's comment that Marcantonio improved upon Bandinelli's composition of the *Martyrdom of St Lawrence*.[25]

In the *School of Athens*, Ghisi's evident desire to create an architecture of figures, organized and modelled so as to achieve a powerful spatial effect, probably means that he was responsible for their greatly increased bulk. The proof states direct attention to the way the gaps between figures are closed up so as to produce a continuous chain of forms modelled by their contiguity. Notice, for example, the alterations to the intervals between "Pythagoras", "Averroes" and the standing figure of the young man immediately behind them. As in the case of the *Nativity* after Bronzino, Ghisi's changes to Raphael's composition may have been partly motivated by his desire to create effects suitable for a fine engraving. He probably required a certain density of light and shade across the sheet, wanting to avoid large areas of empty white paper. But the changes in proportion, both in the vertical and the horizontal axes, were also part of a general desire to give greater prominence to the figures: they formed the principal interest. Comparison with Ghisi's engraving of the *Disputa*, also published by Cock, reveals a similar process:[26] the tiers of figures were brought much closer together so as to eliminate the strip of space between the heads of the earthly figures and the bank of clouds above them. The bulkiness of the figures was also substantially increased so as to compress them together.[27]

These observations may mean no more than that the standards of accuracy expected of reproductive engraving in the sixteenth century were not what they later became. But what I want to argue is that there is nothing to suggest that anyone was expected to read this engraving as a record of Raphael's fresco. As with the *Nativity*, only the indication of Raphael's responsibility for the "invention" recalled that there was a connection with another work. Unlike the *Nativity*, where the changes did not affect the subject-matter, a prominent inscription on the *School of Athens* even transformed the subject, identifying it as Paul preaching on the Areopagus from chapter 17 of the Acts of the Apostles. Jeremy Wood has discussed this point in a stimulating article in the *Journal of the Warburg and Courtauld Institutes*.[28] When Ghisi attached a specific text from the Acts of the Apostles to the engraving, he may or may not have known exactly what the meaning of the original was. There was evidently some confusion about the subject of the fresco, even among well-informed commentators. Vasari, in the 1550 edition of his Life of Raphael, wrote of the Evangelists being present among the philosophers, and stated that the subject was theologians bringing philosophy and astrology into harmony with theology.[29]

It is interesting that all Ghisi's engravings published by Cock have inscriptions referring to their subject-matter. This was not the case with his earlier Italian engravings, where, if there was any lettering apart from the engraver's own monogram, it was to credit the inventor. Other engravings published by Cock also have such inscriptions. For example the *St Paul Baptizing in Ephesus* of 1553, attributed to Coornhert, has a caption identifying Paul's action of baptizing the Ephesians in the name of Christ, from the opening of chapter 19 of the Acts of the Apostles.[30] As Riggs noted, the *School of Athens* is not the only case where such an inscription altered the original subject-matter. The engraving Cock published in 1553 after Andrea del Sarto's *Baptism of the People* from the Scalzo in Florence, was called the "Baptism of Christ".[31] Similarly, the engraved *Disputa* became an "Adoration of the Trinity".[32] The decision about exactly which subject to choose was presumably determined by what the publisher expected his potential audience to be interested in, as well as by what the composition could credibly be read to mean.

In both Italy and the Netherlands during the 1540s, it had become more and more common for single-sheet engravings to appear with indications of the subject-matter. This is evident in Rome among the works published by Antonio Salamanca.[33] In the Netherlands there are many examples: a spectacular one is the *Israelites Carrying the Ark of the Covenant*, published in 1547 and regarded by many as Cornelis Bos's masterpiece.[34] For the most part, these subject prints carried no reference to the "inventor". Other engravings acknowledged the "inventor" without alluding to the subject. The demand in Italy for records of the visual inventions of famous artists was well established by the 1530s: there are many examples among the prints of Antonio Salamanca.[35] Marcantonio's engraving of a figure from the cartoon of the *Battle of Cascina*, with its acknowledgement of Michelangelo as inventor, may have been one of the first symptoms of this, for it was probably made around 1509.[36] In the Netherlands prints of this kind were relatively late in coming. Cornelis Bos's engraving of *Prudence and Justice* of 1537 inscribes Heemskerck's name as "inventor", together with Bos's own monogram; it may be no coincidence that Heemskerck had just returned from Italy when this print was made.[37] With only isolated exceptions, prints from both areas either acknowledged the invention or the subject. What distinguishes Cock's practice is that the name of the "inventor" is invariably accompanied by an indication of the subject-matter; he will have planned this as an effective commercial strategy for his northern clientèle.[38]

If a literary subject-matter was important but to some degree mobile, what was meant by the "invention"? It might be regarded as fraudulent – an indicator of commercial opportunism, not to be taken very seriously. The case of the *Dream of Raphael*, which carries Raphael's name although only one of the figures actually derives from him, apparently indicates that Ghisi was prepared to be unscrupulous in his claims.[39] But even in that case there may have been an honest motive, for Raphael's figure has the central rôle. In the *School of Athens* the subject was transformed into a biblical one, and it is evident that the "invention" with which Raphael was credited must be visual and not literary. The visual "invention", which is preserved in the print, is the figural "invention". Although it is visual, it is not abstract, and must not be confused with the formal properties of the scene. It is relevant here to consider Agostino Veneziano's engraving of the "Pythagoras" group with the fresco of the *School of Athens*. This is identified by the Greek text in an open book as St Luke writing the gospel, and it has an inscription describing Raphael as "inventor".[40] Agostino slightly altered the positions of the figures (note the profile head of the man on the extreme left, for example) in order to create a closed group that could stand on its own. He also created a new background. The transformation of the group may thus be seen both on the formal level – where there were changes to the configuration – and on the subject level. The individual characters with their individual actions and the major components of their psychological interaction are unchanged: they are just redeployed. This is very similar to what happened in the case of Cock's *Baptism* after Sarto, where certain changes were made to the distribution of the figures as well as to the subject-matter.[41]

The visual invention of types and characters, individualized through expression, gesture and movement, and, where there are several figures, manifesting certain psychological relationships one with another, lies at the heart of certain ideas about painting found in sixteenth-century theory. Dolce, for example, in his Dialogue called the *Aretino*, distinguished two aspects of "invention", the subject-matter, which provided the artist with his raw material, and, second, the intellect he brought to bear upon it. What the artist's intellect (*ingegno*) contributed was the way the subject was to be disposed, the finding of appropriate types for its representation, and also "the poses, the variety and (so to speak) the dynamism of the figures . . .".[42] Dolce understood that such figures and their relationships would be created in response to the demands of a particular subject. But the possibility of separating the visual form from the particular subject that had initially motivated it was certainly acknowledged, even if in a disapproving manner. For example, in 1584 Lomazzo used the word *invenzione* to refer to the creation of types and characters who would reveal through their movements the inner dispositions and responses of their souls. He warned against the practice of borrowing such inventions from one composition for use in another.[43]

The prints that were issued to record inventions, from single figures, such as Marcantonio's engraving of Michelangelo's figure from the *Battle of Cascina*, to more complex groups, like Agostino Veneziano's *St Luke* or Ghisi's *School of Athens*, indicate the way that powerfully conceived expressive movements and complex psychological relationships could attract admiration and attention and stimulate new subjects. It is interesting to note that there are analogies with the way pieces of Antique sculpture were studied and used at the time: movements, gestures and expressions were utilized for contemporary purposes, often without knowledge of the original subject. It is probably important that many of the prints of the first half of the sixteenth century present Antique figures and compositions. To this kind of invention we must add allegorical inventions, such as Heemskerck's personifications of Prudence and Justice, where the meaning of the figures themselves was extended by the use of a complex symbolism of attributes.[44] If the printmaker respected these aspects of his model, he could legitimately claim that the invention of the original artist was being preserved, while ignoring the precise nature of the original execution.

To summarize the argument briefly: there is nothing to indicate that purchasers of either the *Nativity* or the *School of Athens* were expected to recognize them as records of particular painted compositions. It may even be doubted whether it is appropriate to continue to call the latter by the name of Raphael's fresco. Ghisi worked from drawings, not from the original paintings, and, in the case of the *School of Athens*, the drawing may not have been his own. He will not have seen his task as that of translating a painting into a graphic language. Some few people, like Vasari, might recognize that the engravings were related to paintings by Bronzino and Raphael, but this was because they knew the paintings independently. The prints were published for an audience who, for the most part, would not have had that knowledge. What they were intended to be was, on the one hand, self-contained subject-prints, which reworked the original images to achieve visual effectiveness in the new medium, and, on the other, by naming the "inventor" they called attention to the emotionally expressive or allegorically significant figures. It might interest artists using a print as an inspiration for their own work to know whose mind lay behind the invention. Amateurs and connoisseurs might value a print primarily because it gave them knowledge of a particular artist's *ingegno*.

To call Ghisi's works for Cock "reproductive" engravings is misleading. The term carries with it the wrong connotations, for it implies a straightforward relationship between the engraving and a specific original. For us today the word resonates with memories of the techniques and functions of photographic "reproduction". As has been seen, prints that were intended to record particular images did exist: The Salamanca print of Raphael's *Fire in the Borgo* of 1545 is an example. These could properly be called prints of "reproduction", or, to use Evelina Borea's term, of "translation". The reason why the distinction between the Salamanca and, say, Ghisi's *School of Athens* has not always been fully understood is, I believe, because in the late nineteenth and twentieth centuries there developed a confusion between the use of the epithet "reproductive" as an aesthetic category – a way of commenting on the status of an engraving whose visual form relied on the invention of another artist – and its use as a description of an historical function. It is essential to use all the available evidence to explore what the intentions of the engravers and publishers of prints actually were. Historians of prints can then begin properly to delineate the early history of "reproduction" alongside the other functions of printmaking, and so escape from imposing on the sixteenth century largely anachronistic aesthetic prejudices.

Notes

An earlier version of this article was presented at the conference of the Association of Art Historians held at Leeds in April 1992. I would like to thank Martin Hopkinson, the session organizer, for having invited me to contribute a paper on this subject. I would also like to thank my colleague Roger Tarr for his careful scrutiny of a draft, and for his many valuable corrections and comments. I am grateful to Antony Griffiths for his help.

1   F. Wickhoff, "Beiträge zur Geschichte der reproducirenden Künste: Marcantons Eintritt in den Kreis römischer Kunstler", *Jahrbuch der kunsthistorischen Sammlungen der allerhöchsten Kaiserhauses*, xx, 1899, pp. 181–94.

2   *Bologna e l'Umanesimo, 1490–1510*, exhibition catalogue by M. Faietti and K. Oberhuber, Bologna, 1988, p. 51.

3   A. M. Hind, *A History of Engraving and Etching*, London, 1923, *passim*.

4   E. Borea, "Stampa figurativa e pubblico dalle origini all'affermazione nel Cinquecento", *Storia dell'Arte Italiana*, II, ed. G. Previtali, Turin 1979, pp. 374 and 380. C. Karpinski, *Italian Printmaking, Fifteenth and Sixteenth Centuries: An Annotated Bibliography*, Boston, 1987, p. xviii, argues that what is needed in the study of sixteenth-century "collaborative" engravings is a case by case comparison with their sources.

5   D. DeGrazia, "Giorgio Ghisi", *Print Quarterly*, iv, 1987, pp. 282ff.

6   In a review of *The Engravings of Giorgio Ghisi*, exhibition catalogue by S. Boorsch, M. Lewis and R. E. Lewis, New York, 1985 (*The Burlington Magazine*, cxxviii, 1986, p. 41).

7   See Boorsch, Lewis and Lewis, *op. cit.*: the *Nativity* of 1553 is no. 14, pp. 71ff., and the *School of Athens* of 1550 is no. 11, pp. 61ff.

8   T. Riggs, *Hieronymus Cock*, London 1977, especially pp. 72ff.

9   G. Vasari, *Le Vite de' più eccelenti pittori, scultori ed architettori*, ed. G. Milanesi, Florence 1906, vii, p. 596: "A Filippo d'Averardo Salviati fece in un quadrotto una Natività di Cristo, in figure piccole, tanto bella che non ha pari, come sa ognuno, essendo oggi la detta opera in stampa". See also R. Borghini, *Il Riposo*, Florence 1584, p. 535. The engraving measures 662 × 454 mm (the painting measures 653 × 467 mm), the engraving thus rivalled the painting.

10 E. A. Carroll, *Rosso Fiorentino: Drawings, Prints and Decorative Arts*, exhibition catalogue, Washington D.C., 1987, p. 94, n. 1.

11 David Landau has drawn my attention to the very precise equivalences between the dimensions of the figures in the painting and those in the engraving. Although they are disposed slightly differently in space, the contours match exactly. Some kind of mechanical method must have been used to transfer the figures from the painting (or, perhaps, the cartoon for it) to the drawing used by the engraver, and thus to the plate.

12 L. Münz, *Bruegel's Drawings*, London, 1961, cat. no. 3, p. 207.

13 The inscriptions are in the circles; they celebrate Mary as the Mother of the Saviour; Boorsch, Lewis and Lewis, *op. cit.*, p. 71.

14 The *Incendio nel Borgo*, published by Salamanca, is inscribed "*RAPHAEL PINXIT IN VATICANO*"; the composition is reversed. See G. Bernini Pezzini, *Raphael Invenit*, exhibition catalogue, Rome, 1985, pp. 54–55 and 333. The anonymous

engraving published by Cock, which is closely related to Bronzino's *Crossing of the Red Sea*, painted within an arched frame in the chapel of Eleanora of Toledo in the Palazzo Vecchio in Florence (1541–42), probably derives from a lost drawing by Bronzino rather than from the fresco itself. Comparison with drawings in Christ Church, Oxford, reveal several features shared with the engraving that are absent from the fresco. The Oxford drawings have been variously judged, either as early designs by Bronzino for the composition of the fresco (Cox-Rearick), or as later variants by Allori (Smyth and Byam Shaw). It has been suggested that Bronzino had a drawing prepared specially for the engraving, perhaps by Allori, but it seems more likely that one of Bronzino's preparatory drawings was used. A similar drawing would have been the point of departure for the draughtsman of the Oxford sheets (it is unlikely to have been the same drawing because there is at least one place where the Oxford sheets relate more closely to the fresco than to the engraving). See J. Cox-Rearick, "Les Dessins de Bronzino pour la Chapelle d'Eleonora au Palazzo Vecchio", *Revue de l'Art*, xiv, 1971, pp. 13–18; C. H. Smyth, *Bronzino as Draughtsman; An Introduction*, Locust Valley, NY, 1971, pp. 19 and 63, nn. 93–96; J. Byam Shaw, *Drawings by Old Masters at Christ Church, Oxford*, Oxford, 1976, i, pp. 69–70, cat. nos. 133 and 134.

15 But it was done in an extremely unintelligent way, it should be said. The designer must, in fact, have felt insecure about his capacities, because he has completely omitted the upper story of the Benediction Loggia, no doubt defeated by the challenge of continuing it without any real clue as to Raphael's idea. It is interesting to compare this with Marcantonio's engraving after Raphael's *Parnassus* (Bartsch, xiv, 200, 247) where the composition is similarly squared off, although the window area is left. Presumably the purpose in that case was, at least in part, to illustrate the invention of the figure group in relation to the window. But it was not felt necessary to preserve the shape of the wall space. See I. H. Shoemaker and E. Broun, *The Engravings of Marcantonio Raimondi*, Lawrence, Kan., 1981, no. 48, pp. 155ff.

16 Bartsch, xiv, 262, 350; Shoemaker and Broun, *op. cit.*, no. 33, pp. 122ff.

17 The practical business of making a drawing of a large-scale fresco like the *School of Athens* should be considered. To make an accurate drawing would have required ladders. For the question of access to the Vatican, see Vasari–Milanesi, vii, p. 13, where Vasari describes his studies in the Vatican in the company of Salviati. Parmigianino's drawing of the *School of Athens* at Windsor was probably made after a modello for the fresco. See A. E. Popham, *Catalogue of the Drawings of Parmigianino*, i, London, 1971, p. 199, no. 666 *recto*.

18 G. B. Bertani, *Gli oscuri e difficili passi dell'opera Ionica di Vitruvio*, Mantua 1558; Paul III died in 1549. Ghisi engraved a template *Last Judgement* after Michelangelo and probably a set of six of the Prophets and Sibyls; however, it is not at all certain that he ever saw the originals, and he may have worked from drawings made by others; see Boorsch, Lewis and Lewis, *op. cit.*, pp. 53–57, and 151–65. For some reason the authors date the Prophets and Sibyls to the early 1570s. It is evident, however, that they show his gradual acquisition of a mature engraving style. The *Ezekiel* and the *Persian Sibyl*, for example, are rather primitive in their handling of form, and Michelangelo's figures are flattened and distorted by the burin. They must be early works. In contrast, the *Jeremiah* and the *Joel* show a sophisticated grasp of how to find equivalents for the swelling of masses of the painted figures.

The date of 1549 that several of them carry seems entirely credible as the year of their first publication, but their execution was probably spread over several years. As David Landau noted in his review of the Ghisi catalogue (see note 6 above), the copying of drawings of Michelangelo's frescoes is well attested in Mantua. In 1547 G. B. Scultori admitted that his series of 59 drawings of the *Last Judgement*, sent to Granvelle, were not made from the fresco but from an existing drawing.

19 Boorsch, Lewis and Lewis, *op. cit.*, pp. 68ff. Riggs, *op. cit.*, p. 50 and 158, thought that Ghisi brought all the drawings with him from Italy; he argued convincingly that the Mantuan engraver was the only likely source for the drawing by the Mantuan G. B. Bertani, used for the *Judgement of Paris* that Cock published.

20 J. Wood, "Cannibalized Prints and Early Art History", *Journal of the Warburg and Courtauld Institutes*, LI, 1988, p. 219, published the proof state of the left half of the *School of Athens* in the British Museum. For the right half, in the Albertina, see Boorsch, Lewis and Lewis, *op. cit.*, p. 62.

21 Boorsch, Lewis and Lewis, *op. cit.*, p. 114. The cross-shaped blank space in the centre is the result of damage to the sheet.

22 The difficulty of successfully engraving a composition of figures in space is implied by the treatment of Ghisi's *Calumny of Apelles*, where refined adjustments between foreground and background are implied in the surviving proof state; see Boorsch, Lewis and Lewis, *op. cit.*, no. 27, pp. 111ff.

23 A single-figure composition too might be approached in the systematic manner of the *Dream*. In the proof state of Ghisi's *Hercules Resting*, the landscape – presumably Ghisi's own invention – is engraved with the body in the foreground, but the background, and the upper parts of the plate, including Hercules's head, are only just begun; see Boorsch, Lewis and Lewis, *op. cit.*, no. 41, pp. 144–45.

24 Bartsch, XIV, 24, 21.

25 Vasari–Milanesi, V, pp. 418–19.

26 Boorsch, Lewis and Lewis, *op. cit.*, no. 13, pp. 68ff.

27 The relative proportions were altered, so that Christ is much larger relative to the others than he is in the fresco. In combination with the closure of the space between the earthly and the heavenly realms, the effect is to reduce the emphasis on the monstrance on the altar and make the Trinity more dominant.

28 See n. 20, above.

29 G. Vasari, *Le Vite de' più eccellenti architetti, pittori e scultori italiani* (1550), ed. L. Bellosi and A. Rossi, Turin, 1986, p. 616.

30 Riggs, *op. cit.*, no. 113, pp. 81 and 339.

31 Riggs, *op. cit.*, no. 181, pp. 160 and 357.

32 The inscription reads: "*COLLAUDUNT HIC TRINI/UNIVSQUE DEI MAIESTATE/COELITES. ADMIRANTVR/AC RELIGIOSE ADORANT/ SACROSANCT/AE ECCLESIAE/PROCERES . . .*".

33 For example, a number by Beatrizet: Bartsch, XV, 243, 8 and XV, 260, 41, and among the Anonymous prints, Bartsch, XV, 13, I and XV, 29, 2.

34 An inscription cites Joshua, ch. 3; S. Schéle, *Cornelis Bos: A Study of the Origins of the Netherland Grotesque*, Stockholm, 1965, pp. 115–16, no. 19. There is no indication of the inventor, which has given rise to a certain amount of argument about who was responsible for the composition; Scorel is the best candidate.

35 Vico's *Entombment*, 1548, Bartsch, xv, 284, 8, and the *George and the Dragon*, Bartsch, xv, 286, 12.

36 Bartsch, xiv, 363, 488, with the inscription *"Iv Mi Ag. Flo."*.

37 S. Schéle, *op. cit.*, pp. 21 and 141, no. 67; it is inscribed *"Martinus Hemskeric inventor"*.

38 See Riggs, *op. cit.*, p. 169; there were precedents for this, but they were quite rare, for example Beatrizet's *Combat of Reason and Love* after Bandinelli, published by Salamanca in 1545 (Bartsch, xv, 262, 44). There are some interesting French cases in the 1540s, as, for example, Pierre Milan's engravings after Rosso; see Carroll *op. cit.*, no. 79, pp. 252ff. and no. 89, pp. 282ff.

39 Boorsch, Lewis and Lewis, *op. cit.*, no. 28, pp. 114ff.

40 Bartsch, xiv, 366, 492; the first state is dated 1523; see Bernini Pezzini, *op. cit.*, pp. 39 and 289; see also Wood, *op. cit.*, pp. 215ff.

41 Riggs, *op. cit.*, no. 181, p. 357.

42 L. Dolce, *Il Dialogo della Pittura, intitolato "L'Aretino"*, Venice 1557; see the edition by Mark Roskill, *Dolce's "Aretino" and Venetian Art Theory of the Cinquecento*, New York, 1968, pp. 128–29.

43 G. P. Lomazzo, "Trattato dell'Arte della Pittura, Scoltura et Architettura", in *Scritti sulle Arti*, ed. R. P. Ciardi, Florence, 1974, ii, p. 99.

44 See n. 37, above.

15

The Historian and the Technique: On the role of Goldsmithery in Vasari's *Lives*

Marco Collareta

Between 1550 and 1568, the two editions of Giorgio Vasari's *Lives of the Most Excellent Painters, Sculptors, and Architects* provided modern artistic thought and modern artistic historiography with their first formulation, derived from the theory of the "three arts of design." Several relatively recent studies have focused on the elaboration of this theory, which concerned the period running from Brunelleschi to Vasari, by way of Alberti and Michelangelo. Despite the sage encouragement of André Chastel, however, scholars have been much less interested in investigating the relationship between various techniques and these three "arts" in the first and second editions of the *Lives*. This is due, in large part, to the fact that the techniques have always been regarded as an undifferentiated group, so much so that only generic, overly general, considerations have been brought to bear on them. No inquiry has yet been pointed in the other direction; none, that is, has been devoted to a particular technique. Before beginning, then, it is legitimate to ask this question: which technique or group of techniques most merits such a consideration? A number of good reasons lie behind my interest in the ensemble of techniques that go under the name of "goldsmithery." This profession, in Vasari's *Lives*, is endowed with a status and a dignity like no other in the arts, with the exception of painting, sculpture, and architecture, in their strictest senses. Reading through the 1550 edition, we often find mention of groups and gatherings composed of painters, sculptors, architects, and goldsmiths,[1] as well as testimony to friendships between goldsmiths, painters, sculptors, and architects;[2] above all, though, and most importantly, we see painters, sculptors, and architects beginning their careers as goldsmiths.[3]

The biography that Vasari devotes to Filippo Brunelleschi constitutes the first significant instance of this, making it a classic example. After reporting the birth of the future architect, the Aretine historian tells of how the happy father, Ser Brunellesco taught little Filippo the rudiments of letters with great care. The child was so gifted and so intelligent that he did not always make much effort, seeming not to worry about his progress, but he appeared very interested in more practical activities. Ser Brunellesco, who wished to see him follow in his own footsteps as a notary or to take up his great-great-grandfather's profession, was very displeased with this. Seeing that the boy was ceaselessly attracted to artistic and manual inventions, he made him learn arithmetic and writing, and placed him as an apprentice with a goldsmith who was one of his friends, in order for him to learn to design, which was to his great satisfaction. Filippo began to assimilate the principles of that art and to put them to use, and, after a few years, he knew how to set fine stones better than the elders of the profession. He practiced niello and sculpture in precious metals [. . .] He also made bas-reliefs with such mastery that everyone could see that his genius was fated to extend the limits of this art.[4]

The model for this knowing literary construction still exists. It is the fragmentary but essential *Life of Filippo di Ser Brunellesco,* written around 1480 by Antonio di Tuccio Manetti. Here is what we read there:

In his earliest youth, Filippo learned to read, to write, and to count [. . .] and also a little literature, because his father was a notary; perhaps he wanted him to be one as well [. . .] From the time he was very small, he instinctively liked drawing and painting: he was taken with them, which is why, when his father made him choose a vocation, as was the custom, he wished to be a goldsmith. His father, being a prudent man, and seeing Filippo's aptitude, consented. In this art, he quickly became very knowledgeable about everything that had to with the fundamental principle of design, which very soon seemed extraordinary. In a short time, he became a master at niello, at enamel, and at the fashioning of reliefs, though he also knew how to prepare, cut, and set any stone; in this art and in others, he made marvelous things, so well that as time passed he no longer appeared to be the age he was.[5]

Comparison of the two texts reveals their considerable differences, yet Manetti and Vasari both preserve the close tie that links goldsmithery to design. At the origin of this is probably the specific character of the goldsmith's techniques: the complexity of procedures and the variety of products obtained from them almost spontaneously reflect a single creative principle – that of knowing "design" – which is at the base of the different arts. It should not be forgotten, however, that consciousness of this phenomenon remains a specific accomplishment of the Florentine Quattrocento. At the moment when Ser Brunelleschi, despite himself, accepted the fact that his second son Filippo was devoting himself to goldsmithery, another Florentine notary, Ser Lapo Mazzei, wrote, regarding one of his numerous sons: "Bruno is with a goldsmith, and design has so gone to his head that [. . .] Niccolò's figures now seem very awkward to him."[6] The contemptuous allusion to Niccolò di Pietro Gerini, a Trecento painter, is most significant. At the dawn of the Quattrocento, design was no longer the prerogative of the bloodless followers of Giotto, but that of the young goldsmiths, who would soon launch a revolution that would be of the greatest importance for the history of Florentine art.

We now understand why, in 1550, Vasari reserved apprenticeship with a goldsmith for artists either contemporary with or later than Brunelleschi. His list includes Brunelleschi himself, Lorenzo Ghiberti, and Masolino da Panicale on the one hand; Antonio Pollaiuolo, Andrea Verrocchio, Sandro Botticelli, Domenico Ghirlandaio, Francesco Francia, and Andrea del Sarto on the other. If the "modern" name of Andrea del Sarto, one of Vasari's teachers, serves mainly to mark a historical connection, the names of the other, older masters allow one to discern two distinct phases of Quattrocento art: the international Gothic at the beginning of the century, and the burgeoning "neo-Gothic," so to speak, of 1460, which even contemporaneous critics considered to be intimately linked. The precision of line, the clear delimiting of form, the impeccable quality of the color and the finish, along with the other characteristics of this style, present in various forms throughout these periods, would be inconceivable without a rigorous apprenticeship under a goldsmith. The Vasari of 1550 might have made a mistake here and there in his accounts, but his perception of goldsmithery's role in the art of the Renaissance is entirely correct, corresponding perfectly with what we learn from the oldest sources and from the works themselves.

I have spoken of the "Vasari of 1550" because things change considerably when we move to the second, 1568 edition of the *Lives*. The reader who peruses only the biographies that supplement the work and bring it up to date, over-looking the author's original intent, will have difficulty in recognizing this fact. The notices dedicated to Timoteo Viti, Baccio Bandinelli, Benvenuto Cellini, Leone Leoni, Francesco Salviati, and Vincenzo Danti only confirm anew the actuality of apprenticeships to goldsmiths for the most diverse arts.[7] But anyone who passes over the biographies added to those already present in the first edition cannot fail to notice some important modifications. I am thinking of the case of Lorenzo di Credi or that of Luca della Robbia. In 1550, Vasari made no allusion to their formation as goldsmiths. In 1568, by contrast, he addresses this matter in great detail.[8] The fact that Lorenzo di Credi descended from an illustrious family of goldsmiths and that Luca della Robbia is referred to in a text from the beginning of the sixteenth century, that of Gauricus, as "*ex aurifice plastes*" – that is, "having passed from being a goldsmith to being a sculptor"[9] – might lead us to believe that Vasari's knowledge had simply deepened. The two artists have a conservative and thus rather negative role in the *Lives*. This is why the reader should not consider the apparent precision of Vasari's information from too literal a point of view, but ought rather to interpret it in terms of its ideological connotations. To clarify this, we might pause over Luca della Robbia. In 1550, Vasari's biography of the sculptor is marked by a devastating comparison with the oeuvre of Donatello. We read:

> Many say that Luca della Robbia collaborated with the most recognized talent of his time, Donatello. This reputation earned him the commission, from the *opera* of

Santa Maria del Fiore, for a few little marble scenes, to be placed on the campanile – allegories of Music, Philosophy, and the Liberal Arts, where he was able to demonstrate his progress. This encouraged the *opera* to commission him to do the marble decoration for the organ above the cathedral's new sacristy. There, with diligence and subtle mastery, he depicted a choir of musicians; though it is situated rather high up, one can see their throats swollen with air, and above their shoulders, the movements of the hands of the one who directs them. In these reliefs, he succeeded in rendering their sounds and their dances in every detail, finishing the ensemble much more carefully than even Donatello himself had: in Donatello's work [that is to say, in the decorations he made for the second organ in Santa Maria del Fiore], one perceives more resolute practice and a more controlled vivacity than in Luca's, despite its perfection and its marvelous finish. With superior artists, sketches always have more force and life than finished works do; the furor of art knows how to render, in one instant, the thought in the artist's mind, which the care and effort expended in the finishing of the works does not.[10]

In 1568, when he evokes Luca della Robbia's past as a goldsmith, Vasari goes further:

> Let us come back to Luca. Once this work, which pleased all, had been completed, he was commissioned to do the bronze door of the sacristy [. . .] The finish and the purity of the ensemble make of it a wonder and prove how useful it was for Luca to have been a goldsmith.[11]

Thus, goldsmithery becomes an index of an "exactitude" (*diligenza*) that, compared to the pre-Michelangelesque "furor" of Donatello, seems irremediably archaic. It is thus not by chance that Luca della Robbia appears in the *Lives* before Donatello, who was his elder, and even before Brunelleschi himself; similarly, it is no accident that the goldsmith who was his teacher is identified as Leonardo di Ser Giovanni, an artist who was active from 1368 to 1371, that is, thirty years before his presumed student was even born.

We now find ourselves nearly at the heart of the problem. The new role, however minor, that goldsmithery plays in the second edition of the *Lives*, can best be understood when we reread the biographies of those artists who precede Brunelleschi; these do not even appear in the first edition. When he added a lengthy account of the Tuscan goldsmiths of the Trecento,[12] Vasari certainly enriched his portrait of the history of medieval art. This account, however, contained one passage that the Aretine historian could not have written without a reason, the passage stating that the Aretine goldsmiths "Pietro and Paolo [. . .] had learned design from the Sienese [sculptors and architects] Agnolo and Agostino, and were the first to succeed in creating important works of goldsmithery."[13] These words reverse, in fact, the link between the arts that we habitually consider to be traditional. Goldsmithery is no longer a métier that forms artists, but an artisanal practice that becomes meaningful only insofar as it is based on more important and established arts. From such a perspective it is not surprising that, in 1568, one passage that disappears from Giotto's biography is that where, in 1550, the renovator of the arts was qualified, significantly, as "very skillful in the art of agriculture [which is an art of design in the tradition extending from Giovanni Santi to Francisco de Holanda], to such a degree that [. . .] the instruments of his profession [. . .] seemed guided by the noble hand of a valiant goldsmith or intaglio engraver."[14]

If a simple comparison of the two editions of the *Lives* suffices to make evident an indubitable deterioration of the image of the goldsmith, we must look to the historical context to explain the cause of this transformation. Vasari conceived his masterpiece in the Rome of the Farnese, where goldsmithery had a very important place in the world of the arts. The biography of Valerio Belli established an explicit link between the glyptic arts and "the happy era in which we now find ourselves";[15] it leaves no doubt on this subject. Very different was the situation in Medicean Florence. There Vasari developed the second edition of the *Lives*; there, the exigencies of duke Cosimo I de' Medici's still young state made themselves violently felt, reclaiming absolute primacy for the monumental arts. It was also necessary to keep the imperatives of representation in mind, not only for the sake of the patrons, but also in relation to the social organization of artists and the reflections on art that resulted from it.

In 1562, the "Company and Academy of the Arts of Design," the world's first art academy, was founded in Florence. The sculptor Giovann'Agnolo Montorsoli (ca. 1507–1563) wanted it to be a second Company of Saint Luke, but the new institution was quickly absorbed in the cultural politics of Vasari and thus in those of Cosimo I de' Medici. With regard to goldsmithery, this seems to have had important consequences. In 1563, the Academy accepted among its members Domenico di Michele Poggini, "who works at the mint, for having made numerous marble sculptures and for no longer working in the profession of the goldsmith [. . .] on condition that he renounces the [goldsmiths'] company and no longer practices this."[16] This must have been an important renunciation for an artist who, in 1554, had inscribed himself as a goldsmith in the silk guild,[17] and who, in 1554 and then again in 1559, had appended the word "aurifex" to his signature on two remarkable marbles. It would seem, however, that Poggini accepted this without perceiving it to be too much of a sacrifice, since he subsequently signed a bronze *Pluto* (1570–1573) for the Studiolo in the Palazzo Vecchio with his name alone, and since he entrusted the copper cornucopia that originally accompanied the statue to a goldsmith who specialized in gilding. It is probable that Poggini dispensed with the cumbersome qualification of "goldsmith" as easily as did an artist whose academic thought is more important, Vincenzo Danti. Danti was born in Perugia in 1530, and in 1548 he joined the goldsmiths' guild in that town. In 1553 he, along with his father, was entrusted with the execution of a bronze statue of Pope Julius III, which still survives. However, in the preface of his treatise *Il primo libro del trattato delle perfette proporzioni,* of which the first and only book appeared in Florence in 1567, he links his original encounter with *disegno* implicitly to his experience as a sculptor, and explicitly to his concomitant knowledge of the works of Michelangelo. Danti writes:

> In truth, I regret infinitely that, because of my age, I cannot devote myself to what I had resolved; because twenty-two years had already passed [this places us back in 1553, the year in which he was commissioned to do the statue of Julius III], that is to say the flower of my early youth was almost already gone, when I decided, after seeing and comprehending the greatness of that man [Michelangelo], to dedicate myself to these arts and to imitate him. I did not reap the benefits that I could possibly have reaped, if things had gone otherwise and if I had imitated his very beautiful manner.[18]

The practice of design and the imitation of a Michelangelo, now canonized, became everything, while the apprenticeship to a goldsmith belonged to a distant past, one that could fade into oblivion.

If we pass quickly from his theoretical account to his executed works, we can refine our observations. Danti's beautiful bronze reliefs, with their sure and elliptical modeling, closely recall Michelangelo's "*non finito*," presenting no visible trace of any long, patient labor of reworking with the chisel. What the inspired sculptor created with his hands, in clay or in silver, seems to have been translated perfectly into bronze. This irresistibly makes us think of the enthusiasm that Vasari expressed in his second edition of the *Lives*: "The procedure now used for founding figures, big or small, is extraordinary; many masters achieve impeccable casts, which require no retouching and which are as thin as knife blades."[19] If we remember that retouching counts among the standard skills of the goldsmith, it is not difficult to read in these phrases yet another attack on the "finish" ("*diligenza*") of goldsmithery. This is key for interpreting the passage in which Vasari, in 1568, describes "the silver altar and retable of S. Giacomo in Pistoia," which he attributes in its entirety to Leonardo di Ser Giovanni:

> There we can admire numerous compositions of figures, above all the Saint James, more than one *braccia* high, which is at the retable's center. He is in full relief and is so highly worked up that he seems to have been cast rather than chiseled.[20]

In his captivating *Autobiography*, Benvenuto Cellini, who was also a goldsmith, treats the metallurgical innovations so welcomed by Vasari as the "veritable practices of madmen."[21] Cellini opposed the academic indifference goldsmiths faced and defended the practice; he did not limit himself to pleading the merits of reworking, which is everywhere evident in his Florentine works. So did he defend the art of the chisel that he endowed it with a status it had never before enjoyed in the history of Renaissance artistic thought. And although his very interesting testimony belongs to a series of texts foreign to the normal "credo" of Italian artistic literature, it should not be underestimated.

The Florentine Accademia del Disegno, like any institution of its kind, needed a coat of arms. The winged ox, symbol of the patron saint of the old Company of Saint Luke, was no longer satisfactory. Numerous people saw in it too marked an allusion to the one art that the evangelist had practiced, painting. It was for this reason that a sort of contest was set in motion in order that a new blazon be found, a contest in which most, if not all, of the academicians participated. No decision was reached in 1563, the date when it was expected, nor in 1571. It was only in 1594 that the matter was settled, in favor of three interlaced crowns, an illustrious and triumphant version of the emblem of the "three circles," which Michelangelo had made his personal seal while working on the New Sacristy.

Of all the projects for the blazon of the Academy that have come down to us, those by Cellini are, without doubt, the most interesting. On a folio now in Munich, one sees the image of Apollo, victor over the Python serpent, inside an elegant oval border, typical of the blazons of the sixteenth century. It would have received the following inscription: "Apollo is the only light/Cosimo is the principal of a great school and its master." The long explanation accompanying this drawing leaves aside the reference to Cosimo I de' Medici but lingers on the figure of Apollo:

> This important star, which is the sun, is the torch of the universe; the Ancients and our ancestors used the figure of Apollo to represent and signify this [. . .] That is why I have drawn it, for I think that our Academy of Design is worthy of this fine emblem, because it is the true inspiration of all actions that men accomplish in all of their professions. There are, in fact, two sorts of design; the first is born in the imagination, and the second, the result of the first, is expressed in line, and this latter has rendered man so fearless that he has made himself the rival of Apollo, his father, who gives life to plants, herbs, flowers, animals, objects so admirable, ornaments of the Earth, a world where man, thanks to design, has conceived grand cities with astonishing palaces, theaters, temples, towers, loggias, houses and bridges, which he has subsequently decorated with admirable figures of animals in marble and in metal; and he ornamented the interior of these marvelous edifices with paintings, then he adorned himself with jewels and gold, and all of this he did it thanks to admirable design; thus, since Apollo is the first master, I have chosen him as an emblem.[22]

If, in this inspired celebration of the creative power of the Sun, goldsmithery discreetly accompanies the monumental arts, Cellini's second "invention" for the Academy's blazon, elaborated more extensively elsewhere, completely overthrows the traditional system of the arts. On a folio in the Calamandrei collection, the first of four distinct folios devoted to this project, we see, inside a quadrangular frame, a figure of *Diana of Ephesus*, flanked by a serpent and a lion. The long explanation accompanying the drawing describes the *Diana of Ephesus* as a personification of Nature; the serpent is an allusion to Cosimo I de' Medici and the lion is "the emblem of our great school," that is, the Florentine artistic

297

tradition. Most interesting for us is what Cellini says about the unusual form of the frame:

> All of the things that exist under these skies are composed of four elements, not one more nor one less, to such an extent that all that man makes reveals itself to be composed of these four elements. For me, sculpture comes first, because God sculpted the first man out of earth, using his divine and immortal hands. Then astonishing and sensual painting was born of this. Thereafter, out of this developed the very useful [art of] architecture. Finally, when man knew and understood that he was the master of the entire earth, when he discovered metals and, among these, the most noble of them, gold and silver, he wanted to execute statues and every sort of thing in these two materials. But [...] he did not want to work them like the copper, tin, and lead that are ordinarily used in casting. These two metals, gold and silver, are worked with the hammer and the chisel; the Ancients called those who practiced this art chiselers. We are thus dealing with four arts, each very different from the other, in relation to the brevity of human life, because each one of them merits that the whole life of a man be devoted to it.[23]

In the sixteenth century, the concept of artistic creation oscillates between two poles: Nature and God. In founding his system of the four arts, including goldsmithery, on the four elements of Aristotelian physics, Cellini directly opposed the Academy, which had extracted a trinitarian theory from Michelangelo and, consequently, divined the three arts of design. We must therefore not be surprised if the Academy fought against Cellini's theoretical and dangerous proposal with all of the weapons at its disposal. This appears very clearly if we consider attentively the two ephemeral pageants that presented the new institution to the public, several years after its foundation: Michelangelo's obsequies in 1564 and the marriage of Francesco de' Medici and Giovanna of Austria in 1565–1566. The first of these events was limited to eulogizing the threefold greatness of the greatest artist of the century. The second, by contrast, was the trial run of a more general and, at the same time, more precise, theoretical elaboration. On the triumphal arch erected at the *Porta a Prato*, meant to present the particularities (*le proprietá*) of Florence to the young foreign bride, Tuscan Language and Poetry had Design as their pendant. This trinitarian iconography, which was described as "a figure [...] with three equal and similar heads,"[24] had as its goal the distinction of painting, sculpture, and architecture from the other artistic practices; the latter were, in fact, placed under the much more modest tutelage of Industry. Among them is found goldsmithery, symbolized by a figure carrying "vases and jars made of silver, gold, and other metals."[25] The art that Cellini had raised to the fourth rank, next to the three canonical arts, is no longer anything other than one of the arts that we, in our day, call "minor" or "applied."

Let us return one last time to Vasari. Among the papers of the Aretine historian that postdate the first edition of the *Lives*, the only allusion to a desire to add supplementary words on goldsmithery dates to 1564, or to the years immediately following.[26] This fact demonstrates that the essentially negative role played by goldsmithery in the second edition of the *Lives* is closely linked to the struggle between Cellini and the Academy over the classification of the arts. The confirmation of this link can be found in one of the frescoes decorating Vasari's Florentine house.[27] There we find, as might be expected, the *Diana of Ephesus* dear to Cellini and the trinitarian representation of design such as was employed during the nuptials of Francesco de' Medici and Giovanna of Austria. While the *Diana of Ephesus* was there to symbolize Nature in its antithesis to Art, the trinitarian iconography of design corresponds to the delicate operation that makes possible the passage from one reality to another. The best commentary on this complex image is found in the long passage devoted to *disegno*[28] that is really the most innovative part of the second edition of the *Lives*. It elevates design to the rank of "father of our three arts, architecture, painting, and sculpture." Goldsmithery is not even mentioned here, and its absence brings to an end one of the most interesting chapters in the Renaissance debate on the arts.

Notes

The text published here exactly reproduces the lecture I gave in the auditorium of the Louvre on the 25th of January 1993. The limits imposed and the particularity of my subject have forced me to limit my annotations to the essential. However, I would like to record all that I owe to the teaching of Paola Barocchi, without forgetting the work of Julius von Schlosser, Nikolaus Pevsner, Paul Oskar Kristeller, Pietro Calamandrei, and Ferdinando Bologna. In the past, I had the opportunity of receiving the advice of John Pope-Hennessy, of Martha Ann McCrory, and of Cornelia Willemina Fock on different versions of this study.

1   G. Vasari, *Le Vite de' più eccelenti pittori, scultori, e architettori*, edited by P. Barocchi and E. Bettarini, Florence, 1966–1987; French edition edited by A. Chastel, G. Vasari, *Les Vies des meilleurs peintres, sculpteurs et architectes*, Paris, 1981–1986. All of the following references will be to the French edition: III, p. 129 (Ghiberti); III, p. 253 (Donatello); VII, p. 245 (Perino).
2   Ibid., III, p. 65 (Dello); III, p. 198 (Brunelleschi); III, pp. 250 and 253 (Donatello); IV, p. 257 (Botticelli); VII, pp. 244–245 (Perino).
3   Ibid., III, pp. 127–128 (Ghiberti); III, p. 153 (Masolino); III, p. 194 (Brunelleschi); IV, p. 22 (Ghirlandaio); IV, p. 243 (Pollaiuolo); IV, p. 257 (Botticelli); IV, p. 285 (Verrocchio); IV, p. 345 (Francia); VI, p. 59 (Andrea del Sarto).
4   Ibid., III, p. 194.
5   A. Manetti, *Vita di Filippo Brunelleschi preceduta de la novella del Grasso*, edited by D. De Robertis and G. Tanturli, Milan, 1976, pp. 52–53. French edition of the life of Brunelleschi in *Filippo Brunelleschi, 1377–1466* (exhibition catalogue), Chapelle de la Sorbonne and École nationale supérieure des Beaux-Arts, Paris, 1979, pp. 58–146.

6   Letter from Lapo Mazzei to Francesco di Marco Datini of January 1408, published by R. Piattoli, "Un mercante del Trecento e gli artisti del tempo suo", in *Rivista d'Arte*, XI, 1929, p. 411.

7   G. Vasari, *Les Vies*, V, p. 298 (Viti); VIII, pp. 18–19 (Bandinelli); X, p. 218 (Cellini); X, p. 122 (Leoni); IX, p. 55 (Salviati); X, p. 224 (Danti).

8   Ibid., III, p. 85; V, p. 345.

9   P. Guarico, *De sculptura*, edited by A. Chastel and R. Klein, Geneva, 1969, p. 251.

10 *G. Vasari, Les Vies*, III, p. 92.

11 Ibid., p. 87.

12 Ibid., II, pp. 137–138.

13 Ibid., p. 137.

14 G. Vasari, *Le Vite*, II, pp. 95–96. For the references in parentheses see L. Bek, "Giovanni Santi's Disputa de la pictura. A Polemical Treatise", *Analecta Romana Instituti Danici*, V, 1969, p. 83; Fr. de Hollanda, *Dialoghi romani con Michelangelo*, edited by E. Spina Barelli, Milan, 1964, p. 48.

15 G. Vasari, *Les Vies*, VII, p. 35.

16 This document has been published by H. W. Frey, *Neue Briefe von Giorgio Vasari*, Burg b.M., 1940, p. 209.

17 This unpublished document can be found in the Florentine State Archives, *Arte della Seta*, 12, c. 18r (2 April 1553; s.f.).

18 "*E per vero dire a me duole infinitamente – scrive infatti il Danti – non più per tempo della mia età essermi di esercitare il disegno risoluto: conciossiachè, avendo già passato ventidua anni [e cioè essendo nel 1553, anno di allogagione della statua di Giulio III] e quasi il fiore della mia prima giovanezza quando, mediante la cognizione e grandezza di costui [cioè di Michelangelo], ad attendere a quest'arti et all'imitazione di lui mi disposi, non ho fatto quel profitto, che averei per aventura potuto fare, se altrimenti fusse avenuto, imitando la di costui bellissima maniera.*" P. Barocchi (ed.), *Trattati d'arte del Cinquecento tra Manierismo e Contro-riforma*, Bari, 1960–1962, I, p. 211.

19 Retouching comprises a series of operations aimed at correcting the faults of a metal work made from a mold, at completing the parts that did not come out well and at polishing remaining irregularities. G. Vasari, *Les Vies* (French edition) I, p. 137.

20 Ibid., II, p. 138.

21 B. Cellini, *Vita*, edited by O. Bacci, Florence, 1901, pp. 343–344.

22 The text and the figures are published by P. Calamandrei, *Scritti ed inediti cellianiani*, Florence, 1971, p. 145 and tables XII–XIII.

23 The text and the figures are published by P. Calamandrei, *Scritti*, pp. 133–134 and plates XIV–XV.

24 D. Mellini, *Descrizione dell'entrata della Serenissima Reina Giovanna d'Austria*, Florence, 1566, p. 6.

25 Ibid., p. 22.

26 Relevant here is the annotation, written by Vasari on the back of a letter that Cosimo Bartoli had addressed to him on 29th April, 1564, in H. and H. W. Frey, *Der literarische Nachlass Giorgio Vasaris*, Munich, 1923–1939, p. 78 (letter CDXL).

27 The fresco is reproduced in P. Barocchi, *Vasari Pittore*, Milan, 1964, plate 73.

28 G. Vasari, *Les Vies*, I, pp. 149ff.

Part V ——————————
Reformations

Introduction

Sixteenth-century Italian culture was shaped, to a remarkable degree, by its reform movements, and a history of the period's art could well be written around these – running, for example, from the effect that Savonarola had on Botticelli and on the young Michelangelo, to the astonishingly diverse syntheses of the century's predominant schools of painting that Barocci, Caravaggio, and Rubens unveiled in a single new church in Rome one hundred years later. That story would look at various artists' rethinking of subject matter and format as well as at their re-forging of styles; it would survey the forms taken by the Church's art-theoretical writings (these, by the end of the century, including dialogues, treatises, and other forms favored by humanist writers in the decades before); and it would introduce the new directions taken by church architecture itself. Attempts to rethink the proper form and role of sacred art, which ranged from the views expressed by local preachers to the more official dogma published by post-Tridentine clerics, are marked more by their variety than by any single unifying interest, but what all do share is a keen eye to the innovations that the Renaissance and Reformation had brought, and a concern for how these might be harnessed, or combated, in a devotional context.

The four pieces in this section aim to convey some sense of the range of interests that reform-minded artists and patrons pursued. The selection by Charles de Tolnay, an excerpt from the last of the five volumes on Michelangelo that de Tolnay devoted most of his career to writing, illustrates that the mechanisms by which early reform took place were not limited to the imposition of dictates, coming down from on high in the Church, but often amounted rather to semi-private exchanges among devout friends – letters, poems, drawings. In Vittoria Colonna, de Tolnay sees both the inspiration and the ideal audience for Michelangelo's new Christocentric imagery of the 1530s and 1540s, an imagery that carries the same message as the poems that both Michelangelo and Colonna penned in the same period. Michelangelo's interaction with Colonna, de Tolnay proposes, informed his thinking about central theological debates of the day –

chief among them the debate over whether salvation was to be achieved through faith or through works. As de Tolnay sees it, Michelangelo's response to this debate, guided by Vittoria Colonna, underlies not only his more intimate drawings but also his monumental undertakings, including the *Last Judgment* he painted in the Sistine Chapel.

Alexander Nagel's article, written almost four decades after de Tolnay's, returns to a similar corpus of material, but directs its attention to the new *function* Michelangelo conceived for religious art in the 1530s. Dwelling on the fact that Michelangelo developed his Christocentric imagery in this period in drawings meant to serve as gifts, Nagel considers the significance of the gesture of withdrawing images from the ritual practices and economic exchanges on which commissioned works usually depended. Offered as gifts, Michelangelo's drawings were not just inspired by the poems Colonna gave him; they were likened to these poems. More profoundly, however, Nagel also argues that Michelangelo's gifts of drawings related closely to their subject, the sacrifice of Christ; that ultimate gift, to follow the reformers in Colonna's circle, uniquely allowed for an individual's salvation. Like de Tolnay, Nagel sees Michelangelo in these years as an artist newly skeptical, even critical, of the idea of justification through works. For Nagel, however, this makes the Virgin's role in Michelangelo's images crucial, for she provides the model for later believers' faith. All of this, moreover, mattered not only for Michelangelo's imagery, but also for the *kinds* of things he made. His commitment to reform led him to reconceive the conventional formats of his day and to generate new *types* of art.

If Nagel's essay encourages us to reflect not just on style or subject, but on the very sorts of objects that sixteenth-century art comprises, James Ackerman's does the same for architecture. Focusing on the origins of the Gesù, the mother church of the newly founded Jesuit order, Ackerman observes the ways that sacred architecture had to be critically reassessed in the wake of the Reformation, even before the Council of Trent reached its end and writers like Carlo Borromeo began to codify their new guidelines for building. Whereas de Tolnay and Nagel highlight the ways that felicitous collaboration could foster innovation, Ackerman by contrast draws attention to the conflicting agendas that different groups involved in a reform undertaking might have – in the case of the Gesù a religious order committed to preaching and to the saying of frequent masses, concerned above all with functionality and suspicious of distracting ornament, and a patron desirous of a monumental showpiece. In this case, the interests of the patrons seem at least as decisive as those of the artists involved: indeed, the essay underscores how tenuous the support for a given architect could be, even on a single given project. Showing how the Gesù, which likewise drew on competing architectural traditions, came to take its final shape, Ackerman's article, though written more than three decades ago, remains an excellent introduction to the origins, in the mid-sixteenth century, of what would become a standard ecclesiastical form.

While de Tolnay, Nagel, and Ackerman look at Roman developments, finally, Charles Dempsey's essay demonstrates how, away from Michelangelo's city, a "reform" of art could look quite different. To whatever degree Michelangelo's own investigations in the middle years of the sixteenth-century were driven by a commitment to reform, the manner he exemplified – and even more so the manner that his followers and admirers cultivated – could seem, to North Italian viewers, a departure from what Vasari called the "devout style," a style identified with earlier Bolognese artists like Francia and with earlier Umbrian artists like Perugino. Church reform, even in its late stages, depended on the memory and on the continuing force of the critiques formulated by late fifteenth-century preachers; what Dempsey demonstrates is that artistic reform could also involve its own retrospective element, one hinging on the recovery of stylistic values that predominated in painting of the same period. Dempsey looks at how, in the interest of finding a style that would be fitting to the new era, the Carracci established a novel curriculum for young artists, one that turned on the study of a canon of masters more inclusive than that which central Italians like Vasari were promoting, and one that aimed at a new degree of naturalism, affect, and grace.

16

Michelangelo and Vittoria Colonna

Charles de Tolnay

During the years Michelangelo was working on the Last Judgment, he was so much absorbed in the problems of mankind's collective guilt and fate and, at the same time, in his own sense of sin and inevitable punishment that he must have felt an intense need for a spiritual helper to give him a firmer base in his anguished moral struggle and deliver him from his solitude. Therefore, it must have been a fortunate circumstance that he became acquainted just at that time with a great, noble woman, Vittoria Colonna.

Vittoria Colonna herself had suffered much in her youth and she had experienced the same religious crises as Michelangelo, but she had overcome them by retiring from worldly life and had attained a serene and balanced outlook. Thus she was well prepared to understand Michelangelo's state of mind; she was able to bring to the master a human concern, warmth, and a tender goodness for which he felt a deep gratitude. Cloaked with the fascinating prestige of the highest, most ancient lineage and family connections of Italy, she was surrounded and worshiped by the spiritual élite of her day. Her incomparable tact and finesse, her noble bearing, which contemporaries confused with beauty, her profound classical and literary learning, a certain gift as poetess, the noble aims and forms of her life, and the aura which suffering had given her spirit and appearance – all this made of her for Michelangelo the personification of human perfection, or rather the incarnation of almost transcendent qualities for which he longed but which he could not attain alone. Perhaps the magic of this woman's presence, its mysterious radiation, was more important for the master than the actual content of her words, letters, or poems directed to him. It was these indefinable, unreachable qualities that raised him to that state of bliss in which he could overcome his inner difficulties and become able to create again.

Vittoria Colonna was descended from one of the oldest noble houses of Italy. Born in 1490, in one of the family castles, Castello di Marino, she was fifteen years younger than Michelangelo. At an early age she was married to Francesco d'Avalos, Marquis of Pescara, but her marriage was not happy: she loved but she

306

was not loved in return. Leading at that time a rather solitary life, she sought the friendship of outstanding humanists and poets like Molza, Castiglione, and later Tasso. Castiglione, in the introduction to his *Cortigiano* (1524), wrote of her as a woman "whose virtue I have always venerated as something divine . . .". At that time she wrote poems inspired by classical authors, especially Ovid. On the death in 1525 of the Marquis of Pescara she renounced the world and retired to convents "to be able to serve God more quietly" ("per poter attendere a servire Dio più quietamente"). She meditated on religious problems and began to write her *Canzoniere Spirituale*, one part of which consists of poems dedicated to the memory of her husband, and the other of religious and moralizing poems. She said: "I write only to free myself from my inner grief." ("Scrivo sol per sfogar l'interna doglia . . .") Her masterwork is not her poetry but her life itself. The greatness of her personality is found in her profound influence. She was connected with almost all the celebrated men and women of her period. She edified all those with whom she came into contact, revealing to them "the solid basis of faith," as Marguerite D'Angoulême, Queen of Navarre, said. "Not only," wrote Cardinal Giberti, "does she surpass all other women, but, moreover, she seems to show to the most serious and most celebrated men the light which is a guide to the harbor of salvation."

But it was Michelangelo who elevated this woman to the rank of Beatrice and Laura, those two great inspirers of spiritual love. While, however, these had to die to be transfigured into angelic beings, into incarnations of Divine Intelligence and Grace in the eyes of their poets, Dante and Petrarch, Vittoria Colonna knew this spiritualization during her lifetime, thanks to the poems of Michelangelo. She is for the artist the instrument of his moral perfection; through her he feels reborn (*rinato*) and his rough soul "of little value" seems to him to be perfected by the virtue of this woman (Frey, *Dicht.*, CXXXIV). She is the bestower of Divine Grace and the mediator between the Divinity and himself (Frey, *Dicht.*, CIX, 82). Michelangelo places her in the heavenly spheres. Her beauty appears to him divine (Frey, *Dicht.*, CIX, 8), her visage angelic and serene (Frey, *Dicht.*, CIX, 46). He asks her aid in climbing the precipitous road which leads up to her, because his own strength is insufficient:

> "A l'alto tuo lucente diadema
> Per la strada erta e lunga
> Non è, Donna, chi giunga,
> S'umiltà non v'aggiugni e cortesia:
> Il montar cresce, e'l mio valore scema,
> E la lena mi manca a mezza via."
> (Frey, *Dicht.*, CIX, 76)

One finds in these verses the Platonic *élan* of the earlier poems of the master written to his friend Cavalieri, but purified of sensual elements. The love for woman here appears to be an image of the love for God. This is a religious attitude reminiscent of the love ideal of the High Middle Ages, the philosophical basis of which is the writings of St. Thomas Aquinas. This attitude found its supreme poetical expression in the *dolce stil nuovo* of the thirteenth and four-teenth centuries. But, whereas in the Middle Ages spiritual love was considered as an absolute ideal, valid in all circumstances, which could be realized only through an asceticism directed against one's own nature, Michelangelo dis-covered the value of this feeling at a period in his life when it harmonized with a stage of his inner personal development. The aged master transferred the role of motherhood to Vittoria Colonna: he found in her that tenderness (*pietà superna*) which the child Michelangelo, who lost his mother when he was only six years old, had missed. He also found in her a spiritual mentor and purifier of his soul. But the fact that Vittoria Colonna played the role of an "ideal mother" is sublimated and almost hidden by the religious adoration in which he held her.

Michelangelo's earlier loves for women are known only through his poems. This poetry shows that he had known passionate love in his earlier years as well as in his maturity and that he suffered because of it. The verses written to the "donna bella e crudele" show that his passion was unrequited. Vittoria Colonna was perhaps the first woman to give him sincere friendship. The poems and letters which Michelangelo wrote to the "Alta Signora" or "Divina Donna," as he called her, are written in a humble, reverent tone. He feels himself unworthy (*indegno*) before this admired being. This humility transcends that which is found in the conventional courtly poetry of the sixteenth century – it is an inner attitude and an expression of Michelangelo's real self-abasement in his pride. The artist does not bow before the socially prominent lady, but before the lofty personality.

In some respects it seems that the artist exaggerated the qualities of Vittoria Colonna. Her "divine beauty" was praised many times during her lifetime, not only by Michelangelo, but also by the Petrarchist poets, especially those of Naples. Such praise at that time was a convention owed to every woman of high birth. The rare authentic portraits of the Marchesa show a woman with a high forehead, a long masculine nose, and a somewhat protruding lower lip. On the whole, it is an energetic face, which was rightly called a "feminine incarnation of masculine strength." Michelangelo indeed exalts in one of his madrigals this masculine side of Vittoria: "Un uomo in una donna, anzi uno dio / per la sua bocca parla . . ." (Frey, *Dicht.*, cxxxv).

The artist is also, like his contemporaries, full of admiration for the Marchesa's sonnets which a contemporary Pirogallo calls "perfect, and full of precepts and inventions" ("perfetti, e pieni di dottrina e di invenzione"). But one may admit that her talent as a poetess does not exceed that of the average conven-tional contemporary poetry derived from Petrarch. Her poetry does not express a personal tone and cadence. The metaphors which she uses are generally rather artificial. No comparison is possible with the glowing quality of Michelangelo's poems.

It is chiefly through Vittoria Colonna that Michelangelo became acquainted with the most important religious current of this period, the so-called "Italian Reformation." After the death of Savonarola, his disciples continued to fight for an internal reform of the Church, which was the great subject of the Council of Pisa (1511) and of that of the Lateran (1512). Men of intense religious feeling founded the *Oratorio del Divino Amore* with the same intention of renewing the faith. Several members of the Oratorium will later play a role in the movements of the Italian Reformation and Counter-Reformation: Sadoleto, Giberti, Contarini and Carafa, who later became Pope Paul IV. After 1527, the year of the Sack of Rome, the Oratorium of the Divine Love was dissolved and a large part of its members fled to Venice, where they met other outstanding ecclesiastics: Cortesi, Priuli, Pole. In 1535, several members of this group were created Cardinals under Paul III and constituted the *Consilium de emendanda Ecclesia*.

Meanwhile the movement of the Northern Reformation penetrated to Naples with Juan Valdés. Coming from Spain around 1531, he lived in Rome until 1534, then, until his death in 1541, in Naples. Before his departure for Italy, Valdés had been influenced by Erasmus, as has been shown by Bataillon. His creed was based on the sentences of St. Paul: "For by grace are ye saved through faith; and that not of yourselves: it is the gift of God" (Ephesians 2:8) and ". . . a man is justified by faith without the deed of the law" (cf. Romans 3:28). This idea, expressed also by Savonarola in his *Trattato dell'Umiltà*, was the point of departure for the doctrine of justification by faith alone.

A small circle of cultivated men and women from high ecclesiastical and secular society gathered around Valdés. After his death, the Naples group transferred itself to Viterbo, to the cloister of Santa Caterina, where the Cardinal Reginald Pole was dominant. We also find in this Viterbo circle Flamini, Carnesecchi, Vittorio Soranzo, Alvise Priuli, and finally Vittoria Colonna.

The essential point of the creed of this group consisted in its conception of salvation. Valdés and his circle believed in justification by faith alone, independent of works and religious practices. This doctrine is a spiritualization of the dogma of salvation. The accent, placed until then on the material fact of the *infusio gratiae* through the Sacraments and through the priest as intermediary, is placed now on the attitude of the believer's soul in his relation to the Sacrifice of Christ. Grace depends on man's faith. The radical manner in which this doctrine was expressed is attested by a small book, at that time much read in Italy, entitled *Del beneficio di Gesù Cristo crocifisso verso i Cristiani*, published anonymously and written by Fra Benedetto da Mantova. In it the following sentence on justification can be found: "The justice of Christ is sufficient to make us the Children of Grace, without any good works on our part; these cannot be good unless we previously make ourselves good and just by faith before executing them, as St. Augustine maintains." At the same time the soul becomes conscious of its powerlessness to save itself through works. It is this pessimistic aspect of the dogma which will play a role in the poems of Vittoria Colonna and of Michelangelo.

Like all the other members of the circle of Valdés, Vittoria Colonna also accepted this doctrine. Some of her poems paraphrase it; for example:

> "Con la croce, col sangue e col sudore,
> Con lo spirto al periglio ognor più ardente,
> E non con voglie pigre et opre lente
> Dee l'uom servire al suo vero Signore."
>
> (V. Colonna, LII)

Another example in which she reaffirms that it is the Will of God that we be saved through faith alone is:

> "Il Padre Eterno del ciel . . .
> Vuol la nostra virtù solo per fede."
>
> (V. Colonna, XXXI)

When Valdés settled in Naples in 1534, Vittoria Colonna left for Ischia and it is not known whether she had an opportunity to meet Valdés personally. If not, she could certainly know his ideas through Ochino, who was spiritual adviser to the Marchesa between 1534 and 1541, or even through Giulia Gonzaga, friend of Vittoria Colonna and ardent disciple of Valdés.

The position of Vittoria Colonna concerning justification by faith alone was defined by Carnesecchi before the tribunal of the Inquisition when he was interrogated in 1566. Carnesecchi said (*Carteggio di Vittoria Colonna*, p. 332): "[Vittoria Colonna] attribuiva molto alla gratia et alla fede in suoi ragionamenti. Et d'altra parte nella vita e nelle attioni sue mostrava di tenere gran conto dell'opere facendo grande elemosine e usando carità universalmente con tutti, nel che veniva a osservare e seguire il consiglio, che ella diceva haverli dato il cardinale [Pole], al quale ella credeva come a un oracolo, cioè che ella dovesse attendere a credere come se per la fede sola s'havesse a salvare, e d'altra parte attendere ad operare come se la salute sua consistesse nelle opere. . . ." This compromise ". . . that she should believe as though only by faith could she be saved and, on the other hand, she should do [good] works as if her salvation consisted of works [alone] . . ." reconciled the external with the internal, the traditional creed with the new ideas. This was also precisely the attitude of Michelangelo.

It is not known precisely in which year Michelangelo became acquainted with Vittoria Colonna but it is supposed that it was in 1536 or 1538. That year Vittoria Colonna lived in the convent of San Silvestro in Capite in Rome, and she usually met Michelangelo on Sundays in San Silvestro a Monte Cavallo, a Dominican convent, where they discussed, among other things, religious problems. These discussions are reported, somewhat freely, by Francisco de Hollanda in his *Four Dialogues on Painting*.

Francisco de Hollanda was a young Portuguese painter, who, sent by his king, was traveling in Italy in 1537–1538 and who made the acquaintance of

Michelangelo during the latter year. About ten years later (ca. 1547–1549) he wrote the *Four Dialogues on Painting* in which he described the meetings between Vittoria Colonna, Michelangelo, Lattanzio Tolomei, nobleman and nephew of the cardinal of Siena, and himself on three successive Sundays in the small Church of San Silvestro a Monte Cavallo and in the adjacent garden of its cloister. (In the fourth dialogue neither Vittoria Colonna nor Michelangelo took part.) These dialogues, although partly fictional, have the merit of evoking the spiritual atmosphere of the day.

San Silvestro a Monte Cavallo is located on the slope of the hill of Monte Cavallo near the entrance to the upper gardens of the Colonna. Little remains today of the inner decoration of the church as it was in the mid-sixteenth century. There remain, however, a few works of art which probably adorned the church around 1538, as for instance a sculptured Virgin of the Duecento, severe and frontal in composition, in the second chapel to the right. The door on the left side of the transept leads to the tiny garden of the convent; this is but the remains of the large original garden which extended in the mid-sixteenth century to the foot of the hill. In this period there opened from the garden a splendid view of Rome up to the Borgo – the same view which one still has today from the Quirinale. Such was the setting for the meetings between Vittoria Colonna and Michelangelo.

According to the *Dialogues* of Francisco de Hollanda, the meetings began with commentaries by Friar Ambrosio on the Epistles of St. Paul, after which they discussed chiefly artistic problems. It should be stressed again that the Epistles of St. Paul were the point of departure for the doctrine of justification by faith alone. The artistic theme discussed in the first meeting was the relationship between Flemish and Italian painting; in the second meeting they made up a list of the more important Italian paintings and of the works of Michelangelo. On the third Sunday, when the Marchesa was absent, Michelangelo spoke of the importance of drawing for war strategy and of religious painting in general; they also discussed the appreciation of painting in Spain and Portugal and finally talked about the so-called grotesque ornaments.

In one of his letters to Vittoria Colonna, probably of 1540, Michelangelo wrote: "[Ho] riconosciuto e visto che la grazia di Iddio non si può comperare e che 'l tenerla a disagio è peccato grandissimo" (Milanesi, p. 514). ("[I have] understood and seen that the Grace of God cannot be bought, and that to hold it in disregard is a very great sin.")

In a sonnet to Vittoria Colonna, Michelangelo expresses his doubt on the value of good works:

> "Chieggio a voi, alta e diva
> Donna, saper, se 'n ciel men grado tiene
> L'umil pechato che'l superchio bene."
>
> (Frey, *Dicht.*, CIX, 97)

("I ask you, high and divine lady, to know whether
in Heaven humble sin has less value than
the supreme good.")

In a whole series of poems of the artist's last period one can find the doctrine
of justification by faith alone:

"O carne, o sangue, o legnio, o doglia strema,
Giusto per vo' si facci el mio peccato."
(Frey, *Dicht.*, XLVIII)

("O flesh, O blood, O wood [of the Cross], O
extreme suffering, through you may my sin be
made just.")

Or:

"Tuo sangue, [Signor], sol mie colpe lavi e tochi."
(Frey, *Dicht.*, CLII)

("May your blood alone, [Lord], wash and touch my sins.")

The same idea is expressed again when he says:

"[Signor], col tuo sangue l'alme purghi e sani,
Dal 'infinite colpe e moti umani."
(Frey, *Dicht.*, CLXV)

("[Lord], with your blood you purify and heal souls
From the infinite sins and actions of men.")

(See also: Frey, *Dicht.*, CXXIII.)

In another poem he paraphrases Valdés' idea that good works do not represent a personal merit, but are only the manifestation of the action of God through
the soul of man.

"Tu sol [Signore] se' seme d'opre caste e pie."
(Frey, *Dicht.*, CLIV)

("Thou alone [Lord] are the seed of chaste and
pious works.")

This concept reverts to St. Augustine and was upheld in the bosom of the
Church itself during the Council of Trent, as Jean Baruzi has shown. One must
not attribute it exclusively to Luther's Reform.

All these verses reveal that Michelangelo knew the doctrine of justification by
faith alone; he has even illustrated this doctrine in the Last Judgment (fig. 16.1).
When Michelangelo conceived the first project for it (ca. 1534), he did not yet

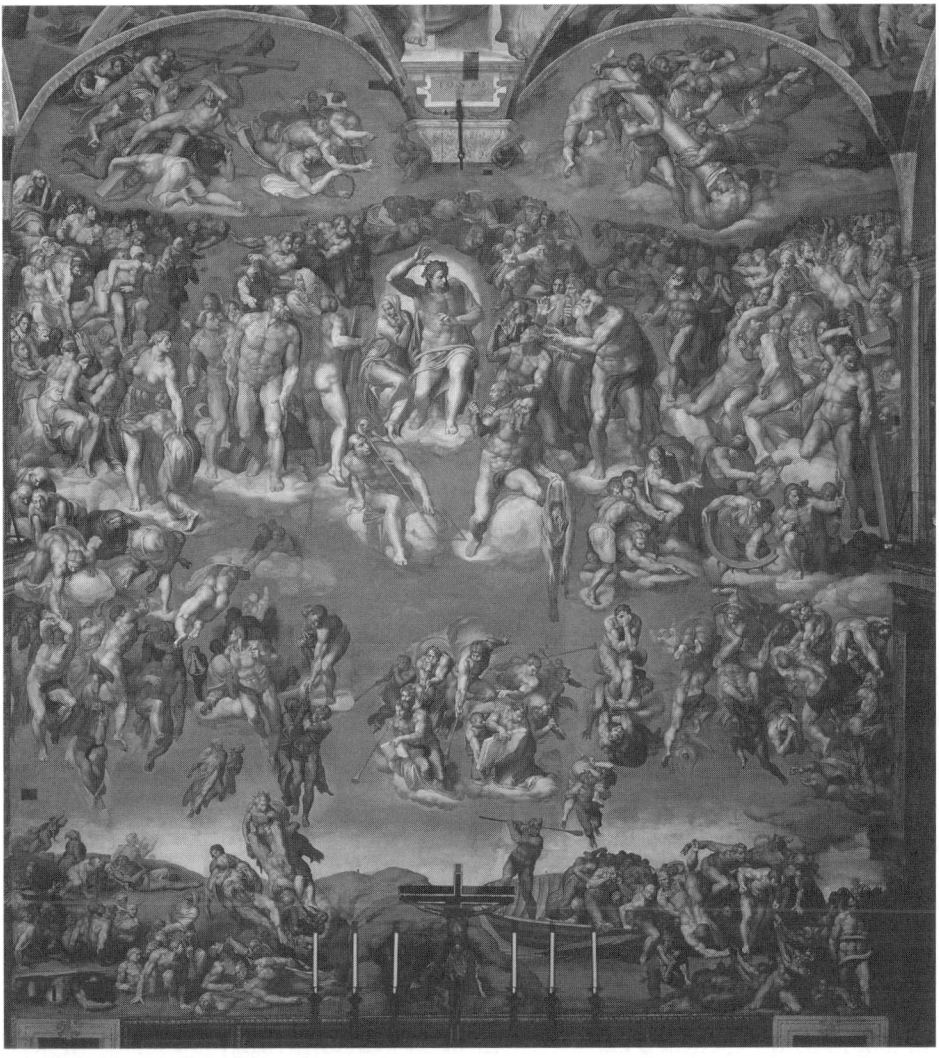

Figure 16.1 Michelangelo (1475–1564), *Last Judgment.* Vatican, Sistine Chapel. akg-images / Electa / Vatican Museums.

know Vittoria Colonna, but during the execution of the fresco he became a friend of the Marchesa, whose spirit left its mark upon the final conception. The influence of the religious ideas of the *spirituali* also seems evident in some details of the fresco.

In the early projects, in the Casa Buonarroti sketch and the Uffizi sketch, the Virgin is shown leading struggling humanity toward heaven, and, in her pose and gestures, Michelangelo still follows the traditional motif of intercession. In the final version the artist represents the helplessness of humanity in the face of *Fatum*, and the Virgin no longer intercedes; she clings to herself in fear and

313

looks down with mercy to the struggling Elect. The Saints around Christ who attempt to stop the execution of the Judgment are also helpless before this Judge: their intercession is vain. Here Michelangelo followed the same conception as Vittoria Colonna: we know from the records of the trial by the Holy Office against Carnesecchi that she believed that "the Saints do not intercede," a detail which Lanckorónska has brought out.

At the left side of the fresco one sees wingless figures floating upwards, partly without help, as if borne up by ecstasy. Some rise by means of the rosary (i.e. prayer), still others by the charity of their fellows, as described above. It is a slow and difficult ascension, carried out by faith and through the magic attraction of the Christ-sun. This motif of the fresco may be directly inspired by the doctrine of justification by faith alone.

In the group of the Rebellious Damned on the right side we have seen the struggle of the souls who, proud of their own strength, do not believe in the power of God. This explains their abandonment by the cosmic forces. Michelangelo expresses the idea that without faith and without God's help even the most powerful are helpless. This is but another aspect of the doctrine of justification by faith alone.

Thus viewed as a religious document, the final version of the Last Judgment becomes an important expression of the basic tenet of the Catholic Reformation.

In the works of art executed by Michelangelo for Vittoria Colonna between ca. 1538 and 1547, which in part are known to us only through copies, the new religious ideas are expressed chiefly by a transformation of the traditional iconographical types. All these changes contribute to emphasize the sacrifice of Jesus Christ – the crucial point of the doctrine of justification by faith. However, their iconographical innovations are still cast into the forms of the earlier works. The figures still belong to the powerful and almost pagan race of the Last Judgment and do not yet fully harmonize with the new spiritual content.

From the Marchesa's letters it is obvious that she was not able to appreciate the boldness of Michelangelo's style. In one of them, written probably in reference to the drawing of the Pietà or the Crucifixion by Michelangelo, she says: "One cannot see a better executed, more lifelike and more finished image." ("Non si può vedere più ben fatta, più viva e più finita imagine.") She especially praises the fact that it is "subtly and marvelously done." She says also: "I have never seen a more finished thing." ("Non vidi mai più finita cosa.") These sentences reveal that Vittoria Colonna appreciated (as Cavalieri had before her) the careful finish of the works of Michelangelo. It must be noted that these works, executed for the Marchesa, as well as those executed before for Cavalieri, are in a somewhat cold, classicizing style. We may conclude from this that Michelangelo made concessions to his beloved's taste. He offered gifts which he knew would please her. Like Cavalieri before her, Vittoria Colonna had therefore a certain influence even on the style of Michelangelo.

One of the works mentioned in the correspondence around 1540, between the artist and the Marchesa (*Carteggio di Vittoria Colonna*, pp. 206, 208), and also described by Condivi (p. 202), was a *Christ Crucified* "in the attitude of a living being, his face turned toward God the Father, and between two angels" (fig. 16.2). These indications suffice to identify the composition with that of the drawing in London and other copies of a lost original. According to the Renaissance tradition, the crucified Christ was shown already dead. Michelangelo represents him still alive as he was represented in the early Middle Ages. Not, as then, in the attitude of a victor with the royal diadem on his head, but as a sufferer with twisted heroic body and eyes turned toward Heaven, saying, "My God, my God, why hast thou forsaken me?" (Matt. 27: 46). Michelangelo wanted to move the Marchesa by his tragic image of Christ. The two angels, like echoes of this suffering, weep beside him, and one of them points to Christ's wound with his hand. Before Michelangelo, these angels had had the function of collecting the blood of Christ in chalices – they usually did not express the suffering and the greatness of his sacrifice. The idea of showing Christ on the Cross, not dead, but undergoing his agony, becomes understandable if we realize that the intention of the artist was to make palpable the greatness of the sacrifice. Attention may be drawn to the contrast in the gestures of the two hands of this crucified Christ: the right shows the palm with the forefinger pointing upward; the left is partly clenched with the fingers curled downward. This may be an allusion to the old symbolism of the right side as the side of good and the left as the side of evil. Michelangelo probably used this motif for the first time in the drawing made for Vittoria Colonna in which the bar of the cross is horizontal. The artist later used the same distinction in the positions of the hands in his late group of drawings in which the cross is occasionally Y-shaped. One cannot, therefore, draw any conclusion as to a significant connection of this motif with a cross of either shape.

In this composition there are empty spaces at bottom to the tight and left, giving the impression that it is unfinished. It may be supposed that Michelangelo wanted to complete the composition with the figures of the Virgin and St. John, as may be seen, in fact, in a painted copy attributed to Marcello Venusti in the Galleria Doria in Rome and in contemporary engravings. Two preparatory drawings, probably by Venusti, one of the Virgin and the other of St. John, are in the Louvre where there is, moreover, a rapid preparatory sketch, possibly by Michelangelo, for the figure of this Virgin.

There exists an alternate version of this composition in which the Virgin, St. John, and the two angels are repeated, but the Christ on the Cross is now dead. Here his head has dropped onto his chest; his arms are extended farther upward; his position is in *contrapposto*, as it was in Michelangelo's earliest Crucifixion in Santo Spirito in Florence. Engravings show the whole composition; the best among them is that of Lafreri of 1568. There is a drawn copy in the Louvre of the Christ alone (Delacre 169) and a miniature in the Missal of

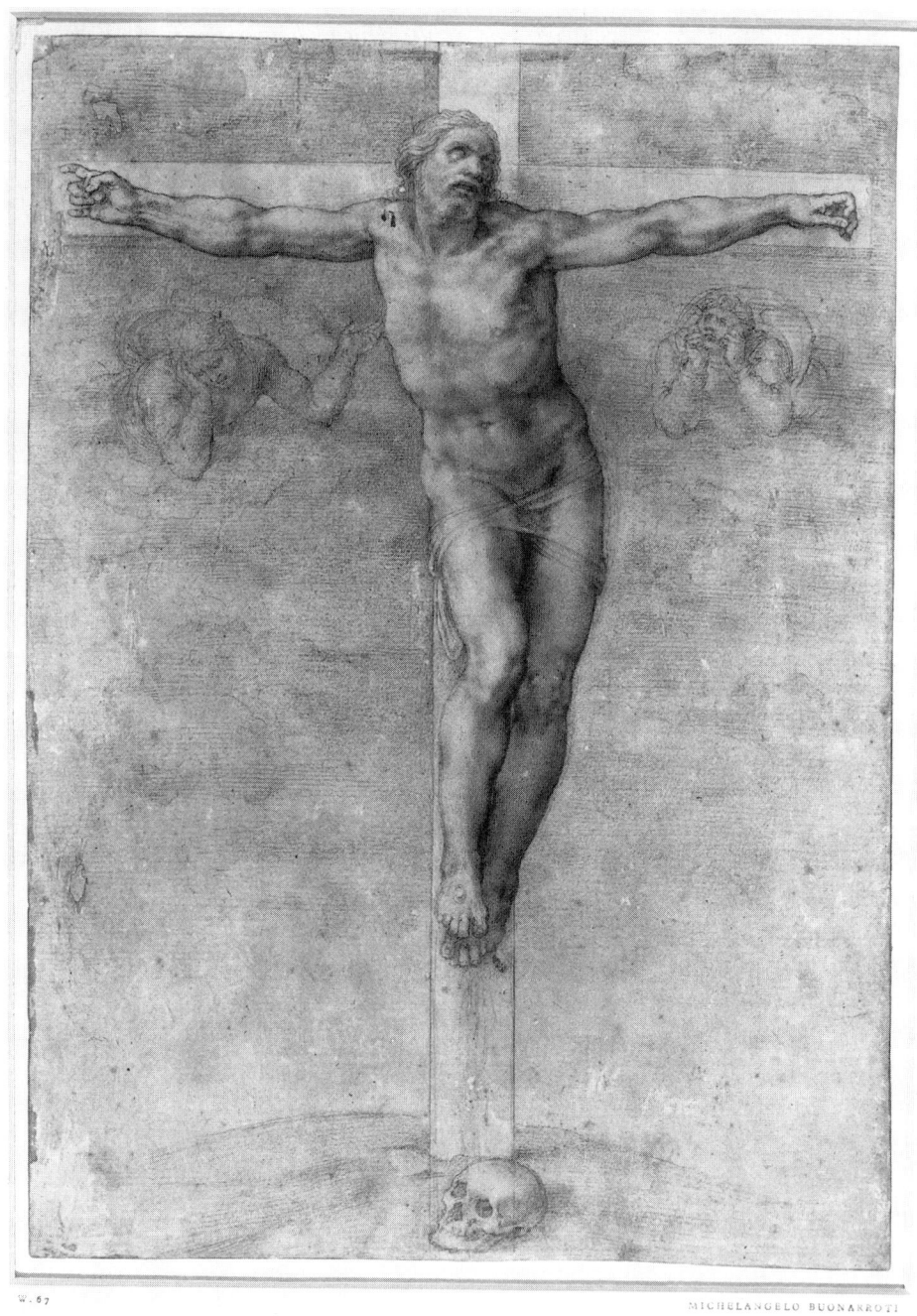

Figure 16.2 Michelangelo, *Christ Crucified between Two Angels.* © The Trustees of the British Museum.

Cardinal D'Armagnac of 1549 – a date which is the *terminus ante quem* for this version.

Since the outlines of the three main figures of the engraving of 1568 correspond to the shapes of the three marble blocks in a sketch by Michelangelo in the Archivio Buonarroti, we may deduce that the master wanted to execute this concept in marble figures larger than life size as the dimensions of the blocks are indicated by Michelangelo. The Crucifixion was to be four braccia high, approximately 2.33 m. and the figures below the cross three and three-quarter braccia, more than 2.20 m. in height. The outline of each of the three figures of the engraving fits well into the shape of its corresponding marble block in the drawing. Although Michelangelo drew the Virgin's block smaller than that of St. John, they are actually planned to be of the same height ($3^3/_4$ braccia each). The reason he drew the left block smaller is that he showed the group in perspective foreshortening. The point of view of the beholder is shifted somewhat to the right.

The character of Michelangelo's handwriting in the Archivio Buonarroti sheet points to the 1540s. It is therefore possible that the idea of making this gigantic marble group came to Michelangelo on the occasion of the death of his friend Vittoria Colonna in 1547.

In any case the type of the living Christ with twisted body and head and eyes pathetically turned upward (i.e. the first version for Vittoria Colonna) became the prototype of the most important later Crucifixion-type in Italy as well as in the North: El Greco's Crucifixion in Paris, Louvre, is a reversed version of it; Guido Reni, Rubens, Van Dyck, and other artists of the seventeenth century followed.

Vasari (1568, p. 249) and Condivi (p. 202) mention another composition which Michelangelo made at the request of the Marchesa: *a dead Christ between the knees of the Virgin* and supported by two little angels (fig. 17.1). On the shaft of the cross behind the group there is an inscription obviously to be attributed to the Virgin, "Non vi si pensa quanto sangue costa" – a sentence taken from Dante's *Paradiso,* XXIX, 91 (and there referring to the Spread of the Gospel). Condivi says that the cross resembles that of the "Bianchi" at the time of the plague of 1348, which was at that time located in the church of Santa Croce. Condivi seems to have made an error as far as the date is concerned, since the religious movement of the flagellants called "Bianchi" appeared in Spring 1399, a year in which there was another outbreak of the plague in North Italy. The Bianchi wandered from town to town, carrying a crucifix at the head of their procession, crying out, "Pace e Misericordia," and the male members flagellated themselves. It is not likely that the Bianchi preferred any particular form of the cross as one would deduce from Condivi's sentence. The miniatures in the Chronicles of Giovanni Sercambi, Lucca, Archivio di Stato, representing scenes of the life of the Bianchi, show crosses with a horizontal bar. The print by Bonasone after Michelangelo's Pietà shows that the cross was here Y-shaped, yet it had a horizontal bar at the top. It is possible that the cross in Santa Croce to which Condivi refers had the same form. That Michelangelo was inspired by the "Croce dei Bianchi" of Santa Croce is not surprising in view of the fact that the artist was at that time greatly concerned with sin and penitence (see his poems), which also played a prominent role with the Bianchi. It should also be borne in mind that Santa Croce was the parish church of the Buonarroti, in the quarter where Michelangelo lived when in Florence, where his family had resided for many generations, and where he bought several houses. Vasari briefly repeated what Condivi had written and in the Life of Marcantonio, mentioned an engraving published by Lafreri and executed by Beatrizet. These descriptions make it possible to identify the composition of which the original as well as numerous copies exist.

In the undated letter to Michelangelo mentioned above, Vittoria Colonna writes about a drawing, which is probably this Pietà, but it could also refer to the Crucifixion just discussed: "I had the greatest faith in God that He would give you a supernatural Grace to make this Christ: then I saw it so marvelous that it surpassed in all ways all my expectations: then, encouraged by your miracles, I desired that which I now see marvelously fulfilled, that is, that it is most perfect from all sides and one could not wish more, nor come to wish so much." ("Io ebbi grandissima fede in Dio che vi dessi una gratia sopranaturale a far questo Cristo: poi il viddi sì mirabile che superò in tutti i modi ogni mia expettatione: poi facta animosa dalli miraculi vostri, desiderai quello che hora meravegliosamente vedo adempito, cioè che sta da ogni parte in summa perfectione, et non se potria desiderar più, nè gionger a desiderar tanto. Et ve dico che mi alegro molto che l'angelo da man destra sia assai più bello, perchè il Michele ponerà voi Michel Angelo alla destra del Signore nel dì novissimo. Et in questo mezzo io non so come servirvi in altro che in pregarne questo dolce Cristo, che sì bene et perfettamente havete dipinto, et pregar voi me comandiate in tutto et per tutto.") This letter clearly indicates the role of Michelangelo's drawings in the religious life of the Marchesa: she believed the works of the artist to be realized by virtue of Divine Grace and considered them as objects invested with divine forces of a miraculous nature which comforted her in her private devotion.

From a letter of the Bishop of Fano of May 12, 1546, to the Cardinal Ercole Gonzaga, we learn that Cardinal Pole – at that time spiritual adviser to the Marchesa – was willing to give his drawing of Michelangelo's Pietà to Ercole when he learned that the latter wanted it. Cardinal Pole said he would not consider this gift as a loss, since he could procure another copy from Vittoria Colonna (K. Frey, *Q.u.F.*, I, p. 139). Therefore, two copies, both by Michelangelo, must have existed.

These two originals seem not to have been identical. The many existing copies form indeed two distinct groups which presumably go back to the two prototypes. The original of the earlier version is, possibly, preserved in a badly damaged drawing in the Isabella Stewart Gardner Museum in Boston. It is a black-chalk drawing on paper turned yellow and cut at top and bottom. Originally the whole cross was visible at the top as described by Condivi. This is a presentation sheet executed with the loving care and soft *sfumato* peculiar to this category of drawings made by Michelangelo for Cavalieri and Vittoria Colonna. The group appears isolated without landscape background: only the rocks emerge in the foreground, forming a kind of pedestal; no horizon is visible. The fluent modeling of the corpse, the inner logic of even the smallest fold, the expressive face of Christ with a broad, firm nose, the dreamy and sad expression of the little angels with half-closed eyes, and the Virgin's face where tragic pain appears without theatrical exaggeration are characteristics of Michelangelo.

The original version of the second drawing is lost. The unfinished marble relief in the Museo Cristiano of the Vatican seems to have been made in the workshop of the master, for the "crosshatchings" executed by a toothed chisel represent a technique characteristic of Michelangelo. However, the modeling is rather weak. An assistant (though probably neither Pierino da Vinci nor Jacopo del Duca, to both of whom it has been attributed) began this relief and perhaps Michelangelo intended to finish it. In any case a drawing, which is now lost, may be supposed to have served as a model for it.

The differences between the two versions are distinct although slight. In the drawing in Boston the hands of Christ hang lifelessly, while in the relief they are stiffly outstretched and the right hand makes the gesture of benediction. In the drawing, the right foot of Christ is visible behind the left; in the relief it can hardly be seen. The hands of the Virgin are outstretched in a gesture of despair in the drawing but in the plastic copy the fingers are spread in the gesture of an *orante*. The Virgin's foot, which is covered in the drawing, is bare in the relief. The angel at the right is seen in profile in the drawing, but is frontal in the plastic copy and the drapery of this putto is also different. On the one hand all the prints and painted copies derive directly or indirectly from the Boston drawing; on the other, all the reliefs and plaques derive directly or indirectly from the prototype of the Vatican relief.

In the Boston drawing the scene is conceived as a symbolic event: it is not unlike a "mystic wine press" made of human bodies with a rotary movement around Christ; in the relief it is a cult image where Christ is more ostentatiously presented to the beholder. We may conclude that the drawing in Boston is the first version and the relief in the Vatican stems from the second version by the master.

The origin of this composition, curious for a Pietà, can perhaps be best explained as a fusion of two iconographic types: the Virgin with the Child placed between her knees and Christ in his grave supported by two angels. In his youth, Michelangelo had made such Virgins which suggest that the Child is still protected in the maternal womb as, for example, the Virgin of Bruges and sketches in London and Paris. In the Pietà for Vittoria Colonna, Michelangelo substituted the body of Christ for the Child and added the small supporting angels, which derive from a tradition especially favored in Northern Italy, such as Donatello's relief in Padua, Santo, and paintings by Mantegna and Giovanni

319

Bellini. The resulting group with the vertical body between the knees of a seated figure and one angel on each side, reminds us at the same time of a Trinity type, for example Dürer's woodcut of 1511 (Bartsch, no. 122), or Agostino Veneto's print of 1516 (Bartsch, no. 40), made after Andrea del Sarto and influenced by Dürer's woodcut. Michelangelo might have felt this resemblance himself since he adapted his later Pietà in the Cathedral of Florence even more to this Trinity type. Looking at this Virgin the beholder is reminded of the words which she is saying in this moment of the Passion, as written in the fourteenth century Franciscan treatise, *Meditazioni della Vita di Cristo*: "E levati li occhi in cielo, con lagrime e con tutto 'l suo affetto disse: Padre eterno, io vi raccomando lo Figliuolo mio e l'anima mia, . . . laquale io lascio co' lui nel sepulcro."

Michelangelo created in the Pietà for Vittoria Colonna a severe, somewhat stiff, symmetrical composition enclosed in a hexagon, accentuating the upward movement of the Virgin's head and arms in contrast to the downward tendency of the body of Christ. The whole pattern presents a cross built of human bodies repeating in the lines of the Virgin's arms the diagonal bars of the "Croce dei Bianchi" of Santa Croce.

The Pietà which Michelangelo created in his youth for St. Peter's showed a traditional composition: the dead Christ lying on the lap of the Virgin. The accent was placed on the Virgin. In both versions of the Pietà for Vittoria Colonna it is Christ who becomes the focal point of the composition. The Virgin shows her grief in her gesture of despair and seems to evoke the immensity of the sacrifice, and the angel-putti are an echo of this grief. The harmonious, balanced, and organic beauty of the group of the first Pietà of St. Peter's is supplanted by a somewhat artificial composition in the Colonna versions. These are of an abstract symmetry and of an almost geometrical regularity. They are no longer the artistic translation into a plastic group of a concrete and human situation, but religious symbols, diagrams of a doctrine. Since the sacrifice of Christ is a fulcrum of the belief of justification by faith alone, it seems probable that Michelangelo now put the body of Christ vertically in frontal view in the center, to create a visual equivalent of this doctrine.

This composition exerted a considerable influence on succeeding generations and had a certain importance for the religious art of the second half of the sixteenth and early seventeenth centuries. The copies made during the lifetime of Michelangelo show the reinterpretation of the master's idea by contemporary artists.

In the mid-sixteenth century there was a reaction against the softness of Michelangelo's late style, and Beatrizet and G. B. Cavalieri "amended" the model according to an intransigent, crude, and hard plastic ideal. In their engravings, the stiffness of the bodies and drapery as well as the hardness of the rocks, is almost metallic: they remodeled this late work into the style of the young Michelangelo of about 1504 (Battle of Cascina). Simultaneously, other artists like Venusti and Bonasone tried to exploit the pictorial possibilities of Michelangelo's late style. It is characteristic from this point of view that Venusti completed the composition by adding a landscape which is here still a relatively discreet background but which becomes later an important setting in the hands of the Flemish artist who made the copy formerly in Gotha. Finally, as late as around 1579, Agostino Carracci in his engraved copy assimilated the soft manner of the aged Michelangelo, adding a preference for rounded forms, following those of Raphael and Correggio.

No one, with the exception of El Greco, has understood the religious depth of the expressions in Michelangelo's Pietà for Vittoria Colonna. All the other copyists have interpreted the Virgin as a pathetic actress and have not grasped the beauty of her lonely, tearless suffering. In his paintings (Philadelphia Museum of Art, and New York, Hispanic Society of America) El Greco has fused Michelangelo's Pietà in the cathedral of Florence with the Pietà for Vittoria Colonna: from the former he took the general configuration of the compact group in the form of a triangle, the body of Christ and the two supporting figures: from the latter he borrowed the lone Virgin at the summit turned toward Heaven with a sorrowful expression. It is not only the composition which is here inspired by Michelangelo but also the spirit of the group. [. . .]

The friendship of Vittoria Colonna and Michelangelo had a common basis in religion. "It was," as Vittoria Colonna said, "bounded by the tie of the Christian knot." Both came from a humanistic, liberal, and highly cultured Catholicism – the Catholicism of the Renaissance. Through the high ethical standards of Valdés, this Catholicism was transformed and became closer in essence to Northern Protestantism, without yet becoming identical with it. On the other hand, it is sharply differentiated also from the militant Catholicism of the Jesuits. The religious influence which Vittoria Colonna exerted on Michelangelo lay precisely in this liberal, deepened Catholicism which was turned toward a reform of the believers' souls and toward the inner reform of the Church.

Both outlived this period. In 1542, with the Inquisition, the Counter-Reformation began. From this moment on, the religious development of Vittoria Colonna and Michelangelo went in different directions. Intimidated by the Inquisition, Vittoria Colonna broke with her religious past and followed closely the trend of the Counter-Reformation. In her fear of being declared a heretic by the Holy Office, she broke with her friends who became Protestants, like Ochino and Carnesecchi, and even turned over Ochino's letters to the Holy Office. She associated with the Jesuits and Capuchins at the end of her life. Michelangelo, on the other hand, whose soul was fortified by Vittoria Colonna's in the early period of their association, remained faithful to his religious ideas. He was almost the only important representative of this older, liberal, and humanistic Catholicism after the establishment of the Inquisition.

Alone among all the notable personalities of the circle of Valdés, Michelangelo was never bothered by the Holy Office nor constrained to choose between the Church and the Reformation. This privileged position was probably due to the universal admiration for his art and to the fact that he was deemed inoffensive in view of his age and of his relatively solitary life. Nevertheless certain malignant rumors accused him of heresy, as for instance, the well-known letters of Pietro Aretino, mentioned above, and an anonymous letter of March 19, 1549 (Gaye II, p. 500). On the occasion of the inauguration of the Pietà by Baccio Bigio in Santo Spirito, Florence, an exact copy of that of Michelangelo in St. Peter's, this unknown person wrote: "There has been unveiled a Pietà in Santo Spirito which has been sent by a Florentine to that Church, and people said that it had its origin in the inventor of filth, saving the art but not the devotion, Michelangelo Buonarroti. All the modern painters and sculptors to imitate such Lutheran caprices paint or sculpt nothing else today for the Holy Church . . . than figures to bury [undermine] faith." ("Si scoperse in Santo Spirito una Pietà, la quale la mandò un Fiorentino a detta chiesa, et si diceva che l'origine veniva dallo inventor delle porcherie, salvandogli l'arte ma non devotione, Michelangelo Buonarroti. Che tutti i moderni pittori et scultori per imitare simili caprici luterani, altro oggi per la Santa Chiesa non si dipigne o scarpella . . . che figure da sotterar la fede.") But the Church, as has been said, paid no attention to these denunciations.

Finally, on the subject of Vittoria Colonna, Condivi had heard Michelangelo say that he "regretted nothing so much as that when he went to visit her at the moment of her passing, he did not kiss her forehead or her face, as he did her hand." Shortly after her death, Michelangelo wrote in one of his letters: "[V. Colonna] felt the warmest affection for me and I not less for her. Death has robbed me of a great friend." (. . . la quale [i.e. V. Colonna] mi voleva grandissimo bene, e io non meno a lei. Morte mi tolse uno grande amico," Milanesi, p. 528.) Symonds observes that Michelangelo uses here the masculine gender, "uno grande amico" and it may be added that he did so perhaps to emphasize that this was a spiritual and not a physical, although intimate, attachment (III, 38). Michelangelo also composed several poems inspired by the death of this friend among which the most gripping begins as follows:

> "Tornami al tempo, allor che lenta e sciolta . . .
> M'era la briglia e'l freno,
> Rendimi il volto angelico e sereno . . ."
> (Frey, *Dicht.*, CXIX)

Bibliographical Abbreviations

Bartsch	A. Bartsch, *Le Peintre Graveur*, Leipzig, 1870.
Condivi	A. Condivi, *Vita di Michelagnolo Buonarroti*, Rome, 1553. Quoted from the edition: *Le vite di Michelagnolo Buonarroti scritte da Giorgio Vasari e da Ascanio Condivi*, ed. K. Frey, Berlin, 1887.
Delacre	M. Delacre, *Le dessin de Michel-Ange*, Brussels, 1938.
Frey, *Dicht.*	K. Frey, *Die Dichtungen des Michelagniolo Buonarroti*, Berlin, 1897.
Frey, *Q.u.F.*	K. Frey, *Michelagniolo Buonarroti, Quellen und Forschungen*, Berlin, 1907.

Gaye — G. Gaye, *Carteggio inedito d'artisti dei secoli xiv, xv, xvi*, 3 vols., Florence, 1839–1840.

Milanesi — G. Milanesi, *Le lettere di Michelangelo Buonarroti*, Florence, 1875.

Symonds — J. A. Symonds, *The Life of Michelangelo Buonarroti*..., 2 vols., London, 1893. Quoted here from the third edition, London, 1901.

V. Colonna — Vittoria Colonna, *Rime e lettere*. Florence (Barbèra), 1860.

Vasari — *Le Vite di Michelangelo Buonarroti scritte da Giorgio Vasari e da Ascanio Condivi*, ed. Karl Frey, Berlin, 1887.

17

Gifts for Michelangelo and Vittoria Colonna

Alexander Nagel

In a study of that central document of Italian Evangelism before the Council of Trent, the *Beneficio di Cristo*, Carlo Ginzburg and Adriano Prosperi noted how far the culture presupposed by this bestseller of 1543 had come from the culture of civic religion so forcefully in evidence in the late Quattrocento.[1] The public processions and liturgies, the miraculous relics and the venerated saints that were taken as symbols of the city, the pomp of private and confraternity chapels – in short, the "ritual setting" studied by, among others, Richard Trexler – stand in stark contrast to the direct relation between the believer and his or her God celebrated in the *Beneficio*. Public rituals, of course, continued to be celebrated in the cinquecento, but the enormous success of the *Beneficio* – a contemporary estimated that between 1543 and 1549 forty thousand copies had been sold in Venice alone[2] – indicates the emergence of deep-seated religious needs that were no longer satisfied by these traditional ritual forms.

This article concentrates less on the causes than on the process of this transformation, which is sharply illuminated by developments in the nature and status of religious images in this period. I concentrate on works by Michelangelo that not only implicitly reveal such a transformation at work but also directly confront and interpret its implications. My purpose is not simply to show in which ways works of art came under the influence of reforming thought in this period. I am more interested in pointing out where developments in the claims of works of art converged with the concerns of reform-minded thinkers. It is my contention that new forms of aesthetic engagement elicited by works of art in this period epitomized and gave interpretative scope to some of the most significant developments in reforming thought at this time – in particular, its subjective emphasis, its preoccupation with the role of the believer's conscience in the movements of faith. The relationship was, I hope to show, mutual: the form of hermeneutic investment demanded by the one activity provided a privileged arena for the development of the other.

324

The work at the focus of this article, a drawing of the *Pietà* that Michelangelo made for Vittoria Colonna (fig. 17.1), belonged to a new category of artwork altogether: it was a drawing made as a finished work in its own right, and offered as a gift.[3] The development runs parallel to the religious developments noted above: the direct and private experience offered by the new category of artwork marks a deliberate retreat from the traditional forms of religious art, such as altarpieces, and from the entire economy of piety – the system of endowments, paid mass-sayings, and ceremonial observances – that such forms served and symbolized. Initially, in the work of Leonardo, Rosso Fiorentino, and Michelangelo himself, the new category had served as a venue for secular and pagan subjects, that is, as an alternative to religious art altogether. Here it was adopted as a means of reforming religious art itself.

In this process the notion of the gift – inherent both in the drawing's subject, the sacrifice of Christ, and in the circumstances of its making and presentation – played a key role. For Michelangelo and Vittoria Colonna, the drawing conceived as a gift was deliberately exempt from the normal economy of art production in the period. Traditional church art typically came with requirements about iconography, or at least about the inclusion of certain patron saints, requirements that were determined by the role it played within a devotional economy.[4] The stipulations that made up the painter's contract, in other words, were a function of the higher system of "contracts" – the economy of vows, dedications, endowments, and mass-sayings – within which religious art worked generally. It was the excessive reliance on this contractual system that reformers, of all stripes, most consistently deplored. The conception of art as a gift elaborated by Michelangelo and Vittoria Colonna was, among other things, an effort to remove it from this economy. For them a liberal conception of art, one that considered art a gift rather than something plied as a trade and under contract, became a privileged model for a more "interiorized" conception of religious faith, one that emphasized the direct relation between divine grace and the believer's conscience. These points are clearly made in the letters between the two that surround this drawing, where we find a highly articulate series of correlations between the claims of art, the protocols of gift giving, and the operations of divine grace.

The Art of the Gift

Michelangelo's *Pietà* drawing for Vittoria Colonna was the result of unprecedented investigations, essays at the limits of Christian iconography. It was a searching effort to interpret the meaning of Christ's sacrifice at a time when this question had become a matter of volatile religious controversy. This circumstance, in turn, reinforced Michelangelo's inclination to pursue such explorations in a private sphere, outside the conventional categories of religious art.

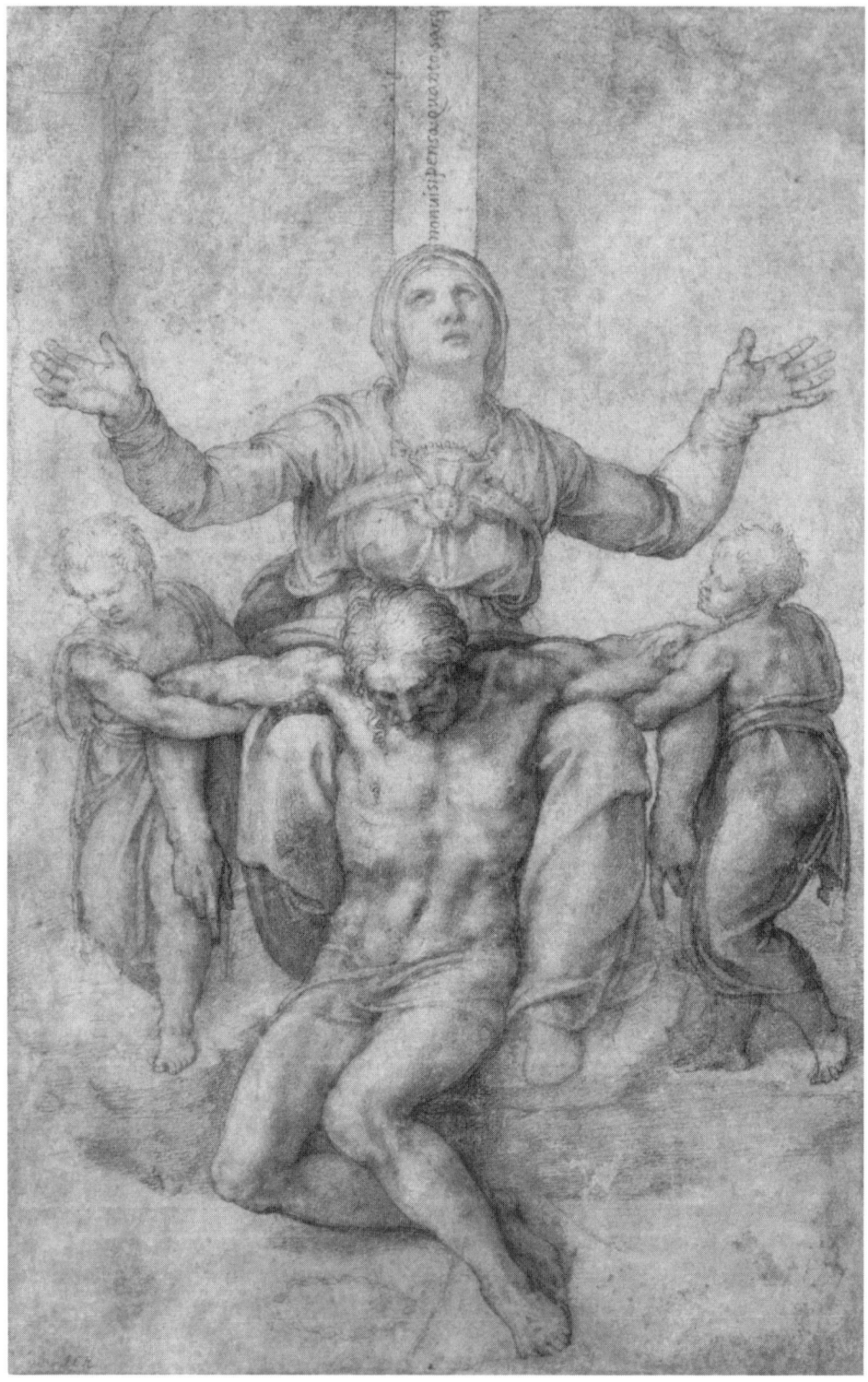

Figure 17.1 Michelangelo, study for the Colonna *Pietà*, early 1540s. Black chalk on paper. Isabella Stewart Gardner Museum, Boston, Massachusetts, USA / The Bridgeman Art Library.

326

The new category of independent drawing he adopted for the purpose was, on the one hand, unlike a preparatory study in that it expressly claimed to be a work of art in its own right. As a drawing, on the other hand, it retained an experimental quality, a freedom from the conventions that controlled finished panel painting in the period – a freedom that, in turn, reinforced the exemption from the conventional practice of making works of art on commission. The claim to freedom of invention, and the consequently heightened demand for hermeneutic engagement on the part of the viewer, was integral to the conception of art as a gift articulated by Michelangelo and Vittoria. These ideas were well suited to the very cultivated circle of reform-minded *letterati* and humanists with which Michelangelo and especially Vittoria were associated.

These reform-minded thinkers shared a sympathy for the doctrine of justification by faith expressed, most canonically, by Saint Paul (Ephesians 2:8): "For by grace are ye saved through faith; and that not of yourselves: it is the gift of God."[5] They also shared a distaste for the notion that salvation could be "earned" through works, insisting on the individual's faith in the redemption freely offered to humankind through the sacrifice of Christ. They were, however, unable to translate their sympathies into a coherent program of Church reform, and they failed to achieve the hoped-for reconciliation with the Protestants at Regensburg in 1541.

One of the primary documents of this milieu, the *Beneficio di Cristo*, appeared at exactly this time: circulated in manuscript at least from 1542, the edition of 1543 enjoyed enormous popularity until 1549, when the book was placed on the Inquisition's Index of prohibited books and, to judge from the number of remaining copies, very effectively suppressed. Written in a first version by a Benedictine monk named Benedetto Fontanini and revised, possibly twice, by the humanist and poet Marcantonio Flaminio, the tract represented the mingled strains of reforming thought in Italy, including the northern Italian Benedictine reforming movement and the Naples circle congregated around Juan de Valdés, to which Flaminio belonged until his relocation in the fall of 1541 to the community gathered around Cardinal Reginald Pole in Viterbo. In Viterbo Flaminio completed his revisions of the manuscript of the *Beneficio*. Vittoria Colonna, also heavily influenced by Valdés, moved to Viterbo in the same year, placing herself under Pole's spiritual guidance.[6]

The tract's title alone gives some indication of the central role that it accords the concept of the gift. In the concluding paragraphs we read a passage that succinctly connects this concept to the tract's main arguments. It can stand as a fair representation of the attitudes that prevailed in the Viterbo circle:

> You will say to me: "I really believe in the remission of sins and I know that God is truthful, but I doubt that I am worthy of such a great gift." I reply to you that the remission of sins would not be a gift and a grace but a payment, if God granted it to you because of the worth of your works. But I repeat that God accepts you as just and does not impute your sins to you through the merits of Christ, which are

given to you and become yours through faith. Therefore, following St. Bernard's saintly advice, do not believe only in general of the remission of sins, but apply this belief to your own case, and believe without doubt that through Christ all your iniquities are pardoned.[7]

Preoccupations with the operations of divine grace were a pervasive part of the culture of the Viterbo circle – so pervasive that even the exchange of courtesies and the practice of gift giving were, semiplayfully, couched in the terms of the debate over grace.[8] The correspondence between Michelangelo and Vittoria Colonna, which draws witty and serious parallels between divine grace and the giving of gifts, specifically the giving of artistic and literary gifts, is one instance of this practice, and deserves closer study.

There are many unanswered questions surrounding these letters. We do not know, for example, their precise date: they are usually dated between 1538 and 1541, but they have also been dated as late as 1545–46. Nor has it been possible to identify with certainty the works to which they refer. My goal in this article is not to resolve these matters – I do not believe it is possible without further empirical evidence – but to pay closer attention to the rhetoric of the letters themselves. The letters may be unclear as to which works are being discussed, but they are extremely eloquent on the question of what makes a gift, and what this has to do with art's religious vocation – questions that are, in turn, basic to understanding works such as the *Pietà* (fig. 17.1). In order, then, to come to a fuller understanding of the conception and reception of the *Pietà* drawing in particular it is necessary to look beyond these letters. In the two sections that follow, I investigate on the one hand, the process by which Michelangelo arrived at this unusual conception, and on the other, Vittoria's own writings on the Passion, which allow us to read the drawing through her eyes.

As we do not know the sequence of the letters, it is best to proceed topically, beginning with a letter of Michelangelo's that offers a brief but cogent state-ment on the nature and ethics of gift giving. The fact that this meditation is elaborated in the language of the theological debate over grace has not been sufficiently recognized, and this oversight has led to misreadings of an important passage in the letter.[9] Having been offered some items (most likely poems) by Vittoria, Michelangelo confesses that his initial impulse was to make something to give her in return, so as to receive her gift less unworthily. He then recog-nized, he says, that to introduce a gift into an economy of exchange violates the very principle of the gift, which he goes on to describe in terms of the opera-tions of divine grace: "then, having recognized and seen that the grace of God cannot be bought, and that to have it with discomfort [*tenerla a disagio*] is a grave sin, I say the fault is mine and willingly I accept these things." The letter, incidentally, confirms an observation of Vasari's, that the artist was loath to accept presents "because it seemed to him, when someone gave him something, that he was put under a permanent obligation."[10] The point of Michelangelo's letter is, however, to announce that he was able to overcome this resistance by invoking the parallel to divine grace. Through this parallel he understands that Vittoria's gift, like divine grace, is already given; it cannot be earned or paid for. To attempt to do so is to deny its unsolicited, gratuitous nature, and thus to resist it as a gift ("tenerla a disagio"). The idea is not far from ideas developed in more elaborate theological terms by Marcantonio Flaminio, coauthor of the *Beneficio* and associate of Vittoria Colonna's. According to Flaminio, divine grace is already there, like the light of the sun. It is not up to the recipient to call it down; instead, it is a matter of not acting to reject it, not putting up an obstacle to the light. And it is faith that allows one to enact this double negative, to abstain from resisting the gift.[11] In not accepting the gifts, in attempting to "buy time" in order first to make something so as to be worthy of them ("to receive them as little unworthily as possible, to make first something for you by my hand"), Michelangelo was in this sense putting up an obstacle to grace, resisting the prevenient claim of the gift. His enlightenment comes in realizing that he cannot actively take possession of them, because he is already possessed by them. Michelangelo expresses this reversal in an elegant transposition: "And I am sure, when I will have them, I will think myself in paradise, not because they are in my house but because I am in theirs."

We are, apparently, far from the conception of the gift proposed in Marcel Mauss's classic study of "archaic" societies, where the gift serves as a token of exchange and an inducement to reciprocity.[12] It is interesting for our purposes that Jacques Derrida's recent critique of Mauss marks exactly this divide. Derrida argues that even within the terms of Mauss's argument the gift resists a system of exchange by always passing "beyond measure," by being in excess of the possibility of repayment – a tendency that Mauss half avows at key points in his argument.[13] The gift, according to Derrida, is "beyond recompense or retribution, beyond economy," effecting a sort of sacrifice of economy itself.[14] Derrida's notion of "the gift" is conceived in abstract terms, separate from a given historical and cultural context. It is not my purpose to determine whether his conception of the gift is right, or to make the letters under discussion an illustration of his theory. Instead, our letters allow us to historicize and contextualize Derrida's theory itself, for in elaborating his extra-economic conception of the gift Derrida draws explicitly on a tradition of Christian thought that is in line with the tradition of reform thought here under study.[15] His debate with Mauss restages a historical debate over reciprocity and gratuitousness in gift giving whose terms were clearly established in the sixteenth century.[16] The rigorous, antireciprocal, Augustinian conception of the gift upheld by Protestant reformers, and elaborated by Derrida, itself had stoical roots, and this relation was in turn reinforced by the popularity of Seneca's *De Beneficiis* in the sixteenth century. According to Seneca, "The logic of gifts is simple: so much is given out. If something is returned it is called gain; if not, there is no loss. I made the gift for the sake of giving."[17] The gift goes in one direction and is not to be understood as a payment for a service or a loan to be repaid. The idea became a commonplace in sixteenth-century debates over divine grace and found clear expression in the *Beneficio di Cristo*:

> And what can man do in order to merit such a great gift and treasure as Christ? This treasure is given only through the grace, favor, and mercy of God, and it is faith alone that receives such a gift and allows us to enjoy the remission of sins. . . . These things cannot be accomplished or done by all the works of all humankind put together.[18]

It is the distinction of the cultivated milieu that produced the *Beneficio* and that constituted its first readership to have reintroduced this theologically exalted conception of the gift into the human sphere of courtesies and of gift giving, that is, back into the secular world of Seneca's *De Beneficiis*. Michelangelo's letter, one example of this tendency, is of special interest in that it applies these ideas to the making and receiving of art.[19] The sonnet included in the letter develops the association in even more explicit terms.[20] In the sonnet, Michelangelo compares his efforts to repay Vittoria's "immense courtesy" by his own works (" 'l mie basso ingegno") to the errors of those who believe mortal works can equal or somehow earn the immensity of divine grace. In the last three verses the analogy is fully "crossed" in a general statement on the inability of human works, specifically works of culture ("l'ingegno e l'arte e la memoria"), to repay a divine gift:

> l'ingegnio e l'arte e la memoria cede:
> c'un don celeste mai con mille pruoue
> pagar può sol del suo chi è mortale.
> (Talent and art and memory surrender: for a heavenly
> gift cannot, even with a thousand attempts, be paid by
> the sole efforts of one who is mortal.)

In another sonnet, also dedicated to Vittoria and probably written in close succession to this one, he makes explicit the theological point. What is there to repay a great benefit, he asks, so that the debtor is let free? Nothing, for such a payment would take away or deny the infinity of the gift, its absolute sovereignty over the one served, denying him the chance of receiving it in the appropriate spirit and thus of serving in return. Therefore, one must risk ingratitude if one is to acknowledge the true power of the giver, one must submit as to a lord, for there is no compensation, no possibility of adequation.[21] As Ralph Waldo Emerson was later to put it, "there is no commensurability between a man and any gift."[22] The overwhelming claims of the gift demand an attitude of submission and trust. This is why for Michelangelo – as for many members of the Viterbo circle – the capacity for faith in divine grace was itself the "gift of gifts [*il don de' doni*]."[23]

Despite its pessimism, Michelangelo's letter implicitly leaves room for a conception of art that would conform to this higher principle of grace: it is a challenge to make works of art that would, so to speak, cease to be "works" and would aspire instead to the status of gifts.[24] What, according to Michelangelo, does it take to make a work of art a gift? A further letter to Vittoria suggests that the decisive criterion is that it be made without or beyond any expectations on the part of the recipient.[25] In this case it is Vittoria, not Michelangelo, who has violated the delicate code of the gift. He scolds her for having left a "Crocifisso" – an unfinished drawing or some form of *modello* – with Tommaso de' Cavalieri so as to prompt him, Michelangelo, to complete the finished work for her. Not only does true love not have need of intermediaries, he tells her, but it consists of a faith that does not need reminders, and that operates in secret: "And although it may have seemed that I had forgotten, I was doing what I wasn't saying, in order to follow through with something unexpected [*io facevo quello che non dicevo, per giungiere con cosa non aspectata*]." Unlike a work made under commission for a client, Michelangelo's gift for Vittoria, actuated by love, is not subject to the usual surveillance: it is meant to be done in silence, and to exceed her every expectation.[26]

It is this claim to a singular and secret relation between donor and recipient that most closely associates the drawings to the sonnets that often accompanied them.[27] This is not to say that the drawings and sonnets were not available to a wider public, but only that on those occasions the public was given access to something understood to be private and secret. As Leonard Barkan has put it: "As genres, presentation drawings and sonnets are quite parallel: both are acts of introspection transferred into privacy *à deux*, but beyond that often circulated within a larger, but still private, coterie."[28] By introducing an intermediary and attempting to intervene in the gift's silent and secret gestation – in what Lewis Hyde calls the "stirring" of the gift[29] – Vittoria violated the gift's condition of secrecy, a violation whose ruinous consequences are summed up by Michelangelo in a deft and bitter pun: "My design [*disegno*: drawing *or* plan] has been spoiled [*È stato guasto el mio d[i]segnio*]." Michelangelo concludes the letter by referring the whole matter to the question of faith, through the quotation of part of a verse from Petrarch: "Mal fa chi tanta fè [sì tosto oblia]": one does wrong to forget so much faith so soon.[30] Petrarch was scolding Laura for doubting his faithful love. In that case, too, the beloved's doubts stemmed from having permitted the intervention of an intermediary, and thus from having broken the secret contract between donor and recipient. (Laura had been made to believe that Petrarch was writing to another woman under her name.) It is characteristic of Michelangelo to have appropriated the Petrarchan topos within the apposite context of an amorous relation, and simultaneously to have expanded its semantic scope to apply both to religious faith and to his work as an artist. In Michelangelo's understanding of the gift the discourses of love, art, and divine grace mingle inextricably.

Elizabeth Cropper has recently argued for a correlation between the emergence of an affective, gendered, subjectivized beholder in High Renaissance painting and a predominantly Petrarchan culture of poetic desire.[31] She argues that new conceptions of picture making in this period, Michelangelo's presentation draw-ings an eminent case among them, invoked relations to the beholder whose closest parallel and cultural model is the relation between lover and beloved, or *io* and *tu*, found in the tradition of the Petrarchan love lyric.[32] In thematizing a relation to something that exceeds the possibility of possession (that resists being treated as "property") the lyrical mode, whether artistic or literary, engages in the dynamic of the gift – a point Michelangelo makes explicitly in the letter discussed above, by invoking Petrarch in the context of the claims of his own artistic gifts.

For Michelangelo, this nexus of aesthetic and amorous claims was also con-nected to a religious discourse of divine grace and faith. It is my contention that, besides the language of the Petrarchan love lyric, the language of religious devotion – which, at least since Saint Bernard's highly influential *Sermons on the Song of Songs*, itself often made use of the rhetoric of amorous love – also served as a means by which the claims of such works were conceived and experienced. These traditions were, indeed, so pervasive that they informed the experience even of nonreligious painting, a fact that is not surprising given that many of the new secular venues for art after 1500 emerged from within the traditional religious categories.[33] To take an example close to our period, the Dominican preacher Girolamo Savonarola explicitly draws the parallel between the beholder's experience of beauty in painting and the believer's experience of Christ's love:

> Love is like a painter. The works of a good painter so charm men that, in con-templating them, they remain suspended, and sometimes to such an extent that it seems they have been put in an ecstasy and have been taken outside of themselves, and seem to forget themselves. This what the love of Jesus Christ does when it is in the soul.

In the same passage, Savonarola explicitly associates both the effects of painting and the effects of the divine with the beloved's effect on the lover. The experi-ence of love, faith, and aesthetic pleasure are thus assimilated to one another:

> Ask a man who is in love with a woman what love paints in the chamber of his imagination. He will respond, "Her face, her eyes, her movements, her clothes," and other such things. And love paints them so well that all his powers remain suspended before these pictures [*tali pitture*] and he is not interested in thinking of anything else, or of contemplating anything other than those pictures . . . If carnal love produces such effects, spiritual love, that is love of Jesus Christ, produces even more powerful ones.[34]

As we have seen, Michelangelo and Vittoria associated the claims of art specific-ally with the operations of divine grace, the crux of religious debate at the time. I suggested above that the association was bound up with the relatively novel practice of presenting drawings as gifts. In Vittoria's eyes, the quality that elevated such works to the status of gifts, in the exalted sense of something akin to divine grace, was their claim to a kind of infinity or inexhaustibility, a claim that, she realized, places a special burden on the viewer as interpreter of the work. The exemption of such works from the normal economy of works made on commission involved a semantic opening: they were not to be explicated by recourse to traditional iconographic conventions, and this meant that they required special interpretative efforts on the part of the viewer.

On receiving a drawing of the "Crucifixo," perhaps the work mentioned in the last cited letter, Vittoria confesses to Michelangelo that she could never fully comprehend its miraculous qualities: "certainly I could never explain how subtly and admirably it is done." The point was of sufficient importance for her to demand to know if the copy intended for her was to be done by Michelangelo or by his assistant, "because knowing the difficulty of imitating it, I would prefer that he [the assistant] do something other than this."[35] The drawing cannot be reduced to its "invention" or "content"; it must be visually realized by the inimitable and unfathomable grace of the master.[36] The corollary of this claim is that it demands to be appreciated by an especially receptive viewer.

A further letter from Vittoria to Michelangelo, acknowledging the receipt of a finished drawing, suggests that these claims go beyond matters of technique. In an effort to describe its effects on her, she immediately turns to the language of divine grace and faith. In an untranslatable phrase, she states in the opening words that his works urge the viewer to new efforts of understanding: "Li effetti vostri excitano a forza il giuditio di chi li guarda." The implications of this aesthetic judgment – that his works stretch the limits of human understanding – move her in the following sentence to make a fully theological pronouncement, a renewed declaration of the very principle of Christian faith: "And I have seen that all things are possible to those who believe." She underscores the shift in discourse by switching into biblical Latin in midsentence: "Et ho visto che *omnia possibilia sunt credenti* [sic]." The words, quoted from Mark 9:23, were originally addressed by Christ to the father of the possessed boy, enjoining him to believe in God's capacity to heal his son. The healing, crucially, happens only after the father squarely confronts the problem of faith: "Lord, I believe; help Thou mine unbelief" (Mark 9:24). Given what we know about Vittoria's religious concerns, it is not surprising that she would quote a biblical passage that placed an emphasis not on God's capacity to perform a miracle but on man's capacity to believe in its possibility.[37] The novel thing about Vittoria's letter is that it invokes this trial of faith in describing the hermeneutic challenges of a work of art that also tests the viewer's capacity to believe and understand. Fittingly, the analogy is completed by the according of a divine grace to the work of the artist: "I had the greatest faith in God, that he would grant you a supernatural grace in making this Christ."[38]

That special claims should be made on the individual's personal resources of belief and understanding is a direct consequence of the workings of grace, because a gift in the sense elaborated by Michelangelo and Vittoria is something singular and secret. As William West has put it, in a recent analysis of the theme of the gift in Derrida and Shakespeare, "when something *means for* someone, it is *meant for* someone."[39] Or, to return to the passage in the *Beneficio di Cristo* quoted above: "do not believe only in general of the remission of sins, but apply this belief to your own case." This belief is possible only when the individual hears the word of God and the promise of redemption addressed to her or him personally and directly. No external assurances from authorities or institutional structures can replace this personal experience of having one's conscience addressed. The true gift, what Michelangelo called "il don' de' doni," is to feel this capacity to believe stir within oneself. At moments like this, Michelangelo and the *Beneficio* are closest in spirit to the thinking of Juan de Valdés, Flaminio's spiritual advisor and an important influence on Vittoria. In the prefatory letter to his *Commentary on Romans*, a copy of which was sent to the community at Viterbo by Giulia Gonzaga (Valdés's primary pupil and the book's dedicatee),[40] Valdés terms this inner certainty "knowledge" – *conozimiento* – which he opposes to mere "opinion":

> It is very true indeed, that the knowledge which they have that Christ is the son of God, who feel not themselves reconciled to God, cannot properly be termed knowledge, being more properly opinion than knowledge: for were it knowledge it would work in them the same effect that it does in others, certifying them of their reconciliation with God, and giving them peace in their consciences.[41]

Elsewhere, Valdés describes this inner conviction and intensity of feeling as "experience":

> The first and principal intent which we who accept the Gospel ought to have, believing that in Christ God has chastised all our sins, is to get the experience of this, to the end that with our faith thus confirmed no man may be able to separate us from it, or make us doubt or stumble in it, as they are able while our faith is not confirmed with experience.[42]

Faith as experience is not a matter of understanding the doctrine propounded by preachers. Still less does it consist of a superstitious belief in the objective power of the sacraments or the virtues of miracle-working images or relics. Nor is it a matter of believing in the objective truth of what is related in the Bible. This is merely "historical faith."[43] Real faith results from the work of the Spirit in making the Word of God speak directly to one's individual conscience.[44] This fundamental belief lies at the basis of the highly private orientation of this group of reformers: they formed exclusive circles in secluded places, and used highly intimate and "secret" means of communication, not merely for fear of persecution but because such practices suited their religious orientation.[45] Theirs was not a doctrine easily adapted to the traditional modes of public dissemination; as several members of the reforming group noted with dismay, it tended to suffer a notable coarsening when it left their privileged circles and was spread to the larger public.[46]

Parallels to issues in religious art come immediately to mind. People with these tastes and this sort of religious orientation would not, one imagines, be inclined to see the commissioning and veneration of religious art as a sort of good work or as an effective means of propitiating God's mercy through heavenly advocates or patron Saints. Nor would one expect them to be interested in images laden with highly doctrinal iconography, or dedicated to the assertion of institutional authority, such as became common in Counter-Reformation imagery. It is also likely that they would have had objections to works that represent Christ's life merely as a historical drama. They would be interested, instead, in Christocentric works that directly addressed the movements of the viewer's conscience, works that inculcated in the viewer the experience of being personally implicated by the immensity of Christ's sacrifice. They would be interested, in other words, in works that made the sorts of claims described by Vittoria in her letters to Michelangelo.

Presentation Drawing and Cult Image

The drawing of the *Pietà* that Michelangelo made for Vittoria Colonna adapted a traditional form of cult image – the Man of Sorrows, or *imago pietatis* – to a new category of art. The image of the Man of Sorrows, transmitted to the West via Byzantine icons imported in the twelfth and thirteenth centuries, typically shows a figure of the dead Christ represented upright but not nailed to the Cross, and thus not attached to any one episode of the Passion narrative.[47] The image fused the upright image of the Christ of the Crucifixion with the image of the recumbent Christ on *epitaphioi*, and in its original bust-length format it also emulated icons of the Pantocrator.[48] This combination of figure types produced a paradoxical image in which Christ is shown dead but standing, pathetic but triumphant. The paradox was sometimes emphasized by "signs of life" in the figure, such as half-open eyes or gestures of self-offering. The combination of death and life in the figure was a means of alluding to the mysterious efficacy of the divine nature within the dead body, and thus of the redemptive power inherent in the sacrifice. The image's affective charge and synthetic quality contributed to its enormous popularity in the West, where it saw a remarkably free and open-ended development.[49]

Michelangelo's lifelong preoccupation with the image of the Man of Sorrows goes back to the unfinished panel of the *Entombment* now in London (fig. 17.2), whose unusual qualities are in part the result of an effort to adapt this cult image tradition to a modern conception of narrative painting.[50] Michelangelo left the painting unfinished, I believe in 1500, and later in life resumed these investigations in a more private sphere, distinctly withdrawn from the traditional categories and practices of religious imagemaking. It is well known that in his later years Michelangelo developed a disdain for "normal" artistic work and for the

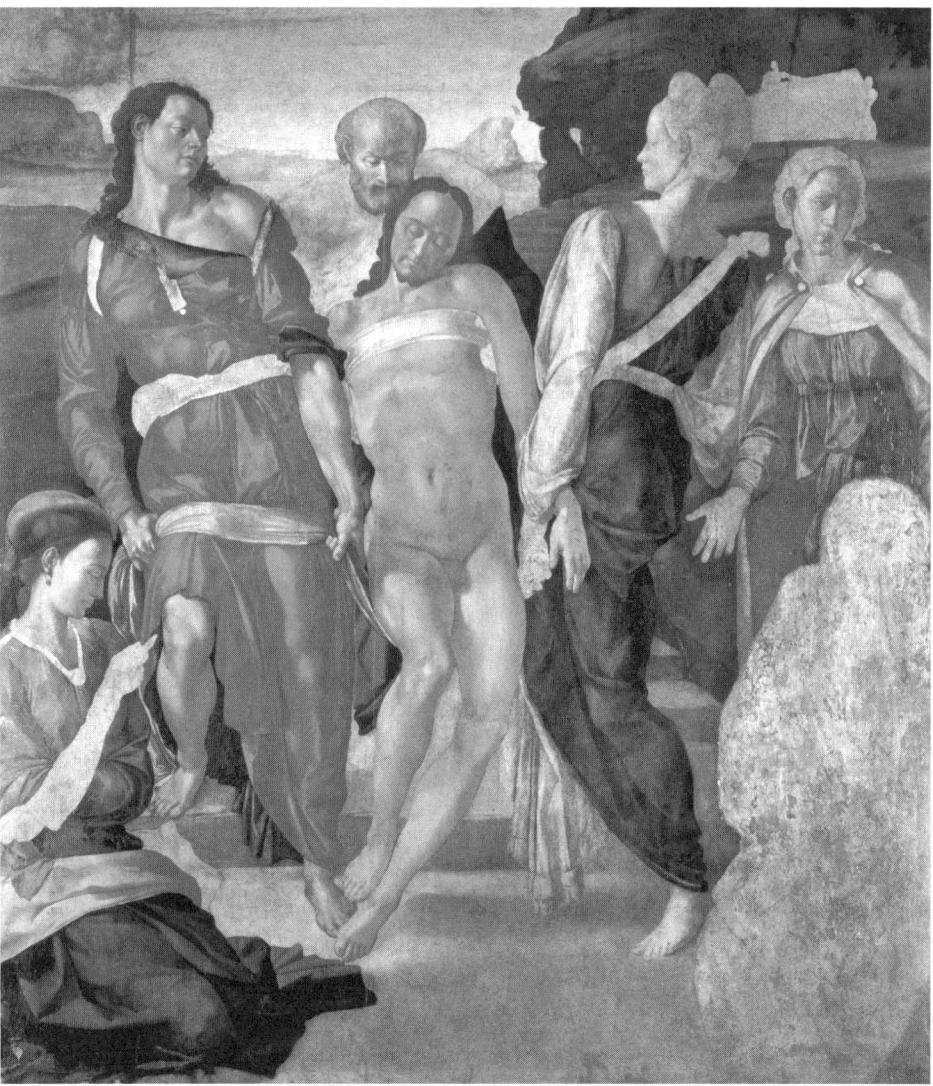

Figure 17.2 Michelangelo, *The Entombment*, unfinished panel. National Gallery, London, UK / The Bridgeman Art Library.

entire practice of making art on commission – a disdain closely linked to the aristocratic claims, familial and otherwise, that preoccupied him later in life. In a letter of 1548 to his nephew, Michelangelo irritably expresses this view, expressing regret even at having had to work for popes:

> Tell the priest not to address me any more "to Michelangelo, sculptor," because I am known here in no way but as Michelangelo Buonarroti, and if a Florentine citizen wants an altarpiece [*tavola da altare*] painted he must find a painter, for I was never a painter or sculptor like the ones who keep a shop. I have always

avoided that for the honor of my father and brothers, although I have served three popes, which has been perforce.[51]

The reference to altarpieces was made in response to a specific request, and thus cannot be taken as a general statement on the issue. Nonetheless, Michelangelo categorically associates the making of altarpieces with the inferior, workaday artist. He does not simply decline the commission; he clearly implies that this *sort* of commission is beneath him, and always has been. Don't come to me for an altarpiece, he says, "for I was never a painter or sculptor like the ones who keep a shop." Of course, he had in fact accepted quite standard commissions for church art, such as the tomb/altar of St. Dominic in Bologna and the Piccolomini altar in Siena. The important point is that toward the end of his life he preferred to think he had never done so.

The new quasi-aristocratic ethos found its clearest expression in the late *Pietàs*. They pursue the reinterpretation of the Man of Sorrows tradition initiated in the early altarpiece of the *Entombment* but abandon the realm of traditional church art altogether. The deliberate withdrawal from the economy and institutions of traditional church art coincided with a time of increasingly heated debate within the Church over the question of reform, and with a time in Michelangelo's life when any implicit affinity he may have felt for reforming trends early in life had grown, as we have seen, into an active engagement with some of the most illustrious proponents of the reform movement, such as Vittoria Colonna and Cardinal Reginald Pole. It is a historically revealing paradox that Michelangelo's efforts to preserve a tradition of religious cult imagery, appreciated precisely for its associations with past forms of public, "communal" religious life, should have been undertaken in a highly rarefied atmosphere of private investigations, new conceptions of art, and exalted claims to artistic originality.

The sequence of drawings that prepares the Colonna *Pietà* continues the effort initiated in the London painting to reinterpret the Man of Sorrows tradition within a modern conception of narrative art. They explore the mystery of the sacramental Christ at the heart of the traditional cult image, but do so within a historically determined conception of the Passion narrative. Of primary interest for Michelangelo was the interval between Crucifixion and Entombment – that is, between the end of Christ's earthly life and the triumph of his divine nature within the tomb. For Michelangelo – and, as we shall see, for Vittoria – the mystery lay in the intimate and animating contact of the dead body of Christ with his attendants, above all, with the Virgin. As in the London *Entombment*, the actors are not simply absorbed in a historical drama of lamentation. The narrative context "motivates" a form of cult to the dead Christ; the historical interval provides the window into the mystery by which the benefits of his sacrifice are transmitted to the faithful. One drawing now in Vienna, datable to the 1530s, shows Christ at the tomb supported by the Virgin (fig. 17.3). The Christ figure is modeled directly on the figure of Christ in the London painting.[52] The elaborate, episodic narrative of the painting has, however, been

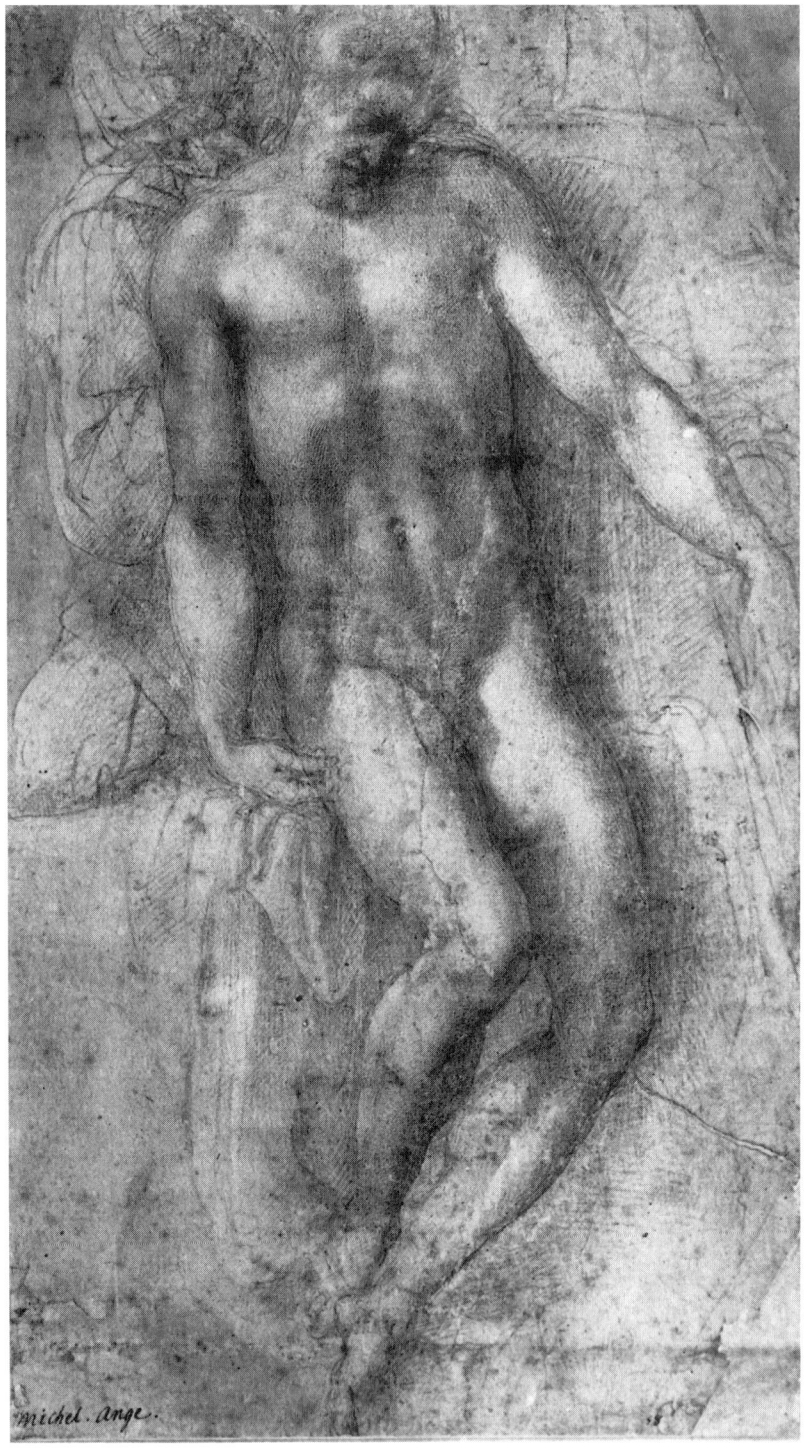

Figure 17.3 Michelangelo (attributed), *Lamentation*. Albertina, Vienna.

abandoned in favor of a stationary two-figure presentation, reemphasizing the link to the Man of Sorrows tradition. The drawing, so to speak, recognized the Man of Sorrows formula at the heart of the London painting and extracted it once again. The resulting arrangement is not unlike the Man of Sorrows compositions of Giovanni Bellini and Antonello da Messina, with the difference that here the figure of Christ is shown in full length.

In drawings closer to the Colonna *Pietà*, Michelangelo pushed this investigation to a more extreme point by increasing the number and animation of the figures even while adhering, doggedly, to the imperative of frontal display that attaches the image to the Man of Sorrows tradition. Michelangelo's preferred means of expressing this intimacy while maintaining Christ's frontal orientation was to show Christ held between the Virgin's legs. This ongoing concern with the front-facing figure of Christ, which is a prevalent feature of Michelangelo's approach to the subject from the London *Entombment* all the way through to the Rondanini *Pietà*, can be understood as a search for a Christocentric alternative to the "other" Pietà type, the *Vesperbild* tradition represented by Michelangelo's early group in St. Peter's, in which Christ lies across the Virgin's lap. That Pietà tradition served a strain of piety that was primarily Marian in orientation: it was a form of the devotion to the Virgin, structured by a parallel to the Virgin and Child image. Just as the Virgin and Child image often incorporated a proleptic reference to the future Passion, the image of the Pietà in the form of the *Vesperbild* is charged with an emotional reminiscence of the image of the Virgin and Child.[53] Not surprisingly, Michelangelo had also adapted the theme of the Virgin and Child in this more Christological direction by placing, in the Bruges *Madonna* for example, a forward-facing Christ Child in between the Virgin's legs.

The three drawings closest to the conception of the Colonna *Pietà* all maintain the front-facing presentation of Christ, while experimenting with a range of configurations. They were probably made in close succession, and are best understood as efforts to grapple with problems to which the Colonna *Pietà* offered a highly effective and condensed solution. A sketch in Bayonne, which can be dated with a great deal of certainty to 1533, shows Christ being hoisted up and separated from the Virgin, a moment in the narrative very close to that conceived for the London painting (fig. 17.2).[54] In the center, Christ is being lifted from the ground by several figures. On the right edge of the drawing, the Virgin is shown swooning and attended to by other figures. The lateral disposition of the figures immediately brings to mind Raphael's Baglioni *Entombment* in the Galleria Borghese in Rome, where the Virgin swoons at the right as Christ is being carried to the tomb at the left.[55] The difference from Raphael's painting lies in the fact that Christ is shown seated on the ground rather than in the process of being carried. In this position his torso can remain in the crucial front-facing orientation – that is, in the configuration that links it to the Man of Sorrows. The posture is, indeed, very close to that developed by Michelangelo for Sebastiano del Piombo's Úbeda *Pietà* (also in 1533), which shows an overt attachment to the Man of Sorrows tradition.[56] It would have been impossible to show Christ's body frontally while he is being carried – that is, not without returning wholesale to the strange solution of the London *Entombment*. So, instead, we have a compromise between Raphael's composition and Michelangelo's recent adaptation of the Man of Sorrows in the Úbeda *Pietà*.

In a drawing in the Louvre, Christ and the Virgin are once again placed in a closer relationship to one another.[57] Christ's head is turned to receive a violently amorous kiss, while his torso is ensconced between the Virgin's legs, a motif that Leo Steinberg has convincingly interpreted as a symbol of filial "issuance."[58] This motif also preserves the front-facing posture that attaches the figure to the Man of Sorrows tradition, and provides a key to Michelangelo's reinterpretation of the traditional cult image. The Man of Sorrows was a symbol of the life-giving efficacy of the dead Christ and thus of the redemptive power of his sacrifice, making it especially common in Eucharistic contexts.[59] The front-facing posture epitomizes this sacramental emphasis, the idea of an offering and a benefit made to the faithful. Michelangelo has refashioned these ideas by incorporating the themes of fertility and regeneration embodied in the motifs of amorous and maternal contact with the Virgin – a reinterpretation that, we will see, was very much in line with Vittoria's interpretation of the subject. This combination of imperatives – the tradition of the front-facing Man of Sorrows and the expression of intimate love – produces a strange, almost untenable configuration, which is not to be understood merely as an awkward transitional moment in the narrative. Rather than working to move Christ to the next stage in the story, the figure above attempts to hold Christ and the Virgin together in their twisted but efficacious union: Christ is front-facing, but also in a rapturous embrace that combines maternal and amorous love. In this sense the drawing represents a movement away from the episodic concerns of the *London Entombment* (fig. 17.2) and the Bayonne drawing.

A larger drawing in Vienna elaborates on these ideas.[60] Christ's body is still in a twisted pose, but now he is upright. The Virgin remains seated below and continues to hold Christ between her knees, but now at the level of his legs. The fully upright extension of Christ's body allows it to be placed in contact with a larger group of figures. This frantic activity is far in excess of the actual physical effort required to sustain a body upright, suggesting that in this contact we are seeing something more than a simple "mechanical" moment in the narrative. The activity has moved beyond the purposeful, beyond even the expression of lamentation, and into the realm of the ecstatic. Christ's body radiates light and seems almost to dance. The bodies of the attendants writhe, as if participating in an exchange of energy flowing both to and from the body of Christ. As in the Louvre drawing, the figures are not engaged in an activity that has a clear "before" and "after"; their efforts do not participate in a forward-moving narrative logic. Instead, they are absorbed in a form of animated cult to the dead Christ, as if their function was none other than to keep him upright, to preserve and celebrate his majesty in death. This understanding of the attendance on the body as a kind of mysterious rite was one shared by Vittoria Colonna, as I will show at length below. Here it will suffice to quote one of her sonnets on the Passion:

> Con la piagata man dolce e soave
> Giogo m'ha posto al collo, e lieve il peso
> Sembrar mi face col suo lume chiaro.
> (With his wounded hand, soft and sweet, he placed a
> yoke on my neck, and his weight seemed to become
> light to me with his clear radiance.)[61]

Like Michelangelo's drawing, Vittoria's poem works within the frame of the Passion narrative but moves beyond the mechanics of carrying and the drama of lamentation. The "yoke" of Christ's limbs, rather than being a burden, becomes a source of light, sweetness, and beauty. It was this emphasis on the life-giving, redemptive, "suprahistorical" qualities of the dead Christ, rather than on the tragedy of his death, that Michelangelo associated with the visual tradition of the Man of Sorrows, or *imago pietatis*, and that he developed in the Colonna *Pietà*.[62]

All three drawings in this group contain highly awkward moments: the untenable pose of the Louvre drawing, the near trampling of the Virgin in the Vienna drawing, and the partly obscured, seated Christ figure of the Bayonne drawing. The near absurdity of aspects of these drawings is, I believe, no argument against their "quality" or autograph status; it instead testifies to the extreme nature of the project, which was an effort to reinterpret the central mystery of the Christian faith in a time of volatile artistic and religious change.

Michelangelo's solution in the Colonna *Pietà* (fig. 17.1) can be understood as an extremely elegant solution to these problems. The crucial move was to introduce a difference in ground level, a feature adapted directly from the Windsor *Children's Bacchanal*, which allows Christ's body to fit neatly into the lower part of the Virgin's body. The yokelike posture of Christ's arms finds its place over the Virgin's knees, and the ground drop allows Christ's legs to be fully displayed. The drawing is thus a reduced concentrate of the physical relations explored in the preceding sheets and is more powerfully focused on the relation between the Virgin and Christ. It also makes explicit the dehistoricizing tendencies present in the drawings, and their lingering attachment to the tradition of the *imago pietatis*, by placing Christ's arms in the care of angels.[63]

The Passion according to Vittoria Colonna

Until now, I have described only in general terms the status of the artistic gifts exchanged between Michelangelo and Vittoria Colonna and the spirit in which they were given and received. I have also described the means by which

Michelangelo arrived at his solution in the Colonna *Pietà*. To come to a fuller understanding of this drawing, and what Vittoria might have made of it, it is necessary to turn to Vittoria's writings on the Passion. The most significant work in this context is her *Pianto sopra la Passione di Cristo*.[64] An extraordinarily personal and innovative attempt to penetrate the significance of the image of the Virgin holding the dead Christ, the *Pianto* presents an approach strikingly close to the approach taken visually by Michelangelo – so close as to arouse the suspicion of a relation between the two. This need not be the case; the text is valuable above all for what it tells us about how Vittoria would have viewed and understood Michelangelo's drawing. The *Pianto* is one of the most consistent expressions of the conviction that most clearly binds Michelangelo to Vittoria Colonna and to the religious thinkers of her circle: that the language of Christian faith needs to be reformed and rediscovered – that it is, indeed, the primary challenge to faith to seek the direct and dependent relation that binds it to the promise of redemption embodied in the Passion of Christ.

In the *Pianto*, Vittoria begins with a physical and affective description of the image of the dead Christ in the lap of the Virgin. Through close attention to its intimate details she draws her own inferences concerning the properties of Christ's body, the nature of the Virgin's relation to it, and, ultimately, the means by which this relation realizes the transmission of divine grace to humankind. This searching investigation and the theologically innovative ideas to which it leads are of exactly the kind that characterize Michelangelo's drawings. As in the drawings, highly intimate relations are described not merely to express the dramatic emotion of grief. We are offered something different from a "historical" scene of lamentation over a dead hero. Physical and affective relations serve, instead, as the path into the heart of the mystery: the effort to sustain the dead Christ in majesty celebrates the efficacy of his sacrifice and the claims made on the believer's faith. This arrival at religious understanding through affective "experience," in turn, parallels the forms of response elicited from the viewer and reader. The *Pianto* provides a language ideally suited to understanding the nature of the *Pietà* and thus warrants an especially careful reading.

Although the title given to the printed text was *Pianto sopra la Passione di Christo*, Vittoria concentrates on only one "episode" of the Passion, the Lamentation of the Virgin over the body of Christ. She begins by proposing to describe the "pious effect of seeing the dead Christ in the arms of his Mother."[65] She emphasizes above all the closeness of their union; Christ lies not simply on her but virtually within her, as in a tomb: she has made "of her nearly dead body a sepulcher in that hour."[66] She gives special emphasis to the means by which the affective relation between the two transforms them reciprocally. The Virgin's love and pain, until this moment modestly held back, are now, at the touch of the sacred body, allowed to flow forth:

> That fire of love and torment . . . that had consumed and penetrated the intimate
> reaches of her soul, now at the touch of the sacred body of Christ spread through

her to its maximum extent, and was released through her eyes in more bitter tears, and through her mouth in more burning sighs.[67]

These effluences have, in turn, an animating effect on the body of Christ, "such as to make him appear truly alive."[68] Vittoria is thus prompted to explain why it is that Christ's body, unlike the bodies of regular mortals, retained its dignity and majesty in death:

> Besides having the divinity which never left him, I believe he had the usual great Majesty, indeed even greater, because whereas in others death is an act of violence and deals them an offence, in Christ who had called for it and desired it with such sweetness, I believe it was an act so soft, sweet, and pious that it softened all hard hearts, and inflamed all cold minds, the ugliness of death being not only beautiful in this most beautiful face but the fierceness becoming a great sweetness.[69]

She goes on to explain how the divine qualities that had animated his features while alive left their "vestigij" on his dead form, even though they had departed with his soul at his death. These qualities were, she argues, still present on the body itself and palpable to those who attended to his body, above all to the Virgin.[70] The Virgin's response is thus more than a mere expression of anecdotal grief. She understands the great benefits that proceed from the sacrifice, and is thus filled with a paradoxical combination of joy and pain. We see her "take pleasure in this pain [*dilettar in questa pena*]," for she is aware that she holds in her arms the source of all grace. Indeed, Vittoria imagines her wishing the whole world to be present to participate in its direct transmission, "to see what she saw so that they may enjoy such immense grace."[71] She thinks above all of those for whom it was possible, historically, to assist at the event but did not. She calls all the Apostles, all those who had known Christ while he was alive, and one by one, describes how they could have benefited from direct contact with the body. She specifically states that their absence was made up for by the presence of angels, who assumed in their place the task of attending to the body: "and if not for the angels who compensated for the ingratitude of man, those who could have been there but were not would feel great sorrow and regret."[72] Thus she includes the attendance of the angels on the body of Christ – an idea that, if not directly adapted from Michelangelo's drawing, may well have been adapted generally from images of the Man of Sorrows supported by angels (the *Engelpietà*) – and explains their presence as the result of a *historical* circumstance.

It is remarkable how strictly this meditative text adheres to what might be called the conditions of historical possibility. The guiding principle of the meditation is that the very transmission of grace to humankind hinges on the virtues of physical contact with Christ in the precise interval *post mortem* and *ante resurrectionem*, and this is what brings her close to Michelangelo's understanding of the subject. A significant portion of the text consists of Vittoria urging those to whom it was possible to come and attend to the body of Christ: "and if you do not all come now it will be impossible again to see him, adore him and thank him. That time is finished that he has deigned to inhabit the earth."[73] She explains that this is the most propitious moment of all, for "even if you have seen him alive, in no other act has he displayed more his humility, indeed all of his excessive graces put together."[74] She describes the privilege enjoyed by the Magdalene, Joseph of Arimathea, and Nicodemus to have been present at the event, but gives them clearly secondary roles. The Magdalene laments Christ and accompanies the Virgin, and Joseph offers his winding cloth and consoles the Virgin.

Nothing, however, mitigates the Virgin's solitude and the greatness and exclusiveness of her burden; she is the one "who alone sustained the faith alive in her holy breast."[75] For this reason, the Virgin gives infinite thanks to the angels "who were there to make up for the absence of man."[76] Then, in a curious conclusion, Vittoria affirms that with the departure of Christ's soul it was left to the Virgin to preserve the honor and majesty of Christ before God:

> Thus the Madonna, seeing the absence of the holy soul of Christ, which alone was sufficient to honor the immense grandeur of divinity, saw that it was up to her to supply such a great debt, and would have wanted to liquefy herself, consume herself to the very limit in the fire of love and in the tears of compassion in order to rid the world and herself of such ingratitude, and to render to God the obsequy and the cult that were due him.[77]

She searches in all of Christ's limbs for a place inhabited by his soul, even though she knows that it is nowhere to be found. All of her greatest virtues, charity, humility, patience, and obedience, are exhausted and overcome in the search. In the end, it is only faith that preserves her: "solo la fede la sostenne in vita," and she in turn is the only one to sustain the faith at a time when it was entirely missing in the world. Through her the world is reinvested with that faith "which if not for her would have been extinguished."[78]

In very naturalistic terms, Vittoria's text finds in contact with Christ's dead body the means by which divine grace is transmitted to humankind. She implicitly argues that it is transmitted by means of the faith sustained at the death of Christ, initially and crucially by that of the Virgin.[79] Christian faith is thus drawn to its origins in the Passion and is specifically forged in relation to the dead body of Christ. This direct link between the Passion of Christ and the emphasis on grace sheds new light on the famous inscription of the verse from Dante on the cross in the drawing: "Non vi si pensa quanto sangue costa." In the original context, this verse alludes to the spread of the Gospel; it occurs in a passage condemning the obfuscation of the original Gospel message by the later inventions of preachers (*Paradiso*, 29, 91–96):

> Non vi si pensa quanto sangue costa
> Seminarla nel mondo, e quanto piace
> Chi umilmente con essa s'accosta.

Per apparer ciascun s'ingegna, e face
Sue invenzioni, e quelle son trascorse
Dai predicanti, e il vangelio si tace.
(They think not there how much blood it costs to sow it in the world, nor how much he pleases who humbly keeps close to it. Each one strives for display and makes his own inventions, and those are treated of by the preachers, and the Gospel is silent.)[80]

By appropriating the verse in the context of the Passion, Michelangelo radicalizes its message in a manner that could not fail to be appreciated by a reform-minded audience: if in Dante the blood refers to the effort expended by preachers and martyrs in the spreading of the Gospel, here the blood springs directly from its source in Christ's sacrifice. The reference to the amount of the blood is not made in the calculating spirit we find so often in late-medieval devotions, where it was common to count and measure Christ's spilled blood with obsessive exactitude. In a late fifteenth-century prayerbook, for example, we find the legend of a nun who, wanting to know the number of drops of blood spilled by Christ, received a vision in which Christ gave her a precise answer: "Whosoever should say 100 Pater Nosters and Ave Marias every day will at the end of fifteen years have prayed a Pater Noster to every drop [of my blood]. This many drops have I spilled for you and all men."[81] The passage is illuminating in clearly revealing the link between this calculating mentality and a numbers-oriented approach to the saying of prayers. This link, of course, also marked the system of indulgences, which had a direct bearing on the image of the Man of Sorrows, one of the most heavily indulgenced images of the late Middle Ages.[82]

The members of the Viterbo circle had nothing but disdain for this entire array of practices, and Michelangelo's drawing was in every sense understood as an alternative. In Michelangelo's drawing the cost and quantity of Christ's blood are invoked in a spirit of grandiose irony, in order to stress the giftlike incalculability of Christ's sacrifice. The "cost" of redemption is beyond reckoning ("non vi si pensa"). There is no way to render it or account for it, as the nun above was able to do through the counting up of prayers. The antinumerical irony is, in fact, very similar to that voiced by Christ (Matt. 18: 21–22) when asked by Peter, "'Lord, how oft shall my brother sin against me and I shall forgive him? Till seven times? Jesus saith unto him, 'I say not unto thee, Until seven times: but, Until seventy times seven.'" In stark contrast to the computing Christ that appeared in the nun's vision, the Christ of the Gospel compounds the digit seven not to correct Peter's calculations but to explode Peter's quantitative reasoning altogether. By such irony Christ points Peter toward the infinite forgiveness proper to divine grace, which Christ goes on to illustrate (in the explicit terms of money and gifts) through the parable of the king who frees the indebted servant of all payment (Matt. 18: 23–35).[83]

Like Vittoria's text, and a host of other writings produced in her circle, Michelangelo's drawing was an effort to establish a direct relation to the source of grace in Christ's sacrifice. The *Pietà* and the *Pianto* have several motifs in common: the centrality of the body of Christ, its enfoldment within the lap of the Virgin, the presence of the angels "who wished to assume the human weight," and finally the special role given to the Virgin. What binds them above all is the emphasis they both place on engendering and amorous motifs, for which they could have found inspiration already in Dante's use of the verbs *seminare* and *accostarsi* to describe the spreading and reception of the Gospel. In both Vittoria's and Michelangelo's interpretations, these metaphors assume a physical immediacy in direct relation to the body of Christ. The series of studies that prepared the way for Michelangelo's drawing for Vittoria are an extremely close visual analogue to Vittoria's passionate and highly erotic rhetoric: "That fire of love and torment . . . that had consumed and penetrated the intimate reaches of her soul . . . was released through her eyes in more bitter tears, and through her mouth in more burning sighs."

The compact solution offered in the drawing for Vittoria (fig. 17.1) replaces the overt rhetoric of physical intimacy with more profoundly figurative allusions to generation and fertility. Christ is nestled deep down between the Virgin's legs, and the lower half of his body is submerged below ground. At a concrete and literal level, such an arrangement effectively displays the heaviness of the dead body and suggests its imminent interment.[84] At a "figural" level, however, Christ's simultaneous embeddedness in the Virgin's body and in the earth combines a figure of birthing with a figure of horticultural growth. There is, in fact, very little emphasis placed on Christ's wounds or the deadness of the body. Instead, the drawing throughout suggests an incipient stirring, a lifegiving energy that contrasts the deathward tendency.[85] The two "senses" in the drawing, deathward and lifeward, are simultaneous, inseparable, and mutually reinforcing. The womb, as Leo Steinberg has put it, is conjoined with the tomb, an idea clearly expressed by Vittoria when she says that the Virgin had made "of her nearly dead body a sepulcher in that hour." Because Christ's death is itself the source of regeneration, the process of entombment, the gift of death, is inseparable from the renewing of life, the giving of birth. His death is a birth, and his dead body ambiguously flickers with signs of life. As Vittoria explained, Christ is dead, but since he "had called for it and desired it with such sweetness" – in the drawing Christ is shown with both hands semiwillfully pointing downward[86] – his body does not show the violence of death but rather a radiant beauty that suggests life. As we have seen, Vittoria was careful to point out that the animated "vestigij" of life that were discernible in the dead body (even before it was "glorified in a better life" in the Resurrection) were not quite objective features: they shine for those who see them, and above all for the Virgin who was closest to him. They shine, that is, for those who see the life in the death, the redemption in the sacrifice.

We are far, here, from the emphasis on Mary's grief found in so many late medieval Passion dramas, and in general we are far from the entire Marian orientation of late medieval piety.[87] The reference to birthing, for example, is not simply a version of the sentimental tradition associated with Pietà imagery, according to which the Virgin remembers having the Child in her lap. The motif insists, instead, on the more profoundly theological point of Christ's death as a source of regeneration. The drawing, like Vittoria's text, is concentrated not on the drama of lamentation but on the mystery of redemption through Christ's sacrifice, and locates it in the stirring of a life force within the dead body. The implied descent tombward simultaneously releases a lifeward energy. Christ's downward-pointing arms are answered by the Virgin's upward gesture, a movement that continued, before the drawing was cropped, up through the arms of the Y-shaped cross. This combination of downward and upward movement is Michelangelo's most consistent "figure" for the paradox of Christ's sacrifice: where the historical blood of Christ's mortal body ran down the cross, the "verse of blood" – the everflowing wellspring of grace – runs up the cross.

Vittoria's letters to Michelangelo, studied above, reveal that for her such a drawing does not merely represent the mystery of the gift: it embodies and enacts it, both through its unfathomable technique and through its figural inexhaustibility. Its meaning is not reducible to an objective doctrinal content but arises through the viewer's experience of the configuration and energy of the drawing. And the viewer's receptivity to the drawing's delicate ambiguities, far from merely being a path to understanding a mystery, is itself an instance of the mystery at work. When Vittoria asserts that Michelangelo's drawings move the viewer to new efforts of understanding ("li effetti vostri excitano a forza il giuditio di chi li guarda"), she is not only making an aesthetic judgment. For Vittoria, to be receptive to the hermeneutic challenge of this kind of art – an art, that is, conceived as a gift – is to engage in the very movements of faith, to open oneself as one does in receiving divine grace. It is to see that "all things are possible to those who believe."

Art and Religion in an Age of Reform

In an illuminating study on books as gifts in the sixteenth century, Natalie Zemon Davis studied the effect of the early modern book market on the medieval tradition according to which knowledge was a gift that could not be sold. "Could such a cultural ideal," she asked, "survive the desacralising technology of the printer's shop?"[88] The problem was, for her, an instance of the larger problem, raised by Mauss, of the decline of a premodern culture of gift exchange with the rise of modern conceptions of absolute property. Davis showed that, although it succumbed to various pressures, the tradition of knowledge as a gift was powerful enough to insure that the book continued to be treated, in various ways, as "a privileged object that resisted permanent appropriation." The book's status as a gift was reaffirmed especially forcefully, she noted, in Protestant circles.[89]

Michelangelo's and Vittoria Colonna's preoccupation with the ethics and aesthetics of the gift was part of a similar backlash. They, too, sought an alternative to the latter-day "economization" of religious devotion, to the prevailing system of works, indulgences, and "endowments" in which art production had become so centrally implicated. And their rejection of these "modern" abuses likewise led to an emphasis on gift giving as a means of restoring originary and thus purer religious values, a project of restoration and reformation that was, in their case, bound up with a distinct reassertion of aristocratic ideals. Their originality was to see in an emerging liberal conception of art, one exempt from the economy of works made on commission, a potential avenue for the reform of the religious image and a privileged model for the type of internal religious experience they espoused.

This convergence of sophisticated aesthetic tastes and reformist ideals belongs to a special moment in Italian religious and cultural history. It is, indeed, one instance of the optimism and hopes for reconciliation that generally mark this earlier, more fluid phase of reform in Italy. But even at this time, even in the midst of the Viterbo circle, there were those who had to admit to a conflict between their artistic tastes and their religious convictions. This is the thrust of a letter of January 23, 1540, from Francesco della Torre to Donato Rullo, both friends of Marcantonio Flaminio and Cardinal Pole:

> I have received from him [Cardinal Pole] verses by Messer Marcantonio [Flaminio], and when I have collected some others I will send you those as well, which in my judgment will satisfy you much more, since they are that much more lovely [*vaghi*] and more beautiful [*venusti*] when they treat of matters that are more capable of loveliness [*più capaci di vaghezza*], for in truth in trying to treat these matters of religion in a lovely manner [*vagamente*] more often than not one merely makes the sacred profane: and I believe it is a difficult thing to do it well, and with dignity. These others are of pastoral and amorous subjects, but be careful not to show them to certain Stoics who are scandalized by everything.[90]

The parting of the ways between art and religion implicitly acknowledged here was already clearly recognized in the north, due to the earlier and more violent impact of the Reformation. In 1522, for example, Luther's protector Franz von Sickingen acknowledged that church images were all too often appreciated for their "art and beauty" rather than for their religious significance, and he suggested that they should be used instead as "ornaments in fine rooms" – that is, in a secular setting – so that the effort and expense that went into them would not be in vain.[91] Sickingen's cultivated and accommodating sense of decorum was, of course, to become a point of doctrine for Calvin, for whom images were inherently in contradiction to the tenets of the Christian religion. As a man of learning Calvin did not condemn image making per se; he believed that it should be cultivated as an art, which he considered a gift from God. The only "pure and legitimate use" of art, for Calvin, was thus as a secular pursuit.[92]

The separation was never so sharply drawn in Italy but, as the letter of Francesco della Torre quoted above clearly shows, there was a clear awareness of an emerging incompatibility. When Federico Gonzaga, in 1524, asked Baldassare

Castiglione to acquire a work by Sebastiano del Piombo, of any kind "so long as it is not about Saints, but rather something lovely and beautiful to look at [*non siano cose di sancti, ma qualche pitture vaghe et belle da vedere*]," it is probable that he was not merely stating an iconographic preference.[93] The phrasing ("ma") implies, quite clearly, that religious images tend not to belong to the category of pictures that are lovely and beautiful to look at. Without leaning too heavily on the phrasing, the main thrust of Gonzaga's comment is clearly that secular subjects offer better opportunities for the display of artistic excellence – that they are, in della Torre's neat phrasing, "*più capaci di vaghezza.*"

By Vasari's time this concern – that religious art is not necessarily compatible with artistic elegance – had become a matter of explicit debate. In a passage that introduces his 1550 Life of Fra Angelico Vasari clearly identifies the issue, referring to paintings made by "men of little belief," which "excite dishonorable appetites and lascivious desires, so that the work is blamed for what is disreputable, while praise is accorded its artistic excellence." Nonetheless, he holds out for the possibility that modern aesthetic ideals can still serve the purposes of religion. People should not, he says, be fooled into thinking that only an awkward, clumsy thing – "goffo et inetto," terms he uses repeatedly to describe medieval art[94] – can be devout, and that modern paintings with more beautiful figures must be more lascivious. By the second edition of 1568 circumstances had changed. With the Counter-Reformation in full force and Michelangelo's *Last Judgment* undergoing "revision," Vasari's earlier optimism concerning the unity of beauty and religion became more guarded. Vasari cautions that he does not want anyone to believe that he approves of "those figures in the churches that are painted practically nude, because in them one sees that the painter has not had the appropriate respect for the place." Again, the pursuit of artistic beauty is not condemned per se, but is relegated to a properly nonreligious sphere. Fra Angelico now assumes a more motivated role within Vasari's historical scheme, representing a pinnacle of Christian art between the artistic deficiencies of the "devout" Middle Ages and the religious indecorousness of the nudes of Vasari's own day, fine and good work though it may be on artistic grounds.[95]

Michelangelo's drawing was an attempt to mend the split – the divorce that, in Vasari's account, had arisen since Fra Angelico's time – and it was produced within a milieu that was especially inclined to appreciate the effort. Michelangelo had initially used the new category of the "presentation drawing" for the exploration of obscure, largely pagan subjects, often with strongly erotic associations. He was now determined to make this most modern of artistic arenas the site of a new kind of religious image, to forge a new link between artistic and divine *grazia* – "a difficult thing to do . . . well, and with dignity," as della Torre says. The result was a drawing that is clearly attached to a medieval cult-image tradition – indeed, is marked throughout by a conscious archaism[96] – even while making the most modern aesthetic claims. The old cult image was thus in a sense preserved, but in a highly rarefied and attenuated form, one that offered a profound introversion of the image's traditional public function and address.

The Man of Sorrows was reinvented as a work of art, and in this way became a privileged model for the understanding of religious faith espoused by Vittoria Colonna and her circle – a conception of faith that, similarly, developed a quite modern psychology of spiritual experience in the name of restoring a purer, evangelical Christian ideal.

This delicate marriage of religious and aesthetic ideals proved as fragile and short-lived as the culture for which it was made. The work's status as a near *unicum* is, in fact, the clearest mark of its tenuous and revealing historical position. The artistic claims that Michelangelo defended and that Vittoria Colonna celebrated – the idea that art is made "liberally" and not plied as a trade, that it results from a free process of invention, that it presents as yet unrealized ideas and thus makes special hermeneutic demands on its viewer – were to become the very basis of a secular conception of art whose primary locus was to be the private cabinet and the picture gallery. Likewise, the notion of art as a gift, far from providing the basis for a reformation and preservation of religious ideals, became the basis for an even more radical marketing of art as a commodity: the claim of the artwork's autonomy and disinterestedness was in fact the corner-stone of a truly free art market, one no longer based on the premodern system of art made on commission. And the same goes for the private address offered by this conception of art: if at first it was bound up in an exalted notion of the gift and couched in an exquisite discourse of aristocratic courtesy, it was ultimately institutionalized in a quite bourgeois conception of art as private property.[97] Before it was definitively inherited by the modern collector, however, such a conception of art emerged as an indeterminate alternative, still without a category and powerfully resistant to appropriation.

Notes

I wish to thank Gadi Algazi, Leonard Barkan, Elizabeth Cropper, Natalie Zemon Davis, Valentin Groebner, Bernhard Jussen, Thomas Lentes, John Paoletti, Christopher Wood, and my two anonymous *Art Bulletin* readers for their comments on this paper. I am also grateful for a Getty Postdoctoral Fellowship during the year 1995–96, which allowed this article truly to develop under the conditions of a gift. All translations are mine unless otherwise indicated; I have included the original texts when they contain significant wordplay or involve matters of philological interest.

1 Ginzburg and Prosperi, 187.
2 The estimate, perhaps exaggerated, was made by Pier Paolo Vergerio; see Fontanini, 444.
3 On the question of drawings made as finished works in their own right, see Johannes Wilde, *Michelangelo: Six Lectures*, Oxford, 1978, 147–58; and Hirst, ch. 10, "The Making of Presents." I follow Wilde and Hirst in describing this type of work as a presentation drawing, and thus distinct from a *modello*, which is a finished design for a project yet to be realized, more often than not in another medium. This is, of

course, not to deny the fact that *modelli* were often deemed worthy of being collected in their own right. I follow Tolnay, 426r., and Hirst, 117, among others, in identifying the Colonna *Pietà* with the drawing now in the Isabella Stewart Gardner Museum in Boston (black chalk, 29.5 × 19.5 cm). An especially strong argument in favor of this attribution is Tolnay's observation of a *pentimento* in the left foot of the left-hand angel. None of the arguments made in this article, however, depends on this attribution.

4   See, for example, the negotiations involved in the making of Francesco Pesellino's Trinity altarpiece, now in the National Gallery, London, which can be reconstructed from the documentation published by Pèleo Bacci, *Documenti e commenti per la storia dell'arte*, Florence, 1944, 113–51. An informative account of the situation in the Venetian context is offered by Peter Humfrey, *The Altarpiece in Renaissance Venice*, New Haven, 1993, pt. 1, ch. 2, "Purposes and Uses." See also Creighton Gilbert, "Peintres et menuisiers au début de la Renaissance en Italie," *Revue de l'Art*, XXXIII, 1977, 9–28; and Charles Hope, "Altarpieces and the Requirements of Patrons," in *Christianity and the Renaissance: Image and Religious Imagination in the Quattrocento*, ed. Timothy Verdon and John Henderson, Syracuse, 1990, 536–71. On the development of the private mass in the late Middle Ages, see Joseph Jungmann, *The Mass of the Roman Rite: Its Origins and Development*, trans. Francis Brunner, I, Westminster, Md., 1986, 103ff.; John Bossy, "The Mass as a Social Institution 1200–1700," *Past and Present*, C, 1983, 29–61; and Jacques Chiffoleau, "Sur l'usage obsessionnel de la messe pour les morts à la fin du Moyen Age," in *Faire croire: Modalités de la diffusion et de la reception des messages religieux du XIIe au XVe siècle*, Rome, 1981, 238–45. On its place within the economy of late-medieval piety generally, see John Bossy, *Christianity in the West 1400–1700*, Oxford, 1985, esp. 3–75. For the specific case of Florence, see Richard Trexler, "Ritual Behavior in Renaissance Florence: The Setting," *Medievalia et Humanistica: Studies in Medieval and Renaissance Culture*, n.s., IV, 1973, 125–44.

5   *The Holy Bible*, King James Version, Nashville, 1970.

6   See Dermot Fenlon, *Heresy and Obedience in Tridentine Italy: Cardinal Pole and the Counter Reformation*, Cambridge, 1972, 70–71. On the northern Italian Benedictine reform movement, with which Pole had early associations (Fenlon, 30ff.), see Barry Collett, *Italian Benedictine Scholars and the Reformation: The Congregation of Santa Giustina of Padua*, Oxford, 1985. The connections between Michelangelo, the Viterbo circle, and the *Beneficio di Cristo* are somewhat more than a matter of inference; they are also indicated by the circumstances described in Francisco de Holanda's *Dialogues on Painting*, in which discussion with Michelangelo and Vittoria Colonna takes place at the church of S. Silvestro al Quirinale, after sermons on Saint Paul by "Fra Ambrogio" – Fra Ambrogio Catarino Politi, the author of an extended critique of the *Beneficio*, in response to which Flaminio made his revisions to the text in Viterbo in 1542. Catarino's text is published in Fontanini, 347–422. For the date of Flaminio's revisions, see Ginzburg and Prosperi, 69–70, where they also entertain the hypothesis that the manuscript of the *Beneficio* reached Catarino's hands through Vittoria Colonna herself. Although the historical reliability of de Holanda's dialogues is still debated, especially with regard to the opinions attributed to Michelangelo, the veracity of these matters of setting and circumstance has been convincingly argued by Deswarte-Rosa, esp. 358. John Bagnell Bury, *Two*

Notes on Francisco de Hollanda, London, 1981, has proposed cogent arguments in favor of de Holanda's reliability with regard to Michelangelo's ideas, a view also strongly, if for the most part implicitly, supported by the study of David Summers, *Michelangelo and the Language of Art*, Princeton, 1981. The most revealing portrait of Vittoria's religious life in these years was offered by Flaminio's friend Pietro Carnesecchi, during his later heresy trial. He remembered that he, Alvise Priuli (also a close associate of Pole's at Viterbo), and Flaminio would visit Vittoria often, and that on matters of dogma they would speak almost exclusively of justification by faith; Manzoni, 269: "I do not remember that on questions of dogma we spoke of anything other than justification by faith, and on this matter I cannot say with certainty where she stood, but suffice to say that she attributed much to grace and faith in her conversations."

7   Quoted after the translation in Gleason, 159. For the Italian, see Fontanini, ch. 6, f. 67v., 81.

8   Examples will be quoted as the argument proceeds. To take one example, however, in a letter of 1541 to Cardinal Pole Vittoria toys, punningly but not entirely playfully, with the analogy; Sergio M. Pagano and Concetta Ranieri, *Nuovi documenti su Vittoria Colonna e Reginald Pole*, Vatican City, 1989, 95: "La supplico che con la sua carità anzi de Christo con la quale ogni molestia suffre, me perdoni de 'l molesto in mandarle certe frascarie, et se ben con San Paulo V.S. suol dire che è più beata cosa el dare che 'l recevere, contentise dare ad me questa beatitudine" (I beg you that with your truly Christlike charity, with which you suffer any annoyance, you will forgive me if I bother you in sending you certain frivolities, and as you like to say with Saint Paul that it is a more beatific thing to give than to receive, then please grant me this beatitude). Pole was directly connected to the focus of gift giving studied here, for he owned a version of Vittoria's *Pietà*. A well-known letter from the bishop of Fano to Cardinal Ercole Gonzaga gives some sense of Pole's attitude toward such gifts, suggesting that he believed that they should be as freely given as they were received; Karl Frey, *Michelangelo: Quellen und Forschungen*, Berlin, 1907, 139: "Monsignor Pole has learned that you would like a Christ by the hand of Michelangelo, and has asked me to confirm discreetly whether this is so: because if indeed it is, he has one by the master's hand that he would gladly send to you; but it is in the form of the Pietà [i.e., the *imago pietatis*], even though the whole body is shown [*ma è in forma di Pietà, pure se gli vede tutto il corpo*]. He says this would not be a loss to him, as he can obtain another from the Marchioness of Pescara [Vittoria Colonna]." On the meaning of the expression "in forma di Pietà" or "in forma pietatis" as a reference to the *imago pietatis*, or Man of Sorrows, rather than to the type we now more commonly describe by the word *pietà* (the *Vesperbild*, with Christ recumbent across the Virgin's lap), see note 63 below. Here the reference is quite clear, as the author felt it necessary to specify that Christ is shown in full length, as opposed to the half-length type of the Man of Sorrows commonly found in Italy. My anonymous *Art Bulletin* reader, who has consulted the original letter in Mantua, kindly informed me that the author of this letter was not Cosimo Gheri, as Frey suggests, but Pietro Bertano, his successor, and that it is to be dated ca. 1546.

9   Barocchi et al., IV, 122: "Volevo, Signiora, prima che io pigliassi le cose che Vostra S[igniori]a m'à più volte volute dare, per riceverle manco indegniamente ch'i' potevo,

fare prima qualche cosa a quella di mia mano; dipoi riconosciuto e visto che la gratia d'Iddio non si può comperare, e che'l tenerla a disagio è pechato grandissimo, dico mie colpa, e volentieri dette cose accecto. E son certo, quando l'arò, non per ave[r]le in casa, ma per essere io in casa loro, mi parrà essere in paradiso. . . ." E. H. Ramsden, *The Letters of Michelangelo*, II, London, 1963, 4, missing the analogy between divine grace and gift giving, offers what I believe to be a flawed translation of the passage: "Then I came to realize that the grace of God cannot be bought, and that to keep you waiting is a grievous sin." Creighton Gilbert, in *Michelangelo: The Complete Poems and Selected Letters of Michelangelo*, ed. Robert Linscott, trans. Creighton Gilbert, New York, 1965, 267, offers a largely similar reading: "[T]hen, having realized and seen that the grace of God is not to be bought and it is a great sin to keep you in suspense. . . ." My reading of the text, where the pronoun "la" refers to "la grazia di Dio" and not to Vittoria, is borne out by the poem included in the letter, which I discuss below. My thanks to Leonard Barkan, Stefano Cracolici, and Brian Stock for discussing the translation of this letter with me.

10 Giorgio Vasari, *Le vite de' più eccelenti pittori, scultori et architettori* . . . (1568), VI, ed. Paola Barocchi and Rosa Bettarini, Florence, 1987, 112.

11 Flaminio introduced the simile in a letter to Gasparo Contarini, probably from 1538, in an effort to clarify a debate over whether the act of faith was itself the result of divine grace or of free will. Quoted in Alessandro Pastore, *Marcantonio Flaminio: Fortune e sfortune di un chierico nell'Italia del Cinquecento*, Milan, 1981, 97: "I say there are two opinions, one of which appears to say that the grace of the Lord is like the sun, which by itself illuminates equally everyone, and thus that putting or not putting up an obstacle to this heavenly light is the mere operation of our free will. The other opinion says that without particular grace and help from God man does not abstain from raising opposition to this divine light. The first opinion is defended by you; the second by Tullio [Crispoldi]." (Flaminio was on Crispoldi's side in the debate.) In a letter to Marguerite d'Angoulême (Ferrero and Müller, letter 112, 186–87), Vittoria Colonna speaks in similar terms of an internal resistance to grace, and like Michelangelo she invokes the divine parallel in the context of an interpersonal relationship of courtesy (in this case, the issue is a hoped-for personal visit). Marguerite's generosity and wisdom is like the celestial manna to the Hebrews, "and if in their case the effect of grace greatly outdid their expectations, in my case similarly the usefulness of seeing your majesty will outstrip all my wishes." She warns, however, that it will require great charity, "because you will encounter in me a resistance in knowing how to receive your graces [*in me troverà resistenza a saper ricever le sue gratie*]."

12 Marcel Mauss, *The Gift: Forms and Functions of Exchange in Archaic Societies*, trans. Ian Cunnison, New York, 1967.

13 Jacques Derrida, *Given Time: I. Counterfeit Money*, trans. Peggy Kamuf, Chicago, 1992, and esp. 1–83. See also the discussion of the gift's "increase" in Hyde, 25–39.

14 Jacques Derrida, *The Gift of Death*, trans. David Willis, Chicago, 1995, 95.

15 This emerges most clearly in Derrida (as in n. 14), which contains an extended commentary on Søren Kierkegaard's conception of faith.

16 See Natalie Zemon Davis, *Gifts and Bribes in Sixteenth-Century France*, Lancaster, Eng., 1995.

17 Seneca, *Moral Essays*, III, trans. John W. Basore, London, 1935, bk. 1, ch. 2, sec. 3, 10–11: "Beneficiorum simplex ratio est: tantum erogatur; si reddet aliquid, lucrum est, si non reddet, damnum non est. Ego illud dedi, ut darem." Seneca's text, which was edited by Erasmus in 1515 and 1529, was translated into Italian by Michelangelo's correspondent and commentator Benedetto Varchi. It is interesting to find that in his version Varchi stresses the "unidirectionality" of the gift and generalizes the message in what could be read as a reformist direction; Benedetto Varchi, *Seneca De Benifizii*, Florence, 1554, 4: "Il modo di dare i benifizii è un solo, perche si danno solamente, se poi te n'è renduto alcuna, questo si chiama guadagno: se nò, non si chiama danno, perchè i benifizii si danno per dare, non per ricevere il cambio." On Varchi's reformist sympathies and affinities with the Viterbo circle, see the very fine analysis of Paolo Simoncelli, *Evangelismo italiano del Cinquecento*, Rome, 1979, ch. 6, 330–95, which proves Varchi to have been a very close reader of the *Beneficio di Cristo*.

18 Quoted after the English translation in Gleason, 128. Fontanini, ch. 6, 29r.–v., 41: "E che cosa può operare l'uomo, che meriti un tanto dono e tesoro quanto è Cristo? Questo tesoro si dà solamente per grazia e favore e misericordia di Dio, e la fede sola è quella che riceve cotal dono, e ci fa godere della remissione de' peccati. . . . Le quali cose tutte le opere, che possono fare tutti li uomini insieme, non potrano conseguire nè fare."

19 The parallel between the gift and the work of art – the idea that works of art are not like other commodities but are giftlike in that their value is irreplaceable and incommensurable – is by now taken quite for granted. Hyde, for example, takes it as the premise of his study. It is, I believe, necessary to historicize this premise and attempt a genealogy of the identification. Hyde's own examples, and his guiding conception of what constitutes "art," implicitly suggest that the identification is a feature of post-Kantian aesthetics. One might argue, in fact, that the very project of marking off and defining the realm of the work of art as such by stressing, as Kant does in the *Critique of Judgment*, its disinterested quality or generally by claiming its exemption from conceptual logic or the logic of "economic" relations – a project served especially well by the notion of the gift – is perhaps the most peculiarly modern feature of modern aesthetics. The case here under study offers one early, experimental moment in the history of this identification, before it received theoretical elaboration, and thus stands as a warning against adopting it as a universal premise.

20 See the variant in Michelangelo Buonarroti, 342–43: "Per esser manco almen, signiora, indegnio."

21 Michelangelo Buonarroti, 86, 343–44: "S'alcun legato è pur tal piacer molto,/ come da morte altrui tornare in vita,/ qual cosa é che po' paghi tanta aita,/ che rende il debitor libero e sciolto?/ E se pur fusse, ne sarebbe tolto/ il soprastar d'una mercé infinita/ al ben servito, onde sarie 'mpedita/ da l'incontro servire, a quella volto./ Dunche, per tener alta vostra grazia,/ donna, sopra 'l mie stato, in me sol bramo/ ingratitudin più che cortesia:/ chè dove l'un dell'altro al par si sazia,/ non mi sare' signor quel che tant'amo:/ ché 'n parità non cape signoria." The sentiment is echoed in a letter from Vittoria Colonna to Marguerite d'Angoulême in 1540; Ferrero and Müller, 185: "Most serene Queen. The lofty and saintly words of your Majesty's most human letter should teach me that sacred silence which in the place

of praise is offered to divine things; but fearing lest my acknowledgment be deemed ingratitude, I will strive, if not to respond, at least not to remain entirely silent. . . ."

22 Ralph Waldo Emerson, "Gifts," in *The Works of Emerson*, I, New York, n.d., 344.

23 The expression appears in Michelangelo Buonarroti, 136: "Non è più bassa o vil cosa terrena." In the terms of Flaminio's letter quoted above (n. 11), this would put Michelangelo in the more radical camp.

24 Summers (as in n. 6), 448, described the association as a basic feature of Michelangelo's thought: "'Grace' also seems to have had a vertical dimension in Michelangelo's mind that distinguished his thought on the subject from the thought of writers such as Alberti or Leonardo, who, like many others, understood the idea and gave it a central place in their discussions of painting. All agree that grace is a desirable characteristic in a work of art. But only if the term is taken literally, seen at its full height as a divine gift, and thus as a means of transcendence and spiritual return, does it cease to be a mere catchword or formula and become the basis for the religion of the beautiful that MA so clearly and so deeply felt through most of his life." I believe the letters to Vittoria Colonna, and the sonnets associated with them, constitute Michelangelo's most explicit statements on this issue.

25 Barocchi et al., IV, 102.

26 On the "discourse of secrecy" surrounding the presentation drawings, see Leonard Barkan, *Transuming Passion: Ganymede and the Erotics of Humanism*, Stanford, 1991, 82.

27 The association was noted, but not analyzed, by Hirst, 107: "The real parallel for these drawings of Michelangelo is love poetry, above all sonnets, actuated by profound personal feeling."

28 Barkan (as in n. 26), 81.

29 Hyde, 48–49.

30 Barocchi et al., IV, 102. Michelangelo is quoting from sonnet 206, "S' i' 'l dissi mai, ch' i' vegna in odio a quella," in Francesco Petrarca, *Le rime*, ed. Giosuè Carducci and Severino Perrari, Florence, 1956, 292–94.

31 See Cropper. See also Cropper's earlier articles, "On Beautiful Women: Parmigianino, Petrarchismo, and the Vernacular Style," *Art Bulletin*, LVIII, no. 3, 1976, 374–94, and more recently, "The Beauty of Woman. Problems in the Rhetoric of Renaissance Portraiture," in *Rewriting the Renaissance: The Discourses of Sexual Difference in Early Modern Europe*, ed. Margaret W. Ferguson, Maureen Quilligan, and Nancy J. Vickers, Chicago, 1986, 175–90. For a cogent summary of these views, see also Elizabeth Cropper and Charles Dempsey, *Nicolas Poussin: Friendship and the Love of Painting*, Princeton, 1996, 177–82.

32 On the lyrical relation of *io* and *tu* as a model for the relation between sitter and beholder in Renaissance portraits, see, besides Cropper, 197–201, the final chapter of Amedeo Quondam, *Il naso di Laura: Lingua e poesia lirica nella tradizione del Classicismo*, Modena, 1991, "Il naso di Laura: Considerazioni sul ritratto poetico e la comunicazione lirica," 291–328.

33 On the secularization of traditional categories of religious images towards 1500, see above all Belting, 1994, esp. chap. 20, "Religion and Art: The Crisis of the Image at the Beginning of the Modern Age." For more in-depth accounts of the genres of portraiture and landscape along these lines, see Joseph Leo Koerner, *The Moment of Self-Portraiture in German Renaissance Art*, Chicago, 1993, esp. chap. 4, "The

Artist as Christ"; and Christopher S. Wood, *Albrecht Altdorfer and the Origins of Landscape*, Chicago, 1993, esp. ch. 1, "Independent Landscape." In Alexander Nagel, "Leonardo and *Sfumato*," *Res: Anthropology and Aesthetics*, XXIV, 1993, 7–20, I argued that through devices such as *sfumato* painting "internalized" modes of concealing and revealing traditionally associated with the presentation of cult images, and with the mysteries of religious cult generally, and thus acquired a quasi-religious mystique in its own right, quite apart from the religiousness of its subject matter – a development in turn presupposed by Kantian philosophical aesthetics and Romantic conceptions of the artist and the work of art.

34 Girolamo Savonarola, *Sermoni sopra il salmo* "*Quam bonus*," in *Sermoni e prediche di F. Girolamo Savonarola*, Prato, It., 1846, sermon 16, 434–35. As this under-studied passage appears in a rare volume and was only partially quoted, in French, by Gustave Gruyer, *Les illustrations des écrits de Jérôme Savonarole publiés en Italie au XVe et au XVIe siècle et les paroles de Savonarole sur l'art*, Paris, 1879, 199, I give the original: "L'amore è come un dipintore. Un buono dipintore, se e' dipigne bene, tanto delettano gli uomini le sue dipinture, che nel contemplarle rimangon sospesi, e qualche volta in tal modo che e' pare che e' sieno posti in estasi e fuora di loro, e pare che e' si dimentichino di loro medesimi. Così fa l'amore di Gesù Cristo quando è nell'anima. . . . Domanda uno che sia innamorato d'una donna, che cosa gli dipinga l'amore nella camera della fantasia; risponderà, la faccia sua, gli occhi e gesti, le veste e simili cose; e tanto bene gliele dipigne, che tutte le potenze dell'anima sua rimangono sospese a tali pitture, e non si diletta di pensare ad altro, nè di contemplare altro che quelle pitture. . . . E se questo fa l'amore carnale, molto più l'amore spirituale, cioè di Gesù Cristo." This passage is followed by a commentary on the Song of Songs.

35 Barocchi et al., IV, 104. The question of the making of copies raised by this letter (as well as by the letter mentioning Pole's version of the *Pietà* drawing, quoted in n. 8) is, unfortunately, not at all clear. It is one of those instances in these letters where, as Hirst, 117, put it, "their language is difficult to interpret." Alexander Perrig, *Michelangelo's Drawings: The Science of Attribution*, trans. Michael Joyce, New Haven, 1991, 48, also admits that "their contents are filled with riddles." The narrative he offers to solve these riddles – which attempts to establish their sequence, the works to which they refer, the purpose of the unfinished drawing mentioned in the letter quoted above, and finally their date – is filled with dramatic supplementation not substantiated by the evidence.

36 The point corresponds to an assertion of Lodovico Dolce, elucidated by Cropper, 177: "Though Alberti had said that invention by itself could be beautiful, Dolce insists that, no matter how beautiful the invention, it requires equally beautiful drawing. In other words, invention must appear, not just in words addressed to the mind but also embodied in visible representation in order to become beautiful to the eye." Cf. Nagel (as in n. 33), 18.

37 Campi, 75–76, stresses the fact that the miracle happened after the Apostles' failed efforts, and thus interprets the quotation as an expression of Vittoria's Christocentrism. He also believes that this letter, which mentions a "Christo" rather than a "Crucifixo," refers specifically to the drawing of the *Pietà*. The argument for this difference in designation appears to be supported by the letter referring to Pole's version of the *Pietà*, quoted in n. 8, which offers Pole's drawing in response to Ercole Gonzaga's

professed desire for a "Cristo di mane di Michelangelo." On the other hand, it is significant that the author of the letter felt it necessary to add the qualification "but it is in the form of the Pietà," as if this is not necessarily what would be expected when asking for a "Cristo." Of course, none of this proves conclusively how Vittoria would have identified her drawing of the *Pietà*. Hirst, 117, believes that Vittoria's letter refers to the British Museum *Christ on the Cross* (Tolnay, 411r.). This question will remain open until further evidence comes to light.

38 For the purposes of clarity I give the uninterrupted Italian text of the passages discussed; Barocchi et al., IV, 105: "Li effetti vostri excitano a forza il giuditio de chi li guarda et per vederne più exsperientia parlai de accrescer bontà alle cose perfette. Et ho visto che *omnia possibilia sunt credenti*. Io ebbi grandissima fede in Dio, che vi dessi una gratia sopranatural a far questo Christo. . . ."

39 William West, "Nothing as Given: Economics of the Gift in Derrida and Shakespeare," *Comparative Literature*, XLVIII, 1996, 11.

40 See Vittoria's letter to Giulia Gonzaga of Dec. 8, 1541, which gives a strong sense of the connections between Valdés and Viterbo, in Ferrero and Muller, 240: "I have understood that you have sent the Exposition on Saint Paul [by Valdés], which was greatly desired, and above all by me who have the most need of it." Our understanding of Vittoria's connection to the thought of Valdés, independently and through the mediation of Bernardino Ochino, Vittoria's spiritual advisor, has now been significantly enriched by Campi.

41 Juan de Valdés, *La Epistola de San Pablo a los Romanos, i la I. a los Corintios* (1556), Madrid, 1856, xv.

42 Juan de Valdés, *Le cento e dieci divine considerazioni del Giovanni Valdesso*, Halle, Saxony, 1860, Considerazione CII, "Che la fede Cristiana ha necessità d'esser confermata con la esperienza; quale è la esperienza e come s'acquista," 376. According to Pietro Carnesecchi's recollection at his heresy trial (Manzoni, 495), during Vittoria's residence at Viterbo Flaminio had with him Valdés's *Considerations*, which he was translating from Spanish into Italian for Giulia Gonzaga, a point that provides further evidence of the connection between Viterbo and Valdés.

43 This theme was taken up in the *Beneficio*; Gleason, ch. 4, 129: "Therefore, when one hears it said that faith alone justifies without works, he should not be deceived and think like the false Christians who drag everything down to the level of carnal life. For them, true faith consists in believing the story of Jesus Christ in the way that one believes those of Caesar and Alexander. This kind of belief is a historical faith, founded on the mere report of men and writings and impressed lightly on the mind through established custom. . . . Faith such as this is a human fantasy; it does not renew man's heart at all or warm it with divine love. . . ." This line of thinking was typical of Christian humanists, and was perhaps a consequence of the fact that as humanists with a developed interest in the study of secular history they were compelled to give renewed critical attention to the question of what distinguished it from sacred history. John O'Malley, *Praise and Blame in Renaissance Rome: Rhetoric, Doctrine, and Reform in the Sacred Orators of the Papal Court*, Durham, N.C., 1979, showed that Renaissance orators at the papal court responded to the problem of speaking about sacred matters in humanist terms by adapting the mode of epideictic rhetoric, which resulted in an enhanced emphasis on sacred history's resistance to logical or rational modes of explanation. O'Malley (45–51) indicated

that the adaptation of epideictic to a Christian context was most clearly theorized by the Augustinian humanist Aurelio Brandolini in his *De ratione scribendi*. It is, therefore, little surprise to find Brandolini applying the epideictic mode in an explicit effort to draw the distinction between sacred and secular history in a sermon delivered in the Sistine Chapel on Good Friday 1496, published as *Delle virtù mostrateci nella Passione dal nostro signor Gesù Cristo*, Rome, 1767, 22–24: "And so we do not deplore, lament or describe the crucifixion of Gavius, as Cicero did, or the assassination of Caesar, as Maro did, or the death of a certain prince, as the ancients have often done, but that Cross, upon which Christ, King of Kings, Prince of Princes, true God, and Son of God, was – by those he had created, whom he had governed with laws, whom he had covered with benefits, for whom he had finally made himself man among men – crucified against all law and all reason." In Nagel, 1993, ch. 2, I argued that Michelangelo also grappled with this issue in the London *Entombment*, in attempting to adapt the principles of history painting to the demands of altar images.

44 Cf. José C. Nieto, *Juan de Valdés and the Origins of the Spanish and Italian Reformation*, Geneva, 1970, 253: "Valdés' hermeneutical principle is rooted in the experience of the word of God as it affects human self-consciousness. Thus, the ultimate hermeneutical question addressed by Valdés to the biblical text is preconditioned by the redemptive and soteriological quest for the text's effect upon his consciousness. The hermeneutical organon is therefore man's own conscience, and whatever does not touch him is passed over with the hope that in some other occasion it will speak to his conscience."

45 This point was aptly emphasized by Susanna Peyronel Rambaldi, "Ancora sull'Evangelismo italiano: Categoria o invenzione storiografica?" *Società e Storia*, XVIII, 1982, 951: "A culture founded on an internal experience that has often been described as aristocratic and individual, whose principles were justification by faith on the one hand and the hatred for superstition and nonspiritual practices on the other, was not a culture that could be easily popularized and become a common patrimony in the Church of the Counter Reformation." The point is close to that made long ago by Delio Cantimori, *Eretici italiani del Cinquecento*, Florence, 1939, 24, who observed that in Valdesianism "the motive of internal reform led to a religion of the individual or of little groups, not equipped to produce or guide a wide movement rooted in all levels of society, as a general reform movement would have had to be." This passage is quoted and discussed by Massimo Firpo, *Tra Alumbrados e "Spirituali": Studi su Juan de Valdés e il Valdesianesimo nella crisi religiosa del '500 italiano*, Florence, 1990, 16 n. 23, and 13–43, who also asserts (28) that the "reserve" typical of the group around Valdés was due not simply to fear of persecution but also to the nature of the piety they practiced.

46 In 1545, Benedetto Varchi noted with amused exasperation that the question of free will was debated "not only by theologians and philosophers, but by all sorts of literati, and even by idiots and uneducated men; and I remember in Padua that even the bakers and fruit vendors, as well as the tailors and shoemakers, had gotten so worked up, after the sermons of some Cappuchin friar [he is feigning not to remember Bernardino Ochino], that they never spoke of anything else, but always debated questions of free will and consequently of predestination, of grace and works, with the result that . . . those dissensions arose that everyone knows about";

Benedetto Varchi, *Lezioni sul Dante e prose varie*, I, ed. Giuseppe Aiazz and Lelio Arbib, Florence, 1841, 49–50. Quoted by Simoncelli (as in n. 17), 342–43. In a letter of 1540 to Giovanni Morone, bishop of Modena, his vicar, Giovanni Domenico Sigibaldi, reported with great alarm: "This entire city (so they say) is sullied [*maculata*], infected by the contagion of various heresies like Prague. In the shops, corners and houses etc. everyone debates questions of faith, of free will, of purgatory and the Eucharist, and of predestination"; quoted in Massimo Firpo, "Gli 'spirituali,' l'accademia di Modena e il Formulario di Fede del 1542: Controllo del dissenso religioso e nicodemismo," *Rivista di Storia e Letteratura Religiosa*, XX, 1984, 47. Already in 1538 Gasparo Contarini, earlier a defender of the public dissemination of reforming doctrine, saw the danger of "[c]ertain preachers who had preached on questions of free will, of predestination, and as a result caused great confusion, having put in the head of many that salvation and damnation were necessary and not contingent, and thus that one could do evil and behave as one wished"; letter to Ercole Gonzaga, Jan. 19, 1538, in Walter Friedensburg, "Der Briefwechsel Gasparo Contarinis mit Ercole Gonzaga nebst einem Briefe Gian Pietro Carafas," in *Quellen und Forschungen aus italienischen Archiven und Bibliotheken*, II, 1899, 185.

47   See Hans Belting, "An Image and Its Function in the Liturgy: The Man of Sorrows in Byzantium," *Dumbarton Oaks Papers*, XXXIV–XXXV, 1980–81, 1–16, and idem, 1981, ch. 5.

48   Erwin Panofsky, "'Imago Pietatis': Ein Beitrag zur Typengeschichte des 'Schmerzensmanns' und der 'Maria Mediatrix,'" in *Festschrift für Max J. Friedländer zum 60. Geburtstag*, Leipzig, 1927, 261.

49   Belting, 1981, chap. 5. The image's freedom of development has been stressed above all by Rudolf Berliner, "Bemerkungen zu einigen Darstellungen des Erlösers als Schmerzensmann," *Das Münster*, IX, 1956, 97–111.

50   The London *Entombment*'s link to the Man of Sorrows tradition was suggested by Michael Hirst, "Michelangelo in Rome: An Altarpiece and the 'Bacchus,'" *Burlington Magazine*, CXXIII, 1981, 589. A comprehensive account of Michelangelo's engagements with the Man of Sorrows tradition, including the Colonna *Pietà*, is offered by Nagel, 1996, from which some of the following observations are drawn. Hirst and I (see Alexander Nagel, "Michelangelo's London *Entombment* and the Church of Sant'Agostino in Rome," *Burlington Magazine*, CXXXVI, 1994, 164–67) have argued that the London *Entombment* was made in response to a documented commission for an altarpiece for the church of Sant'Agostino in Rome in 1500. This is not the place to enter into the debate over the painting's attribution. It is, however, important to emphasize that the work's dubiousness in the history of Michelangelo scholarship has been greatly exaggerated. It was attributed to Michelangelo by, among others, Jakob Burckhardt, Jean Paul Richter, Gustavo Frizzoni, Bernard Berenson, Adolph Goldschmidt, Aby Warburg, Cart Justi, Henry Thode, Adolfo Venturi, Johannes Wilde, Cecil Gould, and in more recent times by Michael Hirst, Howard Hibbard, and John Shearman. The fact that it has receded from attention until recently is due in large measure to the fact that it was excluded from the corpus in Charles de Tolnay's highly influential five-volume study, *Michelangelo*, Princeton, 1943–60. It is worth noting that Tolnay then reversed himself after the picture's cleaning; Charles de Tolnay, *Michelangelo: Sculptor, Painter,*

Architect, Princeton, 1975, 233. The attribution cannot, in the end, be convincingly argued using only narrow stylistic criteria. The aspects of the painting that most strongly suggest Michelangelo's authorship have to do with the work's conception – not only its innovative narrative structure (see John Shearman, *Only Connect . . . : Art and the Spectator in the Italian Renaissance*, Princeton, 1992, 79–86), but also its interpretation of the status of Christ's body between death and resurrection, its reception of the Man of Sorrows tradition, and finally its relation to Michelangelo's late *Pietà*s. I study these aspects of the work in Nagel, 1993, chs. 2, 5, as well as in Nagel, 1996.

51   Quoted after the translation by Gilbert (as in n. 9), 276. For the Italian, see Barocchi et al., IV, 299. Michelangelo's position on this issue is close in spirit to that expressed by Marcantonio Flaminio in a letter of September 25, 1540, to Gasparo Contarini. The parallel to an artist working on commission was, in the case of a humanist such as Flaminio, the work of secretary or chancellor. In both, the resistance to the traditional "offices" is motivated by a claim to freedom of inspiration, and in both the unusualness of the claim is registered in a tone of defiance (in Flaminio mingled with self-pity); Marcantonio Flaminio, *Lettere*, ed. Alessandro Pastore, Rome, 1978, 98–99: "Everything I have written, I have written from certain free motivations [*con certi impeti liberi*], I say free, because it has never been in my power to be able to write every time I have wanted, and as much as I would have liked. My most reverend patron Monsignor of Verona [Gian Matteo Giberti] can attest to this strange nature of mine, for he was never able to make me write any Latin epistle, even though I very much wanted to, and I was embarrassed at denying my benefactor such an honest thing. . . ."

52   Vienna, Albertina, Sc. R. 137, inv. no. 103; Tolnay, 432r.; black and red chalk, 40.4 × 23.3 cm. The drawing's dependence on the London Christ is evident above all in the legs and left arm. Jean Paul Richter, *Italian Art in the National Gallery*, London, 1883, 43–44, convincingly rejected the hypothesis that the drawing could be preparatory for the painting. This view is confirmed by the fact that the drawing begins by closely copying the painting and then diverges from it. The original guiding lines in black chalk, still visible along Christ's (proper) right profile, show a careful and nearly exact copying of the torso in the painting, while the final contour lines in red chalk alter the torso, giving it a more upright position. In Nagel, 1996, 557 and n. 23, I argue that this fact of direct copying, which is at variance with what we know of Michelangelo's working practice (see Hirst's observations on Michelangelo's reuse of previous motifs, 20), is enough to instill legitimate doubt about the authorship of the drawing, a doubt that I believe is reinforced by the drawing's intrinsic qualities. The drawing was, in any case, produced in close proximity to Michelangelo and is closely connected to his *Pietà* studies of the 1530s. Sylvia Ferino Pagden's entry on the drawing, in *Vittoria Colonna: Dichterin und Muse Michelangelos*, exh. cat., Kunsthistorisches Museum, Vienna, 1997, cat. no. IV. 47, 454, also raises some doubts about the drawing's authorship and also suggests a date toward the early 1530s.

53   See Wilhelm Pinder, "Die dichterische Würzel der Pietà," *Repertorium für Kunstwissenschaft*, XLII, 1920, 145–63. See also Nagel, 1996, 555 n. 17.

54   Bayonne, Musée Bonnat, inv. no. 650v.; Tolnay, 337r.; red and black chalk, 20.7 × 30.6 cm. The date of the sheet can be established from the fact that it also contains

studies for the *Children's Bacchanal* in Windsor (Tolnay, 338r.), which dates to 1533–34 (see Hirst, 116, and Nagel, 1996, 552–53).

55   The turbaned figure at the extreme right, turning away from the viewer, is virtually a quotation of Raphael's work. The hypothesis that Michelangelo was specifically remembering Raphael's painting in the Bayonne drawing is further reinforced by the fact that he quoted, and parodied, it in the group of putti carrying the deer in the *Children's Bacchanal* in Windsor, for which the Bayonne sheet contains a preparatory study (see n. 54 above). These recollections, in the midst of studies that also adapt the London *Entombment*, strongly suggest that Michelangelo understood Raphael's *Entombment* in relation to his own, and thus encourage historians to do the same. I have attempted an analysis of the relation between the two paintings in Nagel, 1993, chap. 3.

56   On the Úbeda *Pietà*, commissioned in 1533 from Sebastiano del Piombo by Ferrante Gonzaga as a gift for the imperial minister Francisco de los Cobos, see Michael Hirst, "Sebastiano's *Pietà* for the Comendador Mayor," *Burlington Magazine*, cxiv, 1972, 587. On the connections between the Bayonne drawing and the conception of the Úbeda *Pietà*, see Nagel, 1996, 554.

57   Paris, Louvre, inv. no. 10161r.; Tolnay, 268r.; red chalk; 11 × 9.3 cm.

58   See Steinberg.

59   Ewald M. Vetter, "La iconografia del 'Varón de Dolores': Su significado y origen," *Archivo Español de Arte*, xxxvi, 1963, 218, showed that one of the earliest Western examples of the theme, a miniature in a Roman missal of 1254 in the Museo Archeologico of Cividale (Cod. LXXXVI, f. 167), decorates the canon of the Mass. The Eucharistic associations of the image have been stressed above all by Romuald Bauerreis, *Pie Jesu: Das Schmerzensmann-Bild und sein Einfluss auf die mittelalterliche Frömmigkeit*, Munich, 1931, esp. 3–14.

60   Vienna, Albertina, Sc.R. 136, inv. no. 102r.; Tolnay, 269r.; red chalk; 32 × 25.1 cm.

61   Vittoria Colonna, *Rime di Vittoria Colonna*, Rome, 1860, sonnet 21, 171.

62   I use the term *suprahistorical* in the sense developed by Erich Auerbach, *Mimesis: The Representation of Reality in Western Literature* (1946), trans. Willard R. Trask, Princeton, 1968, 143–73. Auerbach explained that in the figural conception of history that predominated in medieval exegesis each event is understood to have not only a chronological place within the sequence of temporal history but also a place within a scheme of redemption that is above time. The suprahistorical dimension of sacred history thus allowed events such as the Fall of Man or Christ's Passion to be occasions at once for lament and for theologically informed joy.

63   On the specific tradition of the Man of Sorrows with angels, see Georg Swarzenski, "Insinuationes divinae pietatis," in *Festschrift Heinrich Wölfflin*, Munich, 1924, 65–74; Hubert Schrade, "Beitrag zur Erklärung des Schmerzensmannbildes," in *Deutschkundliches – Friedrich Panzer zum 60. Geburtstag überreicht*, Heidelberg, 1930, 178–79; and Gert von der Osten, "Engelpietà," in *Reallexikon zur Deutschen Kunstgeschichte*, v, Stuttgart, 1960, 603. It should be noted that Michelangelo's image conforms particularly to an Italian tradition of the Man of Sorrows with angels, in which Christ is flanked by angels rather than supported from behind by one, an observation made by Panofsky (as in n. 48), 268. Early examples of this type include the relief by Giovanni Pisano in Berlin and the predella of the stone altarpiece by Tommaso Pisano in S. Francesco at Pisa; illustrations in Belting, 1981,

figs. 31, 35. The two types were combined in Andrea del Sarto's lost Puccini *Pietà* (see John Shearman, *Andrea del Sarto*, ii, Oxford, 1965, 229–30). The flanking type was adapted by Rosso in his *Dead Christ* now in Boston, perhaps the most significant parallel to the Colonna *Pietà*. As unusual and "modern" as Rosso's painting is, he himself connected it consciously to the tradition of the Man of Sorrows, or *imago pietatis*, in a letter where he described it as a Christ "in forma Pietatis." See David Franklin, "New Documents for Rosso Fiorentino in Sansepolcro," *Burlington Magazine*, cxxxi, 1989, Document 5, 827. The terms *pietà* or *immagine della pietà*, it should be noted, were more often used to describe what we would call a Man of Sorrows, the *imago pietatis* proper, than the configuration that the term is now generally understood to describe, i.e., the *Vesperbild*. This is the way, for example, Neri di Bicci uses the term, as in, e.g., *Le ricordanze*, ed. Bruno Santi, Pisa, 1976, 60 (f. 26r.): ". . . e nella predella la Piatà e quattro meze fighure da lato." Likewise, the letter to Cardinal Ercole Gonzaga quoted in n. 8 above describes Pole's version of Michelangelo's *Pietà* for Vittoria Colonna as a Christ "in forma di Pietà." See also the illuminating chapter on the meaning of the word *pietas* in relation to the Man of Sorrows image in Belting, 1981, Excursus A, 281–88.

64 The relevance of the treatise to the drawing was observed by Nagel, 1993, 222–30, and by Campi, 49–51. The treatise has been set into the context of reformist writing and concerns over images by Adriano Prosperi, "Zwischen Mystikern und Malern: Überlegungen zur Bilderfrage in Italien zur Zeit Vittoria Colonnas," in *Vittoria Colonna: Dichterin und Muse Michelangelos* (as in n. 52), 283–92. It is written in the form of a letter addressed to a certain "Padre," whose authority is invoked at various points in the course of the text. Simoncelli (as in n. 17), 211–13, showed that several passages, and those in particular that make reference to the "Padre," contain remarkably close allusions to Bernardino Ochino's *Prediche Nove*. On the basis of this evidence, he argues convincingly that Ochino, Vittoria's spiritual advisor from 1534 to 1541, was the addressee of the text. This in turn helps to determine its date: Ochino's *Prediche nove* were delivered in Venice during Lent of 1539 and were published in 1541; in August 1542 he fled to Geneva. Vittoria Colonna thus probably composed her text between 1539 and 1542 – that is, in the same period to which scholars usually date Michelangelo's drawings for her and the correspondence that mentions them. Prosperi, 292, notes that many of these arguments were also made by Eva Maria Jung, "Il pianto della marchesa di Pescara" (1957), *Archivio Italiano per la Storia della Pietà*, x, 1997. On Vittoria's relations with Ochino, who was himself heavily under the influence of Valdés, see Alfred von Reumont, *Vittoria Colonna, marchesa di Pescara: Vita, fede e poesia nel secolo decimosesto*, trans. Ermanno Ferrero and Giuseppe Müller, 2nd ed., Turin, 1892, 151–72, and Campi, 21–54.

65 Colonna, 423.

66 Colonna, 423; "far del suo corpo quasi morto una sepoltura in quella hora." For Vittoria, as for Michelangelo, the lap was the very seat of love. And it was not exclusive to women. In a letter to Pietro Bembo (Ferrero and Müller, 174), for example, she states, "I see your great affection for me, which . . . extends with the ample lap of your warm love. . . . [*Veggo il grande affetto suo verso me, che . . . si spande con la piena falda del suo caldo amore*]."

67 Colonna, 423: "quel fuoco de amor et de tormento che se era desdignato per la grandezza sua mostrarsi tutto di fore, haveva consumato et penetrato l'intimo del'anima, hora nel toccar el sacro Corpo de Christo se allargò con maxima abondantia, et uscì per li occhi con più amare lacrime, et per la bocca con più accesi suspiri."

68 Colonna, 423.

69 Colonna, 423.

70 Colonna, 424: "queste virtù ancor che se ne andassero con l'anima . . . ne restò col santo corpo la impressione in sin la sua resurrettione per viver poi con lui glorificato in meglior vita, sì che tutte rilucevan in quello aspetto visibil più a li altri a la Madonna perchè più ardentemente languisse" (Although these virtues had left with his soul . . . they left imprints on the holy body until his resurrection, when they were again united with him, glorified in a better life, so that they all shone in that visible aspect and especially to the Madonna who yearned all the more ardently).

71 Colonna, 425.

72 Colonna, 425.

73 Colonna, 426.

74 Colonna, 426.

75 Colonna, 426.

76 Colonna, 427.

77 Colonna, 427: "così la Madonna vedendo che non vi era la beata anima de Christo, qual sola era sufficiente ad honorar l'immensa grandeza de la divinità, li pareva che a lei sola appartenesse el grand'offitio de supplire a tanto debito, onde havria voluto liquefarsi, consumarsi anzi farsi ultima nel fuoco del'amore et ne le lacrime de la compassione per toglier al mondo et a se stessa l'ingratitudine, et render a Dio lo ossequio et il colto che li convenia."

78 Colonna, 428.

79 Vittoria thus preserves a role for the Virgin, but subsumes it firmly within a Christocentric orientation, thus offering a "reformed" version of the Catholic tradition of Marian piety, and of medieval Passion literature. Campi, 48–54, offers a sustained analysis of "this silent but vast Mariological reinterpretation [*ridimensionamento mariologico*]," in both the *Pianto* and the *Rime*, and its relations to the thought of Valdés and Ochino. I have attempted to show, both in the analysis of the drawings offered above, and more broadly in Nagel, 1993, 8–89 and 182–247, that the corollary of this shift of emphasis, in the arena of visual traditions, was Michelangelo's shift from the Marian *Vesperbild* to the Christocentric *imago pietatis*.

80 Dante Alighieri, *La Divina Commedia*, ed. G. A. Scartazzini, 2nd ed., Milan, 1896, 988. The translation is quoted from idem, *The Divine Comedy*, trans. Charles S. Singleton, Princeton, 1975, 329.

81 The text, from a prayer book belonging to the convent of Unterlinden in Colmar, was quoted and discussed by Thomas Lentes, *Gebetbuch und Gebärde: Religiöses Ausdrucksverhalten in Gebetbüchern aus dem Dominikanerinnen-Kloster St. Nikolaus in Undis zu Strassburg (1350–1550)*, University of Münster, 1997, 550, 1094–97. On the medieval "piety of counting" more generally, see Arnold Angenendt et al., "Gezählte Frömmigkeit," *Frühmittelalterliche Studien*, xxix, 1995, 1–71.

82 See Émile Mâle, *L'art religieux à la fin du Moyen Âge en France*, Paris, 1908, 93: in the 14th century seven Paternosters, seven Ave Marias, and seven short prayers called the prayers of Saint Gregory obtained a true pardon of 6,000 years from time

in Purgatory; by the 15th century the sum had been inflated to 46,000 years. An intermediate stage in this inflationary process is represented by a highly informative mid-15th-century indulgence panel of the *Man of Sorrows–Gregory Mass* in the Wallraf-Richartz Museum in Cologne (reproduced in Belting, 1981, fig. 108), whose inscription reads that the 14,000 years of true pardon traditionally accorded to worshippers who say the prescribed prayers before this image has since been increased to 27,036 years.

83 This part of my discussion has benefited greatly from conversations with Thomas Lentes.

84 The ground drop that accommodates the lower half of Christ's body was interpreted as a tomb in several copies after the design, beginning with the relief in the Vatican. This point was made by Steinberg, 266–67, who also emphasizes the collapsing of the narrative span from birth to entombment.

85 Steinberg interprets the motif of Christ between the parted legs of the Virgin as a metaphor of parturition and progeniture in the Colonna *Pietà*, as well as in Michelangelo's works and in Renaissance art generally. The interpretative context adduced here serves, I believe, to confirm, and nuance, Steinberg's observations on this and on a number of other points to be noted.

86 A feature noted by Steinberg, 267, who interprets it in this sense.

87 This point is made repeatedly and effectively by Campi, who makes the important caveat (74): "All of this does not to be sure imply the exclusion of Mary from the horizon of faith. In a line of thought evidently close to Ochino's and, in good measure, to Colonna's, the mother of the Lord is represented [in the drawing] not in the act of interceding for humankind, but as one who trusts herself humbly to the salvific initiative of God and faithfully guards in her heart the divine word."

88 Natalie Zemon Davis, "Beyond the Market: Books as Gifts in Sixteenth-Century France," *Transactions of the Royal Historical Society,* 5th series, XXXIII, 1983, 72.

89 More recently, Davis (as in n. 16), has emphasized the tensions between the Catholic emphasis on reciprocity in gift giving and the Protestant emphasis on the gift's gratuitousness.

90 *Lettere volgari di diversi nobilissimi huomini, et eccelentissimi ingegni scritte in diverse materie, Venice,* 1551, bk. 2, 113–113*v.*: "Ho ricevutoli versi di Marcantonio, & quando ne habbia ricuperati alcuni altri che sono in mano d'uno amico mio, io vi manderò anchor quelli, che vi satisferan molto piu à mio giudicio, perche son tanto piu vaghi et piu venusti, quanto che trattano di materie piu capaci di vaghezza che per la verità queste materie della religione à trattarle vagamente si fanno spesso di sante prophane: & credo che sia difficil cosa à farlo bene, & con dignità. Queste altre materie sono pastorali, et amorose: ma guarderetevi di gratia di mostrarli poi à certi Stoici che si scandalizano di ogni cosa. . . ." On della Torre's activities as secretary of Gian Matteo Giberti, see Adriano Prosperi, *Tra Evangelismo e Controriforma: Gian Matteo Giberti (1495–1543)*, Rome, 1969, xv, 150, 164, 184, 188, 196, and passim. Deswarte-Rosa, 358, notes that on January 30, 1540, seven days after the letter quoted above, Francesco della Torre wrote Carlo Gualteruzzi asking to be sent some recent sonnets by Vittoria Colonna, about which he had heard from Lattanzio Tolomei (one of the interlocutors in de Holanda's dialogues), suggesting that his skepticism about the possibility of an elegant religious poetry did not dampen his enthusiasm for it. The connections between Rullo and Flaminio

and Pole were succinctly described by Pietro Carnesecchi at his trial, in Manzoni, 198: "Flaminio and I, coming from Naples to Rome in 1540 or 1541, if I am not mistaken [later in his testimony (211) Carnesecchi confirms that it was the month of May 1541], were accompanied by this Rullo, who had come to know Flaminio in Venice or Padua or Verona or somewhere else as someone who was very much in the service of Giberti bishop of Verona and of Cardinal Pole, both of them patrons of the said Flaminio; and once in Rome, the said Rullo stayed with the Cardinal of England [Pole] as guest. . . . And then when later Flaminio and I relocated to Viterbo . . . we were united again with the same Rullo."

91 Ulrich Oelschlager, "Der Sendbrief Franz von Sickingens an seinem Verwandten Dieter von Handschuchsheim," *Blätter für pfalzische Kirchengeschichte und religiöse Volkskunde*, nos. 37/38, 1971–72, 723: "Ich sorge mich aber, dass solches wenig geschieht, sondern mehr die Kunst und Schönheit und Pracht in ihnen angesehen wird und dadurch das Gemüt und die rechte innerliche Betrachtung im Gebet vom rechten hohen aufsteigenden Weg in Gott abgezogen wird, weshalb sie beinahe meines Erachtens in schönen Gemächern zur Zierde nützlicher wären als in der Kirche, damit nicht der Aufwand und die vergebene Mühe unnütz verloren wären" (I am concerned however that this [taking images of Saints as holy examples] happens rarely, and instead art and beauty and magnificence are seen in them, and in that way the mind and the right inner regard in prayer is diverted from the right and high path in God. For which reason in my view they would be more useful as ornaments in fine rooms than in churches, so that the cost and the trouble expended would not be in vain). The passage was quoted and discussed by Martin Warnke, "Durchbrochene Geschichte? Die Bilderstürme der Wiedertaüfer in Münster 1534/35," in *Bildersturm: Die Zerstorung des Kunstwerks*, Munich, 1973, 73, who believes the suggestion to remove art from the church to the secular sphere of the private room "marks the future career of the artwork in the bourgeois household and the double role that it will play there as object of value and spiritual investment [Verwertungs- und Verinnerlichungsgegenstand]." My attention was drawn to the passage by Belting, 1994, app. 42B, 552, where part of it is excerpted.

92 Jean Calvin, *Institutio Christianae Religionis* (1559), ed. A. Tholuck, Edinburgh, 1874, bk. 1, chap. 11, sec. 12, 81: "Neque tamen ea superstitione teneor ut nullas prorsus imagines ferendas censeam. Sed quia sculptura et pictura Dei dona sunt, purum et legitimum usum requiro: ne quae Dominus in suam gloriam et bonum nostrum nobis contulit, ea non tantum polluantur praepostero abusu, sed in nostram quoque perniciem convertantur" (Despite this superstition, I do not rule out the possibility that images should exist at all. But as sculpture and painting are gifts of God, I require them to have a pure and legitimate use, lest what God has given us, in his glory and for our benefit, be not only defiled by outrageous abuse, but also become our ruin). This and other relevant passages from the *Institutes* are collected in Belting, 1994, app. 41, although with unreliable citations. On the secularizing consequences of the Protestant polemic on images, see also Werner Hofmann, "Die Geburt der Moderne aus dem Geist der Religion," in *Luther und die Folgen für die Kunst*, Munich, 1983, 23–71.

93 Alessandro Luzio, *La galleria dei Gonzaga venduta all'Inghilterra nel 1627–1628* (1913), Milan, 1974, 28; quoted by Michael Hirst, *Sebastiano del Piombo*, Oxford, 1981, 158.

94 On Vasari's periodization and his use of the words *goffo* and *rozzo* to describe medieval art, see Patricia Rubin, *Giorgio Vasari: Art and History*, New Haven, 1995, 281–84.

95 Vasari (as in n. 10), III, 273–74. In his *Commentaria in omnes divi Pauli epistolas et alias septem canones*, Venice, 1551, 645, Ambrogio Catarino Politi, the critic of the *Beneficio di Cristo* who figures in de Holanda's *Dialogues* giving sermons on Saint Paul with Vittoria and (occasionally) Michelangelo in attendance, offered a typical period judgment of Michelangelo when he expresses admiration for Michelangelo's mastery of art but condemns its use for religious purposes: "Commendo artem in facto: at factum ipsum vehementer vitupero ac detestor. Nam haec membrorum nuditas indecentissime in aris et praecipuis Dei sacellis ubique conspicitur" (I commend the art used in the matter, but I vehemently vituperate and detest the matter itself. For this nudity of limbs appears most indecent on altars and in God's most important chapel). The passage was quoted and discussed by Romeo de Maio, "Michelangelo e Pio IV," in *Riforme e miti della Chiesa del Cinquecento*, Naples, 1973, 98; and idem, *Michelangelo e la Controriforma*, Rome-Bari, 1978, 19–20. See also Deswarte-Rosa, 358 and n. 62.

96 On the image's connections to the tradition of the Man of Sorrows, and specifically to the Man of Sorrows with angels, or *Engelpietà*, see nn. 8 and 63 above. A deliberate archaizing impulse is also strongly suggested by Condivi's remark that the Y-shaped cross was based on the cross "which was carried in procession by the Bianchi at the time of the plague of 1348, and afterwards placed in the church of Santa Croce, at Florence," in Michael Holroyd, *Michael Angelo Buonarroti, with Translations of the Life of the Master by His Scholar, Ascanio Condivi, and Three Dialogues from the Portuguese by Francisco Hollanda*, London, 1911, 73. The reference to the medieval past in this image is thus deliberate, even if Condivi's reference to the Bianchi is not entirely accurate: the Bianchi arose in the year 1399 (see Daniel E. Bornstein, *The Bianchi of 1399: Popular Devotion in Late Medieval Italy*, Ithaca, 1993), and their crosses were not Y-shaped (see the illustrations to Giovanni Sercambi's chronicle, in *Le illustrazioni delle croniche nel codice Lucchese*, II, Genoa, 1978, 190–91, 195–202, which shows images of the Bianchi in procession). The important point is, however, that the cross in the drawing was adopted in imitation of a cross in Santa Croce (Michelangelo's parish church), which Michelangelo associated with the history and religious movements of the Tuscan trecento. It is interesting to note, in this connection, that Vittoria Colonna developed a keen interest in the Roman cult images reputed to have been painted by Saint Luke, and that at least one poem of hers on the subject was in Michelangelo's possession. See Deswarte-Rosa, 363.

97 See Pierre Bourdieu, *Distinction: A Social Critique of the Judgment of Taste*, trans. Richard Nice, Cambridge, Mass., 1984, esp. chs. 1, "The Aristocracy of Culture," and 5, "The Sense of Distinction."

Frequently Cited Sources

Barocchi, Paola, Giovanni Poggi, and Renzo Ristori, *Il Carteggio di Michelangelo*, 5 vols., Florence, 1965–73.

Belting, Hans, *Das Bild und sein Publikum im Mittelalter: Form und Funktion früher Bildtafel der Passion*, Berlin, 1981.

Belting, Hans, *Likeness and Presence: A Study of the Image in the Era before Art*, trans. Edmund Jephcott, Chicago, 1994.

Michelangelo Buonarroti, *Rime*, ed. Enzo Noè Girardi, Bari, 1960.

Campi, Emidio, *Michelangelo e Vittoria Colonna: Un dialogo artistico-teologico ispirato da Bernardino Ochino, e altri saggi di storia della Riforma*, Turin, 1994.

Colonna, Vittoria, *Pianto sopra la Passione di Cristo*, in *Evangelismo italiano del Cinquecento*, by Paolo Simoncelli, Rome, 1979, app., Document 1, 423–28.

Cropper, Elizabeth, "The Place of Beauty in the High Renaissance and Its Displacement in the History of Art," *Medieval and Renaissance Texts and Studies*, CXXXII, 1995, 159–205.

Deswarte-Rosa, Sylvie, "Vittoria Colonna und Michelangelo in San Silvestro al Quirinale nach den Gesprächen des Francisco de Holanda," in *Vittoria Colonna: Dichterin und Muse Michelangelos*, exh. cat., Kunsthistorisches Museum, Vienna, 1997, 349–73.

Ferrero, Ermanno, and Giuseppe Müller, eds., *Vittoria Colonna: Carteggio*, 2nd ed., Turin, 1892.

Fontanini, Benedetto, with revisions by Marcantonio Flaminio, *Il Beneficio di Cristo, con le versioni del secolo XVI, documenti e testimonianze*, ed. Salvatore Caponetto, Florence, 1972.

Ginzburg, Carlo, and Adriano Prosperi, *Giochi di Pazienza: Un seminario sul "Beneficio di Cristo,"* Turin, 1975.

Gleason, Elizabeth, *Reform Thought in Sixteenth-Century Italy*, Chico, Calif., 1981.

Hirst, Michael, *Michelangelo and His Drawings*, New Haven, 1988.

Hyde, Lewis, *The Gift: Imagination and the Erotic Life of Property*, New York, 1979.

Manzoni, Giacomo, "Estratto del Processo di Pietro Carnesecchi," *Miscellanea di Storia Italiana*, x, 1870, 187–573.

Nagel, Alexander, "Michelangelo, Raphael and the Altarpiece Tradition," Ph.D. diss., Harvard University, 1993.

Nagel, Alexander, "Observations on Michelangelo's Late *Pietà* Drawings and Sculptures," *Zeitschrift für Kunstgeschichte*, LIX, 1996, 548–72.

Steinberg, Leo, "The Metaphors of Love and Birth in Michelangelo's *Pietàs*," in *Studies in Erotic Art*, ed. Theodore Bowie and Cornelia Christenson, New York, 1970, 231–335.

Tolnay, Charles de, *Corpus dei disegni di Michelangelo*, 4 vols., Novara, It., 1975–80.

18

The Gesù in the Light of Contemporary Church Design

James S. Ackerman

Never has there been any doubt that the Gesù in Rome represents one of the most significant and influential architectural statements of the Renaissance. In fact, it is usually represented as being literally incomparable, as if it had sprung full-grown from the head of Vignola without real precedent or explanation in its environment or background. We see it in a different light, as the first monumental Roman church of a formal and liturgical style adopted as widely in Italy as was the Counter-Reformation itself, and my purpose here is to reconstruct that context. When I say "we see it" this way, I am not being academic, but am acknowledging the fact that when I first presented this problem in a talk, I was only seeing half of its dimensions, and consequently interpreted it wrongly. I was set straight by Professor Milton Lewine of Columbia who, in conversations, in his dissertation of 1960, and in a more recent article, clarified both the Roman background and the liturgical implications.[1]

My theory had been that the sources of the new style were to be found in North Italy, and particularly in Milan.[2] I had two arguments for this. First, I claimed that Milan had not really experienced an architecture of the High Renaissance, so that when the new spirit of the Counter-Reformation encouraged the revival of medieval longitudinal churches with their hall-like naves suitable for preaching, provincial Milan found itself closer to the medieval tradition of liturgy and building than the principal center of religious life, Rome, and unencumbered by the shadow of the great masters of the early sixteenth century – Bramante, Michelangelo, and Raphael. Second, I claimed that the major High Renaissance churches of Rome were centrally planned, notably Bramante's St. Peter's. Humanist thinking had temporarily disrupted the tradition of the longitudinal church for reasons revealed by my great friend and teacher Rudolf Wittkower; architectural theory from Alberti to Palladio insisted on the pre-eminence of the round, polygonal, or Greek-cross plan.[3]

The shock, first of the Protestant Reformation, and second of the sack of Rome in 1527, brought about a revival of pietism and a wave of reform in the

Roman Church that prompted a conservatism in architectural design which, in turn, resulted in a style of church building in what I should call the box style with barnlike naves, flat wooden roofs, a row of side chapels, and a chancel.[4] These examples of the box style serve to show that the change in form was not accompanied by a new architectural vision. Architects of this generation, raised on the tradition of classical antiquity, were unprepared to respond creatively to the new demands, and their large churches were rather uninspired places.

This was the condition of large-scale ecclesiastical building when St. Francis Borgia arrived in Rome in 1550 to find St. Ignatius living and working in squalor and the Jesuits confined to a small chapel entirely inadequate to accommodate the crowds attracted by the import and vigor of their sermons. With his powerful connections in the Curia and Roman nobility, Borgia easily removed the obstacles that St. Ignatius had encountered from the city planners in attempting to gain permission to build a large church and cloister in the vicinity of the Piazza Venezia.[5] Within the same year, 1550, a grandiose scheme was developed for the general area of the present buildings. Fortunately, drawings of this earliest of all Jesuit projects are preserved, together with the hundreds of architectural plans of sixteenth- and seventeenth-century Jesuit buildings in the Bibliothèque Nationale in Paris.[6]

This complex fills a part of the area occupied by the existing buildings; it was not carried out, partly because it provided too little space for living quarters, and partly because wealthy landlords in the area began a fifteen-year battle with the Order to contain its expansion – a battle that ultimately moved from the courts to the streets.[7]

The architect of the Paris plan probably was the Florentine, Nanni di Baccio Bigio (fig. 18.1).[8] Nanni was the right-hand man of Antonio da Sangallo the Younger, who succeeded Raphael as architect of St. Peter's, and who at the time of his death was no longer in the advanced guard of his profession. The selection of Nanni in 1550 implies the expectation of a conservative design, or at least one which might put the needs of the Order above the dictates of high style. The plan supports this interpretation.

While the conventual structures are unexceptional, the church is new in program but without any distinction or modernity architecturally. Indeed, the drawing looks like an amateur's. This is an odd combination: creativity of type is usually accompanied by creativity in design. What we see here suggests that the inventive element is not Nanni's contribution but that of Ignatius and Francis Borgia, that it was they who demanded a cross-plan with entrances in the arms of the cross, a huge open nave without a crossing, an ample apse with plenty of room for dispensing the Eucharist, and a façade flanked by towers in the manner of northern Gothic cathedrals (or should we grant Nanni the towers, under the influence of the Sangallo St. Peter model?). This church could not be vaulted; it required a wooden roof, and we know from later correspondence that Borgia argued vigorously for the wood cover on the grounds that it provided better acoustics for the sermons, since masonry vaulting produced echoes.[9] This plan

369

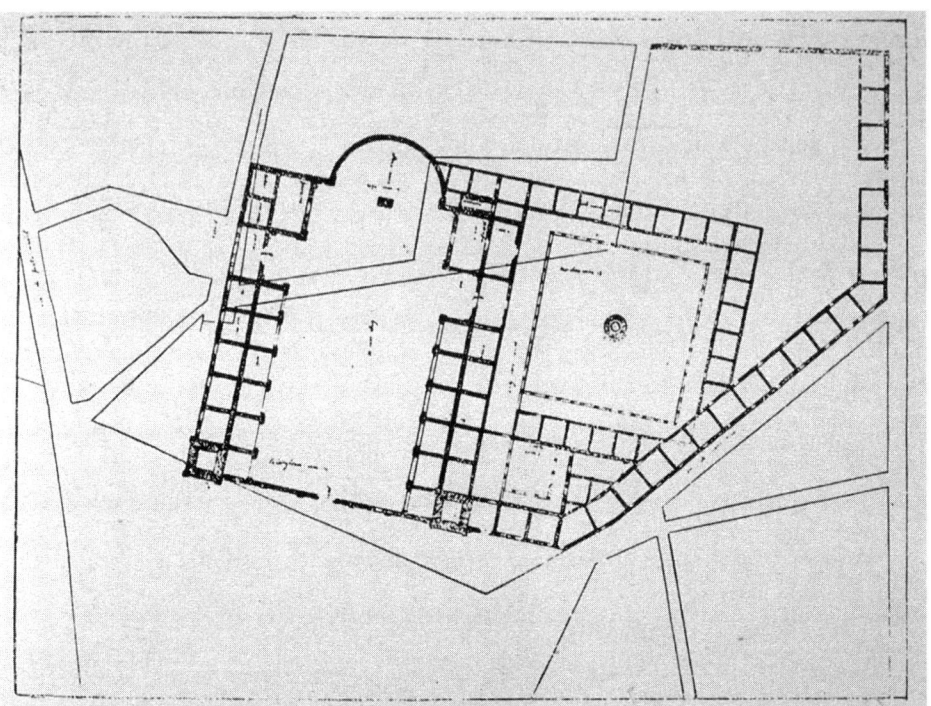

Figure 18.1   Rome, Il Gesù, plan project attributed to Nanni di Baccio Bigio (after Pirri). Paris, Bibliothèque Nationale. From R. Wittkower and I. Jaffe, *Baroque Art: The Jesuit Contribution*, Fordham University Press.

or one like it must have been the one for which a cornerstone was laid in 1550. At the time of its acceptance, the architect Giacomo Barozzi da Vignola, designer of the actual church, was on hand, perhaps as an expert judge;[10] this may indirectly illuminate something of the politics of the situation, as Vignola had become, on Sangallo's death, the favored architect of the Farnese family, and was helping Michelangelo to finish the family palace in Rome (it was the Farnese Pope, Paul III, who chose Michelangelo for St. Peter's).

After the death of St. Ignatius, there emerges a picture of two camps: a Borgia camp committed to the Sangallesque architectural tradition, and a Farnese camp, under Alessandro Cardinal Farnese, supporting Vignola. Borgia must have felt, like many practical men of affairs today, that the important thing was to have a workable plant, and that a minor architect was more apt to listen to reason than a great personality in the arts. The Farnese, like the princes they were, wanted an elegant, avant-garde building by a famous architect – one that would have a Farnese "look." And they ultimately won, because it was they who had the money, and they gave lavishly. Before this happened, however, there was a moment of complete agreement when it appeared that Michelangelo might agree to design the buildings. This was in 1554, and letters of St. Ignatius and

370

Polanco echo the elation of the Order over having secured the services of the greatest artist of the age. It was Cardinal della Cueva who approached the great Florentine, now 79 years of age, who with St. Ignatius was present at the second foundation ceremony on October 6, 1554.[11] The report says that the architect descended into the foundations to lay the stone; it does not say which architect; my guess is that it was not Michelangelo, who was too old, and too vain, to leap into muddy pits. I wonder if Michelangelo even made the design. One drawing has been published several times as his Gesù project.[12] It is identified by a later hand as being for the Gesù, and it has upon it a number of boldly stroked suggestions done in Michelangelo's favored material, red chalk, and with his characteristic bravura. But the architecture is absolutely antithetical to his; it is in the Sangallo tradition, and the ensemble actually is very like the original Nanni scheme: wood-roofed without a crossing, large apse, and short transept arms. This is clearly an alternative design by Nanni or someone close to him, and the chalk jottings, if they are Michelangelo's, are so drastically different in architectural intent that they suggest a master architect correcting the work of an amateur. This is all we hear of Michelangelo and Nanni, and fourteen years pass before the definitive design is accepted (fig. 18.2). What distinguishes the Uffizi design is its broad nave entered by three portals, and its large and simple apse; otherwise it has a poverty of scale and that failure to coordinate parts which characterizes the box style. It is not from this source that Vignola derived his inspiration.

It was for this reason that I was inclined to look outside Rome to find the genesis of the mature Counter-Reformation style, but I learned from Lewine that I was too hasty. He found that some of the most seminal thinking about church design was not going into big parish and conventual churches but, as might be expected, into the small chapels and oratories designed for organizations that were the center of advanced thought and action in the years before and during the Council of Trent. The church of San Giovanni Decollato is one of his major examples.[13] Its significance lies in the fact that the plan is conceived as a sequence of clearly distinguished spaces, each with a distinct function. First, one enters a vestibule marked off from the nave by heavy piers. Then there is a nave with three altar-recesses to a side which again is definitively isolated from the choir or vestigial transept by wall responds, a railing, and a rise of two steps. The chancel is separated again from the altar chapel, which is raised one more step, and finally there is a sacristy behind. This church was started in 1535, the year in which the oratory itself was finished. Obviously the plan was inspired by the simple form of the oratory, but it shows an effort to separate four functions without loss of continuity. The significance of this is apparent when we compare the church to Alessi's San Barnaba in Milan, a church of 1558 to which we shall return later.

Even churches of the box style which did not provide a separation of functions with such clarity began to exhibit features influenced by this kind of thinking. In Antonio da Sangallo's church of Santo Spirito in Sassia in the Vatican Borgo, of the late 1530s, and in many other Roman churches of the period cited by

Lewine, an entrance is provided in the center chapel of the nave, which has the effect of de-emphasizing the longitudinal axis by creating a cross-axis, and this by implication establishes the nave as an autonomous space.

It was clear to both Lewine and me that these changes were not motivated by a new aesthetic of architecture, but by a new concept of the role of the church. The reaction of Rome to the Protestant Reformation and the sack of the city was to initiate a radical reform of the liturgy, the clergy, and the monastic orders. This reform anticipated by several decades the pronouncements of the Council of Trent – it began to take vigorous effect in the 1530s – and it can now be seen that art historians have overestimated the council as the influential force in the Counter-Reformation. Its principal effect was to codify practices and principles that already had been accepted a generation earlier.

Many aspects of the reform demanded radical changes in church design. The need for frequent Masses and dispensing of the Sacrament made obsolete the kind of church that, prior to 1530, had served the majority of the congregation only once or twice a year. Now, many altars were required so that Mass could be said at more than one place at once, and a main altar where the Eucharist could be devoutly enshrined in a distinct area of special holiness. The nave had to be freed from encumbrances such as tombs and screens. Because year-round preaching was seen as the most effective instrument of public reform, and because the previously empty churches began to be filled with crowds of worshippers, the

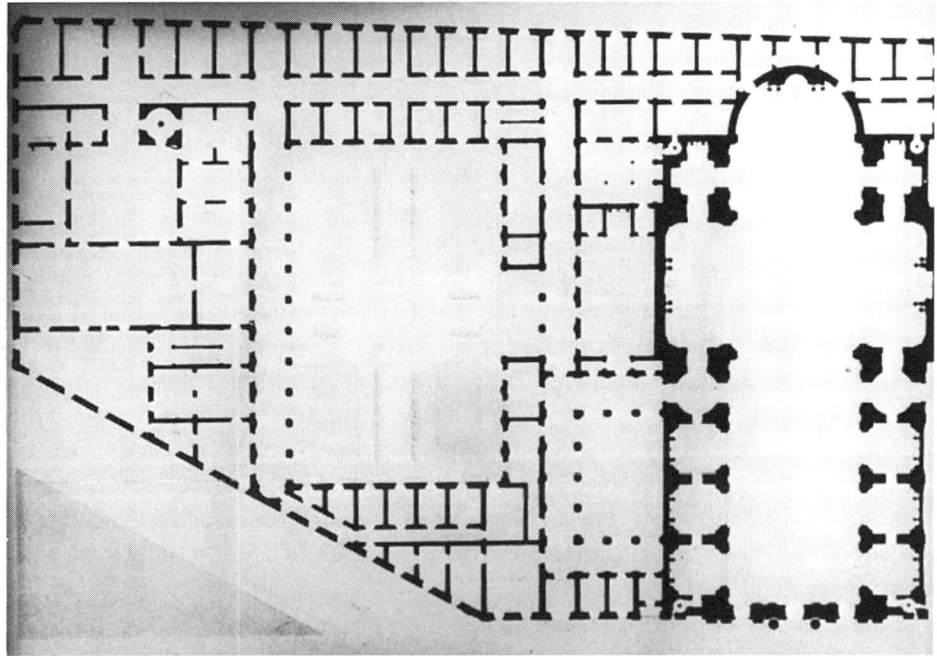

Figure 18.2   Rome, Il Gesù, site plan (after Pirri). From R. Wittkower and I. Jaffe, *Baroque Art: The Jesuit Contribution*, Fordham University Press.

nave also had to become an assembly hall. The logical place for the pulpit was at the end of the nave, and thus the hall acquired a natural terminus that tended to distinguish it from the chancel and crossing.

The preaching function affected not only the form of the nave, but its structure as well, since it stimulated a search for effective acoustical design. At first, the experts claimed that a flat and coffered wooden ceiling provided the best distribution of sound – this was the advice given by Francesco Giorgi to the builders of San Francesco della Vigna in Venice in 1535:

> I recommend that all the chapels and the choir be vaulted because the word or song of the minister echoes better from the vault than it would from rafters. But in the nave of the church, where there will be sermons, I recommend a ceiling (so that the voice of the preacher may not escape, nor re-echo from the vaults). I should like to have it coffered with as many squares as possible with their appropriate measurement and proportions, which squares should be treated in a workmanlike manner with gray paint.[14]

As I have already mentioned, Giorgi's conservative solution was urged for the Gesù by Francis Borgia.

Giorgi's suggestion that the coffering be a uniform gray fits the requirement of the new pietism that the church as well as the clergy be pure and devoid of mundane references or distractions; an asceticism of decoration, particularly in the nave hall, was a significant feature of the new architecture.

The spirit of the Roman reform movement was exported to Northern Italy as early as 1524, when Gian Matteo Giberti was named Bishop of Verona.[15] Giberti's stewardship of this diocese reached into every aspect of ecclesiastical practice; he set out to reform the clergy and the liturgy and to attract and discipline the lay public; his efforts extended even to certain aspects of church design. The principles of his episcopal visits were codified in his *Costituzioni*, published in 1542, a work that strongly influenced the conciliar deliberations. St. Charles Borromeo regarded him as a saint, and when St. Charles arrived in Milan in 1565, he modeled his own pastoral visits and rules on the *Costituzioni*. The design and decoration of churches was the subject of Borromeo's third Provincial Council in 1573, and the regulations decided on at that time were the source of Borromeo's famous book of 1577, the *Instructionum Fabricae et Supellectilis Ecclesiasticae libri duo*.[16] This book and its author have long been identified as a major stimulus to the creation of a Counter-Reformation ecclesiastical style; but a close examination of the North Italian churches themselves proves that he was not the creator of a new style but the spokesman and codifier of a style already fully matured during the third quarter of the century.

My earlier reference to the elimination of decoration from the church interior prompts me to start our North Italian probe close to Giberti's Verona, with the interiors of Palladio's two great churches in Venice, San Giorgio Maggiore of 1568 and the Redentore of 1577 (fig. 18.3), where absolute whiteness prevails.[17] Moreover, at San Giorgio, designed three years before the Gesù, the other new

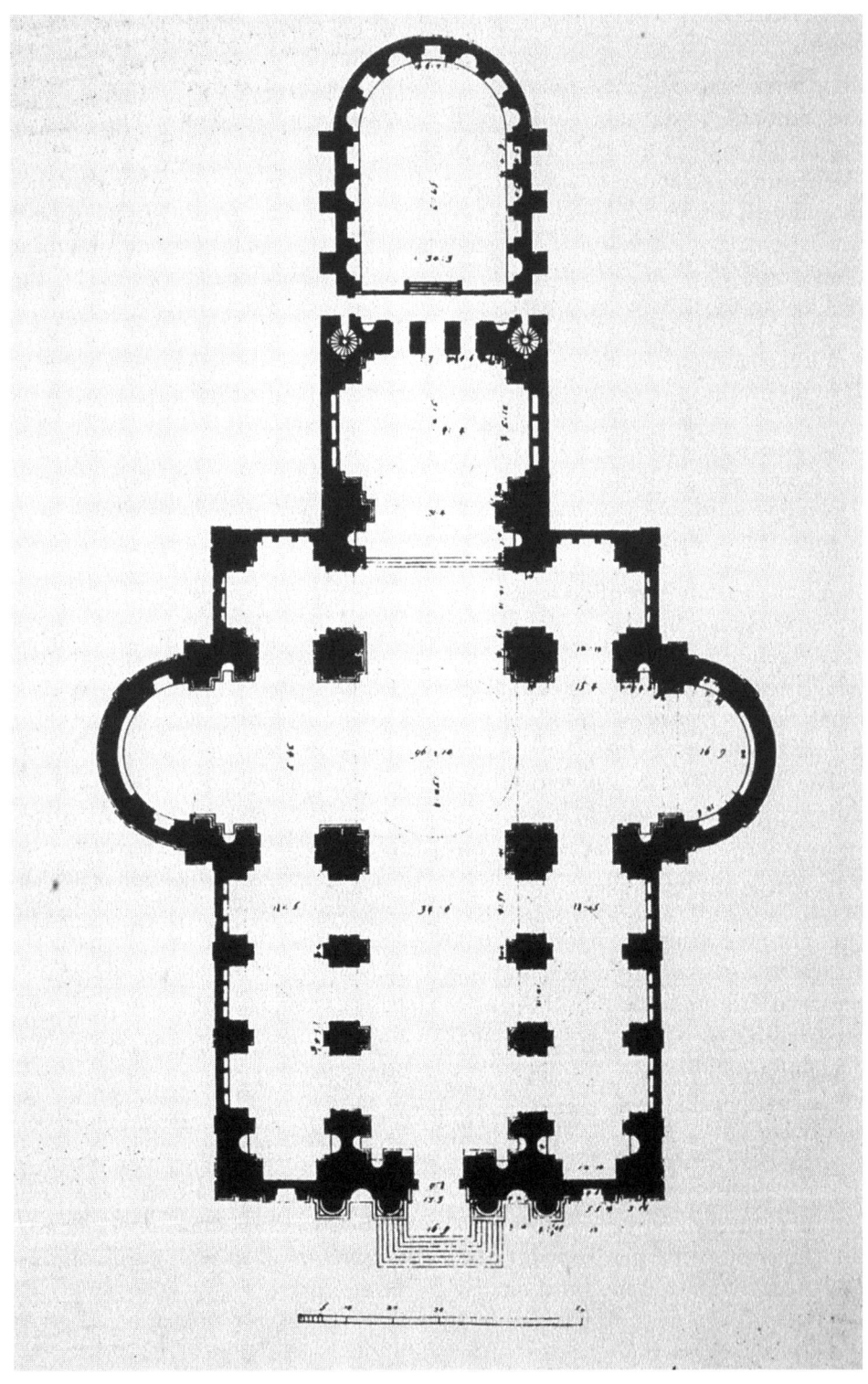

Figure 18.3 Venice, San Giorgio, plan (after Bertotti Scamozzi). From R. Wittkower and I. Jaffe, *Baroque Art: The Jesuit Contribution*, Fordham University Press.

374

tendencies have matured into a design advanced beyond the box churches of the first half of the century. Here the several functions of the church are distinctly separated. There is a distinct nave, with three shallow altar chapels to a side, and a transept with semicircular terminations marked at the crossing by a notably elevated cupola. A chancel or altar-area is elevated three steps above the nave and is structurally self-contained; behind, a columnar screen separates it from the claustral choir designed to keep the monks isolated from the lay public, as they had been earlier in Giorgi's San Francesco della Vigna in Venice. There is an awkwardness in this first attempt to piece together self-sufficient parts which Palladio overcomes in his second experiment in the basilical genre. At the Redentore, the elements are better integrated without compromising the concepts of the separation of functions, but since the later date of that church and its unique votive function remove it from our present concerns, I note only that the nave is literally separate, and that the chapels, raised from the nave floor, are distinct spaces linked by internal passages.

We have already seen that Palladio was not the first North Italian architect to seek new solutions to the new demand. The Perugian Galeazzo Alessi had left home at the age of 24 in 1536 to spend six years in Rome as a member of the household of two cardinals. We know nothing of any architectural training there, but an apprenticeship must be assumed from the fact that he was called for important commissions in 1548 to Genoa and that from the start his work was of a stature to place him alongside his great contemporaries Palladio and Vignola. By 1555 he had begun to spend part of each year in Milan, and was commissioned to design the Palazzo Marino.[18] In 1560 he appears in the documents of the rebuilding of two churches that are central to our present interest: San Barnaba and San Vittore al Corpo.

San Barnaba was designed probably in 1558,[19] the year in which the Barnabites appealed to the city for permission to expand their church slightly into the public right-of-way, since the street on one side and the monastery on the other left a constricted space which explains the peculiarity of the plan. Alessi was forced to invent a dwarfed transept covered by a curious transverse barrel vault with a central lantern. The design is based on the separation of the functions of nave, chancel, and choir, each with a distinct covering in masonry, not coffering. The chancel is raised three steps above the nave and the altar rail is placed on the top step, and the lateral chapels are also raised, as in Palladio's Redentore, which also is anticipated in the narrow passages connecting the chapels. Paul Frankl explained these passages as an aspect of the new aesthetic of the period,[20] in which there was a tendency to create connections among isolated units, but I believe that the motivation is again liturgical, to permit the celebrant to reach his altar without mixing with the laity. These passages are also a feature of the final Gesù design. Finally, the interior is illuminated by windows borrowed from Roman baths, which were adopted by both Palladio and Vignola at mid-century.

Though many individual features of San Barnaba anticipate Palladio, the total configuration of San Vittore al Corpo more effectively conveys the relationship.[21]

The remodeling of the medieval basilica of San Vittore had been in the hands of the local architect Vincenzo Seregni, who built the conventual structures between 1553 and 1559. His numerous projects for the church of 1559–1560 were rejected in favor of Alessi's for reasons that are apparent when we compare one of them with the final Alessi design. Seregni's is retrospective. His attempt to add a nave onto a domed central-plan structure is an effort to solve a problem which Leonardo and Bramante had posed sixty years earlier, notably for the Cathedral of Pavia. Parts are added together ineffectually and without an articulated approach to function. By comparison, Alessi's design is a simple and clear statement of a new program that achieves everything I have ascribed to Palladio: it revives the three-aisled Latin cross, and establishes a four-part division of nave, transept, elevated chancel, and choir. The crossing is dominated by a dome on a high drum supported on four freestanding piers aided by heavy masses in the transept arms. This is the San Giorgio plan in embryo, but a peculiarly mature embryo that achieves a better integration of transept terminations and sacristies, anticipating the Redentore. Palladio, however, far outstripped his predecessor in building on the plan; his shorter nave, ample fenestration, and undecorated creamy surfaces resulted in a moving, light-bathed interior that contrasts with Alessi's cave-like and overdecorated basilica.

Alessi's plan was not entirely unprecedented. The Milanese architect Domenico Giunti, author of the extraordinary Villa Simonetta, designed the church of Sant' Angelo in 1552,[22] in which many of the new elements are anticipated: the linked chapels of San Barnaba, the culminating dome and the distinct transept and choir of San Vittore. Only the cohesion of the whole is lacking.

Features of the new scheme appeared in Rome at the same moment as they were adopted by Palladio. The earliest evidence is in Vignola's unexecuted project of 1565 for Santa Maria in Traspontina, where the nave and transept are of the same design as San Vittore.[23] Although the church was also a monastic foundation, the architect, like his Roman contemporaries, was not interested in the specialization of other functions as the northerners were; it lacks the cloistered choir of the preceding examples. Another Alessian invention which reappears here and in other Vignola designs is the use of a domed area behind the crossing piers to help support the major dome. Alessi put it alongside the chancel, while Vignola moved it forward to the end of the aisles. This project by Vignola – which, incidentally, includes the lateral nave portal we have seen earlier in Rome – is the direct forerunner of the Gesù, to which I shall now return.

Four years after the failure of the second Gesù project of 1554, the Jesuits appointed a member of the Order, Giovanni Tristano, as architect-in-chief for all Italian projects.[24] But when Cardinal Farnese agreed in 1561 to underwrite the costs of the Roman church, Tristano was gently forced into the background by the cardinal's architect, Vignola, who measured the site in 1562. However, the combination of real-estate problems and the cardinal's reluctance to start paying caused another delay. Father Tristano was not recalled from supervising in the provinces to Rome to attend to the new Gesù until 1566, and even then it was two years before the excavations began. Throughout the summer of 1568 a series of negotiations took place between Farnese and Vignola on one hand, and Father General Borgia, Polanco, and Tristano on the other.[25] These resulted in two letters of instruction from the cardinal to Borgia and to Vignola on August 26 which specify, first, that the cost is not to exceed 25,000 scudi; second, that there must be only one nave with side chapels, not a nave with side aisles; third, that the nave is to be vaulted (in answer to Borgia's plea for wood roofing, Farnese says that it is simply not true that masonry vaulting causes echoes, as may be seen in churches of much larger dimensions than this, where one hears perfectly); fourth, that the façade of the church must face west, as it does today; and finally that, these stipulations being met, Vignola is to choose whatever form he thinks best for the church.[26] The cardinal drove a hard bargain, and the only instruction that seems to be a contribution from the Order is the elimination of side aisles. This conflict arose over the orientation and appears from his letter of the same date to Borgia: ". . . the choir and high altar should stand toward San Marco, and thus I instructed the architect; and I wish you would acquiesce and not think about altering my resolution into something different." Two weeks later, Vignola and Tristano again went together to visit the cardinal in his country villa at Caprarola, and thereafter the design of the church proper must have been settled.[27] The façade was still indeterminate; Vignola was paid for a new façade model in 1569, another in 1570, for façade drawings in the same year, and finally, unable to satisfy the cardinal, he was dismissed in 1571.

The plan that presumably was presented to the cardinal does not look precisely like any of those we have seen, but the elements are familiar. From the earlier Gesù projects it preserves the three entrances into a wide nave, and the ample open chancel; the nave, transept, and chancel are clearly distinguished but well coordinated with each other. The transept has flat rather than rounded ends, probably for the same reason as in Alessi's San Barnaba: a street runs along the left side, permitting only a token projection. As in San Barnaba and the Redentore, the nave chapels are linked by passages; they are segregated from the nave not by steps but by low railings. The break between the nave and the transept is marked by a low domed area that is similar to the chapels but serves two entirely different functions: first, it is a passage to the exterior on both sides, like the nave portals we have seen before, and, second, it is part of the buttressing system for the central dome; there is a heavier mass of masonry here than over the chapels: the entrance is much smaller, and the surrounding piers thicker. The great contribution which Vignola has made to the style I have been discussing is in having found a way to create unity without sacrificing the distinctiveness of parts. He uses the domed crossing as a module; the nave is two modules long, the chancel one, and the height of the dome three. The noble cohesiveness of this conception explains why Farnese preferred Vignola to other Roman designers and why the Gesù became the model for most subsequent basilical churches in Rome in the following generations.

This was not Vignola's first and only proposal for the Gesù. Nearly twenty years ago I visited the Siena library to look at a sketchbook of a Sienese architect of the later part of the sixteenth century, Oreste Vannocci Biringucci, and discovered in it a sequence of pages that had been copied from some lost drawings by Vignola. It was in this book that the Traspontina design appeared, and I vividly recall the excitement of turning the page to find a drawing obligingly labeled "Il Vig.ª per il Jesu".[28] There are two drawings on the page, and they draw our attention from the plan to the façade. The lower one, which is the one specifically labeled "Jesu," originally struck me as a fascinating novelty in façade design, but Maria Casotti, in a monograph on Vignola, discovered that this is not really a whole façade but merely the *upper story* of the final Vignola project which was published in a well-known engraving.[29] The upper sketch is much more interesting, as one can deduce from close inspection, because it is for an *oval* church, domed, with a chapel on axis; you can see the flying buttresses all round. Similar oval churches, conceivably planned for the Gesù, appear on another folio of the Vannocci sketchbook. One of these plans has a portico on the façade, a feature which we have seen in Alessi's San Vittore. At first I discounted the connection of the oval projects with the Gesù, arguing that Vannocci's inscription could apply only to the lower of the two sketches, but then Wolfgang Lotz, with whom I published the drawings, pointed out that the façade is almost the same as the one appearing on the foundation medal of 1568.[30] Furthermore, the two-tower elevation is reminiscent of the Ignatian plan of 1550. This project, then, must be close to the medal of June, 1568, but it certainly was done before the instructions were received from the cardinal in August, in which a nave and side chapels are discussed. It probably is the earliest in a series, and it is intriguing because it has nothing in common with the cruciform churches except the façade. I refer to a series, because the foundation medal shows a façade that does not fit the final plan; its two side portals do not lead into the nave, but into the file of side chapels, which must have been designed quite differently if they were to accommodate circulation.

The façades of the drawing and of the medal, with their colossal order below and low attic above, together forming a rectangle crowned by a pediment, are not in the Roman tradition, but revive Michelangelo's unsuccessful project for San Lorenzo in Florence. Roman churches usually had an upper story restricted to the width of the nave and connected to the lower story by the volutes. But the North Italian Serlian or Palladian window in Vignola's medal suggests that a more direct source was a church we have already seen: Alessi's San Barnaba in Milan. Alessi's connection with the Gesù is not merely circumstantial; in January, 1570, a year before Vignola's façade was rejected, Alessi was invited to submit a façade project.[31] The fact that he was asked to do so without being required to visit Rome is evidence of his exalted reputation as a church designer.

Vignola's final façade plan of 1570 was engraved by Cartaro in 1573. Appropriately, the inscription celebrates the imperious cardinal and not the Jesuits. This façade abandons the planar simplicity of the medal project for an intricate, even ambiguous interplay of forms that lacks the cohesion of the inspired plan. It is this, no doubt, that explains the decision of the cardinal to reject Vignola's façade model in favor of one by a young pupil of Michelangelo, Giacomo della Porta (fig. 18.4). The Farnese were not sentimental; they had fired Sangallo in order to get Michelangelo to design the cornice of their palace, and now again they were listening for the *dernier cri*. In both cases they guessed correctly; the shift to della Porta constituted a commitment to the style that became the germ of the Baroque. Vignola was paid 40 scudi compensation and disappeared until his death in 1573.[32] Della Porta also replaced him at the Farnese palace, but perhaps after his death.[33]

Comparing the two façades in engravings, we clearly see that della Porta's is brilliantly knit together in a fashion which focuses attention at the center in a dramatic way. While Vignola's suggests a rectangular center with subsidiary wings, della Porta's creates a crescendo, accentuating the main portal by the invention of a pediment within a pediment, and, by drawing all the niches into the central area, leaving the outer wings bare. His volutes, moreover, softly link the two stories and emphasize their oneness. Of course, della Porta leans on Vignola's ideas in many respects, but simplifies and enriches them in the spirit of Michelangelo.

In subsequent generations, della Porta's solution was tenacious; it impressed itself on church façades throughout the world.[34] Della Porta's façade was finished in 1575, as we can read after the Farnese name on the entablature. In 1577, in accordance with a traditional mason's custom, a grand feast was held on the top of the main vault for the workmen, to celebrate the completion of the nave.[35]

The year in which the façade was finished was the year of Giovanni Tristano's death, which reminds us that he had been on the job as supervisor and co-architect all along. Presumably, he might have made important contributions to the design, in which case his relative obscurity would be unjust treatment, so it is worth examining one of the innumerable independent architectural projects that he designed and built in the period 1556–1557. The largest and finest of these is the church of the Gesù in Tristano's home town, Ferrara, designed in 1570.[36] The façade is the work of a distinct and inventive personality, but it is as somber as penitence itself. The interior is richer and more inventive, but it is disjointed, lacking in cohesive forces, and this can be seen as well in the awkward plan, which is no more mature than those of the '30s and '40s. This is quite characteristic of Tristano's work, and it surely suggests that he cannot have played a significant part in the design either of the façade or of the interior of the Roman church. The examples we have seen also show that it would be impossible to distinguish a Jesuit style; if anything, the examples reflect Tristano's Ferrarese roots. Just how impossible it would be to distinguish a Jesuit style is perhaps best illustrated by reference to a sheet of plan-studies drawn in the '80s by Tristano's successor as chief architect of the Order, Father Giovanni de Rosis.[37] They seem to have almost nothing in common except an unimpeded central space. Even side aisles are now allowed. Vignola's oval was not forgotten; it appears there, again with a vestibule. These plans may have been circulated in

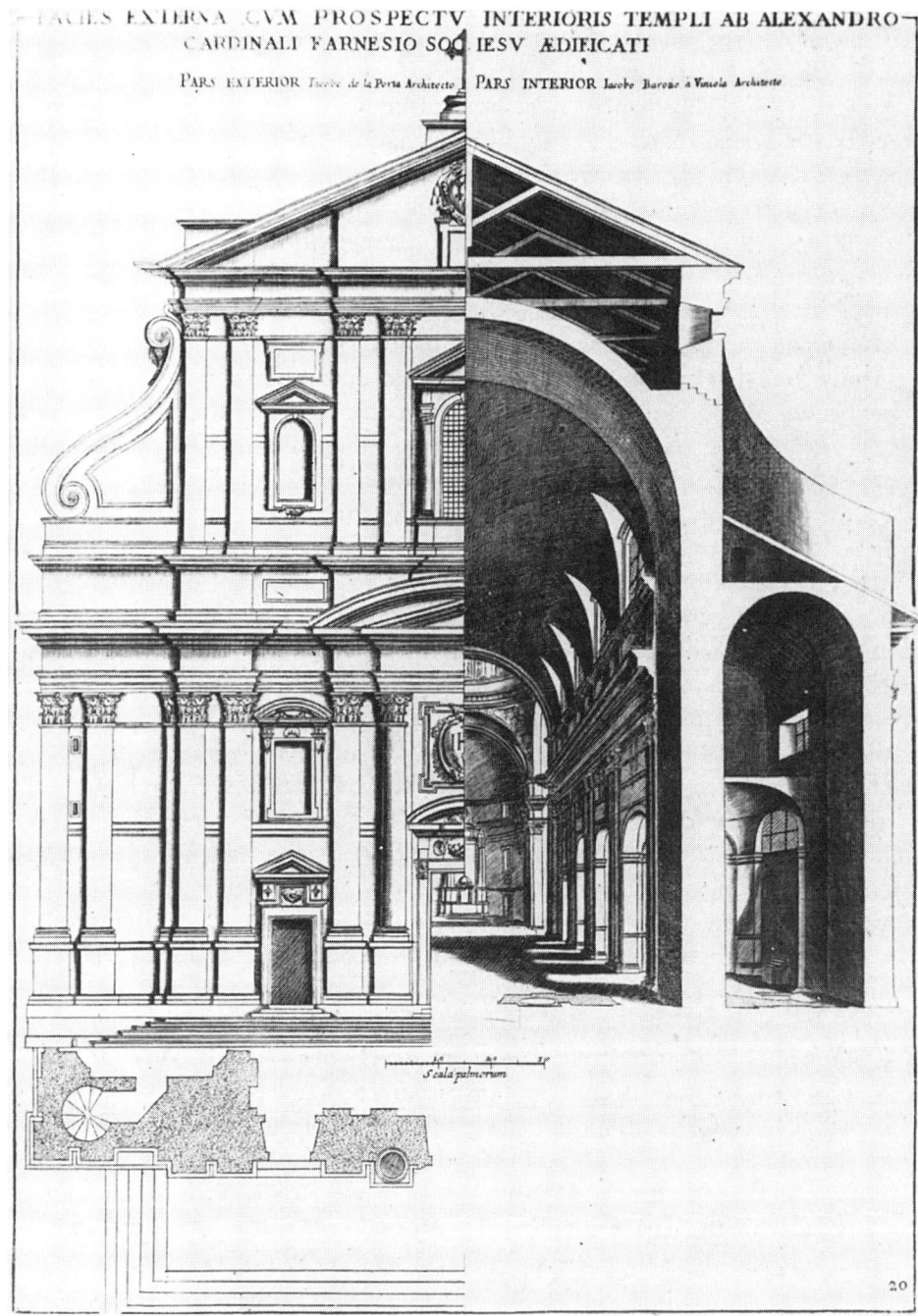

Figure 18.4 Rome, Il Gesù, Della Porta façade project, with nave alteration. From R. Wittkower and I. Jaffe, *Baroque Art: The Jesuit Contribution*, Fordham University Press.

380

the provinces as models to be followed by affiliates without architects of their own. And the variety is characteristic of the great collection of plans in Paris. The freedom of choice was intentional, since, beginning in 1565 on the election of Borgia, it became obligatory for every affiliate to submit for review in Rome any building proposal no matter how small.[38] Since strict control would have been possible within this system, the absence of it must have been purposeful; in Flanders, for example, new churches actually were built in the Gothic style.

It is odd, then, to discover that the architect and painter Giuseppe Valeriani, co-author of the Jesuit College in Rome, composed a treatise on the Jesuit style – "nostra consuetudine," the source says. Another document speaks of the "modo che usa la compania." But this must have been meant only in the most general sense – in short, the characteristic Jesuit church should be on a square accessible to the populace, and yet within the members' living compound; it should dispense with side aisles; where possible, it should have tribunes for private attendance at services on the part of the Fathers within the cloister: screened passages called by the Italians *coretti*, such as those in the Roman church, the first of their kind.[39]

Having returned thus to Rome with the conclusion that the Jesuit style exists, but in so general a sense that it does not affect the significant forms of the architecture, let us conclude with a tour through the mother church, which remained the most imposing of all Renaissance buildings of the Order.

In the engraving after della Porta's project, the interior appears in its original state: austere, even dour, with its great barrel vault crowning the cool classicism of Vignola's design. When we enter the Gesù today we get a quite different experience; Vignola's calm voice is lost in the brilliance of exuberant High Baroque stucco, sculpture, veneer, and painting; it is as if a Palestrina motet had to compete for attention with Vivaldi's *Gloria*. The conflict emerged by degrees; at first the Baroque spirit was applied on festive occasions, such as the splendid celebration of the first centenary of the Order in 1639, portrayed in a painting by Andrea Sacchi and assistants. Here decorations in the form of hangings are simply draped on and over Vignola's orders. The next stage – in which Giovanni Battista Gaulli, called Baciccio, a pupil of the great Bernini, was commissioned to decorate the nave and dome, together with sculptors and stuccoists under Antonio Raggi – came in 1672–1685, and permanently altered the aspect of the interior.[40] In the longitudinal section, engraved while Gaulli was still at work, the dome and apse decorations are still incomplete, but we can see how Vignola's intentions were altered. The spirited mobility of Gaulli's motives is characterized by the detail nearest the observer in the nave, acanthus clusters that leap up the socle of the vault like flames. The formerly sober window frames have been remodeled in the image of altarpieces, as if we should witness actual rather than painted miracles by looking through them into heaven. The fresco at the crown of the vault also does its best to persuade us that the architecture has suddenly dissolved to reveal a vision. The engraving shows at the base of the transept arm a splendid altarpiece with a spectacular sunburst at its crown. This also was erected in the later part of the seventeenth century, together with its companion across the transept, the altarpiece of St. Ignatius, by Father Pozzo. This is vastly different from the one designed for Cardinal Savelli by Giacomo della Porta sometime before 1587 which it replaced.[41] I discovered della Porta's design when leafing through the Italian architectural drawings in the Albertina in Vienna where there is a set of measured drawings taken from the original. It follows the sober spirit of Vignola's design, and shows the versatility of della Porta who also completed much of Michelangelo's work. Of course, this belongs to an era when everyone could remember Ignatius as a quiet priest who probably would have looked with suspicion on images inflamed by passion, no matter how spiritual, and with horror on such an altar dedicated to himself. The causes of differences between the Vignola and the Baroque Gesù could be explained fully only by theologians, but the change illustrates to laymen a fundamental contrast in the concept of religious art between the later sixteenth and the seventeenth century, when the reform character changes to a propaganda character, and the mood of contemplation gives way to a mood of excitation. This change is most evident in painting, and it can be seen in the altarpieces in the several chapels.

Finally, I should like to add that these observations affect the prevailing characterization of the Gesù as it appears in all the handbooks of architecture, where it is represented as the fountainhead of Baroque architecture. It is true that many of Vignola's inventions which were realized here for the first time were accepted by seventeenth-century architects, but I believe that if the Gesù had come down to us in its original simplicity it would have been praised not for its anticipation of the Baroque but for its vigorous statement of the spirit of its own time, when the arts were only beginning to emerge from the shadow of the giants of the High Renaissance, and when the Jesuit Order was just beginning to emerge from its early struggles for survival.

Postscript

This article, written for a symposium organized by Rudolf Wittkower with Irma Jaffe at Fordham University, was the first of several studies I devoted to the influence of reformed liturgy on church planning. My teacher Richard Krautheimer had been a major contributor to the study of the interaction of liturgy and design. The theme of the symposium – "Baroque Art: The Jesuit Contribution" – was a symptom of a tendency in architectural history to reach beyond the characteristically formalistic treatment of buildings to find social, economic, and political motivations for design choices.

The period of the Catholic Reformation and the Counter-Reformation stimulated a profound rethinking of the liturgy, of the participation of the clergy and the congregation in the Mass, of the role of preaching, and other issues that had a potential for radically altering the articulation of spaces within the church. The opportunity to address the design of the Gesù was particularly appealing because it had been so extensively discussed in the purely formal terms of its position in the evolution of Renaissance, Mannerist, and Baroque style.

I'm embarrassed that in this paper I too was still in the thrall of formal interpretation and followed earlier literature on the Gesù in overlooking a fundamental innovation of the Jesuit order with respect to past monastic practice: that Mass is not sung communally. There is no choir and, in the design of churches, no need to provide space for stalls. (Note, however, that Cardinal Farnese, in his letter quoted in the essay at n. 26, refers to the "choir.") This, more than aesthetic preferences, accounts for the simple form of the eastern end of the Gesù, where the expected spatial distinction of presbytery and choir is replaced by a unified space accommodating a single function. Further (and this point had always been emphasized), the church must accommodate resident members of the order by providing sequestered cubicles, out of public view, from which services may be heard. Vignola provided these in *coretti*, chambers behind screens placed in a sort of attic over the nave arcade.

Klaus Schwager's excellent study of the Gesù proposes that Giacomo della Porta made a fundamental change in the design of the interior of the church as well as of the façade. Because della Porta's façade was elevated by 2 meters over that of Vignola, the interior elevation of the nave had to be raised accordingly, which was done by adding an attic over the nave cornice; this attic is clearly delineated in the engraving reproduced in my figure 18.4, and it would have helped to achieve a *meravigliosa vaghezza* (the term used by Alessi, who himself offered more elevated façade designs at this time) on the interior. Below this level, the nave elevation remained as Vignola had designed it.

Schwager was led to this conclusion by an unpublished letter of 1570 addressed to Cardinal Alessandro Farnese (which, curiously, he neither identifies nor transcribes). The letter, he reports, criticizes a design by an unidentified author in which, as in that of Vignola, the entablature of the main façade order is lower than that in the nave. 1570 was also the date at which Vignola produced a *secondo modelo della facciata*, perhaps because Cardinal Farnese was dissatisfied with the initial design, recorded in the medal. We cannot know whether Vignola refused to meet the new demands, or whether the cardinal was dissatisfied with his proposals, but in any case the architect was dismissed in 1571. Clearly, the controversy that culminated in the commission to della Porta for the façade design and the vault elevation was over issues of architectural style (probably relating principally to the appearance of the interior), and did not involve the interests of the Jesuits.

Schwager presents the Uffizi plan – now attributed to Bartolomeo Rocchi – as an awkward reflection of the project by Michelangelo referred to in 1554. I rejected that association except for the pentimenti in red chalk, which I thought to be Michelangelo's effort to control the vast spaces proposed in the drawing. He also brings into consideration a drawing for the cupola from the della Porta workshop that appears to be transitional between Vignola's design and the final project, which, like the nave vault, had to be elevated.

Alan Ceen, in tracing the history of the Via Papalis, shows how the planning of this major Roman street affected the designs of the Gesù. In 1538 the Via Papalis was rerouted at the point at which it reached the Piazza Alteriorum on the west side of the church of Santa Maria Alteriorum – the future site of the Gesù. The new route veered to the right and passed through this square directly toward the Capitoline Hill, crossed the Capitoline piazza, and descended to the Forum. While the church of Santa Maria had faced north onto the old route (which continued past the Palazzo Venezia and San Marco, skirting the Capitoline), the Gesù, as later stipulated in the instructions of Cardinal Farnese, was to be oriented to face west onto the new papal route as it turned toward the Capitoline Hill. Michelangelo was commissioned in 1537 to make the civic center accessible, and this may have encouraged the pope to reroute his triumphal way (thus underscoring his power over the city government) – which ultimately influenced the orientation and the siting of the Gesù.

Notes

1   See Milton Lewine, "The Roman Church Interior, 1527–1580," Ph.D. diss., Columbia University, 1960; "Roman Architectural Practice During Michelangelo's Maturity," *Stil und Überlieferung in der Kunst des Abendlandes*, Acts of the 21st International Congress for the History of Art, 1964 (Berlin, 1967), 20–26.

2   Outlines of the history of Milanese architecture in the first half of the sixteenth century may be found in E. Arslan, "L'architettura milanese del primo Cinquecento," *Storia di Milano*, 7 (1954), 533–563; P. Mezzanotte, "L'architettura milanese dalla fine della signoria sforzesca alla metà del Seicento," ibid., 10 (1957), 559–645; C. Baroni, *L'architettura lombarda da Bramante al Richini* (Milan, 1941).

3   R. Wittkower, "The Centrally Planned Church and the Renaissance," *Architectural Principles in the Age of Humanism*, Part I (London, 1949), and later editions. See also E. Sinding Larsen, "Some Functional and Iconographical Aspects of the Centralized Church in the Italian Renaissance," *Inst. Romanum Norwegiae, Acta*, 2 (1965), 203–253.

4   Churches of this type are discussed by Giuseppe Zander, "A proposito di alcune chiese napoletane anteriori al Gesù di Roma," *Palladio*, n.s. 3 (1953), 41–46. Zander convincingly challenges the proposal by Georg Weise ("Chiese napoletane anteriori al Gesù del Vignola," *Palladio*, n.s. 2 [1952], 148–152) that a group of Neapolitan churches deriving from Spanish Gothic models were influential in the formation of Vignola's plan.

5   P. Tacchi Venturi, "Note storiche e topografiche di Roma nel sec. XVI: Le case abitate in Roma da S. Ignazio di Loyola . . . ," *Studi e documenti di storia e diritto*, 20 (1899), 287ff.; P. Pirri, "La topografia del Gesù di Roma e le vertenze tra Mutio Muti e S. Ignazio," *Archivum Historicum Societatis Iesu*, 10 (1941), 178f.; Tacchi Venturi, *Storia della compagnia di Gesù in Italia*, 2nd ed. (Rome, 1951), 2:546ff.; P. Pecchiai, *Il Gesù di Roma* (Rome, 1952), 3–9.

6   See Jean Vallery-Radot, *Le recueil des plans d'édifices de la compagnie de Jésus conservés à la Bibliothèque Nationale de Paris* (Rome, 1960). Pirri, "La topografia del Gesù," 177ff., discovered the plan of 1550 presumably by Nanni, and published it in the hand-drawn copy reproduced in figure 18.1. I attempted to get a photograph of the original, but the folio cited by Pirri (Paris, B. N., Cabinet des estampes, Cod. Hd-4D, fol. 82) has drawings for other structures, and was obviously misquoted.

7   Pirri, "La topografia del Gesù," 177–204.

8   Pirri, "La topografia del Gesù," and his *Giovanni Tristano e i primordi della architettura gesuitica* (Rome, 1955), 138 and note. A document of 1554 (p. 213) may refer to a later plan by Nanni ("disegno che ho fatto della chiesa nova, che vole fare la comp.ᵃ di Jesu"). The Paris plan is not signed, but since Nanni was the architect at the time, he presumably was the author. On Nanni's active but undistinguished career, see R. Wittkower, "Nanni di Baccio Bigio and Michelangelo," *Festschrift für Ulrich Middeldorf* (Berlin, 1968), 248ff.; M. Lewine, "Nanni, Vignola and S. Martino de' Svizzeri in Rome," *Journ. Soc. Archit. Historians*, 28 (1969), 27ff.

9   Pirri, *Tristano*, 147.

10 Ibid., 138n.; Pecchiai, *Il Gesù di Roma*, 10f.

11 Tacchi Venturi, "Note storiche e topografiche," 326f., and *Storia*, 2:545ff.; Pirri, "La topografia dei Gesù," 20f.; Pecchiai, *Il Gesù di Roma*, 14f.; J. Ackerman, *The Architecture of Michelangelo*, 2nd ed. (London, 1964), 2:145f.; *Michelangelo architetto*, ed. Portoghesi and Zevi (Turin, 1964), 944ff.

12 Uffizi, Arch. 1819, published and first attributed to Michelangelo by A. Popp, "Unbeachtete Projekte Michelangelos," *Münchner Jhb.*, n.s. 4 (1927), 389–477.

13 M. Lewine, "Roman Architectural Practice," 20ff.

14 The text is reproduced in translation by R. Wittkower, *Architectural Principles*, 155ff.

15 On Giberti, see Angelo Grazioli, *Gian Matteo Giberti* (Verona, 1955), esp. 76ff.; E. Cattaneo, "Influenze veronesi nella legislazione di San Carlo Borromeo," *Problemi di vita religiosa in Italia nel Cinquecento*, Atti del convegno di storia della chiesa in Italia, Bologna, 1958 (Padua, 1960), 123–166. Prof. Lewine and Wolfgang Lotz drew my attention to these sources and to Giberti's role.

16 St. Charles's book is most easily accessible in the Italian translation of C. Castiglione and C. Marcora, *Arte sacra, De fabrica ecclesiae* (Milan, 1952). The original is published in *Acta Ecclesiae Mediolanensis* . . . (Milan, II. 1890; III. 1892), ed. A. Ratti (Milan, 1892), esp. 561–638. A richly annotated edition of the Latin text is in Paola Barocchi, *Trattati d'arte del Cinquecento*, vol. 3 (Bari, 1962). See A. Deroo, *Saint Charles Borromée* (Paris, 1963), and C. Baroni, *L'architettura lombarda*, 86ff. Baroni cites the volume *Echi di S. Carlo Borromeo* (Milan, 1937–38) for further commentary on the influence of the Saint on the arts. I have not found this volume. For the Milanese background, see F. Chabod, "Per la storia religiosa dello stato di Milano durante il dominio di Carlo V," *Annuario dell' Ist. ital. per l'età moderna e contemporanea*, 2–3 (1936–37) (Bologna, 1938); C. Marcora, "La chiesa milanese nel decennio 1550–60," *Storia della diocesi di Milano*, 7 (Milan, 1960), 254–501.

17 On Palladio's churches, see W. Timofiewitsch, *Die sakrale Architektur Palladios* (Munich, 1968); G. Zorzi, *Le chiese e i ponti di Andrea Palladio* (Vicenza, 1966), and general observations in my *Palladio* (Harmondsworth and Baltimore, 1967). The peculiar problems involved in the development of the Redentore plan and its possible origins as a central-plan church have been revealed by E. Larsen, "Palladio's Redentore, a Compromise in Composition," *The Art Bulletin*, 47 (1965), 419–467.

18 On Alessi in Milan, see Hanns Hoffmann, "Die Entwicklung der Architektur Mailands von 550–1650," *Wiener Jhb. für Kunstgeschichte*, 9 (1934), 69–73; Giovanni Rocco, "Galeazzo Alessi a Milano," *Atti del IV convegno nazionale di storia dell'architettura* (Milan, 1939), 185–198; P. Mezzanotte, "L'architettura milanese," 577ff.

19 C. Baroni, *Documenti per la storia dell'architettura a Milano nel Rinascimento e Barocco* (Florence, 1940), 1:87ff.; Nancy A. Houghton Brown, "The Church of S. Barnaba in Milan," *Arte lombarda*, 9 (1964), 62–93; 10 (1965), 65–98.

20 Paul Frankl, *Principles of Architectural History* (Cambridge, Mass., 1968), 31ff. (published 1914 as *Entwicklungsphasen der neueren Baukunst*).

21 C. Baroni, *L'architettura lombarda*, 123f.; P. Mezzanotte, "L'architettura milanese," 572ff.

22 C. Baroni, *L'architettura lombarda*, 122; P. Mezzanotte, "L'architettura milanese," 565ff.

23 Vignola's presence at Santa Maria in Traspontina is known only through a drawing of ca. 1580 by Oreste Vannocci Biringucci showing a (competition?) project for the church and inscribed "Trasp.ⁿᵃ Vig.ᵃ," which I published with W. Lotz, "Vignoliana," *Essays in Memory of Karl Lehmann, Marsyas*, suppl. I (New York, 1964), 3–7, figs. 1–2.

24 P. Pirri, *Tristano*, 10ff.; 40ff.

25 The chronology of the design and construction of the church is summarized with reference to the documents and secondary sources by W. Lotz in Ackerman and Lotz, "Vignoliana," 14–18. Cf. the documents in Pirri, *Tristano*, 248ff.

26 The letters are transcribed in Pirri, *Tristano*, 228f., docs. XXIV, XXV.

27 Ibid., p. 249, doc. XLIV; Pecchiai, *Il Gesù di Roma*, 43.

28 Ackerman and Lotz, "Vignoliana," 7–10. The project and the plan mentioned below were first published, with my approval, by Lotz, "Die ovalen Kirchenräume des Cinquecento," *Römisches Jahrbuch für Kunstgeschichte*, 7 (1955), 45–48, and republished by Maria Casotti, *Il Vignola* (Trieste, 1960), 209ff.

29 Casotti, *Il Vignola*, 209ff.

30 Ackerman and Lotz, "Vignoliana," 8f., 18, fig. 7.

31 A. Ronchini, "La chiesa del Gesù in Roma," *Atti e memorie delle RR. dep. di storia patria per le prov. modenesi e parmensi*, 7 (1874), 30; Ackerman and Lotz, "Vignoliana," 16, 19f.

32 Pecchiai, *Il Gesù di Roma*, 43; Pirri, *Tristano*, 252, doc. XLIV: "Sua Signoria s'è resoluta di non fare la facciata secondo il disegno di detto Vigniuola ma pigliare quello di m. Jac.º della Porta."

33 Ackerman, *The Architecture of Michelangelo*, 2:84.

34 See H. Wölfflin, *Renaissance and Baroque* (London, 1964), 93–108 (first ed., 1888); G. Giovannoni, "Chiese della seconda metà del Cinquecento in Roma," *Saggi sull'architettura del Rinascimento*, 2nd ed. (Milan, 1935), 177ff.; W. Lotz in Ackerman and Lotz, "Vignoliana," 22ff.

35 Pirri, *Tristano*, 255, doc. XLIV.

36 Ibid., 118–126, pls. XIX–XXIII.

37 Ibid., pl. VI, from Bibl. Estense, Modena, fondo Campori; Vallery-Radot, *Le recueil des plans*, 7.

38 Vallery-Radot, *Le recueil des plans*, 6ff.; P. Moisy, *Les églises des Jésuites de l'ancienne assistance de France* (Rome, 1958), 1:45ff.

39 Vallery-Radot, *Le recueil des plans*, 7, 68–75; Moisy, *Les églises des Jésuites*, 61ff., 303ff.; F. de Dainville, "La légende du style jésuite," *Études*, 287 (1955), 3ff.; C. Galassi Paluzzi, *Storia segreta dello stile dei Gesuiti* (Rome, 1951).

40 Cf. Robert Enggass, *The Paintings of Baciccio* (University Park, Pa., 1964), 3–74.

41 J. S. Ackerman, "Della Porta's Gesù Altar," *Essays in Honor of Walter Friedlaender*, *Marsyas*, suppl. II (New York, 1965), 1f.

19

The Carracci and the Devout Style in Emilia

Charles Dempsey

When the young Giorgio Vasari arrived in Bologna in 1539, armed with a commission to paint in San Michele in Bosco (fig. 19.1), he arrived there representing the modern manner. This style was above all based on the stupendous and continuing achievement of Michelangelo in Rome, and yet, with the unveiling of the *Last Judgment* only two years later, it was soon to come under direct attack by the forces of the Counter-Reformation as being more concerned with the effects of art than with stirring the souls of the faithful, and indeed even, insofar as it was concerned with the affections at all, as being obscene. It was a style that at that very moment was also being given regional identification, under Medicean patronage and on the basis of the Tuscan Michelangelo's example, with the state style of Tuscany; but which, like the language of Florence and its literature, was also being promoted as the canonical foundation for national expression in the whole of Italy. This is the conception enshrined in the *Lives* Vasari published in 1550 and 1568 under the aegis of the State literary academy of Florence, the Accademia Fiorentina, and it is the foundation for north Italian regional and municipal reaction to the account of the history of art written therein. It is the very origin of the concept of national versus regional style that has so engaged scholarship on Emilian art in particular, and that initiated a polemic still vivid in the days of Malvasia and that had initially made its appearance in the pages of Lamo, Armenini, Ridolfi, and in the *postille* written by the Carracci in the margins of the 1568 edition of the *Lives*.

What Vasari found in Bologna was a group of painters whose works were based on a different model, and to them a powerful one, the *maniera devota* of Francia (fig. 19.2), Costa, and the young Raphael. Francia and Costa were the founders of the first distinctively Bolognese style of painting, a style forged out of Umbrian, north Italian (especially Ferrarese) and Flemish models. Michelangelo had called Francia and Costa «due solennissimi goffi nell'arte», even as he had also called Perugino, the other great master of the *maniera devota*, «goffo nell'arte». It is Vasari who reports, as Previtali has sketched out in his *Fortuna*

388

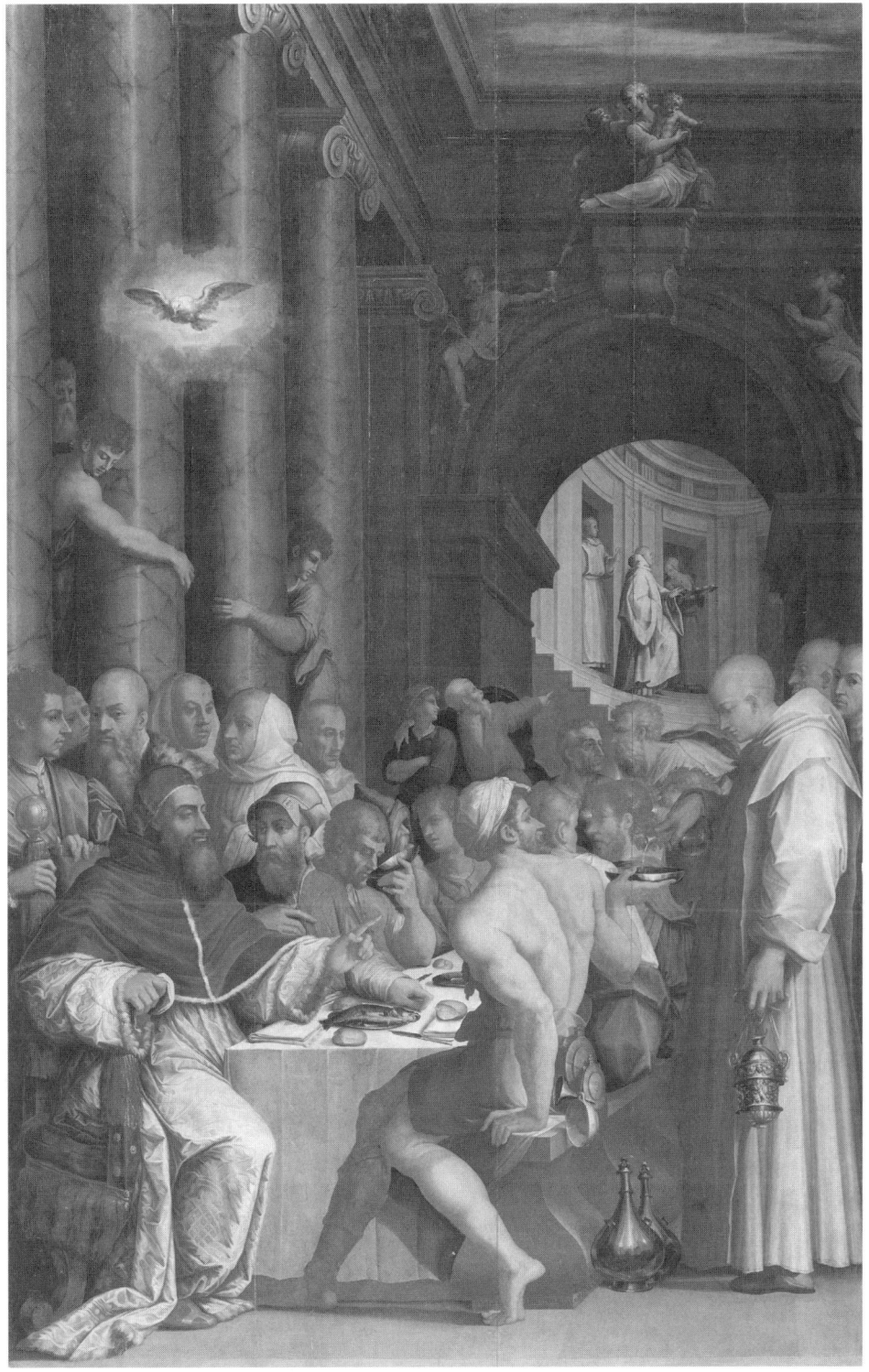

Figure 19.1 Giorgio Vasari (1511–1574), *Supper in the House of St. Gregory.*
Bologna, Pinacoteca Nazionale. © 1990, Photo Scala, Florence – courtesy of the
Ministero Beni e Att. Culturali.

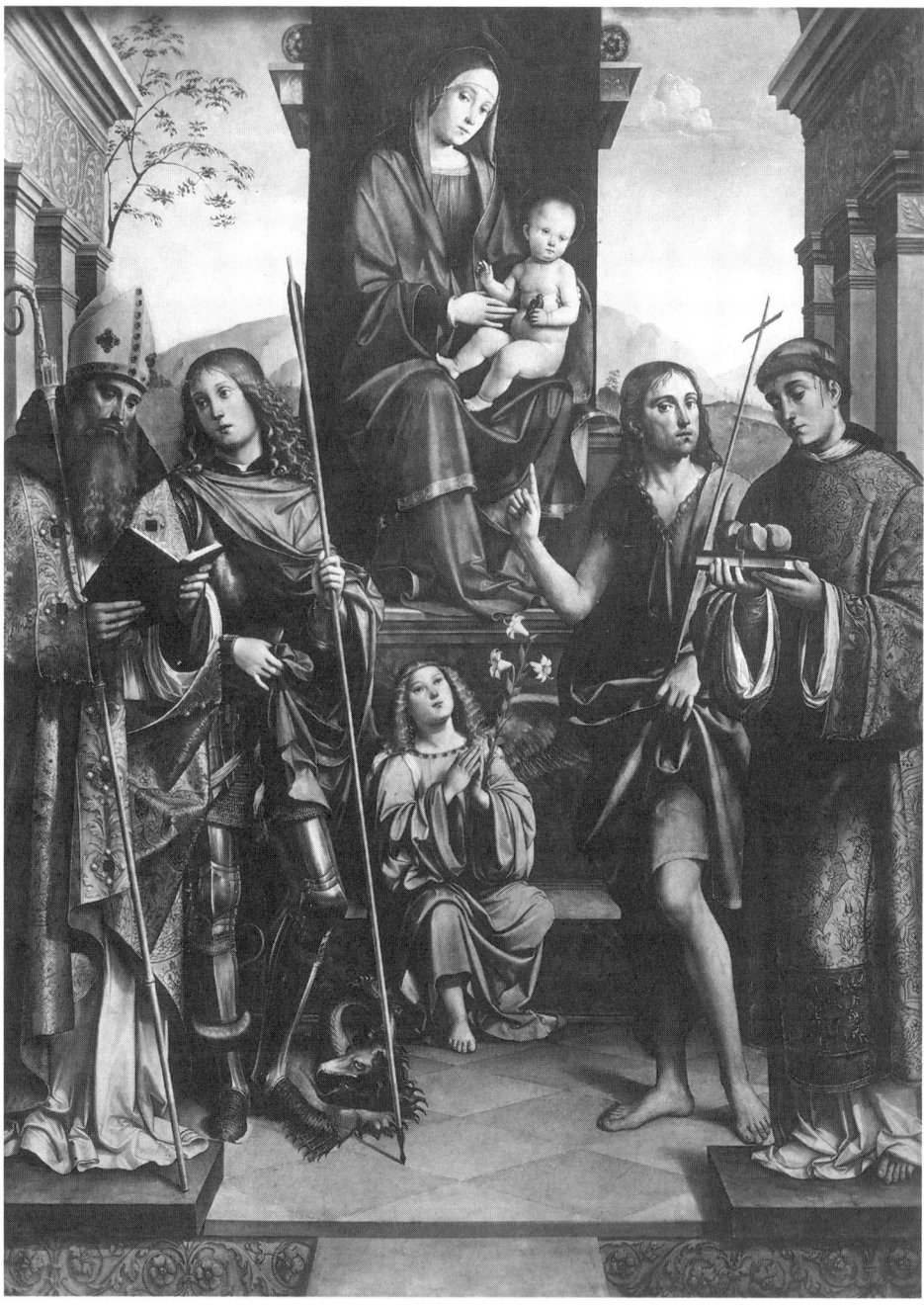

Figure 19.2 Francesco Francia, *Madonna and Child with Four Saints*. Bologna, Pinacoteca Nazionale. Alinari Archives-Florence.

dei primitivi, that this «clumsy and inept» manner was popularly called the «devout style», even though Vasari objects to the term because it implies that the good modern style is incapable of expressing devotion. His characterization of it clearly shows the tensions produced by contemporary Counter-Reformation criticism between the advocates of the modern manner and its detractors, who believed that art should be placed in the service of inspiring devotion:

> I would never wish that anyone deceive himself by interpreting the clumsy and inept as devout; and the beautiful and good as lascivious: as some do, who, when seeing figures of women or youths a little more lovely, or more beautiful and adorned than usual, immediately attack them and judge them lascivious: not realizing how wrongly they condemn the judgment of the painter, who holds that the male and female saints, who are celestial, are as much more beautiful than mortal nature as are the heavens over earthly beauty and our works: and what is worse, they reveal their own souls as infected and corrupt, discovering evil and dishonest desires in those things which, were they truly lovers of honesty, as in their ignorant zeal they would have us believe, should show their desire for heaven, and to make themselves acceptable to the Creator of all things, from whose most perfect and most beautiful arises all perfection and every beauty.

No clearer statement could be wished of the position of an embattled humanist art, with its goal of manifesting an ideal of truth in the forms of an absolutely perfect beauty, set against that of a reformist art, with its goal of touching the earthly passions of the spectator, and thereby invoking a natural yet typical devotional effect that identifies human passion with the divine. Vasari, however, notwithstanding his scorn for the clumsiness of the devout style, also gives clear evidence of its importance, characterizing in the *Lives* a polemic that had arisen earlier in Rome itself between Michelangelo (who had heard the proto-reformist thunderings of Savonarola against lascivious painting) and the «new style» of Francia and Perugino. This style had won great popularity and indeed represented an advance beyond anything that had appeared before, being the penultimate step leading to the emergence of the modern manner. Michelangelo despised it, and associated it (acutely) with Flemish painting, which Francisco da Hollanda reports he also called «devoto» and an art fit only for women, monks and nuns, and clumsy peasants. The vehemence of his reaction attests to the national prominence of Perugino's and Francia's style in Rome when Michelangelo first arrived there, as yet unproven as a painter, and indeed Malvasia, writing a century after Vasari, attests to the many paintings by Francia still hanging in Roman collections. Vasari's account in the *proemio* to the third part of the *Lives* vividly describes the extraordinary acclaim given in Rome to the new style of Perugino and Francia, which he says was because of the sweetness of their unified colors, so lovely that people stopped praising the old and dry style and thronged madly to embrace the new.

The importance of this style, and especially the impact it made in Rome itself before the emergence of the modern manner, at precisely the moment

Michelangelo was beginning work on the Sistine ceiling, has not received its critical due. The reasons for this are complex, and have to do with a modern lack of sympathy (essentially in agreement with Michelangelo) with the pietistic aims, «più chiesastica che religiosa», as Argan put it, of Francia's and Perugino's art; and, on an art historical level, with the obstinate tendency of modern criticism since Morelli to separate and isolate Francia as an artist from Perugino and the young Raphael. They also have to do with the speed with which the devout style was supplanted, thanks to the unveiling of the Sistine Ceiling in 1512, and because of the achievement of the *Stanze* by Raphael – whom Vasari praises for so quickly unlearning the style in which he had been trained by Perugino. The figure of Raphael is indeed crucial to the story, for Vasari also writes that with the painting of the *Sposalizio* in 1504 Raphael had become the greatest master of the *maniera devota*, surpassing even his own master, Perugino. It was as master of that style that he came to Rome in 1508, where he earned Michelangelo's undying antipathy by being promoted as a rival candidate for the commission to paint the Sistine ceiling; and it was Raphael's apostasy, abandoning the style of Perugino and Francia to embrace the modern manner of Michelangelo, that caused the relegation of the devout style from a position of national prominence to a phenomenon of merely regional, and even provincial, interest.

It is important to keep the figure of Raphael clearly in mind at this juncture, for the highly ambiguous claim by Vasari (and yet a correct claim, given the sudden and complete eclipsing of the devout style in Rome) that the devout style represented the most advanced manner in Italy at the beginning of the sixteenth century, yet simultaneously epitomised an awkward and backward-looking provincialism – something that emerges clearly in his venomous account of the painters of the Bolognese school – has yet to be resolved by modern criticism. Primary interest, naturally enough, has concentrated on Raphael's stupendous development from his early training with Perugino in Umbria on to the magnificent achievements in Rome. However, so far as Emilian painters of the sixteenth century were concerned, there was not one Raphael, but two, and the first of these, the greatest master of the devout style, was especially identified with Francia and the school of Bologna. Besides its appeal to pietistic sentiment, the quality especially valued in this style was its sweetness and tenderness of coloring (always an index of naturalistic and affective intent), what Becherucci has seen in Raphael's early works as a Bolognese «strength of colorism that was to restore strength and vigor to the arid range of Perugino's color», and which finds its closest analogies in the vivid and gemlike colors that Francia and Costa inherited from the Ferrarese tradition and attempted to adapt to the atmospheric fusions of Perugino. Her perception has a long history in Bolognese criticism: Malvasia too found Francia's colours «più tenero» than Perugino's, while Cavazzoni, an exact contemporary of the Carracci, wrote at the beginning of the seventeenth that «Francia was a painter without equal in his time, who put all the others on the right path, and whose Madonnas so greatly pleased

Raphael that he admired and contemplated them, abandoning on their account that dryness he had acquired from Perugino».

Raphael is the only painter identified in Vasari's *Lives* as the master of not one, but two styles, and by this Vasari means not personal styles but something grander and more difficult, two generic styles that laid rival claims to national dominance. His fame in Bologna was profoundly based on the first style, which was closely associated with that of Francia, founder of the first school of painting in that city, and master of a style that had attained more than regional recognition. The relations between Bologna and Urbino, between Francia and the young Raphael, remain obscure in modern criticism, being insisted upon only by Filippini, Becherucci, and myself, but suffice it to say that the Bentivoglio, who were driven from the city in 1506, owned no fewer than four early paintings by Raphael – two portraits, an *Adoration*, and a *Baptism* – while Francia himself supervised the decoration of the Palazzo della Viola using drawings sent by Raphael for the project. Agamemnon de' Grassi, brother of Paris de' Grassi, Julius II's chamberlain, owned an early *Annunciation* that had been given him by his other brother Achilles, who was made Bishop of Città di Castello in 1506. I omit mention of paintings from Raphael's Roman period, such as the *Ezekiel* in the Hercolani collection or the *Saint Cecilia*, which Raphael sent to Bologna in Francia's safekeeping, except to note that Raphael's friendship with Francia continued long after he went to Rome and adopted the modern manner, and Francia indeed sent many of his students, Marcantonio and Bagnacavallo among them, to Rome to work with him.

It was indeed this very fact that baffled and enraged Vasari, who vaunted himself as bringing the modern manner to Bologna, but whose work had been ridiculed by the local artists, and who accordingly wrote of Bagnacavallo, Aspertini, Cotignola, Innocenzo da Imola, and all the Bolognese painters, that their «heads were filled with pride and smoke», for they would not «honor the rare masters and studiously imitate them». Instead they remained blindly and xenophobically resistant to painters bringing the modern manner from outside, preferring to adhere to the provincial manner of their master, Francia – whom Vasari, in a famous canard, maintained had died of shock and mortification when the *Saint Cecilia* arrived in the city. What especially baffled Vasari, however, was that:

> All these masters, from having seen the works of Raphael and associated with him (in Rome), had a certain something overall that seemed as if it should be good; but in truth it did not hold to the well-understood particularities of art as it should. But because there were not painters in Bologna in those times who knew more than they did, they were held to be the best masters in Italy by those who governed the city and by the people of that city.

In other words, although the artists Vasari encountered in Bologna had seen the works of Raphael and worked with him in Rome, and so there appeared in their art something that looked as though it should be right – an allusion in it to a pure ideal expressed with reference to the antique, the modern manner, and Raphael's mature style – at the same time, in its scale, in its color and atmospheric fusion, and above all in its naturalistic effects (what Longhi in a famous phrase called the Emilian window opening onto nature), it remained distinctly old-fashioned, appealing to conventional human sentiment as an affective means for attaching the ideal to the particular truth of experience. Though it acknowledged the Roman Raphael, it remained provincial precisely because of its adherence to the spirit of Francia and another Raphael, the Raphael of Città di Castello.

The style of Rome and Vasari would triumph in Bologna in the next generation with those painters – Prospero Fontana, Sabatini, Samacchini, Calvaert, and Passarotti – against whom the Carracci launched their celebrated reform. The initial basis for that reform was a call for a return to the naturalism inherent in the art of the region, precisely in order to make painting again into a means capable of arousing devotion, and especially popular devotion. The call was not theirs alone, but made in response to Counter-Reformation criticism of the arts, which had made of Michelangelo's *Last Judgment* the paradigm of all that was wrong about the *maniera moderna*, and which had stressed that art ought not exalt itself or its own beauties in and of themselves, lest the soul of the spectator be moved only by those beauties, or even be led to lewd speculations. As the *maniera devota* itself had represented an idea of reformist piety, an alternative in fact to the values inherent in humanist art, in the days when Savonarola preached and when the young Luther first visited Rome, and represented moreover an idea that still could be powerfully invoked by clerical critics of Michelangelo's *Last Judgment* long after the particular styles of Francia and Perugino had been defeated and outdated by modern advances, so too did the Carracci in the fullness of the Counter-Reformation return to its critical values and the sensibility inherent in what was, after all, the tradition of their native Emilia. And there can be no doubt that the Carracci were preoccupied, not only with the individual and particular styles of painters in the Emilian, or what they called the Lombard, tradition, but also with the generalized values inherent in that tradition as a whole. We need only recall their appeal to an idea of Lombard *colore* to recognize a concept of distinctive regional excellence that is analogous to recent attempts to characterize what Briganti has now called the «Emilianness» of Emilian art. Indeed, the profound historical and critical consciousness of the Carracci reform really needs no dwelling upon here, beyond recalling that in its beginnings it founded itself in a return to the naturalistic foundations inherent in the traditions of north Italian painting, and that it defined itself in opposition to the too exclusively Tuscan and Roman style championed by Vasari in the *Lives*, a style that had won the day in Bolognese painting of the mid-century.

Paradigmatic of the polemical foundation to their reform was the refusal of Ludovico Carracci to go to Rome in his youth, and his devising for himself and his younger cousin Annibale of a *studioso corso* throughout the cities of north Italy in order to absorb the lessons of the canonical masters there – a canon, incidentally, that Agostino did much to establish throughout the whole of Italy through the medium of reproductive engravings (as Ridolfi acknowledges, the fame of Veronese was greatly increased through Agostino's engravings after his works). And fundamental to the critical consciousness of the reform, as has indeed already appeared from Cavazzoni's precise appreciation of Francia's colorism as being more saturated and less dry than Perugino's, was an attempt to isolate particular values generic to the art of the region, both in the recent and relatively remote past. Indeed, given the historical structure of Vasari's *Lives*, in which the dominant values inherent in Tuscan art were conceived as developing in a coherent and unbroken line from Giotto through to Masaccio and on to the triumph of Michelangelo, such a viewpoint on the part of the Carracci was virtually inescapable. As Elizabeth Cropper has argued in this symposium, once the history of Italian art had been given such a structure, never again was it possible to understand or practice painting without responding to the burden of the past that had thus been created, whether by accepting the canons established by Vasari or by seeking to broaden them to include other possibilities and other values; and this applies with special force with respect to Bolognese painting, which Vasari had consigned to the oblivion of backward provincialism. Accordingly we find Malvasia, in a remarkable passage, writing the following of Ludovico's beginnings.

> Certain it is that Ludovico never saw Rome, save for the few days he stopped there when he was approaching old age and was already a great master, as will have been said below; and that *fare statuina* was not altogether to his own genius, and equally, moreover, it was not entirely to that unlearned Lombard simplicity (*quella inerudita semplicità lombarda*); instead, he sought a mixture that would be neither one nor the other, and would participate in both one and the other. Accordingly, having in the beginning left Prospero, as has been said, he gave himself to studying on his own the beautiful works of two of his countrymen in particular, those of Bagnacavallo for coloring, and those of Tibaldi for *disegno*; because the former set himself, as has been said elsewhere, to imitating Raphael, and though he did not attain that master's *giustezza*, he had still been able to surpass him in a certain Lombard softness and fleshiness (*un certo morbido e carnoso lombardo*), which in that Divine Artificer is the only thing left to be desired; and the latter, following the path of Michelangelo, though he fell short of the *terribilità* of those contours, nevertheless had known how to temper with great grace, and facilitate with much discretion those perilous leaps of the fancy, and hence Ludovico used to call him, as has been said elsewhere, his Buonarroti *riformato*.

The concept of Michelangelo *riformato* is significant, not only in the stylistic sense of attributing to Tibaldi something Michelangelo lacked, a quality of grace and refined judgment in disciplining the unrestrained powers of the imagination, but also (and for these very reasons) it is significant in its linguistic equation of artistic reform and Church reform as an affirmation of the foundation to reformist criticism of the *Last Judgment*. But the important point here is that Ludovico did not reject Michelangelo's art as a model, but on the contrary he accepted it as an essential, though incomplete one. Even more important in the context of our present argument is his attitude toward Bagnacavallo's *inerudita semplicità lombarda* – a phrase that pointedly invokes, and indeed agrees with Michelangelo's and Vasari's equation of the *maniera devota* with clumsiness and provincialism, a *maniera goffa*. For of course, from the standpoint of the 1580s there could be no question of returning literally to the archaic simplicity of Francia and his immediate followers, any more than Michelangelo had it in mind to revive the style of Masaccio when he drew after the frescoes in the Brancacci chapel. What both Ludovico and Michelangelo were instead seeking was an understanding of the fundamental and permanent values inherent in the art of their own respective traditions.

On the other hand, there could be no question either of a literal return to Michelangelo and the *maniera moderna*, not only for the narrowly "campanilistic" reason that Vasari had identified this style with Florence and Rome, nor even entirely because it had degenerated into what the Carracci contemptuously called the cold and naturalistically unconvincing *fare statuina* of the second *maniera* descendants of Michelangelo in Florence and Bologna itself, but fundamentally because the values of that art were incompatible with contemporary religious, political and indeed individual needs and sensibilities. This was true not only of the provinces but also in Rome, where by the death of Vasari in 1574 painting was seen to have spent itself in formulaic and specious repetition of the outward forms of the *maniera moderna*, and sensibilities turned toward a natural yet internalized art capable of touching and stirring the emotions, whether in the devotional context of ecclesiastical art or in secular and highly sophisticated evocations of poetic quality and sentiment.

Nevertheless, how polemical Ludovico's decision not to go to Rome was may be seen by leafing through the pages of Vasari, for whom the only possibility for an artist born in the provinces was to come into contact with the center. From the beginning of the Trecento Florence had been that center, being replaced by Rome in the second decade of the Cinquecento, to which artists were drawn from every part of Italy in order to learn the lessons of the *maniera moderna* first achieved by Leonardo and Michelangelo in Florence. It was with this dual idea of centrality that Vasari sought to identify the national destiny of art with the incorporation of the Accademia del Disegno in Florence in 1563. The centrality of Rome, and the concurrent provinciality of Emilia, was an issue of course that continued to be debated in the pages of Malvasia and Bellori (who revived in just such terms the dispute current at the start of the century over whether Annibale was the better painter in Bologna or Rome, and who differed on the achievement of Ludovico, whom Malvasia bitterly complained was perceived as a painter of only regional importance in Rome), and the debate was framed in terms that had been set by Vasari. Thus, Vasari writes that Niccolò Soggi, «hearing that great things were being done in Rome, left Florence with the idea of advancing his art»; Pierino da Vinci, «having often heard diverse persons discuss and celebrate the art of Rome, was filled with a burning desire to see it»; Battista Franco, «having from his earliest youth devoted himself to *disegno*, as someone who desired perfection in his art betook himself at the age of twenty to Rome»; Giovanni da Udine, while studying as a youth with Giorgione in Venice, «hearing such great praise of Raphael and Michelangelo resolved to go to Rome»; Parmigianino, «having heard great praise of the masters in Rome, especially Raphael and Michelangelo, came upon the desire to go there»; Garofalo, «desperate and stupefied in seeing the grace and liveliness of Raphael's paintings and the profundity of Michelangelo's art cursed the Lombard *maniera* he had labored so hard to learn in Mantua», and after returning to Ferrara «he often recalled with great sorrow his departure from Rome, and resolved to return there at any cost»; Girolamo da Carpi also «often grieved that he had wasted his youth and best years in Ferrara and Bologna and not Rome». In the provincial isolation of the Emilians Garofalo and Girolamo da Carpi, cursing and grieving over the style they had grown up with, we hear the echo of Vasari's praise for Raphael, who overcame his provincial origins, abandoned the *maniera devota* and mastered the modern style; just as we also hear the echo of his bitter condemnation of Francia, Bagnacavallo and the other Bolognese painters for stubbornly resisting the new manner and ignorantly priding themselves on their simple and clumsy style of painting.

And most important in Vasari's enumeration of the painters who did or did not see Rome is, of course, Correggio, the artist upon whom the Carracci especially based fundamental principles of their reform of painting (fig. 19.3), and whom Vasari famously calls «the first in Lombardy who began to paint in the modern manner, and had he only gone to Rome he would have worked miracles». It is undoubtedly on Correggio's example that Ludovico determined not to go to Rome, perceiving that Correggio provided the foundation for a style that deeply drew from the coloristic and naturally affective wellsprings of Lombard painting, and an example that would be neither unconvincingly *statuina* nor provincially *goffa* and *inerudita*. The question of whether Correggio actually did go to Rome is outside the scope of this lecture, but I feel bound to say that, given the importance Vasari attached to precisely the question of just which artists did and did not go to Rome, the pains he took to answer that very question case by case, and the otherwise unimaginable absence of any record of such a visit by so major an artist, in my opinion make it very improbable. Nor do I find the attempts that have been made to find precise points of connection between Correggio's figures and their presumed sources of «inspiration» in works by Michelangelo and Raphael in Rome very persuasive. As Vasari recognized, it is Correggio's understanding of the *maniera moderna* as a generic concept that raises the question of his putative trip to Rome, and not specifically documentable points of figural reference. But for Vasari the wonder and the sorrow of Correggio's art lay in his simultaneous grasp of the modern manner and his inability to perfect it through visiting Rome itself. Even from his Roman viewpoint it was possible (though critics beginning with Mengs, another advocate of the centrality of the capital, have found it inconceivable) to arrive at an

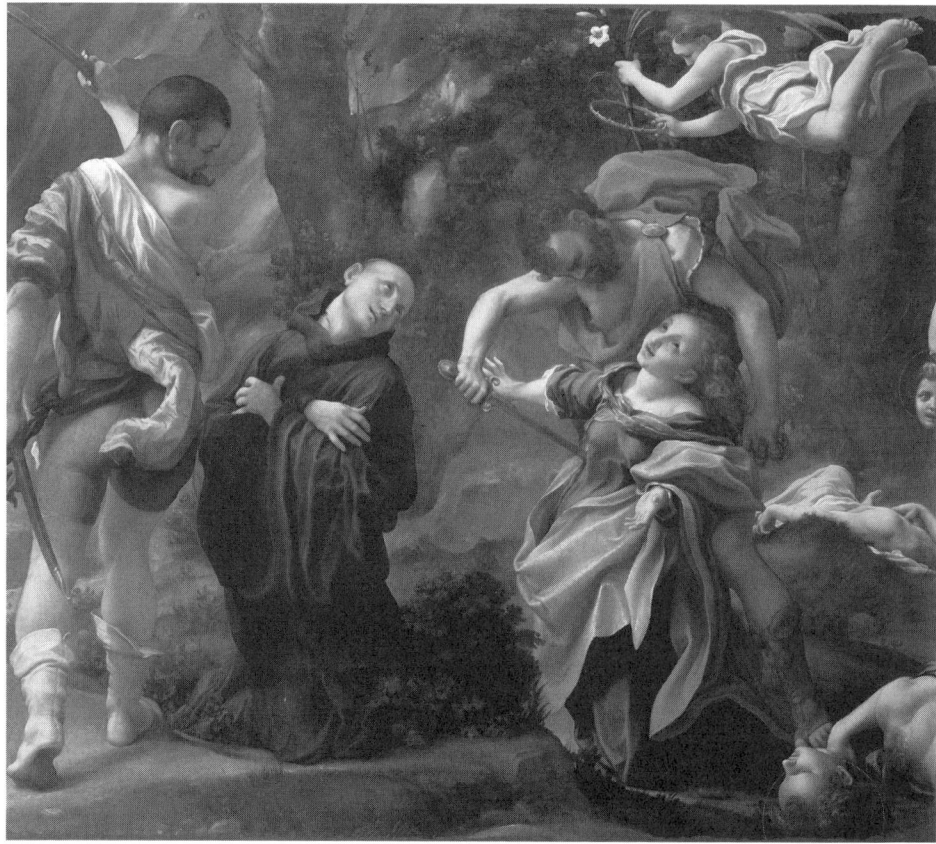

Figure 19.3 Correggio, *Martyrdom of Four Saints*. Parma, Galleria Nazionale. akg-images / Electa.

understanding of the modern manner outside Rome, while indeed going to Rome did not by any means ensure such understanding. Such understanding had eluded Francia and Bagnacavallo in Bologna, Garofalo and Girolamo da Carpi in Ferrara, and Innocenzo da Imola and Marchesi in the Romagna. All of these artists had gone to Rome and known the Roman works of Raphael at first hand, and yet had failed to grasp its essence, in Vasari's view willfully in so far as the Bolognese artists were concerned, who instead diluted what they had seen there with the provincially pietistic and sweetly affective values of Francia's (and the young Raphael's) devout style.

Be that as it may, what the Carracci found in Correggio was a modernization of the devout style, a mode of painting that did not compromise its character-istic sentiment but instead lent the *maniera devota* greater persuasive force by embodying, rather than merely representing, humanly affective feeling in the forms of a pure grace and in the convincing colors of nature itself. They found in him a model, in other words, by appeal to which the perfected ideals of humanist painting could be attached to the realities of nature and individual experience, and the ideal thereby made accessible, poetic fictions or the divine itself appearing as verisimilar extensions of the familiar truths of experience. «No one better ever touched colors», Vasari had said of Correggio, «or with greater loveliness or greater relief painted better». Correggio was incomparable in rendering the softness of flesh, *la morbidezza delle carni*, in Vasari's words, and he describes the *Leda* and the *Danae* as «colored with such softness and worked like flesh in the shadows, so that they did not seem colors but flesh itself» (*sí di morbidezza colorite e d'ombre di carne lavorate, che non parevano colori, ma carni*). Here we have, critically stated by Vasari, a response to exactly the same effects that the Carracci sought to reinstate in their reform, what Malvasia reports they called the *morbido e carnoso lombardo* and sense of *viva carne* that they opposed to the *fare statuina* then prevalent in Bologna. Correggio's mode of color is in one sense a brightening of Leonardo's manner, retaining his softening of contour but without Leonardo's heavy obscurities and smoky darkness of shadow; and in his lucid and clear colors, the very antithesis of Leonardo in their strength and purity of hue, he never abandons the natural strength of colorism practiced by Francia, Costa and the young Raphael, the painters upon whose works his initial style had in large part been founded; but unlike those masters he paints, like Dosso and Lotto, or like the Raphael of the *Saint Cecilia*, with a broad and heavily loaded brush – what the Carracci in their own painting called the *nuovo impasto* – in a manner that, as Vasari lamented, is more direct modeling than it is drawing in the modern manner.

And this mode of coloring can be seen in the Carracci from their beginnings, whether in a painting like the *Annunciation*, painted by Ludovico about 1584 for the Confraternity of the Holy Sacrament at the church of San Giorgio, or in Annibale's *Butcher's Shop*, or in his very different, and much debated *Crucifixion* for the church of San Nicolò di San Felice (fig. 19.4), signed in 1583. The overpowering naturalism of the last painting has led scholars astray in assessing the nature of Correggio's impact on Annibale, for in figural type and stylistic mode it resembles Correggio not at all; but it is precisely its pure, natural colors and bold impasto, scumbled broadly with brush, palette knife, and fingers onto the canvas with an energy and directness that even Courbet might have envied, that betrays Annibale's debt to the vision and techniques not only of Correggio but also the late Titian; and indeed in sheer optical force of illusion (but not idealizing intent), in its rendering of the textures and appearances of rough sackcloth and heavy brocades, it differs not at all from the dazzling illusionism of the much more smoothly finished and sophisticated *Madonna of Saint Louis of Toulouse* for the high altar of Santi Ludovico e Alessio, with its richly oily and impastoed rendering of varied effects ranging from the warmth of heavenly light to the coolness of dawn, or from the dull reflections in polished marble to the gleaming rows of pearls set in the saint's mitre. It is this optical power that distinguishes the *Crucifixion* from Passarotti's pallid *Presentation of the Virgin* of the same year (and displayed in the same room as Annibale's picture

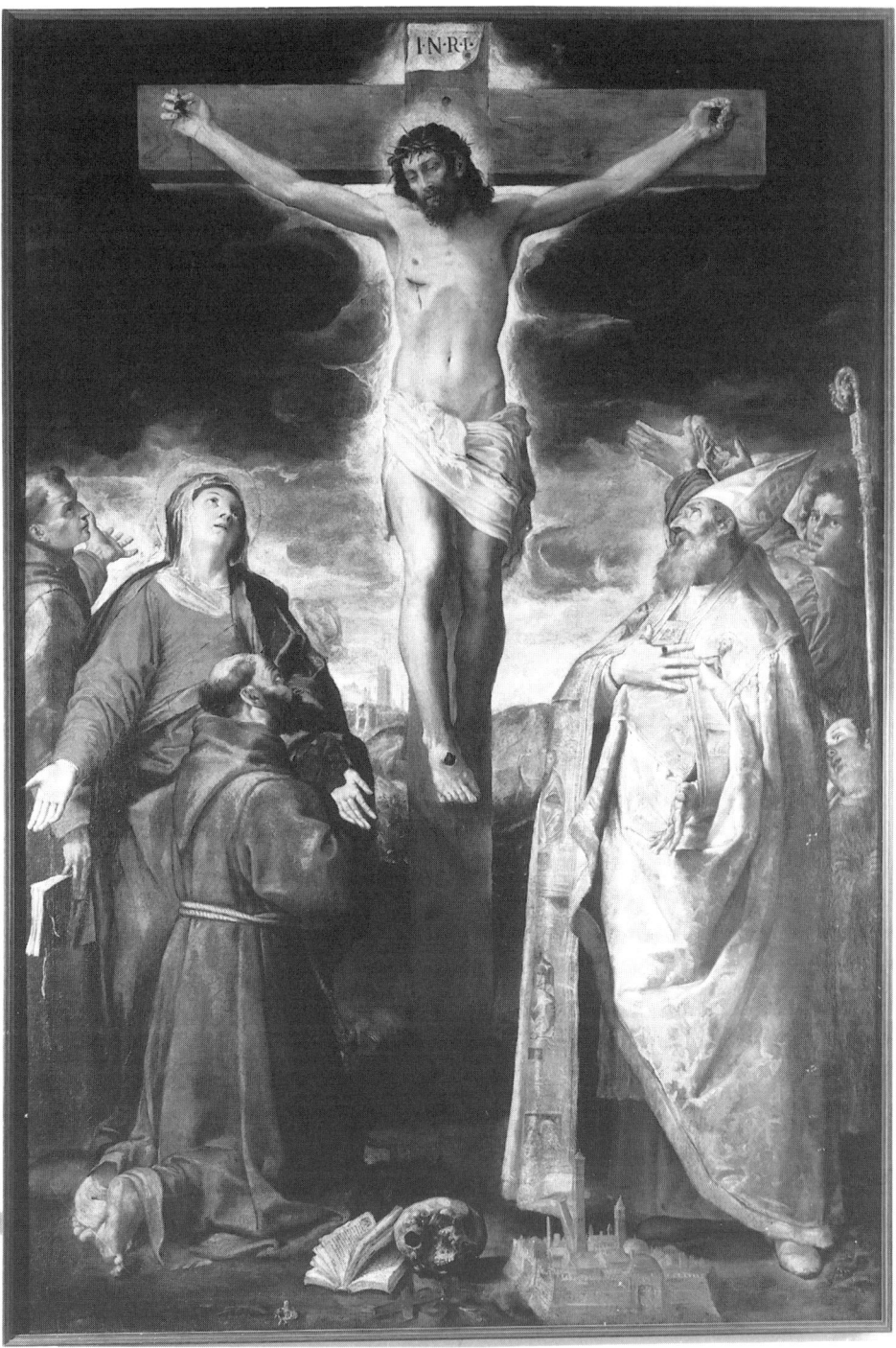

Figure 19.4 Annibale Carracci, *The Crucifixion with the Virgin and the Saints.*
Bologna, Santa Maria della Carità. Soprintendenza P.S.A.D. Bologna, Archivio
Fotografico.

when the present exhibition opened in Bologna), in which colors are applied with a smoothness and lack of differentiation in texture, without descriptive force, more appropriate to the painting of a battleship than to rendering the effects of nature. And indeed it was the raw power of Annibale's naturalism that led Passarotti, who also painted genre themes as a superficial matter of iconography rather than stylistic substance, to complain of pictures like the *Crucifixion* that the breadth of its colorism only concealed an inability to idealize and even to draw. It was a preposterous claim, though not unlike Vasari's similar criticism of Correggio.

The inability of modern criticism to assimilate the *Crucifixion* coherently into an account of Annibale's development as a painter seems to me to derive from an unnecessarily limited concept of the nature of stylistic thinking and absorption. If, in a painting like the *Pietà* Annibale painted for the Capuchins in Parma immediately after completing the *Crucifixion*, his debt to Correggio appears obvious because of its blond harmonies, its figural citation of Correggio's characteristic morphologies, and its evocation of that devotional sentiment Correggio inherited from the painters of the *maniera devota*. This is a matter of expressive purpose as much as technique; as Malvasia indicates, the Carracci could adopt variously Correggio's *colorito suave* or Titian's more heavily chiaroscuroed *colorito forte*, depending upon the affective demands of the subject. The question of when it was that Annibale first became aware of Correggio seems to me a misplaced one, insofar as it would be truly astonishing to find that there could have been a time when he was unaware of the works of the most famous painter of Emilia. Two of Correggio's greatest altarpieces, after all, were no further away than Modena, more were in Reggio, and a *Christ in the Garden* hung with Raphael's *Ezekiel* in the Hercolani collection in Bologna itself. Mannerist painters like Passarotti had copied or closely paraphrased Correggio's figures, a famous example being Niccolò dell'Abate's appropriation of the executioner from the *Martyrdom of Four Saints* in his *Martyrdom of Saints Peter and Paul*. In so doing, however, he reduced Correggio's passionate rendering to mannerist stereotype, either misunderstanding or specifically rejecting the expressive and naturalistic power of his heavily impastoed colorism. And it is precisely the power of Correggio's color, together with Titian's dramatically scumbled chiaroscuro, that makes its appearance with such startling force in Annibale's *Crucifixion*, while his figures deliberately eschew an appeal to Correggio's feminine grace in order to express directly and evoke the strong and humble piety of the poor.

Similarly, in Ludovico's *Annunciation* or his *Vision of Saint Francis* in the Rijksmuseum in Amsterdam, in each of which the tender figure of the heartbreakingly young Virgin is expressed in the flushed tints and softly fleshy forms with which the idea of Correggio's grace found embodiment, we find the emergence of a new *maniera devota*, an art newly designed not to stir admiration but instead to stir human sentiment through an irresistible appeal to psychological response. But this is not to say that the new art sought a simple and unconsidered return to naive simplicity and an escape from history. In the streets of Bologna and in their Academy the Carracci drew on the site and after the model, while simultaneously they took their students through the churches of the city to observe and analyze the traditions of art. With each encounter they put to the test the expressive aims and painterly techniques of the Renaissance masters, from Bagnacavallo and Tibaldi to Correggio and Titian, measuring their effects in *disegno*, color, chiaroscuro, manly force or feminine grace, against the effects of nature itself. In so doing they purged their painting of the superfluous and purely ornamental conventions of the degenerated modern manner, but at the same time they rooted their naturalism firmly in history, both regional and national. And more than that, by turning the powers of art inward, toward the human psyche, they opened up potential wellsprings of authentic expression and response that went far beyond the narrowly defined aims of a merely devotional art. It is for this reason that when Annibale went to Rome in 1595 he arrived not as the representative of a narrowly conceived and limited regional manner, but armed with the secrets of a national and international style that would prevail for the next three hundred years. From that moment even Raphael would speak in Lombard accents.

Part VI

Theory and Practice

Introduction

Sixteenth-century Italian art was a newly literate art. This is evident, in the first place, in the increasingly common phenomenon of the literary artist: a striking number of the major painters and sculptors of the period (Leonardo, Michelangelo, Raphael, Bronzino, Cellini) can be studied for their writings as well as for their visual works. It is equally evident in the rise of what David Summers has called a "language of art": a vocabulary for talking about art and architecture often formulated by dilettanti and amateurs but always in dialogue with the artists themselves. In the sixteenth century, Titian would make paintings that he himself called *poesie*; others would make *istorie*. The workshop master was refashioned as a "professor"; artists' academies, based on the models of earlier writers' associations, would provide new curricula for their students.

Attendant to and sometimes subtending all of this was a new relation between artistic practice and the motley collections of text and ideas that are now sometimes grouped together as "art theory." No previous century provides such a rich array of contemporary literary material relating to its art. Yet both the heterogeneity of sixteenth-century art theory – which includes biographies, poems, discourses, dialogues, treatises, and letters – and the often oblique ways that these texts relate to actual surviving objects, all make the material less than straightforward to study. It was seldom the case that an artwork aimed primarily to illustrate a theoretical claim or that a theoretical text simply expounded on issues raised by a newly unveiled painting or sculpture. Artworks continued, on the whole, to serve the circumscribed purposes for which they had traditionally been commissioned, and the literature of art, written in generic forms that came with their own internal rules and conventional topics, responded as much to earlier writings as it did to new visual works.

The four pieces that follow, therefore, are included not so much for their exegeses of important theoretical texts as for the subtlety and sophistication with which they negotiate the problem of the relation of theory to practice. John Shearman's classic essay, "Leonardo's Colour and Chiaroscuro," gives an account of that painter's revolutionary departure from the color system used by earlier Renaissance painters. At first proceeding empirically, Shearman describes the way that Leonardo's predecessors, employing what the author terms "absolute color," had approached the problem of modeling. Shearman's eloquent and perceptive account of the limitations such an approach entailed sets up Leonardo's alternative as a newly naturalized and rationalized conception of color, one that sacrificed coloristic richness and variety as ends in themselves but that achieved an unprecedented unification of the elements in the canvas by means of light. Additionally, the essay sets its descriptions of Leonardo's achievement against the painter's own writings on the topic, with the result that Leonardo's practice comes to explain his theory. Shearman demonstrates how an awareness of the artist's technological innovations can change the way we think about even the philological issues his writings raise.

Mary Pardo's essay is in many ways an illuminating counterpart to Shearman's, as both the artist and the picture with which it deals are deeply indebted to the Leonardesque inventions Shearman describes. Though Shearman himself raises the topic of how Leonardo's experiments with light and color relate to the content of his pictures – explaining, for example, the dark setting of the *Virgin of the Rocks* in these terms – Pardo makes this a more central problem and in addition takes into account the painting's address of an implied beholder. Central to her reading of Savoldo's *Magdalene* is the artist's clever manner of inserting supernatural events into the "natural" optical space generated by the painting's implied point of view, such that the painting field can stand in for the beholder's perspective and the character in the painting for a vision of the witness who stands before it. The structure, as Pardo shows, has a wide range of implications, from the way the picture plays against conventions of the dramatic close-up as devotional image, to the way that the character in the painting, turning in relation to us as she does, evokes the metaphors of conversion and transfiguration that are central to her story, to the suggestion, in the light itself, of Christ's own presence, beside us, before the image. Where theory enters Pardo's essay is with the metaphors that arise vis-à-vis the picture's central motifs, especially that of the shawl, or veil, that the Magdalene wraps about herself. Whereas Shearman attempted to shed light on Leonardo's theoretical interests by dealing first with the artist's technical experimentation, Pardo uses theory – here construed broadly to include both the literature of art and the poetics to which it closely relates – to add further dimensions to a set of core pictorial conceits.

The third piece, David Summers's essay *"Figure come fratelli,"* begins with a formal issue, the rise of what he calls "three-dimensional symmetry" in late Renaissance painting. Central to Summers's argument is his perception that the sixteenth century saw a general transformation in its principles of pictorial composition: the traditional hieratic organization of the painted surface, according to which planar figures mirrored one another on either side of an axial central element, was gradually outmoded by a different system, one keyed to rotated figures, seen simultaneously from several different points of view. Making painting virtually three-dimensional, this implied a new way of thinking about the relationship between painting and sculpture; that thinking became articulate in textual treatments of contrapposto, or visual antithesis, which characterized three-dimensional symmetry as a means of measuring and displaying technical difficulty, and as a new sort of ornament. In Summers's discussion, bodies – made ever more physical by the new techniques painters were bringing to their work – become devices that allow order. They enable the painter to aspire to something like poetic form, and their reconceived use has implications both for the nature of the religious image and for the subjectivity of the viewer before the image. More broadly, Summers looks to the intersection of theory and practice for a period aesthetics, finding historical language for the qualities that made Renaissance pictures "good."

Finally, Ingrid D. Rowland's study brings out the importance of period antiquarian projects to the development of Renaissance "theory." A crucial model for nearly all Renaissance treatises on the arts was Vitruvius's *Ten Books on Archictecture*, and one of the first attempts to translate the text into the vernacular was that undertaken collaboratively by Raphael, Angelo Colocci, and Marco Fabio Calvo in the late 1510s. The project originated from the assignment Raphael had been given to complete an archaeological reconstruction of ancient Rome; it was also to serve him in his role as chief architect to the Basilica of St. Peter's. The practical impetus behind the philological undertaking, Rowland suggests, helps explain the way Raphael and Colocci transformed Vitruvius's lessons: notably, it was Colocci, in the context of these projects, who codified the incalculably influential idea that architecture has "orders." Raphael, of course, was not merely an architect, and considering his study and reworking of Vitruvius in the context of his diverse and collaborative enterprises allows Rowland to shed light on the artist's movement between different media. Notably, the essay presents Raphael's *Fire in the Borgo* as a "painted treatise," one dealing primarily with beauty, and one that argues through the juxtaposition of human and architectural forms. As Rowland presents it, the relationship between theory and practice is always multidirectional: ancient ideas about architecture inform both modern building and modern painting; at the same time, the experience and practical needs of the modern impresario transform those very ideas, creating a kind of manual for his own successors in the process.

20

Leonardo's Color and Chiaroscuro

John Shearman

It is unfortunately the case that the analysis and interpretation of colour in paintings lags far behind other aspects of formal historical criticism. The subject seems to be in some degree of disrepute, or at the best open to suspicion, and not without reason. It is rare that observations in this field descend from the general to the particular,[1] or from frank subjectivity (even quasi-mysticism) to the admittedly more tedious but ultimately more rewarding objectivity that is, for example, normally regarded as indispensable in modern studies of perspective. The following study was undertaken in the belief that colour (and its dependents, light and chiaroscuro) can just as well be submitted to argument and historical criticism.[2]

The analogy between perspective and colour is not casual. One initial clarification is demanded: light, in painting, is absent, or present, or deployed and characterized in this or that way, always as a result of handling colour, the primary visual constituent of the work, in a certain fashion. This is too often forgotten, and light is discussed as if it were a self-sufficient element which arrived via the artist's brush. Similarly, linear space, in its absence or presence, is the product of the treatment of the perspective of objects. It is not an accident that those artists in the Renaissance who made most discoveries about space also explored and defined the possibilities of pictorial light; the interest in, and understanding of, each problem requires the same state of mind. This is as clear in the art of Giotto as in the words of Alberti; Leonardo is another conspicuous case.

Another clarification must be made. How often has it been said that Leonardo was not interested in colour, but in chiaroscuro or tone? This is a statement that is based on a modern analytical distinction, and no Renaissance text on colour can be understood before the anachronism is removed. For example, in 1504 Ugo da Carpi's "chiaroscuro woodcuts" are called *stampe di legno a 3 colori*.[3] There is in Leonardo's paintings and theoretical writings,[4] as in those of his contemporaries, no opposition between colour on the one hand and light and shade on the other; it is inexact to separate colour – in the customary sense of the chromatic element of *colore* – from chiaroscuro, and to say that he found the former of secondary importance compared with the latter. Leonardo developed both, in new directions and for new purposes. To him they were not separate departments of his art, but were in most respects inseparable; at times they are complementary, at other times their interaction is so complex that they may be regarded, in all but the scientific context, as one medium. It is highly significant that when he talks of colour and chiaroscuro in pictorial, and not scientific, theory, the treatment of light and shade is designated *colore*, as in Alberti. *Dividesi la pittura in due parti principali; delle quali la prima è figura, cioè la linea, che destingue la figura delli corpi e lor particule; la seconda è il colore contenuto da essi termini*; when this division is repeated in all essentials in a second text, *la seconda è detta ombra*.[5]

The development of the handling of colour in Tuscan painting achieves its greatest acceleration between the earliest works of Leonardo and the death of Andrea del Sarto. Its pace may be compared fruitfully to those of plasticity and *disegno* between, say, Filippino and Salviati. It was Leonardo who gave the first impetus in each case, and in colour his contribution is measurably the greatest. It is not my purpose to describe this contribution in all its many aspects, but rather to demonstrate one relatively simple point and to explore its consequences. From the methodological point of view I have taken the obvious opportunity, in the second section, to check observations and interpretations against Leonardo's many notes on the subject; this expresses the assumption that techniques of analysis and terms of reference are most relevant when they can be found in the literary material which is closest to the work of art.[6]

The Tonal Scale of Pigments and the Tonal Unity of Colour

One of the properties of the Absolute Colour of mediaeval painting which most vigorously resisted the realistic tendencies of early Renaissance art was the modelling of forms exclusively in colour. With significant exceptions, most quattrocento painting achieves the relief of form in this way. Generally, a form of a certain colour is defined by variations in the intensity or saturation of this colour; variations in intensity yield automatically a range of tonal differences and these express lighting and relief.

Each pigment, however, in its pure and fully saturated state, has its own specific tonal value; blues are inherently darker than yellows. If, hypothetically, we take the most familiar pigments on the Renaissance palette, fully saturated, it is possible to produce a tonal, as well as a chromatic, scale: from yellow, the lightest, down through cinnobar (or vermilion), apple-green, turquoise, rose-red, to the darkest, lapis lazuli. If an artist works within the convention of colour-modelling these tonal properties of pigments are imposed upon him and lead to certain results.

The awareness of these properties in the Trecento and Quattrocento is demonstrated by the way in which many artists exploit them. An alternative to simple saturation modelling is the phenomenon of colour change; this is the variation of the local colour of a form between its highlight and shadow – a device much favoured for its decorative contribution by many of the Tuscan gothic artists such as Agnolo Gaddi or Lorenzo Monaco, and obviously sympathetic to an age which assessed the beauty of colour quantitatively, both in the sense of variety and of brilliance. Frequently colour changes are no more than decorative, and there is no other logic in the selection of these pairs, but the tonal difference inherently present in the coupling of, say, yellow and blue, may be made to model form. Masolino, in the frescoes at Castiglione Olona, is typical of several Quattrocento artists who consistently select their colour-couples in this way, so that the tonal contrast of pigments alone provides an alternative to variations of saturation.[7]

Another more important fact follows from the tonal scale of pigments. If an artist in this convention paints St. Peter, by tradition clothed in a yellow robe over a blue vestment, with each drapery modelled by saturation-changes and the full intensity of the pigment used for the deepest shadows, then those two forms are bound to be plastically inconsistent. The potential range of tone offered by each pigment cannot be matched, and the modelling of the yellow drapery will be less powerful than that of the blue. The full meaning of this problem may be seen in Masaccio's *St. Anne* in the Uffizi; at this early stage of his career Masaccio worked without modification within the technical tradition of late gothic art. A case where the consequences are least obvious is the relationship between the rose-red and deep blue draperies of the Madonna, for these are pigments close to each other on the tonal scale; even so, if one compares the plasticity attained on the sleeve of the Madonna in red, with that on the knee below in blue, the inevitable disparity is apparent. More striking, however, is the disparity in potential modelling between forms of colours at opposite ends of the scale, between, say, the relatively strong rose-red of St. Anne's robe and the much weaker cinnobar-red of the angel at the top, and most striking of all, if one takes the extremes of the scale between the full saturated yellow of the highlights of the upper left-hand angel and his equally pure, but far deeper blue wing. This angel has a vestment that turns from this full value of yellow to a full cinnobar-red shadow, which is an example of the device of colour-change, used by Masaccio to exploit just the differences of tone in the pigments themselves which pose the problem we are examining.

The *St. Anne* panel introduces a secondary aspect of the problem – modelling forms in paler and darker values of the same colour. Using the technique of colour-modelling, the only possibility is what we have here: the light blue veil of the Madonna is modelled from white to a relatively pale lapis for the full shadow, whereas the dark blue robe has a highlight value of the same pigment already several tones darker than the shadow of the veil, and a full shadow immeasurably deeper again. The same difference exists between the deeper rose-red of S. Anne's veil and the pale red angel below to the right in the same pigment.

The stylistic result of this use of colour is complex, but its main points may be briefly summarized. Firstly, the colour imposes an accent on the linear qualities of the painting; the limits of every object are marked by a sharp transition to a new colour and to a new range of tone values: to a totally different level of plasticity. Consequently the line so created has a special emphasis, and a tendency to insulate each differently-coloured object as an autonomous field on the picture surface; to each individual colour-plane, therefore, this use of colour will introduce a flattening, surface-stressing tendency. In the case of a form like a draped figure, composed of elements of more than one colour, this polychromy will inevitably break up the volume of the whole into planes of varying plastic intensity. In the *St. Anne*, for instance, the total plasticity of the figure of the Virgin – or of the whole figure group – is incoherent, and appreciably less impressive than the really powerful modelling of the forms individually, like the folds over the knees. Because of the tonal scale of pigments, a polychrome object in colour-modelling amounts plastically to much less than the sum of its parts. In the Arena chapel every coloured figure is flatter, and less of a volumetric unit, than the monochrome figures below; to carry the argument a stage further, it is also less fully related to its surrounding forms.

A second result, equally relevant to the style as a whole, is that this use of colour entails the completely finite realization of every part of every form; there is no possibility of varying the sharpness of focus on surfaces right up to their contours, because it is an attitude to colour and form which excludes the notions of atmosphere or of volumes of shadow as universal elements in the painting, whereby the surfaces might become partially or wholly lost to view.

The third point concerns the attitude to *light* which is implied by this handling of colour. By no means, for example, can the colour-change from yellow to red, or green to red, have been thought of in the artist's mind as a rational or naturalistic result of the fall of a stream of light on a coloured form; the same is true of the intensification of the local colour in the more common cases of simple colour-modelling. Neither can he have considered a unity in the reaction of separate coloured forms to a single light: each form makes its own reaction, and this is conditioned in the first place by the intrinsic qualities of the particular pigment in use. Masaccio, of course, even at this early date, was exceptional in his time for the understanding of the action of light in painting. But in the *St. Anne* the impression of light that exists is, so to speak, the sum of a number of individually-lit parts, and the only real difference between this and the light of Cimabue, of Orcagna or even of Lorenzo Monaco, is that on these individual parts there is imposed a unity of direction; all the highlights have been orientated to one side. This step had already been taken by Giotto and Duccio. But it is the lack of unity of response from colours, more than the inconsistencies in direction and cast shadow, that withholds the instantaneous impression of the presence of a true pictorial light, a single, unified element passing through space and conditioning the visibility and invisibility of objects.

The *Annunciation* in the Uffizi forms the best starting-point for a discussion of Leonardo's position in the history of this problem;[8] it is a very remarkable position. In this picture, immature and inconsistent as it is in so many ways, there are already two revolutionary principles of the greatest importance: every form is modelled independently of colour, and every coloured object is invested with a common range of tone.[9]

In fact, the range of colour is as wide as is normal in Florentine painting of the '70s and far wider than that of Masaccio's *St. Anne*; the range which in Lorenzo di Credi, for example, gives rise to a further range of tonal differences, from white through yellow, apple-green, vermilion and rose-red to blue and brown, is used again here, but its effect is completely changed. This change is the result of a new attitude to the relation of colour, light and form.

The modelling of form is achieved by achromatic means – in this case by the addition of black as the object-colour; saturation-change and colour-change are abandoned as ways of achieving the tonal-change which represents relief. In an early *Madonna* by Lorenzo di Credi it is impossible to imagine the chromatic element removed, because that alone generates the form; here, if the chromatic element could be subtracted, every significant form would still remain.

This point is clearest if we compare the angel's white vestment with the small area of pale blue on his collar; tonally these two have an equal range, and in the practical sense the creation of form is precisely the same: each runs through the same sequence of darkening with black. The pale blue becomes darker as the lighting decreases, but it does not become bluer; the local colour has a fixed value in the blue as in the white.

In one sense all colours here are affected by light exactly similarly, and that is the sense which is vital for the continuity of the level of plasticity over each multi-coloured figure: every colour-plane achieves or can achieve, a uniform depth of shadow.

There is one important sense in which colours vary in their reaction to light: the relationship of the saturation of a given local colour to the chiaroscuro depends upon the specific tonal intensity of the pigment. Colours which are by value pale in tone – yellow for instance – are already fully saturated in the highlight, and this continues on an even level into the shadow. This is true also of pale values of richer colours, such as the pale blue already mentioned, and the pale rose-pink floor tiles on the right. On the other hand colours which are inherently deep in tone, rose-red and blue for example, are lightened consider-ably in the highlight and achieve their full value only in the half-tones and the full shadow. Colours of moderate depth of tone, vermilion and apple-green, are lightened a little for the highlight but are already at full intensity in the higher half-tones. The reasons for this apparent inconsistency are two-fold. In the first place a colour plane which is required to be rich in colour, such as the "dark" blue robe of the Madonna (in contrast to the "pale" blue of the angel's collar and ribbons) is already of a depth of tone near to that which will be reached by the blackness of the shadow; if therefore the colour were to remain constant in intensity for dark colours as for light, very little relief would result. It is clear that the new ideal of uniform plasticity requires also that the level of tone of the highlights will be approximately equal. One may also look at this from a rather different view-point, and see that the achromatic modelling implies not only the superimposition on the local colour of a system of darkening with some neutral pigment, in this case black, but also of lightening, if necessary, with white.

The second reason follows from the first: a colour of weak intensity becomes quickly submerged in the chiaroscuro. Consider, for example, the two cases of the Virgin's deep blue robe and its yellow lining; if the yellow followed the same sequence of lightening in the highlights – that is, dilution with white (which would in fact make little tonal difference) the result would be, virtually, mono-chrome; the yellow would be entirely lost in the gathering obscurity of the shadow. The blue, on the other hand, and also the rose of the vestment, have a natural strength which will enable them to colour the form effectively even if they only reach full intensity in the deepest shadow: a power to retain chromatic effect into chiaroscuro which yellow – and apple-green – have not.

Leonardo's solution to this perpetual problem of the different intensities of the palette is not entirely rational; yet, from the aesthetic point of view it is justified. When he varies the treatment of colour over the form – its reaction to light-changes – in relation to the specific qualities of the local colour, this results in some cases in a parallelism of saturation-change to relief, represented by the monochrome element, but it is perfectly clear that these saturation-changes are conditioned by the chiaroscuro, and that they are neutral and inert in the complex processes of the generation of form.

This early, and as yet unsophisticated, reaction to the pigment-problem may be called by what it achieves: Tonal Unity. There are two major consequences to notice. The first, and historically the more important, is the control of the inherently disruptive effects of polychromy upon plasticity. A figure like the Madonna presents now a single, swelling, homogeneously-generated volume in contrast to the inevitably fragmented effects of colour-modelling seen in Masaccio's Madonna. Secondly, and of particular significance for Leonardo himself, light, colour and form are now related in a way that approximates to, and describes, their scientific and naturalistic behaviour. The relation of colour to light has entirely changed.[10] In the relative absolutism of late Quattrocento painting light remained a function of colour; changes in the objective nature of the surface of the form – variations of intensity of colour, or colour changes – created relief, and this relief was the indication of the lighting on the form; the incidence of light on a given part of the form was the result of the objective nature of the colour at that point. Now, colour is a function of light; it appears and disappears according to the lighting conditions, and its specific qualities at a given point are governed by the fall of the light upon it, and not by the properties of the pigment. In other words light is perceived as an exterior force, outside the object and governing the relative visibility of the properties of the object; the colour of the form is now, in the Albertian sense, one of its permanent qualities, rather than temporary or accidental ones.[11]

In the group of early works the concept of tonal unity is always present, though there is a perceptible development. The angel of the Uffizi *Baptism* is in this respect already an exceptional case in Florentine painting of the '70s, yet it is tentative and incomplete. On the other hand the *Madonna* in Munich and the *Portrait of Ginevra Benci*, in the Liechtenstein collection, seem to show a later stage than the *Annunciation*. In the case of the *Madonna* there is a far less perceptible difference in the handling of different pigments than in the *Annunciation*; one is less aware that one group of colours is desaturated in the highlight, or that another is fully intense there. The pale yellow of the robe lining, the blue of the robe, the brick-red of the vestment or the olive-brown of the cushion – even the flesh – seem now to react in unison to light and shade. In spite of the condition of the painting it is clear that this is achieved by a perfection of the method used in the *Annunciation*.

In the Uffizi *Annunciation* the smooth-swelling volume of the Madonna is not only generated in itself, but also with respect to its *ambiente*. The depiction of its background and of the cast shadows in the same tonal range invests the figure in a three-dimensional atmospheric medium which is another personal contribution of Leonardo's: a spatial chiaroscuro, which is a non-linear, tonal, system of coordinates. His achievement of tonal unity brings the possibility of a rich development of this new spatial system, but a series of problems stood in his way. From the proposition that the greatest range of tone in the modelling of a form, say a head, gives the greatest relief, it is a logical step to the realization that this relief is only obtained under certain conditions: in a restricted, focused, light in a dark environment. In any other situation reflected light begins to play in the shadows, and the lighter the object-colour, the more the reflected lights will mitigate the depth of the shadow; flesh is naturally susceptible of reflections. A head, therefore, placed before a landscape raises problems; tonal unity, and also strength of relief, will both be jeopardized if the naturalistic situation is observed.

The problem was initially posed, so to speak, by the Uffizi *Annunciation*; it has an exterior setting, but with lighting variable in intensity and in kind. The variation is not according to naturalistic principles, but in the interests of the clarity of individual objects. Probably the expression of the subject matter made it difficult to invest the head of the angel with the same depth of shadow as his torso and the right arm; two different lighting conditions certainly exist. But the next problem lies in this: that whereas it is the head which is given the lighting appropriate to the exterior setting, and the torso is given that of an interior, it is precisely the torso that is in some sort of atmospheric unity with the dark background, while the head is sharply detached from it, and appears superimposed.

The Colour Problem in Leonardo's Notes

In the whole painted oeuvre of Leonardo the subsequent stages in this problem are naturalistic adjustments of the aesthetic principle of tonal unity. It was a problem which lasted for his entire career and it would be strange if there were no discussion of it in his writings; in fact there is precise confirmation of the objects of tonal unity as they have been deduced from the paintings.

For example, the final considerations in the preceding section are not abstract: Leonardo examined every one of them.[12] As is perhaps to be expected, he is undecided as to which setting he prefers,[13] but no-one was ever clearer on the differences between the two extreme situations: *Grand'errore è di quelli pittori, li quali spesse volte retranno una cosa di rilevo à un lume particulare nelle loro case, e poi mettono in opera tal ritratto à un lume universale de l'aria in campagna, dove tale aria abbraccia et alumina tutte le parte delle vedute à un medesimo modo; e così costui fa l'ombre oscure, dove non po essere ombra, e se pure ella ve è, ella è di tanta chiarezza, che'l è insensibile; e cosi fanno li riflessi, dove è impossibile quelli esser veduti.*[14]

It is hardly necessary to demonstrate that Leonardo had a full understanding of light as an exterior force, and that form is revealed in the dynamic interplay of light and shade; he also distinguished clearly between the local colour and the accidental colour of objects, between the permanent and temporary colouristic properties.[15] Light and shade are temporary phenomena clothing the form: *ogni corpo opaco sia circundato e superfitialmente vestito d'ombre.*[16]

In effect the whole theory of tonal unity follows logically upon these premises. In painting, white and black are not real colours, but are the modifications of colours which indicate their lighting: *nero . . . bianco . . . privatione e generativo . . . in pittura sono li principali, concio sia che la pittura sia composta d'ombre et di lumi, cioè di chiaro et scuro.*[17]

This black/white structure is independent of the local colour on which it is superimposed; it is immaterial whether an object be blue or white if the lighting conditions are the same, for the highlight and the shadow will contain the same quantity of white or black.[18] This observation is followed by a practical recipe for achieving this consistent modelling of relief by the addition of measured quantities to the blue, a recipe which is the perfect counterpart of Cennini's colour-modelling recipes for relief by measured quantities of the object-colour. In another passage the common depth of shadow is clearly stated: *All colours when placed in shadow seem to be equally dark.*[19] Nowhere, in the hundreds of passages on light, shade and colour, is there any contradiction of this fundamental principle.[20]

415

The question of the appearance of the object-colour through this light-shade structure is also discussed in the writings; no definitive solution is reached. Although some passages are contradictory in detail, the approach to the problem corresponds to the analysis of the inconsistencies noticed in the paintings.[21] The difficulty lies in the problem of varying saturation, and whether the greatest brightness, intensity, or simply *bellezza*, occurs in the highlights or in the half-tones; full shadow is naturally out of the question. Generally speaking he is content to accept the conclusions of the Albertian optical theory, that, since light reveals form and shade obscures it, the true colouristic properties will be most visible in the light.[22] The conflict arises from the further observation, more practically linked to painting, that if the object colour remained indeed unchanged in the highlight, light-coloured objects would have a greater range of tone than dark, and greater relief;[23] in the abstract context of optical theory this is assumed to be the case.[24] This difficulty is paralleled by the practical proposition that while shadows in a painting are achieved by the addition of black, highlights are equally to be achieved by white. There is never any statement of the exact nature of the compromise which would solve these conflicts – probably because no stabilized solution was ever achieved – but it seems that the understanding of the different requirements of pigments according to their position on the tonal scale, which was deduced from the examination of the paintings, was in fact in Leonardo's mind. Two passages from the *Trattato* can only be explained in this way: (1) . . . *diverse colore hanno le loro bellezze in diverse parte di se medesimo, è questo ci mostra il nero haver la bellezza nell' Ombre e il bianco nel lume e l'azzurro e'verde e taneto (brown) nell'ombre mezzane, e'l giallo e rosso (cinnobar?) ne'lumi, e l'oro ne reflessi et la laca (rose madder?) nelle ombre mezzani.*[25] (2) *Dove et in qual colore l'ombre perdano piu il color naturale della cosa ombrata? Il bianco, che non vede nè lume incidente, nè nisuna sorte di lume riflesso, è quello che prima perde nel sua ombra integralmente il suo proprio natural colore, se colore si potesse dire il bianco. – Ma il nero agumenta il suo colore nelle ombre e lo perde nelle sue parte aluminate, e tanto piu lo perde, quanto la parte aluminata è veduta da lume di maggiore potenzia. E il verde, e l'azuro agumenta il suo colore ne' l'ombre mezane; et il rosso e giallo acquista di colore nelle sue parte aluminate, e'l simile fa il bianco; e li colori misti partecipano della natura de colori, che compongano tal mistione, cioè, il nero misto col bianco fa berettino, il quale non è bello nell'ultime ombre, com'è'l nero semplice, et non è bello in su lumi, com'è il semplice bianco, ma la suprema sua bellezza siè infra lume et ombra.*[26] White, yellow and red (probably cinnobar or vermilion) are the colours light in themselves, which require little or no adjustment to make an effective tonal contrast to the shadow; on the other hand blue, lake, green (probably the deep copper-green which has now in most cases turned to brown) and brown are the colours which are dark in themselves, and which can therefore appear at full intensity only in the increasing shadow.

The Development of Tonal Unity in Leonardo's Painting

At the conclusion of the first section it was postulated that an unsolved aesthetic problem arose in the *Annunciation*. A naturalistic respect for the exterior lighting conditions in the head of the angel led to a less coherent relation of form to setting than was achieved in a more ideal, or abstract, lighting situation assumed for the rest of the figure. The first stage in the solution of this problem was the exploitation of the second situation, and especially of the dark foil to the figure, with a greater or lesser implication of enclosed space. The aim of these earlier works, up to the first Milanese period, is towards a closer and closer approximation to the complete consistency of tone for the whole figure, flesh and polychrome drapery, and this means at once a greater intensity of lighting and a greater restriction of its direction; the dark foil is a necessary complement to the plastic consequences of this development, and the naturalistic aspect is for the moment ignored. In the more abstract sense there is no conflict in the use of essentially the same pattern of background for both the Munich *Madonna* and the Liechtenstein portrait,[27] for the lighting of the foreground and of the background is unrelated in the naturalistic sense in each case, and the pictorial unity is achieved through the decorative function of the colour. The darkness surrounding the profile of the figure is essential for the atmospheric setting of the form, and in neither case is an enclosure implied which would justify naturalistically the character of the foreground light. It is indeed remarkable that this temporary solution was so systematically applied in the early works; every composition which has been brought to the stage of the chiaroscuro problems shows this dark foil,[28] the function of which is similar to that of the ground in a relief, and if one considers the evolution of the *Adoration* composition it is clear that the half-built choir behind the figures,[29] which provides an apse of shadow behind them, is the answer to an aesthetic, and not an iconographical, problem. It is revealing to see how the purpose of the interior setting of the *Madonna Benois* has been completely misunderstood in Lorenzo di Credi's copy.[30] The *Madonna Benois* is near a consistent and logical solution of this problem; the dark foil is explained naturalistically, the particularized lighting on the figure is justified by the setting, and the strong plasticity of the forms belongs atmospherically to the space of the setting.

Vasari, speaking specifically of these early works, is aware of the limitations of this solution.[31] *È cosa mirabile che quello ingegno, che avendo desiderio di dar sommo rilievo alle cose che egli faceva, andava tanto con l'ombre scure a trovare i fondi de'più scuri che cercava neri che ombrassino e fussino più scuri degli altri neri, per fare che'l chiaro, mediante quegli, fussi più lucido; et infine riusciva questo modo tanto tinto, che non vi rimanendo chiaro, avevon più forma di cose fatte per contraffare una notte, che una finezza del lume del dì: ma tutto era per cercare di dare maggiore rilievo, di trovar il fine e la perfezione dell'arte.*

The next development can best be shown by a comparison between the two versions of the *Madonna of the Rocks*. There is reason to believe that the Louvre version was made in response to the commission of 1483, and is therefore documented as being entirely by Leonardo's hand and finished some time before about 1494.[32] The documents prove without any doubt at all that the National Gallery picture is the one that was destined for the same altar as the 1483 commission but was in an unfinished state when Leonardo left Milan in 1499, and was brought to its present state by him during the second Milanese period. The difference in the conception of the two paintings therefore represents a stylistic advance of about fifteen years and bridges the gap between the *Madonna Benois* and the *Madonna with the Yarn-Winder* (first version), between the *Adoration* and the *Battle of Anghiari*, or between the *Ginevra Benci* and *Mona Lisa*.[33]

Generally speaking, the lighting situation of the Louvre version is that of the *St. Jerome*[34] or of the *Adoration*; that is to say, that the figures are sharply lit, in an exterior setting, before a dark foil. It cannot be too strongly emphasized that this is not a painting of a group in a grotto; there is open sky above the group, conspicuously coloured a clear blue, and no indication of any enclosure; the "grotto" is not really a grotto at all, but the rocky equivalent of the ruined stable behind the figures in the Metropolitan *Adoration* studies.[35] Its pictorial function is the same as the wall in the Uffizi Adoration or the rock behind *St. Jerome*.

In the Louvre version the individual realization of every detailed form, so clearly seen in its drawing, is seen also in the lighting; the dualism of the situation in the *Annunciation* is still unresolved. Only those flesh-forms close to the dark ground achieve a plasticity equal to that of the drapery, even though polychromy in itself no longer presents a tonal problem. In the forms above, more freely enveloped in illuminated space, naturalistic concessions with respect to the "exterior" situation are made – as in the *Ginevra Benci* portrait – so that on the one hand the internal reflections on the flesh deprive heads and hands of plasticity, on the other the persistently clear silhouette of the shadowed side of the forms detaches them from atmospheric union with the setting.[36]

In the London version the dualism is resolved, and this more intensely realized and intellectually meditated conception comes about partly through an apparent change in the actual situation portrayed. The open area of sky above is drastically reduced, and the impression of the enclosure of the figures in a dark space thereby created; it is possible now to read the situation as that of a grotto, since the continuity of the wall of rock is suggested above as well as at both sides. This means that the lighting of the figures may be brought into a rational harmony with their context. A restricted, particularized light enters the scene through such openings as are shown behind but actually from within the spectators' space to the left. The light is restricted not only in the sense of its sharpness of direction, so that the scattered reflections are eliminated, but also in its selective fall: it is a *selective* light seeking out the compositionally and iconographically significant forms and ignoring the rest. In its dynamic qualities of variability and selectivity, in contrast to the static, even, universal light of the Louvre version, it is the light of a new era. By its very restriction the plasticity of every form it touches is augmented, and at the same time the complementary chiaroscuro sets each form in volumetric relation one to another, and each to the grotto, more forcefully than ever before because now the possibility exists of losing a shadowed contour. The "grotto-light" is as objective as *Mona Lisa*'s smile; the naturalistic harmony of the situation is now complementary to the aesthetic harmony.[37]

It is perhaps fair to look upon the London version therefore as the perfected solution of the early problem; what we need to stress here is the role of tonal unity, and what could thereby be achieved. To the independently conceived psychological states of the figures in the first version there is applied a focus of emotional response and physical action which contributes a reflective unity of sentiment. In this dreamlike fusion the interweaving emotional cross-currents become superfluous: the figures do not look at each other, or at us. An integration, parallel in direction and equal in extent, has been applied to the formal constituent of the painting. This is the product as much of a developing treatment of colour, and of its derivative light, as of design. The solution of the initial dualism was not found by abandoning the progress towards unity, but rather by the subordination, first, of naturalistic to aesthetic considerations and then by the invention of a situation in which they could coincide. This common solution to the aesthetic and naturalistic problem in the later years of the Milanese period forms the basis of the final solution whereby the figure could retain its plasticity against either a dark or a bright background, while still preserving its spatial, atmospheric relationship with it. Leonardo's habitual diagonal formal constructions, implying as they do that the setting requires to be in more than decorative harmony with the figures, make the pursuit of this final solution appear inevitable. The new orientation for this pursuit is set initially by the *Last Supper*, which in a very different "naturalistic situation" represents a phase comparable to that of the London *Virgin of the Rocks*.

In the *Last Supper* there could never have been a choice of the setting, yet it is remarkable that even in the very early stages of the conception, in the Venice sketch, the need is felt for the chiaroscuro as a support for the figures.[38] As the painting stands at present it is of course impossible to grasp with any accuracy the original atmospheric effect, but it is clear enough that the figures of the apostles towards the wings are integrated by light with the space behind as in the London *Madonna of the Rocks*. But there are some new features; the chiaroscuro, the three-dimensional dialogue of light and shade, is now so emphatically present as a pictorial reality that it becomes itself expressive directly of the subject matter; this is to be seen not only in the literally dramatic shadow of Judas, but also in the whole *crepuscolo* mise-en-scène, recalling the text: *And it was evening* . . . . So, dependent always upon the tonal unity of the colour, an entirely new expressive medium is given to painting, beyond the means of the Quattrocento. The second feature is the setting of the figure of Christ against the bright background of the view through the doorway onto the open landscape. This is perfectly satisfying only by virtue of the clarity of the lighting-situation; perhaps the point is clearer if we consider the *Mona Lisa* which is in this respect equivalent to the centre portion of the *Last Supper* in isolation.

The *Mona Lisa* must always be visualized with the flanking columns more in evidence than they now are;[39] this therefore, is a portrait in a loggia, with a landscape beginning at an indefinable distance behind it. The stratification of the space therefore justifies logically the unrelated lighting of the figure, restricted and without "scatter", and of the background, limpid and diffuse; this new "situation" should be contrasted with that of *Ginevra Benci*. The figure now stands out by virtue of the strength of its own modelling; it clearly does not belong to the same space-and-light unit as the background either in the aesthetic or the naturalistic sense.

However, the next problem, of the setting of a figure-group in an open landscape, occupied his attention in the same years that were spent on the *Mona Lisa*. This problem was the necessary corollary of the logical treatment of the interior setting of *Mona Lisa* and the *Last Supper*; it was already set by the compromise of the late Milanese cartoon in the Royal Academy, and this was followed by the 1501 *St. Anne* cartoon, the two versions of the *Madonna of the Yarn-Winder*, the *Leda* and the *Battle of Anghiari*; we do not know precisely the stages in the evolution here, only the final result in the Louvre *St. Anne*, but it is clear that one of the elements in the final solution, the greatly enriched penetration of light within the complex group – or, to put it another way, the use of a diffused light without sacrificing plasticity – must have been considerably developed already in response to the special problems of the battle-piece.[40] The other element which is important is the increased role of colour – in the modern sense – in this unity; and here, before considering this in detail, it would be as well to examine the changing functions of the purely chromatic element up to this point, for the *St. Anne* belongs to a phase of Leonardo's development of which Florentine painters were ignorant at least until Andrea del Sarto's journey to Paris in 1518/19.[41]

It seemed worth while to deal with Leonardo's achievement and development of tonal unity at length, because of its great historical importance; of its two functions, the approximation to optical naturalism and the creation of consistent plasticity, it was the latter which was most appreciated in his own day, and which stands so directly in the Florentine monumental tradition; it is no exaggeration to say that this discovery is the essential and inevitable prerequisite for the classic plasticity of the High Renaissance, by which painting achieved the corporeal homogeneity and *relievo* which would rival sculpture. It is impossible to imagine the aims of the early Cinquecento expressed without it. The "sculptural presence" of painted form may well have been among Leonardo's most compelling ambitions, obsessed as he was with the *Paragone*.

420

The judgement of the Cinquecento is on these lines; Vasari's summary of his historical position as a painter, at the end of the *Vita*, is this: *Nell'arte della pittura aggiunse costui alla maniera del colorire ad olio una certa oscurità, donde hanno dato i moderni gran forza e rilievo alle loro figure*[42] and (an independent judgement) a contemporary of Vasari's calls him: *primo inventore delle figure grandi tolte dalle ombre delle lucerne.*[43]

Colour, Chiaroscuro, and Composition

These changes of Leonardo's brought with them two entirely new stylistic characteristics, whereby the actual appearance of the painting is changed; the first concerns the chromatic effect of the picture, the second, the veil of positive, corporeal atmosphere in which the sharpness of the form is lost and found, whereby the tactility of its surface becomes variable.

The "suppression" of colour by chiaroscuro is not a negative attitude to colour; the open clarity, the purity, the brightness of Quattrocento colour are rejected – and progressively more so – and colour speaks only in a dialogue with chiaroscuro, the one infused into the other, but thereby it attains a new resonance and a new depth, and it is this more sophisticated richness which characterized Florentine painting for a generation.

There is a text which is often chosen to show that Leonardo was interested only in the chiaroscuro, and that colour itself meant little or nothing to him:

Qual è di più importantia, o'che la figura abbondi in bellezza di colori, o'in dimostratione di gran rilevo?

Sola lapittura si rende (cosa maravigliosa?) alli contemplatori di quella per fare parere rilevato e spichato dalli muri quel, chè nulla, e li colori sol fanno onore alli maestri, che li fanno, perche in loro non si causa altra maraviglia che bellezza, la quale bellezza non è virtu del pittore, ma di quello, che gli ha generati. E puo una cosa esser vestita di brutti colori e dar di se maraviglia alli suoi contemplanti pel parere di rilevo.[44]

It cannot be too strongly emphasized that *bellezza di colori* does not mean "beauty of colour" in the modern sense, but the harsh brilliance of pure pigment; what Leonardo has in mind is not the choice between a picture brilliantly and subtly coloured (for example, his own *Last Supper*) and a grisaille,[45] but between a painting of, say, Ghirlandaio, and his own: the contrast is between the Quattrocento and the Cinquecento. This is the change of taste which is reflected in the writing of Michiel, Benedetto Varchi, Vasari and Paolo Pino.[46] Leonardo in fact seldom touches on the nebulous subject of colour harmony, but when he does, it is clear that his ideas are those which were given more succinct expression by the greater critical apparatus of Vasari. *Restaci una secunda regola, la quale non attende à fare li colori in se di più suprema bellezza, ch'essi naturalmente sieno, ma che la compagnia loro dia gratia l'uno a l'altro . . .*[47]

Leonardo's personality as a painter is partly conditioned by his "total" vision of a work, which results in the unified conception (in the mature drawings one sees the spontaneous growth of a complex design) and in the necessity of bringing the execution of the whole to a finish simultaneously, an innovation which brought its own difficulties; the traditional fresco technique, for example, was inadequate for his purposes. This simultaneous execution of the whole work is seen in technical terms in the unfinished works and in the evidence we have of the way he actually painted the two wall-paintings: the stories relating to the *Last Supper*,[48] Vasari's description of the adjustable scaffolding for the Battle-cartoon,[49] and the documents describing the scaffolding for the Battle-piece itself,[50] all show how necessary it was to be able to paint, so to speak, the whole work at once. Both for these technical reasons, and for the psychological impetus behind them, it was inevitable, one might think, that Leonardo should have broken the bonds of Quattrocento, quasi-Absolute colour. The clearly defined, mutually insulated, colour-planes imposed limitations like those of *buon fresco*, which the continuously fomenting creativity of his brain could not accept.

We have already seen that in the early Uffizi *Annunciation* colour ceased to play the active role in the creation of form and line; it begins, on the contrary, to be brought into a dynamic relationship with light, parallel to that of form with light. The particular technical characteristics of the chiaroscuro in use up to the time of the London version of the *Virgin of the Rocks* altered the chromatic effect of the painting in two ways: the reduction of the brightness of colour (a suppression of one kind of richness), and its replacement by a homogeneous resonance in a distinctly lower key. In this sense there is already a new unity of colour compared with the Quattrocento; this is a *sfumato* unity achieved by achromatic means.

In the earlier works the compositional function of colour is primarily decorative; that is to say that the colour-links draw the picture-surface into a unity, in the manner sensitive to the reality of the picture surface which is common in the Quattrocento. In the *Annunciation* only the colour-links across the third dimension are exact, whereas those across the plane give the greater stress to the figures; no colour-value is common to both figures, so that each receives accented individuality. The colour-link across the depth is given, for example, by the repetition of the silvery blue of the distant mountains in the ribbons, the collar and wing-roots of the angel. This paler blue, which occurs all over the left-hand half of the painting, in the flowers below and in the sky above as well as in the distant landscape and the angel, is the same blue which occurs more intensely on the robe of the virgin; similarly the glowing ruby-red of the angel's robe is repeated more softly on the bed-cover on the right.

In the *Liechtenstein Portrait* and the *Munich Madonna* the decorative function of the colour answers the essentially different requirements of the format; the consciousness of the depth axis is correspondingly greater, and the necessity of integrating the surface-pattern by repetitions across the plane could be ignored. In the *Madonna*, the olive-brown cushion in the bottom left corner repeats the colours of the middle-distance landscape, while the blue of the robe (softer than in the *Annunciation*) repeats that of the distant mountains. In the *Portrait*, the orange-brown of the middle-distance trees is precisely the same as the highlight on the right shoulder of her gown, and the blue of the lacing on the front is equal to the strongest blue in the landscape, in the distant trees and the church spires.

The colour-composition of the Paris version of the *Virgin of the Rocks* is a development from the Florentine works only in the sense of a greater subtlety and maturity, a new richness of orchestration; the principle is a very fine balance of the still sharply individualized polychromy of the draperies of Virgin and angel. The blue of her robe, for example, by far the most intense colour in the picture and of an extraordinary richness, is given progressively weaker echoes in the distant landscape-vista and the quadrant of sky above, then in the flowers just to the right of her head and in the pale irises beneath the Giovannino, and finally in the cool grey ledges of the foreground parapet of rocks and the feathers of the angel's wings. The warmest patches of rock, ruddy-brown, below Christ on the left and along the very top, seem like reflections from the glowing brilliance of the Angel's robe, and the complementary green of the lining thrown over his left shoulder is softly echoed in the landscape vista, diagonally opposite.

In spite of the disfiguring varnish, and what appears to me to be a considerable quantity of over-paint, all of which adds an artificial degree of unity to the colour-planes, the "separateness" of colour at this stage – a feature which further accentuates the individuality of the forms to which they are fixed – is still apparent; what is also apparent is an intention to use colour as an "accent" on the subject matter, but this has not yet found a new means of expression. The new concept of *crescendo* or focus emerges first in the *Last Supper*.[51]

It is essential to see the *Last Supper* in the correct natural lighting, that is in the late afternoon or early evening when the light comes strongly from above and from the left, and leaves almost a third of the composition in half-shadow on this side. Without this lighting the balance is disturbed. Leonardo has compensated this shadow by a greater strength of colour on the left than on the right, and by stronger contrasts of colour[52] and modelling within the shadow; in comparison, the colour is much softer on the right, with many of the draperies approaching a silvery grey. This increase of plasticity and colour in the more weakly-lit part is a device which he seems to have learnt from Masaccio;[53] it has another function, apart from the balance in the general impression on the spectator, and this is that while the direction and the temporal significance of the actual light has been most subtly re-deployed in the painting, it has been, so to speak, extended to the part of the wall that is actually in shadow.

When the painting is seen in the natural light, therefore, the balance in the chromatic effect from one side to another is perfect, but there is no articulated pattern in its distribution as there is in Ghirlandaio's *Last Supper*: the colour-planes are not unified by repetition. In the present state of the painting[54] it is clearly impossible to say whether there was ever a colour-chain coordinating the colours – perhaps there was; but it is even now possible to see how colours have lost their particularity. No colour-value is exactly repeated anywhere else, yet there is an element of homogeneity, of spontaneous harmony, which runs like a ground-bass beneath the *cantilena* of the individual colours, and is one feature which pulls the whole long composition together. The other is the subordination of the whole to a dominant centre; the figure of Christ, in the colour composition, is isolated by the simplicity of the colour-shapes – a red diamond and a blue equilateral triangle – and also because these two colours, apparently endlessly echoed and re-echoed in the other figures, are the strongest in the whole painting.[55] Moreover, if we are right in reconstructing the rich green of James' tunic as being about equal in intensity to the blue and rose of John's vestment and robe,[56] there was originally a *crescendo* towards the centre, an organic movement in the colour which continuously focuses, even now, the spectators' attention on the quiet figure of Christ.[57]

This "colour focus", distinct from the old method of a particularized accent, is the expressive equivalent of that kernel of formal activity which Leonardo had introduced into the plastic pattern as early as the *Benois Madonna* and the *Adoration*, as a stress on the essence of the subject matter; it may be seen even more plainly, without so many necessary qualifications for condition, in the London version of the *Virgin of the Rocks*.

The change in colour between the two versions is very striking; in the first it is gay, lyrical, finite and wide in range: in the second, brooding, austere, elusive and restricted, virtually, to two impressive chords of deep blue and golden-peach on the Madonna. To see this second picture in a light approximating to a church interior is to realize two things; the first is the futility of the discussions as to whether St. John or the Christ Child is the subject of the painting. The augmented intensity of the blue in these conditions leaves no doubt whatever that it is, in Leonardo's own words, *uno quadro de una nostra dona*;[58] the blue has an overwhelming vitality in the whole composition. The second point is that the robe when seen in this way is as plastically modelled as the head or the yellow lining;[59] this is not normally obvious.

In this case one can be reasonably sure that all the colour in the painting is linked together in a cycle; blue turns to yellow through green, and the yellow returns to blue through brown, warm-grey and cool-grey. The two positive, full-strength, colours are concentrated on the figure of the Virgin, so that She seems to contain the quintessence of the whole chromatic range, and She becomes the true focus of an effect embracing every part of the painting. The flexibility of the colour that is developed at this stage is dependent on the fundamental break with tradition made earlier, when colour was released from its function of creating form. The independent development of form and colour then made possible is in this particular case turned towards the expression of the iconographic content.

Colour therefore, in the fully-developed style of tonal unity, ceases to be a static element, and becomes fluid, surging, dynamic; the dynamic character of this medium, with its new expressive and compositional potential, recalls the similar change in the character of light between the two versions, and distinguishes the High Renaissance artist from the Quattrocento one.

This intensification of the qualities immanent already in the Louvre version, which seems reasonably to be the result of the unusual situation of the artist being required to recreate a work of the same subject for the same altar, profiting from the experience of seeing the first in position, – this intensification is the answer to a specific problem, and it is a little difficult to assess on this basis the general stylistic character of the lost works of the period which is spanned by the execution of the London version. The only painting of this period which does survive is the *Mona Lisa*, and the features these two have in common may be summarized to provide a rough idea of the legacy which Leonardo left to Cinquecento Florentine painting.

It is, of course, notoriously difficult to see any colour at all in the *Mona Lisa*; one's first impression is only of a greenish haze, dimly seen towards the top. One readily perceives, however, what a really essential part colour plays in the whole, how it is vitally present in every particle, if one visualizes its appearance if it were, or rather if it could be, executed in *grisaille*. First, of the functions of this partially-hidden colour, we must not discount the naturalistic evocation of vitality, which form alone cannot give, and which may still be appreciated after long scrutiny in a reasonable light.[60] But two further characteristics must have appeared revolutionary to his contemporaries; the first is the perfection of the plastic consistency through tonal unity (it is quite uncompromising), and the second is the way in which all the colour seems to be infused, as a scarcely tangible element, into tone. The yellow sleeve is a dull glow compared with the ceramic brilliance of Ghirlandaio or Credi, but it is no less yellow. Leonardo now stands, with Titian, on the far side of a dividing line in the history of colour in painting. In Cinquecento painting one does not measure colour, so to speak, in terms of pigment – its refinement or degree of saturation – but in terms of its organic interaction with the tone of the whole picture. Colour is summoned to visibility out of shadow by the action of light; it appears, certainly, as a property of a certain form, but that property is only a particular localized nuance of the continuous, unified colour-material of which the picture is constructed. There is, however, a corollary of this, and that is that as the colour becomes submerged in chiaroscuro, so surfaces disappear also; the two are plainly affected in parallel.

Finally, the last stage in Leonardo's development seen in the *St. Anne* will serve to show that, even to its creator, the colour-system of the period that Florence knew was not a stable thing, but a transition to another system.[61] One of the relative limitations in the style of the London *Virgin of the Rocks* and of the *Mona Lisa* is that each colour plane is in itself homogeneous and "fixed" in value, with the inevitable result that a group of colour-planes remains individualized as far as their colour is concerned, however much this may be tempered by the enveloping chiaroscuro; it is a limited stage of development which

Hetzer still found in Titian's Assunta and he described, in a memorable phrase, its separateness of colour: *fast wie bei einem Glasgemälde.*[62]

The striking characteristic of the St. Anne, in comparison with the other works we have considered, is the much greater softness in all its elements; much of this is beyond analysis and lies deep in the *matière*, but one may discern quite clearly the softening almost to extinction of the differences of colour-planes.[63] All the draperies have a virtually uniform grey, only faintly tinted, for their highlights; the real colour palpitates uncertainly in the half-tones and is lost again in the shadow. The shadow itself is now changed; it is no longer dense, and opaque, for on the one hand light penetrates freely and it is alive with reflections, and on the other it is not black, but – so far as one can see – a chromatic grey. This latent colour in all the shadow is entirely new, and it has this result: the already delicately muted palette – blue-grey, rose-grey, red-brown and lilac-brown – achieves values that are never really stabilized on any form; each "colour-plane" – the expression is hardly adequate any more – is subtly shifting in value all over, and each colour seems potentially present in the next. This development is extremely difficult to define in its precise extent; there is the danger of claiming for Leonardo, in this interpenetration of colours, the achievement of later painters. The approach is fundamentally different in method from the Venetian broken-colour which had already appeared.[64] It is not so much a question of the division of colour, a feature to be expressed in the brushwork, but an instability in its appearance in the three-dimensional light-and-shadow system;[65] its value as a positive factor in the colour-harmony is not to be denied, but it seems also that it is part of the solution of the problems presented by the chiaroscuro-and-space relationship which became critical after 1500.

It is noticeable in front of the original that the construction of the figure-group before the landscape's change of tone from dark to light is achieved without the break in the unity of lighting and atmosphere which has to be justified by the loggia in the *Mona Lisa*. The diaphanous softness of all surfaces and silhouettes is partly responsible for this; there is also a considerable quant-itative change in the proportion of areas of light and shade, in the direction of more light, compared with the London *Virgin of the Rocks* or the *St. Anne* cartoon in the Royal Academy. Sympathetic to this is the raising of the tone of the shadows, which is the automatic result of replacing black by neutralized colour. Furthermore, if colour has re-entered, in a new way compatible with optical rationalism, into the construction of form, then it follows that the fore-ground figures are constructed in the same way as the distance against which they are set. If one could see the Mona Lisa with its filter of varnish removed, there would almost certainly appear the actual change in the quality of the paint between figure and background that is seen in the London *Virgin of the Rocks* (where, of course, the two are not contiguous on the surface, so that the contrast is of small importance); in the *St. Anne*, so far as one may judge through a less dense layer of varnish, the technical means in the whole painting is uniform. This material unity of all colours as of all forms is strikingly paralleled in the developments in technique in the late drawings;[66] entirely new techniques were, in these cases also, invented by Leonardo for the expression of a world of art in harmony with his vision of the continuity and homogeneity in the world of nature.

Context

The development that has been traced in Leonardo's use of colour is not properly assessed in isolation, or simply in contrast to an early panel by Masaccio. There are some interesting precedents for his discoveries and a parallel (but not identical) development took place independently in Venice. In conclusion, therefore, a brief sketch of this situation, and also of the immediate reflexes in Florentine painting, is necessary. In doing this I am not attempting to sketch any sort of development in Florentine colour, but only to round out more fully the character of Leonardo's achievement which, like any other historical phenomenon, gains meaning from a consideration of its context.

It is unlikely that such a profound stylistic change should be unaccompanied by a sympathetic revolution in taste, and some documentation on both counts may make this enquiry seem less like an analytical exercise unrelated to historical events.

The *St. Anne* in the Uffizi represents only Masaccio's starting-point in his handling of colour. It is probable that his last work known to us is the *Cathedra Petri* in the Brancacci chapel, and here the difference is remarkable; the impetus of Masaccio's development was so great that the contrasts exist even between this and his earlier frescoes in the same cycle. The point is simple: not only is there no substantial difference in the plastic intensity of blue and yellow draperies on the figure of St. Peter, but the same is true of flesh-forms and, most remarkably, of the white-habited kneeling figures before him; much of Leonardo's spatial correlation of volumes by tone is also prefigured here, and of course it is in these frescoes (for the same set of reasons) that appears the first instantaneously-felt pictorial light of the Renaissance. However, the extent of Masaccio's adumbration of Leonardo's early use of colour seems to be somewhat exaggerated by the condition of the frescoes; overpainted they certainly are (how much is not clear) and the superimposed dirt and smoke probably give a false impression of an atmospheric chiaroscuro, and obscure one important fact: in those small areas that are free from this distortion[67] it seems that colour-modelling is still predominantly in use. Probably Masaccio modified this only by reinforcing the tonally-weaker pigments with some achromatic addition.[68] It is important that in Masaccio's case no *technical* revolution accompanied this change, for this probably inhibited further development in the Quattrocento, and surely made it relatively easy for this demonstration to be quickly forgotten.[69]

427

It is possible that there were even some precendents in fresco for Masaccio. In Giotto's later chapels in S. Croce there seems to be an appreciably greater control over the properties of pigments than was visible in the Arena chapel.[70] And, on reflection, it is striking how unified in tone is Cavallini's *Last Judgement* in S. Cecilia.[71]

After Masaccio, it seems that only Filippo Lippi attempted to follow him, and that not for long; but Lippi's early colour-style may be significant since it was first of all a translation of the *Cathedra Petri* experiment into panel-painting (a step which, so far as I know, was not taken by Masaccio, and which does in some ways pose the greater technical problem) and secondly because the earlier style of Lippi as a whole is an important part of Leonardo's background.[72]

It is possible that Masaccio's dramatic invention is more than the solution to a practical aesthetic problem and was prompted by theoretical optical conclusions drawn by Brunelleschi. Certainly in Alberti's *della Pittura* the logical counterpart of his perspective theory is a light-shadow system which takes for granted the situation created practically by Masaccio, and this system is entirely based on abstract, optical considerations. Alberti's theory of *colore*[73] bears some relation to the exactly contemporary practice of Filippo Lippi, but I doubt if the relation is one of cause and effect; the perspective theory could fairly easily be converted to workshop practice, whereas the theory of *colore* (in spite of the protestations *parliamo come pictore*) is so totally unrelated to practical problems that it is not surprising that it found no interpreter until, possibly, Piero della Francesca, and Leonardo. It is no longer necessary to demonstrate that Leonardo had digested *della Pittura*,[74] and much of what he says on this subject is a criticism of it; but in his person was presented the unique opportunity for a full, understanding reconciliation of earlier theory and practice, and this critical synthesis is his point of departure in the Uffizi *Annunciation*.

In Venetian painting from the 1470s onwards, in Bellini and Antonello, a development took place which is in some respects similar to Leonardo's; this appears to be prompted by Flemish art, where some of the simpler characteristics of tonal unity appeared at least as early as the mature works of the Master of Flémalle. While the Venetian development seems to be independent of Leonardo, it is more difficult to assess the possibility of Flemish art, especially in its technical solution to the problem, being to some extent a common source of inspiration.[75] While this possibility is not to be excluded, it seems more likely that Leonardo draws the ultimate conclusions from propositions indigenous to Tuscan painting, and certainly his contribution crystallizes the aims and ideals of the local monumental tradition.

Many of the characteristics of Leonardo's colour reappear in the work of Perugino, and this is historically important since Perugino's influence during Leonardo's long absence in Milan in the 1480s and '90s provided to some extent a colouristic substitute for the latter which affects, for example, the earliest works of Fra Bartolomeo and Albertinelli.[76] But Perugino's understanding of the potential of this new use of colour was limited; it went no further than the creation of plastically-coherent simple forms, and exploits none of the volumetric and spatial possibilities, nor the compositional possibilities consequent upon the liberation of colour from the provision of form, and shows no awareness of the rational or naturalistic problems involved. Chronologically assessed, it is clear in any case that Perugino follows Leonardo's first demonstrations in the 1470s.

The first Florentine to explore and develop all the potentialities of Leonardo's colour-style (up to 1508) was Fra Bartolomeo, whose intellectual penetration of that style was remarkable. Fra Bartolomeo's own development cannot be discussed here, but an altarpiece such as the Accademia *Marriage of St. Catherine* (1512) can illustrate what is necessary. The tonal unity of colours is of course complete and is the basis for the homogeneous *rilievo* throughout the work, and at the same time for the instantaneous impression of a powerful light. The presence of this light, and of its complementary shadow, gives the coordinates of the spatial design with practically no assistance from linear constructions. Darkness is the condition of space without light, and the light penetrates selectively and draws out form into visible volume. Fra Bartolomeo at this stage makes full use of the new capacity of the handling of colour to vary the realization, or the tactility, of form, so that the sculpturally-plastic foreground figures contrast with those deep in the half-light of the niche, as insubstantial as shadows. In the earlier quasi-Absolute colour-system a colour-composition automatically created a tone-composition, and the two were indivisible: the tonal composition was the product of colour and line. After the Leonardesque evolution tonal compositions became the product of light, form, and space, so that colour, now independent, was free to surge dynamically over the picture surface, as in the *Last Supper*. In Fra Bartolomeo's altarpiece again the colour-composition is independent of the tonal one, and plays principally the complementary role of articulating, and therefore re-asserting, the surface.

The style of tonal unity in this direct Leonardesque form characterizes Florentine painting in its most vital currents at the end of the first decade of the Cinquecento and for most of the second; it characterizes, for example, not only the School of S. Marco (Fra Bartolomeo, Albertinelli, Sogliani and their followers) but also the rapidly rising and ultimately triumphant rival, the School of the Annunziata, circulating round the figure of Andrea del Sarto. The earliest works of Andrea, of Pontormo, Rosso and Puligo fall within this definition.[77] It was, on the other hand, these artists who progressively formed the most critical reaction to it, and the point of departure for their increasing criticism was a work which was both influenced by, and a protest against, Leonardo's colour-style.

Michelangelo's *Doni Tondo* provided for Florentines an alternative approach to the problem which was very different in character, chromatically more intense, and more directly based upon the Florentine tradition of colour-modelling.

Leonardo's new mode of vision embraced phenomena which were strictly pictorial: light, corporeal space, and chiaroscuro, which brought a subjective flexibility of form, so that its limits and even its substance might be momentarily made less tangible or lost altogether. Michelangelo, by his whole training, saw form in terms of solid *matière*, and was not interested in phenomena outside the envelope of surface. Chiaroscuro would have been anathema to him at this stage, and the workshop practice of his only master in painting, Ghirlandaio, was already on these lines (though indeed with a rather different purpose). The derivation of the chromatic scale of the tondo from Ghirlandaio has often been remarked upon and is precise; but the derivation is selective and suggests that Ghirlandaio's role is that of a channel for the Masacciesque.

In the *Doni Tondo* pure colour creates form; if the chromatic element were removed, all form would cease to exist. Tonal changes, and so modelling, are exclusively provided either by colour-changes or by saturation-changes. It is in character with the ideals of a sculptor that form should be interpreted as modulation of substance, in this case chromatic substance (a quality of the material), rather than as a visual impression of the form, modified by exterior phenomena. The colour retains a degree of Absolutism which is at variance with the optical rationalism of Alberti and Leonardo. A corollary of the sculptural attitude to form is the will for complete clarity, and perfectly sharp and consistent realization, of the surface; so one finds, here, the uniformly precise focus on all forms and a particular emphasis on their limiting outlines.

The colour-changes in the Doni Tondo follow one Florentine tradition in exploiting the natural tonal differences of pigments. Joseph's robe, lying over his knees, is the most striking example: a fully-saturated yellow in the highlights turns smoothly to a pure and luminous coral-red which provides all but the very deepest points of shadow; here, only, the red is reinforced with a little rose-madder and brown. It is easy to find similar passages in Ghirlandaio and Filippino, but it is questionable whether they ever reach such vivid intensity. A second case, however, is in the drapery behind the nudes in the left background: this turns from green to pure rose in the shadows.[78] Both in the case of colour-change, and in the more frequent transition in one chromatic value from a white highlight to a densely-saturated shadow (Joseph's slate-blue vestment, the Virgin's lapis-lazuli robe and rose vestment, and also the flesh-tones), the forcefulness of the plasticity depends upon the strength of the colour; only the practical problems of grinding, purifying, and media set a limit to this plasticity, and this goes a long way towards explaining the really exceptional brilliance of the colour in this painting.[79]

All this is clearly very different from Leonardo's practice; yet the two artists have one vital feature in common in their use of colour, which I believe is an influence of the older upon the younger, however different their methods. This feature is the common and unified ("synchronized") range of tone of all colour planes. An indication of the importance Michelangelo attached to this is the reinforcement of the red shadow of Joseph's robe, which provides an extreme shadow of a depth commensurate with the blues and the rose-red, but which the yellow pigment would not reach. The function of this tonal unity of the colours of the figure-group is also the same as in Leonardo: to provide a uniform development of plasticity throughout.

The subsequent development of early Cinquecento colour in Florence oscillates between the techniques of Leonardo and of Michelangelo. The situation is very confusing, particularly as Michelangelo's later colour seems to have moved significantly closer to Leonardo's.[80] But in general, Andrea del Sarto, Rosso and Pontormo all seem to have reacted against the restraints that Leonardo placed upon the purely chromatic attributes of painting, and each of them, from about 1520 onwards, varied at will the proportions of colour-modelling or of chiaroscuro in their works. However, no artist who was trained in the Tonal Unity of High Renaissance painting could afford to forget its formal and expressive potential, and the many adjustments that follow Leonardo do not contradict, but on the contrary develop further, his fundamental aesthetic principles.

In 1522 a group of artists discussing the frescoes in the Carmine admired Masaccio's *maniera si moderna . . . nel colorito*.[81] It is probable that – at least in part – they were commenting upon the advanced tonal unity of his colour, as Vasari did when he remarked: *dipinse le cose sue con buona unione e morbidezza, accompagnando con le incarnazioni delle teste e degl'ignudi i colori dei panni . . . come fa il vivo e naturale . . . .*[82] This remark is a compression of his advice in his *della Pittura*: *Nè si debbono vestire gl'ignudi di colori tanto carichi di corpo, che dividano le carni da'panni, quando detti panni attraversassino detti ignudi; ma i colori dei lumi di detti panni siano chiari simili alle carni, o gialletti, o rossigni . . . (etc.), purchè tragghino allo scuro, e che unitamente si accompagnino nel girare delle figure con le lor ombre: in quel medesimo modo, che noi veggiamo nel vivo . . . .*[83] Aretino, in his letter to Tintoretto of February 1545, on the *Apollo and Marsyas*, had already appreciated the same point: *. . . lo intende il vostro spirito intendente il dove si distendono i colori chiari e gli oscuri. Per la quale intelligenzia le figure ignude e vestite mostrano se medesime nei lor propri rilievi.*[84]

Vasari on another occasion explains that *. . . colori . . . carichi di corpo, siccome usavano di fare già alcuni pittori* make the figures too obviously painted with pigments and prevent them being *di rilievo e naturali*.[85] More acutely still, he observes that sharp contrasts of pigments make a painting *più presto un tappeto colorito, o un paro di carte da giocare, che carne unita, o panni morbidi o altre cose piumose, delicate, e dolci*.[86] Carpets and playing-cards do indeed preserve, naturally, the qualities of Absolute Colour.[87]

In the Cinquecento, beauty of colour is no longer the quantitative *bellezza*. Dolce makes this point clear: *Né creda alcuno, che la forza del colorito consista nella scelta de'bei colori; come belle lache, bei azzurri, bei verdi, e simili; perciochè questi colori sono belli parimente senza che e'si mettano in opera; ma nel sapergli maneggiare convenevolmente . . . . Altri . . non sanno imitar la diversità delle tinte de panni, ma pongono solamente i colori pieni, come essi stanno, in guisa che nelle opere loro non si ha a lodare altro che i colori.*[88] Pino, characteristically, had already made the same point more pungently: ... *non pero intendo vagghezza l'azzurro oltra marino da sessanta scudi l'ontia, ò la bella lacha, per ch'i colori sono ancho belli nelle scatole da se stessi.*[89]

Before Pino, even, Aretino had made the same point in 1537: ... *i miniatori tengono del disegno dei mastri de le finestre di vetro, e il far loro non è altro che una vaghezza di oltramarini, di verdi azzurri, di lacche di grana e d'ori macinati, studiandosi in una fragola, in una chiocciola e simili novelluzze. Ma l'opra vostra è tutta disegno e tutta rilievo ... ogni cosa è dolce, sfumata, come fusse a olio.*[90] This point of view is already seen in the passage of Leonardo's quoted above (p. 421): *li colori sol fanno onore alli maestri che li fanno.*

This reversal of taste, which from the literary evidence is as true of Venice as of Florence, has two facets: that true beauty does not lie in material richness, and that the proper business of painting is the pursuit of light and shade, or *rilievo*. It seems probable that both ideas may reflect the influence of classical aesthetics. The first proposition is to be found already in Alberti's *della Pittura* in a form that presupposes an antique source.[91] Pliny's description of Apelles's painting must have been particularly important since it is the only extended passage whereby the style of an antique painting could be visualized in colouristic terms: the final process was a glaze to prevent the brilliance of colour offending the sight, and from a distance subtly to give *austeritatem* to over-vivid colour.[92] Paolo Giovio's appreciation of Raphael's colour is expressed in these Plinian terms.[93] Another remark by Pliny may be part of the foundation of the second proposition: *Quod inter haec (lumen) et umbras esset appellarunt tonon* ... (The relation of light and shade they called the strength of painting.[94]) This may explain Alberti's summary of *colore* as *ricevere il lume* and Dolce's *la principal parte del colorito (è) il contendimento, che fa il lume con l'ombra.*[95]

Just as Leonardo's effective revolution in colour was prefigured in Masaccio, so the general change of taste in the Cinquecento was foreshadowed in the Quattrocento, most obviously in Alberti. When Alberti says, in the introduction to the *della Pittura*, that in Masaccio's painting he found a standard recreated which was not exceeded by that of antiquity, he could only have assessed the latter on the literary tradition. I believe that what he meant, at least in part, was the rediscovery of *austeritatem* (Manetti's *puro, sanza ornato*) and of *rilievo* or *ricevere il lume*. It is undoubtedly true that Leonardo expressed these two propositions with even greater effect. It is a possibility, then, that Leonardo's colour-style was not only the consummation of a tradition within the monumental art of Tuscany, and of the inheritence of optical theory, but also of an ideal derived from the literature of antiquity.[96]

Leonardo's greatest contribution to Florentine art was energy, both formal and psychological. His development of tonal unity of colour goes far beyond its simplest result: a coherence of plasticity in the painted form which may rival that of sculpture; it gives energy to light and colour, and through the dynamic variability of tactility, or plastic force, it contributes to the energy of forms.

Notes

1   It is a pleasure to recall two distinguished exceptions, the more so since I feel incalculably but profoundly indebted to them: H. Siebenhüner, *Über den Kolorismus der Frührenaissance*, Leipzig, 1935, and T. Hetzer, *Tizian, Geschichte seiner Farbe*, Frankfurt, 1948 (2nd edition).

2   This article is a condensed and re-arranged version of one chapter from my thesis, "Developments in the Use of Colour in Tuscan Painting of the Early Sixteenth Century", delivered at London University in 1957; the substance of it was given as a Public Lecture at the Courtauld Institute in the Summer of 1958. During the initial work, and in many subsequent conversations on this subject, I have been fortunate in, and most grateful for, the guidance and inspiration of Johannes Wilde.

3   From the inscription on a portrait in the Castello dei Pio, Carpi, reproduced in L. Servolini, *La Xilographia a chiaroscuro italiana . . .* , Lecco, 1930.

4   References to the various publications of Leonardo's writings have been abbreviated as follows. – The Trattato, or Libro della Pittura (Codex Vaticanus 1270), as "Trat."; the numbers refer to the paragraphs in the edition by H. Ludwig, *Lionardo da Vinci, Das Buch von der Malerei*, Vienna, 1882. "McC.", followed by a number refers to the page in E. McCurdy, *The Notebooks of Leonardo da Vinci*, London, 1938 (2 vols.). "Richter", followed by a number refers to J. P. Richter, *The Literary Works of Leonardo da Vinci*, Oxford, 1939 (2nd edition).

5   Trat. 111 and 133. In one of the *Paragone* texts (Trat. 31a) he says, speaking of sculpture, *Questa anchora non è imitatrice de' colori, per li quali il pittore si affatica a trovare, che le ombre sieno compagne de' lumi . . .* , which is very close to Alberti's broadest definition of *colore: ricevere il lume*. Alberti, defining the three parts of painting, states: *Ultimo, più distinto determiniamo colori et qualità delle superficie, quali ripresentandoli, ché ogni differenza nasce da lumi, proprio possiamo chiamarlo receptione di lumi.* (*L. B. Alberti, della Pittura*, ed. L. Mallè, Florence, 1950, p. 82.)

6   This was the method used with striking results by Siebenhüner, loc. cit., for the analysis of earlier Quattrocento painting. Another line of enquiry, which for practical reasons I have had to omit, is the changes in the use of colour brought about by changes of technique.

7   One example: the St. Ambrose (M. Salmi, *Masaccio*, Paris, 1934, pl. CLXXIX) wears a robe with turquoise highlights and deep wine-red shadows, and a lining turning from yellow to red. The principle is applied to architecture as well as to figures. Colour-changes are frequently interpreted as shot-silk, which is very seldom correct in Renaissance painting.

8   A new analysis of the origins of this painting is given by G. Passavant, "Beobachtungen am Verkündigungsbild aus Monte Oliveto", *Mitteilungen des Kunsthistorischen Institutes in Florenz*, February 1960, pp. 71ff: that the composition was by Domenico Ghirlandaio, and largely overpainted by Leonardo. This hypothesis seems to me convincing. The colour remains in all essential parts Leonardo's, and is unimaginable in Ghirlandaio.

9   With the exceptions, especially in the flesh in some parts, mentioned below, p. 22 and n. 35a.

10   I hope is clear that in this analysis "colour" means the chromatic constituent of the wider complex which Leonardo would have called *colore*, which would include, of

course, the neutral chiaroscuro. From his point of view (in the synthesis, as opposed to the analysis) these elements remain indivisible.

11 Cf. *della Pittura*, ed. Mallè, p. 56.

12 (I) For the different types of lighting, cf. for example MS. B. N. 2038, 29r. (McC. II, 265). (II) The different degrees of contrast produced: Trat. 120, 86, 712 (B. N. 2038, 33v.) and E 32v. (McC. II, 346). (III) The necessity of using a light appropriate to the environment: Trat. 94, 498, 414 (MS. B. N. 2038, 33r., McC. II, 272–3), G 33v. (McC. II, 352) etc. (IV) No reflections in a dark environment: Trat. 157.

13 Cf., for example, E 32v. (McC. II, 346) and Trat. 712. No opinion seems to be datable through the MSS.

14 Trat. 110.

15 Cf. Trat. 454 and 886 (MS. G 24r., McC. II, 297).

16 MS. C. A. 250a (Richter, I, 111). The whole passage, a *Proemio* to the projected books on light and shade, is particularly relevant to this discussion.

17 Trat. 213 (cf. also 207).

18 Trat. 433, 514 and especially 703, where colour-changes are excluded and black alone is to provide the *vera ombra de colori*. cf. also Trat. 706: *Del colore de' l'ombre, e quanto si scurano. Si come tutti li colori si tingono nell'oscurità delle tenebre della notte, cosi d' l'ombra di qualonche colore finisce in esse tenebre, adonque tu, pittore, non osservare, che nelle ultime tue oscurità s'abbia à conoscere li colori . . .*

19 MS. E 17v. (McC. I, 258; see also Trat. 201).

20 Two apparent exceptions: (I) Richter I, 265: "A shadow is always affected by the colour of the surface on which it is cast", is a mistranslation of W. 19076a: *L'ombra participa sempre del color del suo obbietto. Obbietto*, in the optical theory of Alberti and Leonardo, means an object placed opposite the surface in question; this is therefore one of many texts on reflected colour in shadows. (II) Trat. 592 (MS. E 30v., McC. II, p. 343): *Qualita dellonbre. Infralle equali alleviatione diluce tal proportione sia da osschurita asschurita delle generate onbre Qual sara daosschurita asschurita delli cholori dove tali onbre sichongiunghano.* (From the facsimile in C. Ravaisson-Mollien, *Les Manuscrits de Leonardo de Vinci*, C, E, K, de la Bibliothèque de l'Institut, Paris 1888.) *Generate onbre* are cast shadows, not body-shadows, and this text refers to their apparent change in value according to the relative darkness or lightness of adjacent surfaces, an abstract optical problem which need not concern us here.

21 See above, p. 406.

22 E.g., Trat. 207, and MS. B. N. 2038, 33r. (McC. II, 273–4). In the same MS., however (31v., McC. II, 272), it is stated that the part which is between the light and the shadow is *più colorita*. (Both these texts were included in the Trattato, 210 and 419 respectively.) MS. B. N. 2038 is datable c. 1492. The first conclusion is repeated in the much later Arundel MS. (B. M. 263, 169r., McC. II, 379) and in numerous other places.

23 MS. B. N. 2038, 26a (McC. II, 258) and Trat. 492.

24 E.g. Trat. 713b.

25 Trat. 206.

26 Trat. 692; for the use of the word *bello* here, see n. 44.

27 At first sight the setting of this head against the dark background is deceptively like the Angel's silhouette in the Annunciation. But in this case the light falls full on the face from the right, with the purpose – one imagines for personal reasons – of reducing shadow to a minimum; the dark foil does not delineate the profile of the head, as in the angel, because the head is at no point actually in contact with it. On the contrary, the enclosing hair is related tonally to the dark foil.

28 For example, the most advanced stages of the *Madonna with the Cat* (A. E. Popham, *The Drawings of Leonardo da Vinci*, London, 1947, Nos. 9A, which shows a window behind, and 9B, which simply has a dark background). The dark foil is designated *campo* by Leonardo: see Trat. 120.

29 Which may also be, as it is sometimes interpreted, the Virgin's Cloth of Honour.

30 The two are reproduced together in E. Hildebrandt, *Leonardo da Vinci, der Künstler und sein Werk*, Berlin, 1927, pp. 244–5.

31 Vasari, *Vite* . . . , 1568 edition, ed. Milanesi, IV p. 26; the reference comes between comments on the *Madonna of Clement VII*, and the *Adoration*.

32 This is not a suitable place for yet another discussion of these documents. For the point of view expressed here, see G. Castelfranco in *Raccolta Vinciana* XVIII, my comments in the *Burlington Magazine*, November 1961, p. 475, and the ensuing correspondence between Cecil Gould and myself in the *Burlington Magazine*, January 1962. If, as I believe with Castelfranco and others, the documents establish that two paintings were made in response to the contract of 1483, then the first (the Louvre version) must be *la dicta nostra dona facta a olio per lo dicto florentino* mentioned in the *Supplica* of the early '90s.

33 For the provenance of the London version see M. Davies, in the *Catalogue of the Earlier Italian Schools*, National Gallery, London, 1951, pp. 211ff. In spite of the unusually positive documentation that the London version is Leonardo's work, this is denied in many quarters. My acceptance is based partly on the documents and partly on a visual estimate of its quality; moreover, it differs in style, compared with the Louvre version, in a way that is consistent with Leonardo's development between 1483 and 1508 (as I hope I can demonstrate partly here) and I do not see how these stylistic advances can logically be attributed to Leonardo's followers. See also note 58.

34 This comparison is suggested by the small sketch at Windsor (Popham, op. cit., 160) which seems to come between the two.

35 Popham 159.

36 It will be noticed that the unity of tone is frequently broken in the flesh; two possible explanations for this appear in the notes. Leonardo quotes the flesh of young people as a case in which heavy shadows should be avoided, apparently as an exception to the regular depth of shadow (Trat. 419, B. N. 2038, 31v., McC. II, 272). According to his optical theory, reflections will be most effective on the pale surface of flesh (Trat. 160 and 162–3) so it follows that only in a very restricted light will the degree of relief be unaffected, and equal to that of darker drapery. His painting becomes progressively more logical in this sense. Alternatively, another observation may apply in the *Annunciation* and in the Louvre *Madonna of the Rocks*: no reflected lights will appear in shadows, even in the open air, near *corpi ombrosi, come . . . prati di varie altezze d'herbe* (Trat. 157). In the *Annunciation*, according to Passavant's analysis (above, n. 8), the Angel's

head was less repainted by Leonardo than, for example, his left hand; it is questionable how much, in that case, this was consciously an application of the principles mentioned here.

37 The design of the original *ancona* is far from clear, but it seems probable that it provided for the central panel a setting which was, in a sense, cavern-like. The Madonna was enclosed by shutters (in the National Gallery); moreover I believe that the *absidem . . . que vadit ante imaginem beatissime virginis marie ad modum incastri* (from the payment to the carpenter del Maino, 7th August 1482) was a baldacchino (Du Cange, *Absides*, in *Glossarium Mediae et Infimae Latinitatis*), like the vaulted canopies fairly frequently found in North Italian elaborately-carved *ancone* (such as Foppa's polyptych in S. Maria in Castello, Savona) and often placed over the image of the Virgin. A baldacchino is mentioned as part of the ancona in question in the inventory of 1781. I wonder if Leonardo did not exploit such a situation in the second version having seen the first in position.

38 Popham 162. This drawing has been described as a fake by A. M. Brizio in *Raccolta Vinciana* XVIII; I believe it is either an authentic, but routine, drawing by Leonardo, or a pupil's copy of one (see the *Burlington Magazine*, November 1961, p. 475).

39 Bodmer, *Klassiker der Kunst, Leonardo*, 1931, p. 362/3.

40 There are a few references in the notes to this three-dimensional aspect of chiaroscuro, of which the most notable are MS. G 19r. (McC. II, 283–4) and Trat. 440, which is virtually a text for the chiaroscuro of the *Battle of Anghiari*.

41 In the version that we know; at the same late date Leonardo drew the extreme conclusions from the dark setting in the Louvre *Baptist*, in which it appears to me that the shadowed profile is in some places physically non-existent on the panel.

42 Vasari, ed. Milanesi, IV. p. 50.

43 Sabba da Castiglione, 1554; compare Paolo Giovio, *Leonardi Vincii Vita* (soon after 1527): *Plasticem ante alia penicillo praeponebat, veluti archetypum ad planas imagines exprimendas*, and the anonymous sonnet appended by Vasari to the 1550 edition of the *Vite:*

> *Perspicuas picturae umbras, oleoque colores,*
> *Illius ante alios docta manus posuit.*

44 Trat. 123.

45 On the contrary, cf. one of the *Paragone* texts (Trat. 45): *Se il bronzo rimano nero e bruno, questa pittura è piena di vari e vaghi colori.* For other examples of *bellezza* in this sense, cf. Trat. 191 (in which stained glass is said to give maximum *bellezza*) and MS. E 18a (Richter I, 286). Naturally Leonardo still uses *bellezza* as beauty (for example Trat. 36). Michelangelo also uses the word in the first sense; at the commencement of the Sistine Ceiling he writes to Frate Jacopo of the Gesuati, in Florence: *m'è di bisognio di cierta quantità d'azzuri begli . . .* and particularly insists *che sieno begli* (Milanesi, Lettere, p. 379); this was quoted by Tolnay, *Michelangelo*, II, Princeton 1945, p. 185, but I feel sure that *begli* should be translated "pure" or "brilliant", rather than "beautiful".

46 See below, p. 41.

47 Trat. 190 a.

48 Cf. Bandello's eyewitness report reprinted in *Leonardo da Vinci, La Vita di Giorgio Vasari*, ed. G. Poggi, Florence 1919, pp. 21–2.

49 Vasari, ed. Milanesi, IV, p. 43.

50 G. Gaye, *Carteggio Inedito . . .*, Florence 1840, II, p. 89. Leonardo's invention defied description in normal bureaucratic terms: . . . 4 *ruote per fare il carro a Lionardo da Vincio overo ponte.*

51 The *Last Supper* seems always to have been considered unusually "colourful"; cf. Carlo Torre, *Il Ritratto di Milano*, 1674, p. 164 (. . . *veggonsi ancora vivi sembianti, figure in iscorsi sforzosi, colori risplendente . . .*).

52 On the left, green against red, yellow against blue, etc., on the right, soft blues, pink-greys, lilac etc.

53 Compare the two ends of *The Raising of the King's Son* in the Brancacci Chapel, the right third of which is normally in shadow (and would have been from the original window). Leonardo would have remembered this fresco without its portions by Filippino, so that the contrast would have been at its most obvious.

54 For estimates of the original colours remaining, compare F. Wittgens, *Il restauro del Cenacolo di Leonardo, Atti del convegno di studi Vinciani*, Florence, 1953, p. 39, and Arturo Bovi, La visione del colore e della luce nella Cena, *Raccolta Vinciana* XVII, 1954, p. 315.

55 Bovi judged that the blue is still somewhat overpainted, whereas Wittgens inferred that this had been removed; my personal impression, from the ground, is that there is a good deal of old and new paint remaining.

56 Cf. Bovi: *Frammenti di colore si scoprono dello sfacello della veste . . . e risplendono del verde chiarissimo originario che si riflette nei toni delle argentee stoviglie sul tavolo.*

57 The setting around the figures is predominantly neutral in colour, but the whole palette, with special emphasis on the reds and greens, is repeated in the wreaths in the lunettes above. The distant view in the centre (which is said to be free from overpaint), seems also to pick up the paler blues and greens of the figures in the normal way.

58 From the undated *Supplica* of the early '90s; Leonardo's authorship may be deduced from its phraseology. In this case he was referring, I believe, to the Louvre version, but it is clear from the documents that there was no change of subject between the two versions, since both were made in response to the same contract, without amendments.

It is already true of the Louvre version that, when it is seen in a light approximating to that for which it was intended, the increased relative intensity of the blue makes the Madonna the true subject of the picture, but the intensification of this effect, and the sacrifice of all inessential decorative colour in the second version, is yet another example of Leonardo's deeper appreciation of the painting's destination.

The explanation of the changed appearance of the paintings in lower illumination is to be found in what is known as the "Purkinje effect" (C. Ladd-Franklin, *Colour and Colour Theories*, London, 1932, p. 58); the importance of this for the study of paintings seems not to have been appreciated. The decrease of illumination on a complete colour-scale results in a shift of emphasis (or of *relative* intensity) from the red end of the spectrum towards the blue. In paintings, therefore, the

437

distortions of modern gallery-lighting may affect the symbolism of colour, the relative plasticity of colours, or a finely-balanced colour-composition.

59 The painting of this lining to the robe is worth special attention. In Leonardo's notes it is observed that a coarse texture (like the blue robe) will have no "lustre"; the extreme highlight of a smooth silk-texture will be entirely lustre, and the highlight proper will be introduced, along with the colour, around this. The colour-reflections will appear to intensify the local colour in half-shadows where they are reflected from one part of a form to another part of the same (Trat. 223–4, etc.). In the London version, the fluctuating value of the colour in the silk lining is remarkably sensitive in its exact analysis of the source, nature, and colour of the light falling on its sharp folds. It is a measure, as true as the notes, of the completely three-dimensional perception of light at this stage. It seems to me that details like these support the attribution to Leonardo of this version; not only is the practice intimately related to the novel analysis in the notes, so that we seem to see one mind at work, but also no work by any pupil that I have ever seen displays a comparable intellectual grasp of such problems.

60 See the evocative description in Sir Kenneth Clark's *Leonardo da Vinci*, Cambridge, 1952, p. 116. In fact the impression of vitality given by the *Mona Lisa* (and, one must imagine, the *Leda*) became an important factor in the style of Andrea del Sarto and of his followers.

61 In the case of the *Leda* and of the *Madonna of the Yarn-Winder*, both compositions in an exterior setting, we may infer in the lighting a respect for these conditions partly from the copies, and partly from a consideration of the converse of the argument about *Mona Lisa*. Exactly how this was done cannot be determined, but that it was done in the second Florentine period is historically important.

62 Hetzer, op. cit., p. 133. Leonardo's departure from this point was not, of course, so complete or so important as Titian's.

63 The condition of this painting, in some ways unusually satisfactory, requires a little mental reconstruction, not only in those unimportant parts where the degree of finish is uncertain. The most important change is in the Virgin's robe, which has lost its tonal qualities owing to the phenomenon of "Ultramarine sickness". It may be reconstructed as tonally unified, also in the shadow, with the other draperies, on the basis of the Uffizi copy; the tone of the highlights has changed little, if at all. There is considerable overpaint on this drapery, especially on the hip, and this attempts to rectify the loss of the shadows.

64 Perhaps the most important early example is Bellini's S. Zaccaria altarpiece, though it had already appeared in some parts of the Pesaro *Coronation*, and in Carpaccio's painting of the '90s. Fra Bartolomeo brought back this device from Venice, among other Venetian influences, and it is to be found spasmodically used in altarpieces by him and by Albertinelli from 1509; the Florentine who first exploited its potentialities was Andrea del Sarto. Michelangelo also uses it in the second half of the Sistine ceiling.

65 For example St. Anne's left sleeve: grey, variable over a short range from yellowish to bluish; its exact value is never established, but it makes an effective continuity with the lamb and with the hills in the left background.

66 E.g. the studies for the Trivulzio Monument, or the *Windsor Allegory* (Popham 102, 123).

67 For example, the small area revealed by removal of the baroque altar-frame, reproduced in M. Salmi, *Masaccio, Cappella Brancacci*, Milan (U. N. E. S. C. O.), 1949, pl. XVI.

68 The increasing rationalism of Masaccio's light is seen in the progressive rejection of colour-change in modelling; in the earlier frescoes yellow is often shaded with red, whereas in the later ones it is shaded towards grey-brown.

69 How completely it was forgotten can be seen in the Brancacci Chapel itself, comparing Masaccio's frescoes with Filippino's of the 1480s. It is impossible for me to mention here all the many exceptions to colour-modelling that exist even within Florentine painting of the Quattrocento. None of them, to my knowledge, anticipate Leonardo in any significant way, with the possible exception of the technique of the Pollaiuoli which, while not being directed towards tonal unity, may have been important as a precedent for the infusion of neutral pigment into colour. There may well be a technical link between such works as the *Mercanzia Virtues* and the Angel in the *S. Salvi Baptism* (Uffizi).

70 Again, this is seen partly in the rejection of colour-modelling between the Arena and Bardi Chapels.

71 I owe this comment to John White.

72 Compare, for example, the Angel in the *S. Salvi Baptism* with the left kneeling Saint in the Barbadori Altarpiece; similarly, Fra Bartolomeo's debt to this source is demonstrated by the relation of his mature drapery-style (for example in the 1509 S. Marco Altarpiece) to Lippi's in the S. Lorenzo *Annunciation*. One of the Angels in the Barbadori Altar is exactly repeated in an early Ridolfo Ghirlandaio, an *Adoration* once in Berlin (S. Freedberg, *Painting of the High Renaissance in Rome and Florence*, Cambridge, 1961, II, fig. 278).

73 The most thorough analysis is still Siebenhüner, op. cit.

74 See, most recently, V. P. Zoubov, Léon-Battista Alberti et Léonard de Vinci, *Raccolta Vinciana* XVIII, 1961.

75 Leonardo's interest in Northern technique is shown by his note on Jean Perréal, MS. C. A. 247r. (Richter 1379; for the date – either 1494–5 or 1499 – see G. Calvi in *Raccolta Vinciana*, III, p. 99).

76 E.g. the *Annunciation* in the Duomo at Volterra, 1947, by Fra Bartolomeo, or the *Holy Family* tondo in the Pitti by Albertinelli of about the same date.

77 For Andrea, the *Noli me tangere* of *c.* 1510 in the Uffizi; for Pontormo, the *Madonna* from Poggio Imperiale (now in the Uffizi, Mostra Pontormo, 1956, No. 14), *c.* 1515; for Rosso, the *Madonna* in the Staedel Institute, Frankfurt, *c.* 1515 (K. Kusenberg, Le Rosso, Paris 1931, Pl. XII); for Puligo, the *Magdalen* in the Johnson Collection, Philadelphia (also. *c.* 1515).

78 This example is particularly close to the upper-right angel in Masaccio's *St Anne*. I have not mentioned in the text the colour-change on the lining of the Virgin's robe, which is an exemplary though rare case of the description of shot-silk.

79 Michelangelo was insistent on the perfection of his materials in painting as well as in sculpture; cf. the letter mentioned above, n. 44.

80 The direction seen in the later parts of the Sistine Ceiling was probably continued in the *Leda* of 1530; to judge from the probable influence of the latter upon Pontormo's *Noli me Tangere*, this was the case. For an assessment of the pictorial qualities of the

Leda see J. Wilde, Notes on the Genesis of Michelangelo's "Leda", *Memorial Essays for Fritz Saxl*, London, 1957, p. 279.

81   *Vita* of Perino del Vaga, Vasari ed. Milanesi, V, p. 604.

82   Vasari, II, p. 288.

83   Vasari, *della Pittura*, Cap. IV, ed. Milanesi, I, p. 180.

84   Aretino, *Lettere sull'Arte*, ed. F. Pertile and E. Camesasca, Milan, 1957, II, p. 52.

85   Vasari, *della Pittura*, Cap. IV, I, p. 179.

86   Vasari, loc. cit.

87   The same is inevitably the case with tapestry; Armenini (II, 2 and 7) condemns the colours of tapestries as confusing and jarring. cf. already Giulio Romano in his letter to the Steccata, 1541 (F. Hartt, *Giulio Romano*, New Haven, 1958, p. 249).

88   L. Dolce, *Dialogo della Pittura (1557)*, ed. P. Barocchi, Bari, 1960, pp. 184–5.

89   Paolo Pino, *Dialogo di Pittura*, Venice, 1548, p. 18.

90   Aretino, ed. cit., I, p. 45.

91   Alberti, *della Pittura*, ed. Mallé, p. 76.

92   K. Jex-Blake and E. Sellers, *The Elder Pliny's Chapters on the History of Art*, London, 1896, p. 132. If it seems improbable that a text in Pliny can affect Renaissance style, this at least was not the view held in the Quattrocento. Facio (De Viris Illustribus, before 1457) claimed that Jan van Eyck learnt the *proprietates dei colori* from reading the ancient authors, especially Pliny: see J. Schlosser Magnino, *La Letteratura Artistica*, 2nd ed. Florence and Vienna, 1956, p. 110.

93   V. Golzio, *Raffaello nei documenti . . .*, Città del Vaticano, 1936, p. 192.

94   Pliny XXX, 50; Jex-Blake and Sellers, p. 96. The word *tonos* cannot really be translated: "tone" is certainly inadequate, and "relative strength" may be nearer.

95   Dolce, ed. cit., p. 183.

96   Bandello, as an eye-witness, records a conversation between Leonardo and the Cardinal of Gurk, on the possibility of modern paintings rivalling those of antiquity *che tanto da i buoni scrittori sono celebrate* (Poggi, op. cit., p. 22). Leonardo was compared with Zeuxis and Parrhasius as early as 1497; see Luca Pacioli, *de Divina Proportione*, ed. C. Winterberg, Vienna, 1896, p. 41.

21

The Subject of Savoldo's *Magdalene*

Mary Pardo

In important respects, the essay that follows is a gloss on the striking assertion with which Panofsky concluded his epochal contribution to the study of perspective, "Die Perspektive als 'symbolische Form' ":[1]

> Through the distinctive transferral of artistic objectivity to the sphere of the phenomenal, the perspectival view severs religious art from the realm of the magical, where the work of art is itself the miracle-worker, and the realm of the dogmatic-symbolical, where it attests to or predicts the miraculous. But the perspectival view opens to religious art something entirely new, the realm of the visionary, where the miracle becomes the beholder's immediate experience, in that the supernatural events break – as it were – into his own seemingly natural visual space, thus enabling him to apprehend directly their miraculous nature; and perspective opens to religious art the realm of the psychological in the deepest sense, where the miracle takes place now only in the souls of those represented in the work of art.

As Panofsky indicated, traditional religious imagery in particular was utterly transformed by the Renaissance adoption of a "perspectival view," with its valorization of the individual beholder and his "natural" perceptual sphere. It is the consequence of this transformation that I wish to consider through a close reading of Giovanni Gerolamo Savoldo's half-length *Magdalene* (fig. 21.1) – a cinquecento *invenzione* whose interpretation hinges to an unusual degree on the particular, optically determined relationship between the individual viewer and the image. If it is approached both as a "vision" (in Panofsky's sense), and a virtual demonstration of pictorial artifice in the "perspectival" mode, Savoldo's painting sheds light on an entire dimension of Renaissance artistic thinking – the dimension, to be precise, in which the perceiving subject and the object of his attention are both united and disjoined by a device of fictive projection.

Savoldo's image survives in several autograph variants (fig. 21.1), two of which include the ointment jar by which the saint is identified.[2] They are all thought to have been painted sometime between 1520 and 1536.[3] In each version, the

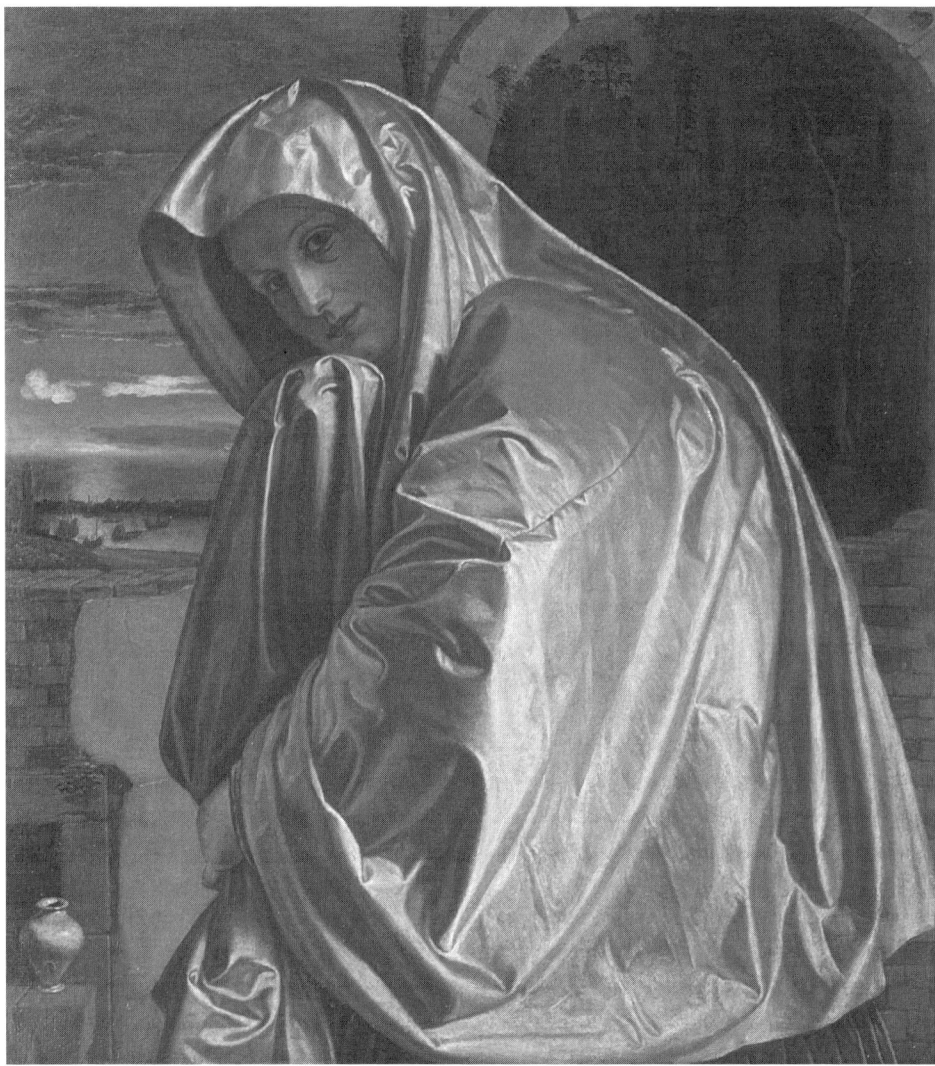

Figure 21.1 Giovanni Girolamo Savoldo, *St. Mary Magdalene Approaching the Sepulchre*. National Gallery, London, UK / The Bridgeman Art Library.

Magdalene's pose is the same: a contrapposto (underscored by the gesture of the arms) that sets the orientation of the torso against that of the face, with its three-quarter turn toward the viewer. The figure's heavy, lustrous shawl dominates the picture surface, and is the occasion for a virtuoso display of illusionistic skill. This reflective envelope is both a magnet to the viewer's eye and a shield blocking direct access to the image's interior. Compositionally, it fulfills the double function of clarifying the volumetric extension of the pose while assimilating it – by breadth and simplicity of contour – to the plane of the canvas. The luministic rendering of the shawl adds a further level to the play of contrapositions:

against the somber background, the fabric appears simultaneously fractured and bound together by an effect of momentary illumination, which in turn offsets the suggestive shadow veiling the saint's face, whose gaze appears fastened on the world outside the picture.

The figure's allure, its promise of interaction with the spectator, as well as its sheer sensory appeal, are appreciatively noted in the modern literature on the paintings. This same literature has posited an ambivalent or even subversive relationship between Savoldo's apparent subject (a female saint depicted, on the face of it, to satisfy a devotional purpose) and its mode of presentation. Already Vasari had said of the painter that he was "capriccioso e sofistico," fanciful and artful, and worthy of much praise for the work he undertook in minor genres.[4] For most of its recent interpreters, the seductive-seeming *Magdalene* is indeed "capricious," but in the sense that Savoldo disregarded the decorum governing traditional religious images, in order to pursue an essentially "naturalistic" vision of female enchantment. This view originated in the later nineteenth century, when Savoldo's oeuvre was reconstituted after a period of neglect; it deserves a moment's attention, since it still dominates the discussion of the *Magdalene*'s subject.

The eighteenth century marked a drastic decline in Savoldo's critical fortune.[5] Earlier, his work had enjoyed a stable reputation in the art-collecting circles of the Veneto; the *Magdalene* in particular was popular from the outset (as the authentic variants attest), and its fame lasted well into the next century: in his *Maraviglie dell'arte* of 1648 Ridolfi identified the version then in Brescia as "a figure of the Magdalene – wrapped in a cloak, and holding the alabaster jar – on her way to the Sepulcher, a famous painting from which many copies have been made."[6] No significant critical assessment followed Ridolfi's until Crowe and Cavalcaselle's description in 1871 of the Berlin variant, which they accepted (perhaps because it is signed) as Savoldo's original formulation of the theme:

> The hour is sunset. The shape is that of a woman, young, warm, and impulsive. Her form, half-hid in a mantilla, glides round the corner of a ruin. The light just tips her nose and leaves the rest of the face in gloom, the right hand concealed in the silk which it lifts to the chin. The left hand clutching the skirts, the furtive archness of the glance, the twilight in which the scene is shrouded, are full of mystery.[7]

The Berlin picture lacks the traditional ointment jar, whence its secular title. Comparing it to the one subsequently acquired for London (fig. 21.1), Crowe and Cavalcaselle found the latter less "mysterious," with its distant view of the Venetian lagoon, and the addition of "a table with a vase" (the ointment jar on a stone ledge!). By taking the London *Magdalene* as the earliest version, Adolfo Venturi restored the primacy of the religious subject in his volume of the *Storia dell'arte italiana* of 1928, but in ekphrastic passages destined to a long afterlife, he also certified the figure's status as a romantic invention along the lines of the Berlin variant.[8]

443

The subsequent literature has echoed this characterization, at times dwelling on the figure's seductiveness, at others on its evocative surroundings, and usually dissociating the image from its religious pretext.[9] This has led to particular assumptions about its patronage, most recently reiterated by Monika Ingenhoff-Danhäuser, who considers Savoldo's *Magdalene* a courtesan portrait, with the sitter in the guise of her repentant New Testament counterpart – but wearing the cloak prescribed by Venetian law for prostitutes going out in public.[10] This reading has the merit of addressing the socio-historical context, but it sheds no light on the *Magdalene*'s position in the body of Savoldo's work, the bulk of which is religious in subject.[11] The artist's other religious images typically evoke a poignantly reverential mood – associated, as in the *Magdalene*, with setting and time of day, but always in a contemplative key appropriate to the subject. A nuanced reading of the *Magdalene* should reconcile its apparent sensuality (which seems undeniable) with Savoldo's characteristically introspective approach to devotional themes. Most important, it should do so by acknowledging Savoldo's remarkable exploitation of the means of pictorial illusion.

In his dissertation of 1955, Creighton Gilbert had already sought to free the *Magdalene* from association with courtesan imagery, arguing instead that it was adapted from a serving maid in Savoldo's lost *Continence of Scipio*, known through later copies.[12] The saint's "air of the world" could thus be considered an accidental consequence of its derivation from a secular model. Gilbert eventually rejected this hypothesis on chronological grounds; but elsewhere in his thesis he proposed a far more productive line of inquiry, addressing larger issues of representational strategy.[13] Assessing Savoldo's innovations, Gilbert noted how "in synthesizing the figure-painting into a restricted form, in widening the portrait out to a narrative implication," the artist had narrowed the gap between the two genres.[14] In addition, he referred to the *Magdalene*, by analogy with Savoldo's portraits, as "the transformation of an image into a story."[15] It is precisely this "narrative implication" – already fully acknowledged in Ridolfi's seventeenth-century remarks on the *Magdalene* – that will be taken here as a guide to the subject of Savoldo's invention.

As will be seen, Savoldo's image gains in vividness and complexity once it is "read into" and recast as a story with the aid of the appropriate Gospel text. At the same time, the text is to be read in light of the image's most telling visual characteristics: the contrapposto structures (tonal no less than figural) articulating the composition. The interpretive remarks that follow primarily concern the visual reciprocity between the saint's shadowed expression and the shawl's incandescence – each, in its way, simultaneously inviting and deflecting our entry into the figure's world, each reminding us of the difficulty of seeing clearly in conditions of excess, whether of darkness or light. Further, the significance of the chiaroscuro may be linked to the Magdalene's turning pose, which produces the illusion of a momentary gesture caught in the act of unfolding (so that the viewer finds himself engaging an event rather than a static figure).

This momentary quality – which seems crucial to the "seductive" immediacy of the figure – is enhanced by an added detail of illumination in the two versions of the *Magdalene* that appear the best preserved and most consistent in quality, those in London and Florence (fig. 21.1).[16] Both include a natural light source – the sunrise – in the landscape behind the figure: the saint's active pose is thus associated with a transitional time of day. Moreover, this faraway radiance appears in counterpoint to the strong light that shines on the figure from our side of the picture. The juxtaposition seems anything but accidental; in his era, Savoldo was noted for his mastery of fugitive and unusual light effects.[17] Like the coupling of shadow and light in the *Magdalene*, the distinction between ambient and figure illumination seems to invite something beyond a merely naturalistic interpretation.[18]

Since I consider the light effects to be intrinsic to Savoldo's theme, I will confine my remarks in the rest of this paper to the London and Florence *Magdalenes* (which for the present purposes may be treated as interchangeable).[19] In both, the sunrise (especially in juxtaposition with the somber ruin at the saint's back) can be broadly taken as a conventional allusion to the Resurrection.[20] In the London catalogue, Cecil Gould has suggested that the Resurrection account in John 20 provides the likely Gospel source for Savoldo's image, since it alone has the Magdalene approach the tomb unaccompanied. The chapter opens as follows: "And on the first day of the week Mary Magdalene cometh early, when it was yet dark, unto the sepulchre, and she saw the stone taken away from the sepulchre."[21]

At first sight this raises a difficulty, since the sunrise and the ointments destined for Christ's body are absent here, but present in the synoptic Gospels, which give no special prominence to the Magdalene. However, the image need not be taken as a textual illustration at the level of its literal furnishings – it is too highly compressed. The ointment jar is in any case the saint's normal attribute, while the dawn sky evokes the event without necessarily singling out a textual source. In visual terms, what shapes our response to the image, next to the illuminated shawl, is the momentary quality of the pose, with its simultaneous inward rotation of the body and outward turn of the face. And this action provides the key to a narrative reading by suggesting a later passage in the Gospel of John, verses 11–16, which tell of the events following Mary Magdalene's return alone to the tomb after having informed John and Peter of the removal of Christ's body (late enough in the narrative, incidentally, for dawn to have broken). The scene is set in verse 11:

But Mary stood at the sepulchre, without, weeping. Now as she was weeping, she stooped down, and looked into the sepulchre,

12. And she saw two angels in white sitting, one at the head, and one at the feet, where the body of Jesus had been laid.

13. They say to her: Woman, why weepest thou? She saith to them, Because they have taken away my Lord; and I know not where they have laid him.

14. And when she had thus said, she turned herself back, and saw Jesus standing, and she knew not that it was Jesus.

15. Jesus saith to her: Woman, why weepest thou, whom seekest thou? She, thinking that it was the gardener, saith to him: Sir, if thou hast taken him hence, tell me where thou hast laid him, and I will take him away.

16. Jesus saith to her: Mary. She, turning, saith to him, Rabboni (which is to say, Master).[22]

Twice in this passage (at verses 14 and 16) the Magdalene, who had been peering disconsolately into the tomb, turns away to look at Christ, who has appeared behind her. The first time, it is uncomprehendingly; in the ensuing dialogue her error about Christ's identity is rectified by his affirmation of her own (*Dicit ei Iesus: Maria*). At the sound of her name, she turns a second time and simultaneously expresses recognition, as if turning and understanding were the same process. Like her Gospel counterpart, Savoldo's figure has been crying: she holds a cloaked right hand before the lower part of her face in a gesture clearly derived from a well-established convention for weeping mourners at the scene of Christ's death; but here the wrapped fist is not pressed to the eyes, and the saint gazes out as if acknowledging a momentary interruption.[23] The suspension of weeping, together with the turning pose, precisely illustrates the query, "Woman, why weepest thou," spoken successively by the angels and Christ, and followed by the phrases, "she turned . . . back . . . She, turning . . . ," of the Gospel account. In keeping with the image's narrative pregnancy, its quality of duration, I would suggest that the painted Magdalene's turning represents both verse 14 and verse 16 in John 20, with the viewer imagining the temporal interval they bracket, in the course of which a mere gardener at the saint's back metamorphoses into a resurrected deity.[24]

We might say, then, that the figure's ambiguous and "veiled" facial expression is meant to register something unpaintable, a transition – from blindness to sight, from loss to restitution, from mortal to supernatural reality – that the viewer projects or constructs, prompted by visual metaphors suggestive of temporal unfolding: dark passing into light, the body turning on its axis, dawn spreading at the horizon.[25] To use the language of the Vulgate (*conversa est retrorsum, conversa illa*), the Magdalene depicted by Savoldo is experiencing an aspect of conversion, both literally and on a plane that redefines (and fulfills) the very modality of her role as Christian example: repentant sinner, convert.[26] Savoldo's metaphorical wit calls upon our awareness that painting is indeed mute poetry: it is the viewer's task to supply the text and its exegesis, so to speak writing these into the Magdalene's withdrawn and shadowy face. It may well be that Savoldo's figure has accommodated a secular reading as easily as it has because it is not demonstrative, but rather asks to be "made up."

If the Magdalene's face is, in a sense, a *tabula rasa* awaiting inscription, the light that renders her visible and transfigures her garment may be interpreted as the bodiless yet irrefutable manifestation of the resurrected Christ's presence – answering, from outside the picture, the dawn light at the farthest distance within it. This radiance is an effect whose cause, again, is imagined by the viewer, this time by projecting an effulgent being in his own space, but to the side, as suggested by the oblique path of the light across the Magdalene's cloak. It seems crucial that the reflective garment reveals the general position – and not just the presence – of the light source; the apparition's specificity, and our involvement in it, hinge on this.

Assuming one stands directly in front of the canvas, the figure of Christ should be imagined to the right, since the light burns brightest against the Magdalene's hood and her jutting arm as their surfaces tilt rightward into the picture space (the effect is equally evident in the modeling of the ointment jar). Despite its broad sweep across the shawl, it is not a full frontal illumination: its course is broken by the wedge of the Magdalene's elbow projecting directly forward. At the same time, the highlighted ridges veining the shawl presuppose – like all highlights – a viewer in a position of angular reciprocity to the incidence of light, which is to say, in a determinate location with respect to the light source.[27] In the terms of the geometry of optics (the proper object of traditional *perspectiva*), the "mirror-writing" of the highlights reaches the viewer's eye along a radial path, as does the saint's gaze directed outward from the shadows. The viewer is effectively caught up in a triangular relationship with two fictive entities – the painted figure returning his glance and the imagined figure ensnaring it in a net of reflections.

By providing the Magdalene with a text (indeed, a dramatic script), the beholder is empowered to decipher her pictorial message and breathe life into the fixity of the image. He becomes the painter's accomplice, but also his creature, assuming an essential role in the space between two fictions. Properly speaking, the "subject" of Savoldo's *Magdalene* is as much the viewer as the saint or the Gospel narrative. This brings us to the psychological effect of the image, which resides in its explicit specularity. In reflecting upon the shawl's reflections, the beholder undertakes a complicated projective exercise with respect to the painted figure. At one level, as he awakens to the implications of the radiant form before him, he undergoes something analogous to the unfolding process of enlightenment chronicled in John 20, so that the real and the painted person become psychic correlates. At another level, this identification is checked by the awareness of a radical difference in the kinds of reality contributing to our experience of the *Magdalene*.

Paradoxically, the asymmetrical interlocking of a real with a fictive situation – and of both with the sacred text that certifies their significance, yet depends upon them for actualization – enhances the devotional possibilities of the image. To give an example: in the painting (and the Gospel account) the saint cannot "see" until she recognizes Christ – a recognition figured here by the fullness of light toward which she turns, as her blindness is figured by the shadow still clouding her face. Each of these moments is a kind of absolute state of being. By contrast, we "see" the miracle in "mixed" light, by decoding the composite and allusive structure of chiaroscuro depiction. Literally, what is whole for the narrative's Magdalene is divided as it reaches us (mediated by representation as by the historical interval elapsed since the original event). At the same time, our partial seeing comprehends – in the mere image to which it lends life – something like the condition of its own transcendence.

With the viewer primed to impart to the Magdalene's figure an affective immediacy derived from his own concurrent experience of "quasi-conversion," she becomes more like a living person. And this is essential to the image's significance, since the Magdalene was present outside Christ's tomb as the first mortal witness to the Resurrection. In the Gospel of John, the passage immediately following the moment of recognition narrates Christ's charge to the Magdalene that she testify to the significance of what she has seen:

> 17. Jesus saith to her: Do not touch me, for I am not yet ascended to my Father. But go to my brethren, and say to them: I ascend to my father and to your Father, to my God and your God.
> 18. Mary Magdalene cometh and telleth his disciples: I have seen the Lord, and these things he said to me.[28]

To the extent that the fictive Magdalene comes alive for the viewer, the original occasion for her testimony is reenacted in the here and now of the viewer's experience. But since her eyes remain in shadow, we may suppose that she has not yet seen what she has begun to know. The viewer – who sees what she does not, the light of Christ on her garment – has the opportunity in a way to precede her as the Resurrection's first witness. He sees only a reflection, however, which is all that a painting can be; but it is a cunning reflection, for it literally expresses the saint's role in the Gospel account, which is to affirm the reality of the Resurrection as an event of this world, to mirror it (even in spite of herself).

Jacobus de Voragine's etymological preface to the saint's life in the *Golden Legend* is to the point in connection with Savoldo's use of the reflective shawl to evoke a double process of enlightenment – the Magdalene's and ours: "Mary signifies 'bitter sea,' or 'light-giver' [*illuminatrix*] or 'enlightened' [*illuminata*]. . . . Inasmuch as she chose the excellent portion of contemplation, she is called light-giver, because she received eagerly what she afterwards gave back abundantly: she received the light with which she then enlightened [*illustravit*] others."[29] At the same time, the device of the light-imprinted cloak conveys the sense of the *noli me tangere*, since it withholds (as mirrors must) the physical source of its image. Even more radically than the historical Magdalene, we remain at an unbridgeable distance from the mystery we seem to witness.

We may now reassess the "seductiveness" of Savoldo's figure, since its pictorial function goes beyond evoking the vestigial sensuality of a beautiful but repentant fallen woman. Certainly the homiletic and devotional literature on the saint consistently emphasized the Magdalene's amorous nature.[30] This aspect of her spiritual profile put her outside the bounds of ordinary propriety even after conversion – and undoubtedly served in a general way to justify the sensual inflection of so many depictions of the Magdalene, including Savoldo's. However, the latter is open to a more particular reading. If it is justifiable to posit a radiant Christ on the viewer's right, then the Magdalene's gaze implicates us in her process of awakening by momentarily escaping the narrative frame (where Christ is the proper object of her attention). In narrative terms, it is by chance that we intercept her glance while standing before the painting; but in devotional terms it is by necessity, since our attention literally endows the painted image with life. By seeming to see us she solicits this cooperation.

In pictorial terms, then, the poetic intimacy of the Magdalene's demeanor seduces us to take part in a fictive exercise; there is something potentially transgressive about this, but it leads to the deeper apprehension of the saint's devotional significance, since she is a model of unconditional attachment to the Redeemer as a physically real person. Whatever additional roles the Magdalene may have played in Christian thought, she was first of all Christ's most cherished female follower. The encounter at the tomb was habitually allegorized in light of this bond of affection; to take a widespread example, in block-book editions of the typological *Biblia pauperum* (ca. 1460–65), the *Noli me tangere* illustration is flanked by an image of the encounter between the Bride and Bridegroom of the Song of Solomon. Scrolls with apposite quotations issue from the mouths of the Old Testament protagonists – the Bride's a fitting expression of the fulfillment anticipated in the mute gaze of Savoldo's figure: "[I found him whom my soul loveth:] I held him: and I will not let him go" (Cant. 3:4).[31]

So far I have spoken of a generic "viewer" as the necessary agent in Savoldo's pictorial *invenzione*; but it has been my assumption that this reading of the *Magdalene* is congruent with expectations about the work of art (in contradistinction to the image of devotion) that are specific to the Renaissance.[32] These must now be examined at some length, but not before establishing the *Magdalene*'s pedigree in religious painting of the late quattrocento and early cinquecento. Savoldo's invention is not an isolated phenomenon. It crowns a historical development in which the half-length format, through the representational devices opened up by the "perspectival view," became the vehicle for an unprecedented interaction between the viewer and the painted image.

In a fundamental study, Sixten Ringbom traced the contours of this development, arguing that narrative additions to the traditional iconic image *en buste* produced a novel sort of fifteenth-century meditation picture – the "dramatic close-up" – distinguished by its immediacy (a function of the newly established means of optical realism), but also by its symbolic or exegetical allusiveness.[33] In a subsequent analysis of "ostensive" devotional images of the sort culminating in the dramatic close-up, Hans Belting added the important specification that, with the advent of an optically based theory of art in Renaissance Italy, artistic values proper achieved autonomous status in the context of religious representation.[34]

Thus, to the degree that they were perspectively regulated, dramatic close-ups brought together (without necessarily harmonizing) an earlier focus on empathetic appeal and a more modern expression of the artistic will embodied in the image's construction as a "window view." The *Magdalene* certainly fits Ringbom's category of amplified iconic "portraits" endowed with a heightened suggestiveness for the worshipper. But, in line with Belting's observations, it also indicates how, as they became more comprehensively illusionistic, images inviting the viewer to spiritual absorption increasingly presupposed a kind of expertise about pictorial illusion itself. The specific pictorial type to which Savoldo's image belongs (with its eloquent, and potentially ambivalent, artfulness) can be traced back by at least a half-century.

As Ringbom's survey demonstrates, North Italy had played an important part in the rise of the dramatic close-up.[35] In the last quarter of the fifteenth century, the region was visited by two highly original artists whose successive experiments with the half-length religious picture seem to have had a direct impact on Savoldo: Antonello da Messina and Leonardo. Antonello quite probably invented the sort of narratively "charged" yet introspective figure from which the *Magdalene* is descended.[36] Leonardo, in turn, took up and refashioned the half-length image (over a range of genres extending from the portrait to the multi-figure religious narrative) as the vehicle for a dynamically conceived fusion of tonal and bodily contrapposto. I will briefly take up each artist's contribution.

Toward 1475 – about the time of his Venetian sojourn – Antonello painted two remarkable images of the Virgin Annunciate, neither of which includes the angel; instead, Mary faces the viewer across a kind of desk-top closely associated with the bottom edge of the panel.[37] In the more famous image, in Palermo (fig. 21.2), the cloaked Virgin, her torso pivoted towards the viewer's right, displays a subtle but unmistakable contrapposto. She raises a foreshortened right hand as if to acknowledge the powerful light that shines down on her from front and left; though her face has assumed a hieratic frontality, the lowered eyes complete the rotational movement toward the incoming light. Ringbom traces this unusual image to icons of the praying Virgin amplified with elements from Annunciation scenes; most scholars agree that it puts the viewer in the position of "impersonating" the announcing angel.[38] Given the lighting's strong directional quality, it seems more appropriate to place Gabriel (as the implied light source) somewhere above the viewer's left shoulder – or simply to interpret the light as both a visual substitute for the angelic greeting and an emblem of Christ's Incarnation.[39] In either case, the dynamics of the composition, as defined by the fall of light from without and the Virgin's answering foreshortened gesture, unfold orthogonally in relation to the viewer, directly soliciting his imaginative complicity in the event's enactment.

For its narrative quality and suggestive use of an extrapictorial light source as the apparent cause of the painted figure's reaction, the Palermo *Annunciate* is a worthy forerunner of Savoldo's *Magdalene*. Versions of it may have circulated in North Italy; certainly Leonardo's design for a half-length *Angel of the Annun-*

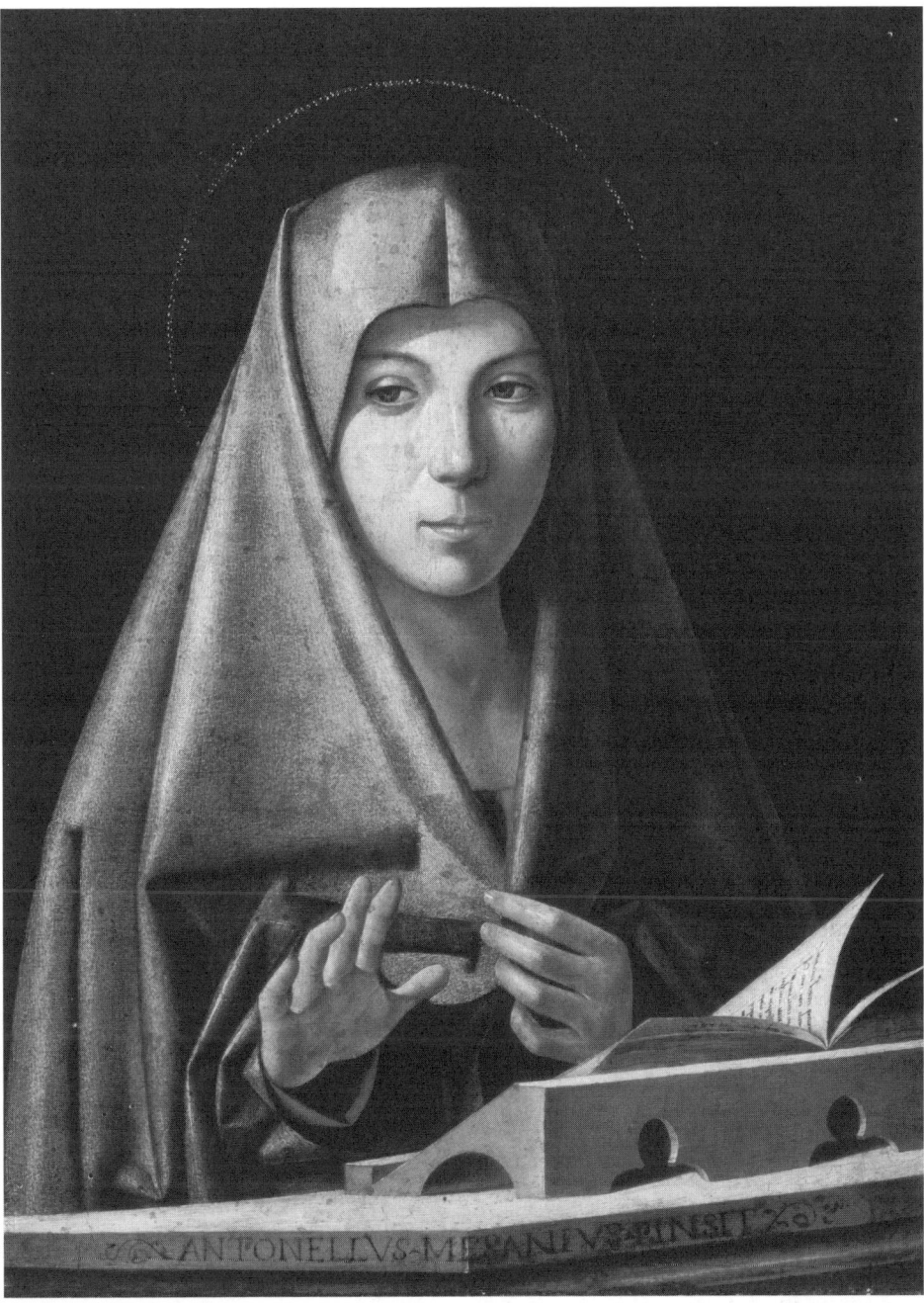

Figure 21.2 Antonello da Messina, *Virgin Annunciate*. Palermo, Galleria Nazionale. Bridgeman / Alinari Archives-Florence.

ciation seems deliberately complementary to Antonello's *concetto* (Windsor 12328r).[40] Leonardo's original painting is lost, but various replicas have been identified on the strength of Vasari's description: "the head of an angel who raises in the air an arm projected forward and foreshortened from shoulder to elbow, and whose other arm is brought up with the hand to the chest."[41] A vivid impression of the original is conveyed in the remarkable pen drawing (ca. 1514) by the youthful Baccio Bandinelli.[42] Most probably, the painting was executed in Florence between 1500 and 1507: a near-contemporary reference has been discerned in Albertini's mention in 1510 of "uno Angelo di Leonardo Vinci" at S. Salvi.[43]

The lost *Angel*, and its close relative, the later *John the Baptist* in the Louvre, deserve a moment's attention; among Leonardo's final essays in the half-length figure, they are almost programmatic in their exploration of the metaphorical suggestiveness of contrapposto.[44] In this sense, they articulate the conceptual basis for Savoldo's approach to the design of the *Magdalene*. Both the *Angel* and the *Baptist* emerge from (rather than stand against) a palpable darkness, rotating away from it to face our world, yet insisting through gesture that we fix our gaze on another "unseeable" space above the figure, outside the painting. In both, the rotational effect creates the sensation that, by continuing along the arc of its motion, the figure will return to the darkness from which it was bodied forth. The concrete irreality of a pictorial method in which insubstantial-seeming light-toned glazes conjure a phosphorescent apparition out of the panel's inky ground, enacts at a literal level the transcendent "impossibility" of the message of Incarnation.[45]

In the Louvre *Baptist*, however, the right arm brought across the chest effectively confines the gesture to its own painted world and is in tension with the magnetism of the glance; in this sense the figure's contrapposto is assimilable to the traditional gesture of the pointing Baptist.[46] In the *Angel* the device of the foreshortened upper arm (coordinated with the path of the light falling on the figure from front and left) created an emphatic orthogonal link with the viewer's space, akin to the foreshortened hand in Antonello's *Annunciate*. The emblematic compression and psychological immediacy of the gesture – locked into a spatial reciprocity with the beholder – were unprecedented. The piercing of the frontal plane through foreshortening became a visual metaphor for the direct intrusion of the divine into the realm of the human, and an effective means of implicating the viewer as the receptor of a message of Incarnation.

Savoldo was working in Florence when Leonardo's *Angel* was put on display.[47] To be sure, he did not have to be there to learn about the Tuscan master's inventions in contrapposto of the early 1500s, since their impact was equally great in North Italy, where Leonardo had actually begun his study of the half-length format well before 1500.[48] Savoldo's period of Veneto-Lombard apprenticeship (between the mid-1490s and ca. 1505) overlapped Leonardo's Milanese sojourn. This was the very period of Leonardo's experimentation with the type of over-the-shoulder "turning pose" evident in the *Magdalene*. It had become a Venetian specially – particularly in the field of half-length portraiture – by the time Savoldo took it up.[49] Giorgione, Palma Vecchio, and Sebastiano all exploited it for psychologically charged effects – often with the aid of brilliantly rendered illusionistic textile embellishments.[50] These Venetian images are the *Magdalene*'s immediate precursors in the actual disposition of the figure.

Still, as the codifier of the *figura serpentinata*, Leonardo provided the essential foundation for a mastery of "rotational" contrapposto such as we find in Savoldo's *Magdalene*.[51] For this reason, it is of particular interest that, around 1500, Leonardo actually made an influential contribution to the iconography of the half-length Magdalene – one in which the "turning pose" is the source of the figure's expressiveness. This is recorded in a drawing that has been dated as early as ca. 1480 and as late as 1509.[52] The figure turning to look over her right shoulder (an action offset by the gesture of the hands supporting and uncovering the ointment jar) is studied from two different viewpoints, as if it were derived from a three-dimensional *modello* in which the angle of arms and head had undergone slight modifications. Following fifteenth-century preference, the Magdalene is fashionably clothed; the nearest prototype in half-length format would be something like Roger van der Weyden's splendid figure in the Braque Triptych, whose pose (if not her garb) approximates that of trecento half-length Magdalene images.[53]

By rethinking its spatial possibilities, Leonardo transforms this "holy portrait" of traditional, and even archaistic, complexion into a kind of dynamic narrative slice – realized in the continuous torsion of head, arms, and body, and the suspension of the gesture in mid-course. The more fully developed design at the top of the sheet, where the figure turns away to look behind herself, strongly suggests that the theme of *conversio* (in Savoldo's sense) is being embodied in the rotational structure of the pose.[54] The impact of Leonardo's *concetto* is documented in paintings by his Milanese successors – chief among them Bernardino Luini's serenely opulent *Magdalene*, dated to about 1525.[55] The overall pose reflects Leonardo's earlier design (especially in the sacramental deliberateness of the gesture), which suggests that a more developed model than the rapid sketch just examined made its way to the Lombard *ambiente* during the early 1520s.[56]

There are, then, at least two kinds of earlier – yet distinctively "modern" – pictorial inventions converging in Savoldo's *Magdalene*: a thematic one (the "orthogonal" dialogue, with the viewer more or less substituting for one of the protagonists); and a formal one (chiaroscuro and figural contrapposto as vehicles for the bodying forth of the inward, or the ineffable), with a special subcategory (the contrapposto of the figure looking over its shoulder, both inviting and closing out the viewer). A final, essential element in Savoldo's formulation remains to be placed in this brief genealogy: the saint's garment, which so exceeds its usual status as a decorative accessory.

As was seen in connection with Leonardo's sketch, the preference after 1400 was for half-length images of the Magdalene in contemporary dress.[57] Savoldo's figure, in contrast to those typical of his day, is cloaked like a mourner in a "scenic" representation of the Entombment – though in Renaissance paintings this garb is far more usual for the Virgin than the Magdalene. More particularly, the type of cloak depicted by Savoldo – even as it restores the trecento veiled Magdalene type – is closer in weight and fullness to the hooded garments worn by the *pleurants* in early fifteenth-century Northern Entombment sculptures.[58] Whatever its ultimate filiation, the shawl is singular by virtue of its structural role in the design, which is partly a matter of scale and partly of optical richness. Resembling metal beaten to a shell-like thinness, the very quality that makes it mirror-like and elusive, it differs noticeably from the more fictile drapery in the majority of Savoldo's paintings. The choice of a surface specifically suited to luministic effects underscores the *Magdalene*'s ties to recent Venetian tradition, since an innovative approach to the formal possibilities of reflective fabric characterized the early paintings of Titian and Sebastiano.[59] It may not be a coincidence that Titian himself introduced a similarly foil-like mourner's cloak in the faltering Virgin of the Louvre *Deposition*, dated to the mid- to late 1520s and therefore contemporary with Savoldo's invention.[60] Though one artist's precedence over the other cannot be established, the visual affinity is suggestive, given Titian's extraordinary authority at the time. What is certain is that, by reconceiving the image of the Magdalene as a virtuoso demonstration of luministic surface description, Savoldo unlocked thematic possibilities of remarkable scope.

In constituting the image as a virtual mirror, the Magdalene's shawl leads the viewer from the visualization of specularity to a speculative process of some complexity. In fact, this envelope may be regarded as the picture's effective "content," to the degree that it collapses the paradoxical experience of visionary immediacy and inaccessible otherness into a single incandescent surface. As a visual cue to meditation, the shawl points up the difference between Savoldo's *invenzione* and the more typical Renaissance means of engaging the viewer in a devout reading of the painted image. In late medieval and Renaissance illustrations, for example, a figure of the Magdalene kneeling before the resurrected Christ might also – in her gestures and expression – illustrate for the viewer the proper attitude in which to contemplate the miracle; moreover, such an image might include a donor figure experiencing the same apparition as the saint, and thus bearing contemporary witness to the Resurrection.[61] The particular effectiveness of Savoldo's *Magdalene* – like that of Antonello's *Annunciate* and Leonardo's *Angel* – depends on factors that put us on the other side of the imaginative threshold that is acknowledged, but not crossed, in the more standard images. Savoldo's picture does not explicitly encode a doctrinal message or exemplify devout behavior. Instead, it is activated by a disorienting narrative asymmetry, with depicted and real persons converging at the center of a fictive enactment. The asymmetry comes from the fact that the beholder, though "really" exterior to the representation, is yet the key to its completion, and thus singularly free to determine its efficacy.

Without doubt, the "ostensive" religious images (such as the *Ecce Homo* or Man of Sorrows) and their derivatives analyzed by Ringbom and Belting had answered the devout beholder's habit of imaginative participation from the thirteenth century onwards – and nurtured that habit increasingly as the range of pictorial illusion grew to dissolve the apparent boundaries between actual and painted world. The *Magdalene*, like Leonardo's half-length figures, represents a mutation within this development in the way that it engages our self-conscious awareness of pictorial artifice. By 1500, chiaroscuro, contraposition, and fore-shortening commanded specialized critical attention as key elements in a lan-guage of pictorial illusion, and functioned as demonstration subjects in their own right. If I am correct about the importance of the aesthetic to the devotional experience of Savoldo's painting, then it is possible to say that the *Magdalene* affirms its own critical dimension – which is that of artistic problem-solving – even as it opens the way for higher contemplative activity.

With this in mind, we can turn to the Renaissance discourse on artifice in order to single out both a metaphor and a category of artistic performance justifying – but also represented by – the idea of veiling for the purpose of revealing. In this critical perspective the *Magdalene* is, first and foremost, a pictorial demons-tration piece: its subject is the art of painting. To see how this is so, it will be necessary to go backwards in time and take at full value some of the more familiar commonplaces of the *ut pictura poesis* tradition.

Concerning Savoldo's choice of an expanse of cloth as stand-in for the appa-rition of the resurrected Christ, the visual pun on veiling-revelation deserves a closer look. The particular wit of the Magdalene's shawl is that it conceals what it discloses – inward (the saint's figure) and outward (the source of light). It concretizes a miraculous experience by vividly stating its inaccessibility. Late in Savoldo's life, his pupil Pino wrote that "painting is poetry itself, that is to say invention, which makes that which is not, appear to be"; consequently, he added, one ought to observe the poets' procedures, and practice conciseness – *brevità* – in one's inventions.[62] The *Magdalene*, as an extreme demonstration of brevity in the "far apparere quello che non è," exemplifies Pino's advice, which in turn may be put in a wider and more suggestive context.

Except for the reference to brevity, Pino's phrase is a virtual abridgment of Cennino Cennini's definition of painting in the opening chapter of the *Libro dell'arte*, written before 1435: "And this is an art called painting, for which one ought to have fantasy and skill of hand, to find things not seen [*trovare* (equival-ent to the Latin *invenire) cose non vedute*], hidden in the shadow of natural ones [*cacciandosi sotto ombra di naturali*], and retrace them [*fermarle*] with the hand, thus demonstrating that that which is not, is [*dando a dimostrare quello che non è, sia*]. And rightly does it deserve to be enthroned in the second degree to science, and to be crowned with poetry [*e coronarla di poesia*]."[63] These words, which can reasonably be considered a trecento workshop commonplace, articulate the broad endeavor of the Renaissance tradition, Northern and Southern, beginning with Giotto and Duccio, whose comprehensive mastery of pictorial illusion fatefully redirected the possibilities of Christian image-making. However, they apply to the *Magdalene* in a more particular way, as becomes apparent from a closer examination of the passage.

Cennini's definition has the merit of linking together the magical results of illusionistic painting (making the invisible visible in the guise of natural appearance – clearly a prescription tailored to the ends of religious painting), and its formal means (chiaroscuro or "shadow"-rendering, which makes that which is not, appear to be – a flat surface appear a body).[64] Especially noteworthy is the fact that the "things not seen" figured forth by the painter's hand are "hidden" in the "shadow" (the material semblance) of natural objects and must be discovered by an imaginative act. We are being explicitly told that natural appearance is not the goal of pictorial skill, but rather an instrument in the evocation of that which lies beneath, as under a veil. For its part, the chiaroscuro technique, which miraculously transforms flat surfaces into bodies and space, meets the inventive fantasy part-way, since its images are nothing but immaterial projections, shadow tracings re-embodying the solid objects of sense in a different dimension.

Paradoxically, then, representation can only embody that which exists in imagination by "concealing" it in the borrowed garment of a natural appearance. No doubt Cennini would have exemplified this pictorial commerce between invisible and visible, suggestion and depiction, by reference to the legacy of Giotto.[65] But also in Savoldo's time, and especially in the context of religious representation, that mysterious leap from the illusion of the natural to the intimation of something beyond remained a central concern of painting, whatever its style. The *Magdalene* only stands apart in the almost programmatic manner by which it embodies the essential lesson of Cennini's definition.

Across the century-long interval that separates them, Cennini and Pino agree that the painter's "inventive" endeavor is of a piece with poetic artifice.[66] In effect, both refer to a theory of fiction formulated for Italy during the second half of the trecento, and encoded in the poetic theory of the quattrocento: its chief exponent was Boccaccio, who drew directly on Petrarch's celebration of his own calling.[67] In the apologia for the art that takes up the closing chapters of his *Genealogiae deorum gentilium*, Boccaccio defined poetry as

> a sort of fervid and exquisite invention and expression, in speech or writing, of that which the mind has invented [*est fervor quidam exquisite inveniendi atque dicendi seu scribendi quod inveneris*] . . . This fervor of poesy . . . impels the soul to a longing for utterance; it brings forth far-fetched and unheard-of inventions [*peregrinas et inauditas invenciones*] of the mind; it composes these meditations in a fixed order, adorns the whole composition with unusual interweaving of words and thoughts; and thus it covers truth with a comely veil of fable [*meditatas ordine certo componere, ornare compositum inusitato quodam verborum atque sentenciarum*

contextu, velamento fabuloso atque decenti veritatem contegere] . . . [Its detractors]
will say that it is rhetoric which the poets employ . . . I will not deny it in part, for
rhetoric also has its own inventions. Yet . . . among the disguises of fiction rhetoric
has no part, for whatever is composed as under a veil, and exquisitely devised, is
poetry and poetry alone [*verum apud tegumenta fictionum nulle sunt rhetorice
partes; mera poesis est, quicquid sub velamento componimus et exquiritur exquisite*]
(XIV, vii).[68]

The point of interest here is that Boccaccio's definition observes the etymological bond between "textile" and "text": poetic composition, represented as
the weaving of a garment, assembles and combines mere words in such a way
that from them an opaque, embellished fabric of sense is conjured up – though
it is a purely illusive surface, *fabula* or *fictio*. Boccaccio and Petrarch, following
Dante, claim for secular poetry something of the deep content that medieval
exegetical method had uncovered in Holy Writ; but Scripture has a true literal
sense as well, while secular poetry begins as "fable" at a remove from ordinary
truth, even as it stops short of the transcendental.[69] In this poetics, an imagistic
or figurative envelope screens off the poem's meaning, yet is also the only
form of access to it. As has been seen, it is the same with painting in Cennini's
definition: the chiaroscuro image – comparable to a written page in that it is
made up of mere pigmented marks on a flat surface – lends an apparently
tangible fictive body to an invisible sense. In Savoldo's *Magdalene*, the shawl
illustrates this insight about illusionistic painting's relationship to "true" content
in a form that turns out to be the very emblem for poetic expression from late
antiquity through the Renaissance.[70]

According to Boccaccio, the "disguises of fiction" are, properly speaking,
poetic when a text is composed *sub velamento*. By this I take him to mean that
in a poem the "argument" (the *compositus* into which the invention is structured) – no less than the specific diction, meter, and turns of phrase (the *ornatus*
woven upon this plot structure) – appears as a fictive projection.[71] Indeed, the
poetical veil was more often identified as subject – the self-contained *fabula*
"hiding" a deeper meaning – than as style (the "garment" of embellished language). The latter constituted rhetorical ornament proper, which, since it was
legitimately applied to "real-life" arguments, necessarily stopped short of pure
fictional utterance. The implication, then, is that for Boccaccio a poem – no
matter how abstract or how "natural" its sense – always began imagistically (in
peregrinas et inauditas invenciones), as a figurative statement. More coolly and
concisely, Cennino suggests as much for pictorial artifice, with the fantasy (like
the poet's "fervor" finding unheard-of things) "inventing" the unseen thing
concealed in a figure of nature, that the hand may then encode it in a figural
projection.

The ornaments of rhetoric, underplayed in Boccaccio's definition, provided a
natural bridge from the textile to the pictorial analogy for poetry. Petrarch
himself sheds light on this:

The task [of the poet] is to feign, that is to say, compose and adorn [*fingere, id est componere atque ornare*]; and to adumbrate with artful colors [*artificiosis adumbrare coloribus*], and cover with a veil of delightful fictions [*velo amoenae fictionis obnubere*] the truth of things, whether human, natural, or any kind whatsoever; for truth uncovered is all the more pleasant, the more difficult its quest has been.[72]

In this passage – which resembles Cennini's in its suggestion that the realm of experience provides the stimulus toward embodying hidden truth in artistic illusions – the pictorial "adumbrating with artful colors" is equivalent (but not identical) to the textile "covering with a veil of pleasant fictions"; the "colors" without doubt stand for the figures of speech, the basic ornament of rhetoric. These figures "adumbrate" the truth of things in the sense that they give language relief, make it vivid, just like Cennini's chiaroscuro, which draws solid objects out of shadow.[73] But since the thing to which the *colores* lend tangibility is already a fictive argument masking truth, we must regard them as superficial illusions upon the veil of fable, enticing the reader to the more arduous task of looking within.

Savoldo's *Magdalene* seems radically "poetic" in precisely the sense of Boccaccio's and Petrarch's definitions (which I believe lie behind Cennini's), for it presents itself as neither more nor less than a sensuously compelling fictive veil, enticing the viewer to seek the hidden truth that, properly speaking, it cannot embody. In this regard, it is appropriate that the saint's figure is doubly veiled, since the shadow across her face obscures or distances her expression, even as the shawl's brilliance stops us at the picture's surface.[74] The image – a bereaved woman seeking an absent body, a penitent soul seeking unearthly beatitude – is perfectly suited to this paradoxical admission of the subject's "unpaintability." This is not to say that the resurrected Christ could not be painted; he was, often and movingly. Rather, I mean that Savoldo creates in us a sense of the ineffability of his theme precisely by pouring the resources of a considerable artifice into a device of indirection, as if to lead us to say: if this is Christ's reflected splendor, what must the source be like? More important, the larger indirection of letting the viewer supply the narrative unveils the real locus of the story's unfolding, which is the viewer's psyche. As Petrarch suggests, this truth is valorized by the circuitous path one has had to follow in order to discern that it is not to be found, after all, in the poetic fiction itself. The inventiveness of poetry, in effect, is to make an inventor (with all the attendant pleasures of discovery) out of its reader.

Renaissance art theory, in the measure that it drew upon the theory of rhetorical embellishment, articulated a "veiled figure topos" which sheds further light on the critical frame of reference for Savoldo's *invenzione*. In tracing its outline, we are brought back to the *pleurants* who recur in Renaissance Passion representations, as if embodying the more introspective extremities of grief. In connection with John 20:11, we may recall that Savoldo's Magdalene, with her cloaked hand held close to the face, has just ceased to be such a figure: though still in shadow, she is no longer buried in the folds of the shawl. We learn from Cardinal Paleotti's Counter-Reformation treatise on painting (1582) that as a *pleurant* in a larger composition, a figure such as Savoldo's would have had a precise rhetorical function:

> ... Let us recall that there is a kind of, so to speak, perfect imperfection, and a diminution with augmentation, in the form of that figure called by the rhetoricians *aposiopesis*, which through suppression signifies greater things. Thus, in the art of painting things may, and often should, be depicted in such a manner that, by one's leaving something out and only alluding to it deftly, the viewer will of his own imagine greater things. . . . Whence the fame of that device used by the painter called Timanthes, of which the same Pliny speaks: for, having painted Iphigenia about to be sacrificed in the presence of many, and among them her uncle and her father, and feeling unequal to the task of fully expressing the father's sorrow, he covered the latter's face with a veil [*le coprisse la faccia con un velo*] . . . which example we often see judiciously followed by worthy painters who, in representing the Maries at the foot of the crucified Christ – and wishing to express the greatness of their sorrow – will depict some of them with the head bowed to the breast, and with hands and cloak covering the face, signifying their greater sorrow and inexpressible bitterness.[75]

Paleotti's reference to the *Iphigenia* was not by chance, for it was indeed a famous demonstration piece. The painting was the key example in Pliny's characterization of Timanthes as the master who stood for the artistic virtue of *ingenium*; appropriately, both Cicero and Quintilian cited it as a model of resourcefulness for the orator, who must be allowed verbal and formal licenses (figurative expression, unusual arrangement) in handling the problematic variables of a case.[76] Pliny's qualifying remarks on Timanthean *ingenium* are suggestive, and enable us to go beyond Paleotti's reference to *aposiopesis*: "Indeed Timanthes is the only artist in whose works more is always implied than is depicted, and whose artifice, though consummate, is always surpassed by his *ingenium* [*atque in unius huius operibus intelligitur plus semper quam pingitur et, cum sit ars summa, ingenium tamen ultra artem est*]." The key point in this passage is that the painter's *ingenium* – his resourcefulness or inventiveness elevated to quasi-technical status – is a skill that enables him actually to exceed the apparent scope of pictorial skill.[77] It does so by devising means of calling upon the viewer's *ingenium* to supply what is not shown: in the case of the *Iphigenia*, the individual participants at the sacrifice exhibit a crescendo of emotion, until the father's "indescribable" grief is reached. The viewer's comparative skills have been engaged in a steady progression up to the critical moment, where he is left to invent for himself the culmination of the series.

Because it concisely set forth the special attainments of the art, Pliny's chapter on painting was constantly cited in the Renaissance; certainly his praise of the veiled figure simultaneously affirming and transcending the limits of representation lurks in the background of Savoldo's "ingenious" solution to the far more challenging task of depicting a supernatural apparition. Like the *Iphigenia*, the *Magdalene* makes its expressive point through a veiled figure, but by an inversion of the Timanthean device: the veil is lifted to reveal the passing of sorrow, yet continues to challenge us to look beyond – and not just, like Agamemnon's cloak, to an expressive climax, but to the very core of the sacred narrative. The primacy of a spiritual content is symptomatic of the Christian image's purpose; but in the more general sense of seeming to transcend the possibilities of artifice, Savoldo's fiction addresses psychological assumptions implicit in Pliny's account of the *Iphigenia*. Indeed, we seem to witness in the *Magdalene* a deliberate *paragone* with the pictorial wit of the ancients.

The evaluation of Timanthean *ingenium* was also recast in a Renaissance mold before Savoldo's time, in the fundamental paragraphs on expression at the heart of Leon Battista Alberti's *De pictura* of 1435. As is well known, this treatise pioneered the integration of rhetorical and pictorial approaches to artifice (bearing its richest fruit in Leonardo's theory and practice).[78] The Timanthean example is cited – in a composite version from Pliny and Quintilian – at the crucial point in the treatise where Alberti defines the supreme pictorial achievement, the *historia*. The latter is the exemplar of a visual rhetoric, its figures broadly analogous to verbal ones in bearing the work's chief burden of illusionistic embellishment. But like Petrarch's decorated fictive veil, the *historia's* exterior of full-bodied and lively protagonists is there solely to engage us in the production of an "invisible" sense; and this is primarily achieved by making the figures – as vehicles for an inner, affective life – suggest more than is shown:

> It is extremely difficult to vary the movements of the body in accordance with the almost infinite movements of the heart . . . All these things, then, must be sought with the greatest diligence from Nature. The more expressive things should always be imitated, and those preferred in a painting which leave more for the mind to imagine than is seen by the eye.[79]

Following this paraphrase of Pliny's "intelligitur plus semper quam pingitur," Alberti makes it clear that *ingenium*, the ingenuity that goes beyond artifice, is (like Cennini's *fantasia*) the faculty that extracts from nature appropriate and suggestive semblances. First, he gives an example of his own *ingenium* by introducing the concept of a figure that mediates between *historia* and viewer; only then does he proceed to the *Iphigenia* as an exemplar of visual suggestiveness:

> They praise Timanthes of Cyprus . . . because, when he had made Calchas sad and Ulysses even sadder at the sacrifice of Iphigenia, and employed all his art and *ingenium* on the grief-stricken Menelaus, he could find no suitable way to represent the expression of her disconsolate father; so he covered his head with a veil, and thus left more for the onlooker to imagine about his grief than he could see with the eyes [*ut quique plus relinqueret quod de illius dolore animo meditaretur, quam quod posset visu discernere*]. They also praise in Rome the boat in which our Tuscan painter Giotto represented [*expressit*] the eleven disciples struck with fear and wonder at the sight of their colleague walking on the water. . . .

Alberti is not so much citing the Plinian text as altering its focus: by juxtaposing Giotto's *Navicella* with the *Iphigenia* he not only suggests that the Tuscan master was the "new Timanthes," but also subtly points up the essential difference between the ancient and the Christian *historia* – a tragic mythical event is answered by a miraculous lesson on faith, the veiling of the "supreme sorrow" of mortality by the revelation of an incarnate reality. It seems no accident that Giotto's mosaic showed one of the awestruck Apostles burying his face in his mantle.[80]

The "mediator" figure bracketed between Alberti's two allusions to Timanthean *ingenium* deserves a moment's attention in light of *De pictura's* repeated emphasis on the depiction of inner life. This personage prompts us to identify with the action of the *historia* and, more important, functions as a kind of artificial mirror to our psychic response:

> Let me here, however, speak of some things concerning movements, partly made up from my own thoughts, and partly learned from Nature [*partim fabricavimus nostro ingenio, partim ab ipsa natura didicimus*]. . . . I like there to be someone in the *historia* who tells the spectators what is going on, and either beckons them with his hand to look, or with ferocious expression and forbidding glance challenges them not to come near, as if he wished their business to be secret, or points to some danger or remarkable thing in the picture, or by his gestures invites you to laugh or weep with them. [This is followed by the *Iphigenia* and *Navicella* references.][81]

This herald or mediator is like an "ostensive" figure in traditional devotional representation, but adapted to the new function of securing the orthogonal linkage between the viewer and the perspectivally deployed *historia*. He still invites participation in the reality of the image, but not by an act of direct absorption; rather, he underscores the fact that our access to the painted event is now channeled through a particular viewpoint, encoded in the spatial construction: the distance between viewer and vision is marked by the very gestures signaling us to traverse it.[82] Savoldo's Magdalene – like her numerous precursors in the "activated" or dramatic half-length figuration of Leonardo and the Venetan painters – is the sophisticated descendant of the Albertian figure precisely in the measure that she grants access to an optically defined – a perspectival – realm. If these images as a class do not exhibit the dramatic gesturing recommended in *De pictura*; if, more important, they turn the viewer's attention to a *historia* within his psyche, nonetheless they draw on Alberti's essential achievement, his resourceful appropriation of rhetorical models.

Indeed, apart from suggesting, with her cloaked form as well as the suspenseful "readiness" of her hand gesture, the figure of *aposiopesis*, Savoldo's Magdalene is structurally akin to a variety of other rhetorical figures: as the protagonist from whom we deduce a larger scene, *synecdoche*, in which the part may stand for the whole; as an Albertian "herald" gazing directly at the viewer, *apostrophe*; and as an image whose turning pose and luminosity represent conversion or enlightenment, *metaphora*.[83] But, as has been seen, the Magdalene is above all a pictorial

461

demonstration of the figure of *antithesis* (Latin *contrapositum*), which was central to Alberti's and later to Leonardo's compositional theory.[84] In this regard, the "turning pose" itself, with its structural kinship to the canonical *figura serpentinata*, assumes an emblematic status. In Quintilian's discussion of rhetorical ornament, the figures of eloquence had been defined with a comparison to bodily movement:

> The first point for consideration is, therefore, what is meant by a figure [*quid accipere debeamus figuram*]. For the term is used in two senses. In the first it is applied to any form in which thought is expressed, just as it is to bodies which, whatever their composition [*quoquo modo sunt composita*], must have some shape [*habitus*]. In the second and special sense, in which it is called a *schema*, it means a rational change in meaning or language from the ordinary and simple form, that is to say, a change analogous to that involved in sitting, lying down on something or looking back [*sicut nos sedemus, incumbimus, respicimus*].[85]

This passage precisely complements that in which Quintilian illustrated his justification of figurative expression by a series of notable visual *exempla*, chief among them the Timanthean *Iphigenia*, and – as the very analogue to the rhetorical concept of the *schema* – Myron's *Discobolos*, with its continuously shifting axis.[86]

Savoldo's *Magdalene* departs from the "ordinary and simple form" of an antecedent "holy portrait," and in so doing signals to the viewer an aspect of her meaning as a figure for conversion (conversion itself being a kind of spiritual trope). The pose is a rhetorical super-*schema* in much the same way that the shawl is a *velamentum fabulosus* about an event in which the garment of the body becomes the manifestation of triumphant divinity. Quintilian said of the *Discobolos* that it could not be appreciated by viewers lacking a grasp of artifice. If, as Ridolfi claims, the *Magdalene* was famous, one can also believe Paolo Pino, who lamented that while Savoldo was *raro nell'arte*, he never achieved popularity and "spent his life on few works."[87] Even so gorgeous a painting as the *Magdalene* seems to presuppose a restricted audience of fellow-painters and sophisticated patrons willing to savor its mirror play of sense and surface.[88]

It seems likely that, in calling Savoldo *capriccioso e sofistico*, Vasari was targeting the Brescian master's ironic reserve, his pleasure in putting grand artistry into modestly scaled, isolated images.[89] The *Magdalene* is especially suited to the display of artifice: since it does not pretend to "contain" truth, only to reflect it, its ostensible content is wholly exterior to it. Yet the resultant "emptiness" is also a kind of limitless potentiality (since it holds the viewer in thrall), and guarantees the painter's essential autonomy in spinning out his fiction. The gleaming shawl "re-represents" the pigmented and brush-imprinted canvas surface in terms of illusion, and thus invites us to contemplate on its own terms that other content, the artistic process itself.[90] It is an extraordinary sleight-of-hand.

Savoldo's *invenzione* synthesizes a range of possibilities offered in the vanguard traditions of North Italian painting, and exemplifies the kind of self-assured dialogue with Central Italian art which gave a particular edge to the Venetan "difference." Like the better-appreciated artists of his day, Savoldo approached issues of religious representation with a sound awareness of the implications of fictive embellishment, an awareness that rooted him, as it rooted them, in an effort of illusionistic discovery two centuries old; and beyond that, in an ancient aesthetic preserved (almost miraculously) by a few texts and damaged relics. In its acknowledgement of illusion's "superficiality," but also of metaphor's capacity for intimating absolute truth, the *Magdalene* addresses traditional Christian beliefs on the role of the image. But it also asks to be considered in light of ancient painting's fabled remembrance, and the rich store of poetical and rhetorical borrowings to which that remembrance led the creators of a modern art of painting. In this sense, too, it is a resurrection: Savoldo's saint, turning in gladness to disclose herself together with the painting's meaning, revives as she redeems the lost art of the ancients, Agamemnon's sorrow.

Notes

A partial outline of this paper was delivered at the 1983 Annual Meeting of the College Art Association in Philadelphia. The paper is dedicated to Charles Mitchell, who had kind words for it then. I have since benefited from the good advice and criticism of friends and colleagues; special thanks are due to Andrea Bolland, Ann Peterson, Mary Sheriff, David Summers, Winifred Woodhull, and the anonymous reader of the *Art Bulletin*.

1   See Panofsky, *Vorträge der Bibliothek Warburg*, 1924–25, 290–291, repr. in E. Panoksky, *Aufsätze zu Grundfragen der Kunstwissenschaft*, Berlin, 1964, 99–167. I thank Professor Walter Cahn for his idiomatic transposition of the anonymous typescript translation into English, a typescript available by permission from the Institute of Fine Arts, New York University.

2   The variants – all in oil on canvas – universally considered authentic are no. 1031 in the National Gallery, London (in which the figure wears a silvery cloak, in contrast to the other versions, where the fabric is golden); no. 307 in the Gemäldegalerie, Berlin (the only one that bears Savoldo's signature); and Contini Bonacossi no. 17 in the Uffizi, Florence (on deposit at the Pitti Palace Meridiana). A fourth version, formerly at Warwick Castle, has been rejected as a "badly repainted copy" by Gilbert, 493, cat. no. 104; its authenticity is tacitly admitted by Gould, 236, and in the *Catalogue of Paintings, Berlin Picture Gallery*, Berlin, 1978, 400, where it is considered the predecessor of no. 307 (but see also n. 16, below). The ex-Warwick painting was in the Leonard Koetser Gallery's exhibition of Old Master paintings in the spring of 1971 (advertisement with color reproduction in *Apollo*, XCIII, April 1971, 83); in reproduction, the execution of the wall and attribute, the figure, and in particular the shawl (which is a true variant, not a copy of the others), seem wholly convincing – except, perhaps, for the lower right portions of the shawl. Discussion and analysis of the other *Magdalenes* may be found in Gilbert, 163–164 (cat. no. 2), 171–172 (cat. no. 14), 175 (cat. no. 19), 367ff., 378–379, 390–391, 540–542, 546, 551–552, and 555–556 (for the latest revision of his dating).

3 None of the paintings bears a date, and opinions differ on the order in which they were produced. A. Boschetto, *Gian Gerolamo Savoldo*, Milan, 1963, pl. 24, dates the Florence version to shortly after 1520, and the London version (his pl. 45) to before 1530, with the Berlin picture coming last – an order accepted in the Berlin catalogue (but with the ex-Warwick version inserted in the penultimate position). Gilbert dates them as follows: Berlin, 1527–28; London, 1528–30; Florence, 1533–36. In *Gli Uffizi: Catalogo generale*, Florence, 1979, 472, the dates proposed by both Gilbert and A. Venturi (1527–33) are cited for the Contini painting.

4 Vasari, VI, 507: "Ma perchè costui si adoperò solamente in simili cose [nocturnes and *cose di simili fantasie, delle quali era maestro*], e non fece cose grandi, non si può dire altro di lui, se non che fu capriccioso e sofistico, e che quello che fece merita di essere molto comendato." For *sofistico's* connotation of "artfulness" (derived from the cleverness of sophistic argumentation), and its use by Vasari as a term of praise for artful inventiveness, see D. Summers, *Michelangelo and the Language of Art*, Princeton, 1981, 237–238, and 522, n. 14. See also n. 62, below, for a definition of painting as sophistic on account of its illusionism. On Vasari's use of the term *capriccio* to designate artful and extravagant invention, see A. Rathé, "Le *capriccio* dans les écrits de Vasari," *Italica*, LVII, 1980, 239ff. One model for Vasari's characterization of Savoldo seems to be Pliny's account of the too-diligent Protogenes, who painted little, and preferred more personal and playful subjects to heroic ones: "Aristotle used to advise the artist to paint the achievements of Alexander the Great. . . . The impulse of his mind, however, and a certain artistic capriciousness [*impetus animi et quaedam artis libido*] led him rather to the subjects mentioned" (*NH* xxxv. 106). I associate the "non fece cose grandi" with this (rather than translating it as "he did not make large pictures") in light of Pliny's distinction between painters of major and minor subjects. The latter include the landscape, genre, still-life, and light-effect specialists (see *NH* xxxv. 112ff., and esp. 138).

5 Gilbert, 207ff. and 495ff.

6 Ridolfi, I, 271: Savoldo left a worthy memory of himself in Brescia "in casa Averolda in una figura della Maddalena involta in drappo, col vase dell'alabastro, incaminata al Sepolcro, celebre pittura, dalla quale si sono tratte molte copie."

7 J. A. Crowe and G. B. Cavalcaselle, *A History of Painting in North Italy*, III, ed. T. Borenius, 2nd ed., London, 1912, 317–318. This treatment of the *Magdalene* is echoed in such casual references as W. Friedlaender's in *Caravaggio Studies*, 1955, repr. New York, 1969, 94, where – as often in the Savoldo literature – the issue is the artist's role as mediator for the Lombard, and ultimately Flemish, components of Caravaggio's *verismo*: but for the "diminutive ointment jar . . . [Savoldo's Magdalene] might be a romantically veiled beauty whom one could have seen in the streets of Venice." Friedlaender's characterization is based on G. Nicco Fasola, "Lineamenti del Savoldo," *L'arte*, XLIII, n.s. 11, 1940, 57.

8 Venturi, IX, iii, 764–765: "Later, in the Berlin painting, her form is almost lost in the silken rustling of the shawl; here it seems foursquare and sturdy beneath the silvery cloth, which now evens out, as on the shoulder, into broad planes of cold shadow and effulgent light, now again ripples like a sheet of water grazed by the wind on a moonlit night. And into mysterious distances does the romantic landscape deepen around the figure who passes garbed in magical nocturnal splendors,

concealing in the shadows her pensive eyes." (Venturi's actual cadences are untranslatable.) The reference to moonlight has made so deep an impression that it is cited or adapted in virtually every discussion of the *Magdalene*.

9   Boschetto (as in n. 3), text to pl. 24, exemplifies this outlook while discussing the Florence *Magdalene*, his candidate for the first version: "The little ointment jar within an opening in the wall, at the lower left, most frequently has led to the subject being identified as a representation of the Magdalene approaching the sepulcher at daybreak. However, the marvellous figure in its cloak of greenish golden silk seems little enough moved and inspired by the hour's gravity."

10 Ingenhoff-Danhäuser, 59, 70, and nn. 71–74 (citing J. S. Held, "Flora, Goddess and Courtesan," *De artibus opuscula XL. Essays in Honor of Erwin Panofsky*, New York, 1961, 216, n. 81): the argument primarily depends on assimilating the gold or bronze tonality of most of Savoldo's variant shawls to the yellow of the prostitutes' official garment (though one would suppose the shape and material to be likewise relevant); no explanation is given for the fact that the London figure, which is among the finest, is cloaked in white. Other possibilities should be checked before imposing on the saint a specific 16th-century "uniform": it is of interest that the liturgical colors for the Magdalene's feast were white and/or gold (the latter designating the Contemplatives) until at least the late 15th century (see Saxer, 320–322). Ingenhoff-Danhäuser's study emphasizes the contributions of Leonardo and Titian, and focuses on the dialectical tensions arising from the confluence of Christian, Classical, and secular types and meanings in the standard image of the Magdalene. However, Savoldo's *invenzione* is conspicuously out of place in her visual documentation of the overlap between courtesan and Magdalene images: alone among the numerous half-length paintings reproduced, it lacks the appropriate marks of carnality or secularity. In order to explain the figure's modest and introspective appearance, Ingenhoff-Danhäuser dates its invention unjustifiably late (at the very end of the 1530s, but preferably in the early forties), and associates it with early Counter-Reformation demands for a penitential imagery. I cannot agree with this interpretation, though I concur with Ingenhoff-Danhäuser's criticism of T. Fomiciova's view of the Savoldo *Magdalene* as a pure genre image, in "Giorgione e la formazione della pittura di genere nell'arte veneziana del XVI secolo," *Giorgione, Atti del Convegno Internazionale di Studio per il 5⁰ Centenario della Nascita (Castelfranco Veneto 1978)*, Venice, 1979, 163.

11 Gilbert, 444–445, gives a convenient tabulation of Savoldo's subjects.

12 Gilbert, 368, but see also 363–368, 449–453, 516 (cat. 16bis), 544–546, and pl. 41. Marcantonio Michiel saw the *Continence of Scipio* in the Andrea Odoni Collection in Venice in 1532. Gilbert is responsible for identifying the subject of the painting, which is now in a private collection in Florence, and which has been dated to the late 16th century. In 1955, Gilbert did not attribute to a specific source the view of the *Magdalene* as a courtesan portrait; he may have had in mind observations akin to Friedlaender's in *Caravaggio Studies* (see above, n. 7).

13 In 1985 Gilbert changed his opinion (correctly, I think) about the dating of the *Scipio* and the *Magdalenes*, and dropped his initial argument for the latter's derivation from the former; see Gilbert, 544–545. I cannot help feeling uneasy with the *Scipio* in the form in which it has come down to us. The two principal figures in the foreground are unmistakably Savoldesque, but the three subsidiary personages, strung

at equal intervals along a single background plane, are uncharacteristically arranged. The ineffectual silhouetting of the light-toned "Magdalene" against a light strip of background is especially curious, and suggests the possibility that the picture is, in part at least, a pastiche.

14 Gilbert, 323.

15 Ibid., 376.

16 The Berlin version – though it seems to bear an authentic signature – departs from Savoldo's usual descriptive care in the rather coarsely delineated background wall. Dr. Erich Schleier of the Staatliche Museen, Berlin, has kindly informed me that the painting was apparently restored in the 19th century, and is "covered by a heavy layer of discoloured varnish," in addition to showing evidence of damage and abrasion in the figure's face (E. Schleier, letter of July 1988). Is it possible that the background has been partly painted over, and that the ledge and ointment jar (and possibly a dawn landscape) lie concealed under the present surface? In support of this conjecture, I would call attention to a recently published late 18th-century etching preserving the appearance of yet another seemingly authentic *Magdalene* variant. R. Stradiotti, in "L'opera del Savoldo attraverso la grafica," *Giovanni Gerolamo Savoldo*, 132–133, reproduces and discusses Zocchi and Lorenzi's high-quality illustration (with an attribution to Veronese) of the *Magdalene* then in the collection of the Marchese Gerini in Florence. As Stradiotti indicates, the figure's shawl is extremely close to the Berlin version in the fluidity and disposition of the folds. However, the Gerini picture's setting is closest to the ex-Warwick version in the configuration of wall and landscape on the left side, and in the particular detail of an arched – rather than square – niche behind the saint's attribute. The most significant difference is the Gerini *Magdalene's* dawn sky, which (as Stradiotti notes) recalls the Uffizi *Magdalene's*. As I mentioned in n. 2, above, the ex-Warwick picture has been considered the predecessor to the one in Berlin – except that the shawl is terse and voluminous, as in the other versions. The Zocchi print fits neatly in the gap between these two. The links among variants support the likelihood that the Berlin *Magdalene* originally had a background more akin to the others.

17 Savoldo's pupil Pino observed: "Messer Gerolamo of Brescia was most learned in this part: I once saw by his hand certain sunrises with solar reflections, certain nocturnes with a thousand most ingenious and rare particularities [*alcune aurore con rifletti del sole, certe oscurità con mille discrizzioni ingeniosissime e rare*], all of which render a truer image of things themselves than do the Flemish." See Barocchi, I, 134, and – for Savoldo's mastery of *quadri di notte e di fuochi* – Vasari, VI, 507.

18 Inspired by Venturi's beautiful description (see n. 8 above), explanations of the lighting on the Magdalene's shawl are generally limited to the suggestion that it comes from an (otherwise unaccounted-for) full moon. See, for instance, S. Freedberg, *Painting in Italy: 1500–1600*, Harmondsworth, 1979, 343.

19 The two paintings, with their nearly square format, have practically the same dimensions (London: 86.4 × 79cm; Florence: 84 × 77.5cm). In this they are closer to one another than to either the Berlin (92 × 73cm) or the ex-Warwick (99.1 × 80cm) *Magdalenes*, which are more vertical. The London version is almost certainly the one recorded in the Averoldo Collection, Brescia, in 1620; see Gould, 236–237. The Florence version was acquired in 1932 by the Contini Bonacossi from the Giovanelli Collection in Venice; its earlier provenance is not noted in the Uffizi

catalogue. The London *Magdalene*, which is cooler in tonality, shows a view of the Venetian lagoon, with a sky in which sparse clouds float above the column of pale gold light visible through the mists at the horizon; the Florence picture is more somber, with a variegated sky over a rustic inland scene. Both backgrounds fall under Pino's category of *aurore con rifletti del sole*, with the lower clouds becoming incandescent at the approach of the sun, and the higher ones, of a smoky hue, turning ruddy along their bottom edges.

20 See P. Wilhelm, "Auferstehung Christi," *Lexikon der christlichen Ikonographie*, I, Rome, 1968, 203: the sunrise is commonly associated with images of the Resurrection from the 15th century onwards. The combination of low wall and vaulted ruin in the *Magdalene* does not seem to have a counterpart in traditional Resurrection iconography. As a rule, the 15th- and 16th-century scenes include Christ's sarcophagus (or some reference to it), sometimes locating it in the excavated rock setting specified by the synoptic Gospels. Often this rock becomes an imposing cavern integral to the topography of the garden specified by John 19:41. Savoldo alludes to the cavern setting in his several Lamentation scenes (see Gilbert, pls. 2, 38, 39); on the other hand, he depicts a ruined architecture of comparable scale and character to the *Magdalene*'s in his Pesaro and Dubrovnik *Flights into Egypt* (see Gilbert, pls. 30 and 73). Similar structures are silhouetted behind the figures in his Turin and Hampton Court half-length paintings of the *Virgin and Child* (Gilbert, pls. 32, 33), and his Milan and Rome *Adorations* (Gilbert, pls. 56, 64). In all of these paintings, the ruins are used to designate a rustic setting. More important, they evoke a symbolism of decay and renewal traditionally associated with Nativity and Infancy scenes, but not incompatible with the Resurrection theme.

21 The Vulgate reads: "Una autem sabbati, Maria Magdalene venit mane, cum adhuc tenebrae essent, ad monumentum; et vidit lapidem sublatum a monumento."

22 In the Vulgate: "Maria autem stabat ad monumentum foris, plorans. Dum ergo fleret, inclinavit se, et prospexit in monumentum: 12 et vidit duos angelos in albis, sedentes, unum ad caput, et unum ad pedes, ubi positum fuerat corpus Iesu. 13 Dicunt ei illi: Mulier, quid ploras? Dicit eis: Quia tulerunt Dominum meum: et nescio ubi posuerunt eum. 14 Haec cum dixisset, conversa est retrorsum, et vidit Iesum stantem: at non sciebat quia Iesus est. 15 Dicit ei Iesus: Mulier, quid ploras? quem quaeris? Illa existimans quia hortulanus esset, dicit ei: Domine, si tu sustulisti eum, dicito mihi ubi posuisti eum; et ego eum tollam. 16 Dicit ei Iesus: Maria. Conversa illa, dicit ei: Rabboni (quod dicitur Magister)."

23 The veiled hand pressed to the eyes as a sign for weeping has an ancient Roman pedigree, and appears repeatedly in Christian art of the later Middle Ages; see M. Barasch, *Gestures of Despair in Medieval and Early Renaissance Art*, New York, 1976, 11 (and n. 11), 23, and figs. 31, 44, 47. Belting, 37 (fig. 10), and 50 (fig. 20), reproduces two works – Mantegna's *Entombment* engraving, and a *Lamentation* drawing by Jacopo Bellini – in which the gesture is used in a context of mourning directly relevant to the *Magdalene*. For a striking 15th-century Northern example of the gesture, see the Magdalene figure on the left panel of Roger van der Weyden's Vienna (Kunsthistorisches Museum) Crucifixion Triptych (repro. in L. Campbell, *Van der Weyden*, New York, 1980, 48–49, pls. 22, 230). For an example from the North Italian *ambiente* of 1500–25, see Andrea Solario's *Pietà* in the National Gallery, Washington, discussed by F. R. Shapley, *Complete Catalogue*

of the Samuel H. Kress Collection: Italian Paintings XV–XVI Centuries, New York, 1968, 139, no. K2061, fig. 332. Savoldo's Magdalene figure is recognizably cited in the role of a full-length "weeper," wholly analogous to those just mentioned, in Veronese's Louvre *Crucifixion* of the 1570s (see the reproduction in R. Pallucchini, *Veronese*, Milan, 1984, 95).

24 If, in light of the Gospel passage, the *Magdalene*'s figure is seen as engaged in an uncompleted action that will bring her to a full- or right-facing pose, then one might visualize her as initially facing toward the arched ruin at her back. In such a case, the grotto-like architecture would stand for the enclosure for Christ's tomb.

25 The most comprehensive discussion of contraposition as both conceptual and formal principle (equally relevant to luministic and spatial-figural design) in Renaissance art is in Summers, 336–361. Later in this essay it will become apparent how fundamentally indebted I am to Summers's analysis; in the present context, Summers's remarks (pp. 349–350) on the metaphysical resonance acquired in medieval religious literature by the devices of contraposition, have a bearing on the sort of meaning I ascribe to such devices in the *Magdalene*. D. Rosand, *Painting in Cinquecento Venice*, New Haven, 1982, 69–75 (ch. 2, pt. 3: "Titian's Light as Form and Symbol"), emphasizes how Bellini and his successors, in their relentless investigation of tonal painting's properties, devised ever richer metaphorical associations for depicted light. Savoldo is in the mainstream of this development.

26 A convenient summary of the medieval tradition on the Magdalene as an exemplar of conversion and penitence – a notion incorporated in the saint's liturgy – is in Saxer, 328–334. Saxer notes that in this capacity, the Magdalene became the protectress both of religious establishments dedicated to rehabilitating prostitutes and of contemplative orders pursuing an eremitical ideal.

27 My remarks on the lighting are prompted by E. H. Gombrich's invaluable observations on the localizing and particularizing functions of modeling and highlights, in both "The Heritage of Apelles" and "Light, Form and Texture in Fifteenth-Century Painting North and South of the Alps," *The Heritage of Apelles*, New York, 1976, 3ff. and 19ff. As Gombrich points out, highlights (luster) differ from graduated passages of light into shade (illumination) in that – rather than revealing form as lit from a constant direction – they consist of minuscule mirror-images specific both to the curvature (and surface properties) of the illuminated object, and to the observer's position. As determined by the optical laws of reflection, highlights "follow" the viewer as he moves before the reflective surface (by contrast, the ratio of illuminated to shadowed surface alters markedly, since it is governed by the fixed position of the light source). In the *Magdalene*, given a fixed viewing position before the life-size image of the saint, and allowing for the angular displacement and curvature of her form, one could – theoretically – extrapolate an approximate position for the source of light (based on the angle at which the viewer's gaze appears to meet the highlighted surfaces). I thank David Summers for calling my attention to the relevance for my argument of the optics of reflection.

28 In the Vulgate: "Dicit ei Iesus: Noli me tangere, nondum enim ascendi ad Patrem meum: vade autem ad fratres meos, et dic eis: Ascendo ad Patrem meum, et Patrem vestrum, Deum meum, et Deum vestrum. 18 Venit Maria Magdalene annuntians discipulis: Quia vidi Dominum, et haec dixit mihi." Because of Christ's explicit charge to her, the Magdalene came to be known, in medieval commentary, as the

Apostle to the Apostles; see Saxer, 342–345 (and esp. p. 343 for Odo of Cluny's comparison of the Magdalene to the Virgin, on the grounds that at the close of Christ's earthly life she was a vehicle for transmitting to the world the splendor of the Resurrection, as the Virgin was for the glory of the Incarnation at the beginning).

29 See Voragine, 407 (cap. xcvi).

30 Gregory the Great's *Homilia* xxv (on John 20:11–18) opens with Christ's words to the repentant Magdalene in Luke 7: "Many sins are forgiven her, because she hath loved much" (Luke 7:47); they prompt an extended analysis of the believer's amorous quest for the Redeemer, paralleling the process of enlightenment depicted in John 20. For a 13th-century characterization of the saint, see Ragusa and Green, 172–174 (ch. xxviii), where the scene of the Magdalene's conversion concludes with the exhortation to imitate her loving-kindness. Pope Gregory's *Homilia* xxv and *Homilia* xxxiii (on Luke 7:36–50) were the basis for all later depictions of the Magdalene as typifying the convert and lover of Christ, and as a figure for both the true Church (that of the converted Gentiles) and the individual Christian soul, as represented in the allegorical Bride of the Song of Solomon. See Saxer, 328, and *Pat. lat.*, LXXVI, 1188ff. (*Hom.* xxv) and 1258ff. (*Hom.* xxxiii). It should be mentioned that Gregory also certified the "composite" Magdalene venerated in the Western Church, whose story conflated various Gospel episodes involving either sinful women, or women named Mary; for a succinct discussion of the sources, see V. Saxer, "Maria Maddalena," *Bibliotheca sanctorum*, viii, Rome, 1967, cols. 1078–79. As Saxer, 328, points out, the Magdalene as a figure for Ecclesia receives greater emphasis in the Early Christian period, while her exemplification of personal redemption through love assumes a growing importance in later medieval commentary.

31 The full passage, for which the *Biblia pauperum* gives an abbreviated tag, reads: "Inveni quem diligit anima mea, / Tenui eum, nec dimittam, / Donec introducam illum in domum matris meae, / Et in cubiculum genitricis meae." In the illustration, the Bride and Bridegroom are "impersonated" by the same figures of the *noli me tangere* image. It is of interest that the "touch me not" of the main illustration is reversed in the embrace and utterance ("Tenui eum, nec dimittam") of its Old Testament counterpart. See the illustration in E. Soltesz, *Biblia pauperum*, Budapest, 1967, pl. 31 (also in Büttner, text fig. 31). For bibliography on the dating of the blockbooks, see J. Snyder, *Northern Renaissance Art*, New York, 1985, 528 (n. 102). The 13th-century *Meditations on the Life of Christ* (see Ragusa and Green, 361–363 [ch. lxxxviii]) visualize the initial encounter at the tomb in pointedly psychological terms, which yet are a recasting of the amorous quest in the Song of Solomon: "When she cried and paid no attention to the angels, her Master for love could not hold back any longer. . . . And she, like an inebriate, not yet recognizing Him, said, 'Lord, . . . tell me where you have laid Him . . .' Look at her well, how with tearstained face she entreats Him humbly and devoutly to lead her to Him whom she seeks; for she always hoped to hear something new about her Beloved." It should be noted that this text – as befits a manual of devotional practice – assumes the reader's imaginative participation in the narrative, and includes a prompting to imitate the saint in order to dispose the soul to a redemptive experience. Ambrogio Lorenzetti's Magdalene in the S. Petronilla Triptych (Siena, Pinacoteca; ill. in P. Torriti, *La Pinacoteca Nazionale di Siena: I dipinti dal XII al XV secolo*, Genoa, 1980, fig. 77) is of special interest in light of this devotional

literature. The saint gazes at the Christ Child in the central panel; a gold nimbus on her breast bears the miniature image of the adult Christ's face, as if picturing the imprint of divine love. M. Anstett-Janssen, *Maria Magdalena in der abendländischen Kunst. Ikonographie der Heiligen von der Anfängen bis ins 16. Jahrhundert*, diss., Albert-Ludwigs Universitäts, Freiburg i. Br., 1961, 191–192, calls this an adaptation of the Eastern Platytera icon of the Virgin. Lorenzetti's saint "stamped" with the image of her beloved has a counterpart in medieval homiletic literature; see below, n. 70, for a widely translated sermon that analyzes the Magdalene's absorption in Christ's physical appearance before and after the Resurrection.

32 A comparable attention to the spectator's role in constituting the fiction is proposed, in connection with the secular iconography of Titian's reclining *Venuses*, by D. Rosand, "*Ermeneutica amorosa*: Observations on the Interpretation of Titian's Venuses," *Tiziano e Venezia*, Vicenza, 1980, 377–378, where Rosand cites his own earlier contribution to this argument, "Art History as Criticism: The Past as Present," *New Literary History*, v, 1973–74, 435ff. (See also the stimulating essay by C. Ginzburg, "Tiziano, Ovidio, e i codici della figurazione erotica nel '500," likewise in *Tiziano e Venezia*, 125–135; Ginzburg points to the shared psychological territory of Renaissance erotic and religious visualizations – in either case a matter of the efficacy of sight as an incitement to action.) J. H. Marrow, in an essay addressing the role of the beholder in Northern Renaissance art, makes an especially strong case for the importance of pictorial devices directly implicating the viewer in the representation; see his "Symbol and Meaning in the Northern European Art of the Late Middle Ages and the Early Renaissance," *Simiolus*, xvi, 1986, 150–169.

33 In particular, see Ringbom, 11–71 (ch. i: "The Devotional Image"). Ringbom's "dramatic close-up" category is developed from the definition of the private devotional (as opposed to public liturgical) image proposed by E. Panofsky in "Imago Pietatis," *Festschrift für M. J. Friedländer z. 60. Geburtstag*, Leipzig, 1927, 261ff. (but see n. 34 below). According to Ringbom, in the course of the 15th century certain iconic types (Madonna and Child, Man of Sorrows, Salvator Mundi) were amplified by the addition of figures drawn from "scenic" narrative images. The dramatic close-up with which he is concerned is not an abridged narrative scene, but an "enriched" icon, which thus retains the portrait-like presence (and meditational effect) of its antecedent. See also by Ringbom, "Devotional Images and Imaginative Devotions: Notes on the Place of Art in Late Medieval Private Piety," *Gazette des beaux-arts*, LXXIII (ser. VI), 1969, 159–170.

34 Belting, *Das Bild und sein Publikum in Mittelalter*, Berlin, 1981, and especially ch. IV ("Realismus und Bildrhetorik"), 69–104, and 105ff., where he corrects Panofsky's original distinction between public and private devotion by demonstrating that collective (and liturgically based) devotional practices informed even the most intimate forms of private worship well into the Renaissance. For Belting, the illusionism of 15th-century painting is more problematic than it is for Ringbom, who treats it as a direct aid to psychological identification with the Christian redemptive story. In particular, Belting considers the perspectival aesthetic a "closed" system of organization, imposing a new type of psychological distance on the previously "open," cultic-affective relation of worshipper and image (see his ch. III ["Funktionen mittelalterlicher Bilder"]). See also Ringbom, 212ff. ("Author's Postscript"), for a response to Belting's terminological criticism, and a reassertion of the

devotional appropriateness of pictorial realism. Although I tend to echo Ringbom's view of illusionistic representation, I agree with Belting's conclusion that a valorization of the artistic means as such introduced a different order of response to the work of religious art.

35 The Veneto in particular contributed novel images of this type from the mid-15th century onwards. See, for instance, Ringbom, 72ff., for Mantegna's and Bellini's development of a half-length Presentation in the Temple/Circumcision type. R. Goffen, "Icon and Vision: Giovanni Bellini's Half-Length Madonnas," *Art Bulletin*, LVII, 1975, 487–518, examines the devotional implications of the half-length format for Bellini, whose Madonnas emerge as particularly successful modernizations of hallowed Byzantine prototypes. More recently, Belting has investigated the implications of Bellini's transformation of iconic models in half-length representations of the *Pietà* (see Sources).

36 On Antonello, particularly in relation to the Flemish tradition that inspired his half-length images, see J. Wright, "Antonello da Messina: The Origins of His Style and Technique," *Art History*, III, 1980, 41–60; Ringbom, 171–175; and M. T. Bonaccorso, "Il tema iconografico del Salvator Mundi e dell'Ecce Homo," *Antonello da Messina*, Rome, 1981, 128ff.

37 One version, usually dated to 1473–75, is in Munich, Alte Pinakothek, no. 8054; the other, considered slightly later, is in Palermo, Galleria Regionale della Sicilia. The Palermo panel measures 45 × 34.5cm, virtually the same dimensions as no. 8054 in Munich. See *Antonello*, 148, no. 31, and 184–186, no. 41; and L. Sciascia, *L'opera completa di Antonello da Messina* (*Classici dell'arte*, X), Milan, 1967, 94, no. 40, and 99–100, no. 65.

38 See Ringbom, 63–65. The image might be associated with representations of the Virgin at prayer in the Temple, were it not that they normally show her as a young girl, with head uncovered and hair unbound. See G. Schiller, *Ikonographie der christlichen Kunst*, IV, pt. 2 ("Maria"), Gütersloh, 1980, 72ff. and 165ff. A more conventional reason for the angel's omission is given by F. Zeri in "Un riflesso di Antonello da Messina a Firenze," *Paragone*, XCIX, 1958, 19–20; he suggests that both of the *Annunciates* are right halves to dismembered diptychs, and originally were paired with an angel – but the view has not gained currency (see the objections in *Antonello da Messina*, 148). Baxandall, 1972, 55 (but see also 51), considers this type of *Annunciate* to represent the Virgin's act of thanksgiving after the angel's departure, as explicated in Fra Roberto Caracciolo's late 15th-century sermon on the Annunciation. I think the image is a great deal more ambiguous than the enactment proposed in the sermon (as indeed seems to be the case with the more conventional *Annunciations* to which Baxandall applies Fra Roberto's other divisions of the Angelic Colloquy). In particular, the specificity and force of the lighting, together with the Virgin's gesture, suggest a moment of drama rather than recollection.

39 On the incarnational symbolism of the light in Annunciation images, see M. Meiss's fundamental "Light as Form and Symbol in Some Fifteenth-Century Paintings," *Art Bulletin*, XXVII, 1945, 175–181, repr. in *The Painter's Choice*, New York, 1976, 3–18.

40 An old copy of the Palermo *Annunciate* in the Accademia, now ascribed to a pupil (and initially considered the original), was recorded in Venice in 1809; see, again, *Antonello*, 148, and Sciascia (as in n. 37), 99–100. The Windsor angel figure – on

a sheet with studies for the *Battle of Anghiari* – is by a student, but partly corrected by Leonardo himself. C. Gould, *Leonardo: The Artist and the Non-Artist*, Boston, 1975, 122–124, suggests that Leonardo may have known Antonello's *Annunciates*, and considers the *Angel* an invention of specifically North Italian inspiration; he emphasizes Leonardo's concern during this period with half-length images that directly address the beholder (such as the lost "young Christ" commissioned by Isabella d'Este, and echoed in a series of Leonardesque paintings), and calls the design of the *Angel* a foreshadowing of Baroque modes of communication with the beholder.

41 Vasari, IV, 26: "Una testa d'uno angelo, che alza un braccio in aria, che scorta dalla spalla al gomito venendo innanzi, e l'altro ne va al petto con una mano." The same figure as in the Windsor drawing (with the wings omitted) appears, modified into a John the Baptist and with more of the torso exposed, in three painted copies, the best of which is said to be the one in Basel. All three are discussed and illustrated by E. Möller, who recognized their derivation from a Leonardo prototype other than the Louvre *Baptist*; see his "Leonardo da Vincis Brustbild eines Engels und seine Komposition des S. Johannes-Baptista," *Monatshefte für Kunstwissenschaft*, III, 1911, 529–39. Möller cited Amoretti's notice of 1804 that in the Casa Anguissola in Milan there was an "angelo in atto d'annunziare M. V." by Leonardo, but disagreed with the identification of the subject, arguing instead that it was an image of the Guardian Angel. As far as I can tell, in all of the current literature it is considered an Annunciation figure.

42 It has been published and discussed by Kathleen Weil-Garris-Posner, *Leonardo and Central Italian Art: 1515–1550*, New York, 1974, 39–40, and fig. 48. In spite (or because?) of its strong individual flavor, this copy – made after the prototype reproduced on the Windsor sheet – is by far the most faithful to Leonardo's handling of form and expressive physiognomy.

43 This is suggested by M. Kemp, *Leonardo da Vinci: The Marvellous Works of Nature and Man*, Cambridge, MA, 1981, 218; but in his bibliographical notes (p. 353, no. 44) he mentions the more usual identification of the angel with the figure in Verrocchio's *Baptism*, which was also at S. Salvi. I think the first alternative preferable, because Albertini's catalogue of notable works in Florence seems quite precise about indications of joint authorship, and is especially well-informed about works produced from the last quarter of the 15th century onwards. Albertini's complete statement reads: "Lascio in sancto Salvi tavole bellissime et uno Angelo di Leonardo Vinci"; it might translate as "I omit certain most beautiful panels at San Salvi, and [the panel of] an Angel by Leonardo . . ." (as in "In the Angeli there are many panels by the hand of Fra Lorenzo, a monk of theirs, and [the panel of] a Last Judgment by Fra Giovanni [Angelico]" – *et uno iuditio di fra Iohanni*). I cannot find an instance of Albertini singling out for separate mention a figure in a larger composition. See Francesco Albertini, *Memoriale de molte statue et picture . . .* (Florence, 1510), n. pag. (sig. a.iiii–4r), in *Five Early Guides to Rome and Florence*, Westmead, 1972. The sheet with the student drawing after Leonardo's *Angel* has been dated to ca. 1505; see Popham, 140, no. 202, and Kenneth Clark, *The Drawings of Leonardo da Vinci . . . at Windsor Castle*, 2nd rev. ed. with C. Pedretti, London, 1968, I, 27, no. 12328r. Following Möller, W. Suida, *Leonardo und sein Kreis*, Munich, 1929, 154–155, noted the general relationship between the *Angel*

and Rustici's bronze *Baptist* (commissioned in 1506 for the Florentine Baptistery, and linked to Leonardo in the sources). He also indicated its unequivocal reflection in the John the Evangelist in Piero di Cosimo's *Immaculate Conception* (Uffizi, inv. no. 506).

44   It seems no accident that Vasari's description of the *Angel* is directly followed by his evaluation of Leonardo's chiaroscuro: "It is a thing to be marvelled at how that *ingegno*, wishing to impart the greatest relief to the things he made, so endeavored with dark shadows to achieve the darkest backgrounds, that he sought out blacks which might shade and be blacker than other blacks, so that by such means the lights should be brighter; and in the end this manner turned out so inky [*tinto*] that – there being no light tones left – they looked rather like things made to copy a nocturnal effect, than a refinement on the light of day: but it was all from seeking to impart greater relief, to attain the end and perfection of the art" (see above, no. 41). Möller (as in n. 41), 537, calls the *Angel* an artistic paradigm, and cites Leonardo: "Il chiaro e lo scuro co'li scorti è la eccellenzia della scienza della pittura."

45   J. Rudel, in "Bacco e San Giovanni Battista," *Leonardo: La pittura*, Florence, 1985, 121–124, focuses on the *Baptist*'s insistent gaze and smile as manifestations of *grazia* (comparable to the emergence of light from darkness as a manifestation of the divine).

46   The evolution of angel into Baptist in Leonardo's designs was facilitated by traditional associations. These are clarified by M. A. Lavin, "The Joy of the Bridegroom's Friend: Smiling Faces in Fra Filippo, Raphael, and Leonardo," *Art the Ape of Nature*, New York, 1981, 193ff. – but esp. 201–203, where Lavin explains the iconographic link between Leonardo's *Angel* and *Baptist*. Lavin establishes the doctrinal background for representations of smiling angels in images of the Madonna and Child, by indicating their dependence on the commentary tradition of the Song of Solomon. In addition to comparing the betrothal of Bride and Bridegroom to that of the Virgin/Ecclesia and Savior, the commentaries identified the ecstatic "Friends of the Bridegroom" with the angelic host celebrating the fulfillment of the Salvation promise. (The Song of Solomon has already been cited in this paper as an allegorical prefiguration of the Magdalene's reunion with the risen Christ – see nn. 30 and 31, above; since in Savoldo's painting we are the event's chief witnesses, to some degree we must also be playing the part of the "Friends of the Bridegroom.") In its turn, the Gospel of John has the Baptist expressly identifying himself as the "friend of the bridegroom" rejoicing at the sound of the latter's voice; this, and Christ's reference (in Matthew 10:11) to John as his "Angel" or messenger, constituted the authority for elevating the Baptist beyond ordinary mortal sainthood. For a popular medieval source discussing the Baptist's angelic status, see Ragusa and Green, 182–183 (citing the interpretation ascribed to Bernard of Clairvaux). John's likeness to the angels is also explained, with considerable amplification, in the no less popular *Golden Legend*: see Voragine, 356, 358, 359–60 (Cap. LXXXVI).

47   The earliest surviving document for the Brescian painter is the record of his matriculation in the Florentine painters' guild in December 1508; moreover, it is highly likely that Savoldo was the "Ieronimo dipintore da Bressa" in Florence who had been turned down as an assistant for Michelangelo's Sistine project in October of the same year. See G. Vezzoli, "Gian Girolamo Savoldo a Firenze,"

Giovanni Gerolamo Savoldo, 39ff. Vezzoli cites a letter to Buonarroto Buonarroti in Florence from Piero d'Argenta, a *garzone* of Michelangelo who was intimate with the Buonarroti family between 1497 and 1529. D'Argenta was in Rome with Michelangelo when he wrote: "Hora io ti prego che tu dia la lettera che sarà in questa al nostro maestro Ieronimo dipintore da Bressa et racomandami a lui. Io volevo che Michelangiolo lo tolessi, ma io non cii vego ordine. Non altro." As Vezzoli points out, the tone of the letter suggests that "Ieronimo da Bressa" was more than casually acquainted with Buonarroto.

48   The surviving painted replicas of the *Angel* are all from the Lombard *ambiente* (see Möller, as in n. 41 above). A recently rediscovered painting by Savoldo, the *Annunciation* now on deposit at the Pordenone Museum, suggests that he knowingly adapted the *Angel*'s gesture. Savoldo's painting is convincingly attributed in a fine article that is also a review of the artist's critical fortune: see V. Sgarbi, "Savoldo tra Giorgione e Caravaggio: *L'Annunciata* di San Domenico di Castello a Venezia," *Paragone*, no. 409, 1984, 62–69, pl. I, and fig. 58. Savoldo's treatment of the narrative is highly unusual: it is a nocturnal full-length Annunciation in which the angel and the Virgin in the foreground are side by side and frontally posed, though they incline their heads toward one another. The viewer consequently faces them, as if he/she were the recipient of both the angelic greeting and the Virgin's reply. The angel's right arm is raised precisely like Leonardo's (the left holds out a lily and is equally foreshortened). With some difference in the placement and spacing of the figures, this is also the form of Lorenzo Lotto's wonderfully eccentric *Annunciation* in the Museo Civico, Recanati, though the angel's raised arm does not precisely echo Leonardo's, and his middle-ground position gives Mary's response the greater immediacy for the viewer. Lotto's North Italian formation was comparable to Savoldo's, and he too was working in Central Italy before 1510. I do not know how one might determine which of their *Annunciations* has priority as an invention (later, Veronese returned in several *Annunciations* to the basic disposition of Savoldo's figures). There seems to be great unanimity in dating the Lotto to about 1526–27 (see Zampetti's review of the dating in P. dal Poggetto and P. Zampetti, *Lorenzo Lotto nelle Marche. Il suo tempo, il suo influsso*, Florence, 1981, 310, cat. no. 73, with reproduction). Sgarbi, 67, dates the Savoldo between 1530 and 1535, which I think too late (admittedly on no better evidence than the reproduction). The foreshortened hands seem closest in their plasticity to those of the figures in the Turin *Virgin and Child with SS. Jerome and Francis*, which Gilbert (pp. 521–522, no. 39, fig. 32, and pp. 533–534, 555) dates to before 1520 (perhaps a bit early).

49   Pedretti has pointed out that as early as the 1480s, with a "rotational" figure such as the angel in the *Madonna of the Rocks*, the formula for the "turning portrait," or *ritratto di spalla*, was already synthesized – and would be reused by Leonardo toward 1500 in the drawing for a half-length *Christ Bearing the Cross* (Venice, Academy; Popham, no. 171B), an image clearly related to the novel and dramatic half-length *Portacroce* at S. Rocco (1508), alternately attributed to Giorgione and Titian; see C. Pedretti, "Ancora sul rapporto Giorgione-Leonardo e l'origine del ritratto di spalla," *Giorgione: Atti del Convegno* (as in n. 10), 181ff., and esp. 181–183. On the S. Rocco *Cristo portacroce*, see F. Valcanover's contribution in *Giorgione a Venezia*, Milan, 1978, 148–153.

50   See J. Anderson, "The Giorgionesque Portrait: From Likeness to Allegory," *Giorgione: Atti del Convegno* (as in n. 10), 153ff., with a succinct discussion of the *ritratto*

di spalla and its varied progeny, noting particularly the innovative fusion of history and portrait painting achieved by Giorgione. In pose, Savoldo's figure is very close to that in Palma Vechio's *Portrait of a Young Lady* (Vienna, Kunsthistorisches Museum; Anderson's fig. 120).

51 See D. Summers's excellent study, "Maniera and Movement: The *figura serpentinata*," *Art Quarterly*, XXXV, 1972, 269ff.

52 It is no. 80 in the Princes Gate Collection, bequeathed to the Courtauld Institute in 1978; see A[ntoine] S[eilern], *Italian Paintings and Drawings at 56 Princes Gate . . .*, London, 1959, text vol., 23, and pl. XXXIV. The traditional early dating has been challenged by C. Pedretti, *Leonardo*, Berkeley, 1973, 104; he finds the closest analogies to the bold abbreviations of the drawing in sketches securely dated to 1508–09, and relates the type of the Magdalene to that of the Virgin in the Burlington House cartoon. Pedretti, 134, suggests that the Seilern sketch may be our only record of a more finished project, a Leonardo cartoon described in the Pompeo Leoni estate inventory as "a little over a *braccio* in which is reproduced from a living model a lady Saint shown from below the waist, in black chalk, with a perspective of buildings." Pedretti also sees a reflection of the lost cartoon in Raphael's *Saint Catherine of Alexandria* (London, National Gallery). However, the Raphael, like Leonardo's monumental figures of the period around 1508–09, exhibits a compact sinuousness rather different from the stereometric articulation of the Seilern figure. Whatever the latter's date, its impact was in evidence about the time of the composition of Savoldo's *Magdalene*.

53 For most of the 15th century, half-length images of the Magdalene are rare on either side of the Alps. See the survey by Anstett-Janssen (as in n. 31), and especially 196ff. (on the trecento half-length type) and 366ff. (for the quattrocento). The archaizing character of the Braque Triptych is discussed by B. G. Lane in *The Altar and the Altarpiece*, New York, 1984, 122–128; and also in "Early Italian Sources for the Braque Triptych," *Art Bulletin*, LXII, 1980, 281–284. One aspect of Roger's Magdalene deserves notice: tears run down her cheeks, bringing into the hieratic composition of the triptych allusions to both her conversion and her mourning at the Tomb.

54 Moretto's beautiful full-length *Magdalene* (Art Institute of Chicago; Ingenhoff-Danhäuser, fig. 72) is also in this category of image: she holds the ointment jar in both hands and turns away from the viewer, but looks back over one shoulder as if attending to a sudden interruption.

55 See Shapley, 142–143, no. K2159, fig. 338. The Kress Collection owns another painting of the same subject and design, a Giampietrino dated to ca. 1521 (K1021, in the Portland Art Museum; Shapley, 136, fig. 330); see also K1230. Ingenhoff-Danhäuser, 13ff. (following Anstett-Janssen, as in n. 31, 365ff.), analyzes the range of Leonardesque half-length *Magdalenes* related to either the Seilern sketch or nude variants of the *Mona Lisa*. Luini adapted the figure in a half-length *Martha and Mary* (The Timken Foundation, San Diego) that has been associated with other examples of imagery of the active/comtemplative life by F. Cummings, "The Meaning of Caravaggio's 'Conversion of the Magdalene,'" *Burlington Magazine*, DCCCLIX, 1974, 575–576.

56 Perhaps such a design was among the studio properties bequeathed to Melzi by Leonardo. As Popham, 19, has noted, Leonardo's invention also has a Transalpine echo in paintings (contemporary with Luini's) from the circle of Metsys, where the

gesture of the hands, in particular, is taken up. Popham also cites, and with good reason rejects, B. Haendcke's proposal of 1924 of a link between the *Mona Lisa* and Roger's Magdalene of the Braque Triptych – though certainly the latter, in the perfection of its design, points the way to Leonardo's concern with images of similar format. A *Magdalene* by Metsys of the Leonardesque type is reproduced by Snyder (as in n. 31), 406, fig. 474; see also M. J. Friedländer, *Early Netherlandish Painting*, Leyden, 1967–76, VII, pls. 76/89, 80/100–101, 124/suppl. 178 and XII, pl. 41/83. The Northern popularity of the Leonardesque type suggests that studio variants may have been produced as early as 1517–19, during Leonardo's final years in France.

57 For a concise survey of Magdalene types from the Middle Ages to the modern period, see the richly illustrated catalogue, *La Maddalena tra sacro e profano*, ed. M. Mosco, Florence, 1986, and esp. 67–151 ("La mirrofora," "La devota"), which cover the figural and narrative types relevant to this discussion. Savoldo's *Magdalenes* are discussed on pp. 128–129, in a catalogue entry that gives prominence to Ingenhoff-Danhäuser's interpretation.

58 Heavily draped hooded mourners were a specialty of the life-size, free-standing Burgundian Entombment groups in the Sluter tradition. A fine example of this widespread type is the *Entombment* at Tonnerre, dated 1454: in it, all but one of the Holy Women customarily present alongside the sarcophagus appear as hooded *pleurants* in a majestic display of grief. See W. H. Forsyth, *The Entombment of Christ: French Sculpture of the Fifteenth and Sixteenth Centuries*, Cambridge, MA, 1970, 65ff., figs. 88–92. This invention has been plausibly associated with high and late medieval Easter plays and funeral practices; I would also relate its emergence to an interest in the Plinian devices discussed below, and in n. 77. Savoldo, whose wife was Flemish (see *Giovanni Gerolamo Savoldo*, 15), may have been directly acquainted with the Northern *pleurants*, and not just Italian adaptations.

59 The attention to textile surfaces in a painting (and more generally to materials whose optical properties deflect the glance and keep it in motion over a surface) shaped in a special way the modes of contrapposto figuration shared by the Venetian masters with Leonardo and other Central Italian painters of the *terza maniera*. The mysteriously abridged quality of Venetian pictorial design begins in a paradoxical continuity between the surface tension of texturally uniform, colored elements, and the opposing gravitational pull of depths opened up by chiaroscuro and the rotation of figural elements. Titian in particular combined resonantly colored – and often reflective – surfaces with emphatic contrapposto. In his London *Portrait of a Man* (the so-called *Ariosto*; National Gallery, no. 1944), dated to about 1510–12, the "turning portrait" schema is monumentalized by the imposing, luministically complex expanse of sleeve, which both snares the viewer, and shields from his gaze the shadowy space out of which the figure looks (and into which the bulk of his torso is set). The effect is comparable to that of the Magdalene's shawl.

60 Titian's Louvre *Entombment* is dated 1526–32 by H. E. Wethey, *The Paintings of Titian*, I, London, 1969, 89, no. 36. The Magdalene's shawl is also to be compared with the voluminous patterned silks on the foreground figures (and the gold cloak about Saint Peter's hips) in Titian's *Pesaro Madonna* (1519–26). I am inclined to view Savoldo's figure as a knowing emulation of Titian's example. However, the mirror-like fabric makes a contemporaneous appearance in the work of Savoldo's fellow Brescian, Romanino, in a series of paintings spanning the period 1524–ca.

1530: the *Feast in the House of the Pharisee*, S. Giovanni Evangelista, Brescia (the Magdalene's gold cloak); the *Nativity* in the Pinacoteca Tosio-Martinengo, Brescia (the Virgin's silver cloak); and closest in effect to the Savoldo, the half-length tondo of *Christ Bearing the Cross*, Pinacoteca Tosio-Martinengo (Christ's silver sleeve). See G. Panazza, *Mostra di Girolamo Romanino*, Brescia, 1965, figs. 40, 90, and 91. It may be, after all, that this sort of display is more of a Lombard contribution.

61 See Frank O. Büttner, *Imitatio Pietatis*, Berlin, 1983, 165ff., and esp. 172–173, figs. 197–198 (manuscript illustrations from France ca. 1495, and Venice ca. 1430–40, respectively). Büttner focuses on book illustration because it naturally integrates image and verbal commentary, but his observations are easily transferable to half-length panels of the type discussed by Ringbom, where secondary personages often model for the viewer the appropriate attitude before a holy narrative. On the Renaissance habit of devout visualization, which made of the viewer an active contributor to, rather than a spectator of, religious pictures, see also Baxandall, 1972, 40–48, and 157, n. 4.

62 Barocchi, I, 115. J. Anderson [Pau], "The Imagery of Giorgione," Ph.D diss., Bryn Mawr College, 1972, 6–24, assimilates Pino's *brevità* to Giorgione's aesthetic of the allusive image with composite significance. In connection with Pino's remark, Benedetto Varchi's near-contemporary paraphrase of certain arguments for the superiority of painting over sculpture deserves quoting: "... painting foreshortens figure[s], makes them appear round and in relief on a flat surface, making it dissolve and appear distant, with all of the resemblances and enticements one may desire; it gives all of [the painters'] works their lights and shadows, properly observed according to the lighting and its reflections, which they take for a most difficult thing; and, in sum, they say that they make that which is not appear to be, something requiring infinite labor and artifice." See Barocchi, I, 38. This is glossed from the sculptors' standpoint in a subsequent passage: "[The sculptors] add that painting is, so to speak, sophistical – that is to say, apparent and not real, virtually indistinguishable from the way that figures are seen in mirrors"; Barocchi, I, 41. See n. 4 above, for Vasari's praise of Savoldo as *sofistico* on account of his luministic renderings.

63 I translate from Cennini, *Il libro dell'arte*, ed. F. Brunello, Vicenza, 1971, 3–4. In rendering *fermarle* ("fix" or "set them") as "retrace them," I have tried to convey the technical action implicit in the term, as it emerges from Cennino's chs. X (after drawing with the stylus, the contours can be gone over – or set – with ink [*ferma con inchiostro ne' luoghi stremi* ...]), and XXX (after drawing in charcoal, the contours and chief folds can be gone over in silverpoint and the charcoal dusted off, *e rimarrà il tuo disegno fermato collo stile*). Since Cennino consistently describes contour in terms of shadow or spatial recession, his *fermare* suggests grasping a three-dimensional object by "stabilizing" its contour.

64 Cennini's definition is structured in such a way that *fantasia* and "finding things not seen" (invention) are conceptually paired, as are "skill of hand" and "shadow-rendering." The passage closes with a clarification of the role of fantasy: it "composes," by recombining forms, figures both natural and nonexistent, and is identified as the *scienza* of both poet and painter. The remainder of Cennini's manual is about "skill of hand," which – unlike fantasy – can be systematically taught.

65 In Giotto's art, the solidity and gravity of the figures, and the humanity of their gestures, invariably serve an "unpaintable" content. Thus, in the Arena Chapel *Raising of Lazarus* the dynamics of the composition come to a focus in the preg-

nant gap between Christ's illuminated blessing hand and the foreshortened hand of the youth whose sweeping gesture leads straight to Lazarus. That crucial hiatus, a carefully defined volume of space, is Giotto's way of suggesting the miraculous nature of Christ's bestowal of life – an invisible act as distinct from its corporeal effect.

66 The discussion that follows is indebted throughout to chs. I ("Laurel") and II ("*Quello che non è sia*") in Summers (as in n. 4), 33–55.

67 The tradition is surveyed by C. C. Greenfield, *Humanist and Scholastic Poetics, 1250–1500*, East Brunswick, NJ, 1981; it is evident from her discussion that the concept of poetry as a "fictive garment" was a hoary commonplace since late antiquity, but was given a particular relief and weight by Petrarch, Boccaccio, and Salutati (who brings together all of the trecento topics). In the 15th century, the Neoplatonist writers took over this legacy, but granted a heightened philosophical status to vatic inspiration and "mysterious" utterance. Toward the close of the century a more philological and classicizing poetics coexisted with the Neoplatonist variety. As Greenfield, chs. 10 and 11, illustrates, the 15th-century North Italian *ambiente* contributed to the formulation of poetical theory (it had originated there with Mussato and Petrarch), though the more ambitious texts came out of Florence.

68 I cite the translation by C. G. Osgood, *Boccaccio on Poetry*, 1st ed. 1930, repr., n.p., 1956, 39 and 42; the Latin is taken from J. Reedy, ed., *Boccaccio: In Defence of Poetry*, Toronto, 1978, 34–36. The *Genealogiae* – which received ten printings between 1472 and 1532 – remained a standard interpretive handbook of mythology through the 16th century. For information on the editions, see G. Boccaccio, *Genealogiae deorum gentilium libri*, ed. V. Romano, Bari, 1951, II, 802, n. 1.

69 The medieval theories about the allegorical "veiling" of truth, secular and religious, are cogently reviewed in E. de Bruyne's *Etudes d'esthétique médiévale*, II, Bruges, 1946, 302ff. For an account of the notion of the poetic *integumentum* or *involucrum* (wrapping, shell, or cover, as well as veil) and its medieval application, see H. Brinkmann, "Verhüllung ('Integumentum') als literarische Darstellungsform im Mittelater," *Der Begriff der Repraesentatio im Mittelalter* (*Miscellanea Mediaevalia*, VIII), Berlin, 1971, 314ff. See also H. de Lubac, *Exégèse médiévale*, II, Pt. 2, Paris, 1964, 182ff., with numerous examples of the use of *integumentum* in the sense of deliberate concealment or obscuring.

70 Savoldo was certainly acquainted with the notion of Christian exegesis as the unveiling of Scripture. As pointed out by Gilbert, 533, his paintings of the adoration of the infant Christ frequently show the luminous child drawing aside the veil that covered him – in illustration of the Pauline concept of the Word Incarnate as revealing to the Christian convert the radiant truth veiled in the letter of the Old Law. The Christ prefigured throughout the Old Testament is the justification for the Christian reading-into of Scripture. A fine discussion of Saint Paul's doctrine of conversion/re-velation is found in J. Freccero, *Dante: The Poetics of Conversion*, Cambridge, MA, 1986, 121–123. Apart from the typological schemas popularized by the *Biblia pauperum*, an example of allegorical unveiling in connection with the Magdalene's visit to the Sepulcher is in Gregory the Great, Hom. XXV (as in n. 30), 1548B and C, where the mystical truth of the Magdalene's literally false identification of Christ as gardener is pointed up by a metaphorical reading: "Indeed, was he not a spiritual gardener, who sowed in her breast out of love for her the seeds of the plants of virtue?" Pope Gregory's interpretation is doctrinal, and not merely

"poetic," because by the logic of Christian interpretation Christ's identity could only be purposely veiled or concealed – the Magdalene's was not a simple misperception. This point is elaborated in a celebrated 13th-century homily (traditionally – if erroneously – ascribed to Origen) on John 20, translated into Italian by the 14th century: "Oh Lord Jesus Christ, what is this you are doing? Do you think she can know you while you wish to remain concealed? . . . Oh miserable sorrow, oh marvelous love! This good woman, beside herself and shrouded with pain as with a cloud, did not know the Sun she was seeing, and with whom she was speaking; and she felt such longing from the love of Jesus, and such ardor, that this longing and desire to see him caused a mist and a fog to settle over her heart . . . But in truth, Mary, I have seen the reason why at first, perhaps, he withheld himself from you and would not show himself to you, and did not let himself be known by you . . . And this is because he would not have shown himself in the way in which you were asking for him." As this sample makes evident, the sermon develops a psychological imagery congruent with Savoldo's visualization. See M. H. Hansel, "Die Quellen der bayerischen Magdalenenklage," *Zeitschrift für deutsche Philologie*, LXII, 1937, 363ff. The Italian version I cite is printed as an appendix to *Lo specchio della vera penitenza di Fr. Jacopo Passavanti* . . . , Florence, 1725, 290–292.

71   In a 12th-century poetics that was still being consulted in the quattrocento, the *Poetria nova*, Geoffrey of Vinsauf described both the arrangement and verbal embellishment of the poem with (among others) textile metaphors. See J. J. Murphy, ed., *Three Medieval Rhetorical Arts*, Berkeley, 1971, 41–42, 60–61. Patz, 283 and n. 104, points out that Gasparino Barzizza, who seems to have taught Alberti, still cited Geoffrey as an authority.

72   *Epistolae seniles* XII. 2, as cited in W. Tatarkiewicz, *History of Aesthetics*, III, The Hague, 1974, 10. This seems a gloss on Isidore of Seville, *Etymologies* VIII. vii: "Officium autem poetae in eo est ut ea, quae vere gesta sunt, in alias species obliquis figurationibus cum decore aliquo conversa transducant." Isidore's "oblique figurations" parallel Petrarch's "artful colors," while the "different form" into which true things are changed matches the "veil of fiction."

73   The classification of figures as *colores* was a commonplace of medieval literary theory (see E. Faral, *Les arts poétiques du XIIe et du XIIIe siècle*, repr. Geneva-Paris, 1982, 48ff.). Petrarch, whose taste as a collector of painting was highly sophisticated, must have used this pictorial terminology with a real sense of its illusionistic applications. In both his poetry and his literary theory, Petrarch showed a particular concern with "adumbration," which he related (in explicit reference to pictorial practice) to atmospheric illusion and effects of resemblance. See the famous Canzone 129 ("Di pensier in pensier, di monte in monte"). For a discussion of *aria* and *ombra* as literary terms in Petrarch, see T. M. Greene, *The Light in Troy: Imitation and Discovery in Renaissance Poetry*, New Haven, 1982, chs. 5 and 7, 81ff. and 127ff.

74   D. Summers, *The Judgment of Sense*, Cambridge, 1987, 121, discusses Petrarch's use of the painter's term *aria* to designate both the artist's style as an intangible personal quality, and the traces of that quality – which register as an in-spiriting or animation – in the artist's work. According to Petrarch, a pictorial example of *aria* is the shadow about the face (and especially the eyes) that betrays the kinship between father and son, and is the quality to be emulated in portraiture (rather than literal resemblance). Savoldo's *Magdalene*, with her shadowy face, has the kind of

elusive animation that depends on our willingness to follow Petrarch in interpreting an atmospheric effect as evidence of the maker's presence in his creature.

75 See Barocchi, II, 381–382. *Aposiopesis* is described under the figures of *emphasis* in the *Rhetorica ad Herennium* IV. liv. 67. *Emphasis* (*significatio*) is defined as "that which leaves more to be suspected than has been actually asserted [*quae plus in suspicione relinquit quam positum est in oratione*]" (IV. liii. 66).

76 See Pliny, *NH* XXXV. 73f., as well as Cicero, *Orator* 69–74, and Quintilian II. xiii. 8–14. For Renaissance art theory, the passage in Quintilian, with its wealth of examples drawn from the visual arts, was the most important. See also below, n. 86.

77 J. J. Pollitt, *The Ancient View of Greek Art*, New Haven, 1974, analyzes the key ancient passages on *ingenium* as a specifically artistic virtue (deriving from the term's broader meaning of "native talent" – on this, see D. Summers, as in n. 74, 99ff.). However, his explanation of artistic *ingenium* (pp. 387–388) does not wholly clarify the Plinian sense: "The ingenium of Timanthes, it is clear, meant the imaginative, subtle touches he inserted into the narrative subject matter of his paintings"; Pliny "seems to mean, not that Timanthes' technique was inadequate for his ideas, but that in his paintings subject matter was always of greater interest than technique"; Quintilian's reference to *ingenium* in Apelles is puzzling, since "the paintings of Apelles do not appear to have been famed for . . . ingenious, unconventional features of subject matter." By placing the emphasis on subject matter, Pollitt devalues the specifically psychological dimension of works that make one "see" things not actually depicted, or (more literally) in excess of the space available for them. This is not only the common feature in the Timanthean works, but also of Pollitt's examples no. 5 (great artists brought ingenious skill to the painting of famous prodigies – which is to say phenomena outside natural experience), and no. 10 (Phidias managed to accommodate monumental narratives in even the smallest left-over spaces of his large works). Quintilian's reference to Apelles ceases to be puzzling if one takes into account how he "painted the unpaintable" (lightning and thunderbolts personified), or created a vivid likeness with just a few strokes of charcoal, or made one "see" the features of an averted face (*NH* XXXV. 89, 94, 96). The point of interest in these examples is that subject matter is transformed for the purpose of enhancing the imaginative suggestiveness of the work. Pollitt's wonderful book, with its philological approach to a broad range of Greek and Roman art critical terms, is also a useful guide to the Renaissance understanding of Pliny's terminology, since much of the latter was explicated then by reference to the standard texts still consulted by modern classicists.

78 An excellent discussion of the use of rhetorical principle in Book II of *De pictura* is to be found in chapter III of Baxandall, 1971, 121–139. More recently, Patz has surveyed the entire literature on the question, and proposed certain correctives to Baxandall. D. R. Edward Wright, "Alberti's *De pictura*: Its Literary Structure and Purpose," *Journal of the Warburg and Courtauld Institutes*, XLVII, 1984, 52–71, has demonstrated that *De pictura* is particularly dependent on the structure and pedagogical recommendations of Quintilian's *Institutio oratoria*. However, Wright's interpretation of *De pictura's* purpose as the elementary instruction of very young (Book I) and adolescent (Book II) painters (with "postgraduate" tips for adult practitioners in Book III), seems drastically reductive – even if one agrees with him that Alberti was not producing a comprehensive *ars* to cover the theory and practice

of quattrocento painting. The major emphasis in *De pictura* falls on stylistic practice and its implications (as correctly noted by Summers, 339ff., 344–345, 350–351, 353–354 and 360), a matter left out of account by Wright, who dedicates one paragraph (on p. 65) to the bulk of *De pictura's* Book II.

79 "Idcirco diligentissime ex ipsa natura cuncta perscrutanda sunt, semperque promptiora imitanda, eaque potissimum pingenda sunt, quae plus animis guod excogitent relinquant, quam quae oculis intueantur." This and the following quotations are from Alberti-Grayson, 80–83 (para. 42). I have modified Grayson's translation of *promptiora*. He renders it as "the more visible things," but in this context Alberti is referring specifically to movement, in relation to which the vernacular art-critical term *pronto* denoted readiness, a vivid potentiality – and, by extension, suggestiveness; see Baxandall, 1972, 145–147. Patz, 282–285, indicates that Alberti conflated Quintilian and the *Ars poetica* in his recommendations on expression; she also underscores the centrality of the *historia's* expressive mission. It is worth nothing that Alberti himself used the veiling-depicting analogy with characteristic wit in Book I of *De pictura*, where line, contour, plane, visual rays, visual pyramid, are all "pictured" through textile similes (respectively, thread, hemline, woven fabric, colored threads gathered into bundles or attached to the "hem" of an object). This prepares the way for Alberti's gridded tracing device in Book II, the *velum*, which is presented as an analogue to the picture plane-as-window, and serves to trace the contours (or embroider the "hemlines") of the *historia's* expressive figures. Since the *velum* facilitates the construction of foreshortened organic forms, with their complex relation of undulant contour to depth projection, it is a tool for figural embellishment, in the proper rhetorical sense. By the logic of *De pictura*, Alberti's tracing-veil is like a literal version of its counterpart in poetics.

80 Baxandall, 1971, 129–130 (and see pls. 3 and 5[a]), points out that Giotto's *Navicella* is the only modern composition praised by Alberti, and may represent his advocacy of a neo-Giottesque standard for contemporary painting. The celebration of Giotto's *ingegno* in the illusionistic rendering of "living Nature" originates – close to the master's lifetime – with Boccaccio; see E. Falaschi, "Giotto: The Literary Legend," *Italian Studies*, XXVII, 1972, 6–8. Alberti's *Navicella* reference may be inspired by Filippo Villani's late trecento *De origine civitatis Florentiae et eiusdem famosis civibus*, which brings together the several strands of the "Giotto legend." There, Giotto is the exemplar of modern artistic *ingenium* who, in his quest for universal reputation, takes care to leave important works in the major cities of Italy – and chiefly the *Navicella* in Rome, which will be seen by pilgrims from all over the world. This passage is translated in Baxandall, 70–71 (and 146–147 for the Latin). It is tempting – and perhaps not inappropriate – to see in Giotto's art explicit recreations of Plinian pictorial virtues: the Arena Chapel *Lamentation* makes striking use of "Timanthean" veiled foreground mourners seen from behind.

81 This figure is the equivalent, at the level of elocutionary elaboration, of the man who provides the three-*braccia* yardstick in the perspective construction schema of Book I. One is the mensurational, the other the psychophysical projection, onto the fictive window of the painting, of a counterpart to the viewer.

82 Alberti's attention to the viewer's psychic entry into the painting brings us back to Northern Italy, with its tradition of dramatic close-ups. In a stimulating analysis of Bellini's Brera *Pietà*, H. Belting argues that the Venetian master both adapted

and inverted Alberti's humanist requirement of a high narrative eloquence, by assimilating it to the devotional format of the icon (see Belting, 31–48). Belting cites Mantegna's classicizing *Entombment* print of ca. 1460 as properly Albertian, and contrasts it with Bellini's spatialization and psychic enlivening of the traditional icon; in both images Saint John the Evangelist is the Albertian "mediator," but in Mantegna's he stands – a sorrowing onlooker – at a remove from both the viewer and the narrative core of the scene. Belting's concept of the Albertian *historia* seems rather strict, given the very wide range of pictorial exempla adduced in *De pictura*. I think that, rather than advocating one particular pictorial genre, Alberti offered an ideal scheme whose rules could be adapted to every genre, from the portrait to the heroic narrative (and from the traditional to the classicizing religious narrative). *Historia* would then designate a "composite" horizon of possibility, rather like Cicero's ideal orator. See Patz, 285–287, who points out that a full definition of Alberti's *historia* will have to take into account the medieval, and not only the classical sources incorporated in *De pictura*.

83 See Quintilian VIII. vi. 4ff., 19ff.; IX. ii. 38ff. Quintilian classifies *synecdoche* and *metaphora* as tropes, separating them from figures of thought and speech; however, in Bk. IX he also argues that tropes and figures, as departures from normative usage, are fundamentally the same. Isidore of Seville's *Etymologies* I. xxxvi–xxxvii, and II. xxi present a concise survey of tropes and figures.

84 See Summers, 347ff., for the fundamental analysis of *antithesis*/contrapposto, including a review of the classical literary models. Alberti's principle of *varietà* – crucial to the articulation of the *historia*, from the shaping of the bodies to the production of transitory light effects – is based on antithetical construction. For *varietà* and the pictorial effects that distinguish the *Magdalene*, see Alberti-Grayson, 90–93 (paras. 47 and 48; modeling and coloring; the use of highlights in vitreous and metallic objects).

85 Quintilian IX. i. 10–11.

86 Quintilian II. xiii. 8ff.: ". . . in all his pleadings the orator should keep two things . . . in view, what is becoming and what is expedient. But it is often expedient and occasionally becoming to make some modification in the time-honoured order. We see the same thing in pictures and statues . . . The body when held bolt upright has but little grace, for the face looks straight forward . . . and the whole figure is stiff from top to toe. But that curve, I might almost call it motion [*flexus ille, ut sic dixerim, motus*], . . . gives an impression of action and animation [*dat actum quendam et adfectum*] . . . Some figures are represented as running . . . , others sit or recline, some are nude, others clothed . . . Where can we find a more . . . elaborate attitude than that of the *Discobolos* . . . ? Yet the critic who disapproved of the figure because it was not upright, would merely show his utter failure to understand the sculptor's art . . . A similar impression of grace and charm is produced by rhetorical figures. . . . For they depart from the straight line and have the merit of variation from the ordinary usage. . . . So, too, in speaking, there are certain things which have to be concealed, either because they ought not to be disclosed or because they cannot be expressed as they deserve. Timanthes . . . provides an example of this . . ."

87 Barocchi, I, 99.

88 Not surprisingly, for the main speaker in Pino's *Dialogo* it is impossible to judge painting if one lacks a knowledge of its principles; his interlocutor agrees by citing

Savoldo as an example of misunderstood artistry (see Barocchi, I, 98–100). As an image for *intendenti* to "unveil," the *Magdalene* also calls to mind another famous Plinian anecdote, Parrhasios's deception of his fellow-painter Zeuxis with a painted curtain (*NH* xxxv. 65). Gilbert, 540–542, has a very seductive hypothesis for the *Magdalene*'s original ownership: in 1527, Savoldo was commissioned to do a *Saint Jerome* (very probably the painting in London, National Gallery, no. 3092) for Giovan Paolo Averoldi, a member of the prominent Brescian family (see C. Boselli, "Nuovi documenti sull'arte veneta del secolo XVI nell'archivio della famiglia Averoldi di Brescia," *Arte veneta*, xxvi, 1972, 234ff.). The archives show that G. P. Averoldi – whose relative Altobello Averoldi commissioned Titian's brilliant SS. Nazzaro e Celso *Resurrection* polyptych in the early 1520s – regularly invested in vanguard Venetian painting. The London *Magdalene* was recorded in the Averoldi Collection by 1620 (see n. 19, above); perhaps it had been there, like the nearly contemporary *Jerome*, since the cinquecento. If it had, it was indeed painted for an audience of cognoscenti.

89 The most remarkable such image by Savoldo is the so-called *"Gaston de Foix"* (Paris, Louvre; see Gilbert, pl. 46), a *paragone* picture of a half-length figure in armor (also in a "turning pose," but with daring foreshortenings) positioned between two mirrors.

90 See David Rosand's astute remarks (as in n. 25), 18–19, on the Venetian appreciation of the canvas ground as a kind of arena for the visible display of brushwork caught in the process of creating an illusionistic world.

Frequently Cited Sources

Alberti, L. B., *On Painting and On Sculpture: The Latin Texts of "De pictura" and "De statua,"* trans. and ed. C. Grayson, London, 1972.

Antonello da Messina, ed. A. Marabottini and F. Sricchia Santoro, Rome, 1981.

Barocchi, P., ed., *Trattati d'arte del Cinquecento*, 3 vols., Bari, 1960.

Baxandall, M., *Giotto and the Orators*, Oxford, 1971.

—— *Painting and Experience in Fifteenth-Century Italy*, Oxford, 1972.

Belting, H., *Giovanni Bellini: Pietà*, Frankfurt-am-Main, 1985.

Biblia sacra iuxta vulgatam clementinam, ed. A. Colunga, and L. Turrado, Madrid, 1965.

Büttner, F. O., *Imitatio pietatis: Motive der christlichen Ikonographie als Modelle zur Verähnlichung*, Berlin, 1983.

Gilbert, C., *The Works of Girolamo Savoldo: The 1955 Dissertation, with a Review of Research, 1955–1985*, New York, 1986.

Giovanni Gerolamo Savoldo pittore bresciano: Atti del Convegno (21–22 maggio 1983), ed. G. Panazza, Brescia, 1985.

Gould, C., *The Sixteenth-Century Italian Schools (National Gallery Catalogues)*, London, 1975.

Holy Bible, Douay-Rheims ed., 1889, repr. Baltimore, 1971.

Ingenhoff-Danhäuser, M., *Maria Magdalena, Heilige und Sünderin in der italienischen Renaissance: Studien zur Ikonographie der Heiligen von Leonardo bis Tizian*, Tübingen, 1984.

Patz, K., "Zum Begriff der 'Historia' in L. B. Albertis 'De Pictura,'" *Zeitschrift für Kunstgeschichte*, XLIX, 1986, 269ff.

Pliny, *Natural History*, trans. and ed. H. Rackham, 10 vols., Cambridge, MA, 1958–62.

Popham, A. E., *The Drawings of Leonardo da Vinci*, New York, 1945.

Quintilian, *The Institutio oratoria*, trans. H. E. Butler, 4 vols., Cambridge, MA, 1966–69.

Ragusa, I., and R. B. Green, trans. and ed., *Meditations on the Life of Christ: An Illustrated Manuscript of the Fourteenth Century* (*Princeton Monographs on Art and Archaeology*, XXXV), Princeton, 1961.

Ridolfi, C., *Le maravigle dell'arte* (Venice, 1648), ed. D. von Hadeln, 2 vols., 1914–24, repr. Rome, 1965.

Ringbom, S., *Icon to Narrative: The Rise of the Dramatic Close-up in Fifteenth-Century Devotional Painting*, 2nd ed., Doornspijk, 1984.

Saxer, V., *Le culte de Marie Madeleine en occident*, Paris, 1959.

Shapley, F. R., *Complete Catalogue of the Samuel H. Kress Collection: Italian Paintings XV–XVI Centuries*, New York, 1968.

Summers, D., "Contrapposto: Style and Meaning in Renaissance Art," *Art Bulletin*, LIX, 1977, 336–361.

Vasari, G., *Le vite de' più eccellenti pittori, scultori ed architettori*, ed. G. Milanesi, 9 vols., Florence, 1878–85.

Venturi, A., *Storia dell'arte italiana*, 11 vols., Milan, 1901–40.

Voragine, Jacobus da, *Legenda aurea*, ed. T. Graesse, 1890, repr. Osnabrück, 1969.

22

Figure come fratelli: A Transformation of Symmetry in Renaissance Painting

David Summers

> Vegniamo al fatto et al punto principale, che la natura non ha se non una veduta per volta . . .
>
> Nasce bene in queste arti la maraviglia . . . quando queste arti faccin cose che passino la natura di quel subietto . . .
>
> Vincenzo Borghini[1]

According to Giorgio Vasari, Giotto rescued the art of painting from the stagnant waters of the *maniera greca* and began a sustained development which culminated in the art of Vasari's own time. His thesis accounts logically and economically for events in Italian art from 1300 to 1550, and no doubt Vasari still participated in the tradition of intentions that had guided and unified the generations of progress he recorded; but at the same time, Vasari's viewpoint involved a systematic lack of concern with ways in which the renaissance of Italian art was a continuation of its own long past. Vasari was avowedly interested in precisely those characteristics that distinguished the new art from what had gone before, in characteristics reflecting the historically unique aspirations and achievements of a more cultured age. Accordingly, he presented the *terza maniera* – to us, the High Renaissance and its aftermath – as having begun its boyhood, like the heroes of myth, without a real father, claiming instead the paternity of divine antiquity. Such a view, if fruitful in some respects, is less so in others, and however much Vasari may have meant to favor Italian art by separating it from the larger tradition of which it was an episode, the depth of the transformation brought about by Italian artists remains concealed by such a treatment.

One of the major pictorial means the High Renaissance style shared with its predecessors – and indeed with most styles of world art – was bilateral symmetry used as a basic mode of composition. Yet this survival – or continuation – was not simply the persistence of a more or less universal organizational principle, and bilateral symmetry, so ancient and so deeply rooted in the human imagination, underwent a change in the hands of Renaissance artists that radically altered the use and significance of symmetry in the centuries that followed. We may begin our discussion of this transformation of symmetry with a review and closer examination of a series of paintings that E. H. Gombrich has used to illustrate his argument for the survival of normative symmetry into Italian Renaissance painting from the preceding tradition.[2]

As an example of the traditional use of bilateral symmetry in Italian art Gombrich cites the Duecento *Madonna and Saints* from Panzano. Bilateral symmetry is evidently much more than incidental in this painting, and Gombrich's brief formal discussion can be pushed without difficulty to the point where an inextricably close bond between simple formal construction and significance becomes apparent. If we consider the preconditions of bilateral symmetry, a vertical axis and a plane surface, it is clear that these elements are also the preconditions of the *centrality* and *frontality* of the Madonna; that is to say, purely formal categories may be interchanged for categories that have implications for the meaning of the image. Thus formal description, which may seem at first to have little to do with the image as such, in fact supports its significance. The Virgin occupies the visually privileged central vertical axis, assuming the eidetic fullness of completely frontal presentation.[3] The symmetrical disposition of the two saints – a single shape turned about the central axis through the 180 degrees of the plane of the painting – may also be described with reference to the same conditions of vertical axiality and planarity. Their symmetry, moreover, implies the *generic identity* of Peter and Paul – surely intended – which is stated with perfect visual economy by the two figures' nearly unbroken reflection of one another about the central vertical axis and about the "central" figure of the Virgin.

The fusion of significant elements of visual order with explicit meaning – what will be called hieratic symmetry, since the term denotes precisely this fusion – is remarked again by Gombrich in Piero della Francesca's *Madonna del Parto* (fig. 22.1). The same elements are present once more, but the almost unconditioned response of the earlier image to the picture plane is now altered by the movement of a virtual or fictive – but in its visual consequences, very real – ground plane, which, at the same time that it can be read as simple passage in depth, can also be seen as the introduction of a second plane, equivalent and perpendicular to the plane surface of the painting itself. For the sake of illustration we might describe the illusion of the presence of the Virgin and angels as the resolution of the forces of these two coordinate planes. The artistic problem has now become location of figures on the virtual plane as well as position on the real plane of the painting; that is, not only must the figures be realized as two-dimensional *shapes*, as were for the most part the Duecento saints, but now they must to a much greater degree be realized also as three-dimensional *forms*.

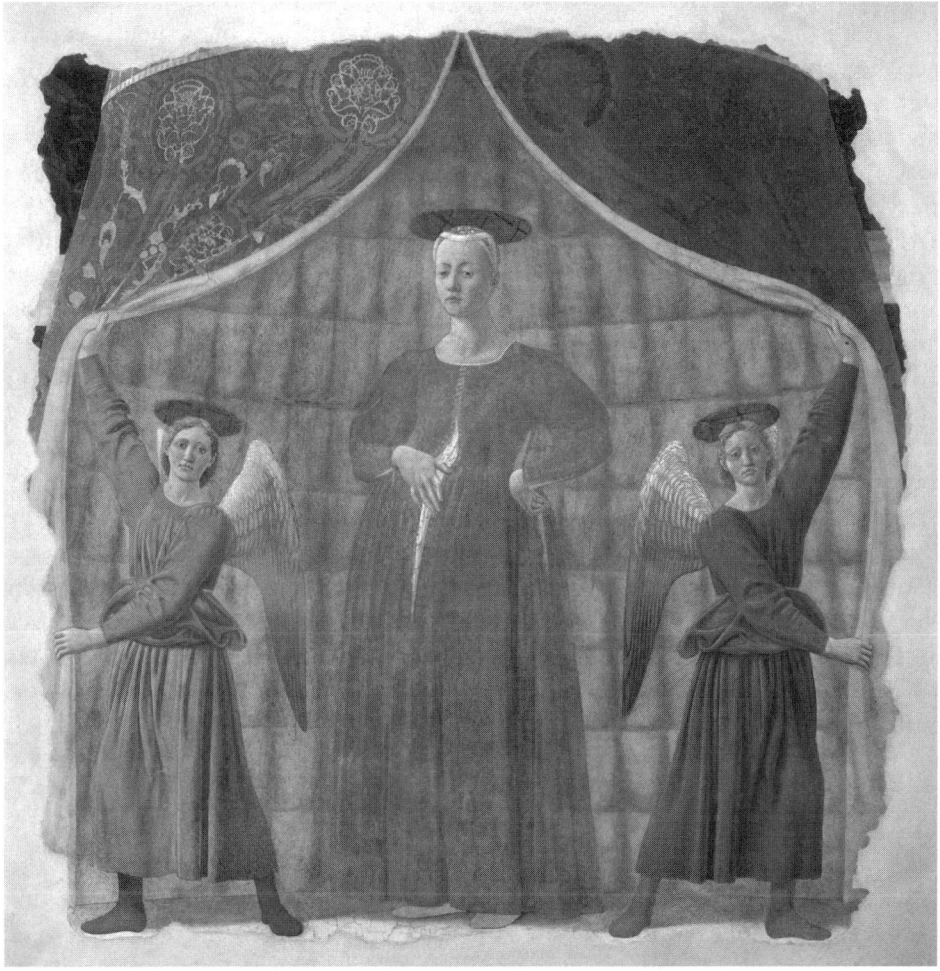

Figure 22.1 Piero della Francesca, *Madonna del Parto*. Fresco, transferred onto wood. Monterchi (Arrezzo), Cappella del Cimetro. Alinari Archives-Florence.

It is important at this point to stress the equation of the real and virtual planes if we are to understand a transference of what had been exclusively two-dimensional order into three-dimensional order of a similar kind. Planarity, of course, is modified by the addition of a second, coordinate plane. But all the other factors – frontality, axiality and symmetry – will undergo changes which can only be described beginning from the original two-dimensional situation. And the meanings correlative to these formal factors will also change.

In Piero's *Madonna del Parto* the new virtual plane is stated by the ground upon which the figures are placed, but it is more emphatic in the round pavilion projected in three dimensions within which the Virgin stands. Almost to the extent that she herself has become clear volume – echoing in her formal purity the purity of the circle above her – she departs in a pregnant, mild, Gothic sway

487

from the central vertical axis, which is nonetheless very much in evidence. Not only does the axis determine her position and control her movement, lending her the central, hieratic importance she had in the Duecento painting, but the axis is now active in two and in three dimensions, being the visual pitchpole of the pavilion and, more simply, the central line around which the cylinder of space revolves. The Virgin still commands the two flanking angels symmetrically arrayed on either side of the axis, much as Peter and Paul were deployed in the earlier painting. As Gombrich points out, Piero seems to have followed the simple procedure of reversing these angels, and by doing so he has imposed upon his image a hieratic symmetry made all the more powerful because of the uncanny intrusion of the angels' perfect, reflected identity into a world which, however abstract it might be in its own terms, is still – as an expressive correlate of the virtual plane – a world of space, light and palpable form.[4]

In Gombrich's third example, Benozzo Gozzoli's *Martyrdom of St. Sebastian*, a vertical axis is again dramatically and symbolically dominant. An arrow-riddled St. Sebastian stands atop a pedestal occupying the terrestrial half of an axis extending from bottom to top, most of whose upper half is the radius for a semicircle filled with seraphim symmetrically arrayed about Christ and the Virgin Mary. Beneath this semicircle, the angels holding the crown of martyrdom over St. Sebastian's head are treated in the same way in which Piero treated his angels or the anonymous Duecento painter treated his two saints. Both angels on either side mirror, with only the slightest variations, their counterpart; and all four could have been made (and probably were made) as Piero's angels were, by simply reversing a single cartoon on either side of the central axis.

It is beneath the calm, nearly frontal head of St. Sebastian that hieratic order ceases to govern and is replaced by a relative formal complexity analogous to the visual complexity of the real world, the world of his bodily suffering. In this lower realm Gombrich notes a new kind of formal arrangement, closely related to the earlier images in that the vertical axis is still the paramount principle of the composition but different from them in that it is made to imply three-dimensional forms rather than two-dimensional shapes. The two pendant archers on the extreme right and left – the "same" figure as regards their position on the plane with respect to the central vertical axis – are shown in the same posture, but turned through 180 degrees. The objection that a right-handed archer can only be shown at his work in a small number of ways is more than adequately met by the next example, Pollaiuolo's *Martyrdom of St. Sebastian*, painted some nine years later. Pollaiuolo has taken the opportunity afforded by a number of nearly identical figures to play what is obviously a highly conscious game of formal manipulation, the implications and relations of which this paper will trace.

In Pollaiuolo's *Martyrdom of St. Sebastian*, the right and left foreground archers – very similar to Benozzo Gozzoli's – are also semicircular rotations of a single figure; but if the relationship of these two archers to earlier procedures of creating hieratic symmetry by the reversal of a single pattern seems at first to be distant, in fact it is close. Seen as two-dimensional shapes the archers are nearly identical and could have been created by reversing a single cartoon, if only the outline were transferred. Since it is not possible to tell from which side a pure silhouette is seen, Pollaiuolo could distinguish each shape as front and back merely by filling in the outline with the appropriate details. This simple 180-degree rotation of a single figure based on the community of two-dimensional shape had the advantage of satisfying the demands of the surface of the painting, and bilateral symmetry still commands the position of the figures just as it did in the earliest of our examples, the Panzano *Madonna and Child*. At the same time, consistent with more modern aims, it provided a well defined format within which problems of foreshortening could be solved, or, beyond this, within which facility in foreshortening could be displayed.

The three-dimensional implications of the repetition of a single figure are extended in the third archer in the right background; for while this figure is substantially identical with the two archers in the left and right foreground, it could not have been made by the same mechanical means and would have required either a sculptural model or an extraordinarily developed spatial imagination.[5] The two figures bending over their crossbows in the center foreground should dispel any doubt that Pollaiuolo was aware of what we have described, or that he was aware of it in about the same terms. These two figures, strongly foreshortened, and not reducible to flat shape, as are the figures flanking them, are not-quite-precise 180-degree reversals of one another.[6]

Like their brothers farther to the left and right, these bending archers are still reversed by rotation with respect to the central axis, which has itself, like the figures it governs, become more active in the third dimension, at the same time remaining consistent with its traditional two-dimensional role. In Piero's *Madonna del Parto* a certain ambiguity was apparent in the role of the central axis. It was no longer governed solely by the surface as it had been in the Panzano *Madonna*. This ambivalence is still more clearly developed in Pollaiuolo's *Martyrdom of St. Sebastian* – the central axis now functions visually as the line on either side of which shapes are arranged, and at the same time fixes the central point of a circle projected on the ground plane from which the trunk to which Sebastian is bound rises, and around which the three-dimensional forms of the four standing archers can be seen to revolve. In its two capacities the axis now commands pictorial order in two and in three dimensions. Two-dimensional hieratic symmetry, by a simple, visible process, has thus been translated into what will be called *three-dimensional symmetry.*[7] Forms in virtual space may now be ordered with the same clarity as two-dimensional shapes and may be ordered in such a way by formal means clearly related to traditional pictorial organization.

To summarize, hieratic symmetry began to undergo the change described in the preceding paragraphs when a virtual coordinate plane – a third dimension – was added to the system for which symmetry had been a principal organizing force. The new three-dimensional symmetry existed alongside its parent; but even though there are many examples of constitutive symmetry in Renaissance painting after the changes just described had taken place, the inherent two-dimensionality of symmetry numbered its days, at the same time that it passed on certain characteristics to the first perfection of the new modes of visual order. On the level of correlative meaning there is also a change. The abstract identity of bilateral symmetrical figures has become concrete identity, that is, three-dimensionally symmetrical forms are nothing more than the same figure seen simultaneously from different points of view. Taken together, two or more such forms body forth a reality equivalent to sculpture. This was true in a theoretical but also in a simple practical sense. It has already been noted that three-dimensional models would have been necessary to draw the two archers loading their cross-bows in Pollaiuolo's *St. Sebastian*, and sculpture in fact played an integral part in the beginnings of three-dimensional symmetry.

At the very end of *De Statua* Alberti states in perhaps the barest geometrical terms possible the relation of drawn contour to three-dimensional form. The passage contains clear recollections of the famous story of the invention of painting from the tracing of shadows, but the tale has been greatly abstracted and, more than that, brought into the context of the geometry of vision.

> It is also very important to understand how we observe the outlines of the body by sections. For, if someone cuts an upright cylinder so that the part you can see is divided from the part you cannot see from the same position, two bodies are made out of this cylinder, though their base remains equal and the same, and they are still contained in four lines and circles. The same is true of our observations by sections of the body. There is the outline at which the surface we see from a particular viewpoint ends and is separated from the other we cannot see by virtue of the part that stands between; and this outline, if it were done properly on a wall, would produce a figure exactly like the one a shadow would make by interception of light, if the source of light were placed at the same point in space where the eye of the observer had been before. But this theory of observing sections and outlines is more a matter for the painter than the sculptor.[8]

That Alberti ended his treatise on sculpture with observations about three-dimensional forms of more use to painters than sculptors should not surprise us, and it indicates that the inextricable and essential union of painting and sculpture was at the heart of the Tuscan tradition of painting and its accompanying theory. The most succinct restatement of Alberti's argument – or demonstration – is to be found in Leonardo's *paragone* notes, now turned to the purpose of proving the superiority of painting over sculpture. Leonardo wrote simply that two points of view, diametrically opposed, were sufficient to make all of a sculpture visible;[9] these points of view would meet – ideally speaking – in a single contour. The painter, by showing this contour twice, was able to show us everything that sculpture was able to show us and – so the argument runs – could show it to us in the same moment, an achievement sculpture could not hope to equal. In this way the arguments of Alberti and Leonardo turned a single attitude toward vision and form to two different purposes. If such arguments seem like mere humanist gimcrackery, it must also be admitted that they had practical consequences, as we shall see in many instances. It should be noted too that the stress on contour running through all these ideas is perfectly consistent with the ancient and still living practice of reversing cartoons. Pollaiuolo adapted long-established shop procedures to the study of sculpture (or of three-dimensional forms understood sculpturally), and the equivalent of sculpture resulted from the manipulation of forms first clearly evident in his *St. Sebastian*. It is important to stress again that Pollaiuolo, in turning to sculpture, remained wholly within the Florentine tradition: Alberti recommended that artists learn from sculpture and Vasari wrote that the formulation of the *terza maniera* was the immediate result of such study.[10] The basic critical category of *rilievo* was also metaphorically dependent upon the art of sculpture and was certainly rooted in the evident intention of Florentine painters to realize the illusion of sculptural reality – it would not be an exaggeration to say that of all practical critical standards, *rilievo* was the *sine qua non* for Central Italian painting for at least two hundred years.[11] On the other hand, the achievement of the illusion of three dimensions in painting had a dialectical sister in the equally prevalent notion that sculpture was prismatic, made up of a definite number of aspects, and therefore, in that its very definition involved fixed points of view, was a kind of multiple painting.[12]

Pollaiuolo's study of the problems of representing three-dimensional forms by such means was recorded and clearly elaborated by Albrecht Dürer. Panofsky noted that two figures in a copy by Dürer of a drawing for a Rape of the Sabines by Pollaiuolo are in fact a single figure.[13] In this case, the second Sabine-bearing nude was made, not by reversing a single outline pattern, as Pollaiuolo himself might have done in the outer arches of the National Gallery *St. Sebastian* or his engraving of *Nude Men Fighting*, but rather by transferring the contour without reversing it, as if to repeat figures in a frieze moving from left to right. Accordingly the two figures are not identical, since only reversal of the pattern creates the equivalent of moving around a single three-dimensional form; but the primacy of contour and the practice of beginning to realize figures from contour is clearly evident. Pollaiuolo, in Panofsky's words, "provided only an outline which Dürer filled with plastic volume and functional energy."[14] Clearly, this contour was the basic element of the invention, and Dürer completed it with details which defined it as seen from one side or the other. Dürer used a similar contour, also apparently derived from Pollaiuolo, which he developed from two points of view in his only mythological painting, *Hercules Killing the Stymphalian Birds* (1500), and in a design for another classical theme, a woodcut of *Apollo and Daphne* printed in 1502.[15] Panofsky has convincingly argued that Dürer got his figures from Pollaiuolo and that he did not directly know their classical source, statues or reliefs of *Hercules and the Erymanthean Boar*.[16] At any rate, the important point is that these figures unquestionably had their origins in the study of sculpture, and it seems likely that Dürer thought that in studying Pollaiuolo's drawings he was in some way or another studying classical sculpture.[17] In 1494 Dürer drew a *Death of Orpheus*, following the model of a Mantegnesque engraving. In the central figure of Orpheus the allusion to classical sculptures of fallen warriors is clear, and the degree of its spatial complexity compares favorably with Pollaiuolo's foreshortened central bowmen in the *Martyrdom of St. Sebastian*. The women flanking Orpheus on either side are precise repetitions of one another, and a kind of disguised but visually operant symmetry is created by these two figures. In the quotation from classical form in the Orpheus and the creation of the equivalent of sculpture in the two women, a whole meditation upon the theme of sculpture, consistent in character with Pollaiuolo's transmission of classical sculpture to Dürer, is carried through.

Like pictorial relief, *figure come fratelli* are possible only in the context of a specific understanding of the relations between painting and sculpture. As we have noted, the critical blurring of the distinction between the two arts found pointed expression in the *paragone* dispute, illustrations for which comprise a special strain of three-dimensionally symmetrical figures.[18] The quarrel over the relative importance of the two arts of painting and sculpture seems mostly to be regarded by modern scholars as a dusty, inconsequential skirmish on the borders of the real history of Italian Renaissance art. But however much it may have been an intellectual game, and however quickly its moves and rules may be mastered, the contest was often joined with real passion, sometimes cresting in near-violence. Artists of the first rank joined the fray. Giorgione, in order to counter the boasting of certain sculptors, is supposed to have painted a St. George standing next to a clear pool in which he was reflected. Behind him on either side were mirrors which showed his back. Giorgione, as Paolo Pino recounts the story, thought he had routed his opponents not only by showing a single figure from several points of view, thus equalling sculpture, but also, by making these several views visible from a single vantage point, argued that he had surpassed the possibilities of sculpture.[19] As is well known, Leonardo da Vinci considered the question of the *paragone* at length, partly with the intention of establishing his art among the liberal arts, but also for its own sake as a theoretical question that seems to have had an urgency for him that surprises us now.[20] After its major florescence in the early Cinquecento, the dispute died down, to be rekindled nearly fifty years later by Benedetto Varchi, who polled a number of Florentine artists on the matter and himself penned a lengthy consideration of the various issues involved.[21] Michelangelo responded to Varchi's *inchiesta* with a short-tempered reply apparently favoring sculpture, although he does not seem to have felt deeply enough about the question to have refused to supply Daniele da Volterra with a design for a painting of David and Goliath, which, showing the same group on both sides of a single panel, presumably illustrated the ability of painting to equal sculpture.[22]

Three-dimensionally symmetrical figures were at all times a display of artistic skill, a *difficultà*, which, like *figure serpentinate, chiaroscuro*, counterposed color, foreshortening or *rilievo*, was understood and repeated as conscious pictorial embellishment. There was, moreover, an important textual precedent for the inclusion of such figures among the *difficultà* related to the all-important *disegno, rilievo* and *scorci*. Pliny describes a Hercules seen from behind, thought to be by the hand of Apelles, drawn in such a way that, "a most difficult thing, the picture seems not only to suggest, but actually to give the face" (. . . quod est difficilimum, faciem eius ostendat verius pictura quam promittat).[23] In the Renaissance mind this passage must have been connected immediately with Pliny's characterization of the masterly drawing of Parrhasios of Ephesos, which had so many echoes in Renaissance art theory and was particularly applied to *tour de force* drawing. "For the outline ought to round itself off and establish such limits that it suggests other things behind it and reveals even what it hides" (Ambire enim se ipsa debet extremitas et sic desinere ut promittat alia post se ostendatque etiam quae occultat).[24] Three-dimensionally symmetrical figures of course displayed all they promised, and the emphasis on contour in relation to the description of three-dimensional form, as well as the definition of skill in such terms, relates them to the lost marvels of painting recorded by Pliny.

Now *figure come fratelli* could be worked up as a particular mode of pictorial embellishment or turned to the ends of the *paragone* debate; one way or the other these figures, simultaneously visible front and back, were instances of *contrapposto*, in themselves a major means to the achievement of *varietà*.[25] Juxta-position of figures front and back was common in composition and decoration, and figures so arranged were of course not *figure come fratelli* unless they clearly repeated a single posture. So Titian wrote to Phillip II that "because the Danae, previously sent to your majesty, had appeared entirely from the front, I wished [in the present Venus and Adonis] to show the opposite side, to the end that the chamber where [these pictures] will hang, may became more delightful to see."[26] *Contrapposto* thus fulfilled the universal demands of *varietà*, although it did not necessarily meet the definition of *figure come fratelli*. Certainly the two themes reinforced one another, and it is sometimes hard to distinguish them. Three-dimensionally symmetrical figures not only satisfied the psychological requirements of *varietà*, but also touched upon the implicit perceptual basis of Renaissance painting and sculpture, while at the same time giving evidence of artifice and clear separation from observable nature. One of the interlocutors in Giovanni Andrea Gilio's *Degli errori dei pittori* – a defender of the *maniera* – cites a painting deriving from the tradition of Giorgione's *paragone* painting which is, equally, a *contrapposto*, both works being linked to the *ingegno* of the artist understood in the crucial sense not of natural talent, but of personal invention apart from imitation.

> Truly, the imagination (*ingegno*) of man is great, and all the more so when, with charming and beautiful inventions (*vaghe e belle invenzioni*), men sometimes do

with art what nature is not able herself to do. And to this point I understand that a panel – or canvas – was taken to Francis, the king of France, in which an armed man was to be seen that showed his whole back; and the prudent and ingenious artist wishing to show also the front part, not being able to do so, charmingly painted a mirror in his hand, in which he showed his face, with his chest and all the rest, with so much charm (*vaghezza*) that that generous king paid many hundreds of *scudi* for that figure.[27]

The appearance together in this passage of artificial (*varietà*, *contrapposto*) and theoretical (*paragone*) concerns is entirely consistent and indicates an intersection of complementary intentions often met in practice. The most powerful fusion of *contrapposto*, its structure accommodated to the demands of colossal narrative, with reinforcing sculptural meaning is Michelangelo's *Creation of the Sun and Moon* on the Sistine Ceiling. The impact of the image is multiplied by the altered but identical foreshortened form, coming and going, which states God's wholeness and the completeness of his power conceived as physical power. The conditions of his eidetic physical plenitude are the conditions of the inevitable sequence of his acts; at the same time the fresco should also be regarded as a visible expression of *ingegno*.

The formal theme of *contrapposto* turned to entirely different expressive ends, this time linked to conceptual antithesis in strict analogy to the embellishment of poetry, also underlies the Medici Chapel *Day* and *Night*. Here, of course, we are dealing with sculpture, but the figures are similar enough to be more than *contrapposti* and raise the question of identity implicit in three-dimensionally symmetrical figures. Riegl remarked that Michelangelo's figures of *Night* and *Day*, although bound by almost identical contours, were exact reversals of one another, and that this resulted in a feeling of rotation: it appears, he wrote, that *Day* recedes and *Night* comes forward.[28] Riegl's description precisely coincides with the conditions of simple three-dimensional symmetry, if the sense of rotation in the viewer is replaced by the imaginary rotation of the figures themselves through 180 degrees. To *contrapposto* is thus added implied identity, and in this regard Condivi's praise of (and, presumably, Michelangelo's pride in) the Times of Day becomes most interesting. "Although all [the allegories] were of one intention and form, nonetheless the figures are all different, and in different movements and actions." For our purposes we may restate this remark as follows: although both are times of day, and therefore in a certain sense identical, both *Day* and *Night* are as different as they can be while still maintaining visible identity.[29] The figures are, in other words, symmetrical, but inherent in their symmetry is the inescapable physicality of the stone out of which they are oppositely carved. As *Day* and *Night* are time, their allegorical representations are one; and the conditions of their polar opposition are the conditions of their identity.

With the advent of the *terza maniera*, bilateral symmetry took its place among a number of formal devices of the same degree of clarity, and, perhaps more important, continued to act as a defining norm for other kinds of formal relations which approached the rightness of symmetry without actually achieving it. Albertinelli's *Crucifixion*, in the Certosa outside Florence, still displays at the top angels only slightly inflected from simple mirror symmetry; but for the most part such one-to-one relations are concealed in the interests of *varietà*, the whole of a painting tending toward an adjustment of forms and shapes unique to each composition. Nevertheless, bilateral symmetry was essential at several levels of pictorial construction, and traditional hieratic symmetry finds a place in the upper part of Raphael's last Florentine work, the *Madonna del Baldacchino*.[30] Symmetrical angels, again only slightly inflected from a single pattern, take up their anticipated positions in a strongly symmetrical governing structure, whose parts have been carefully varied.

That the visual order so splendidly realized in Raphael's *Disputa* and the *School of Athens* is dependent upon norms of planarity, axiality and symmetry hardly needs repeating. Raphael also developed and elaborated, together with bilateral symmetry, three-dimensional symmetry, with an understanding and degree of clarity not approached by other Renaissance artists.[31] The upper portion of the San Severo *Trinity*, for instance, is an essay in multiplied three-dimensional symmetry. The angels flanking Christ are, excepting the permissible variation of the heads, three-dimensionally symmetrical, one figure being the other turned through 90 degrees, so that they cannot be seen as symmetrical shapes, even though they occur in a hieratic circumstance in which one would expect to find such surface symmetry. The putto on the left echoes the angel below. His counterpart on the right – damaged, but surviving sufficiently to preserve the point – is turned through 90 degrees also, but in the opposite direction, into the space, so that he faces dead opposite the angel below him. Thus, all possibilities of location are included except the thematically irrelevant option of looking away from the main figures. In the three putti above the head of the Farnesina *Galatea* Raphael used a related device, three-dimensional symmetry about the vertical axis, reminiscent of that used in Pollaiuolo's *Martyrdom of St. Sebastian*. Such symmetry is also evident in the angels closing either upper corner of the fresco of the *Sibyls* in Sta. Maria della Pace. This composition is clearly the result of a most intensely abstract study of the possibilities of organizing three-dimensional forms around a normative central axis and within the stricture of a carefully exploited plane. As Raphael repeatedly used this new mode of achieving symmetry-like clarity in the relation of three-dimensional forms, the formula of exact opposition of front and back softened and varied, functioning, like bilateral symmetry, as a visual norm which strictly governs but is not itself apparent, as it had been obviously apparent in Pollaiuolo's bowmen. In the Sta. Maria della Pace *Sibyls* not one figure in a rigorously symmetrical composition conforms exactly to its counterpart, but rather answers it in size, posture (which can be read as planar shape) and relative harmony of parts; the major forms also tend toward, but are inflected with respect to, a pure three-dimensional symmetry that is most closely approached in the flanking angels. The two seated angels atop the arch are not just nearly symmetrical in two dimensions as shapes – they are, correspondingly, very nearly rotations of the same form through 180 degrees. As we have seen, such simple rotation is the kind of three-dimensional symmetry most responsive to the plane, since it is the repetition of a single shape. The equivalence implied by mirror symmetry diminishes as the arch descends on either side. At the extreme, the angels with scrolls close the composition if it is read as a progression across the wall and complete a rotation around the central axis in three dimensions, adding the implied sequentiality of passage in space, and therefore in time, over prismatically conceived sculptural form.

Perhaps complete organization of represented forms in two and three dimensions was most purely realized by Raphael in the lunette of the *Virtues* in the Stanza della Segnatura (fig. 22.2). A shallow pyramidal dais, clearly stepping up and into depth to the profiled figure of *Prudence*, provides the basis for two- and three-dimensional order. The rhythm across the surface of small and large shapes, the putti and the allegories, the syncopation of the series and the reversal of the putti between *Fortitude* and *Prudence*, is finally unified by the three-dimensionality of the flanking virtues. The rotation of these two lower virtues is more freely inflected than in any example of such organization previously considered. *Prudence*, whose profile echoes the plane and closes the recession into depth, is herself not much different in form from her sister virtues. A remarkable

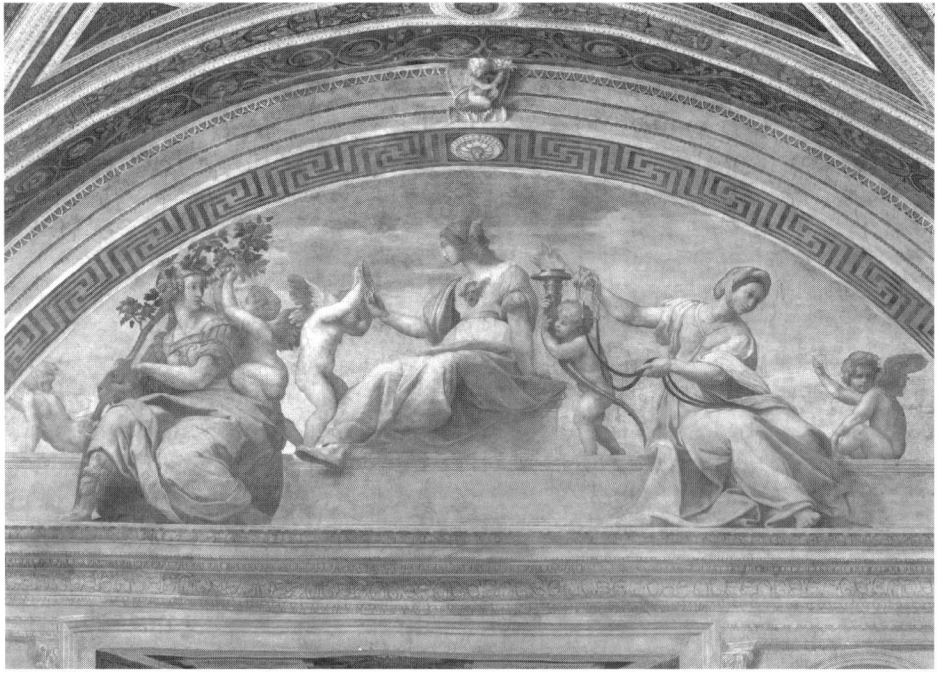

Figure 22.2 Raphael, *Cardinal Virtues*. Vatican, Stanza della Segnatura. © 1990, Photo Scala, Florence.

balance is achieved between freedom and the salience and apparent pervasiveness of normative visual elements.

The sequential symmetry and identity of Raphael's *Virtues* are not empty categories and suggest that the results of a formal description of Raphael's paintings are more than simply formal. The relationships described, to the extent that intentional formal harmony is in itself meaningful, bear meaning. But, more important, the identity implied by repetition is wedded to significance. The *Virtues* as depicted are irrefragably beings of the same kind, and this equality is as economically stated by their symmetry in three dimensions as the equality of Peter and Paul was stated in two dimensions in the San Panzano panel.

It was argued earlier that the connection between bilateral symmetry, three-dimensional symmetry and sculpture is identity. The identity of figures repeated in a single painting is comparable to the three-dimensionality of sculpture prismatically conceived, inasmuch as the facets of a sculpture (since they all belong to the same figure) are in an obvious sense identical with, although at the same time different from, one another, difference being determined by point of view and by the composition of the figure itself. A clear and simple example of such identity in repetition is Leonardo's analytical method of showing the parts of the body from three or four cardinal points of view.[32] As we have seen, hieratic symmetry provides the possibility of stating identity within minimal conditions of difference. And insofar as it states identity, symmetry may be significant in itself: we noted in the discussion of the Panzano *Madonna and Saints* that the symmetry of Peter and Paul implied equivalence. Weyl cites the example of a Byzantine paten bearing a representation of the Eucharist in which Christ is shown twice, stemming symmetrically from the central axis, on one side giving bread and, on the other side, wine, to the disciples. As Weyl notes, symmetry in this case is more than formal, and the basis of its significance is once again identity. This possible significance was not forgotten by artists of the High Renaissance.[33]

When Michelangelo in 1516 designed the *Flagellation* for Sebastiano Veneziano's Borgherini Chapel, at the same time that he subjected his figures to a degree of formal sublimation only equalled by the Palazzo Vecchio *Victory* and the *Resurrection* drawings of the late '20s and early '30s, he used three-dimensional symmetry. The theme of the *Flagellation* was traditionally treated more or less symmetrically, often with two figures flanking the central figure of Christ at the column. Michelangelo varied this pattern and at the same time produced its equivalent: he turned the figure on the left through 90 degrees in order to make the figure on the right (or vice versa). The result is in an abstract sense symmetrical, but, once again, only if the three-dimensionality of the forms is given. Thus *varietà* is achieved by the introduction of diagrammatically clear three-dimensional order as an element in the composition. Once the identity of the figures is recognized, a continuity is also evident which gives the group a grace of movement less evident in the movement of the shapes in two dimensions. Three-dimensional sequence has become a kind of dance.[34]

Such organization was not characteristic of Michelangelo. The skeleton of the Sistine Chapel is governed throughout its major compositional and decorative elements by strict bilateral symmetry, and it seems to have been mostly through the school of Raphael that three-dimensionally symmetrical figures became part of the stock-in-trade of Cinquecento decoration. As a fully developed example of such a construction from the school of Raphael, we might consider Giulio Romano's scroll-bearing figures above allegories flanking St. Peter and the portrait of Leo X as Clement I in the Sala di Costantino: all four figures are symmetrical in a pattern ABBA, as well as three-dimensionally symmetrical in pairs. Here, the organization is baldly evident, lacking the careful inflections we have seen Raphael himself give to similar groups of figures.

If the formal development of three-dimensional symmetry was most consistently explored by Raphael, its capacity for significance was also most clearly understood by him: almost contemporary with Michelangelo's cartoon for Sebastiano, and of an even greater purity of abstraction, was the *St. Michael* painted for Francis I. This painting, one of the most mysteriously beautiful of the Cinquecento, and, like Michelangelo's *Flagellation*, a kind of epitome of the definition of the *maniera*, can be better understood in the context of form and meaning under discussion here. The frankly decorative energies of the centrifugally inflected swastika of St. Michael's arms and drapery – recalling the angels in the *Madonna del Baldacchino* – are identified with the archangel's weightless action and its silent effects. With a degree of clarity comparable to this decorative swastika the vertical axis, pronounced by the format of the canvas itself, supports, abstracts and lends inevitability to suspended movement. The union of virtual physical form with perspicuous formal devices gives the painting much of its transcendental quality. Once again a kind of uncanniness is achieved by the introduction of artificial repetition and regularity into a recognizably "real" landscape world. A similarly abstract purity extends into the third dimension. St. Michael stands flush in the plane, as already noted, along the full length of the central axis, about which the limbs and movement of his body organize themselves. This clear insistency upon the two-dimensional plane is precisely mirrored by the conceptually pure statement of the virtual coordinate (three-dimensional) plane. The figure of the saint is repeated in the figure of the devil, which, if compared limb for limb and movement for movement with the figure above him, is the same. Only the attributes differ, the horrid wings and contorted face of the Evil One dialectically mirroring the radiant, ideal face of the archangel. The fact that a plane projected in three dimensions rises as it recedes provides the necessity for foreshortening and the opportunity for a display of the ability to cast one figure along two axes. But more important, and more closely bound to the significance of the image, is the identity of the archangel and the fallen angel implied by the formal equivalence of the axes along which they are cast, and by their only slightly inflected three-dimensional identity. Once the three-dimensional clarity of the basic composition becomes apparent, then the whole image is seen to partake of formal and decorative energies of the same kind. The arms of St. Michael are organized in both two and three dimensions about the pivotal face. St. Michael and the Devil are the same figure by the very conditions of their visibility, yet by those same conditions – the absolute perpendicularity of their informing coordinates – they are eternally separated from one another, meeting only at the junction of the two planes. A clear and irresolvable mystery is created, stated in terms of a rich interplay of reinforcing structures of form and meaning, similar to that evident in Michelangelo's allegories of Day and Night.[35]

The painter who understood most clearly the nature of these compositions was Jacopo Pontormo. Already in the *St. Veronica* of 1514 he replaced the customarily hieratically symmetrical angels with three-dimensionally symmetrical ones. His lunette at Poggio a Caiano, if not an essay in three-dimensional organization of the kind we are considering here, is an exercise in formal manipulation of the same degree of self-consciousness.[36] In the Pitti version of his *Martyrdom of the Ten Thousand*, organization of a geometrically or decoratively describable kind is once again dominant. The isolated composition of crucified figures in the upper right hand corner of the painting, reminiscent of Michelangelo's Cascina cartoon or of the discrete, episodic compositions of the Sistine Ceiling *Deluge*, is perhaps the most complex essay in three-dimensional symmetry in all Renaissance painting (fig. 22.3). Since the similarity of nude, crucified men was given (and Pontormo made no attempt to distinguish them) he turned them as if they were a single figure, which he repeated with numerous spatial variations in a composition that is closed at the bottom and side. As if the schematic purity of the result were not clearly enough stated by the polished order of the figures themselves, Pontormo precisely and regularly punctuated the series with faces at waist height.[37]

In the context of such formal manipulation, one of Pontormo's great anti-classical works of the late 1520s, the Carmignano *Visitation*, can be more fully understood and can be seen to belong to the same order of images as Raphael's *St. Michael*, to which it is remarkably similar in its significant formal aspects. Once again there is pronounced verticality. Pontormo created this verticality not, as did Raphael in the *St. Michael*, by extending his figures along a central axis whose visual salience is amplified by the shape of the painting itself, but by allowing his figures to multiply fully equivalent vertical axes. In Pontormo's *Visitation* (as in the group of crucified figures in the *Martyrdom of the Ten Thousand* considered as a composition in itself) there is no central axis. But the primacy of the plane in both the *Visitation* and the *St. Michael*, implicit in the clear maintenance of the axes and explicit in the treatment of the figures – which in both paintings press close to the plane and extend nearly the whole length of the surface – marks the two compositions as variations on the same basic elements. Pontormo's Mary and Elizabeth in fact move flush along the plane, sustained by their plumb vertical axes and subjected to formal sublimation of a

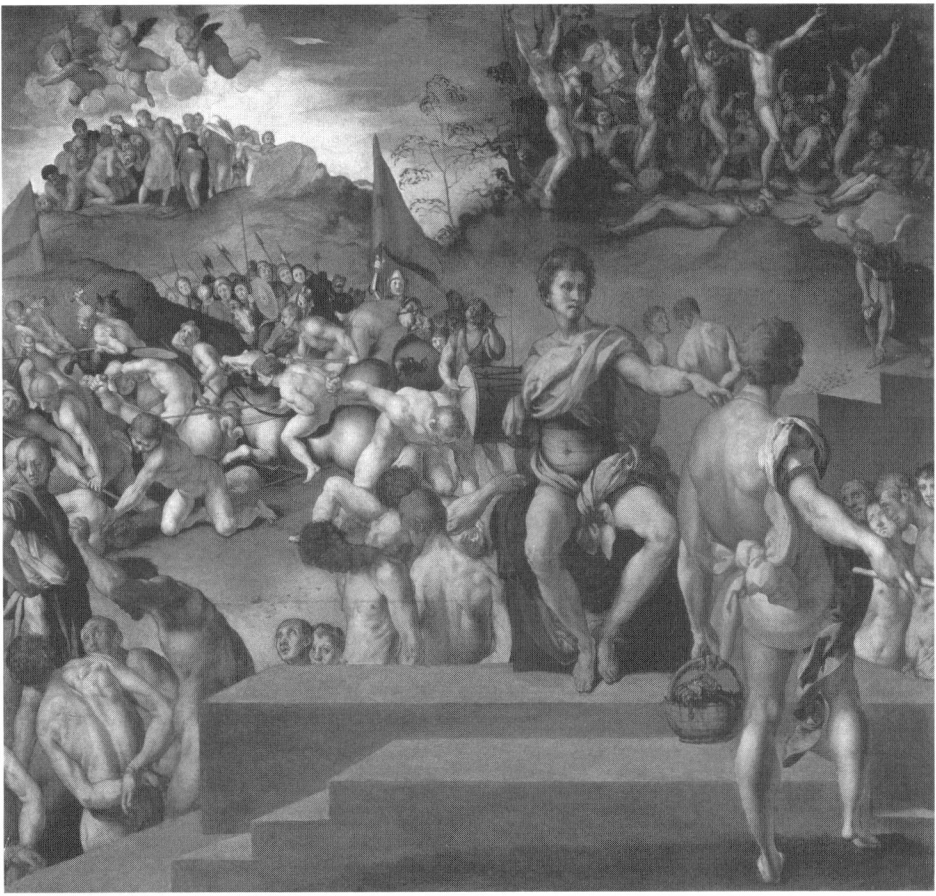

Figure 22.3 Pontormo, *Martyrdom of the Ten Thousand* (detail). Florence, Pitti Palace. AKG-images / Rabatti – Domingie.

degree consistent with the preservation of the visual force of these axes. The figures are also determined by the plane in being shown in pure profile; this sets them in the starkest possible opposition to similar but full-face figures, which seem to advance along vertical planes perpendicular to the picture plane itself. These figures in the coordinate dimension of the painting are not precisely identical to those in the plane, as was the case in Raphael's *St. Michael*; but they are strikingly – even hauntingly – close variations. Pontormo, like Piero della Francesca or Raphael before him, has allowed organizational elements signifying equivalence not merely to have a place in, but to be an essential part of, what is ostensibly an image of the real world. The result is an uncanniness (heightened, of course, by the complementary characteristics of the image) which results from the occurrence, in a recognizably real world made up of forms situated in space and light, of ordering elements possessing manifestly artificial regularity and clarity. Pontormo has shown us the same event twice at one viewing, an image of impossible equivalence. As had always been implicit in the traditional use of similar hieratic symmetry – from which the kind of visual order we are discussing had its rise and to which it remained essentially related – absolute equivalence is a mode of the transcendent and the artificial, not of the real. By the time in which Pontormo painted, all images were understood to be defined by point of view; and only painting, the art which made possible the fullest description of the world from a point in space and time, could transcend this temporal horizon to possess the whole concrete object, unfaceted by accidents of time and place.[38]

We may carry the implications of this argument further. One-point perspective involved a fixed point of view as to height and distance, and prismatic sculpture implied a sequence of similarly fixed viewpoints: the sculpture was assumed to cohere at the center of a number of radii which controlled point of view. Taking this notion of sculpture as a model, the time in which the sculpture is seen is understood as a series of views, all of which are congruent, but whose object differs (unless the object were the same on all side – a line, column, cone or sphere developed with respect to a central axis). According to such an understanding of sequence, timelessness is only possible as a series of identical objects of vision, tantamount to stasis. This is to say nothing more than that perspective painting and prismatic sculpture – the latter developed in the direction of maximum variety, which reinforced its temporal potential by distinguishing ever more strongly the moments comprising the sequence of views – are based upon assumptions about the kind of perception to be shaped by art which are similar to those underlying central planning. In the case of architecture, the centrality of the viewer and the equivalence of the segments of vision within the circumscribed plan (as well as the prismatic treatment of the exterior of the building) created an image of eternity not only in symbolic but also in concrete perceptual terms.

With these clarifications in mind we may return to our consideration of painting and begin to gather some general conclusions about the nature of Renaissance images. It is often noted that Renaissance painting placed divine personages in real space, or in the same space in which all other things were also shown. This change had constitutively important consequences not only for the general significance of religious images and their meaning but for the formal tradition of conceptual imagery, of which symmetry and its attendant planarity and axiality were mainstays. Perspective created the problem of making divine personages visible from a point of view, by the conditions of their visibility calling into question their divine identity (again, only a small number of perfect forms were self-identical in this sense) and denying the transcendent wholeness which a planar statement of images had clearly manifested. In that three-dimensional symmetry showed all of a form at once – responding to a sense of the tangible (as the real) – one might argue that it was truly transitional between old and new meanings, preserving the visibility of wholeness of conceptual images in the context of all-inclusive illusion. Interestingly, when a contemporary religious writer addressed this problem, he did it precisely in the terms discussed here.

> An intervening object does not impede the vision of the blessed . . . If Christ, even though himself in heaven after his ascension, saw his dear mother still on earth and at prayer in her chamber, clearly distance and the interposition of a wall does not hinder their vision. The same is true when an object's face is turned away from the viewer so that an opaque body intervenes . . . Christ could see the face of his mother when she was prostrate on the ground . . . as if he were looking directly at her face. It is clear that the blessed can see the front of an object from the back, the face through the back of the head.[39]

With Raphael's *St. Michael* and Pontormo's Carmignano *Visitation* pictorial organization formally comparable to hieratic symmetry, and similar in its economy of means and relation to meaning, is once again evident. But now it is based on the introduction of a virtual coordinate plane, which, as the formal condition of the pursuit of the reality of sculpture in painting, intervened between these paintings and their earliest antecedents, fundamentally changing the order and the significance of the order informing them. Such expressive use of three-dimensional symmetry was confined to the early mannerist period, developing a form invented in the years immediately preceding. The invention of the theme of the repeated figure – closely linked to sculpture as it was – provided a set problem through which problems of spatial representation, and especially fore-shortening, could be mastered and this mastery displayed. It is important to stress that the development had little to do with perspective, being concerned with figures and not with the relations among them; rather, *figure come fratelli* should be regarded as adjunct to perspective as a means of ordered construction in three dimensions, solving a different problem arising from the same impulse to complete spatial realization of images. It was finally the force of the general development of the spatial imagination itself which led to the abandonment of forms whose ancestry in parent two-dimensional symmetry was obvious. The destruction of symmetry was thus carried out on various fronts, and after the Renaissance bilateral symmetry ceased to have the widespread and apparently unconscious necessity it had had in earlier periods of European art.

The preceding development may be viewed as a rather simple variation within a confined range of artistic practice and concern. Bilateral symmetry, however, occupies a special position in the history of images, and since it has governed so many of them, any structural modifications in its workings are of great import-ance. In the case of the art of the Renaissance this transformation is, I think, unusually significant, since the Renaissance – and especially the High Renaissance – formulated the modern notion of pictorial composition. In Raphael's *School of Athens* or Leonardo's *Last Supper* bilateral symmetry is the basis of a per-vasive order, the character of which is now no longer objective – in the sense that symmetry had been considered proper to the image itself – but rather must be understood as subjective – derived from the artist – and therefore aesthetic.

Once the principle of *giudizio dell'occhio* had been established – and in its broadest sense this idea is the core of Vasari's *terza maniera* – then bilateral symmetry became simply one of a potentially infinite number of aesthetically satisfactory visual orders. When Pontormo painted the San Michele Visdomini altarpiece, for example, he began to work toward a kind of painting in which relationships among parts were not determined by preexisting normative structures – certainly chief among which was bilateral symmetry – but rather by his own *giudizio*. Still, it is important to stress that bilateral symmetry occupied an important position in the development of the idea of visual composition. It was necessary to come to a full aesthetic awareness of symmetry as a principle of pictorial construction in order to pass beyond it to freely derived composition. The artists of the Italian Renaissance subjected symmetry to a kind of critical scrutiny to which it had not been subjected previously, and in this way traditional forms provided the starting point for what, in its consequences, amounted to both a transformation of the visual imagination and a radical change in the relation between image and viewer.

It might finally be argued that there was a direct correlation between the transformation and destruction of symmetry and the increasingly subjective constitution of the art object. The destruction of symmetry – and the advent of purely aesthetically derived composition – is one of the stages in the completion of the change in the relation of object to artist-viewer that is first clearly signalled by one-point perspective. Further, this fact implies that symmetry is not only a way in which things are a reflection of ourselves but also a way in which, at the same time they are similar to us, they are absolutely other than we. Symmetrical things, it might be said, have their own right and left, and these cannot be transformed without the object's losing its integrity. As a simple index of the change toward a completely subjective constitution of the object which we have described, it may be noted that, some time after the Renaissance, the present-day convention emerged of describing works of art in terms, not of the right and left of the image, but rather of our right and left. It may also be that, at the beginning of modern art, when the relation of art object and artist-viewer changed once again, painters such as van Gogh and Cézanne found object and painting to have their own right and left, irreconcilable with the organizing demands of their visions. That is to say simply that they deeply felt the iconic objectness, not only of shoes and apples, but of the painting itself.

Notes

1   P. Barocchi, *Scritti d'arte del Cinquecento*, Bari, 1960, I, p. 642.
2   E. H. Gombrich, *Norm and Form. Studies in the art of the Renaissance*, London, 1965, p. 95.
3   The phrase "in maestà", which may be used to describe any full-face figure quite apart from iconographic significance (see L. Pacioli, *De divina proportione*, ed. C. Winterberg, Vienna, 1889, p. 132; L. Dolce, *L'Aretino*, in P. Barocchi, *Trattati*

d'arte del Cinquecento, Bari, 1960, I, p. 179) recognizes such an overlapping of the formal and iconographic value of frontality.

4   Ibid., p. 95. Gombrich also notes Andrea del Castagno's reversal of cartoons. This is no doubt a venerable means of creating symmetry. Piero's definitions of *disegno* and *commensuratio* (P. della Francesca, *De Prospectiva pingendi*, ed. G. Nicco Fasola, Florence, 1942, p. 63) imply the same preeminence of two-dimensional considerations in the organization of fictive three-dimensional forms apparent in the Monterchi Madonna: "Desegno intendiamo essere profili e contorni che nella cosa se contene. Commensuratio diciamo essere essi profili et contorni proportionalmente posti nei luoghi loro". Repetition of pattern becomes part of a much more subtle *numerositas* in Piero's Arezzo frescoes, as noted by K. Clark, *Piero della Francesca*, London and New York, 1969, p. 46.

The definition of *disegno* as profile or contour, which was widely held, will become more important as the argument unfolds. Michelangelo reversed cartoons throughout the Sistine Ceiling frescoes for his auxiliary decorative figures, the putti-caryatids at the sides of the prophets and sibyls and the reclining bronze figures above the spandrels. He also used this procedure in the facing *ignudi* flanking the first history, the *Drunkenness of Noah*, creating a kind of opposition by subjecting both figures from the same cartoon to light from a single source. He quickly abandoned this device for the more complex *contrarietà* of the remainder of the series of *ignudi*.

5   E. H. Gombrich, *Art and Illusion*, Princeton, 1969, pp. 153–4, has also suggested that the many dogs in Paolo Uccello's *Hunt* in Oxford were drawn by turning a single model. It seems reasonable to suppose that sculptural models were used by many Quattrocento painters, and their use becomes more evidently likely as artists addressed themselves to more and more complex figural problems. A *Trinity with Saints* by Filippo Lippi and Pesellino in the National Gallery, London, from around 1455–60, displays angels rotated around the central vertical axis about 30° with respect to the picture plane. Repetition of the angels as shapes is minimized where rotation is not governed by the picture plane. In this case the use of a three-dimensional model seems necessary. It is interesting to note here that the painters must have thought of two views of a single figure as equivalent to the traditional hieratic symmetry of flanking angels. Leonardo's Vatican *St. Jerome* is repeated in a drawing in Windsor Castle (K. Clark and C. Pedretti, *The Drawings of Leonardo da Vinci in the Collection of Her Majesty the Queen at Windsor Castle*, London, 1969, II, 12571 recto), suggesting a three-dimensional model common to painting and drawing. See also F. Hartt, *Giulio Romano*, New Haven, 1958, pp. 53–54, where it is noted that the *Holy Family* called "La Perla" in the Prado and the *Madonna della Gatta* in Naples were drawn from a single model turned through about 45°.

6   The derivation from Pollaiuolo of Michael Pacher's use of a precisely similar group in his *Attempted Stoning of Christ* for the Wolfgang Altar, dated 1481, is remarked by N. Rasmo, *Michael Pacher*, London, 1971, p. 144.

7   The term "virtual coordinate plane" has been used in order to establish the conditions for the construction of clear relations in three dimensions at a formal level more basic than perspective construction. In this context, the term rotational symmetry has not been used to describe the behavior of virtual three-dimensional forms because their movement is properly rotational only from a position taken

above the virtual plane, which would be an airy perch indeed; to use the term "three-dimensional symmetry" is simpler, and preserves the whole system of visual order. It is sometimes difficult to distinguish such symmetry from the slight inflection for decorative purposes of bilaterally symmetrical figures, where Peter and Paul have opposite legs forward and back; and indeed H. Weyl, *Symmetry*, Princeton, 1952, p. 9, does distinguish between these arrangements and true symmetry. In another example of such decorative practice, a *Madonna Enthroned with Angels* by the Master E. S. (*Die Kupferstiche des Meisters E. S.*, ed. M. Geisberg, Berlin, 1924, T. 64), the putti at the top of the throne holding the curtain are developed point for point in opposition to one another, but it is difficult to imagine that the artist had any further end in view than making a maximum formal variety within the strictures of the format. Whatever other uses three-dimensional symmetry might have had, it was certainly always desirable for its *varietà*. See notes 25 and 26 below.

8 L. B. Alberti, *On Painting and On Sculpture*, ed. and tr. C. Grayson, London, 1972, p. 139.

9 I. A. Richter, *Paragone: A Comparison of the Arts by Leonardo da Vinci*, London, 1949, p. 107. "Dice lo scultore, che non pò fare una figura, che non ne faccia infinite per l'infiniti termini, ch'hanno le quantità continue. Rispondesi, che l'infiniti termini di tal figura si riducono in due mezza figure, cioè una mezza indietro, e l'altra mezza dal mezzo inanzi, le quali sendo ben proporzionate, compongono una figura tonda". See also ibid., p. 98. The primary importance of contour implied by such a view again recalls Pliny's often related story of the invention of painting as the circumscription of shadow (K. Jex-Blake and E. Sellers, *The Elder Pliny's Chapters on the History of Art*, Chicago, 1968, pp. 84–5). This tale is echoed with considerable elaboration by Cellini in his fragment, "Sopra l'arte del Disegno" (*La Vita di Benvenuto Cellini seguita dai Trattati dell'Oreficeria e della Scultura e dagli Scritti sull'arte*, ed. A. J. Rusconi and A. Valeri, Rome, 1901, p. 794). "Noi pigliavamo un uomo giovane di bella fatta, di poi in una camera, dove fussi imgiancato, posto il detto giovane a sedere o ritto con diverse attitudini, con le quali noi potessimo vedere e più difficili scorci; da poi messogli un lume a ragione di dietro non troppo alto, nè basso, nè troppo discosto da lui, lo mettevamo con quella discrezione che ci mostrava il più bello et il più vero. E. veduto quell'ombra che esso faceva nel muro, facendolo star fermo, prestamente si proffilava la detta ombra; da poi facilmente si faceva passare alcune linee le quali non mostrava l'ombra; perchè nella grossezza del braccio alcune pieghe che sono nella piegatura del gomito, così nella spalla drento e fuora, così nella testa, in alcune parte del corpo, nelle gambe, nelli piedi e nelle mani non si possono vedere. Adunque questo modo del disegnare è quello che hanno usato i migliori maestri, con il qual si fa la mirabil pittura: e fra i migliori pittori che noi aviamo mai conosciuti, Michelagnolo Buonarroti . . . è stato il maggiore". Or see, again, Leonardo (J. P. Richter, *The Literary Works of Leonardo da Vinci*, London, 1883, I, pp. 332 and 661).

10 L. B. Alberti, *Della Pittura*, ed. L. Mallè, Florence, 1950, p. 109: "Et se pure ti piaci ritrarre opere d'altrui perché elle più techo anno patienza che le cose vive, più me piace a ritrarre una mediocre sculptura che una ottima dipintura, però che dalle cose dipinte nulla più acquisti che solo sapere asimiliarteli ma dalle cose scolpite inpari asimiliarti et inpari consciere et ritrarre i lumi". G. Vasari, *Le Vite de' più eccellenti pittori, scultori ed architettori*, ed. C. Milanesi, Florence, 1906, IV, p. 10:

"Bene lo trovaron poi dopo gli altri, nel veder cavar fuora di terra certe anticaglie citate da Plinio delle più famose . . . le quali nella lor dolcezza e nelle lor asprezze, con termini carnosi e cavati dalle maggior bellezze del vivo, con certi atti che non in tutto si storcono, ma si vanno in certe parti movendo, e si mostrano con una graziosissima grazia, e' furono cagione di levar via una certa maniera secca e cruda e tagliente che, per lo soverchio studio, avevano lasciata in quest'arte Pietro della Francesca, etc. . . ."

11   See, for example, Alberti, *Della Pittura*, pp. 109–110; or Leonardo (Richter, I, p. 17, n. 17): "La prima parte della pittura è che li corpi con quella figurati si dimostrino rilevati". Or Cellini, "Sopra l'arte", p. 794: ". . . e la maggior lode che si dà a una bella pittura e' se gli gli dice: la par propriamente di rilievo". Or Michelangelo (Barocchi, *Trattati*, I, p. 82): "Io dico che la pittura mi par più tenuta buona quanto più va verso il rilievo, et il relievo più tenuta cattivo quanto più va verso la pittura; e però a me soleva parere che la scultura fussi la lanterna della pittura . . ."

12   E. Panofsky (*Studies in Iconology*, New York, 1962, p. 175) discusses the question of multiple points of view, considering the notion of double relief (see above, nn. 8–9) as High Renaissance, the "multiview" as "manneristic". The latter is evidently an extension by multiplication of the former principle. As Panofsky notes, Cellini is the spokesman for the manneristic view, arguing sometimes that sculpture should have eight views, sometimes "a hundred or more". In a single paragraph ("Sopra l'arte", pp. 794–5) Cellini could write, "La pittura è una parte delle otto parti principali a che è obbligata la scultura", a few lines later of the "quattro vedute principali", the "non tanto otto vedute le sono più di quaranta" and triumphantly conclude his reflections by saying that sculpture is "venti volte maggiore e più degna della pittura".

13   E. Panofsky, *Meaning in the Visual Arts*, Garden City, 1955, p. 245.

14   Ibid., p. 245.

15   Ibid., pp. 244–7; compare text figures 13 and 16.

16   Ibid., p. 246, n. 29.

17   Panofsky (ibid., figures 69 and 70) illustrates a statue of Hercules from P. Apianus, *Inscriptiones sacrosanctae vetustatis*, 1534, shown front and back in two nearly identical profile views. A drawing by Antonio Federighi in L. Steinberg, "Picasso: Drawing as if to Possess", *Artforum*, October, 1971, p. 47, fig. 8, also shows classical sculpture, in this case the *Three Graces* in Siena, from front and back. They do not share a common contour. Parmigianino clearly made use of a similar device of reversing a figure within a contour – again related to the mechanical process of reversing a cartoon – in decorative figures in his Sta. Maria della Steccata frescoes: see A. Ghidaglia Quintavalle, *Gli Ultime affreschi del Parmigianino*, Milan, 1971, figs. 70–73. Parmigianino also reversed figures within a single contour, as Pollaiuolo did in the drawings preserved by Dürer in studies for the prophet in the *Madonna of the Long Neck*. See K. T. Parker, *Catalogue of the Collection of Drawings in the Ashmolean Museum*, II, Oxford, 1956, n. 440.

18   I. A. Richter, *Paragone*, provides a sound history of this dispute in the Renaissance. J. White, "Painting and Sculpture", *Art, Science and History in the Renaissance*, ed. C. S. Singleton, Baltimore, 1967, pp. 43–110, has treated the subject most recently. On Cellini's near-fistic insistence on the supremacy of sculpture, see R. and

M. Wittkower, *The Divine Michelangelo: The Florentine Academy's Homage on his Death in 1564*, London, 1964, pp. 18–21. C. Seymour, Jr., *Sculpture in Italy, 1400–1500*, Harmondsworth and Baltimore, 1966, p. 184, has connected three-dimensionally symmetrical figures with the *paragone* dispute.

19 P. Pino, *Dialogo di Pittura* (1547), in Barocchi, *Trattati*, I, p. 131 with notes. R. W. Kennedy, "Apelles Redivivus", *Essays in Honor of Karl Lehmann*, Locust Valley, 1964, p. 161, connects Titian's early so-called *Schiavona* in the National Gallery, London, with the *paragone* dispute, characterizing it as an amusing commentary on the debate without recourse to Giorgione's mirrors. Titian's introduction of a painted profile relief of his sitter in the full-face portrait is more related to the Central Italian definition of the debate than Giorgione's lost St. George, which, with its mirrors and reflections, has a decidedly Flemish flavor, recalling similar devices used by Flemish artists from the van Eycks onwards. An interesting and perhaps related sub-theme is *St. Luke painting the Virgin*; compare Maerten van Heemskerk's treatment of the subject with Giorgio Vasari's version in the Cappella di San Luca in the Santissima Annunziata, Florence.

20 Richter, *Paragone*, pp. 12–17.

21 Varchi's own "Della Maggioranza delle Arti", published in 1549, has been republished in Barocchi, *Trattati*, I, pp. 1–82, together with the replies to his request for opinions on this issue from a number of Florentine artists.

22 For Michelangelo's letter, see Barocchi, *Trattati*, I, p. 82. Daniele da Volterra's *paragone* paintings, now at Fontainebleau, are discussed by J. Holderbaum, "A Bronze by Giovanni Bologna and a Painting by Bronzino", *Burlington Magazine*, XCVIII, 1956, pp. 441–2. See Vasari, *Vite*, VII, p. 61. "Avendo monsignor messer Giovanni della Casa, fiorentino ed uomo dottissimo . . . cominciato a scrivere un trattato delle cose di pittura, e volendo chiarirsi d'alcune minuzie e particolari dagli uomini della professione, fece fare a Daniello, con tutta quella diligenza che fu possibile, il modello d'un Davit di terra finito; e dopo gli fece dipignere, o vero ritrarre in un quadro, il medesimo Davit, che è bellissimo, da tutte due le bande, cioè in dinanzi ed il di dietro, che fu cosa capricciosa". Daniele's paintings are variously connected with Michelangelo's Sistine Ceiling pendentive (G. Barnaud, in *Le XVI Siècle Européen: Peintures et Dessins dans les Collections publiques françaises*, Paris, Petit Palais, 1965, no. 110, accepting the date 1546–9) and with Michelangelo's compositionally similar but much later drawings in the Pierpont Morgan Library (C. de Tolnay, *Michelangelo: The Final Period*, Princeton, 1960, pp. 199–200, pl. 179–183). De Tolnay dates Michelangelo's drawings 1542–5. To the example of such painting by Bronzino discussed by Holderbaum should be added the bizarre bowing skeleton by Bronzino's pupil Alessandro Allori, *Mostra di disegni dei fondatori dell'Accademia delle Arti del Disegno*, ed. P. Barocchi, A. Bianchini, A. Forlani, M. Fossi, Florence, Uffizi, 1963, nos. 52 and 53.

23 Jex-Blake and Sellers, *Pliny*, pp. 130–131.

In the mid-Cinquecento, Bartolommeo Maranta (Barocchi, *Scritti*, I, pp. 871–2) praises precisely the artifice of such drawing, invoking Pliny: "avendo Tiziano voluto mostrar *la grandezza del suo ingegno*, non voluto mostrar dell'angelo se non mezzo il volto, ma di sì bel modo fe' spiccar la bocca in atto di parlare, che in vederne quel mezzo solo vi par vedere anco tutto quello che si nasconde". Such *difficultà* is immediately likened to polyphony in music.

24 Ibid., pp. 110–113.

25 D. Summers, "*Maniera* and Movement: The *Figura Serpentinata*", Art Quarterly, XXXV, 1972, pp. 274–5.

26 Quoted in Steinberg, "Drawing", p. 46. Of many examples of such straightforward *contrapposto*, we may mention Perino del Vaga's *sovraporta* figures for the Sala Paolina in the Castel Sant'Angelo (B. Davidson, *Mostra di disegni di Perino del Vaga e la sua cerchia*, Florence, Uffizi, 1966, no. 53 with notes) or Tintoretto's foreground *figure serpentinate* in the *Gathering of Manna* in the Scuola di San Rocco. An interesting example of a clearly related two-dimensional manipulation of decorative figural groups (within which are *contrapposti* of the kind here described) is provided by the shield-bearing *ignudi* at the corners of the main scene in Vincenzo Danti's Sportello relief for Cosimo I de'Medici in the Bargello, Florence: here, two patterns, top and bottom, are turned through a little less than 90°. The result is a kind of permutational *varietà* clearly dependent upon the repetition of similar patterns.

27 Barocchi, *Trattati*, II, p. 17.

28 A. Riegl, *Die Entstehung der Barockkunst in Rom*, Vienna, 1923, p. 33.

29 A Condivi, *Michelangelo. La Vita raccolta dal suo discepolo Ascanio Condivi*, ed. P. d'Ancona, Milan, 1928, p. 135. An emphatic statement of the critical standards at work here is found in S. Serlio, *Tutte l'opere d'architettura et prospettiva*, Venice, 1619, facsimile, Ridgewood, N. J., 1964, Libro VII, ff. 92 and 94: "La varietà delle cose è di gran contentezza all'occhio humano, & di sodisfattione all'animo"; and, more to Condivi's point (p. 94), "Gran cosa è veramente il voler variare in quelle cose, c'hanno in se pochissimi termini".

30 For Albertinelli's *Crucifixion*, see S. J. Freedberg, *Painting of the High Renaissance in Rome and Florence*, Cambridge, Mass., 1961, II, pl. 41. In its use of symmetry, as in other compositional aspects, Raphael's *Madonna del Baldacchino* recalls Filippino Lippi's *Madonna degli Otto* in the Uffizi. Similarly, Raphael's Sta. Maria della Pace *Sibyls* recall the altar wall of Filippino's Strozzi Chapel in Sta. Maria Novella, where Filippino made use of two- and three-dimensionally symmetrical angels (A. Scharf, *Filippino Lippi*, Vienna, 1935, taf. 81): the two standing shield-bearing angels in the center are simply symmetrical, but the outer, kneeling angels were made by passing the same figure through approximately 90°. This is a significant example (see also note 5 above), since the appearance of both kinds of symmetry in close conjunction suggests that Filippino recognized the derivation of such three-dimensional organization from two-dimensional symmetry and, more important, thought of them as equivalent.

31 An early Cinquecento *Resurrection* in Sao Paolo, sometimes ascribed to Raphael, is rigidly axial, and the sleeping soldiers in the foreground are three-dimensionally symmetrical in a way recalling Pollaiuolo's *St. Sebastian* (see Perugino's *Martyrdom of St. Sebastian* in San Sebastiano, Panicale, of 1505: C. Castellaneta and E. Camesasca, *L'Opera completa del Perugino*, Milan, 1969, no. 95). The *Resurrection* does not seem to be by Raphael, but that he had a hand in its design is indicated by a drawing in the Ashmolean Museum (Parker, *Catalogue*, nos. 505–6). See also the early sixteenth-century Umbrian *Flagellation* in the National Gallery, Washington (F. R. Shapley, *Paintings from the Samuel H. Kress Collection. Italian Schools, XV–XVI Century*, London, 1968, p. 106, fig. 253). Related *contrapposto* within the order of symmetry was also used by Raphael in the Stanza della Segnatura

Parnassus; the large figure of Homer closing the group of Apollo and the Muses on the left is answered by a symmetrically corresponding female figure on the right. They face in opposite directions. Thus, the opposites male-female and back-front vary a symmetry that is still intact and still in control.

32   For example, see A. E. Popham, *The Drawings of Leonardo da Vinci*, New York, 1945, nos. 170, 189, 217–222. Michelangelo followed a generally simpler but basically similar procedure in studies for or after sculpture – for example, in the Medici Chapel River God drawings in the British Museum (J. Wilde, *Italian Drawings in the British Museum, Michelangelo and his Studio*, London, 1953, no. 35); studies for the Medici Chapel *Night* (Parker, *Catalogue*, 309 verso), and studies connected with the Rondanini *Pietà* (ibid., 339). Parker considers the two sketches at the left of the last sheet to be variant compositions. I believe them to be the same group seen from a shift in angle of about 45°. See also C. de Tolnay, "Sur des Vénus dessinées par Michel-Ange à propos d'un dessin oublié du Musée du Louvre", *Gazette des Beaux-Arts*, LXIX, 1967, pp. 193–200.

33   Weyl, *Symmetry*, p. 10. A. Parronchi, *Le Opere giovanili di Michelangelo*, Florence, 1968, pp. 29–37, has noted the similarity of the figures in Pollaiuolo's *Nude Men Fighting*, arguing from their formal identity to their iconographic identity. Whatever the merits of his interpretation after the first point, the inference from identity is consistent with the arguments put forward here.

34   See the criticisms of Sebastiano's painting by the Counter-reformation writer G. A. Gilio (Barocchi, *Trattati*, II, p. 40). On Michelangelo's drawing, see J. Wilde, *Italian Drawings*, no. 15. The order is preserved in Sebastiano's final painting, and echoed in the outermost figures of the apostles in the *Transfiguration* above the *Flagellation*. In the *Pietà* for Vittoria Colonna, a hieratically symmetrical pair of angels is made three-dimensionally various by rotating a reflected figure through 90°. This interesting variation, similar to Michelangelo's earlier *Flagellation* in that the rotation is along two coordinates, differs from other examples, since the figures are not identical in the same sculptural sense.

35   It will have been noted that angels, whose hieratic significance goes without saying, are consistently informed by clear variants of simple symmetrical relationships. Raphael's *St. Michael* perhaps belongs to this tradition. The idea raises the further possibility of a consciously spiritual mode of composition, or a hierarchy of kinds of composition along a scale of increasing clarity of decorative or conceptual formal basis. Bronzino's *St. Michael*, in the Chapel of Eleanora of Toledo in the Palazzo Vecchio, which is so inconsistent with the other figures in its departure from illusionistic order, might be explained by such an hypothesis. C. H. Smyth, *Mannerism and Maniera*, Locust Valley, 1963, p. 18, has made a similar observation about Bronzino's *St. Michael*.

36   K. W. Forster, *Pontormo*, Munich, 1966, p. 90, relates drawings seen back and front, connected with the lost decorations at Castello, to an old Florentine tradition, which he illustrates with Pollaiuolo's *St. Sebastian*, noting that Pontormo has differentiated his figures to a higher degree than did his Quattrocento predecessor.

37   H. S. Merritt, "The Legend of St. Achatius: Bachiacca, Perino, Pontormo", *Art Bulletin*, XLV, 1963, p. 262, where the figures are described as "rather dully organized in trochaic pentameter". Pontormo's organization is perhaps traceable to the school of Raphael through the cartoon by Perino del Vaga for the *Martyrdom of*

the Ten Thousand done in Florence in 1523 (J. Shearman, "Maniera as an Aesthetic Ideal", *Studies in Western Art. Acts of the Twentieth International Congress of the History of Art. II. The Renaissance and Mannerism*, Princeton, 1963, pp. 216–17).

38   The repetition of one form in a single time (based on that same assumption about the perception of painting and sculpture underlying the *paragone* dispute) here defies the sequential nature of time, since recognizably similar figures (permutationally varied by counterposed color) are repeated in the same time (of the viewer). Repetition as a mode of the uncanny is brilliantly discussed by S. Freud, "The Uncanny", *On Creativity and the Unconscious*, New York, 1965, pp. 122–161. There is a precise and apposite contrast between experiential time – the region of incessant, indivisible and irreversible change – and conceptual time, the idea of pure succession, of which change is not necessarily a part and within which, in contrast to experiential time, doubling, true repetition, and continual identity are possible.

39   From Bartholomeus Rimbertinus, *De deliciis sensibilibus paradisi*, Venice, 1498, quoted and translated by M. Baxandall, *Painting and Experience in Fifteenth Century Italy*, London, 1972, p. 104.

23

Raphael, Angelo Colocci, and the Genesis of the Architectural Orders

Ingrid D. Rowland

When Raphael died in 1520, he left behind a staggering amount of unfinished business. Even with an active workshop to help him, and a laudable ability to delegate projects, Rome's favorite artist was hopelessly overextended. Some commissions would probably have remained unfulfilled in any case: the *Triumph of Bacchus*, for instance, about which Duke Alfonso d'Este had nagged him for three years.[1] Raphael, he had hoped, would supply a painting for his palace in Ferrara, its size, program, and iconography subject to his own rigorous control, there to contend with trophies from other renowned painters already bent to the patron's will. Though Raphael entertained Duke Alfonso's commission, he seems to have done nothing further about it.[2] Instead, the Raphael workshop generated large-scale designs, not only for Pope Leo X, to whom Duke Alfonso could not but pay homage, but also, against any traditional notions of social superiority, for such secondary characters as businessmen, especially the great banker Agostino Chigi, who had masterminded the destruction of Ferrara's salt beds on behalf of the Papacy in 1512.[3]

That Raphael respected money himself can be shown beyond doubt by his *modus vivendi*: he chose his company carefully, making stylish outings to the countryside with Pietro Bembo and other humanists, flirting with marriage to a cardinal's niece, painting pictures for kings, and investing in real estate along the via Giulia and in the Borgo, where Agostino Chigi's money was certain to procure him better terms than any that Duke Alfonso might extend. Like many of his well-placed friends in Rome, the artist had become a speculator almost as a matter of personality. As the fifteenth century had progressed into the sixteenth, the entrepreneurial aspect of Roman life had spilled over from the world of property and finance to the world of the arts: humanists discovered the printed book, painters the engraving, architects the illustrated treatise, all of them economical, infinitely reproducible versions of their work, objects at once physically and socially mobile. In keeping with this general tendency, Raphael, a shrewder operator than most, had fashioned himself from a consummate painter into a general designer in all media, the time-honored *artes* as well as the newer techniques of mass-produced creation. The diversified nature of his workshop allowed him to produce designs while leaving the execution of such manual tasks as engraving to Marcantonio Raimondi, frescoed garlands to Giovanni da Udine, or sculpture to Lorenzetto.[4] In an ultimate instance of delegation, Pope Leo X's Sistine Chapel tapestries, their cartoons originated in the Raphael workshop, were sent to Flanders for their actual weaving.[5]

Raphael's transformation from an independent artist to the head of a large-scale cultural operation seems to have occurred under the reign of Pope Leo X. To a certain extent this process simply represents the natural course of the artist's own increasing maturity; the painter of the *Disputa* and the *School of Athens* had been a boy wonder, who with those two works created his reputation in Rome as an established professional and hence the impetus for his *bottega*. The particular course of his trajectory has more to do, however, with a similar shift in the practice of a whole series of professions in Leonine Rome.

In the first place, division of labor in Raphael's diversified workshop is a different phenomenon from the virtuosity in a variety of media that defines many quattro- and cinquecento artists as "Renaissance men" *par excellence*. Thus Leone Battista Alberti, whose treatises toy with mass dissemination of artistic ideas, actually produced works of art that were jealously one-of-a-kind. The works of artists like Brunelleschi, and even Leonardo and Michelangelo, are appealing unavoidably for the way in which their own hands can be seen to have made them. The viewer is impressed that the same eye that guided the hewing of a *Pietà* from marble assessed with equal sensitivity how best to build up the cross-hatched pigments of the Sistine Chapel ceiling.

Raphael belonged to another world altogether. His workshop was a commercial enterprise that traded on his name, to be sure, but more significantly, on a set of immediately recognizable, reproducible artistic principles. These principles sometimes found expression in techniques to which Raphael himself never put a hand (sculpture in particular), but the imprint of his imagination is unfailingly present nonetheless in composition, choice of imagery, and the characteristic style that he himself called his *maniera*.[6] In one sense, the Raphael workshop can be seen in modern terms as a corporation with a distinct marketing strategy, but more essential to the real meaning of his enterprise is the way in which, in the terms of his own age, it channelled Raphael's own creativity and made it available to an immense public.

Medieval craftsmen, like their ancient predecessors, had made wide use of pattern books in the generation of design.[7] Renaissance classicism subjected these patterns to a set of increasingly demanding rules, both for the form of individual elements and for the sequence of their combination; the most obvious of these rules was the insistence on proportion, abetted by contemporary innovations in the practice of arithmetic.[8] Whereas fifteenth-century art and architecture largely generated their own rules for form and proportion, Raphael and his contemporaries refined their perception of classicism by direct reference to ancient precedent, through the study of archaeological remains and the analysis of ancient theoretical texts. Pattern books were replaced by treatises, in which the basic units of art (*membra*) were subject to a critical study and emendation analogous to the operations of humanistic philology, and the syntax of their arrangement (*ordines*) became a rigorous grammar subject to verification by calculation.[9]

That intertwining of art and learning for which we so admire the Renaissance stems in great measure from the fact that its art, speaking, and writing subscribe to a single aesthetic, this itself rooted in Greco-Roman antiquity. The analytical vocabulary for art and rhetoric is one entity: not that the classical strain in Western culture is logocentric, for by a reciprocal action words themselves function as visual entities, as Frances Yates's work on the "classical art of memory" has revealed to illuminating effect.[10] Rather, the Horatian dictum *ut pictura poesis* cuts both ways, especially if one translates the phrase so as to take its parallel construction into account: "what goes for painting goes for poetry," and what goes for these arts had originally gone for rhetoric, the sovereign art form in the ancient word. Humanist classicism revived the ancient world's preoccupation with rhetoric and with style.[11] Thus Raphael practiced a literary art because he practiced art; his learned friend Angelo Colocci, of whom more shall be said presently, perceived measure equally in the spatial length of the Roman foot and the temporal length of the iambic foot, and was expert about both. This fundamental sense of the unity of human creative force explains why, in the end, Raphael refused to specialize as an artist, why he dabbled as a poet, and why he ultimately found himself deeply embroiled in archaeology for its own sake.

What saves Raphael's archaeological and philological researches into artistic form from arid pedantry is the combination of his critical synthetic power and the sheer exuberance of his imagination; he was drawn to observe everything around him, classical, medieval, or contemporary, lofty or raw, and he absorbed it all with an eagerness that led an irritated Michelangelo to call him nothing more than an imitator.[12] An imitator he was, of Leonardo and Bramante as well as Michelangelo, but also of the ancient Romans, the early Christians, and the mosaicists of medieval Rome.[13] Like his contemporaries, moreover, he regarded his classical predecessors with a good dose of skepticism. Vitruvius and Horace, for example, deplored the wild fancies of early Imperial Roman painting, yet this is the precise style that the Raphael workshop chose in 1514–18 for Leo X's Logge Vaticane, at a time, furthermore, when Raphael himself was deeply engrossed, as will be seen, in the study of Vitruvius. However classical the formal *ordines* of the Raphael workshop may have been, they were also unmistakably his own, and he spent his creative time in testing each of those *ordines* to its limits. It is no wonder that this restless, enterprising spirit found one of its most congenial customers in the financial *magus* Agostino Chigi.

A second important aspect of Raphael's later career is the ambiguity of his social status. The scope of his workshop and its demands on his talents meant in turn that he no longer operated within the traditional purviews of a professional artist; the guild to which his father had belonged, and under whose rules he had undergone his apprenticeship to Pietro Perugino, was never designed to deal with the problems of an international corporation.[14] In a position between that of artist and that of executive (and the Curia was full of these, so the term is not so anachronistic), with his personable manner and receptivity, however apparently unobtrusive, to intellectual debate in its most rarefied form, Raphael was able to move with some ease through the ranks of Rome's fluid, aggressive society. In his movements, moreover, he met other souls whose social status was as negotiable as his own.

The contact between Raphael and Chigi, another social anomaly, provides a particularly illuminating example of the effect that mass marketing and economic speculation were beginning to produce on the culture of papal Rome, and contemporanously on Europe as whole, and how this effect became clearer than ever during the pontificate of Leo X. Indeed, the pattern of Chigi's activity under Leo parallels that of Raphael in significant ways: like the gifted painter, who came to trade on a whole new set of social and intellectual skills, Chigi, the brilliant speculator in alum, who built his fortune on manipulating the international cloth markets, transformed himself after 1513 into a man-about-town whose status was, for any practical purposes, unique: to the greatest extent possible, he withdrew from active participation in finance and plunged himself into the world of culture, not only as a patron, but also to entrepreneurial ends.[15]

For Chigi, the impetus to withdraw stemmed in some important measure from the passivity of the pope himself. For Raphael, this same passivity affected his work with the pope in quite different ways.[16] The Vatican continued to act as the artist's primary patron, but the quality of the demands put on his ingenuity changed dramatically. As the decorative program for the suite of papal apartments called the Stanze Vaticane continued, Leo initiated a series of tapestries for the Sistine Chapel; these, given the pope's own humanistic training, tended toward the same sort of meticulous programmatic messages that destined the *Triumph of Bacchus* for Duke Alfonso d'Este to eternal incompletion. The tapestry cycle called, in effect, for a set of illustrations from the Acts of the Apostles. This set of strictly circumscribed tales left relatively little play for Raphael's own powers of invention, whose phenomenal energy emerges more clearly in Leo's less restrictive program for the Vatican Logge.

Another papal project, however, allowed Raphael room to imagine freely, while offering in addition the hopes of a remarkable advancement to his career, as well as the prospect of a lucrative venture into publishing. This was a combination he predictably found irresistible.

Raphael describes Leo's initial charge to him as follows:[17] "Your Holiness commanded that I draw ancient Rome, or as much of it as one can know from what can be seen today, with those buildings which show sufficient preservation to enable infallible reconstruction on true principles of their original state, making those elements which are entirely ruined or barely visible correspond to those still standing and visible."

The guidelines for archaeological reconstruction to be used in drawing ancient Rome are strict: material evidence should be "sufficient," the principles of reconstruction "true" (*vero argomento*), the results "infallible." The word "draw," *disegnare*, leaves a tantalizing ambiguity as to the look of the pope's envisioned final product, for in sixteenth-century Italy, one "draws" many things, among them maps, plans, cartoons, frescoes, and geometrical exercises. Indeed, virtually anything wrought by pen or brush on any surface whatsoever, virtually anything but a written text, can be a *disegno*.

What emerges unequivocally from this commission, however, is Leo's demand for the highest professionalism. For Raphael, almost by definition, such an enterprise implied a team of specialists; when the reigning criteria for the project are as generalized as sufficiency, truth, and infallible results, the specialists involved in bringing these infallible results about may – and must – be sought in every walk of Roman life and at every rung of its social ladder. Thus, for example, Raphael entrusted final composition of his presentation letter for the project to the gracious aristocrat Baldassare Castiglione, his own sense of that elegant man evident in the portrait of 1516 that is now in the Louvre.[18] Though Raphael's text is composed in the first person, and in the comparatively humble idiom of the *volgare* (the only language he commanded), this gesture toward social modesty is belied by the supple, euphonious phrases supplied him by his learned consultant.[19]

Significantly, however, the longest, and clearly the latest, copy of Raphael's presentation letter to Pope Leo X was written, not by Castiglione, but by another elegant and worldly noble, the papal secretary Angelo Colocci.[20] The Vatican Library preserves an unusually extensive sample of Colocci's script, ranging over half a century of activity, from some of his youthful annotations to the very last, tortured signature he put to his will on his deathbed. The letter to Leo X represents some of his better writing, of which some of the most characteristic traits, for better or worse, are the thick stroke, the sprightly leftward swing of the letter "g," the tendency of the letter "h" to open, and the predilection for simple, spare forms. It is not a particularly easy script to read, and it is a highly distinctive one with an unusually large range of samples; into these the Munich manuscript, and the various watermarks of its paper, fit seamlessly.[21]

A native of Iesi in the Marches, Colocci first came to Rome in 1498 in his late teens. In 1513, at the very end of Julius II's papacy, he bought a garden property near the Trevi Fountain that quickly became a focal point for the revival of Pompeo Leto's long-struggling Roman Academy.[22] From 1511 onward, he had worked in the Vatican as one of the apostolic secretaries, a demanding job that put the humanist firmly at the center of Roman social life even as it decimated his scholarly output. A wealthy man to begin with, Colocci amassed one of the most impressive libraries of his time, its holdings indicative of an extraordinarily wide-ranging mind.[23] Furthermore, these manuscripts were furnished to other learned Romans, and provided a source of illumination for the humanists' community on myriad fronts. Even after the Sack of Rome wrought unspeakable havoc on Colocci's collection, as we know from a chilling report by his close friend Antonio Tebaldeo, its remaining manuscripts in the Vatican Library numbered nearly two hundred.[24] Still more were spirited away to the Bibliothèque Nationale in Paris in Napoleon's wake, because Colocci was one of the earliest scholars to collect Provençal and other Romance lyrics. In the remnants of Colocci's library and in his voluminous notebooks, one may begin to unravel the reasons for his involvement in Raphael's paper reconstruction of the glories of Imperial Rome.

An autograph *minuta* by Baldassare Castiglione in the Castiglione family archives in Mantua confirms that humanist's partial authorship of the letter's early paragraphs, which lament the destruction of classical Rome by Goths, Vandals, and, pointedly, by ignorant contemporaries.[25] This lament for Rome's bygone wonders imitates a significant precedent: Fra Giocondo da Verona's preface to a sylloge of ancient inscriptions compiled for Lorenzo de' Medici, Pope Leo's father.[26] In 1516, Fra Giocondo was only recently deceased, his legacies as Raphael's co-architect of St. Peter's and as editor of the Aldine Vitruvius of 1511 still central to the architectural program of the papal court.

After its high-flown exordium, the letter switches its tone to promote a modern drawing method, by means of which the measurements of buildings may be left intact: the letter calls it "bussola della calamita" or "magnetic compass." We call it drawing by plane-table intercepts. This highly technical discussion certainly reflects Raphael's own participation: he had personally corrected Colocci's redaction of the text.[27] However, it is most unlikely that Colocci, the wealthy curialist, acted only as Raphael's scribe. By the time he drafted this expansion of the letter from Castiglione's nucleus, sometime between 1518 and 1520, he was well ensconced in the Vatican bureaucracy and served as toastmaster, as we know, of a revivified academic community from his vantage in his *Horti Colotiani* by the Trevi Fountain. Years later, he would recall this time under Leo's reign as an idyllic period of intense and relatively uninterrupted antiquarian study.[28] His garden, meanwhile, seems to have been the setting in which he proudly displayed his collection of ancient weights and measures, including his prized exemplars of the Roman foot, whose accuracy he had tested against an inscribed ten-foot column in the Lateran Palace and many other ancient columns besides:[29] "Add that among my monuments in the little garden by the Aqua Virgo there was a cask-shaped tombstone of the architect Agathangelus, and in the stone on the left side architect's tools were sculpted; there was also a little one-foot measure. Immediately I had my servants make a copy of this and I sent it off to the little [ten-foot] column in the Lateran and likewise to various other monuments." A *vero argomento* for archaeological reconstruction of more tangible immediacy could hardly have been sought in Leonine Rome, or, as Colocci remarks himself, anywhere else in Italy.[30]

The avid collector was an even more avid student of his collections. Indeed, Angelo Colocci was the reigning expert in his day on ancient weights and measures. Endless notes to a never-completed treatise *De numeris, ponderibus, et mensuris* are our only, if copious, testimony to what had been a lifelong obsession with that one particular aspect of ancient culture.[31] Nor was the topic itself so narrow as it might seem. In an accurate understanding of ancient weights and measures Colocci felt that he had found the key to the secrets of classical proportion, and this conviction spurred him on to serious study of technical treatises from the ancient and the contemporary world. The easily miscopied Roman numerals that had so vexed the researches of earlier scholars like Leone Battista Alberti struck Angelo Colocci somewhat differently: he saw them instead as a problem to be solved. As a result, Colocci's calculation of the Roman foot would hold for generations of archaeological investigation and classically inspired Renaissance architecture.[32] The hand that drafted Raphael's letter to the pope was the hand of Rome's chief authority on many of the issues faced by the reconstruction project, and it is difficult to believe that his notoriously poor handwriting was his greatest contribution to the effort.

Angelo Colocci had a further motive for investigating ancient weights and measures, and this even more fundamental drive shows up in the very organizing principles of his notebooks. The apocryphal biblical Book of Wisdom proclaims that God "arranged all things in terms of number, measure, and weight."[33] The categories that head Colocci's lists of citations from the ancients preserve this biblical order: *numeri, mensurae, pondera*. His deep religious faith is attested also in his decision to take holy orders after the death of his wife in 1518.[34] Proportion, then, carried for Colocci a spark of divinity, an idea he could find confirmed in Plato, Ficino, Luca Pacioli, and Egidio da Viterbo, among authors of particular interest in his own day and in his own circles.[35] In accurate measurement lay the revelation of absolute truth.[36]

Thus Colocci's interest in Raphael's new drawing method would have been far deeper than an academic curiosity, particularly because the method's chief selling point was its preservation of accurate measurement. "Now that we have clarified which buildings of ancient Rome are the ones we wish to show and how it is an easy matter to distinguish them from the others, it remains to demonstrate the method that we have adopted for measuring and drawing them, so that whoever wants to turn his attention to Architecture will know how to carry out the one and the other without error."

The practice of measurement and drawing by "magnetic compass" was, as the letter states, current among contemporary architects:[37] "The method of measuring by means of magnetic compass, the method which we use ourselves, I imagine to be an invention of modern times."[38] Raphael must have learned it in the company of a professional practitioner of the art like Bramante or Antonio da Sangallo. It is not wholly out the question that Colocci himself had some knowledge of it; in conjunction with his study of measure he had amassed an impressive collection of ancient surveying manuals, the *Corpus agrimensorum*, and pored over their techniques, as his marginal notes attest.[39] In fact, the early paragraphs of the letter to Leo X seem to present a portrait of Colocci at work as much as Raphael.[40] "Because I have been extremely interested in these antiquities, and have spent no little care in examining them minutely and measuring them painstakingly, and in always reading the excellent Authors and comparing the monuments with their writings, I believe that I have attained some little acquaintance with this ancient architecture."

As befits his station as papal humanist, Colocci's influence upon Raphael's letter goes further than a generic concern for number and proportion. His library, too, must have been at Raphael's disposal for their joint endeavors. Raphael's letter to the pope calls particular attention to two textual sources for his antiquarian investigations. His basic approach to Rome, on the scale of wholesale urban planning, looked to a treatise called *De XIII regionibus urbis Romae*, which he attributes to one "Publius Victor."[41] This text, handed down from Constantinian times, had been much elaborated in the fifteenth century by the Roman academics in the circle of Pomponio Leto. Colocci himself owned an attractive fifteenth-century text of this augmented "Publius Victor," from which he had a second copy made by one of his professional scribes.[42]

"Publius Victor" supplied a region-by-region list of ancient Roman buildings, from great temples to humble workshops; each entry ended by measuring the perimeter of the region in Roman feet. Fragments of the ancient marble plan of Rome, the *Forma urbis*, had already begun to emerge in the area of the Forum in the early sixteenth century, as the letter to Leo X makes clear.[43] "Even though I have extracted what I intend to demonstrate from many Latin authors, nonetheless I have principally followed Publius Victor, who, by virtue of his being among the latest Roman authors, can give more detailed information about the last remains of antiquity, though not omitting those which are more ancient. And it can be seen that in describing the Regions he agrees with some ancient marbles on which likewise they are depicted."

This ancient text, then, supplemented by the *Forma urbis*, would provide the general framework on which the drawn city would eventually be laid out. Furthermore, the *De XIII regionibus* was hardly more than a list. Raphael, who had at best little Latin, could have understood the booklet reasonably well on his own, particularly if he were helped in his researches by the graphic evidence of the *Forma urbis* and the literary skills of his humanist friends.

For reconstructing the buildings themselves, the chief ancient guide for Raphael and his expert colleagues was, necessarily, the *Ten Books on Architecture* composed for the emperor Augustus by Vitruvius: no other writer on ancient architecture had survived antiquity. By contrast with "Publius Victor" and his spare lists of buildings, however, Vitruvius presented ten books of carefully wrought Golden Latin prose. To read *De architectura* with any comprehension, Raphael would have needed help. And expert help, as he well knew, was ready to hand all around him.

Angelo Colocci's draft of the letter from Raphael to Leo X came to its present quarters in Munich in the company of three other manuscripts.[44] One of these (Cod. It. 37c) is a fragment from a treatise on the formation of Roman capital letters, composed by Fra Giocondo.[45] The other two manuscripts are both from the hand of Angelo Colocci and both considerably longer.[46] One (Cod. It. 37) is a translation of Vitruvius, whose colophon reports that it was made in Raphael's house, and at Raphael's insistence, by Marco Fabio Calvo of Ravenna, a venerable but impoverished humanist perpetually in search of money and intellectual stimulation around the papal court.[47] This text, all written in Colocci's hand, has been corrected and annotated by Colocci himself and by Raphael; it seems to indicate, therefore, that the papal secretary actually served as Calvo's scribe. (It also contains a little drawing by Colocci of a column capital. Calvo's own important scholarly work included a translation of Hippocrates, a treatise on numbers in the ancient world, and, after Raphael's death, the editing of Jacopo Mazzocchi's *Antiquae urbis Romae simulachrum* of 1527. Given Colocci's own eclectic interests in the ancient world, and his particular obsession with weights, measures, and numbers, his participation in the translation project of Calvo and Raphael is not entirely surprising, though the undertaking is not a trivial one for someone in his position, with a terminally sick wife (Girolama Bufalini Colocci died in 1518 after a long illness) and myriad obligations to a uniquely demanding employer.

Like Colocci's draft of the letter to Leo X, the Italian Vitruvius in Munich is quite clearly Raphael's own working copy; marginalia in the artist's own hand display a variety of inks and writing styles that indicate his repeated study of Books III and IV in particular, the sections of Vitruvius that deal with the proportions of ancient temples. Clearly, in his annotations Raphael is seeking out a systematic understanding of classical architecture – Doric, Ionic, Corinthian, and Tuscan. But so, importantly, was Angelo Colocci, whose marginalia to the manuscript are far more numerous. In general, these notes seem to be directed toward helping the artist understand what exactly lies written in the original Latin, and what is implicit in its content.

Both Calvo's translation and Colocci's annotations to Calvo's text follow closely on the Latin of Fra Giocondo's superb illustrated Vitruvius of 1511, printed in Venice by Giovanni de Tridino. Colocci's own copy of this attractive book, much scribbled upon by its enthusiastic owner, still survives in the Vatican Library (fig. 23.1).[48] His marginalia to this manhandled Fra Giocondo Vitruvius often parallel his marginalia to Calvo's translation, for in addition to this fine printed book, Colocci had access to manuscript exemplars of the two main Vitruvian textual traditions; these he collated diligently with Giocondo's text.[49] Other corrections to Calvo's text concerned its literary style. As a committed proponent of the vernacular, Colocci strived to inject a degree of elegance into Calvo's workmanlike prose; Vitruvius himself had striven to attain a decorous

Latin and such personages as Petrarch had appreciated his success.[50] Thus the manuscript and its annotations suggest that Calvo had furnished Raphael with a working draft of Vitruvius in Italian, for which enterprise at some stage Colocci had acted as amanuensis. On subsequent rereadings of this original text, Colocci had given its straightforward *volgare* some linguistic polish. (This fact suggests that the text may have been destined for a wider audience than Raphael alone, or that the idea of a wider distribution emerged shortly after Calvo had completed the work of translation.) More important to Raphael as a practicing artist, however, the papal secretary drew upon his expertise in ancient technology to supply emended numbers for the dimensions that Vitruvius so frequently gave when he discussed ancient Roman buildings – emendations needed because Roman numerals are particularly susceptible to mistranscription, especially by scribes whose interest in ancient statistics was probably minimal.[51] As a practicing architect, Vitruvius reveled in numbers, and as a student of numbers, Colocci felt the same pull; it may have been the opportunity to study the Vitruvian text in such expert company as that of Calvo and Raphael that led him to undertake the task of scribe, which he normally delegated to professionals.[52] Raphael's own notes to his Italian Vitruvius often parallel Colocci's, and continue Colocci's search for the tangible: accurate numbers, reliable identification of building materials, clear translation of Latin terms, and a surprising interest in timber.

The second manuscript in Colocci's hand to accompany his draft of the letter to Leo X is a partial transcript of the corrected Calvo Vitruvius (Cod. It. 37a). Nearly all, though not absolutely all, of Colocci's corrections to Calvo's text have been incorporated into this second version, which proceeds rather neatly for four books. Thereafter, however, the writing becomes large and hasty; Colocci, for some reason, was suddenly in a tremendous hurry. The manuscript breaks off in the middle of Book v; Colocci never completed it. Its margins, up to the beginning of Book v, contain, carefully numbered, a list of projected illustrations to accompany the *volgare* text. The text is accompanied by a small collection of drawings, some by Colocci himself and others by another amateur artist, as well as a list of technical vocabulary drawn up according to Colocci's characteristic practice of "tabulation." One of these, Colocci's composite drawing for Book v, combines Vitruvius's prefatory disquisition on perfect numbers with the first chapter's suggestions for creating a well-planned forum.[53] Here, the humanist displays a certain degree of graphic ingenuity in his attempt to combine numerology and city planning in a single image. This ingenuity testifies to more than the exhilaration of collaborating with the endlessly inventive Raphael; it testifies as well to Colocci's own efforts to clarify, through drawing, a particularly opaque section of the Vitruvian text.

The profusion of projected drawings and their content suggest that from a translation whose initial purpose must have been to supplement Raphael's archaeological studies, we have moved once again into the area of entrepreneurship: this second Vitruvius surely outlines a printed book in the style of Cesare Cesariano's illustrated *volgare* Vitruvius, which was issued in Como in 1521.

With any luck, Raphael, Calvo, and Colocci might have reached the market before him.

Thus Leo X's charge to Raphael to "draw ancient Rome" apparently led him into generating two diverse and ambitious projects, one, a set of archaeological drawings, and, the second, a *volgare* version of Vitruvius. The Vitruvius, as has been seen, was surely destined for eventual publication as a printed book, with the close involvement of Angelo Colocci. Christof Thoenes has suggested that the Raphael workshop's drawings of ancient Rome were to have met a similar fate.[54] The Munich draft of Raphael's letter to Leo X, he postulates, is in fact a version of Raphael's preface to the presentation copy of his *Roma antica disegnata*, which must therefore have been significantly on the way to completion; indeed, Thoenes would identify some drawings by Antonio da Sangallo with this project. The revisions made to Castiglione and Raphael's original text, Thoenes observes, point to a printed version of the *Roma antica disegnata*, which would in turn have been directed toward a wider audience.[55] That the original letter acted as the preface to a corpus of drawings is beyond doubt; prefaces in this period, and indeed for centuries before, had been couched in the form of letters to the patron.[56] As Thoenes observes, the Munich revisions to Castiglione's text of the letter elevate personal references to the pope to more general, and generic, terms. As with the Vitruvius, the person actually responsible for the transformation from private commission to publishing project was Angelo Colocci, again acting as scribe for Raphael, his own text again bearing Raphael's notes. If Raphael himself was a canny operator, in Colocci he had found his match.

The spirit of entrepreneurship is one with which Colocci had long been familiar; he invested with great success in real estate, as Raphael would attempt to do at precisely this same time. Publishing and real estate were also two realms in which another curial fixture, Agostino Chigi, decided to expand his venture capitalism in these same years. The great merchant's contacts with Raphael in this period are made manifest in a whole series of artistic endeavors, but it is hardly necessary that art had been the only subject they ever talked about.

Thus two apparently disparate, and extremely ambitious, projects brought Raphael into close contact with Angelo Colocci, and simultaneously with several new worlds of endeavor: on the one hand, the heady business atmosphere in Leo's otherwise somewhat acephalous Rome, on another the realm of archaeological investigation, operating all the while in an apostolic court that continued to move ahead by fits and starts upon the ideological momentum of its late pope Julius.

The letter to Leo X pays distinct homage to Rome's enduring spiritual mission and to the way in which careful study of antiquity might contribute to it: "In preserving the living paragon of the ancients, may your Holiness endeavor above all else to equal, and even surpass them. This you may do with grand buildings, by nurturing and favoring the virtues, reawakening talents, rewarding valiant effort, sowing the holy seed of Peace among Christian princes . . . this is to be a true Clement Pastor, and Father to all the world."

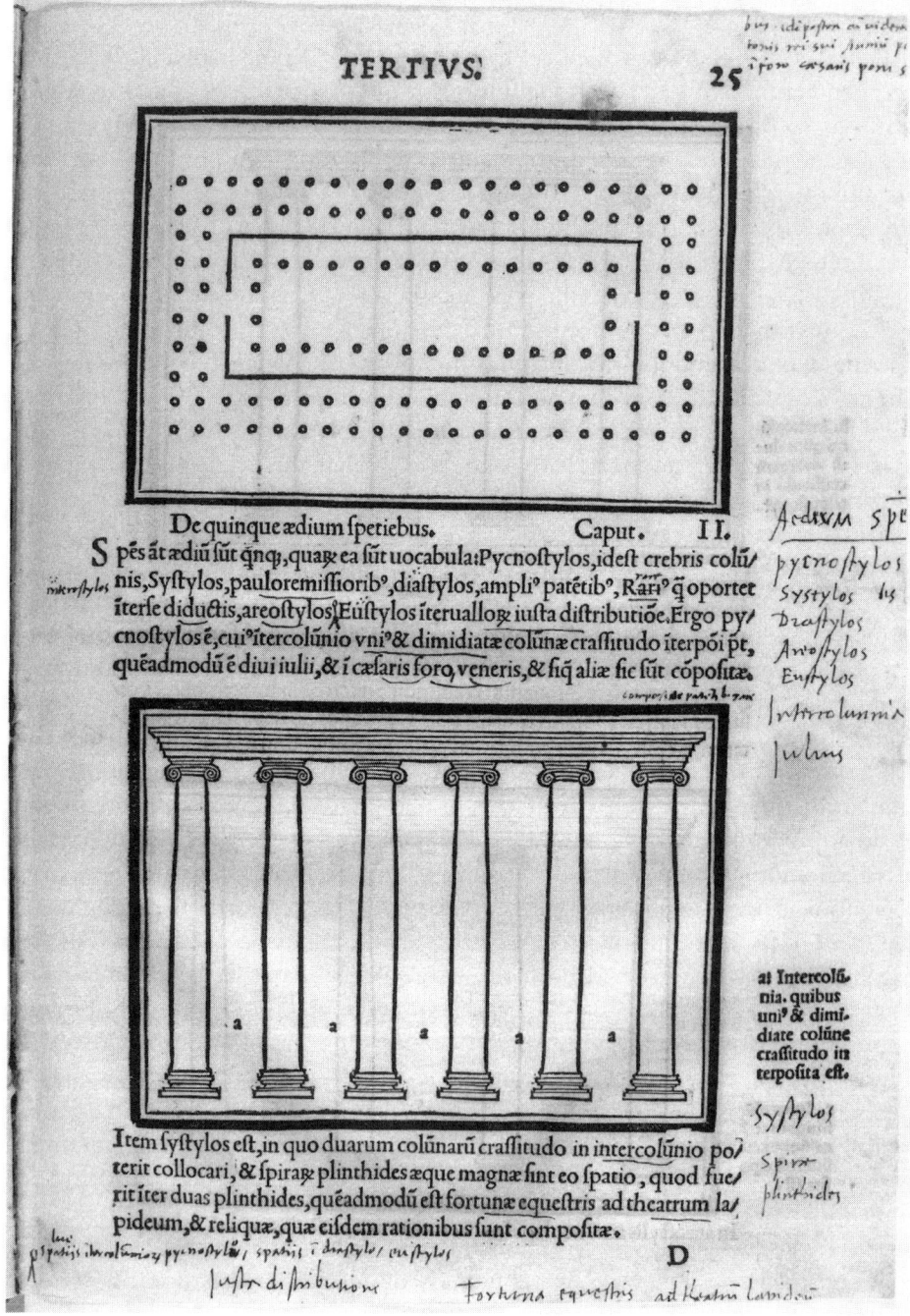

Figure 23.1 Vitruvius Pollio, *De architectura*, Venice, 1511, edited by Fra Giocondo da Verona, copy owned by Angelo Colocci with his annotations. Biblioteca Apostolica Vaticana, Stampati R.I.III.298, fol. 25r (courtesy BAV).

More pointedly still, the letter goes on:

> The modern buildings are extremely well known, both because they are new and because they have not yet attained the excellence of the ancient ones in all respects; neither have they arrived at that immense expense which one may see and contemplate among the ancients. Thus, even if it so happens that architecture has been awakened from its slumbers in our day and come very close to the style of the ancients, as one sees in many beautiful works of Bramante, nonetheless the ornaments are in less precious material than those of the ancients, who, it seems, with endless expense put into effect exactly what they imagined, and their will alone toppled every obstacle.

Therefore, the real point of the pope's antiquarian exercise in reconstructing ancient Rome was to lend Rome's new buildings the full charge of *gravitas* and *auctoritas* once mustered by the structures of the Imperial city. Accordingly, Raphael's studies of ancient Rome and her architecture must have served yet another ulterior purpose, for in 1514, on the death of Donato Bramante, he had been appointed architect to St. Peter's.[57]

The relationship between Raphael's Vitruvian studies and his designs for St. Peter's were made patent in a fresco executed for Pope Leo X in that same crucial year of 1514, *Fire in the Borgo* (fig. 23.2).[58] In many respects, this is the last of Raphael's complex iconographies for the Vatican Stanze; it is also the last time in his career when he has anything substantial to gain from any pope by displays of brilliant inventiveness.

Fire in the Borgo, like all Raphael's great paintings for the papal quarters, is many things at once, but on one of its most significant levels it is a treatise on beauty, on architectural beauty in particular. As part of the Stanze Vaticane, it takes papal authority as its chief theme; this is made manifest in Pope Leo IV's ability to quench a raging fire in the Vatican's surrounding neighborhood of the Borgo by making the sign of the Cross. A secondary theme, one of several, concerns the nature of beauty, which Angelo Colocci and many other contemporaries regarded on good Neoplatonic evidence as a revelation of God. "Beauty," Colocci writes in one of his notebooks on measure, "is, as it were, the antechamber of divine goodness."[59]

In effect, beauty and the Church accomplish the same task, that of bringing God into contact with humanity; hence, in strictly utilitarian terms, a beautiful new St. Peter's will also be an efficient new St. Peter's, presumably more efficient than the medieval building whose façade is visible in the background of Raphael's painting. (It is worthwhile here to remember that *goffo*, the adjective by which Raphael's letter to Leo X describes medieval style, is the direct ancestor of our own pejorative "goofy.") A building more in tune with the divine harmonies of number, weight, and measure would serve as a more fitting conduit for the divine encounters of prayer, communion, and salvation.

Like the rest of the frescoes in the Vatican Stanze, *Fire in the Borgo* is highly literate; that is, it makes explicit allusions to a body of literary texts known in

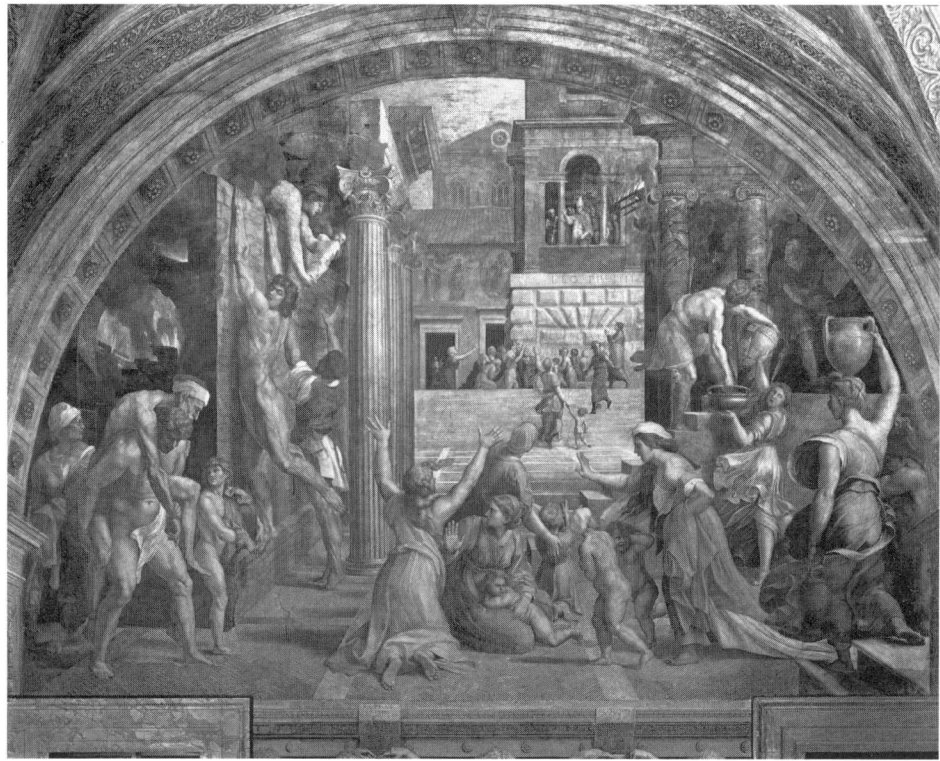

Figure 23.2 Raphael and workshop, *Fire in the Borgo*, 1514–15. Musei Vaticani, Stanza dell'Incendio. Alinari Archives-Florence.

common by learned members of the papal court, in terms of which, in fact, they have formulated their own aspirations for and representations of Leo's papacy. Leo himself was as deeply involved in devising this complex of imagery as his curial aides. Visual citations of these texts in the official art of the papacy also serve to strengthen by reminder the interdependence of all the arts and sciences in the vibrant mix of early sixteenth-century curial culture; failure to catch such allusions would serve at once to identify and to intimidate a less *au courant* outsider.

The ancient textual sources for *Fire in the Borgo*'s painted treatise are not difficult to discern: they are virtual commonplaces of humanist aesthetics, yet the way in which Raphael combines them has much to do with his companionship in these years with Baldassare Castiglione and Angelo Colocci.

In the case of *Fire in the Borgo*, Raphael leads us to think of beauty in the abstract by showing the juxtaposition of a statuesque water carrier and an Ionic colonnade. The Platonic dialogue *Hippias major* (its authenticity taken for granted in the period under discussion here) provides the first key to the artist's choice of imagery. This disquisition on beauty begins by discussing the beauty of a vase, which resides both in elegant form and useful function, proceeding thence to the beauty of women, and ending with a glimpse of beauty absolute. Absolute beauty is ineffable (therefore, also resistant to visual portrayal), but in the figures of women and vases, the primary stages of the *Hippias major*'s ascesis are shown clearly enough.[60] Beauty in architecture raises another set of issues, with the architect's need to reconcile aesthetic principles with the hard facts of structure. As with a beautiful vase, a beautiful building must simultaneously perform a mundane physical function, and do it well. The *Hippias major* does not address architectural beauty per se (the Platonic corpus spends little time on architecture at all); instead, the Ionic colonnade of *Fire in the Borgo* makes reference to the aesthetic precepts of Vitruvius, who lodges the proportions of the Ionic *genus* – not yet an order[61] – in the figure of a stately matron (IV.1.7). The male nude hanging so conspicuously from a crumbling wall to the left of Raphael's fresco poses no less meaningfully next to a Composite column, forcing the Vitruvian analogy between architectural proportion and human proportion for the male figure as well (IV.1.6).

This excursus on Platonic and Vitruvian beauty by no means exhausts the painting's references to the Greco-Roman classics. The family group in the left foreground, piggyback grandfather, young father, and son, recalls the flight of Aeneas from burning Troy, his lame father Anchises on his back and his son Ascanius at his side. Like the Troy of Virgil's *Aeneid*, which was sacrificed in order that Rome might rise, Raphael's painted world of classical beauty is also burning up, presumably in order to become something else: a rejuvenated Borgo, a rebuilt Rome, a new Constantinople? Whatever the answer (and it is probably a combination of all three possibilities), the anachronistic Aeneas escaping these local Roman fires makes the future's bright certainty clear enough, and what that future means to become is surely something like the middle ground of the fresco, the prominent, unscathed building from which Pope Leo IV launches his mighty blessing.

Significantly, not one of the colonnades depicted in *Fire in the Borgo* follows Vitruvian prescriptions. Raphael's Ionic columns lack flutes; Vitruvius assumes that the Ionic *genus* features fluted shafts (III.5.14–15). The ancient author evinces no knowledge of the Composite *genus*, which probably had yet to be invented, nor of the arched entablature, which certainly had been. If absent from the ancient world's sole surviving architectural treatise, unfluted columns in exotic stone and arched entablatures find ample exempla among the standing ruins of ancient Rome. Raphael is caught *in flagrante* using his eyes and his archaeological imagination, reading Vitruvius carefully but with equally careful independence from the limitations of that ancient handbook. At the same time, the sheer volume of Raphael's columns reflects how, when it comes to their proportions, assiduous study of the ancient monuments works in perfect harmony with the Vitruvian text.[62] Only with Bramante's arrival in Rome had Renaissance columns begun to take on such substantial, and truly classical, dimensions; in the hands of Bramante and his protégé, a spirit akin to Angelo

Colocci's obsession with measurement bore palpable fruit in an altered architectural aesthetic.

Caught between the façade of Old St. Peter's in the background and the elegant but threatened classical colonnades in the foreground, Pope Leo's benediction loggia also serves as the focal point for the fresco's compositional structure, a formal device that Raphael had already exploited brilliantly in his *Disputa* next door in the Stanza della Segnatura. The painting's essential meaning resides in the center of its composition, and that center for *Fire in the Borgo* is not a person, but a building, a rusticated papal benediction loggia. This loggia, like the classical colonnades in front of it, belongs to a *genus* that is known to Roman archaeology but absent from Vitruvius, namely a Tuscan colonnade with Doric entablature, including the arched motif known as "Palladian" or a "Serliana," which terms both do grave injustice to Bramante, its first great advocate in the Renaissance.

This Tuscan-Doric combination was still visible in Raphael's day on the façade of the Basilica Aemilia in the Roman Forum. Bramante had used the same *genus* for his Tempietto at S. Pietro in Montorio, and from that moment on there seems to be at least a vague association between this Tuscan Doric and the Papacy.[63] Certainly there is such an association here, with a powerfully gesturing pope placed between Tuscan-Doric columns much as the heroic male nude and the statuesque female water-carrier stand next to Composite and Ionic columns at the painting's left and right. By a process already seen at work in the letter to Leo X (and visible also in the Stanza della Segnatura), this placement of the papal loggia between symbolic representations of the classical and Christian past seems to make a comparison between the style and spirituality of each age, combining them to effect a new synthesis of what is best in each. At exactly the same time, and for the same pope, Egidio da Viterbo had written:[64] "There were things written before in a holy fashion (*sancte*), but with less elegance; and those written elegantly (*eleganter*), but without holiness. Now these same things are written with holiness (*sancte*) and with elegance (*eleganter*) at one and the same time."

Fire in the Borgo makes the same point in images about the new architecture of the Leonine age. The pope, and his Church, shall henceforth be housed both *sancte* and *eleganter*. The Tuscan Doric arch under which Leo IV appears represents, in every sense, a new order.

In the preface to his never-completed *De numeris, ponderibus, et mensuris*, Angelo Colocci had once written: "And because a great project was undertaken on the proportions of columns, based on Vitruvius, I began to examine columns." One member of that great project was Raphael, as has been seen; another was Fabio Calvo. Others can probably be added to the list: Andrea Fulvio, who produced a book of literary testimonia about ancient Rome in 1527, or the artists in Raphael's équipe: Giulio Romano, certainly, and Antonio da Sangallo the Younger. Fra Giocondo, editor of the marvelous Venetian Vitruvius of 1511, was also present in Rome during this flurry of studious activity. A letter to Aldus Manutius of August 2, 1514, presents him as a grumpy old monk who speaks a great deal about money, a fair amount about Pope Leo, and a bit about books.[65] Yet Angelo Colocci also reports that the old man was a great friend of his, as well as an active participant in his own endless search for ancient weights and measures, and to Colocci Fra Giocondo seems to have willed many of his books, particularly on those subjects.[66] It was this same old man who had been appointed in 1513 to join Bramante in the design of new St. Peter's.

Curiously, when Raphael's letter to Leo X makes its transition from the passages composed by Castiglione to the passages drawn up with the help of Angelo Colocci, it switches voice, from "I" to "we."[67] The makeup of this "we" is probably quite close, if not identical, to those who, in Colocci's abortive preface, undertook the great project on Vitruvius. In the letter to Leo X, it is "we" who have measured the buildings with magnetic compass, "we" who have substituted for the three Vitruvian modes of architectural drawing (plan, elevation, *scaenographia*) a new series of three: plan, elevation, and orthographic projection of the interior. It is even "we" who:

> have – over and above the three modes of architecture set out above – also included perspective drawings of some of the buildings that to our mind required it, so that the eye might see and evaluate the beauty of the images for the beautiful proportions and the symmetries of these buildings, something which is not self-evident in the measured architectural drawings . . . for, even if this mode of perspective drawing is more properly the province of the painter, still, it is useful for the architect as well.

The Munich Staatsbibliothek preserves an important trace of the extent to which this "we" truly reflects the intensity of Angelo Colocci's collaboration with Raphael, and the extent to which the scattered Colocci and Raphael marginalia to Fabio Calvo's translation of Vitruvius represent a genuine conversation (in which the long-dead Vitruvius, in his own way, must have held up his own end admirably).[68] A final section of the presentation letter to Leo X exists only in the Munich copy, that is, the copy in Angelo Colocci's own hand.[69] Here, for the first time in the history of architecture, the varieties of classical columns – Doric, Ionic, Tuscan, Corinthian, and the Renaissance invention, Attic – take the name "orders."[70] They have kept the name ever since, even though Vitruvius, Alberti, Francesco di Giorgio, Fabio Calvo, Cesare Cesariano, and indeed every writer on classical architecture before about 1519 used the rhetorical term *genus* or one of its derivatives to classify these architectural styles:

> Just as for a painter it is useful to have some acquaintance with architecture to know how to make well-measured ornaments with their proportions, so an architect should know perspective because through that exercise he may better depict the entire building outfitted with its ornaments.
>
> About these there is no need to say anything, except that all of them derive from the five orders which the ancients used, that is, Doric, Ionic, Corinthian, Tuscan, and Attic. . . .

> We, as the need arises, shall explain the orders of all [five], presupposing what Vitruvius says.

In essence, the shift in terminology from *genus* to *ordo* reflects two forces: one mundane, the other sublime. There is a common Renaissance Italian usage of the word *ordine* to denote instructions. We see it very clearly in the phrase "li ordini di tutte" in the second passage just cited. *Ordine* also means: how to build a cannon in Vannoccio Biringucci's treatise on pyrotechnics, or how to ship ricotta in Agostino Chigi's business correspondence, or, in the case of Colocci's glosses for Raphael on Calvo's Vitruvius, how to draw a classical façade. The list of projected illustrations to the Colocci-Calvo-Raphael Vitruvius uses *ordine* in precisely this same sense when its draws up the "order" of systyle, pycnostyle, and diastyle temples. In essence, the "ordine del systylo" is a "how-to" chart.

The term also takes on a meaning close to that of *genus* in defining a class of objects; Christof Thoenes suggests persuasively that an analogy with contemporary religious orders might lead naturally to regarding any group with a family resemblance as an order.[71] This is roughly the sense in which the word appears so portentously in the first citation above from the letter to Leo X. Yet it supplants *genus* so swiftly as a term of classification because of an altogether different set of connotations.

Bramante, and Raphael after him, approached the practice of architecture in the classical mode with unsurpassed precision. This precision is visible in their sense of mass when they proportion columns; it also emerges in their attempts to subject the inherent flexibility of the classical idiom to stricter control, by limiting themselves to those forms of Doric, Ionic, Corinthian, Tuscan, and Composite which had clear ancient precedents, and by inventing an "Attic order" by which to classify square piers.

Vitruvius himself put no such limit on the numbers of architectural *genera*; he simply confessed that there were only four for which he knew the names (IV.8.4–6). Bramante and Raphael, coming after decades (if not centuries) of experimentation with classical forms, are after something very different, and are certainly in search of strict definitions. In a sense, they are performing the same kind of operation on the formal vocabulary of architecture that contemporaries like Bembo seem to be performing on the use of Latin, or Egidio da Viterbo on monastic living. Their schemes of classification for the architectural *genera* are more rigorous, and more binding, than they had been hitherto. "Order" is a classification whose connotations are more defined, more absolute than the loose kinship suggested by *genus*, and this binding categorization fits the temperament of papal Rome, which deals by vocation with eternal verities.

"Order" in papal Rome is never an entirely neutral word, because order derives from God and serves to define the trace of God's presence.[72] Vitruvius himself declares that a proportioned building strikes a harmony, down to its minutest detail, with the measure of the universe.[73] The Raphael who produces the blending of religion, revelation, proportion, and architecture that animates

Fire in the Borgo cannot feel too differently. His frescoed intimations of the designs underway for the new St. Peter's are, as has been seen, couched in a more general, even theoretical, rumination on what precisely constitutes beauty, for humble implements like water jugs, for the human body – of all ages and both sexes, if we look at the huddled women and the Aeneas group in that light – and, finally, for sacred architecture, the kind of architecture that Vitruvius claimed (III.1.4) as paradigmatic for all others. The essential contribution to result from such ruminations, visible in the Vatican Stanze in a completed fresco, and in the Vatican Library among Angelo Colocci's inchoate notes, lies embodied, but still not wholly accounted for, in the invention, here and now in the Roman High Renaissance, of the classical orders.

If the beauty expressed in proportion offers us a glimpse of God, then the sequence of forms and actions by which an artist releases the power of such beauty itself constitutes a kind of liturgy. Raphael and Colocci's marginal notes to Vitruvius use "order," *ordine*, in exactly this sense, too; *ordo* refers, as they both well knew, to the proper sequence of sacred ritual. Plato's image of the inspired artist, whose art is unequivocally a revelation of the divine, certainly provides them with an eminent precedent for perceiving their work as a holy act, not least because the ceiling of the Stanza della Segnatura next door bears four painted *tabulae* alluding to four different expressions of just such an idea. The few years that had passed between the time when Raphael painted those four inscriptions for Julius II and his maturity under Leo X brought with them a sea-change in his understanding of order, artistry, and, one can only presume, of God. Yet, ironically, just when Raphael had reached the point where he seemed at last to grasp the cosmic amplitude of his own talents, he assigned execution of this painted treatise on beauty to his assistants, prominent among them Giulio Romano, eventual heir to Raphael's Vitruvian papers and to Angelo Colocci's draft of the letter to Leo X. Little, if any, of *Fire in the Borgo* bears Raphael's own touch; he was too busy resurrecting ancient Rome for the same pope. His own thoughts must be traced now in the clumsier figures of his workshop, fallen embodiments, in true Platonic vein, of the master's divine vision.[74]

The reconstructed marvels of ancient Rome and the illustrated Italian Vitruvius have been left even more tragically incomplete than the vision of beauty propelling *Fire in the Borgo*; the realization of these more massive projects was made suddenly impossible by the great artist's death. Shortly after April 8, 1520, Baldassare Castiglione penned an elegy on the untimely loss to Rome of this remarkable creative spirit – which is preserved, appropriately enough, among the papers, and in the hand, of Angelo Colocci.

By Baldassare Castiglione[75]
Forth from the waters of Styx, once came Hippolytus, summoned
That his torn body be healed by the physician's art.
One of Asclepius's snakes sank in the Stygian billows;
That was the price of new life, paid in by the life-giver's death.

529

You also, Raphael, patient, with wonderful insight
Gathered the scattered limbs of your parent and set them to rights.
You restored Rome's broken corpse, victim of blade, fire, and ages,
Bringing it back to life, back to the splendor of old.
Death was outraged at your skill in summoning souls long departed –
Therefore you died, to appease the jealousy of the gods.
How could you make rise again what long slow ruin had accomplished?
Only by open contempt for the force of mortality's laws.
So now, poor friend, you fall, cut off in youth's early blossom;
Shall we then also be slain – we and all that is ours?

Notes

Thanks to Christof Thoenes, Joseph Connors, Richard Brilliant, and Thomas N. Howe for their generously offered expertise. Thanks also to the staff of the Handschriftenabteilung of the Bayerische Staatsbibliothek, Munich, and to the Biblioteca Apostolica Vaticana.

1   Golzio, 53ff.
2   Ibid.
3   Gilbert, 88–90.
4   Nicole Dacos addresses the composition of the Raphael workshop in Dacos, XVII–XXXII and 81–119, and in her "Il Trastullo di Raffaello," *Paragone*, No. 219, 1968, 3–29.
5   J. Shearman, *Raphael's Cartoons in the Collection of Her Majesty the Queen and the Tapestries for the Sistine Chapel*, London, 1972. Flemings were, of course, the acknowledged masters of tapestry.
6   J. Shearman, "Maniera as an Aesthetic Ideal," in *Acts of the Twentieth International Congress of the History of Art*, II, Princeton, 1963, 200ff.; idem, *Mannerism*, Harmondsworth, 1967, esp. 15–22.
7   Dacos, 114–119, details how Raphael modified this practice.
8   See, e.g., M. Baxandall, *Painting and Experience in Fifteenth-Century Italy: A Primer in the Social History of Pictorial Style*, Oxford, 1972; C. Hulse, *The Rule of Art*, Chicago, 1991.
9   Like Church reform, artistic reform was to be creation by purgation. The letter to Leo X mourns the loss of *arte*, *misura*, and *gratia* as components of *buona maniera*, along with *ragione*. See discussion above, pp. 523–525.
10 *The Art of Memory*, Chicago, 1996; see also P. Rossi, *Clavis universalis, Arti mnemoniche e logica combinatoria da Lullo a Leibniz*, Milan, 1960; M. Carruthers, *The Book of Memory: A Study of Memory in Medieval Culture*, Cambridge, 1990.
11 M. Baxandall, *Giotto and the Orators: Humanist Observers of Painting in Italy and the Discovery of Pictorial Composition, 1350–1450*, Oxford, 1971.
12 Golzio, 298: "ciò che aveva dell' arte, l'aveva da me."
13 Dacos provides perhaps the most detailed proof of this catholicity.
14 The most obvious analogy to Raphael is probably Titian; see M. R. Fisher, *Titian's Assistants during the Later Years* (Harvard dissertation, 1958), New York and London, 1977; D. Rosand and M. Muraro, *Titian and the Venetian Woodcut*, Washington, D.C., 1976, 17–23.

15 Gilbert, 97–99.

16 The idea that Leo's pontificate marked Rome's Golden Age was proclaimed by such influential humanists as Castiglione and Angelo Colocci. William Roscoe's monumental *Life of Leo X* has enshrined this position charmingly. Meanwhile, other contemporaries of Castiglione and Colocci, like Antonio Tebaldeo, preferred the papacy of Julius II. The idea that Julius provided the intellectual impetus for High Renaissance Rome was argued forcefully by D. Gnoli, "Secolo di Leone X?" in idem, *La Roma di Leone X*, Milan, 1938, 341–384. Both Ludwig von Pastor in his *History of the Popes*, and Bonner Mitchell, in his *Rome in the High Renaissance: The Age of Leo X*, Norman, Okla., 1973, portray Leo as a fundamentally unattractive character.

17 Though this letter from an artist to a pope explicitly mentions neither by name, its attribution to Raphael and Leo X has been generally accepted for a long time. With the discovery of an autograph *minuta* of the first parts of the text in the hand of Baldassare Castiglione (in the Castiglione family archive!), that humanist's contribution to its redaction, also a matter of consensus, was made entirely secure. As will be seen below, Raphael's autograph correction to one text of the letter confirms what was already an exceedingly strong case for his authorship. The analysis by Thoenes is concise and superbly documented; pp. 373–381. See also H. Burns and A. Nesselrath, "Raffaello e l'antico," in C. Frommel, S. Ray, and M. Tafuri, eds., *Raffaello architetto*, Milan, 1984, 379–452.

18 For the date of the painting, see Golzio, 42–43. For its significance, particularly in the present context, see J. Shearman, "Le Portrait de Baldassare Castiglione par Raphaël," *La Revue du Louvre et des Musées de France*, xxix, 1977, 261–276.

19 The letter is published (with some inaccuracies) by Golzio, 78–92, and in an extremely useful annotated edition (though still with significant textual inaccuracies) by R. Borelli, "Lettera a Leone X," in *Scritti rinascimentali di architettura*, Milan, 1978, 459–484. For the history of the letter and the identification of its authors, see Thoenes, 373–381; Morolli, 51–64. For the identification of Angelo Colocci as scribe, see Rowland. I am much indebted to Christof Thoenes for discussing the letter; his projected annotated edition of all three versions will treat many of these issues at length.

20 For Angelo Colocci's life, see Fanelli, 1969; Fanelli, 1979; *Dizionario biografico degli Italiani*, Rome, 1982, 105–111, s.v. *Colocci, Angelo*.

21 Rowland, 218ff.

22 Fanelli, 1969, 42–43; Fanelli, 1979, 91–134; P. B. Bober, "The *Coryciana* and the Nymph Corycia," *Journal of the Warburg and Courtauld Institutes*, xl, 1977, 223–239. The Neapolitan humanist Girolamo Borgia celebrated the garden with an "Ecloga Felix" dedicated to Colocci, Julius II, and his daughter Felice della Rovere Orsini, BAV, Cod. Vat. lat. 5225, 1013v–1015v.

23 The breadth of Colocci's intellectual interests emerge plainly in the papers compiled for *Atti*.

24 Tebaldeo's report can be found in BAV, Cod. Vat. lat. 4104, fols. 78r–80r, November 20, 1527. See, e.g., fol. 79r: "Quando io fui a casa vostra li soldati erano partiti et la massara vostra era morta, ond' io andai con la Philippa vostra Comadre, et trovai ne la camera di sopra a tetto li libri vostri, et li cominciai a mettere in ordine, et in questa tornò il Capitaneo spagnolo, et mi percosse, ond' io non li potei più andare: di poi è venuto tutto l' exercito in Roma, et altra gente è entrata in Casa

531

vostra, Tal che è stato uno altro Saccho, et credo che tutti li libri siano andati in la mala hora non potrò intendere quel che sia successo, se li soldati non vanno fuora, come si spera, in breve," and 79v: "Non so come serà andata quella casa, perchè li soldati brusano tutto il legname de le case in modo che tutte le Case sono vóte dentro, e se tornarete trovarete Roma disfatta."

For the library, see S. Lattès, "Recherches sur la bibliothèque d' Angelo Colocci," *Mélanges d'archéologie et d'histoire*, XLVIII, 1931, 308–344, now supplemented by the work of Rossella Bianchi and other scholars.

25 Thoenes. A reproduction of the Castiglione *minuta* is to be found in *Raffaello architetto*, 437.

26 The presentation copy is BAV, Cod. Vat. lat. 10228; another copy is in Verona, Biblioteca Capitolare 270. See the discussion in Morello 101–102. Thanks to Michael Koortbojian for bringing this parallel to my attention.

27 The corrected passage is cited in Appendix I. The formation of the "p" is unusual for Raphael, but the shapes of "a," "r," "e," and the ligature "te" all compare closely with the marginalia to Munich It. 37 and with BAV, Cod. Borg. lat. 800; in addition, they differ significantly from the hands of such collaborators as Giulio Romano and Antonio da Sangallo.

28 In a letter to Pier Vettori of April 17, 1543, Brit. Lib., Add. MS 10 265: ". . . Vorrei hormai riposarmi et attendere alli studi, il che dalla morte di Leone in qua non ho possuto fare."

29 BAV, Cod. Vat. lat. 3904, fol. 272v: "Adde quod in monumenti mei[s] in hortulo ad Virginis aquaeductum erat Agathangeli architecti cupa et in saxo a latere sinistro instrumenta architectonica erant insculpta erat etiam ibi podismi mensura statimque facta copia famulis meis misi ad lateranum columellam et sic in varios."

30 BAV, Cod. Vat. lat. 3904, fol. 300r, in which he laments the fact that Leonardo da Porto (whom he mistakenly calls "Ludovico") has published a treatise on weights and measures long before he has. Because Da Porto speaks of him in flattering terms, his feathers are not wholly ruffled; nonetheless, he notes to himself that the Venetian writer implies that there are things scattered throughout Rome that are really to be found only in Colocci's own possession. ("Et ille grato erga me animo in germe fassus est illud ex monumentis meis habuisset nisi et aliud adiecisset pro mensura humana multis esset in locis Rome reperiri quod nullibi nisi penes me et vere aliud inveniatur.")

31 S. Lattès, "A proposito dell'opera incompiuta 'De ponderibus et mensuris' di Angelo Colocci," in *Atti*, 97–108.

32 H. Günther, "Die Rekonstruktion des antiken Fußmaßes in der Renaissance," *Sitzungsberichte der Kunstgeschichtlichen Gesellschaft zu Berlin*, N.S. XXX, December 18, 1981, 8–12. My thanks to Christof Thoenes for this reference.

33 See L. Pacioli, *Summa de arithmetica*, Venice, 1494, fol. 68v: "E però la divina sapientia (commo dice Augustino in sua laude e commendatione) Omnia fecit deus in numero: pondere: et mensura: cioè che a ogni cosa dette la sua debita exigentia: considerata secondo el peso: el numero: e la mesura. In le quali tre cose: sempre se à retrovare la proporzione: secondo la quale (commo summo opefice) cuncta bene disponit."

34 A bishopric was already reserved for Colocci in 1521, thanks to his connections in the Vatican. Clearly he understood his decision to take holy orders in a sense typical of his age, for in 1526 he legitimized his two-year-old son Marcantonio, whose

mother, Bernardina, was married to someone else; *Dizionario biografico degli Italiani*, 106, s.v. *Colocci, Angelo.*

35 See Pacioli, *Summa de arithmetica*, fol. 69r: "Commo di sopra habiamo detto non solamente in lo numero e misura se retrova la proportione ma etiam in li suoni: e in li luoghi: e in li tempi: e in li pesi: e in le potentie si commo [P]lato vole e afferma in suo [T]hi[me]o."

36 See a note by Colocci, Cod. Vat. lat. 3903, fol. 68r: "Philon Deus Intelligibilis atque incorporeus/omnibus numeris absolutus/ego ex [P]hilone Quodsi partes eius sunt corporeae et corpus mensurabile est vel sub mensura cadit. tum mundum praecipue quod corpus omnium corporum maximum est quippe quod aliorum corporum congeriem in sinu suo tanquam proprias praeter gerit. quod ab ipso igitur incipiendum, esse divinus ad quem mensurandum deveniemus si a minoris mundi mensura progrediamur."

37 "El modo del misurare con la bussola della calamita, el quale modo noi usiamo, estimo che sia inventione de moderni."

38 The magnetic compass seems to have appeared in China, the Islamic world, and Europe sometime around the year 1100; see G. Sarton, *An Introduction to the History of Science*, II, London, 1931, 509–510 and *passim.*

39 Colocci's agrimensorial texts are: BAV, Cod. Vat. lat. 3132, 3353, 3893, 3894, 3895, 4498, 5394, and the Codex Arcerianus at the Herzog August-Bibliothek in Wolfenbüttel. For Colocci's studies of surveying, see G. Martines, "Gromatici veteres' tra antichità e medioevo," *B.S.A. Ricerche di storia dell'arte*, III, 1976, 3–23; idem, "Hygino gromatico: Fonti antiche per la ricostruzione rinascimentale della città vitruviana," *B.S.A. Ricerche di storia dell'arte*, I–II, 1976, 277–284; idem, "La scienza dei gromatici: Un esercizio di geografia astronomica nel *Corpus Agrimensorum*," in *Misurare la terra*, I: *Centuriazione e coloni nel mondo romano, città, agricoltura, commercio: Materiali da Roma e dal suburbio*, Bologna, 1984; Pagliara; J. N. Carder, *Art Historical Problems of a Roman Land Surveying Manuscript: The Codex Arcerianus A. Wolfenbüttel*, New York, 1978; C. Thulin, "Humanistische Handschriften des Corpus Agrimensorum romanorum," *Rheinisches Museum für Philologie*, n.s. LXVI, 1911, 419–422; O. A. W. Dilke, *The Roman Surveyors, An Introduction to the "Agrimensores,"* Newton Abbot, 1971, 130.

40 "Some little acquaintance" translates "qualche notitia," a term with explicit connotations in the Roman humanist lexicon; it means knowledge that can be quantified.

41 An excellent discussion of Publius Victor is to be found in R. Valentini and G. Zucchetti, *Codice topografico della città di Roma*, I, Rome, 1940, 63–257. In Colocci's notes on measure compiled in BAV, Cod. Vat. lat. 3906, the phrase "P. Victor de regionibus urbis multa de mensuris" appears three times, fols. 79v, 138r, 186v.

42 The copy of Publius Victor is now bound into BAV, Cod. Vat. lat. 3353, fols. 310r–311v; the decorative 15th-century codex, once wrongly attributed to Pomponio Leto, is Cod. Vat. lat. 3191.

43 Discovery of the *Forma urbis* is generally put later in the century, under the pontificate of Pius IV (1559–65); see R. Lanciani, *The Ruins and Excavations of Ancient Rome* (New York, 1897), repr. New York, 1979, 94–98.

44 The intermediary through whom they passed from Italy to Munich was the Florentine humanist Pier Vettori, whose papers are now in the Bayerische Staatsbibliothek. They are supposed to have come to Vettori by way of Giulio Romano. The Sack of

Rome by Swiss mercenary troops in 1527 presents as plausible an occasion as any other for the papers to have changed hands; Angelo Colocci sent parts of his library to Florence for safekeeping before the Sack, and others may have done the same.

45 L. A. Ciapponi, "A Fragmentary Treatise on Epigraphic Alphabets by Fra Giocondo da Verona," *Renaissance Quarterly*, XXXII, 1979, 18–40.

46 The identification of Colocci as scribe was made in Rowland. The reliance of previous identifications on forged material, particularly the purported letter of August 15, 1514, from Raphael to Fabio Calvo (modeled on the genuine BAV, Cod. Borg. lat. 800), is discussed there.

47 The text of Cod. It. 37 has been published by V. Fontana and P. Moracchiello, *Vitruvio e Raffaello*, Rome, 1975. The transcription, unfortunately, is not reliable, though some of the accompanying information is extremely useful. For Fabio Calvo, see also Morolli, 47–51; Pagliara; Morello, 102–105.

48 BAV, Stampati R.I.III.298.

49 These two traditions are termed H and G after their two oldest exemplars, Cod. Harleianus 2767 of the British Library and Cod. Guelferbytanus Gudianus 69 of the Herzog-August Bibliothek, Wolfenbüttel. Colocci mentions a "codex vetustissimus" and another codex in the marginalia to his Fra Giocondo, and seems to distinguish his readings from each.

50 L. A. Ciapponi, "Il *De architectura di Vitruvio* nel primo umanesimo," *Italia medievale e umanistica*, III, 1960, 59ff; P. N. Pagliara, "Vitruvio da testo a canone," in S. Settis, ed., *Memoria dell'antico nell'arte Italiana*, III, Turin, 1984, 4–82.

51 Calvo's interest in numbers, attested by his small treatise in Colocci's library, BAV Cod. Vat. lat. 3896, would suggest that he might be well qualified to attend to the numerical problems of Vitruvius. In fact, he simply uses the dimensions supplied by Fra Giocondo's edition of 1511; it is Colocci, in annotating Fra Giocondo and the Calvo text, who emends some of the numbers.

52 See his letters to Pier Vettori in February and March of 1538, Brit. Lib., Add. MS 10,265, fols. 264r–265r; fol. 266r.

53 For tabulation, see L. M. Tocci, "Dei libri stampati appartenuti al Colocci," *Atti*, 84, and esp. 92–93.

54 Thoenes, 374.

55 Thoenes, 374–375; see also Morolli, 51–52, n. 70.

56 Fra Giocondo's sylloge of inscriptions for Lorenzo the Magnificent, mentioned above, again supplies an illustrative precedent.

57 Golzio, 33–34. Fra Giocondo, appointed in 1513, also remained in that position; Golzio, 32.

58 For Vitruvian echoes in Raphael's work, see also R. Brilliant, "Intellectual Giants: A Classical Topos and *The School of Athens*," *Source*, III, 4, 1984, 1–12.

59 Cod. Vat. lat. 3903, fol. 120v: "Pulchritudo ut divinae bonitatis vestibulum." The sentiment derives from Proclus.

60 Compare Angelo Colocci's notes in BAV, Cod. Vat. lat. 3903, fols. 131r–132r; fol. 140r.

61 See infra, 528–529.

62 C. Thoenes and H. Günther, "Gli ordini architettonici: Rinascita o invenzione?" in M. Fagiolo, ed., *Roma e l'antico nell'arte e nella cultura del cinquecento*, Rome, 1985, 261–310; C. Thoenes, "Bramante und die Säulenordnungen," *Kunstchronik*,

xxx, 1977, 62ff; and, with excellent bibliography, A. Bruschi, "L'Antico e la riscoperta degli ordini architettonici nella prima metà del quattrocento: Storia e problemi," in *Roma, centro ideale della cultura del antico nei secoli XV e XVI, da Martino V al Sacco di Roma, 1417–1527*, Milan, 1989, 410–434.

63   First proposed by Ackerman, 15–18. Alberti, in *De re aedificatoria* VII.2, makes the patriotic suggestion that the Italic god Janus was the true inventor of architecture in Italy, and attributes both sacred architecture and Doric architecture in particular to the Etruscans (VI.3 and VII.6), probably with reference to the medieval Roman tradition that Janus was the Hebrew patriarch Noah in another disguise. The late 15th-century forgeries of Annius of Viterbo made explicit the connection between Janus and the Papacy; these became even more public with the preaching of Egidio da Viterbo, and there is good reason to suppose that this Tuscan-Doric style carried with it, at least in early 16th-century Rome, Etruscan connotations.

64   *Historia viginti saeculorum*, Rome, Biblioteca Angelica, Cod. lat. 351, fol. 248 (245): "Et erint ut complaceant eloquia oris mei. Quae enim sancte prius: minus eleganter: quae eleganter non sancte scribebantur: nunc eadem simul sancte eleganterque scripti sunt."

65   BAV, Cod. Vat. lat. 4104, fol. 50r.

66   Cod. Vat. lat. 5349 is a Giocondo autograph annotated by Colocci, probably in the period of the latter's collaboration with Raphael. Thanks to Michael Koortbojian for information on the fate of Giocondo's library.

67   Thoenes, 374, sees this shift as a sign of the transition to an editorial "we" for the printed text.

68   The letter purportedly written from Raphael to Castiglione of 1514, in which he says "mi porge una gran luce Vitruvio, ma non tanto che basti," comes from Pietro Aretino, not a source above suspicion.

69   Cod. It. 37b, fol. 87v.

70   Ackerman, 18, n. 12, seems to have been the first to notice this. See also Morolli, 69.

71   Private communication, 1991.

72   See I. D. Rowland, "Abacus and Humanism," *Renaissance Quarterly*, 48, 1995, 695–727.

73   He does not do so in a single lapidary sentence, but the interconnections of human (III.1.1, III.1.9), celestial (III.1.5; VI.1.2; IX, *passim*), harmonic (V, *passim*), and architectural proportion are the basic contention of his treatise, with nature acting as architect of the whole cosmos (IX.1.1).

74   D. Redig de Campos. *Le stanze di Raffaello*, Florence, 1950, finds even the design of *Fire in the Borgo* tired; p. 55: "Non è più il linguaggio ispirato di prima, e par di sentire in ogni cosa la stanchezza del pittore, la sua difficoltà ad elevarsi dal piano illustrativo della realtà a quello trasfigurante della poesia." Leo X was no Julius II; he inspired archaeology, not invention.

75   This is a slightly different version of the text transmitted in Vasari's *Life* of Raphael; Golzio, 232. BAV, Cod. Vat. lat. 2836, fol. 55r; better copy on fol. 119r–v.

Baldassar Castilion.
Quod lacerum corpus medica sanaverit arte
Hippolytum stygiis ex revocavit aquis.

Ad Stygias raptus serpens epidaurius undas
Sic pretium vitae mors fuit artifici.
Tu quoque discerpta Raphael dum membra parentis
Componis miro sedulus ingenio
Atque urbis lacerum ferro igni annisque cadaver
Ad vitam antiquum restituisque decus.
Moristi superum invidiam indignataque mors est
Te dudum extinctis reddere posse animam.
Et quod longa dies paulatim aboleverat, hoc te
Mortali spreta lege parare iterum.
Sic miser heu prima cadis intercepta Juventa
Deberique mones nostraque nosque neci?

Frequently Cited Sources

Ackerman, J., "The Tuscan/Rustic Order: A Study in the Metaphorical Language of Architecture," *Journal of the Society of Architectural Historians*, XLII, 1983.

Atti=Lattès, S., ed., *Atti del Convegno di Studi su Angelo Colocci, Jesi, Palazzo della Signoria, 13–14 settembre 1969*, Jesi, 1972.

Dacos, N., *Le Logge di Raffaello: Maestro e bottega di fronte all' antico*, 2nd ed., Rome, 1986.

Fanelli, V., 1969, *Federico Ubaldini, Vita di Mons, Angelo Colocci (Barb. Lat. 4882)* (*Studi e testi*, CCLVI), Vatican City.

—— 1979, *Ricerche su Angelo Colocci e sulla Roma cinquecentesca* (*Studi e testi*, CCLXXXIII), Vatican City, 1979.

Gilbert, F., *The Pope, His Banker, and Venice*, Cambridge, Mass., 1980.

Golzio, V., *Raffaello nei documenti*, Vatican City, 1936.

Morello, G., *Raffaello e la Roma dei Papi*, Rome, 1986.

Morolli, G., *"Le belle forme degli edifici antichi"; Raffaello e il progetto del primo trattato rinascimentale sulle antichità di Roma*, Florence, 1984.

Pagliara, P. N., "La Roma antica di Fabio Calvo. Note sulla cultura antiquaria e architettonica," *Psicon*, VIII–IX, 1977, 65–87.

Rowland, I. D., "Angelo Colocci ed i suoi rapporti con Raffaello," *Res publica litterarum/ Studi umanistici piceni*, XI, 1991, 217–225.

Thoenes, C., "La 'lettera' a Leone X," in *Raffaello a Roma: Il convegno del 1983*, Rome, 1986, 373–381.

Index